Warman's
PAPER

Volumes in the Warman's Encyclopedia of Antiques and Collectibles

Harry L. Rinker, Series Editor

Warman's Americana & Collectibles, 6th Edition,
  edited by Harry L. Rinker

Warman's Country Antiques & Collectibles,
  by Dana Gehman Morykan and Harry L. Rinker

Warman's English & Continental Pottery & Porcelain, 2nd Edition,
  by Susan and Al Bagdade

Warman's Furniture,
  edited by Harry L. Rinker

Warman's Glass,
  by Ellen Tischbein Schroy

Warman's Oriental Antiques,
  by Gloria and Robert Mascarelli

Warman's Paper,
  by Norman E. Martinus and Harry L. Rinker

Warman's
PAPER

NORMAN E. MARTINUS
HARRY L. RINKER

Wallace-Homestead Book Company
Radnor, Pennsylvania

Published in Radnor, Pennsylvania 19089, by Wallace-Homestead,
a division of Chilton Book Company

Manufactured in the United States of America

Library of Congress Cataloging in Publication Data

Martinus, Norman E.
    Warman's paper / Norman E. Martinus and Harry L. Rinker.
      p.   cm. — (Warman's encyclopedia of antiques and
collectibles)
    Includes bibliographical references and index.
    ISBN 0-87069-672-6
    1. Printed ephemera—United States—Catalogs. 2. Printed
ephemera—Collectors and collecting—United States—Catalogs.
3. Advertising specialties—United States—Catalogs. 4. Advertising
specialties—Collectors and collecting—United States—Catalogs.
I. Rinker, Harry L. II. Title. III. Series: Encyclopedia of
antiques and collectibles.
NC1284.U6M27   1994
741.6—dc20   93-38523
                                          CIP

1 2 3 4 5 6 7 8 9 0   3 2 1 0 9 8 7 6 5 4

CONTENTS

INTRODUCTION

Welcome to *Warman's Paper*, the seventh volume to be published in the Warman's Encyclopedia of Antiques and Collectibles. Those who regularly use *Warman's Antiques and Collectibles Price Guide* and other volumes in the Warman's Encyclopedia series are already familiar with the Warman format—category introductions featuring history, references, periodicals, collecting hints, and reproduction and copycat information complemented by detailed, accurate listings and values. You will find these features and more in this book.

The paper market is one of the hot, trendy collecting markets of the 1990s. Collectible paper is everywhere, from the poster dealer at a major antiques show to the individual selling a copy of the JFK assassination edition of *Life* at a garage sale. The growth potential for the paper market is unlimited.

Paper collecting has international roots dating back to the late 1500s. The first paper collectors were sixteenth and seventeenth century English gentlemen, e.g., John Selden (1584–1654), Samuel Pepys (1633–1703), and John Bagford (1650–1716). Throughout the eighteenth, nineteenth, and early twentieth centuries, these Englishmen and several key Continental collectors and dealers determined what paper topics were collectible and how they were to be collected. Much of the emphasis was literary: books, bookmarks, prints, and paper itself (e.g., samples of paper from different historical periods or watermarked paper) were the principal mainstays. American collectors followed the lead of their European counterparts.

This changed significantly in the 1960s and 1970s when twentieth century collectibles became a major part of the antiques marketplace. American collectibles collectors were pioneers in areas considered weird, strange, and kitsch by the more sophisticated European collectors. Much of what was collected included paper-related items.

Assembling large collections is one of the principal driving forces in the American collecting philosophy. In order to achieve this goal, objects must be affordable and plentiful. Paper meets both of these criteria. Paper collectors frequently own over a hundred times more objects than they display. They live in a pile–and–sort environment.

Although paper collecting did not gain universal recognition as a field unto itself until the 1980s, its sophistication grew in the post–World War II decades. One result is that four specialized paper markets—books, comic books, post cards, and sports cards—split off from the paper market and now operate independently. Occasionally some of these specialized dealers, especially post card dealers, participate in general antiques and collectibles paper shows. However, their principal buying and selling take place within their own specialized markets.

Warman's Paper does not include comic books and sports cards. If you need information on these topics, we recommend Alex G. Malloy's *Comic Values Annual: The Comic Books Price Guide*, published annually by Wallace–Homestead, and *Sports Collectors Digest Baseball Card Price Guide*, edited by Jeff Kurowski and published annually by Krause Publications. Coverage of books is limited to out–of–print books written about antiques and collectibles. Book prices can be researched in the annual volumes of *American Book Prices Current*, published by Brancroft/Parkman, Inc., and *Huxford's Old Book Value Guide*, published approximately every eighteen months by Collector Books.

A post card category is included in *Warman's Paper* in recognition of the continued strong link between the post card and paper markets. Besides, we never fail to find something to buy when perusing the offerings of post card dealers at a paper show.

IS IT EPHEMERA OR IS IT PAPER?

If we were traditionalists, the title of this book would be *Warman's Ephemera* instead of *Warman's Paper*. Our problem with "ephemera" is twofold. First, the word is incredibly pretentious and snobby. If you meet any of the individuals who tout themselves as ephemerists, you will understand what we mean and why we object to the term.

We are not aristocrats, but common men—to the ephemerists a failing, but to the vast majority of American paper collectors a sign that we are in tune with them. We love paper solely because it is paper, not because it is a certain type or classification of paper. Fast food paper excites us just as much as eighteenth century billheads. Ours is not to discriminate, but simply to relish finding, collecting, displaying, and talking about paper.

Second, what is ephemera? *Webster's Ninth New Collegiate Dictionary* defines ephemera as "matter of no lasting significance, esp.: collectibles (posters, broadsides, and tickets) that were orig. intended to have only ephemeral value." (Someday we plan to tell the Webster people what we think of definitions that make one go to another definition to understand them.) Ephemeral is defined as something "lasting one day only; lasting a very short time."

The Webster people need to rethink their definition of ephemera. They obviously have never been to a modern paper show. If they had, they would quickly realize that a large number of posters, broadsides, and tickets survived far longer than a day. Many have lasted years, decades, and even centuries. Also, many of these objects have a monetary value that promises to be infinite rather than ephemeral. Time for the Webster people to lift their heads from the pages of their dictionary and discover the real world.

The difficulty with ephemera is that few collectors view it as a collecting category. There are no general price guides for ephemera as defined by the ephemerists. When considering collectors' club listings for categories in the Warman's titles, we frequently wrestle with the problem of whether or not to include The Ephemera Society of America in some categories. Until a paper ephemera category was added to *Warman's Antiques and Collectibles Price Guide*, advertising was the only category in which The Ephemera Society of America was listed.

The best definition for ephemera that I found is in Maurice Rickards' *Collecting Printed Ephemera* (Abbeville Press, 1988). Rickards suggests that ephemera is made up of the "minor transient documents of every life," material destined for the wastebasket, but never quite making it. Ephemera includes your old driver's licenses, copies of restaurant menus that you took as souvenirs, or a collection of your old business cards. The definition sounds surprisingly close to the material found in this book until you realize that it is a definition for "printed" ephemera.

The Ephemera Society of America holds its own trade show once a year. In addition, many of its dealer members participate actively in the paper show circuit. Difficulty arises when you examine the objects offered for sale in their booths. Many are not made of paper.

The truth is that not all ephemera is paper. The terms are not synonymous. An advertising wooden ruler is just as much a piece of ephemera as is an advertising blotter. There are plenty of 1990s plastic objects that are clearly transient in nature, e.g., fast food drinking cups.

Why confuse the issue with a term that is difficult to understand and which the vast majority of collectors and dealers cannot pronounce properly? **Paper is paper**.

Warman's Paper contains objects made primarily of paper and paper-related products, e.g., cardboard and poster board. Over ninety–five percent of the objects that we chose for listings and illustrations are made only of paper. A few objects have metal clasps or attachments made from something other than paper. When this intrusion is minor, we see no reason to exclude them from the listings.

A SALUTE TO OUR PREDECESSORS

No general price guide develops in a vacuum; rather, it builds upon the successes and learns from the failures of its predecessors. Likewise, its foundation stones are the numerous specialized guides written about specific market segments. *Warman's Paper* is no exception.

One of the earliest attempts at defining the paper market was Robert D. Connolly's *Paper Collectibles: A Collector's Identification and Value Guide*, published by Books Americana. The second and last edition appeared in 1982. Connolly's work exhibited an excellent command of the marketplace. We value our copies highly. Had the title continued and responded to changing market trends, *Warman's Paper* might never have been written. Perhaps even more tragic is the fact that Books Americana's latest publication in this field, Gene Utz's *Collecting Paper: A Collector's Identification and Value Guide*, chose a different route rather than build upon the base Connolly had already prepared.

The Official Price Guide to Paper Collectibles, Fifth Edition, from the editors of House of Collectibles, was published in 1986. Like many other books in the House of Collectibles line in the mid-1980s, it was compiled by adding information from specialized sales lists to already existing paper listings from other House of Collectibles titles. After Random House acquired House of Collectibles, the title was abandoned.

Over the past ten years, numerous coffee table books and specialized price guides have been published on paper topics or subjects. These references are listed in the category introductions in the topical section and with their appropriate subjects in the subject section. These specialized publications, along with the trade papers, are most responsible for creating the strong, vibrant paper market of the 1990s. Writing *Warman's Paper* would have been far more difficult without them.

ORGANIZATION OF THE BOOK

General Approach: *Warman's Paper* is organized into three sections—a mini–collector's guide to paper, paper organized by topic, and paper organized by subject. The first is designed to increase your collecting enjoyment and provide information on some common pitfalls encountered in paper collecting. The second and third sections represent the two basic paper collecting methods.

A collector's guide to paper is badly needed. The only two books that touch upon the subject are John Lewis' *Printed Ephemera: The Changing Uses of Type and Letterforms in English and American printing* (Antique Collectors Club, 1990) and Maurice Rickards' *Collecting Paper Ephemera* (Abbeville, 1988). Both are by British paper scholars. The approach is extremely traditional, concentrating primarily on eighteenth and nineteenth century paper objects. While a few American examples are included, the bulk of the text and illustrations is European.

Although The Ephemera Society of America is leading the fight to encourage American collectors to mimic their British counterparts, the American spirit of independence has made it impossible to keep the troops in line. American paper collectors are a breed apart. They collect everything and anything. In fact, their influence now extends abroad. Each year the British "ephemerists" are forced to retreat further and further behind their traditional bastions. Long live the cereal premium, fast food, and toilet paper collectors of the world.

The American paper collecting market is filled with the same unbounded enthusiasm as the twentieth century collectibles market. Almost every auctioneer, collector, or dealer is involved with paper in some fashion or another. Paper interfaces with other collecting categories across the antiques and collectibles spectrum.

Two of the most common reasons for buying antique and collectible paper are: (1) decorative and (2) research purposes. A large number of people buy paper because of its graphics. It looks terrific framed and hanging on a wall. Collectors and dealers acquire paper because it provides important research clues in respect to date, manufacturer, and model variations. Some extend their search to locate paper items that merely picture their favorite antique or collectible objects.

Because of this, many paper buyers are neophytes, outside their element when attending a paper show and encountering a piece of paper that matches their wants. It is for this reason that the first portion of *Warman's Paper* is a mini–collector's guide to the American paper marketplace. It is a starting point, not an ending point. Once you have read it, your next task is to locate and review the publications found in the **Reference** portion of the introductions of the topical and subject categories that relate to your wants. These books contain in-depth information.

The mini–collector's guide consists of six parts: (1) collecting keys, (2) caring for paper, (3) keys to spotting reproductions, copycats, and fantasy items, (4) a state of the market report, (5) a list of auction houses and mail order sellers with a strong paper focus, and (6) a list of the major American paper shows along with approximate date, location, and the name, address, and telephone number of the show promoter. Each of these sections could easily have been three to four times its present size. Remember, *Warman's Paper* is first and foremost a price guide to paper. Even though it's relatively small when compared to the listings and prices, we hope you will find the mini–collector's guide an unexpected bonus.

Paper is bought, sold, and collected in two basic ways–by topic and subject. The topical approach focuses on what the paper object is, e.g., arcade card or magazine. The subject approach focuses on the image found on the paper, i.e., an electrical appliance or pin–up.

Deciding which is more important, topic or subject, when evaluating an object is not easy. Most paper objects fit neatly into one specific topical category. On the other hand, they often contain an image or other features that would qualify them for inclusion in half a dozen subject categories.

Topical collectors dominated the American paper market until the mid–1970s. As the 1980s advanced, subject collectors grew more and more important in paper sales. The 1990s market is balanced between these two groups. It is for this reason that *Warman's Paper* uses a dual approach.

The topical approach appears first because it reflects the more traditional paper collecting market. It also provides the best opportunity to focus on history, collecting hints, references, periodicals, and other pieces of information needed by the collector to better understand the paper market.

Those who collect by subject or seek paper for research and collection enhancement are well advised to take the time to learn the intricacies of the topical paper categories in which they plan to buy. Advantage in the antiques and collectibles field rests with those who know. *Warman's Paper* provides the informational keys. Please take time to read them.

When deciding upon the organization of this book, we carefully considered using only a topical approach for the price listing section and dealing with subject through an exhaustive index, but such an approach is too limiting. Like other books in the Warman's Encyclopedia of Antiques and Collectibles, *Warman's Paper* is designed to serve the general, as well as the collecting, public. The general public is subject oriented. As a result, a section of this book is devoted to collecting by subject. As this book expands in subsequent editions, so will the subject section.

History: The principal purpose of the history section of a topical category introduction is to provide a sense of the historical development of the object type. It is designed to answer such questions as: when was the object first made; how did it evolve; who were the principal manufacturers; how was it used; and why is it collected. We hope it will encourage you to learn more, to become more actively involved with the objects that you purchase and/or collect.

There are two additional pieces of information that you will find in the history section. The first is collecting hints. In several cases, some information applies to that category alone, e.g., how value is affected for a punched out versus an unpunched punchboard. We note where cross-category collecting and outside factors are critical in pricing. The second informational focus is on specific reproductions, copycats, and fantasy items as related to that category.

You will note differing amounts of information in the history sections of the topical categories. The authors' role in *Warman's Paper* is primarily that of compilers. The introductory material builds on research done by others. In several instances researchers have not as yet published an article or book dealing with the history of that category. When information was lacking, we drew upon our own personal experiences in life and among the trade. As new research is published, this information will appear in future editions of this book.

In addition to understanding the historical evolution of specific paper collecting topics, it is equally important to understand the historical evolution of paper collecting itself. Maurice Rickards' *Collecting Paper Ephemera*, mentioned earlier, contains an excellent chapter on the pioneers of paper collecting.

Special Note: Histories with their collecting hints and reproduction, copycat, and fantasy information are found only in the topic section; references, periodicals, and collectors' club information are found in both the subject and topic sections. The reason is that many of these subject references, periodicals, and collectors' club publications include pricing information. Since any general price guide can provide only a sampling of prices, we think it important that you be aware of additional sources in case you cannot find the information that you seek or want more detailed information than we provide.

References: A few general references are listed which include author, title, most recent edition, publisher (if published by a small firm or individual, "published by author" is used), and a date of publication. This provides more than enough information for you to order the books from your local book shop or a book dealer within the trade.

When possible, we listed books that are available in print or through direct purchase from the author. If a book is out–of–print, the reference information provides the information needed by your local reference librarian to obtain a copy through interlibrary loan. This also is an excellent way to review a book before deciding if you want to acquire a copy on the used book market.

Finding the books listed may present a problem. The antiques field is blessed with a dedicated core of book dealers who stock these specialized publications. You will find them at flea markets, malls, antiques shows, and through their advertisements in leading publications in the field. Many dealers publish annual or semi–annual catalogs. Ask to be put on their mailing list. Books go out–of–print quickly. Some have been reprinted. Do not forget to haunt the used book dealers in your area for these critical reference sources.

Periodicals: There are two general trade periodicals devoted exclusively to antique and collectible paper: *P.A.C. (Paper & Advertising Collector)*, PO Box 500, Mt. Joy, PA 17552, and *P.C.M. (Paper Collectors' Marketplace)*, PO Box 128, Scandinavia, WI 54977. These trade periodicals feature two to three articles about specific topics or subjects per issue, report regularly on auctions and shows, and have a large number of display and classified advertisements from sellers and buyers. Of the two, our favorite is *P.C.M.*

Among the paper market's greatest strengths are the collectors' club newsletters and periodicals that focus on a specific collecting topic or subject, e.g., *Postcard Collector.* These are listed in their appropriate topic or subject category.

The two general trade papers that most frequently report on developments within the paper market are *Antique Week*, PO Box 90, Knightstown, IN 46148, and *Maine Antique Digest*, PO Box 358, Waldoboro, ME 04572. We highly recommend both papers. *Antique Week* is ideal for those individuals whose paper interest is oriented toward collectibles and contemporary paper. *Maine Antique Digest* serves the middle and upscale side of the market.

The best sources for understanding trends in the paper market are catalogs from America's leading auction houses and mail auctions. Find the catalogs that contain the type of paper that you purchase and invest the money to acquire them. Make certain that any catalog that you purchase also supplies you with a "prices realized" list, otherwise the catalogs are worthless.

Transferring the prices from the "prices realized" sheet to the catalog forces you to concentrate on which objects sold and which did not and how much was paid (do not forget to add in the buyer's penalty). Learn to analyze the results: ask yourself what each price means; and mentally compare these prices to those that you have seen elsewhere.

Finally, do not ignore these catalogs once you have completed your initial review. Refer to them occasionally. Adhering to this approach helps you keep a historical perspective on market development.

Collectors' Clubs: Collectors' clubs add vitality to any collecting category. Their publications provide knowledge that often cannot be found elsewhere. Many of these clubs are short–lived; others are so strong that they have regional and local chapters. Support those clubs that match your collecting interest.

If your paper collecting interests are traditional, you should consider joining one or more of the following ephemera societies: The Ephemera Society of America, PO Box 224, Ravena, NY 12143; The Ephemera Society of Australia, Inc., 345 Highett Street, Richmond, Victoria 3121; The Ephemera Society of Austria, Landstrasse 22, A-6971 Hard, Austria; The Ephemera Society of Canada, 36 Macauley Drive, Thornhill, Ontario L3T 5S5; or The Ephemera Society of England, 12 Fitzroy Square, London, W1P 5HQ.

Among its many activities, The Ephemera Society of America offers an ephemera book service: Ephemera Books (PO Box 37, Schoharie, NY 12157). Ephemera Books sells books at select paper shows and through the mail. Books are sold at list price with an added fee for shipping if ordered through the mail. The Ephemera Book catalog fails to list publishers, a deliberate attempt to force you to buy from them instead of through your favorite book store or one of the general antiques and collectibles booksellers. Since many of the general antiques and collectibles booksellers offer discounts to the trade, you may want to check with them before buying at full price and paying additional shipping charges.

Museums, Libraries, and Historical Societies: The best way to study a specific field is to see as many documented examples as possible. Unlike more traditional antiques and collectibles, many of the great paper collections reside in libraries and historical societies as opposed to museums. Often these collections are open to collectors and scholars, but not on display to the general public.

We have chosen to use **Museum** in the category introduction as a generic term for the trio of historical society, library, and museum. Before visiting any of these institutions, call in advance to check hours and accessibility to any collections that you wish to see.

The following two museums deserve special mention: The Smithsonian Institution, Museum of American History, Washington, D.C., and the Margaret Woodbury Strong Museum, Rochester, New York. Their collections are outstanding. Gaining access to the study collections of the Strong Museum is far easier than gaining access to those of the Smithsonian. However, if what you seek is part of the Smithsonian's collection, persist. In every instance, we have found that persistence pays handsomely.

Reproduction Alert: Reproductions (exact copies) and copycats (stylistic copies) are a major concern. Unfortunately, many of these items are unmarked. Newness of appearance is often the best clue to spotting them. Where **Reproduction Alert** appears, a watchful eye should be kept within the entire category.

Reproductions are only one part of a growing problem; outright fakes (objects deliberately meant to deceive) are another. Be especially alert for fakes in all categories, especially where paper and folk art are linked in a single piece.

Listings: We have attempted to make the listings descriptive enough so the specific object can be identified. Most guides limit their descriptions to one line, but not those with *Warman's* in the title. We have placed emphasis on those items actively being sold in the marketplace. Nevertheless, some harder-to-find objects are included in order to demonstrate market spread.

Several of the listings in the topical categories are divided into more than one section. The reasons for the division differ from category to category. In one instance, dating may be the important consideration. In another, it may be object type. The important point is that we have tried to present each category in the manner by which it is usually collected, not force every category's listing to fit one standard mold. Users of volumes in the Warman's Encyclopedia of Antiques and Collectibles have indicated that this flexible approach is one of the series' most valued features.

Warman's Paper is not the only Warman title in which you will find paper listed. We have made every effort to make the objects listed in this book different from those found in the current edition of other Warman titles. However, in several categories, e.g., post cards, a type listing approach has been developed. Great care was taken to develop a representative type list. However, change for change's sake makes absolutely no sense (since one list would be definitely inferior to the other), hence, there is listing duplication in a few topical categories.

Illustrations: *Warman's Paper* is rich in illustrations. One of the principal pricing components in paper is "displayability." While words alone can suffice in most instances, there are occasions when a piece of paper must be seen to be fully appreciated. Illustrations involving a large amount of text have been made larger than other illustrations in the book so that they can be read.

The illustrations reflect material readily available in the market. Eighty percent of the illustrations came from "for sale" stock. The balance came from private collections, but always with a sensitivity to seeing the identical object offered for sale in the paper market during the past year. Nothing is gained in any book by featuring illustrations of objects that are unobtainable.

When you examine the illustrations in this book, do not just look at them in respect to the topic or category to which they have been assigned. Study their crossover potential. Learn to identify other subject categories to which they also might have been assigned. When looking at the illustrations in the subject area, pause and identify the topic category to which they belong. We have purposely selected illustrations that have strong crossover characteristics.

The wonderful thing about many topic categories, e.g., cigar labels, magazine advertising, and jigsaw puzzles, is that one could easily have used examples from any one of them to illustrate over half of the subject categories. In selecting the illustrations for the subject categories, we have tried to achieve a balance among possible topical choices.

PRICE NOTES

Pricing in the paper market is erratic. In some traditional categories, e.g., post cards, pricing is stable. In others it fluctuates wildly, e.g., cigar labels, often due to either increasing collector interest or deliberate market manipulation by a few speculators and dealers.

The situation is further complicated by paper arriving in the market in hoards. When it does, extreme differences in price may be encountered depending on: (1) who is selling the item and (2) whether or not the seller and/or buyer knows of the existence of the hoard. This is why it is common to see the same paper item at a paper show priced at $2.00 in one booth and $25.00 in another.

In order to achieve reliable pricing in *Warman's Paper*, we chose the following pricing philosophy. The prices in this book are collector prices, not decorator prices. The prices are retail, i.e., what you would have to pay as a collector if you purchased the object from an established and knowledgeable paper dealer at a paper show or through the mail.

Our pricing is based on an object being in fine condition. In other words, the object is crisp, clean, and free from any surface blemishes or tears. Only minor wear is acceptable; and, ideally, this should be along the edges or in a location that does not infringe upon the central motif. Another way to describe this is that the object must be ready for display and framing without any cleaning or restoration work.

We accepted fine condition as the basis of our pricing because we dislike pricing based upon near-mint or mint condition. While it is true that some paper items have survived in near-mint condition, the truth is that most were used in some fashion or another and show evidence of that use when examined. We feel that some of the signs of use are what give a piece its charm. Again, these are acceptable only if they do not seriously affect the overall displayability of the piece.

Each object is priced solely on the value of the object itself. It is a common practice among paper dealers to enhance the value of the paper they offer through matting, framing, or grouping. We realize that these are perfectly valid marketing approaches and, when properly done, do enhance paper's displayability. However, once accomplished, the final product is focused toward the decorator, not collector, market. When encountering an enhanced piece of paper, collectors must discipline themselves to look past the value of the enhancement and concentrate on the value of the piece of paper alone.

As the number of special interest collectors grows, a single object may appeal to more than one buyer, each of whom has their own idea of the object's value. In preparing prices for *Warman's Paper*, we assigned value based upon our opinion of an object's worth to a collector of the category in which the object is listed. Therefore, if the same object appears in more than one subject category, it may have two different prices.

We have ignored local and regional considerations in our pricing, opting in favor of a national pricing consensus. A national consensus has formed for most paper items as a result of the publication of specialized price guides, collectors' club newsletters, magazines, and newspapers.

Many paper items have a local or regional flavor. When sold on their home turf, they can, and often do, bring premium prices. However, few sellers have either the time or inclination to take advantage of this situation. In most cases, selling based on subject, rather than region, more than compensates for ignoring regional pricing considerations.

One final point has to be made. **Not all paper is collectible**. Actually the percentage of collectible paper is very small, probably less than ten percent. Condition alone eliminates a large majority. Other paper items are discarded and destroyed because of lack of collector interest in subject matter or topic. Identifying and separating collectible paper from non–collectible paper in a large lot is time consuming.

Warman's Paper includes only those paper items for which we were able to determine prices either in the field, through direct sale catalogs and classified advertisements, or at auction. In essence, we have saved you time and trouble by culling available paper and reported only on items that have established their value through sale. It is important that you understand this. Do not make a mistake and read more into what has been selected for inclusion than you should.

RESEARCH

Research into paper topic and subject categories is continual. Each month brings new revelations. This is perhaps one of the most exciting aspects of being involved in the paper market. Paper researchers, amateur as well as professional, deserve credit for their attention to scholarship and the skill by which they have assembled their collections.

Listings and prices come from many key sources—dealers, publications, auctions, collectors, and field work. The generosity with which auction houses, mail auctions, and mail catalog sellers have given advice is a credit to the field. Everyone recognizes the need for a guide that is specific and accurate in its pricing. In addition, listings and prices were taken from magazines, newsletters, newspapers, and other antiques and collectibles publications. All of them are critical to understanding what is available in the market and for what price. Collectors' club newsletters and magazines that discuss and report prices deserve special recognition.

We have been ably assisted throughout this project by the Rinkettes, the staff of Rinker Enterprises, Inc. They are constantly in the field checking trends and prices. Further, we have sought and received input from several members of Warman's Board of Advisors. Finally, private collectors have worked closely with us, sharing their knowledge of price trends and developments unique to their specialties.

BUYER'S GUIDE, NOT SELLER'S GUIDE

Warman's Paper is designed to be a buyer's guide, a guide to what you have to pay to purchase an object on the open market from a dealer or collector. **It is not a seller's price guide to prices**. People frequently make this mistake and are deceiving themselves by doing so.

If you have a large lot of unorganized paper, e.g., hundreds of old magazines or boxes of old correspondence and greeting cards, and wish to sell it to a paper dealer, expect to receive between 10 cents and 15 cents on the dollar. If the material is common, expect to receive even less.

To someone who does not understand the paper market, these figures will seem low, perhaps grossly unfair. The truth is simple: The paper market is labor intensive. Paper buyers spend a great deal of time evaluating, sorting, and preparing paper for sale. As indicated earlier, more than half of a general paper lot that they buy will be discarded as unsalable.

In addition to the time they spend, paper dealers also must make a substantial inventory commitment. For every item that they sell at a paper show, they have three to five hundred times more in inventory. Some items simply never sell; no dealer guesses right all the time. It is for this reason that there is a high resale markup on paper. Paper dealers need it to achieve an adequate return for the time and dollars that they invest. In this way, the paper market differs substantially from other antiques and collectibles markets.

If you understand the paper market and are willing to invest your time in separating the collectible from non–collectible paper, you will increase the amount you receive when you sell. Even under the best of circumstances, dealers can rarely justify paying more than 35% of retail value.

While it is true that private collectors pay more than dealers, they know enough not to pay full retail to a private seller. They also expect to buy at bargain prices, otherwise they might as well buy at full retail from their established dealer sources.

Knowing who will buy an object is worth 50% or more of its value. Buyers are specialized. Dealers spend years developing a list of collectors who will pay top dollar for an item. One extremely useful source for such information is David J. Maloney, Jr.'s *Maloney's Antiques and Collectibles Resource Directory*, published biannually by Wallace–Homestead.

Finding a specialized collector does not mean that you have found a buyer. What you really need to find is a specialized collector who does not own an example of the object that you are trying to sell. Considering the amount of time it takes to realize a few extra selling percentages, most private individuals are best advised to sell to a dealer.

Examine your paper item as objectively as possible. If it is something from your childhood, try to step back from the personal memories in evaluating its condition. As an antiques appraiser, I spend a great deal of my time telling people their treasures are not "gold," but items that are readily available in the marketplace, have limited collector interest, or are in such poor condition that collectible value is nonexistent.

In respect to buying and selling, a simple philosophy is that a good purchase occurs when both the buyer and seller are happy with the price. Don't look back. Hindsight has little value in the antiques and collectibles field. Given time, things balance out.

COMMENTS INVITED

Warman's Paper is a major effort to deal with a complex field. Our readers are encouraged to send their comments and suggestions to Rinker Enterprises, Inc., 5093 Vera Cruz Road, Emmaus, PA 18049.

ACKNOWLEDGMENTS

We wish to thank the many auctioneers, collectors, dealers, publishers, and others who supplied information for the data bank used to prepare the listings in this book. We hope our effort justifies the support extended to us.

Kudos to the Rinkettes, the staff at Rinker Enterprises, Inc., for contributing their talents to the development of this book. We appreciate their willingness to allow our names to appear on the title page without animosity.

Warman's Paper, like other Warman's titles prepared at Rinker Enterprises, Inc., was a group effort. Terese J. Oswald, Research Associate, was the mainstay behind this book. She served as project coordinator and researched, authenticated, and keystroked most of the descriptions and listings. Dana N. Morykan, Assistant Research Associate, coordinated the selection and captioning of the photographs. As the book neared completion, she waded into paper "feet first" and became actively involved in doing sections of the subject listings and prices. We are proud to welcome Terese and Dana to the growing ranks of paper experts.

Ellen T. Schroy, Director of Publications and Research, managed our time so that we met our continuing obligations for articles, books, and columns in a timely fashion while we worked on this book. Nancy M. Butt, Librarian, was responsible for the reference and periodical listings. Harry L. Rinker, Jr., Art Director, served as photographer for the project.

The staff at Chilton Books, parent company of Wallace–Homestead Book Company, accepted our proposal with enthusiasm, supported us during the preparation of the manuscript, and applied their professional expertise to the design, layout, and printing of this book. Special thanks to Edna Jones, Managing Editor, and Troy Vozzella, Developmental Editor, for shepherding yet another new Warman's title.

Finally, our thanks to those of you who bought this book. We trust you will find your purchase more than justified. If you have complaints, send them to Harry. If you have praise, send it to Norman. That's part of the deal we made when we agreed to work together on this book.

NORMAN'S TWO CENTS

I think I dreaded writing the acknowledgment section of this book more than any other part. Like many first time authors, I began making a list of customers, dealers, and friends who supported and influenced my involvement in paper. I wanted to thank them all personally.

As the list kept growing and growing, I began to panic. No matter how hard I tried, I was certain that I was going to skip someone. I called Harry. "What am I to do?" Harry faces this "no win" situation several times a year. "Write a note of general thanks and keep your special acknowledgments short," were his recommendations.

Following Harry's advice, I want to extend my appreciation to everyone who helped me along the way. Our friendship and business relationship is not based upon their names appearing on these pages. You know who you are; and, so do I. Thanks.

If you know Harry as well as I do, you probably guessed that he could not resist one more piece of advice. "You had better write something terrific about me." Since I know Harry quite well, I really panicked. If I told the truth, who would believe it?

I felt honored when Harry approached me a year-and-a-half ago about writing *Warman's Paper*. It has been a learning experience. Harry's drive, enthusiasm, intellect, and wonderful (perhaps I should have used "warped") sense of humor made long hours and tedious tasks pass quickly. He was the glue that held this project together when it came unstuck. In fairness, *Warman's Paper* is his vision. My role was that of a back seat driver.

As a paper dealer, I have made some special friends within the dealers' community. Thanks to Jon Alk of Green Bay, Wisconsin; Steve and Linda Alsberg of Skokie, Illinois; Chuck Barger of Willow Valley Antiques, Mansfield, Ohio; John Whiting of Whiting's Old Paper, Hanover, Virginia; and Sherman Sackheim in Florida for supplying me with some great paper that more than made my customers happy.

Mary and Bill Smith of Super Flea in Greensboro, North Carolina, and Susie Clodfelter and Bob and Alice Adams of Antiques Extravaganzas of North Carolina helped me establish myself in the show circuit. Thanks for the time and effort you spent.

Behind every great man is a great woman. In my case, the opposite sex numbers four— no, not wives, members of my immediate family. My three daughters, Noreen, Karen, and Lee Ellen, show their support for Dad by proudly displaying the paper that I frame and mat for them on the walls of their homes and offices. They have even allowed me to inflict their children with my love of paper.

My final thanks is reserved for the most important person of all, my wife Elizabeth; without her tolerance and support my paper collecting would have ended years ago. She is a continual source of help.

As this book goes to press, Elizabeth, Lee Ellen, and I are about to realize one of my life long dreams, my own frame shop and paper gallery. What man could ask for more, surrounded by the things and people he loves. Hopefully, the Nostalgia Gallery will last a long, long time.

HARRY'S TWO CENTS

How am I going to top Norman's comments? I am probably a fool to try.

I first met Norman and Elizabeth in the mid–1980s at an *Antiques Week* seminar in Lebanon, Ohio. We hit it off immediately. To our surprise, the more contact that Norman and I had with each other, the more similarities we found between ourselves. It is frightening. I keep asking Norman for his family history. Somewhere in our blood lines there must be a common ancestor.

Another positive note is that Connie, my wife, has finally found someone who sympathizes and fully understands what it means to be married to someone like me. Just as Norman and I have become friends, so have Connie and Elizabeth. Thanks to these friendships, Connie and I are now frequent visitors to North Carolina Outer Banks. After each visit, we return home with the aromatic scent of the sea and its surroundings vividly impressed in our minds.

Although I cannot prove it, I think one of the first items I ever collected had to be a piece of paper. I have saved and collected paper items for as long as I can remember. I still have my homework assignments from high school neatly preserved in files. You make your own judgments about the meaning of this.

I never met a piece of paper I did not like. *Warman's Paper* was created because I have complained for years about the need for a general guide to the paper market. It is my hope that this book will turn even larger numbers of people on to paper. The field is so vast that there is room for everyone. Jump in and enjoy yourself.

Norman E. Martinus   Harry L. Rinker
Nostalgia Gallery   Rinker Enterprises, Inc.
148 Marlin Drive   5093 Vera Cruz Road
Kitty Hawk, NC 27949   Emmaus, PA 18049

August 1993

Part I
Mini-Collector's Guide

KEYS TO COLLECTING PAPER

Paper collectors are fanatics. Their cars have not seen the inside of a garage for twenty years or more. Their collecting is governed by key premises, among which are: (1) one can never own enough paper; (2) I will sort through this new pile of paper as soon as I get home or tomorrow if I am too tired to do it today; (3) I am not certain if I own one of these so I had better buy it; and (4) I will sell my duplicates and other excess paper one of these days, which, as you may have already guessed, never happens. It is for this reason that there is a similarity in appearance between a scrap paper junk yard and the home of a serious paper collector.

While you may consider taking the path of least resistance just like most paper devotees, we urge you to think twice, three or four times, or however many times it takes to narrow your paper collecting focus from the beginning. Keep your collection manageable. Your spouse or significant other, children, and friends will thank you while you are alive and not speak your name in vain and with disdain after you die. If paper collecting is possible without going off the deep end, you must prove this yourself. Do not look to us for role models.

The quantity of available paper is limitless. The first thing that paper collectors learn is that they are never going to own it all. Even when concentrating on one topic, e.g., jigsaw puzzles, the same applies. No one will ever own one example of every puzzle made. The only way to maintain control is to narrow your focus. When you think you have the issue in hand, narrow it even further. When the number of possible examples is in the hundreds, not thousands, you have achieved your goal.

Expect to change your focus frequently when you first start collecting paper. This happens to every paper collector—the more paper you see, the more you find that catches your eye. Even if you spend several months studying the paper market, there is no way you can understand and appreciate its depth until you are actively involved in it.

As you identify and define your collecting focuses, develop checklists of specific paper items that you have seen in other individuals' collections or as illustrations in books. Remember, this material represents only a small portion of what is available. With a few exceptions, e.g., magazines, some post card series, and major illustrators, collecting check-lists are not available. You have to create your own. Carefully prepared want lists in a checklist format provide measurable collecting goals as well as a means of communicating with paper sellers.

What you pay for paper depends entirely on how much time and effort you are willing to invest in the hunt. Paper is found everywhere: church rummage sales, community and local garage sales, flea markets, auctions, general antiques and collectibles shows, specialized paper shows, homes of friends, relatives, and business associates, and even in the closets, basement, attic, and garage of your own residence. Acquisition costs range from ''you can have the stuff if you just get it out of my attic'' to retail market price.

The key is to make your wants known. The two best sources for doing this are seeker advertisements in trade periodicals and carefully crafted want lists. Because paper can be shipped with a minimum of difficulty, most paper dealers willingly conduct business via mail and telephone.

You probably are familiar with the phrase ''the weight of knowledge.'' If you collect paper, you will quickly learn the true meaning of this phrase. Piles and boxes of paper become weighty in a hurry. Neither of us are ideal physical specimens. We grunt and groan when we haul paper. Sooner or later if we do not take better care of ourselves, our backs will no longer allow us to indulge in the quantity side of our affliction.

Similar physical considerations are involved in the buying process. Muscle aches and paper shows go hand in hand. One constantly bends over or sits for long periods examining paper. Two years ago I bought Norman's exercise bicycle. For some strange reason, the mileage on it remains identical to the day it arrived in Vera Cruz. My waist line and stamina at paper shows tell me it is time to start pedaling and pumping iron if I want to keep collecting. Mañana.

VALUE CONSIDERATIONS

Almost every paper item is mass produced in quantities often numbering in the hundreds of thousands or millions. There are exceptions, e.g., hand drawn art work, family letters, and business journals. There is no question about their individual uniqueness. However, the wise collector always places them within a larger context. For example, the paper market is saturated with letters written home by Civil War soldiers. No two are the same. Yet, as a group, they represent a specific type of letter. Content determines value, not the fact that the letter has survived from the Civil War period.

Most collectors and dealers underestimate the survival level of paper. They never saw one before. Therefore, it must be scarce. The vast majority of paper items are common, extremely common. Why should they not be? Force yourself to remember production quantities.

Whenever goods are available in quantity, it makes sense to shop around—not only for the best price, but also for the best condition. Disciplining yourself not to buy is one of the hardest things to do. Many buyers find it impossible to resist the "I see it; I want it" mentality.

When examining a piece of paper, identify its value points. Note the paper's topic and subject categories and decide what each specific collector might pay. Next determine its value as a display piece to someone other than a collector. When all this is done, ask yourself one question: what are *you* willing to pay for the item? This is the only answer that counts— not the seller's price, not the price that you think someone else might pay, and not the price that you find listed in a price guide. Value, like beauty, rests in the eye of the beholder.

Develop an eye for paper. Whether you collect topically or by subject or are buying solely for decorative purposes, learn to look at the surface image aesthetically. Understand what you like and what excites the public. We are amazed at the illustrator collectors who pay a premium price for every illustration that they can acquire by their favorite artist. Not every picture is a masterpiece, yet they pay masterpiece prices for everything. Every artist has bad days. Aesthetics and discrimination go hand in hand.

Almost everyone in the antiques and collectibles trade is familiar with the "good, better, best" concept. The only problem with this approach is that it has no downside. Use the following seven-step scale when examining paper: landfill, junk, poor, ordinary, good, better, and best. Now, think of availability in the form of a pyramid with a geometric progression used to determine how much space to assign to each unit, e.g., landfill (64), junk (32), poor (16), ordinary (8), good (4), better (2), and best (1). What this means is that less than six percent of all available paper is aesthetically collectible. This makes sense to us; we hope it does to you as well.

We fully recognize that not all paper is collected for aesthetic reasons. As a result, other value considerations, e.g., regionalism, subject, support material for another collecting category, etc., must be factored into the equation as well. However, in the final analysis, the most desirable paper, whether movie posters or magazine advertisements, always has a strong aesthetic component.

CONDITION CONSIDERATIONS

The Introduction deals briefly with the issue of condition. It is time to examine the issue in detail. There is a continuing argument in the paper community as to whether condition or surface image is the most important consideration in pricing. Who cares? Avoid the debate. Do not buy damaged paper.

Force yourself to set high condition standards from the beginning. This is easy to say and hard to do. Only buy paper that is in fine or better condition. A piece of paper in fine condition has no defects of any kind in the surface image and only minor evidence of wear elsewhere.

Use the arm's length test. Hold the paper at arm's length. If you can detect any problems, e.g., tears, surface blemishes, or crease lines from folding, the paper is not in fine or better condition. Be critical.

Do not buy paper that has been water damaged. Staining is very difficult to remove. It is virtually impossible, without a great deal of expense, to separate pages of paper that have been stuck together through water damage. Water damage also wrinkles paper. Again, these wrinkles are difficult to remove.

Most sellers downplay the importance of tears, creases, and surface dirt. Why not? It is in *their* best interest to do so. Do not accept the argument that all you have to do to restore the paper to fine condition is take it to a paper conservator. Paper conservators can work wonders; they are highly skilled but expensive. Justifying their cost is often difficult. Frequently, even a trained paper conservator cannot save the piece.

MATTED AND FRAMED

There is no question that matting and framing enhance the presentation of many paper items. However, they also can hide serious defects and, improperly done, can create serious long term problems. Sellers of fakes and reproductions often use framing to disguise their handiwork.

When you encounter a piece that has been matted and/or framed, you have to make a decision as to whether you are comfortable buying the piece without examining it outside the mat and frame. If the piece is pressed against the glass of a frame, i.e., there is no mat separating the paper from the glass, always ask to have the paper removed from the frame. You will be surprised how often the paper is stuck to the glass.

A piece's value is affected negatively if the object has been cut down for framing, dry mounted or glued to the backboard, gained an unsightly brown line due to the use of acidic matting, or been discolored from the backing material. If you suspect any of these possibilities, insist on inspecting the piece with the mat and frame removed. A professional paper dealer will have no objections to such a request. More than likely he will have the requisite tools available to accomplish this task quickly and efficiently.

Just because you asked to have a piece taken out of its mat or frame does not imply an obligation to buy even if the piece checks out properly. However, in fairness to paper dealers, a dematting or deframing request should be made only when it is the final factor in your determination on whether or not to buy.

Many matted and framed items are sold for their displayability, not their collectibility. Assuming that you find the presentation satisfactory, there is no reason to request that the frame or mat be removed. When a person buys a matted or framed piece of paper for display purposes, the issue of resale should be a minor or a complete non–factor in price consideration. The piece should be viewed in the same vein as any decorator item purchased in a large department store or specialty shop. When its decorative value ceases, discard it.

More and more paper dealers who sell matted and framed material are providing source and historical information about their items. While it is well and good to receive a guarantee that the object is over a specific number of years old, knowing something about the origin and history of the item is far more exciting, especially if you purchase it as a conversation piece.

Take the time to develop a working relationship with a skilled professional matter/

framer. While your local frame shop may suffice for some items, a trained professional should mat and frame your most valuable paper. Search until you find a dealer whose presentations meet your standards. If the dealer does not do the framing himself, ask if you can contract for your framing through him.

Finally, when you purchase a matted or framed object as a collector, make certain you understand how much value rests in the object and how much rests in the mat and/or frame. With increasing collector interest in frames, more often than not the real value of a framed print or etching from the turn of the twentieth century rests in the frame and not in the artwork.

SOME FINAL THOUGHTS

Collect what you like—do not be swayed by the opinions of others. When collecting something is no longer fun, switch. The paper market is so huge that you are certain to find something that strikes your fancy.

Take pride in what you collect. Show it off. Do not be embarrassed if it is a little out of the ordinary. Three cheers if it has shock value.

Finally, interact regularly with your collection. Add to it systematically and regularly. Remember, you can never have enough quality material. There is always something more to buy. If you need a good divorce lawyer or the name of a friendly bank loan officer, drop us a line. We understand.

CARING FOR PAPER

Whether you paid a few cents or hundreds of dollars for paper, learn to properly care for it. You are only a temporary custodian for your paper, a caretaker until it passes to its next owner. Adopt the Boy Scout mentality—leave the campsite in better shape than you found it. When paper finally leaves your care, hopefully it will be in as good or better condition than when you purchased it.

There are two books with which every paper collector should be familiar: Anne F. Clapp's *Curatorial Care of Works of Art on Paper: Basic Procedures for Paper Preservation*, published in 1987 and available from Nick Lyons Books (31 West 21st Street, New York, NY 10010) and A. Bruce MacLeish's "Paper: Care and Conservation" chapter in *The Care of Antiques and Historical Collections, Second Edition*, published in 1985 and available from The American Association for State and Local History (530 Church Street, Nashville, TN 37219). AASLH publications have much to offer individuals in the antiques and collectibles field. If you are unfamiliar with the AASLH publications, write for a catalog.

Paper is subject to a wide variety of hazards—light, water (moisture), rapid temperature changes, dirt and other environmental concerns, Scotch tape and other objects applied to paper, packaging, insects and rodents, and humans. The only way to avoid these problems is through precautions and proper care.

Prolonged exposure to light causes fading in ink and other colors applied to paper. Sunlight and fluorescent light, both rich in ultraviolet radiation, are the principal culprits. However, indirect light also produces long term fading. Excess heat, whether from a light or heat source, can cause paper to become brittle. The answer is to rotate your display pieces every four to six months. Not only does this help preserve them, it adds variety to your display.

Light is both an enemy and a friend to paper. Storing paper in a dark, damp environment invites mold. Light helps kill mold. As a paper collector, it is up to you to find the proper balance.

Paper requires moisture to survive. The ideal humidity level for paper is between 40% and 50%. The key is to keep a constant humidity level. Of greatest concern is excessive moisture which can cause weakening of adhesives, water stains, blurred inks and paints, mold growth, and even a change in the dimensions of the paper. A key preventative measure is to conduct a quarterly check of your stored paper.

If necessary, invest in humidifiers and dehumidifiers. In most cases the problem is too much, not too little, humidity. When using a dehumidifier, carefully consider its placement. Unless you are fortunate enough to have a drain in your storage area, you are going to have to empty your water pan every day or two. Everything is lost if you accidentally trip in a narrow spot and spill the pan of water on your paper goods.

Brown, spotty staining on paper is known as "foxing." It is caused by either a chemical reaction involving fungi and the iron salts in paper or the decomposition of cellulose interacting with fungi in a damp environment. Once it occurs, the only solution is to enlist the services of a paper conservator.

If you encounter mold, there are some preventative measures that you can take. First, if the paper is dry, brush off the mold with a very soft brush. A photographer's blow–brush will also work provided the object is not a charcoal or pastel piece of art work. After removing the mold, expose the paper to an hour or two of direct sunlight, making certain that the paper has adequate ventilation on all sides. Second, you can build an air–tight box and place the paper inside along with thymol or ortho–phenyl–phenol crystals that are allowed to fume. A few days of fuming should kill the mold.

Attempting to remove water stains is fraught with risks. Better to do nothing. Water baths, even with distilled water, may cause irreversible damage by removing stabilizing chemicals in paper. There is only one safe method to remove water stains—professionally. Professionals are trained in the techniques required to bleach out spots and stains. You are not.

Avoid rapid changes in temperature and humidity. If you display framed paper on an outside wall, constantly check the temperature behind the frame. Most framers now add small rubber or fabric disks to the back of frames to make them stand out from the wall in order to allow circulation behind them. Carefully check your heat sources in relationship to displayed paper. A surprising number of collectors hang framed paper directly over a heat source. This should be avoided.

Consider the environment in which you display, work on, and store your paper. Many work areas, especially if they are in a garage, are heated with wood or coal stoves or kerosene heaters. These heat sources generate unwelcome quantities of oily soot. Before you put any piece of paper down, check the surface on which it will rest for harmful substances.

Dirty paper is unattractive. The first tendency when encountering any piece of paper that is dirty is to clean it. For years antiques and collectibles dealers touted the effectiveness of rolled fresh bread as an eraser of dirt, forgetting the fact that it left behind a residue that attracted insects. It is time to trash these "old time remedies" and do things correctly.

Test a small corner of any piece of paper before proceeding to work on the whole. Opaline or Scum–X, powdered erasers, will remove most freshly fallen surface dirt on *hard* surface papers. Work in the margins and blank parts of the design on the reverse side of the paper. Artists' soft vinyl or kneaded erasers work. Again, confine your efforts to the margins and reverse side. Work gently. If not, you will tear or abrade the paper. If at all possible, avoid working directly on the surface image. If the image area has major problems, seek professional help.

There is a special place reserved in hell for individuals who repair paper with Scotch tape. The reason is simple. Most commercial adhesives are acidic. Once applied, they begin reacting chemically with paper immediately. Removing the dark stains left behind from Scotch tape is nearly impossible. MacLeish's *The Care of Antiques and Historical Collections* recommends a formula that might help to lessen the effect.

Try a hair dryer to warm the residue on old tape as a means of getting it loose. Many paper collectors are accustomed to liberally using acetone to loosen tape. Besides being flammable, overuse can cause serious damage. Whenever possible, avoid buying paper that has tape, recent or old, applied to it.

Shrink wrapping can do more harm than good when the back board is cardboard or another paper product with high acidity or the shrink wrap contains chemicals that are not inert. If shrink wrapping is too tight, paper crinkles. Further, paper and plastic need to breathe. Shrink wrap should have slits along some of the edges to allow air to enter.

Beware of inexpensive plastic sleeves and pocket pages. Many of them are not of archival quality, i.e., they contain plastic chemicals that can seriously harm their contents. Further, many of them trap and retain moisture, especially when exposed to air in the early morning hours of an outdoor flea market. If you want to store paper in plastic sleeves or pocket pages, should you spend the extra money for archival quality products? The only answer is "yes."

Storing paper objects on top of each other can cause problems. Ink and colors that may look stable often are not, especially when exposed to high humidity. It is common to find ghost images on personal correspondence, newspapers, and a host of other paper materials. Weight alone causes the objects on the bottom to bend and curl. If stacked paper becomes damp, it can "felt" (physically bond together). The same is true if moisture gets inside paper.

Store your most valuable paper in acid free sheets or envelopes. The expense is minor compared to the potential damage done by improper storage. Also insist on the use of acid free mats when matting is done.

An excellent source of supply for archival material is a large local or regional art supply store. Your area library, historical society, and museums use archival material. If your needs are small, they may be willing to sell you what you need. They may even allow you to combine your order with their order, hopefully resulting in savings to you both.

You also can order archival quality materials from Conservation Resources International (8000-H Forbes Place, Springfield, VA 22151), Hollinger Corporation (PO Box 6185, Arlington, VA 22206), Light Impressions Corporation (PO Box 940, Rochester, NY 14603), TALAS (Technical Library Service, 130 Fifth Avenue, New York, NY 10011), and University Products, Inc. (PO Box 101, Holyoke, MA 01040). Be forewarned. Archival supplies are expensive.

Beware of archival material advertised for sale in the trade papers and offered for sale at paper shows. We have handled a great deal of archival material and much of what we see does not measure up to our standards.

Never store paper with any form of metal fasteners, e.g., paper clips or staples, attached to it. Even in the best of situations, these items rust and leave a residue on paper that is impossible to remove without doing serious damage to the paper's integrity. Do not be fooled into using plastic fasteners as a substitute. These cause permanent creases when left on paper for an extended period of time.

Perhaps the most overlooked potential dangers are insects and rodents. Learn to recognize damage caused by silverfish, crickets, flies, mice, and rats. Thinning and loss of paper, especially on the surface, chew marks along the outer edges, black spots, and droppings are visible signs of danger. Just because you do not see these creatures does not mean that they are absent. While most collectors check their paper storage area quarterly, if you suspect insect damage, check monthly.

Keep paradichlorobenzene moth crystals in your storage area as a precaution (naphthalene moth crystals are ineffective). If you have a major problem, call a professional exterminator. This is one situation you do not want to get out of hand.

Many collectors store newly acquired material in an area that is separated from the rest of their collection until such time as they can carefully inspect, clean, and house their new acquisitions. This step is a definite must if you buy a large paper lot that has been stored in an attic, basement, garage, or shed for more than a year. Some collectors build an air–tight tent in which they place all new acquisitions along with some paradichlorobenzene moth crystals for a two-to-four-week period.

There remains just one final matter to discuss in respect to matting and framing—encapsulation. While single and double strength glass can be used for glazing, serious paper collectors prefer to invest in acrylic plastic, e.g., Plexiglas, made from an ultraviolet–filtering formula. Do not use this material for charcoal or pastels because it can develop an electrostatic charge that pulls the charcoal or pastel from the surface. Frosted non–glare glass is rarely used any longer. There is no need to replace it in an already framed piece unless you find it offensive.

Framers often make a capsule that consists of UV–3 filtered Plexiglas, an acid free mat, the object, and acid free backing board. This is sealed around the edges with clear tape. Two slightly overlapping pieces of Mylar are put on the back. This allows the piece to breathe while providing protection. Mylar on the back helps prevent water damage from occurring during the fighting of a fire. Several collectors have lost pieces because water drained down walls or bounced off a wall and soaked through the backing board of a frame.

Another form of encapsulation is to store a piece of paper between two sheets of inert polyester film (Mylar, Melinex, etc.) sealed along three of the edges with 3M–brand No. 415 double–sided tape. Allow plenty of space between the edge of the paper and the edge of the film. The main gain from this approach is less damage through handling.

Which brings us to the final threat to paper—YOU. It is up to you to learn how to properly handle, display, and store paper. Knowing about the techniques does little good if you do not practice them. Proper care is work. There is little fun involved. If you care about your paper, you have no choice.

Some tips: Your hands are oily and can easily transmit dirt. Wash your hands thoroughly before and after handling paper. If you are handling large quantities of paper, wash your hands several times during the handling period.

Avoid liquids around paper. Drink your coffee or soda somewhere else. Why tempt fate? We have learned the hard way. Now you will find no liquid in our work or storage areas.

Neither of us smoke, but many paper collectors and dealers do. Aside from the health hazards, consider the risks of fire and smoke. The only place in the paper field where smoking and paper should mix is when tobacco advertising and paper products are offered for sale.

When you have a problem involving the preservation of paper and need a professional, how do you find help? The easiest method is to contact the Foundation of the American Institute for Conservation of Historic and Artistic Works, 1400 16th Street, N.W., Suite 340, Washington, D.C. 20036 (phone [202] 232–6636, fax [202] 232–6630). This organization's Referral System provides a systematic, consistent method to identify and locate professional conservation services across the country including the selection of the most appropriate and qualified conservation professional.

Paper care can be learned. You have to make a conscious commitment in the beginning. Within a short period of time, it becomes second nature. The reward will be a valuable, well-preserved collection.

SPOTTING RESTRIKES, REPRODUCTIONS, COPYCATS, FANTASIES, AND FAKES

Given the endless supply of period paper, why is the field plagued by restrikes, reproductions, copycats, fantasies, and fakes? The answer is summed up in one word–GREED. Greed is everywhere. Collectors want and want and want. They want what their rivals have and want what no one else has. Little wonder fakers do so well. Reproduction, copycat, and fantasy manufacturers want a piece of the lucrative paper collectibles market. Hence, they produce goods in quantity, the principal effect of which is an undermining of market confidence. Sellers want the dollars involved from supplying rarities or selling in quantity.

While some of the difficulties rest with commercial manufacturers and wholesale importers who do not indelibly mark their products, the real culprits are private individuals. The camera, color photocopier, and computer with a color laser printer are just tools; the act to misuse them is a human decision.

Before discussing techniques used to spot restrikes, reproductions, copycats, fantasies, and fakes, it is necessary to define these terms as they relate to paper. Consider the distinctions carefully, then incorporate these words into your vocabulary for future use.

A *restrike* is a later example made from period plates or dies. If the printing technique is identical to that used during the original period of production, restrikes can be very difficult to spot. The critical question to ask yourself is: What is the possibility that the period separations or plates survived? The percentages are higher than you think.

A *reproduction* is an exact copy of a period piece. The most common tools used are the camera and photocopy machine. Using a camera, precise size duplication is possible. The good news is that some sharpness of image is lost. However, loss of sharpness that was easy to spot in reproductions done prior to the 1980s is now more difficult to spot due to the quality of today's cameras and films. Examples duplicated on a photocopy machine have a very slight reduction, even when copied at one hundred percent.

A *copycat* is a stylist copy. It has an image that strongly suggests a specific illustrator, period decorative motif, or shape. In the area of paper, it is used to create variants, objects that differ in some way, e.g., color or imagery, from commonly found examples. In paper, it really is an image oriented fantasy.

A *fantasy* is a topical paper item that did not exist during the initial period when a specific item or group of paper items was first introduced or when a personality or character was in their prime. Consider the following examples: a hand fan picturing a person long deceased; a post card set utilizing pictures of period trade cards; and, a cereal box with an altered image. Probably one of the most tasteless examples in the current market is the infamous "Last Breakfast Cereal" computer generated Wheaties cereal box containing a picture of Jesus Christ on the front cover.

Most restrike, reproduction, copycat, and fantasy items start life honestly. The manufacturers and wholesalers who sell them make no attempt to hide what they are. Again, it is worth acknowledging that they also do not go out of their way to permanently mark them for what they are. The problem rests with auctioneers, dealers, and others who buy these items, remove any markings that do exist, and attempt to pass them as period pieces.

One of the most common methods of marketing this material is through the advertisement of "warehouse" finds. A few object groups pictured in the advertisement may indeed have been found in an old warehouse, but the vast majority of paper items have a warehousing history that is measured in days and weeks rather than years and decades.

Fakes are deliberately meant to deceive. They are a major problem in the autograph, manuscript, and original art categories. They are a major contributing factor to the current decline of the sports card market. Fakes range in quality from those that only an expert can spot to examples that are outright laughable. However, there is nothing laughable about being deceived by a fake.

There are three steps that you need to take to protect yourself from restrikes, reproductions, copycats, fantasies, and fakes. First, constantly question the authenticity of what you are examining. Second, learn a few basic "alarm bells" that when they ring in your mind, you stop and look more closely. Third, know your selling source and get proper documentation.

Developing a questioning mindset is not as easy as it sounds. When you encounter a piece that you like, you really want to believe, not question. There is no fun in finding out that something is not what it pretends to be.

The good news is that, unlike some categories, e.g., furniture, most paper is right. This may also be the biggest problem. It is extremely easy to become lulled into complacency. The only safe approach is to be constantly on guard.

The key is to develop an alarm bell mentality. You look at a piece of paper. Without initially knowing why, an alarm bell sounds in your mind. Something is not quite right. The only way to stop the alarm from ringing is to examine the paper up close. These alarm bells are a collector's sixth sense. Once a bell rings, trust it. While you will experience a few false alarms, the vast majority of the time there will be a fire.

The first alarm bell is crispness of image. Images that are copied often appear muddy, losing resolution along the edges. Examine print type edges. Is there loss? Do lines that should connect actually connect? Does the same degree of ink consistency appear throughout the document? Loss of line detail in lettering is one of the best methods of spotting later copies of Currier and Ives prints, broadsides, and historical documents.

Make a study of print technology no matter what type of paper you collect. It is important for you to know the difference between a chromolithograph and four color separation printed piece. Most early prints were hand colored. A chromolithograph is done by placing layers of color on top of one another one at a time. Four color separation uses an overlapping four color, dot matrix system to achieve color tone. A nineteenth century paper item that reveals dot matrix printing under examination with a magnifying glass is a later copy.

The second alarm bell is paper itself. Take time to study paper types. Learn the differences between laid and wove, rag and pulp paper. Concentrate on understanding when certain paper types and styles were popular and when they fell out of favor. Read books that deal with paper technology. If you are friends with a local printer, ask for a mini–course in paper.

As you handle period paper objects in your collecting area, develop a feel for paper, i.e., its surface texture and heft. Study how it ages. Smell it. Old paper should have an inherent musty smell. Recently printed examples, even if they appear old, will smell of chemicals.

Different historical periods favored different paper sizes. In the eighteenth and nineteenth centuries when paper was expensive, sheets were halved, quartered, and eighthed to save money. As the size of the standard paper sheet differed, so also did the size of the division. An 1820s document on the wrong size paper should set off the alarm bells.

Development in printing press technology also influenced paper size. Each printer tries to design the size of their finished products to achieve maximum use of the printing sheet. Trim has to be paid for as does the paper used in the final product.

Paper collectors during the first half of the twentieth century often included among their holdings a study collection of period papers in order to understand composition, size, and typography. This practice has been abandoned by current paper collectors. It is a major oversight.

Often restrikes, reproductions, copycats, and fantasies are done on lesser quality paper than the period pieces they are mimicking. However, the opposite also is true. Again, the key is knowing what paper type is most likely to be encountered for a specific image or paper topic. Do not get frustrated. You will learn these subtleties in time.

The third alarm bell is ink. The chemical content of household and printer's ink changes continually. Consider household correspondence. Eighteenth century writers used a quill pen dipped in highly acidic oak gull ink. Late nineteenth and early twentieth century writers used fountain pens filled with blue inks. The ball point pen and flare tip are the common writing instruments of the later twentieth century.

Use good judgment and common sense. When examining an autograph album and all the signatures appear to have been written with the same pen, off go the alarm bells. If the signatures all look like they have been signed by the same hand, walk away.

The fourth alarm bell is typography and handwriting styles. Each historical period has its favorite type faces. Learn to identify them. An early nineteenth century document printed with a sans serif face is trouble. John Lewis' *Printed Ephemera* is a starting point, but only a starting point. It is up to you to memorize type faces and relate them to a specific date.

Those who were subjected to continual grade school handwriting exercises understand the importance that was placed on proper and legible script writing in the eighteenth, nineteenth, and first half of the twentieth centuries. We continue to hold in high esteem those individuals who wrote using fancy Spencerian script. Group handwriting styles by historical periods: 1700 to 1820; 1820 to 1880; 1880 to 1920; 1920 to 1940; 1940 to 1960; and post-1960. Whenever you handle a piece of manuscript from one of these periods, take a few seconds to study the hand. Before long, you will recognize identifiable style differences.

When working with handwritten documents, study the slope and letter formation of the hand. Over and over again in the antiques and collectibles field, consistency is taught as one of the primary keys to knowing if a piece is correct. The hardest problem handwriting fakers face is to maintain consistency of letter slope and formation. In addition, a hand that is too perfect should also trip the alarm bells.

The fifth alarm bell is color tone. Advances in printing inks accompanied by differing color tone period preferences are an excellent way to determine if a piece is authentic. Of all the alarm bells, this is perhaps the most difficult to learn if you do not have a discriminating, artistic eye. The best argument that we can make to encourage you to take the time to learn the color palette of different historical periods is that there is a correlation between printing color tones and those used in fashion, ceramic, glass, jewelry, and other decorative accessories for the same period. Learn the correct colors in one area and then apply what you learned with ease to other areas.

Color tone is helpful in spotting images produced by computer laser printers and color photocopiers. Examples done on these two machines tend to be brighter, i.e., have more vivid color. Take a few pieces from your collection to a color photocopier and make copies. Compare the two. You will quickly learn to make the necessary distinctions.

Price is the sixth alarm bell. When the price seems low, too low, check the piece. A condition problem may be the reason for the lower price. No matter, you need to know this as well in order to make an intelligent purchasing decision. If the condition is perfect, then think restrike, reproduction, copycat, or fantasy. If none of the other alarm bells sound, you may have found what every collector loves to brag about—a bargain.

Alarm bells have to be manufactured. They are made by critically handling thousands upon thousands of pieces of paper. When I wanted to learn how to identify period Frakturs, I asked one of the leading experts what his secret was to authentication. What he told me has been my work methodology for over twenty years. He said, "Handle and examine five hundred good objects. Once you do, you will never have any trouble spotting the bad material." How right he was.

Protect yourself by buying from reliable sources. Make certain that every seller supplies you with their name, full mailing address, and telephone number. Do not let them bully you by saying that they do not like to give out this information for security purposes. As a customer, you have a right to this information.

Further, ask the seller for a "money back, no questions asked" guarantee. Anything short of this is unsatisfactory. Nothing is gained by either party becoming involved in a "yes, you will"/"no I will not" return it argument. The one thing to remember is that if you ask to return an item, it must be the same item and in the same condition as when you acquired it. One of the reasons why many paper dealers resist returns is that unscrupulous customers switch a lesser example from their collection with the one they bought and then try to return the lesser example for a full refund.

Insist upon a receipt. The receipt should contain the full name, address, and telephone number of the seller. The item should be described fully, including: date, description, size, date of manufacture, any pre–existing condition problems, price you paid, and any applicable taxes. It makes no difference whether you pay by cash or check, which, by the way, is not an adequate receipt of your purchase. You have the right to an actual receipt.

Create a study collection of the restrikes, reproductions, copycats, fantasies, and fakes that you bought. Use them to educate yourself and others. Many collectors purposely acquire these items and place them beside period pieces as a constant visual reminder to be on the alert. Above all, do not send your mistakes back into the market. If you cannot live with them, trash them.

It is our hope that these hints help you avoid some of the pitfalls involved in buying paper. Do not expect to avoid them all. As experienced as we are, we still get fooled occasionally. However, we learn from our mistakes, hopefully making it much harder to fool us the next time. We survive because (1) we never know all there is to know and (2) we never stop learning. This is the real lesson of this chapter.

STATE OF THE MARKET

The paper market has reached early adulthood—mature, but still exhibiting a fair amount of youthful exuberance. It is willing and able to party at the drop of a hat, yet responsible enough to be trusted by collectors and dealers with a conservative bent. It has assumed its place as a primary antiques market. Its second fiddle days are over.

After a conservative childhood, the paper market experienced a rip–roaring youth. Early paper collectors made their home among the antique elites and academic community. They were mostly male and focused heavily on business and literary related paper. Paper with a female flare was collected as Victorian niceties. Nowhere is this more evident than in the categories covered in Maurice Rickards' *Collecting Paper Ephemera*—admission tickets, billheads and letterheads, book labels, dance programs, Flag Day emblems, handbills, labels, playing–card stationery, poster stamps, rewards of merit, sale notices, scraps/diecuts, toll/turnpike tickets, tradecards, valentines, and watchpapers. You will find less than half of these categories in *Warman's Paper* either because they are not defined collecting categories in the American paper marketplace or the number of American collectors is extremely small.

Let's give credit where credit is due. Early paper collectors did pioneering research in the areas of paper technology, the printing process, and typography. It is one of the great tragedies of the present paper market that few collectors and dealers care about these subjects. Paper technology, printing, and typograpy provide many of the clues necessary to identify restrikes, reproductions, copycats, and fakes. Ignorance of the past is one of the prices that has been paid for moving paper collecting into the mainstream of the modern collectibles market.

The American paper market owes a tremendous debt of gratitude to the advertising, advertising trade card, and post card collectors and dealers for laying the foundation stones upon which the present market is based. As the paper market progressed in the 1980s, it slowly consumed advertising, jilted the advertising trade card, and willingly watched post cards amble off and create their own market. Advertising collectors and dealers are in the process of regrouping in an attempt to establish their own specialized marketplace. Advertising trade cards have staged a comeback as a high ticket collectible in the 1990s. Post cards continue to keep one foot in and one foot outside of the mainstream paper marketplace.

The 1970s and 1980s brought a period of profound change in the American paper market. First, the number of collectors grew exponentially, drawn by paper's availability and affordability. Second, several key paper items, e.g., baseball trading cards and comic books, became hot trendy commodities. Third, market manipulators recognized and took advantage of opportunities in paper. A major market manipulation of stock and bond certificates took place between 1975 and 1985. Like all such manipulations, the bubble finally burst. Fourth, interior decorators and designers discovered paper. Paper now has two values: (1) collectible and (2) decorative.

However, this period's most important development was the arrival of the collector and dealer of paper. The initial attraction was paper items related to their collecting specialty. For example, William Boyd as Hopalong Cassidy licensed a large number of paper related material, ranging from coloring books to personal stationery. A Hoppy collection that does not contain these and other Hoppy paper items is incomplete.

As collectibles collectors became more familiar with the paper market, they began to realize that there was a wealth of supporting paper material that complemented their collections. Press kits for Hopalong Cassidy movies, promotional catalogs for Hopalong Cassidy merchandise, or the instruction sheet to build a Hoppy sales corral in a department store now became desirable to the Hoppy collector. These are utilitarian paper, not the traditional licensed or consumer products that constitute the bulk of most collections.

Further, collectors turned to paper in search of images of their favorite collectible, character, or personality. Hoppy's picture on the cover of *Life* and *Look* became "must have" items. Magazine tear sheets showing Hoppy promoting Motorola televisions, Chicken of the Sea, and other products were eagerly sought and purchased. In the 1980s, collecting grew in complexity, and the increasing role played by paper was one of the principal reasons.

The first signs of market fragmentation occurred in the 1970s as specialized post card publications and shows developed. The trend accelerated in the 1980s as sports trading cards, led by baseball trading cards, and comic books split off and created their own market. The Ephemera Society of America, through its annual and regional shows, continues to attempt to segregate the traditionalist paper categories from what they consider to be nouveau riche paper categories, e.g., cereal, radio, and television premiums, comic books, and non–sport and sport trading cards. Thus far, their efforts have only partially succeeded.

The main purpose of this historical account is to demonstrate that it is impossible in 1993 to talk about "a" paper market. There are many paper markets, each an entity unto itself. Further, the paper market is not restricted to paper aficionados any longer. It is home to crossover collectors, interior decorators, and market manipulators as well as serious paper collectors. In other words, it is just like the mainstream antiques and collectibles markets.

In fact, the paper market is healthier in 1993 than either the general antiques or collectibles market. The paper market benefited from the recession of the late 1980s and early 1990s. Its affordability attracted many individuals who were turned off elsewhere. The only problem is that it attracted the bad as well as the good.

At the end of the 1980s, a feeling developed among many paper dealers that their goods were underpriced. They raised prices, slowly at first and then more rapidly. The influx of new collectors and the competition it created fueled these price increases. Prices in most categories doubled or tripled in the five year period between 1989 and 1993.

In 1994 a growing resentment toward these higher prices is developing among established collectors. There is grumbling in the ranks that scarce material in many sectors of the paper market is very much overpriced. Post cards crashed through the $10,000 barrier, movie posters through the $50,000 barrier, and animation cels through the $100,000 barrier in the last several years. These are not prices that the average collector can afford. These are investor and speculator prices. Times are changing.

Collecting paper is fun only when the best items in a category are within reach of a collector with limited funding. When the best is no longer attainable because of cost, many collectors become discouraged and turn their attention elsewhere.

The paper market is at a crossroads. If it can maintain its affordability, it will keep its large collector base. It is one of the few markets where collectors significantly outnumber dealers. If prices continue to rise, paper's collector base will narrow, and it will find itself facing the same crises that currently are sapping much of the strength from the 1990s antiques and collectibles markets. The next three to four years are critical.

One of the strengths of the paper market is its show circuit. Instead of four to six major paper shows a year, there are now strong regional paper shows almost every week. Paper dealers also are a major component in the flea market circuit.

Initially paper shows were promoted by local dealers and collectors. Their success attracted the attention of several national antiques show promoters. At the moment the main thrust of these national promoters is to add paper dealers to their established show circuit. However, several are considering promoting their own paper shows.

Until the early 1990s, the two principal buying sources for paper were paper shows and mail order. The arrival of the paper mail auction threatens to change this picture significantly. Mail auctions have proven to be a surefire way to manipulate prices upward. They pit the greed of one collector against another in the privacy of their own homes. The mail auctioneer, who usually is a leading dealer, no longer has to wrestle with the dilemmas of how much to charge and to whom among his or her many clients should the piece be offered. Under the fairness guise, they put their best pieces up for bid. While they may gain some friends doing this, they make enemies of many of their long-time customers.

Mail auctions work only if they focus on the best pieces available in any specialty category. A mail order auction that features common pieces fails. In every instance, mail auctions are unlicensed and unregulated. Most are honestly run, but a few are not. Look for the mail auction trend to become even stronger as the 1990s progress.

In the 1980s, the paper market became literature rich. The arrival of *P.C.M.* on the scene gave the paper market a quality national periodical, a role that *P.A.C.* does not fill adequately. Numerous coffee table books and price guides on specific paper subjects were published. In many areas, e.g., movie posters and paperback books, multiple price guides are now available. Add to this niche targeted periodicals and collectors' club newsletters. Overall the paper market's support literature is among the best in the antiques and collectibles field. Only the comic book, sports card, and toy markets exceed it.

Exercise caution when relying upon specialized paper price guides. Publishing a price guide with unrealistic high prices is a favorite tool of the market manipulator. Misinformation, either deliberate or through ignorance, abounds. It is dangerous, plentiful, misinterpreted, and difficult to counter once it appears in print. A recent publication contained the following: "Instead, big money has invaded the game as exclusive puzzles, mounted once again on wood, and hand cut, are designed by specialists for corporate or private customers. For one of these one–of–a–kind pieces $2,000 may be a low figure." If the author is talking about older puzzles, he is whistling in the dark. Within the past year, I have purchased several puzzles that match the description given above for less than $100 each. If he is talking about modern Stave puzzles, some of which do retail for $2,000 plus, he certainly does not make that clear. The end result is that the author has confused the public and created the illusion of gold where only fool's gold exists. When someone writes and offers me a puzzle for $2,000, I am going to send them the name and address of the author of that book and strongly suggest that they ask him to buy it.

There is a need for a national paper collectors' organization that focuses on the concerns, desires, and needs of the ordinary collector. The Ephemera Society of America is not the answer. It is elitist. The programs are entirely too academic and out of touch with major collecting currents in paper. Its membership size clearly reflects this lack of responsiveness.

Further, the Society refuses to sell books about paper that list prices on the grounds that discussion of pricing degrades paper. Yet, its leadership is in the vanguard of individuals who are attempting to manipulate market prices upward. In our opinion, the simple reason that they do not want prices reported is that they do not want the public to know what they charge their customers for fear that their cheap buying sources will vanish and that their customers will find that they can buy the same quality items at far lower prices from someone else.

Given what we have said about The Ephemera Society of America and its leadership, it is obvious that we do not expect a ringing endorsement from this Society for our efforts. Nothing we have said is new. Many collectors and dealers have been talking about the Society this way for years. We are ready for the windstorm. Let it blow.

One of the major trends in the antiques and collectibles market is the growing internationalism of these markets. With some exceptions (e.g., posters), the American paper market remains primarily American. In this respect, it is behind the times. There are signs of change, but they are modest. When European and Japanese collectors finally do discover the American paper market, expect a ripple price effect of major proportions.

The biggest area of growth in paper in the 1990s focuses on the illustrator. In the 1980s, the number of collectible illustrators was less than twenty–five. In the 1990s, the number is in the hundreds, including such names as Anthony Cucchi, Edward M. Eggleston, Philip R. Goodwin, John Henry Hintermeister, Francis Tipton Hunter, and William M. Thompson.

Illustrator collectors are possessed. They will buy anything, just so it has artwork by their favorite illustrator; and, they usually are willing to pay higher prices than collectors who would be attracted to the same paper item for other reasons. Many of these illustrator collectors are reluctant to make their wants known or publish articles about their favorite artist for fear of attracting competitors and driving up prices. If they surface, it is most likely through seeker advertisements in trade papers.

The increasing emphasis on illustrators is symbolic of the growing complexity of the paper market in the 1990s. It has reached the point where it is virtually impossible for a single individual to keep track of all the market components. Paper generalists are an endangered species.

Warman's Paper fills the gap. It is the generalist source the market needs and upon which it can depend for guidance. Hopefully, when we write the state of the market chapter in a future edition, we will face the pleasant task of noting how *Warman's Paper* played a role in defining and providing an understanding of the paper market much as *Warman's Americana & Collectibles* did for twentieth century collectibles.

AUCTION HOUSES
AND DIRECT MAIL SOURCES

The following auctions and direct mail sources have provided catalogs and price lists to Norman E. Martinus or Rinker Enterprises, Inc. This information was used to prepare *Warman's Paper*. This material is most appreciated.

AUCTION HOUSES

American West Archives
Warren Anderson
PO Box 100
Cedar City, UT 84720
(801) 586-9497

Antebellum Covers
PO Box 3494
Gaithersburg, MD 20878
(301) 869-2623

W. Graham Arader III
1000 Boxwood Court
King of Prussia, PA 19406
(610) 825-6570

Kit Barry
143 Main Street
Brattleboro, VT 05301
(802) 254-2195

Robert F. Batchelder
1 West Butler Avenue
Ambler, PA 19002
(215) 643-1430

Michael Bennett Auctions
Pickering Road
Dover, NH 03820
(603) 335-1694

Cohasco, Inc.
PO Box 821
Yonkers, NY 10702
(914) 476-8500

Collectors' Emporium
Susan and Marty Weiner
800 W. Chaminade Drive
Hollywood, FL 33021
(305) 966-2220

Herman Darvick Autograph
   Auctions
PO Box 388
Rockville Centre, NY
   11571-0388
(516) 766-0289

William Doyle Galleries,
   Inc.
175 East 87th Street
New York, NY 10128
(212) 427-2730

Robert Edward Auctions
PO Box 1923
Hoboken, NJ 07030
(201) 792-9324

Grandma's Trunk
The Millards
PO Box 404
Northport, MI 49670
(616) 386-5351

C. E. Guarino
PO Box 49
Denmark, ME 04022
(209) 452-2123

Hake's Americana and
   Collectibles
PO Box 1444
York, PA 17405
(717) 848-1333

Dave Inman
424 Geneseo St.
Storm Lake, IA 50588
(712) 732-3372

Michael Ivankovich
   Antiques
PO Box 2458
Doylestown, PA 18901
(215) 345-6094

Howard Lowery
3818 W. Magnolia Blvd.
Burbank, CA 91505
(818) 972-9080

Miscellaneous Man
George Theofiles
PO Box 1776
New Freedom, PA 17349
(717) 235-4766

G. E. Moore
PO Box 414
Yucca Valley, CA 92286
Fax: (619) 365-9668

New Hampshire Book
   Auctions
Woodbury Rd.
Weare, NH 03281
(603) 529-1700

Postcards International
PO Box 2930
New Haven, CT
   06515-0030
(203) 865-0814

R. Niel & Elaine Reynolds
Box 133
Waterford, VA 22190
(703) 882-3574

Secondary Merchandising
  Specialists
2701 Arthur
Des Moines, IA 50317
(515) 263-9396

Robert W. Skinner Inc.
Bolton Gallery
357 Main St.
Bolton, MA 01740
(508) 779-6241

Swann Galleries, Inc.
104 E. 25th St.
New York, NY 10010
(212) 254-4710

The Old Paperphiles
PO Box 135
Tiverton, RI 02878
(401) 624-9420

Victorian Images
Russell S. Mascieri
PO Box 284
Marlton, NJ 08053
(609) 985-7711

Vintage Cover Story
PO Box 975
Burlington, NC 27215

DIRECT MAIL ORDER SOURCES

Steve and Linda Alsberg
9850 Kedvale
Skokie, IL 60076-1124
(708) 676-9850

American Resources
Larry L. Krug
18222 Flower Hill Road,
  Suite 299
Gaithersburg, MD 20879
(301) 926-8663

Charles Amery
PO Box 201
Peoria, IL 61650

Books West
PO Box 417760
Sacramento, CA 95841
(916) 331-4746

Cairns Antiques
Lorie Cairns
PO Box 26
Lemoncove, CA 93244
(209) 564-2158

Casterbridge Books
Peter K. Lennon
720 S. Dearborn, #601
Chicago, IL 60605

Cerebro
PO Box 1221
Lancaster, PA 17603
(800) 695-2235

Edward J. Craig
PO Box 3909
Newport, RI 02840
(401) 847-6498

Historic Originals
4424 Trescott Drive
Orlando, FL 32817-3158
(407) 677-5444

Timothy Hughes Rare &
  Early Newspapers
PO Box 3636
Williamsport, PA 17701
(717) 326-1045

Denis Jackson
PO Box 1958
Sequim, WA 98382
(206) 683-2559

Ira S. Mesbane
PO Box 356
Plainview, NY 11803
(516) 935-7977

Ken Pierce Books
PO Box 332
Park Forest, IL 60466

Rebecca of Sunny Brook
  Farm
Rebecca Greason
PO Box 209
Hershey, PA 17033
(717) 533-3039

Ken Ritchie
3825 Bowen Ave.
Memphis, TN 38122
(901) 323-6195

Harry S. Ross
Soitenly Stooges
PO Box 72
Skokie, IL 60076
(708) 432-9270

Brian Russell
PO Box 1734
Royal Oak, MI 48068
(313) 544-3373

Kenneth E. Schneringer
271 Sabrina Ct.
Woodstock, GA 30188
(404) 926-9383

Gary Snover
PO Box 9696
San Bernardino, CA 92427
(909) 883-5849

Star Shots
5389 Bearup Street
Port Charlotte, FL 33981
(813) 697-6935

The Card Coach
PO Box 128
Plover, WI 54467
(715) 341-5452

The Paper Soldier
Barbara and Jonathan
   Newman
8 McIntosh Lane
Clifton Park, NY 12065
(518) 371-9202

Tibbetts Corner
PO Box 1449
Lexington, VA 24450
(703) 464-4326

Gordon and Diane Totty
347 Shady Lake Parkway
Baton Rouge, LA 70810

Valley Books
199 N. Pleasant
Amherst, MA 01002
(413) 256-1508

Harry A. Victor
1422 18th Ave.
San Francisco, CA 94122
(415) 664-4286

Westwood
P O Box 455
Holyoke, MA 01041-0455
(413) 533-5481

Willow Valley Antiques
392 Twitchell Rd.
Mansfield, OH 44903
(419) 529-8787

SHOWS

The following list provides you with information regarding paper shows throughout the country. We regret that this list is not more comprehensive, but acknowledge that it is a starting point. For more information, check current issues of *P.C.M.* and *P.A.C.*

ALABAMA

Birmingham
Postcard Show/early September
Parliment Hotel, 420 South 20th St.
Promoter: Charlie McCoy
(706) 335-3976

ARIZONA

Phoenix
Phoenix Paper Collectibles Show/mid
February, late July
Tower Plaza, 38th and Thomas Rd.
Promoter: Jack Black Shows
PO Box 61172
Phoenix, AZ 85082
(602) 943-1766

Sierra Vista
Roadrunner Stamps Club Stamp, Coin and
Collectible Show/late October
Sierra Suites, 391 E. Fry Blvd.
Promoter: Douglas Syson
300 E. Vista
Bisbee, AZ 85603
(602) 432-7096

ARKANSAS

Little Rock
Arkansas Postcard Club Show/late March
Arkansas Livestock Show Grounds, Arts &
Crafts Bldg.
Promoter: Jim Pfeifer
#15 Piedmont Lane
Little Rock, AR 02174
(617) 646-3576

CALIFORNIA

Arcadia
Greater San Gabriel Valley Postcard &
Paper Collectibles Show/late March,
early November
Masonic Hall, 50 W. Duarte Rd.
Promoter: Nick Farago
PO Box 217
Temple City, CA 91790
(818) 281-3390

Culver City
Western National Antique & Collectable
Show & Sales/mid March
Veteran's Memorial Building, 4117
Overland Ave., Culver City
Promoter: Western National
John Nutting
1309 Pauline Way
Las Vegas, NV 89104
(702) 382-7043

Fresno
Fashion Fair Mall Sports Card &
Collectibles Show/late January
Fresno Fashion Fair Mall
Promoter: Cal Bellini
41593 Camino Lorado
Temecula, CA 92592
(714) 676-0524

Fullerton
Second Sunday Stamp, Postcard & Paper
Collectibles Show/mid March, April,
June, July, August, September, October,
November, December
Days Inn, 91 Freeway at Raymond Ave.
Promoter: E. Swonger
Box 847
Anaheim, CA 92815-0847
(714) 535-2794

Hemet

Hemet Valley Mall Antique & Collectibles
 Show/late Dec-early January
Hemet Valley Mall
Promoter: Cal Bellini
41593 Camino Lorado
Temecula, CA 92592
(714) 676-0524

Mission Hills

14th Annual Paperback Collectors Show &
 Sale/early April
Mission Hills Inn
Promoter: Tom Lesser
(818) 349-3844

Montecito

Santa Barbara Postcard and Paper
 Collectibles Show/early May
Mira Mar Hotel, 1555 So. Jameson Lane
Promoter: R & N Postcard Company
Nick Farago
PO Box 217
Temple City, CA 91790
(818) 281-3390

North Hollywood

Hollywood Collector's Show/mid January,
 early April
Beverly Garland Resort Hotel, 4222
 Vineland
Promoter: Ave. Ray Courts
PO Box 5040
Spring Hill, FL 34606
(904) 683-5110

Palm Springs

Palm Springs Mall Antique & Collectible
 Show/late January
Palm Springs Mall, Farrel & Tahquitz
Promoter: Cal Bellini
41593 Camino Lorado
Temecula, CA 92592
(714) 676-0524

Pasadena

Greater LA Postcard & Paper Collectibles
 Show/early February, early June, late
 September, early October
Elks Hall, 400 W. Colorado Blvd.
Promoter: Nick Farago

PO Box 217
Temple City, CA 91790
(818) 281-3390

Pasadena

Nostalgia & Collectibles Show & Sale/
 early January, mid June, early October
Pasadena Convention Center, 300 E.
 Green St.
Promoter: Doug Wright
PO Box 69308
West Hollywood, CA 90069
(213) 656-1266

Pasadena

Rose Bowl Flea Market/mid Jan, Feb,
 March, April, May, June
Rose Bowl
Promoter: R. G. Canning Attractions
PO Box 400
Maywood, CA 90270
(213) 587-5100

Pomona

Movie & Entertainment Memorabilia &
 Collectibles Show & Sale/mid
 December
Fairplex La County Fair & Exposition
 Complex
Promoter: Bob Sass Productions
PO Box 56268
Sherman Oaks, CA 91413

Sacramento

Seventh Annual California's Capital Show/
 mid January
Scottish Rite Temple, 6151 H St.
Promoter: Natalie Schafer
2820 Echo Way
Sacramento, CA 95821
(916) 971-1953

San Diego

Greater San Diego Postcard and Paper
 Collectibles Show/early December, late
 April
Al Bahr Temple, 5400 Kearny Mesa
Promoter: Nick Farago
PO Box 217
Temple City, CA 91790
(818) 281-3390

San Francisco

American's Largest Antiques & Collectible
  Sales/mid February, late May
Cow Palace
Promoter: Christine Palmer
4001 NE Halsey
Portland, OR 97232
(503) 282-0877

San Francisco

San Francisco Bay Area Postcard Sale/late
  January, mid February, mid July
Holiday Inn-Foster City Blvd., 1221 Chess
  Drive
Promoter: Jan Banneck
PO Box 26
San Ramon, CA 94583
(510) 837-7907

San Francisco

26th California International Antiquarian
  Book Fair/mid February
San Francisco Concourse, 8th & Brannon
Promoter: Cynthia Traina
116 New Montgomery St., Suite 106
San Francisco, CA 94105
(415) 495-0100

San Rafael

Marin Paper and Ephemera Extravaganza/
  late January
Marin Civic Center, Exhibition Hall
Promoter: Kingsbury Productions
4555 N. Pershing Ave., Suite 33-138
Stockton, CA 95207
(209) 467-8433

Santa Cruz

7th California Central Coast Postcard &
  Paper Memorabilia Show/early April
Holiday Inn, 611 Ocean St.
Promoter: Mike Rasmussen
PO Box 726
Marina, CA 93933
(408) 384-5460

Stockton

The West Coast Americana Paper Show/
  late May, late October
Scottish Rite Temple, 33 W. Alpine Ave.

Promoter: Kingsbury Productions
4555 N. Pershing Ave., Suite 33-138
Stockton, CA 95207
(209) 467-8438

West Covina

Eastland Mall Antique & Collectibles
  Show/early January
Eastland Mall, Citrus at Workman
Promoter: Cal Bellini
41593 Camino Lorado
Temecula, CA 92592
(714) 676-0524

COLORADO

Denver

Postcard and Western Paper Show/mid
  July
Promoter: Giorgian Zekay
3003 Valmont Rd.
Boulder, CO 80301
(303) 442-2469

CONNECTICUT

Bristol

3rd Paper Quest/late November
Bristol Eastern High School
Promoter: Show Coordinator
140 Maxine Rd.
Bristol, CT 06010

Hartford

Papermania and Papermania Plus/early
  January and late August
Hartford Civic Center
Promoter: Hillcrest Promotions
PO Box 152
Wethersfield, CT 06109
(203) 529-7582

Litchfield

15th Annual Litchfield Post Card Show/
  late September
Litchfield Fire House, 258 West St.
Promoter: Peter Maronn
180 Goodwin St.
Bristol, CT 06010
(203) 589-6984

Manchester

Annual Central Connecticut Postcard
    Show & Sale/early October
East Catholic High School
Promoter: Herb Stevenson
PO Box 555
Manchester, CT 06040
(203) 649-7560

Meriden

Connecticut Postcard Club's 12th Annual
    Postcard Bourse/late April
Ramada Inn, 275 Research Parkway
Promoter: Peter Maronn
180 Goodwin St.
Bristol, CT 06010
(203) 589-6984

Old Greenwich

Ephemera Thirteen/mid March
Hyatt Regency Greenwich, 1800 East
    Putnam Ave., Old Greenwich, CT
Promoter: Jacqueline Sideli Antique Shows
Box 67
Malden Bridge, NY 12115
(518) 766-4968

Ridgefield

Annual SW Connecticut Antiquarian Book
    Fair/early October
East Ridge Middle School
Promoter: Deer Park Books
609 Kent Rd.
Gaylordsville, CT 06755
(203) 350-4140

FLORIDA

Fort Lauderdale

Miami Stamp Expo early January
Boward County Convention Center, 1950
    Eisenhower Blvd.
Promoter: Alvin Krasne
PO Box 6279
Hollywood, FL 33021
(305) 987-1104

Jacksonville

Dixie Lane Extravaganza Collectibles
    Show/mid January

Morocco Temple Center, St. John Bluff Rd.
    South
Promoter: Chip Nofal
(904) 641-4821

Jenson Beach

20th Annual Port St. Lucie Stamp, Coin,
    Postcard Show & Sale/late March
Jensen Beach American Legion Hall, 3195
    NE Savannah Rd.
Promoter: David Ulian Larson
1342 SW Patricia Ave.
Port St. Lucie, FL 34953-4903

Lakeland

Collectorama Show/mid March
Lakeland Civic Center, 700 W. Lemon St.
Promoter: Collectorama Shows, Inc.
Nick: (813) 647-2052; Ed: (407) 368-7422
3425 S Florida Ave
Lakeland, FL 33803

Miami

IPAFEST mid January
Holiday Inn, LeJeune Centre, 950 NW
    LeJeune Rd.
Promoter: Connie Skillman
PO Box 617
Milford, OH 45150

Orlando

Postcard Show/late January
Las Palmas Hotel, 6233 International Dr.
Promoter: Postcard Society, Inc.
PO Box 1765
Manassas, VA 22110

Palm Beach Gardens

Palm Beach Stamp, Coin & Baseball Card
    Festival/late June, late July, late August,
    late September, late October, early
    December
MacArthur Holiday Inn, PGA Blvd, I-95
Promoter: Joseph Banfi
Cove Shopping Center
5965 SE Federal Hwy.
Stuart, FL 34998
(407) 283-2128

Pompano Beach

TROPOBEX Annual Antique Post Card
  Winter Show/early January
Pompano Beach Civic Center, 1801 NE 6
  St.
Promoter: Ben Ladin
(407) 483-5600

St. Petersburg

10th Paper Collectibles & Postcard Show
  & Sale/late February
National Guard Armory, 38th Ave.
Promoter: Evans Events
31 W. 5th St.
Pottstown, PA 19464

St. Petersburg

12th Annual Antiquarian Book Fair/mid
  March
St. Petersburg Campus, Acitivity Center
Promoter: Larry Kellogg
(813) 525-0422

Tampa

Sunshine Postcard Clubs 17th Annual
  Postcard Show/early February
IBEW Hall, 5621 Harney Rd.
Promoter: Sunshine Postcard Club
PO Box 1232
St. Petersburg, FL 33731

Winter Haven

Universal Antique Show/early January
Florida Citrus Blvd, Nora Mayo Hall
Promoter: Roberta & Charlie Barnes
5416 Milan Dr.
Orlando, FL 32810

GEORGIA

Atlanta

12th Annual Georgia Postcard Club Show/
  early March
Atlanta Sheraton Airport Hotel, 1325
  Virginia Ave.
Promoter: Don Skillman
6646 Shiloh Road
Goshen, OH 45122
(513) 625-9518

Atlanta

Postcard Show/early November
Castlegate Hotel, I-75 Howell Mill Rd.
Promoter: Charlie McCoy
(706) 335-3976

Macon

Middle Georgia Coin, Stamp, Postcard
  Show/late January
Macon Colesium, I-16 at Colesium Dr.

HAWAII

Honolulu

Hawaii All-Collectors Show/late July
Neal Blaisdell Exhibition Hall
Promoter: Ilene Wong
PO Box 61704
Honolulu, HI 96839-1704
(808) 941-9754

ILLINOIS

Bloomington

CORNPEX mid November
Scottish Rite Temple
Promoter: CBPS
Janice Jenkins
PO Box 625
Bloomington, IL 61702-0625
(309) 663-2761

Collinsville

4th Metro-East Postcard Show/early April
VFW Hall, 1234 Vandalia St
Promoter: Holger Danielsen
PO Box 630
O'Fallon, IL 62269
(618) 632-1921

Collinsville

17th Annual Gateway Postcard Club
  Show/early September
VFW Hall, 1234 Vandalia St
Promoter: Holger Danielsen
PO Box 630
O'Fallon, IL 62269
(618) 632-1921

Evanston

15th Annual Evanston Postcard Show &
   Paper Collectible Bourse/early
   November
Levy Center, 1700 Maple
Promoter: Louis Berman
(708) 256-4161

Hillside

Greater Chicago Postcard Show/late April,
   late November
Holiday Inn, I-290 and Manheim
Promoter: Susan Brown Nicholson
PO Box 595
Lisle, IL 60532
(708) 964-5240

Peoria

D-J Postcard Show/late June
Holiday Inn, 4400 Brandywine Dr.
Promoter: D-J Postcards Shows
Jerry Andreen
PO Box 2301
Rockford, IL 61131
(815) 397-3100

Rockford

Rockford Illinois Fall Postcard Show/early
   December
Ken-Rock Community Center, 3200 11th
   St.
Promoter: D-J Postcards Shows
PO Box 2301
Rockford, IL 61131
(815) 397-3100

Rockford

Rock Valley Post Card Club Show/mid
   April
Promoter: Molly Crocker
PO Box 2722
Rockford, IL 66132
(815) 282-5166

Rock Island

Blackhawk Post Card Club's 10th Annual
   Post Card Show/late March
Knights of Columbus Hall, 420 23rd St
Promoter: Black Hawk Post Card Club
1325 45 St.

Rock Island, IL 61201
(309) 786-1335

INDIANA

Evansville

6th Annual Twin Bridges Postcard & Paper
   Collectibles Show/late March
Vanderburgh Auditorium Convention
   Center, 717 Locust St.
Promoter: Mike Finley
RR1, Box 847
Tell City, IN 47586
(812) 836-2747

Indianapolis

Crossroads of America Postcard Show/
   early October
Indiana State Fair Grounds, SE Pavillion
Promoter: George Mitchell
2154 N. Talbott
Indianapolis, IN 46202
(317) 924-0712

Indianapolis

Indianapolis Postcard Club's 18th Annual
   Postcard Show and Sale/early May
Indiana State Fairgrounds, SW Pavilion,
   1202 East 38th St.
Promoter: John McDonough
5881 Downing Dr.
Indianapolis, IN 46208-1635
(317) 290-9276

South Bend

Maple City Postcard Club Show/late
   March
Hedwig Hall, 700 Western St.
Promoter: Dave Long and Diane Allmen
(219) 264-0013

IOWA

Cedar Rapids

Cedar Rapids Post Card Club Show/late
   October
Sheraton Inn, 525 33rd Ave., SW
Promoter: Vivian Rineaberger
4548 Fairlane Dr., NE
Cedar Rapids, IA 52402
(319) 393-6743

Clive

Postcard & Paper Show/late September
Des Moines West Travelodge, 11001
    University Ave.
Promoter: Hawkeye Postcard Club
PO Box 4683
Des Moines, IA 50306
(515) 279-5418

Dubuque

D-J Postcard Show/late August
Midway Best Western, 3100 Dodge
Promoter: D-J Postcards Shows
Jerry Andreen
PO Box 2301
Rockford, IL 61131
(815) 397-3100

KANSAS

Wichita

Wichita Postcard Club Show/mid October
All Saint's Gymnasium, 3313 Grand
Promoter: John Pittman
3900 N. St. Clair
Wichita, KS 67204
(316) 838-3038

KENTUCKY

Louisville

Postcard Show/late August
Hurstborne Hotel, 9700 Bluegrass
    Parkway
Promoter: John McClintock
PO Box 1765
Manassas, VA 22110
(703) 368-2757

MAINE

Portland

Fifth Annual Postcard Show and Sale/mid
    August
Verrillo's Convention Center, 155
    Riverside St.

Portland

Third Annual Maine Paper Americana
    Show/mid July
Portland Exposition Building
Promoter: Oliver & Gannon Assoc.
PO Box 131
Altamont, NY 12009
(518) 861-5062

MARYLAND

Baltimore

Greater Baltimore Collectors Mart/late
    March, mid November
Pikesville Armory
Promoter: Annapolis Marketing Inc.
6506 Pyle Rd.
Bethesda, MD 20817

Baltimore

PIKPOST late October
Days Hotel, I-83, exit 17
Promoter: Perry Judelson
PO Box 7675
Baltimore, MD 21207
(410) 655-5239

Baltimore

Suburban Washington/Baltimore Coin
    Show/late March
Baltimore Convention Center, Festival Hall
Promoter: Edward Kuszmar
(407) 368-7422

Havre de Grace

Chesapeake Postcard Fair/mid April
Policeman's Community Center
Promoter: Mary Martin
4899 Pulaski Highway
Perryville, MD 21903
(410) 575-7768

Towson

Towson Postcard & Paper Show/early
    March, early May
Quality Inn, Hampton Room, 1015 York
    Rd.
Promoter: Dee Delcher
413 E. Lake Ave.
Baltimore, MD 21212
(410) 433-1532

MASSACHUSETTS

Barrington
Berkshire Antiques Show/late July
Barrington Fairgrounds, Rt. 7
Promoter: Bernice Bornstein Show
PO Box 421
Marblehead, MA 01945
(508) 744-2731

Barrington
Searles Castle Antiquarian Book Fair/early
   August
John Dewey Academy, Main St., Rt. 7
Promoter: Bernice Bornstein Show
PO Box 421
Marblehead, MA 01945
(508) 744-2731

Boston
The New . . . New Year's Show at the
   Castle/early January
Park Plaza Castle
Promoter: Bernice Bornstein Show
PO Box 421
Marblehead, MA 01945
(508) 744-2731

Boxborough
Paper & Collectibles Show/early February/
   late September
Boxborough Host Hotel
Promoter: Bernice Bornstein Show
PO Box 421
Marblehead, MA 01945
(508) 744-2731

Brimfield
Brimfield Postcard & Ephemera Show/late
   June, mid September
White House Field, Route 20 West
Promoter: Alan Grab, (305) 372-4107
Harris Gray, (506) 867-7210

East Watertown
Card-O-Rama Show/mid April
Armenian Cultural and Educational
   Center, 47 Nichols Ave.

Promoter: Bill Crane
898 Massachusetts Ave., Apt. 6
Arlington, MA 02174

Marlborough
Big Paper & Collectible Show/early
   December
Royal Plaza Trade Center
Promoter: Bernice Bornstein Show
PO Box 421
Marblehead, MA 01945
(508) 744-2731

Peabody
Boston-Peabody Classic/early April, late
   August, mid December
Holiday Inn, Route One
Promoter: Joel Hall
25 Mystic St.
Arlington, MA 02174
(617) 646-7757

Westford
Boston Antique Photographic Image Show/
   late March
Westford Regency
Promoter: Russell Norton
PO Box 1070
New Haven, CT 06504
(203) 562-7800

West Springfield
Eastern States Ephemera, Book,
   Advertising and Post Card Show & Sale/
   early November
Eastern States Exposition Center, 1305
   Memorial Ave.

MICHIGAN

Berkley
Marty Raskin Postcard & Paper Show/mid
   August
Knights of Columbus Hall, 2299 W. 12
   Mile Rd.
Promoter: Marty Raskin
PO Box 48153
Oak Park, MI 48237
(313) 968-5910

Kalamazoo

SW Michigan Postcard Club Postcard
  Bourse/mid April, mid October
Kalamazoo County Fairgrounds, 2900
  Lake St.
Promoter: Sue Hodapp
1415 Seminole St.
Kalamazoo, MI 49006
(616) 344-2545

Lansing

16th Michigan Antiquarian Book and
  Paper Show/early October
Lansing Center, 333 E. Michigan Ave.
(517) 332-0112

MINNESOTA

St. Paul

Twin City Postcard Club Spring Show/late
  March, mid September
The Kelly Inn, I-94 at Marion St
Promoter: W. R. Everett
111 Marquette #1202
Minneapolis, MN 55401-2029
(612) 333-2219

MISSOURI

Hannibal

Post Card Show of the Mark Twain Post
  Card Club/mid October
Holiday Inn, Hwy. 61 South
Promoter: Sally Polc
24 Brown Estates
Hannibal, MO 63401
(314) 248-1216

MONTANA

Helena

Montana Postcard & Paper Show & Sale/
  mid September
Colonial Inn, 2301 Colonial Dr.
Promoter: Tom Mulvaney
PO Box 814
East Helena, MT 59635
(406) 227-8790

NEBRASKA

Omaha

Postcard and Paper Show/late March, late
  August
Ramada Inn Airport, Abbott Dr. and
  Locust St.
Promoter: David Edwards
PO Box 3402
Omaha, NE 68103
(402) 292-2646

NEVADA

Las Vegas

Western National Antique & Collectable
  Show & Sales/late March
Hacienda Hotel & Casino
Promoter: Western National
John Nutting
1309 Pauline Way
Las Vegas, NV 89104
(702) 382-7043

Las Vegas

Western National Antique & Collectable
  Show & Sales/late November
Cashman Field Center
Promoter: Western National
John Nutting
1309 Pauline Way
Las Vegas, NV 89104
(702) 382-7043

Las Vegas

Western National Antique & Collectable
  Show & Sales/mid May
Union Plaza Hotel & Casino
Promoter: Western National
John Nutting
1309 Pauline Way
Las Vegas, NV 89104
(702) 382-7043

NEW HAMPSHIRE

Hudson

Granite State Post Card Show & Sale/mid
  June, early October
Lions Hall, Lions Ave.

Promoter: David Sysyn
Box 341
Hancock, NH 03349
(603) 827-3654

Portsmouth
Strawberry Bank Antiquarian Book Fair/
    early October
Portsmouth High School
Promoter: Bernice Bornstein Show
PO Box 421
Marblehead, MA 01945
(508) 744-2731

NEW JERSEY

Belmar
10th Annual Jersey Shore Post Card Show/
    early March, early November
John Taylor Pavilion, Front Ocean and 5th
    Ave.
Promoter: John McGrath
(201) 363-3121

Cherry Hill
Film Collectors Expo/late February
Holiday Inn, Route 70
Promoter: JD Productions
PO Box 726
Cherry Hill, NJ 08003
(609) 795-0436

Hackensack
The Great Paper Chase/mid February, mid
    August
Rothman Center, Fairleigh-Dickson Univ.
Promoter: America Shows Ent., Inc.
PO Box 538
Round Lake, NY 12151
(518) 899-6190

Hasbrouck Heights
BEPEX late February
Holiday Inn, 283 Route 17 South
Promoter: L. Liebowitz
PO Box 412
E. Brunswick, NJ 08816
(908) 247-1093

Jersey City
Liberty Collectibles Expo/late June
Liberty State Park

Promoter: Stella Show Management Co.
163 Terrace St.
Haworth, NJ 07641
(201) 384-0010

Mahwah
Great American County Fair/late April
Ramapo College
Promoter: Stella Show Management Co.
163 Terrace St.
Haworth, NJ 07641
(201) 384-0010

Mt. Laurel
POCAX/early April
Budget Motor Lodge, Route 70 &
    Fellowship Road
Promoter: David Grubbs
212 Kathy Dr.
Yardley, PA 19067

Mt. Laurel
Postcard Show/mid February, mid July,
    mid September, early December
Budget Motor Lodge, Route 70 &
    Fellowship Road
Promoter: Postcard Society, Inc.
PO Box 1765
Manassas, VA 22110

Parsippany
33rd Annual Garden State Post Card
    Collectors Club Post Card Show/mid
    October
P. A. L. Center, 33 Baldwin Rd.
Promoter: Dolores Kirchgessner
421 Washington St.
Hoboken, NJ 07030
(201) 659-1922

Ramsey
America Antiques & Craft Show/early
    March
Don Bosco Prep School
Promoter: Stella Show Management Co.
163 Terrace St.
Haworth, NJ 07641
(201) 384-0010

Somerville

Garden State Spring Stamp Fair/late April,
mid August
Holiday Inn, Route 22 East
Promoter: L. Liebowitz
PO Box 412
E. Brunswick, NJ 08816
(908) 247-1093

Wayne

Garden State Stamp Show/early January
Wayne Manor, Route 23
Promoter: L. Liebowitz
PO Box 412
E. Brunswick, NJ 08816
(908) 247-1093

NEW YORK

Albany

18th Annual Albany Institute of History &
Art Antiquarian Book & Ephemera Fair/
late November
New Scotland Ave. Armory
Promoter: Oliver & Gannan Assoc.
PO Box 131
Altamont, NY 12009
(518) 861-5062

Clayton

14th Annual Thousand Islands Stamp,
Coin, Postcard and Collectibles Show/
late July
Clayton Arena
Promoter: Shayne Robbins
PO Box 676
Cape Vincent, NY 13618
(315) 654-2571

Clinton

16th Annual Central New York Postcard
Club Show/mid September
Clinton Arena, Kirkland Ave.
Promoter: Ruth Weimer
RD 2, Box 173
Canastota, NY 13032
(315) 697-7157

Corning

Annual Corning National Postcard Fair/
mid June

Corning Glass Center
Promoter: Mary Martin
4899 Pulaski Highway
Perryville, MD 21903
(410) 575-7768

Fredonia

Annual Stamp & Postcard Show/early
October
Fredonia Days Inn
Promoter: W. Sedimayer
45 Curtis Place
Fredonia, NY 14063
(716) 679-7936

Huntington

Great Long Island Paper, Book &
Ephemera Fair/late January, late October
New York State Armory, 100 E. 5th St.
Promoter: Shows by Ruth
Ruth Kleckowski
15 Richmond Place
Commack, NY 11725
(518) 499-7586

Kingston

Kaaterskill Post Card Club Show/early
April, early August
Ramada Inn, Thruway Exit 19
Promoter: Nancy Foutz
2182 Lucas Turnpike
High Falls, NY 12440
(914) 687-0175

Levittown

16th Annual Postcard & Paper Ephemera
Show/early April
Israel Community Center, 3235
Hempstead Turnpike
Promoter: LI Postcard Club, Charles
Huttunen
(516) 261-4031

New York

New York Coliseum Antiques Show/late
March
New York Coliseum, Columbus Circle
Promoter: Stella Show Management Co.
163 Terrace St.
Haworth, NJ 07641
(201) 384-0010

New York

16th International Post Card Bourse/late
   April, mid November
Days Inn, 440 W. 57th St.
Promoter: Leah Schnall
67-00 192nd St.
Flushing, NY 11365
(718) 454-1272

New York

Paper Collectibles & Movie Memorabilia
   Show/mid March
St. Frances Xavier, 30 W. 16th St.
Promoter: Bob and Paul Gallagher
72-39 66th Place
Glendale, NY 11385
(718) 497-6575

Rochester

D-J Postcard Show/mid July
Midway Best Western, Rt. 52 and Rt. 14
Promoter: D-J Postcards Shows
Jerry Andreen
PO Box 2301
Rockford, IL 61131
(815) 397-3100

Schenectady

Upstate NY Postcard Club Show/late
   September
Shaughnessy Hall, 1 S. Church St.
Promoter: James Davis
5 Cutter Dr.
Johnstown, NY 12095

NORTH CAROLINA

Durham

1993 Postcard Society Sales/mid April
Holiday Inn-Durham West, 3460
   Hillsborough Rd.
Promoter: John McClintock
PO Box 1765
Manassas, VA 22110
(703) 368-2757

OHIO

Ashland

Johnny Appleseed Postcard Club Show/
   mid June

Ashland Senior High School
Promoter: James Perkins
PO Box 132
Ashland, OH 44805

Cincinnati

Don Skillman's 1st Annual December
   Postcard Show/early October, early
   December
Ramada Hotel, 5901 Pfeiffer Rd
Promoter: Don Skillman
6646 Shiloh Rd.
Goshen, OH 45122
(513) 625-9518

Cleveland

Saturday's Child Nostalgia Comics &
   Cards Show/mid August, early October
Harley House Independence, 5300
   Rockside Rd.
Promoter: Joe Tricarichi
2520 Ashurst
Cleveland, OH 41118
(216) 932-8596

Columbus

Columbus Paper Fair/early January, mid
   April
Veterans Memorial Convention Center,
   300 West Broad St.
Promoter: Columbus Productions, Inc.
3280 Riverside Dr., Suite 18
Columbus, OH 43221
(614) 459-7469

Columbus

Heart of Ohio Post Card Club Show/mid
   September
Quality Inn Airport, 4801 E. Broad St. &
   Hamilton Rd.
Promoter: Ron Hilbert
PO Box 67
Unionville Center, OH 43077
(614) 873-4552

Dayton

Dayton Ohio Postcard Show/late March,
   late September
Holiday Inn, Englewood
Promoter: Dave Long, Diane Allman
(219) 264-0013

New Philadelphia

2nd Annual Tri-County Post Card Club
Postcard & Paper Show/early April
Riverfront Antique Mall & Auction Center
Promoter: Ray Ferrell
332 St. Clair Avenue
Cadiz, OH 43907
(614) 942-3465

Sandusky

Stamp & Postcard Show/early March, mid
April
Sheraton Sandusky Inn, St. Rt. 250 at
1119 Sandusky Mall Blvd.
Promoter: L. Smith
PO Box 421
Cleveland, OH 44146
(216) 943-4468

OKLAHOMA

Tulsa

T-Town Postcard Club Show/late May
Holiday Inn South, 145th & Broken Arrow
Expressway
Promoter: Leroy Hatchett
PO Box 70034
Tulsa, OK 74170
(918) 743-1854

OREGON

Hillsboro

The Great Northwest Americana Paper
Ephemera & Book Fair/late March, mid
April
Washington County Fairplex, 872 N. E.
28th St.
Promoter: Kingsbury Productions, David
and Katherine Kreider
4555 N. Pershing Avenue, Suite 33-138
Stockton, CA 95207
(209) 467-8438

Oak Grove

2nd Annual Willamette Valley Postcard
Club Show & Sale/mid September
Oak Grove Community Club, Cedar &
Maple

Promoter: Cathy Clark
P. O. Box 135
Lake Oswego, OR 97034

Portland

America's Largest Antiques & Collectibles
Sale/early March
Portland Expo Center
Promoter: Christine Palmer
4001 NE Halsey
Portland, OR 97232
(503) 282-0877

Portland

Fall Post Card Show and Sale/mid October
Italian Heritage Center, Outer Congress St.
Promoter: J. Vierra
PO Box 6815
Portland, OR 04101

Portland

Greater Portland Postcard and Paper
Collectibles Show/mid October
Portland Scottish Rite Temple, 709 SW
15th at Morrison St.
Promoter: R & N Postcard Co.
Roger LeRoque
PO Box 217
Temple City, CA 91790
(818) 281-3390

Portland

Webfooters Postcard Club Show and Sale/
late April
National Guard Armory, 500 NE Division
St.
Promoter: Doris Brockell
5014 NE 25th
Portland, OR 97211-6315
(503) 282-2130

PENNSYLVANIA

Allentown

Great Eastern U. S. Antique Book & Paper
Advertising Collectibles Show/late April
Agricultural Hall, 17th & Chew St.,
Allentown Fairgrounds

Promoter: Joyce Heilman, Manager
R. D. 2, Box 141
Zionsville, PA 18092
(610) 967-2181

Allentown

Matchcover Swapfest/late October
Hilton Hotel, 9th & Hamilton St.
Promoter: Bill Hollman
604 Laurel Ct.
Bensalem, PA 19020
(215) 639-5312

Denver

Matchcover Swapfest, mid July
Holiday Inn, Lancaster Co., Exit 21 PA
  Turnpike
Promoter: Bud Shappell
109 Wood Lane
Reading, PA 19606
(610) 779-0733

Lancaster

Lancaster Rare Book and Paper Fair/early
  June
Farm and Home Center, Route 72 and US
  Route 30
Promoter: ABC Shows
343 West Mark St.
York, PA 17401
(717) 845-7577

Philadelphia

Premiere Colossal Show & Sale/early
  October
Philadelphia Civic Center
Promoter: Nadia Promotions, Inc.
PO Box 156
Flourtown, PA, 19031
(215) 643-1396

Pittsburgh

Postcard & Paper Show/mid April
Mt. Lebanon United Methodist Church,
  3319 West Liberty Ave.

Promoter: Richard Campbell
PO Box 25313
Pittsburgh, PA 15242

Trevose

Matchcover Convention/mid August
Ramada Hotel, 2400 Old Lincoln Way
Promoter: John Williams
1358 Surrey Rd.
Vandalia, OH 45377
(513) 890-8684

Trevose

Philly Non-Sports Show/late October
Ramada Hotel, Rt. 1 & Old Lincoln Hwy.
Promoter: Frank Reighter
10220 Calera Rd.
Philadelphia, PA 19114

York

York International Postcard Fair/late
  November
Promoter: Mary Martin
4899 Pulaski Highway
Perryville, MD 21903
(410) 575-7768

York

Vintage Paperback Show/mid March, late
  October
Historic York Book & Paper Fair, York
  Fairgrounds, Old Main Building
Promoter: ABC Shows
343 W. Market St.
York, PA 17401
(717) 845-7577

SOUTH CAROLINA

Fort Mill

9th Annual Heart of Dixie Postcard
  Collectors Show/mid September
Carrowinda Holiday Inn, 225 Carrowinda
  Blvd
Promoter: S.C.P.C.C.
PO Box 10648
Rock Hill, SC 29731
(803) 324-5820

TENNESSEE

Knoxville

Tennessee Postcard Assoc. Show/late November
Holiday Inn, NW, 1-75 and Merchants Rd.
Promoter: Paul Garland
1919 Rosemont Circle
Louisville, TN 37777
(615) 970-3271

Memphis

Science Fiction Convention/late March
Promoter: Sylvia Cox
PO Box 22749
Memphis, TN 38122

Nashville

3rd Annual Nashville Postcard Show/late March
Quality Inn Airport Opryland
Promoter: Postcard Collector Magazine
PO Box 337
Iola, WI 54945
(715) 445-5000

TEXAS

Austin

2nd Annual Capital of Texas Post Card Club Post Card Collector Show & Sale/ mid February
Howard Johnson Plaza-Hotel North
Promoter: Bob Fesler
PO Box 202471
Austin, TX 78720

Dallas

Dallas Metroplex Postcard Club Show/late March
Holiday Inn Park Central, 8102 LBJ & Coit Rd.
Promoter: Jack Thornhill
(214) 276-3089

Dallas

TSDA Stamp Fair/mid January, early April, late September, late November
Holiday Inn, Coit Rd., LBJ Freeway & US 75

Promoter: Ken Kerruish
3216 W. Park Row
Arlington, TX 76013
(817) 265-8645

Houston

Greater Houston Postcard Society Annual Show/late October
Holiday Inn, 7611 Katy Freeway
Promoter: Dick Pendergrast
12403 Rip Van Winkle
Houston, TX 77024
(713) 464-3486

Houston

12th Annual Houston Post Card Club Show/mid March
Holiday Inn, 7611 Katy Freeway
Promoter: Hazel Leler
12327 Windjammer
Houston, TX 77072
(713) 933-3557

Houston

TSDA Stamp Fair/early January, late March, late November
Holiday Inn, 7611 Katy Freeway
Promoter: Phil Cordes
PO Box 223
Seabrook, TX 77586

San Antonio

TSDA Stamp Fair/late January, late October
Oak Hills Motor Inn, 7401 Warbach Rd.
Promoter: Phil Cordes
PO Box 223
Seabrook, TX 77586

VERMONT

Woodstock Village Green

Antiquarian Book Fair/early August
Pomfret School, Pomfret Rd.
Promoter: (802) 899-4447

VIRGINIA

Arlington

DC Antique Photographic Image Show/
late March
Rosslyn Westpark Hotel, 1900 N. Ft. Myer
Dr.
Promoter: Russell Norton
PO Box 1070
New Haven, CT 06504
(203) 562-7800

Chantilly

Postcard Show/mid March, mid July
Dulles Airport Marriott, Dulles Access
Road
Promoter: Postcard Society, Inc.
PO Box 1765
Manassas, VA 22110

Harrisonburg

Shenandoah Valley Postcard Show and
Sale/late July
Holiday Inn, Route 11
Promoter: Jeff Bradfield
(703) 879-9961

WASHINGTON

Kent

Greater Seattle Postcard & Paper
Collectibles Show/late January, late June
Kent Commons, 525 4th Ave.
Promoter: R & N Postcard Co.
Nick Farago
PO Box 217
Temple City, CA 91780
(818) 281-3390

Seattle

Seattle American Paper Ephemera & Book
Fair/early May
Flag Pavillion, 305 Harrison St.

Promoter: Kingsbury Productions
4555 N. Pershing Ave., Suite 33-138
Stockton, CA 95207
(209) 467-8438

WISCONSIN

Green Bay

D-J Postcard Show/early August
Holiday Inn Civic Center, 200 Main St.
Promoter: D-J Postcards Shows
Jerry Andreen
PO Box 2301
Rockford, IL 61131
(815) 397-3100

Madison

Madison Collectible Paper Show & Sale/
mid July
South Towne Mall, 3401 West Broadway
Promoter: Hank Luttrell
108 King St.
Madison, WI 53703
(608) 251-6226

Milwaukee

Milwaukee Postcard Show and Sale/late
October
Gonzaga Hall, 1441 South 92nd St.
Promoter: Frank Greicek
3041 N. Humboldt Blvd.
Milwaukee, WI 53212
(414) 264-0225

Milwaukee

National Postcard Collector Convention/
early April
MECCA Convention Center
Promoter: Nat'l Postcard Collector Conv.
PO Box 337
Iola, WI 54945
(715) 445-5000

ABBREVIATIONS

The following are standard abbreviations used throughout this edition of *Warman's Paper*.

3D	= three dimensional		mfg	= manufactured
4to	= approximately 8 x 10"		MIB	= mint in box
8vo	= approximately 5 x 7"		MIP	= mint in package
12mo	= approximately 3 x 5"		MOC	= mint on card
ADS	= autograph document signed		mkd	= marked
adv	= advertising		n.d.	= no date
ALS	= autograph letter signed		NE	= New England
AQS	= autograph quotation signed		No.	= number
C	= century		orig	= original
c	= circa		oz	= ounce
CS	= card signed		pat	= patent
circ	= circular		pc	= piece
cov	= cover		pcs	= pieces
d	= diameter or depth		pgs	= pages
dec	= decorated		pkg	= package
dj	= dust jacket		pr	= pair
DS	= document signed		PS	= photograph signed
emb	= embossed		pt	= pint
ext.	= exterior		qt	= quart
FE	= first edition		rect	= rectangular
Folio	= approximately 12 x 16"		sgd	= signed
gal	= gallon		sngl	= single
ground	= background		sq	= square
h	= height		teg	= top edges gilt
hp	= hand painted		TLS	= Typed Letter Signed
illus	= illustrated, illustration, illustrator		unp	= unpaged
imp	= impressed		vol	= volume
int.	= interior		w	= width
l	= length		wraps	= paper covers
lb	= pound		yr	= year
litho	= lithograph		#	= numbered
LS	= letter signed			

Part II
Collecting Paper by Topic

ADVERTISING

History: Advertisers have traditionally relied on colorful product labels, magazine and broadside advertising, and giveaways to promote their products. Containers appealed to buyers by the use of stylish lithographs and bright colors. Many periodical advertisements contained an illustration of the product itself so that even illiterate buyers could identify it. Advertising giveaway premiums continue to be a favorite form of promotion.

Advertising is an excellent way to document changing tastes, whether aesthetic, fashion, or social. Perhaps more than any other topic, advertising provides a detailed chronicle for each generation.

References: Al Bergevin, *Drugstore Tins and Their Prices,* Wallace–Homestead Book Company, 1990; Al Bergevin, *Food and Drink Containers and Their Prices,* Wallace–Homestead Book Company, 1988; Leslie and Marcie Cabarga, *Trademark Designs of the Twenties,* Dover, 1991; Douglas Congdon–Martin, *America For Sale: A Collector's Guide to Antique Advertising,* Schiffer Publishing, 1991; Everett Grist, *Advertising Playing Cards: An Identification and Value Guide,* Collector Books, 1992; Ted Hake, *Hake's Guide To Advertising Collectibles,* Wallace–Homestead, 1992; Bob and Sharon Huxford, *Huxford's Collectible Advertising,* Collector Books, 1993; Jerry Jankowski, *Shelf Life: Modern Package Design 1920–1945,* Chronicle Books, 1992; Ray Klug, *Antique Advertising Encyclopedia,* Vol. 1 (1978, 1992 value update) and Vol. 2 (1985), L–W Promotions; Ralph and Terry Kovel, *Kovels' Advertising Collectibles Price List,* Crown Publishers, 1986; L–W Promotions (ed.), *Antique Advertising Handbook and Price Guide,* L–W Book Sales, 1988; Alice L. Muncaster, Ellen Sawyer and Ken Kapson, *The Baby Made Me Buy It!,* Crown Publishers, 1991; Robert Opie, *The Art of the Label: Designs of the Times,* Chartwell Books, 1987; Robert Opie, *Packaging Source Book,* Chartwell Books, 1989; Dawn E. Reno, *Advertising: Identification and Price Guide,* Avon Books, 1993.

Collectors' Clubs: The Antique Advertising Association, PO Box 1121, Morton Grove, IL 60053; The Ephemera Society of America, PO Box 37, Schoharie, NY 12157.

Periodicals: *National Association of Paper and Advertising Collectibles,* PO Box 500, Mount Joy, PA 17552; *Paper Collectors' Marketplace,* PO Box 128, Scandinavia, WI 54917.

Note: This is a catchall topic. The category is organized first by form and then by company. Technically it does not belong in this section since it is not a type of object, e.g., business card, game, pulp, or sheet music. However, it does not fit in the subject section either. Advertising, along with topics such as erotic and illustrator material, has achieved a level among collectors where it is treated as an object class.

Activity Book, Gold Dust Twins At Work and Play, 1904, 20 pgs, full color cover, 5 x 7"	50.00
Bag, Old Plantation Coffee, Negro loading boat, 1930s, 4 x 8"	8.00
Book, Hires Root Beer, *The Animals' Trip to Town,* 1920s, 12 pgs, full color cov, 3 x 5"	15.00
Booklet	
Arm & Hammer Baking Soda, *Successful Baking For Flavor & Texture,* 1938, 38 pgs	8.00
Burma–Shave Jingle Book, 1939, 16 pgs, 2¾ x 2¾"	12.00
Cracker Jack Riddles, 1920s, 42 pgs, 2¾ x 5"	50.00
Hires Household Extract, 1920s, 12 pgs, cartoon character images on cover, 3½ x 5"	15.00
Hood's Sarsaparilla, Handsome Is That Handsome Does, 1890, 16 pgs, full color cover, 3⅕ x 6"	25.00
Kerr Glass, Home Canning Book, National Nutrition Edition, 1943, 56 pgs	9.00
Quick Meal Steel Ranges, Ringen Stove Co, c1904, Buster Brown and Tige on cov, 3 x 5"	35.00
Bookmark	
Antikammia Tablets, The Antikammia Chemical Co, St Louis, two color	6.00
Climax Catarrah Cure, woman with fur coat, multicolored	10.00

Needle Packet, Town Talk, 3 x 4½", $6.50.

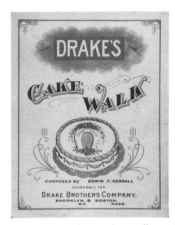

Sheet Music, *Drake's Cake Walk*, Drake Bros. Co., Brooklyn, NY, black and white, red logo, 10½ x 14", c1909, $30.00.

Daggetts Chocolates, Clapsaddle girl, emb butterfly, multicolored . . **10.00**
Hood's Sarsaparilla, 1900, full color children holding books illus, 2½ x 7" **10.00**
Hoyt's German Cologne, diecut, multicolored **6.00**
James Fitzgerald, Bookseller & Stationer, MA, rural scene **6.00**
Peters Weatherbird Shoes, 1930s, black, red, and yellow, 3¾" l **10.00**
Box
  English Ovals Cigarettes, 1940s **8.00**
  Globe Chalk, 1920s **3.00**
Calendar
  1930, A C Stram Groceries, URMA Brand, Green Bay, full pad, 10 x 16" **20.00**
  1931, August Wichman Work Clothes & Hosiery, Wear–U–Well Shoes, Seymour, WI, full pad, 10¼ x 16¾" **10.00**
  1941, Rosseau Shoes, Rubbers, Repairing–Men's & Women's Hosiery, Shiocton, WI, full pad, 8½ x 14" **8.00**
Can
  Dixie Kid Cut Plug Tobacco, cardboard, baby label, screw lid, 5 x 5" **550.00**
  H & K's Mighty Good Coffee, cardboard, person wearing night clothes, holding cup of coffee, square **210.00**
Canister, Bigger Hair Tobacco, cardboard, black woman label, 5" d, 7" h **115.00**
Catalog
  Bailey & Farrell Bathroom Fixtures, 1921 . . . . **75.00**

Bastian Bros Co, Badges, 1908, 36 pgs, 4½ x 11" **50.00**
General Electric Refrigerator, 1939, black and white photo, 8½ x 11" **15.00**
John Wilkinson Co, 1885–86, 56 pgs, wood working implements . . **35.00**
Victor Hawaiian Records, 1916, full color illus on cov, 8 x 11" **20.00**
Coaster, Reddy Kilowatt, 1950s, black, white, and red illus, 3½" d **15.00**
Coupon, Mirro Aluminum Bake Pan, printed black on pale orange paper, double–sided coupon offers 20 cents off a 55 cent bake pan when presented to your local grocer, Lundt & Co Moline, IL, c1920, never used, 6 x 3" **3.00**
Decal, Lucky Strike, Lucky "Green" pack illus, 1931, 6" sq **15.00**
Display, cardboard
  Adam Hats, diecut, easel type, Baby Snooks, miniature hat box, 17" . . . **25.00**
  Alka–Seltzer, Speedy, easel type, full color, c1950, 5 x 12" **125.00**
  American Pencil Co, three–dimensional, roadster shape **85.00**
  Austin's Dog Bread, In Use Over Fifty Years, diecut, dog illus **20.00**
  Cliquot Club Beverages, figural, easel type, full color, 1930s, 3 x 6" . . **35.00**
  Dr Miles Nervine, girl pouring dose with two customers, 36 x 51" **240.00**
  El Principal Cigars, "The Taste Pleases," diecut, cardboard, two cigar boxes, blue background, 25 x 38" **20.00**
  Heinz Rice Flakes, 1933–34, easel type, full color Col Roscoe Turner illus, wings pins premium offer, 20 x 22" **150.00**
  Hinds Cream, "For Chapping, Windburn," trifold, portico with ladies and product, 34 x 59" **60.00**

Store Hanger, Salada Tea, double sided, 7½ x 11", $7.50.

Peters—The Old Timer's Standby, 1930s, easel type, 14 x 18" **75.00**

Quaker Oats, 1950, diecut, easel type, Roy Rogers, "I Was Raised On Quaker Oats," 60" h........ **1,000.00**

Fan

Buster Brown Shoes, Brown's 5—Star Shoes, cardboard, 1910, 7 x 8" ... **35.00**

Gold Dust & Fairy Soap, Gold Dust Twins overlooking 1904 World's Fair, 8" d **70.00**

Kool Cigarettes, Tune In Every Wednesday Night, Tommy Dorsey, diecut, full color penguin illus, 1930s, 7 1/2 x 10 1/2" **30.00**

Moxie, full color man pointing finger, 1921, 6 x 8" **50.00**

Phillips 66, Van's Service Station, Downtown Fairbury, IL, shield shape, wood handle, 14 x 8 1/2" ... **20.00**

Putnam Dyes, cardboard, litho, Gen Putnam and British Dragoons dec **20.00**

Tip—Top Bread, colorful loaf illus, 1940s, 9 x 13" **8.00**

Figure, Red Goose Shoes, 1930s, full color, cardboard, wood stand, 2 1/4" h **15.00**

Flour Sack, ER Heller Milling Co, rooster pulling child in wagon, 10 x 20" **18.00**

Hat, Cracker Jack, red, white, and blue, 1930s, 7 x 14" **35.00**

Horn, Red Goose Shoes, 6" l, unused **10.00**

Kite, Buster Brown Shoes, unused, 1940s **25.00**

Label

Cigar

Frontier Cigars, two hunters with buck, snow scene with cabin, 6 x 9" **125.00**

Garcia Lopez Cigars, 1882, man and two white statues, 6 x 9" **5.00**

Habana Cigars, fan, tulips, and leaves illus, 6 x 9" **5.00**

Lucky Bill Cigars, young boy wearing knickers, 5 x 5" **3.00**

Orange, Gold Buckle, 1930s, orchards encircled by belt, 10 x 12" **4.00**

Leaflet, Buick, full color illus, 8 1/2 x 11" **30.00**

Magazine, *Best Buick Yet,* 1940, September, 14 pgs, full color illus, 8 1/2 x 11" **12.00**

Mask

Buster Brown Shoes, c1905, diecut, full color half mask, 7 1/2 x 10" **75.00**

Chevrolet, diecut winking face, full color, 8 1/2 x 11" **35.00**

Kellogg's, Rice Krispies, Snap, 1933, diecut, full color, 11 x 14" **25.00**

Matchbook, Carstairs White Seal Blended Whiskey, oversized match-

book, blue gold and red printing, seal balancing ball on his nose, matches also illustrate the seal, never used, c1940, 3 1/2 x 4 1/2", opens to 8 1/4" **10.00**

Memorandum Book, "Pierce's Memo And Account Book," designed for farmers and mechanics, World's Dispensary Medical Association, Buffalo, NY, elaborate black printing on heavy brown paper cover, 48 pgs of testimonials and advice on the use of products plus monthly calendar for 1924, 3 1/2 x 4 1/2" **6.00**

Menu Cover, Anheuser—Busch, Drink Budweiser/King of Bottled Beer, full color design, c1930, 7 x 11 1/4" **15.00**

Napkin, Red Goose Shoes, 1930–40.. **3.00**

Needle Holder, Hires Condensed Milk, cardboard, diecut, full color, 1899, 1 1/2 x 2 1/2" **20.00**

Newspaper Advertisement, Chase & Sanborn Coffee, September 19, 1937, *This Week,* full page, W C Fields and Charlie McCarthy promoting product, 10 1/2 x 16" **15.00**

Notepad

Arm & Hammer Brand Soda, Saleratus & Sal Soda, calendar cov, 3 1/2 x 5" **20.00**

Cream of Wheat, "Don't Forget Cream of Wheat," black chef illus on leather cover, 1910, 4 x 6" **30.00**

Fleischmann's Yeast, full color lady illus on front cov, black and white slogan on back, orig attached pencil with string, 1908, 2 x 3" **25.00**

Hamilton Watch, 1907, black and white cover railroad illus, 3 x 5" .. **20.00**

Paint Book, Ceresota Flour, *The Adventures of Ceresota,* 1912, 6 x 8" **35.00**

Playing Cards, Maull's Barbecue Sauce, red bottle of product, red and gold border **8.00**

Pocket Calendar, Swift's Premium Ham and Bacon, 1918, full color celluloid cover, 1 3/4 x 3 1/2" **20.00**

Post Card

C D Kenny, Smile and Be Happy, 1906, spinner disk changes facial expression, 4 x 5 1/2" **10.00**

De Laval Cream Separator, The World's Standard, full color image, 1914, 3 1/2 x 5 1/2" **20.00**

Poster

Eastman Kodak, Vest Pocket Autographic Kodak, black, white, and red, 1920s, 12 x 18" **75.00**

Four Roses Tobacco, elegant women with four roses litho, 12 x 16", orig frame...................... **325.00**

Hannis Distilling Co, Hannisville

Distillery, Martinsburg, WV, factory scene, 20 x 18", framed, orig mat **450.00**

Kissel's Garage, two trucks, circular background, 22 x 17" **20.00**

Orphan Boy Tobacco, full color illus, 1930s, 12 x 18" **15.00**

Satin Skin Cream, 1903, 25 x 38" . . .   **70.00**

Puzzle Book, *Quaker Oats Puzzle Pictures,* 1900, full color, 3 x 6" **15.00**

Sheet Music

Cliquot Club Eskimos, 1926, black, white, and orange cover, 9 x 12" . .   **12.00**

Take Me On A Buick Honeymoon, 1922, full color automobile scene on front cover, back with Buick engine, 9 x 12" **35.00**

Sign

Adriance Farm Machinery, 1902, paper on cardboard, vignette of children on horse and machinery, 28 x 21", framed. **225.00**

A J Stillwell Ham, 16", wood frame   **150.00**

Allens Root Beer Extract, Donaldson Brothers, paper with metal strips, woman distilling extract for cherubs, 20 x 14", framed **650.00**

American Tobacco Co, 1899, pub master smoking cigar, 26 x 18" . . .   **50.00**

Angelus Marshmallows, 1930s, diecut, full color, boy and product, 8 x 11" **250.00**

Arrow Collars, cardboard, young man with head turned right. **270.00**

Babbitt's Soap, 1892, little girl riding tricycle, 14 x 28" **400.00**

Beech–Nut Mints, girl serving mints to two men, 18 x 28", framed **100.00**

Big Smith Shirts, standup, cardboard, WWII airplane illus. **40.00**

Blackberry Punch, cardboard, barefoot boy, bottle of punch, and bucket of blackberries illus, 5½ x 14" **45.00**

Boston Belting Co, factory scene and rubber gathering vignettes, 25 x 21", orig mat, framed **250.00**

Brillo Pads, cardboard, diecut, product box with skillet being hand scrubbed, 17 x 15" **100.00**

Clark's Mile End Spool Cotton, mother holding daughter on rail, 17 x 29", framed **50.00**

Colgate–Palmolive, The Palm and Olive Oil Soap, cardboard, diecut, full color, 1930s, 10½ x 12¼" . .   **50.00**

Cracker Jack, 1930s, full color, diecut, girl, dog, and product, 7 x 11"   **300.00**

Crosman Bros Seeds, New Crop, Rochester, NY, smiling farmer with pipe, 17 x 24" **325.00**

Dental Sweet Snuff, "How Did You

Know I Use," couple seated on ground by car, 12 x 16". **35.00**

Dingman's Soap, crawling baby, 13 x 15" **150.00**

Everhardt & Ober Brewing Co, colorful factory, logo, and company name, 32 x 46" **400.00**

Fairy Soap, little girl atop soap bar, 11 x 21". **50.00**

Gold Dust Washing Powder, 1900, orange, black, and white illus, 8 x 11" **75.00**

Golden Rod Ice Cream, "Keeps Youth In Health," diecut, girl wearing sailor outfit, holding ice cream cone, 27 x 17" **70.00**

Golden's Blue Ribbon Cigars, 5½ x 9¼", blue and white, 1930s **5.00**

Heinz Cream of Tomato Soup, 1930s, full color image, 10 x 20"   **100.00**

Heinz Mince Meat, 1930s, full color image, 12 x 22" **75.00**

High Grade Cigarettes, cardboard litho, man and two women wearing costumes, 14 x 8", framed. **130.00**

Howe Scale Co, 1889, printed by Donaldson Bros Litho, woman standing on platform scale, 29 x 15" **300.00**

Iron Clad Hosiery, 1920s, cardboard, flapper girl illus, 10¼ x 13"   **15.00**

Kis–Me Gum, American Chicle Co, cardboard litho, diecut, girl sitting in fancy chair, 11 x 10", framed . .   **500.00**

Kitchen Kleanzer, cardboard, product illus **45.00**

Knox Gelatin, 18 x 27" **170.00**

Ladies Short Smokes, cardboard litho, two gentlemen wearing top hats, standing in front of theater, 25 x 36", framed **100.00**

Lava Soap, 1910, full color illus, 8 x 8". **20.00**

Window Card, Greenville Ice & Fuel Plant, black lettering, yellow ground, 9 x 9", $7.50.

Little African Licorice Drops, 1910–1919, black and white black baby crawling and alligator illus, 11½ x 14½".....................   **250.00**

Manitou Table Water, "All Use It," bottle with Indian label, people using product vignettes, 29 x 22"   **500.00**

Minneapolis Underwear For Children, cardboard, diecut, happy and sad toddlers **90.00**

Moline Wagon Co, c1890, double sided, angel with scythe, sitting in tree, Moline wagons and buggies on reverse, 10 x 7".............   **70.00**

Mother's Oats, 1902, American Lithographic Co, child with pipe wearing men's clothes, 17 x 24". .   **145.00**

Moxie, Drink Moxie, 1920s, diecut, stiff cardboard, man pointing finger, 20 x 20" **150.00**

National Dry Hop Yeast, girl holding fan and product, 19 x 12" **20.00**

New Home Sewing Machine Co, family, dog, and sewing machine, 18 x 24", framed **125.00**

New York Daily News, paper litho, newsboy running, busy street scene background, matted and framed......................   **280.00**

Old Virginia Cheroots Tobacco, cowboy smoking cigar, blue background, 23 x 15".............   **300.00**

Order Sack of Pride of the Rockies Today, red, white, and blue, flour sack shape, 5 x 10" **6.00**

Packard's Black 'O' Shoe Polish, cardboard, oval with boy pointing at product, 7 x 11"............   **95.00**

Palmolive Soap, paper, green, black, and white, 1930s, 14 x 22" **20.00**

Penn Beverage Co, bathing beauty and floating beverage case illus, framed......................   **85.00**

Philip Morris, 1940s, textured paper, full color illus, 18½ x 23½" **75.00**

Pillsbury Cake Mixes, 1950s, full color Art Linkletter illus, 11½ x 22" **20.00**

Polly Parrot Shoes, 1930s, boys and girls illus, 15" h **100.00**

Putnam Horse Shoe Nails, c1888, "The Only Safe Nail To Drive," horsedrawn carriage image, 26 x 33", matted and framed.........   **200.00**

Quaker Oats, 1950, Roy Rogers autographed souvenir cup offer, full color, 15 x 22"................   **200.00**

Remington UMC, multicolored scene of Remington bears sign at top of gun cabinet, 14 x 20" **450.00**

Rising Sun Stove Polish, A Thing Of Beauty Is A Joy Forever, 1880s,

woman leaning on banister, 13 x 29".........................   **650.00**

Sandwich Mfg Co, Hay Press & the New Way Large Bale, 23 x 29", matted and framed **125.00**

Sharples Tubular Cream Separators, The Right Now Separator, girl wearing bonnet using product, 27 x 18".......................   **1,100.00**

Snow King Baking Powder, c1930, cardboard, 12 x 26" **40.00**

Sonny 5¢ Cones, 1920s, 8 x 19"....   **10.00**

Swastika Pears, 1930s, 5 x 10" **5.00**

Toiletine, Don't Forget Toiletine, Unequalled For Sunburn, cardboard, diecut, smiling man wearing lettered top hat, 9 x 6".......   **15.00**

Union Mills Flour, 1910, full color illus, child lying in basket, 15 x 19", framed **250.00**

Value Cigarros, c1900, two men stealing money and cigars from safe, 16 x 25", matted and framed   **200.00**

Walk–Over Shoes, The World's Greatest Fine Shoe Plant, factory view and two product insets, 20 x 26" **55.00**

Wilbur's Stock Tonic, beer wagon with six horses, 15 x 32" **60.00**

Winchesters Arms, Columbus Day Values, 1966.................   **12.00**

Wolf Co Flouring Mill Machinery, child wearing floppy hat and machinery, 13 x 21", framed **175.00**

Zu Zu Ginger Snaps, The Snappiest Ginger, clown with product, light blue background, 15 x 12" **190.00**

Songbook, Sharples Cream Separator, color cover of man and woman, 1920s, 6 x 8½" **20.00**

Souvenir Book, Firestone, 1933 Century of Progress Exposition, 32 pgs, 5 x 8" **10.00**

Trade Card

Adams Pepsin Tutti Frutti Chewing Gum, 1890s, full color, 4½ x 6½"   **25.00**

Chase & Sanborn, 1886, red, white, and blue illus, 3 x 5" **15.00**

Gold Dust Washing Powder, 1890s, diecut, full color illus of two children sitting in tub, 3 x 3½" **35.00**

Horlick's Malted Milk, 1890s, full color woman and cow, 3 x 5"....   **30.00**

Lion Coffee, c1895, full color boy holding dog portrait, blue and white free pocket knife premium, 3½ x 5½" **10.00**

McLaughlin's Coffee, girl playing teacher **5.00**

Moxie, Learn To Drink Moxie, 1910, diecut, full color illus, 7" l.......   **30.00**

Quaker Oats, 1900, full color

Quaker illus on front, housewives
message on back, 2³/₄ x 5¹/₂" **20.00**
Whistle, Cracker Jack, Blow For More,
red, white, and blue stiff paper,
1930s, 1¹/₄ x 3" **25.00**

ADVERTISING TRADE CARDS

History: The advertising trade card first appeared
around 1700. From the beginning, trade cards
used visual appeal and wit to attract customers'
attention. Initially, American trade cards were
modeled after English examples. Eighteenth century trade cards promoted luxury goods made by
skilled craftsmen and were targeted to a sophisticated group of consumers.

By the beginning of the nineteenth century,
American printers developed imaginary new approaches to advertising trade cards. The printing
of trade cards spread to the countryside from the
large urban printing centers of Boston, New York,
and Philadelphia. Business clients wanted quick,
local access to their printers.

In the 1820s lithography challenged engraving
as the principal commercial printing medium.
Large press runs at low cost were possible. When
the ability to print in several colors occurred in
the 1860s, lithography printing of trade cards became dominant. A leader in this movement was
Louis Prang.

The Golden Age of the advertising trade card
was the 1880s and 1890s. A collecting craze
developed. Albums were created to hold the
cards. Manufacturers issued cards in series as a
means of continuing to attract customers. Ex-
changes among friends took place nationwide.

Although advertising trade cards were used internationally, they reached their greatest development in America. In the last quarter of the
nineteenth century America enjoyed a favorable
balance of trade with the world. America moved
from fourth to first in manufactured goods worldwide between 1860 and 1894, at which time it
out–produced England, France, and Germany
combined. Enormous growth in consumer goods,
improved transportation, new inventions, and
consumer demand led to a marketing bonanza.

The newspaper and periodical literature of the
era still printed primarily in black and white.
Many had a very conservative advertising policy.
Advertisers preferred posters and trade cards because of their great visual appeal as well as freedom from editorial constraints.

Individuals obtained trade cards either at
point–of–purchase (i.e., they were included in
the packaging) or directly from the shopkeeper. In
many cases the shopkeeper had his address
printed on a stock card or added it with a rubber
stamp.

By the mid–1890s the Golden Age of the advertising trade card was ending. The postal service reduced second class mail rates, opening the
door to mass distribution of magazines and other
periodicals. By 1900 the 160 leading monthly
magazines enjoyed a circulation of over 157,000.
Advertising in these periodicals increased by hundreds of percent in the 1880s and 1890s. By the
end of the 1890s many manufacturers were in-
serting full page, colored lithograph prints in periodicals. Increased magazine advertising, coupled
with the trend to monopolies, replacement of the
small shopkeeper by large department stores, and
the growth of mail order, ended the advertising
trade card era. In addition, the American lithography industry was undercut by German printers.
By 1900 advertising post cards, many printed
abroad, played a far more important role than
advertising trade cards.

Advertising trade cards have always enjoyed
strong popularity among paper collectors. After a
period of strong interest in the late 1970s and
early 1980s, the advertising trade card market
quieted. It remained so until 1992 when Russell
Mascieri launched Victorian Images (PO Box
284, Marlton, NJ 08053), an advertising trade
card mail auction. Kit Barry (143 Main Street,
Battleboro, VT 05301) and other dealers in advertising trade cards have climbed aboard the mail
auction bandwagon. The end result has been a
significant increase in value in harder to find advertising trade cards and a renewed public interest.

References: Kit Barry, *The Advertising Trade
Card, Book 1* , Iris Publishing, 1981; Robert Jay,
The Trade Card In Nineteenth–Century America,
University of Missouri Press, 1987; Jim and Cathy
McQuary, *Collectors Guide To Advertising
Cards*, L–W Promotions, 1975; Murray Card (In-
ternational) Ltd., *Cigarette Card Values: Murray's
1992 Catalogue of Cigarette & Other Trade Cards*,
Murray Cards International Ltd., 1992.

Clothing and Accessories
American Woolen Mills, engraved tai-
lor vignette. **50.00**
Automatic Shoe Heel Co, diecut,
black shoe, brown sole **42.00**
Ball's Health Preserving Corsets, mul-
ticolored **10.00**
Brown The Shoe Dealer, gold center
panel, green, white, and pink **10.00**
Celluloid Corset Clasps **25.00**
Draper & Maynard Co Gloves &
Mittens, plant vignette on reverse . . **10.00**
Edward Kakaas Furs. **14.00**
Fisk, Clark & Flaggs Gloves, two gen-
tlemen, gold background. **8.00**
F T Gray Hat & Bonnet Bleachers,
1883, sepia, Paris The Opera on re-
verse **65.00**

C. A. Coutant & Co., Chicago, Corset Department, color litho, 3 x 5", $5.00.

Jacob Reed's Finest Clothing, Philadelphia	12.00
Joseph Juel Dress, Driving & Coaching Gloves, black and white	15.00
Leigh & Prindle Clothes, black and white	10.00
New Globe Patented Shirts, caricature illus, sepia and black	18.00
R P Kenyon & Co Hats, Caps, Furs, engraved, black and white	35.00
Solar Tip Shoes, wise man, foolish man story	15.00
Taylor & Rogers Clothing, black and green, vignette	26.00
USA Grain Shoes, multicolored vignette	24.00
William Barton Hatter & Furrier, vignette	34.00

Food

Allen's Root Beer Extract, multicolored	16.00
AMC Cereal, woman using telephone	25.00
Ariosa Coffee, "A Misconstruction," two men illus	16.00
Cleveland's Baking Powder, granny baking biscuits	28.00
Colburn's Philadelphia Mustard, arctic scene	16.00
Fleischmann's Yeast, Buckwheat Cakes	30.00
Heinz Apple Butter, diecut, pickle	33.00
Highland Brand Evaporated Creme, diecut, vignette	28.00
Huyler's Cocoa, diecut, cocoa bean shape	12.00
Joseph Hurst & Co Groceries & Provisions, black and white	44.00
Knapp's Root Beer, multicolored, diecut	22.00
Pillsbury's Best, two black children	26.00

Sanford's Ginger, black girl holding baby in watermelon	30.00
Sterling Baking Powder	14.00
Stickney & Poor Vanilla	22.00
Warner's Safe Yeast, multicolored	10.00

Health and Beauty

Arophene Mfg Co Tooth Powder, black and white	44.00
Ayer's Cherry Pectoral	18.00
Campbell's Hair Cutting & Shaving Saloon, black and blue	42.00
Colaine Headache Powders, puzzle on reverse	38.00
Dr Kilmer's Female Remedy, two women and girl	28.00
Radway's Ready Relief, Stops Pain, two girls	40.00
Trix Breath Perfume, bold design	22.00
Viola Cream Skin Soap, folder, skin care information	15.00

Household

Adams Steam Carpet Cleaning, gold dec, dark green background	15.00
Canton Ladder Co, Century Washboard, red illus, buff ground	8.00
Colton & Ruggles Cabinet Furniture, brown and white	10.00

Music

Clarendon Pianos, little girl holding tennis racket and ball, 3 x 5"	5.00
C M Loomis, Proprietor of the Temple of Music, black and gray	11.00
Fairbanks & Cole Banjo Makers, red banjo, black and white letters	35.00
Misfit Parlors, girl playing mandolin	8.00
R D Gardner Organs, black illus, light green ground	14.00
Weaver Organ Factory, multicolored	26.00
Vose & Sons Pianos, Boston, MA, woman playing mandolin	15.00

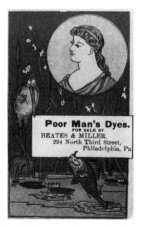

Poor Man's Dyes, color, text on back, 3 x 5", $4.00.

Sewing and Thread

Brook's Spool Cotton, whale scene . . .   **22.00**
Chadwick's Six Cord Cotton, monk
    sewing **24.00**
Clark's O.N.T. Spool Cotton, The Electric Building illus **16.00**
Domestic Sewing Machine, family scene, father playing with children   **15.00**
New Home Sewing Machine, "A New Home or a Divorce Take Your Choice Sir" **12.00**
Packards Sewing Machine Needles, case photo pasted on card **16.00**
Standard Sewing Machine Co, bicycle wheel form rotary shuttle **8.00**
Wakefield Shuttle and Needle Co, plant vignette on reverse **8.00**
White Sewing Machine, double sided   **15.00**
Williamatic Thread, "The Peoples favorite hobby" **16.00**

Soap

Dreydroppel's Soap, "True Story of the White Elephant," blue and white . .   **22.00**
Fairbank's Gold Dust Twins **50.00**
Lavine for Washing, folder, engraved   **12.00**
Lifebuoy Soap, woman holding life preserver with boy, boy holding product **22.00**
Maypole Soap, For Home Dying, three girls dying different colors **18.00**
Scourine, Arrest All Dirt. **8.00**
White Swan Soap, black boy **22.00**
Williams Yankee Soap, red, white, and blue flag, beige background **100.00**

Stoves and Ranges

Acorn Stoves & Ranges, diecut acorn, range illus **18.00**
Co–operative Foundry Red Cross Stoves & Ranges, folder, range directions on interior **16.00**
Excelsior Cook–Hot Blast, Victorian ladies cooking illus **22.00**
Florence Oil Stoves, restaurant kitchen scene **38.00**
Lustro Nickel Stove Cleaner **15.00**
Model Stoves & Ranges, large illus . . .   **15.00**
Monarch Vapor Ranges, diecut, loaf of bread **45.00**
New Hub Range, black scene of people mobbing store to buy new range   **20.00**
Raven Paste Stove Polish, black dog looking at his image in range **12.00**
Rising Sun Stove Polish, folder, rising sun **18.00**

Tobacco

Allen Nichols & Co, whimsical image of frogs **20.00**
Capudora "The Bath," woman smoking cigar, blue, green and black **14.00**
Harry Clinton Tobacco Dealer, children holding long cigar, man smoking **12.00**

Wise's Axle Grease, full color, 3 x 5",
$3.00.

Liggett & Meyers **34.00**
Red Cross Plug Tobacco, knight on horse illus **33.00**
Target Plug Tobacco, multicolored . . .   **22.00**
Weyman & Bro Copenhagen Snuff, good design **26.00**

Transportation

Chicago North Western Railway, blue and gold **25.00**
Columbus Buggy Co, diecut **30.00**
Hingham Hull and Downer Steamboat, time table, and Hotel Pemberton illus **45.00**
Mallory Line, rates for shipping oranges **45.00**
National Line Steamships, *SS England*   **120.00**
Stonington Line, time table **35.00**

Travel

Bruna's First Excursion to Cape May, 1878, time table, blue and white . . .   **70.00**
Ryder's Grand Excursion Steamer, *Columbia*, New York to Coney Island and Rockway **170.00**

World's Fair and Expositions

Grand National Industrial Expo, New York, 1882 . . . .   **24.00**
Paris Expo, 1878, American Co, Russell & Erwin MFG, New Britain, black and white **20.00**

ANIMATION CELS

History: Film historians credit Winsor McCay's 1909 "Gertie the Dinosaur" as the first animated cartoon. Early animated films were largely the work of comic strip artists. The invention of the celluloid process (a "cel" is an animation drawing on celluloid) is attributed to Earl Hurd. The technique reached perfection under animation giants Walt Disney and Max Fleischer. Ub Iwerks, Walt Lantz, and Paul Terry at Columbia and Charles Mintz at Screen Gems, MGM, Paramount/Famous Studios, UPA, and Warner Brothers also did pioneering work.

Leonard Martin's *Of Mice and Magic: A History of American Animated Cartoons* (A Plume Book/New American Library: revised and updated 1987 edition) provides an excellent historical background. Although Bob Bennett's *Collecting Original Cartoon Art* (Wallace–Homestead, 1987) contains a chapter on animation art, it concentrates far too heavily on historical and production information and far too little on the criteria needed to successfully judge and value animation art.

One second of film requires over twenty animation cels. If you multiply the length of a cartoon in minutes times sixty times twenty–four, you will achieve a fair idea of the potential number of animation cels available from any given film. Scarce is a word that must be used cautiously.

The vocabulary involving animation cels is very specific. The difference between a Courvoisier, Disneyland, master, key production, printed or publication, production, and studio background can mean thousands of dollars in value. Sotheby's and Christie's East, the two major auction houses selling animation art, do not agree on terminology. Read the glossary section of any animation auction or sales catalog very carefully.

Most importantly avoid limited edition serigraphs. A serigraph is a color print made by the silk screen process. Although they appear to be animation cels, they are not.

As the value of cels rises to astronomical heights, animation collectors are turning to secondary material, such as animation drawings, storyboard drawings, inspiration sketches, background drawings or layouts, and character model statues. Bargains abound in these areas.

References: Bob Bennett, *Collecting Original Cartoon Art*, Wallace–Homestead, 1987; Richard DeThurin, *The Official Identification and Price Guide to Movie Memorabilia*, House of Collectibles, 1990; Leonard Martin, *Of Mice and Magic: A History of American Animated Cartoons*, Plume Book/New American Library: revised and updated 1987 edition; Tom Tumbusch, *Tomart's Illustrated Disneyana Catalog and Price Guide, Condensed Edition*, Wallace–Homestead, 1989; Jerry Weist, *Original Comic Art: Identification and Price Guide*, Avon Books, 1992.

Periodical: Original Art Collector, 210 Fifth Avenue, Suite 1102, New York, NY 10010.

Alice In Wonderland
  Alice, framed, Walt Disney Studio, 7
    x 4½" **1,760.00**

Tweedledum and Tweedledee, framed, Walt Disney Studio, 6 x 6" **1,760.00**
All The Cats Join In, Make Mine Music, blond bobby soxer and her fellow, framed, Walt Disney Studio, 1946, 6 x 7½" **825.00**
An American Tail, Fievel, Don Bluth Studio, 7 x 13", framed **825.00**
Augie Doggie and Doggie Daddy, pr, tempera background sheet, framed, Hanna–Barbera Studio, c1960, 8 x 10" **1,870.00**
Bambi
  Bambi and butterfly, airbrush background, framed, Walt Disney Studio, 7 x 7½" **4,840.00**
  Bright eyed wood mouse, Walt Disney Studio, 1942, 8½ x 11" **7,700.00**
Bugs Bunny
  Ghostly hands lead floating Bugs, tempera background, framed, Warner Brothers Studio, c1946 .. **3,520.00**
  Holding carrot in hand, Warner Brothers Studio, 7 x 3"........... **2,310.00**
  Rabbit Rampage, Warner Brothers Studio, framed, 7¼ x 7" **1,870.00**
Charlie Brown and Woodstock, Schulz, 3 x 3½"................ **125.00**
Chip and Dale, carrying hobo sacks, framed, Walt Disney Studio, 1960s, 4 x 8½" **1,045.00**
Cinderella
  Cinderella holding broom, Walt Disney Studio, 7½ x 4"............ **2,310.00**
  Jaq and Lucifer, pr, framed, Walt Disney Studio, 10 x 13"........ **1,210.00**
Donald Duck
  Donald's Penguin, Donald and Tootsie, airbrush background, trimmed to outline figures, framed, Walt Disney Studio **2,970.00**
  Test Pilot, wearing mechanic's cap and aviator jacket, framed, Walt Disney Studio, 5½ x 4" **935.00**
Dumbo, portrait, label on back ''prepared by Courvoisier,'' Walt Disney Studio, 1941, 6 x 7"............. **2,640.00**
Fantasia, baby blue pegasus, airbrush background, framed, Walt Disney Studio, 7 x 8".................. **2,640.00**
Fat Albert and the Cosby Kids, tempera background sheet, framed, Filmation Studio, 1970s **880.00**
Foghorn Leghorn, full figure, framed, Warner Brothers Studio, 1950s, 6 x 4½"......................... **880.00**
Horton Hears A Who, Dr Suess elephant, tempera background, framed, MGM Studio/Chuck Jones **1,650.00**
Jetson, Elroy and Astro, elevator pad, 5 x 3" **80.00**
Lady and the Tramp, Tramp and Tony,

Ursula, *The Little Mermaid,* Walt Disney, gouache on celluloid, $2,000.00.

Tramp licking Tony's face, Walt Disney Studio, 5¹/₂ x 6". **1,760.00**

Lonesome Ghosts, Mickey Mouse, Donald Duck, and Goofy, black, white, and shades of gray painted, framed, Walt Disney Studio, 6 x 4¹/₂" **2,310.00**

Make Mine Music, Alice Bluebonnet and Johnny Fedora atop horse's head, Walt Disney Studio, 5¹/₂ x 5" **1,100.00**

Melody Time, two young lovers in horse drawn sleigh, trimmed to outline figure, framed, Walt Disney Studio **715.00**

Mickey Mouse
Mickey and the Beanstalk, pr, Mickey escaping hand of Willie the Giant, framed, Walt Disney Studio, 1947, 9¹/₂ x 11¹/₂" **2,970.00**

Mickey's Christmas Carol, Mickey as Bob Cratchit, line print background, Walt Disney Studio, 9 x 8" **1,210.00**

Satchmo, Mickey playing trumpet, framed, Walt Disney Studio, 1958, 6¹/₂ x 6¹/₂" **1,980.00**

Tricks of Our Trade, Mickey raising fishing pole, framed, Walt Disney Studio, 8¹/₂ x 4" **1,870.00**

Mother Goose Goes Hollywood, Oliver Hardy as Pieman, Walt Disney Studio, 7¹/₂ x 7¹/₂" **1,650.00**

101 Dalmatians, Cruella de Vil at wheel of roadster, framed, Walt Disney Studio, 8 x 10" **2,530.00**

Pepe Le Pew, Pepe with lettle luff bundle, framed, Warner Brothers Studio, 1950s, 4 x 7¹/₂" **3,520.00**

Peter Pan
John and Lost Boys, cheering for fearless leader, framed, Walt Disney Studio, 1953, 6 x 6¹/₂". **1,540.00**

Mrs Darling, Michael, and John, Disney, 7 x 5" **275.00**

Wendy's little brother Michael, Walt Disney Studio, 7 x 3". **800.00**

Pinocchio, Wily J Worthington Foulfellow, Walt Disney Studio, 5¹/₂ x 4¹/₂" **1,210.00**

Pluto, portrait, expressive features, framed, Walt Disney Studio, 1950s, 11¹/₂ x 7¹/₂" **1,540.00**

Porky Pig, Porky's Last Stand, pr, framed, Warner Brothers Studio, 1940, 7¹/₂ x 10". **2,200.00**

Punkin Puss and Mush Mouse, 1964, Hanna–Barbera, 7 x 9". **365.00**

Red Hot Riding Hood, framed, MGM Studio, 1943, 8 x 7". **3,080.00**

Robin Hood, pr, Sheriff of Nottingham and bodyguard Trigger, framed, Walt Disney Studio, 7 x 11" and 9¹/₂ x 8¹/₂" **990.00**

Road Runner and Coyote, pr, hand inked, framed, Warner Brothers Studio, 1970s, 4¹/₂ x 3¹/₂" and 5 x 6¹/₂" . . **2,090.00**

Saludos Amigos, Jose Carioca and Donald Duck, Walt Disney Studio, framed, label on back "Prepared by Courvoisier," 7 x 7" **3,080.00**

Sleeping Beauty
Aurora and two feathered friends, color print background, Walt Disney Studio, 10 x 9" **2,310.00**

Merryweather and Fauna, Walt Disney Studio, 8 x 10" **1,485.00**

Song of the South, set of 2, Brer Rabbit with Tar Baby; and Brer Rabbit, Fox, and Bear, Walt Disney Studio, framed, 10¹/₂ x 14¹/₂" **2,640.00**

Star Trek, Spock and Captain Kirk, 6¹/₂ x 6¹/₂" **285.00**

Sword in the Stone, Merlin, 1963, 9 x 7¹/₄". **775.00**

The Adventures of Ichabod and Mr Toad, Ichabod bowing, framed, Walt Disney studio, 1949, 6¹/₂ x 5¹/₂" **880.00**

The Great Mouse Detective, pr, Basil
and Dr Dawson, Ratigan and Hiram
Flaversham, laminated, framed,
Walt Disney Studio, 1986, 8 x 13"
and 10 x 14" **1,320.00**
The Jungle Book
Baloo, full figure, unframed, Walt
Disney Studio, 6½ x 4" **880.00**
Baloo with tiger by the tail, Walt Dis-
ney Studio, 8½ x 11". **1,210.00**
The Little Mermaid, Ursula, framed,
Walt Disney Studio, 6 x 11" **2,310.00**
The Reluctant Dragon, full figure ep-
onymous, framed, Walt Disney Stu-
dio, 8 x 9" **1,760.00**
The Rescuers, portrait, Madame
Medusa, framed, Walt Disney Stu-
dio, 7½ x 10½". **825.00**
The Sword in the Stone, Wart, Merlin,
and Archimedes, tempera back-
ground sheet, trimmed to outline fig-
ure, framed, Walt Disney Studios,
1963 . . . .   **2,090.00**
The Three Caballeros, full figure
Aracuan Bird, framed, Walt Disney
Studio, 1945, 5 x 2½" **470.00**
Tom and Jerry, 1950s, sword fight,
hand ink, 6 x 7" **185.00**
Toot, Whistle, Plunk, and Boom, cigar
chomping female dancer, Walt Dis-
ney Studio, 8 x 6½". **825.00**
Tweety's Circus, Sylvester on high
wire, framed, Warner Brothers Stu-
dio, 1955, 5½ x 12" **1,760.00**
Who Framed Roger Rabbit, movie
scene, Walt Disney Studio, 8½ x
11½". **1,760.00**
Winnie the Pooh and a Day For Eeyore,
Pooh holding honey jar, Walt Disney
Studio, 6 x 3½" **1,045.00**
Winnie the Pooh, Christopher Robin
and Eeyore, 6 x 8" **195.00**
Wynken, Blynken, and Nod, riding in
wooden shoe boat, airbrush back-
ground, framed, Walt Disney Stu-
dios, 1938, 9½ x 11" **2,090.00**
Yellow Submarine, John Lennon and
Ringo Starr, King Features/Heinz
Edleman, 7½ x 9" **2,200.00**

ARCADE CARDS

History: Arcade cards were distributed in coin
operated vending machines in "Penny Arcades"
and other locations before the electronic game
era. They are generally ¹/₁₆" thick, a thickness
necessary to accommodate the coin operated machines.

A typical arcade card measured approximately
3³/₈" x 5¹/₄", roughly the same size as a golden age

post card. In fact, many arcade cards had post
card backs to enhance their appeal to tourists.

Arcade Machine and Supply Company's pin–
up style, 1901–07 era post cards are recognized
as the first arcade cards. Around 1910 the Meyer
Printing Company, Chicago, Illinois, produced
their first series of pin–up arcade cards. Meyer
Printing Company evolved into the Exhibit Supply
Company of Chicago.

Exhibit Supply Company introduced a sepia–
tone arcade card Movie Stars set featuring post
card backs around 1919. The set's popularity led
to a market explosion. By 1921 series relating to
baseball stars, boxers, cowboys and Indians, fortunes, horoscopes, and myriad novelty topics
were offered. The Exhibit Supply Company continued to produce numerous arcade card series
on a variety of subjects through the seventies. The
company ceased operations in 1979.

International Mutoscope Reel Company was
Exhibit Supply Company's main competition
from the 1930s through the 1950s. Mutoscope
issued a variety of topical cards, but is best known
for its pin–up series featuring drawings by illustrators such as Rolf Armstrong, Elvgren, Earl Moran,
and Zoe Moran. These pin–up sketches are fine
examples of American lithography. Because each
card contains a distinct title (e.g., "A popular
number" or "Datable"), a checklist can be created, thus enhancing their collectibility. The Exhibit Supply Company did counter with a pin–up
series of its own early in 1950, which is much
harder to find.

Arcade card collectors are fortunate. Unlike
gum and tobacco card collectors who deal with
isolated sets, arcade card collectors can pick a
subject and find almost fifty years of unbroken
issues. Many collectors focus on a particular subject—baseball players, boxers, cowboys, historic
cards, movie stars, etc. Their primary goal is to
collect an entire series spanning the decades.
However, many are content to assemble several
annual sets.

Dating arcade cards is a science. In a few instances the cards are dated by copyright, e.g., the
boxers of the 1920s. More often it is necessary to
rely on clues such as size or position of a "MADE
IN USA" or "Printed in USA" inscription. Generally cards marked "MADE IN USA" are from the
forties, "Made in USA" are from the early fifties,
and "Printed in USA" from the late fifties onward.

Because of the breadth and depth of arcade
subjects, arcade card collectors often have to
compete with crossover collectors from other
fields. Fans of Muhammad Ali covet the 1963
"Cassius Clay" card, the only card produced of
Clay while he was an active boxer, quite a con-
trast to the Tom Mix collector who has over one
hundred different views from which to choose.
Nearly every celebrity from Charlie Chaplin to Ty
Cobb to Astronaut John Glenn has been portrayed
on an arcade card.

Key Cards and Sets: Sports related arcade cards, especially those focused on baseball, have attracted the attention of sports memorabilia collectors. The most valuable are 1920s issued baseball cards featuring Hall of Fame players, e.g., Ty Cobb and Lou Gehrig. These cards can bring several hundred dollars depending on condition. The most valuable card known is that of Babe Ruth dressed in a suit used to promote *The Babe Comes Home,* a movie in which he starred. It recently was offered for $3,000.

The 1925 and 1948 Sports Champions sets are also highly prized by collectors. Each set includes a selection of champions from a variety of sports. The 1948 set even includes Ben Sklar, the national champion marble shooter. The 1948 George Mikan, the first "big man" in basketball, card is valued at $200 plus.

Marilyn Monroe arcade cards command the most attention among movie star collectors. The three different cards produced during the 1950s sell in excess of $100 in near mint condition. John Wayne is king of the cowboy stars. Henry Winkler's card from Exhibit Supply was among the last of the star cards. It has a market value of $10.

Aviation buffs prize the sixteen card Lindbergh set and the "American Aces" set featuring record breaking flights, both from the late 1920s. Individual cards sell in the $15 range.

In the Mutoscope series, the hardest to find cards is "My Diver's License" from the Earl Moran "Hotcha Girl" set. Most examples were removed before the set was distributed. Value exceeds $100.

The most enigmatic set is the sixteen card Mussolini set from around 1927. It sold poorly, thus making it one of the most difficult sets to find.

Collectors' Club: Arcade Collectors International, 3621 Silver Spur Lane, Acton, CA 93510.

REPRODUCTION ALERT: On any given day, perhaps twenty percent (20%) of the arcade cards being offered for sale at a flea market, shop, or show are forgeries. Many sellers simply do not know the difference.

Until approximately 1966, Exhibit Supply Company used a consistent cream color stock that turns a darker tan with age. Forgeries do not duplicate this original stock. Most have stark white backs, often of a poor quality stock flecked with black impurities.

Post 1966 Exhibit Supply Company sets do have a lighter colored stock, thus creating some confusion. Continue to look for a cream colored caste (pure with no strands of black) and higher quality half tones to distinguish the Exhibit cards from the forgeries. Forgeries often have muddy and light half tones.

Exhibit did not necessarily change a successful set each year. Often the company "reprinted" a set for several years. This occurred more readily

in the late sixties when the company experienced financial difficulties and less money was available for new product development. Legitimate reprint cards are collected as though they were first year issue cards. However, because of their large numbers, values for cards from these sets are often low.

Advisor: R. J. Schulhof, 3621 Silver Spur Lane, Acton, CA 93510.

Price Notes: Like most paper collectibles, value is based on condition, scarcity, and desirability. Grading is similar to that used in gum cards— Near Mint (NR MT) is virtually a perfect card; Excellent (EX) has some wear at the corners; Very Good (VG) is still attractive, almost no visible defects, and rounded corners; and Good is really used for cards in such a condition that no serious collector will collect them.

In the listing below, "Normal Grade" means the best grade normally accessible to collector. Going up one grade, e.g. excellent to near mint, increases value by 50% to 100%. Going down one grade, e.g., excellent to very good, decreases values by 25% to 50%.

Value is the retail price for a single card. It is customary to discount complete sets approximately 20% below the total of the individual card prices.

Set numbers are from J. R. Burdick's *The American Card Catalog: The Standard Guide On All Collected Cards and Their Values,* reprinted in 1988 by Nostalgia Press, Inc., of New York, which assigned arcade cards the numbers W401 to W470. Remember, post–1966 cards are distinguished by their near white backs.

W401 to W405, Movie Stars

1919–1940, Normal Grade: Very Good to Excellent

Common card.............	**3.00–5.00**
Star card	**10.00–15.00**

1940–1957, Normal Grade: Excellent to Mint

Common card.............	**2.00–3.00**
Star card	**5.00–10.00**

1958–1966, Normal Grade: Near Mint

Common card.............	**1.00–3.00**
Star card.....................	**5.00**

1966 and later, Normal Grade: Near Mint

Common card	**1.00**
Star card.....................	**3.00**

Premier Card

Chaplin, excellent	**20.00–30.00**
Gable, near mint..........	**10.00–20.00**
Harlow, excellent..........	**20.00–30.00**
Pickford, excellent	**20.00–30.00**
Taylor, near mint	**10.00–20.00**
Valentino, excellent	**10.00–20.00**

Girlie, woman wearing lingerie, 3¹/₄ x 5¹/₄", 1950s, $9.00.

W409, Radio & TV Stars
1930–1940, Normal Grade: Very Good to Excellent
  Common card............ **3.00–5.00**
  Star card................. **5.00–10.00**
1940–1958, Normal Grade: Excellent to Mint
  Common card............ **3.00–5.00**
  Star card **5.00–10.00**
1958–1966, Normal Grade: Near Mint
  Common card............ **1.00–3.00**
  Star card................. **5.00**
1966 and later, Normal Grade: Near Mint
  Common card **1.00**
  Star card................. **3.00**
Premier Card
  Amos & Andy, excellent to mint ... **10.00**
  Lucille Ball, excellent to mint **10.00**
W410 to W419, Western Stars
1922–1940, Normal Grade: Very Good to Excellent
  Common card **5.00**
  Star card **8.00–12.00**
1940–1957, Normal Grade: Excellent to Mint
  Common card............ **3.00–5.00**
  Star card **8.00–10.00**
1958–1966, Normal Grade, Near Mint
  Common card............ **1.00–3.00**
  Star card................. **5.00**
1966 and later, Normal Grade: Near Mint
  Common card **1.00**
  Star card................. **3.00**
Premier Card
  Chuck Conners **5.00**
  William S. Hart, excellent **12.00**

Tom Mix, excellent **12.00**
Jayne Russell (cowgirl)........... **15.00**
John Wayne, excellent........... **20.00**
W423, Pin–ups
  Note: Most pin–up cards portray anonymous models. Exhibit Supply cards that feature recognizable movie stars are worth a premium.
1910–1920, Normal Grade: Very Good to Excellent
  Common card............ **1.00–3.00**
  Star card.................. **NA**
1920–1940, Normal Grade: Excellent to Near Mint
  Common card............ **3.00–5.00**
  Star card.................. **10.00**
1940–1957, Normal Grade: Excellent to Near Mint
  Common card............ **3.00–5.00**
  Star card.................. **10.00**
1958–1966, Normal Grade: Near Mint
  Common card **3.00**
  Star card **5.00–10.00**
1966 and later, Normal Grade: Near Mint
  Common card **1.00**
  Star card.................. **NA**
Premier cards
  Betty Grable................. **10.00**
  Marilyn Monroe .... **100.00 +**
  Jayne Russell **15.00**
W424, Artist Lithographs
  Note: Artwork signed by Armstrong, Elvgren, Moran, and Mozert. Produced in 32 or 64 card sets.
Exhibit Supply–slightly larger than a Mutoscope card, no inscription, 1950–1955
  Near Mint **15.00–25.00**
  Excellent to Mint.......... **10.00–20.00**
Mutoscope, always inscribed "A MUTOSCOPE CARD," 1940–1950
  Near Mint **8.00**
  Excellent to Mint **5.00**
Premier cards
  Golden Hours **25.00**
  My Diver's License **100.00**
W451 to W453, Historic Cards, series
Air Aces, Normal Grade: Excellent, 1929 .... **15.00**
Astronauts, Normal Grade: Near Mint
  1963–1966.............. **3.00–5.00**
  1966 and later............ **2.00–3.00**
Automobiles, Normal Grade: Near Mint
  1951–1966.............. **3.00–5.00**
  1966 and later **1.00**
Jet Planes, Normal Grade: Near Mint, 1951–58 .... **3.00–5.00**
Lindbergh, Normal Grade: Excellent, 1927 until early 1930s **10.00–12.00**

John Mack Brown, real photo, green tone, 3¼ x 5¼", 1950s, $9.00.

Roger Mackay, wrestler, real photo, sepia tint, 3⅜ x 5⅜", 1940s, $7.50.

Mussolini, Normal Grade: Excellent, 1927 .... **20.00**
W460–W464, Baseball Players
1920–1929, Normal Grade: Excellent
  Common card **15.00**
  Hall of Fame card **50.00**
1929–1938, Normal Grade: Excellent to Near Mint, four on one card
  Common card **30.00**
  Hall of Fame card **100.00**
1939–1946, Normal Grade: Near Mint
  Common card **4.00**
  Hall of Fame card **10.00**
1946–1963, Normal Grade: Near Mint
  Common card **3.00**
  Hall of Fame card **10.00**
Premier cards
  Earl Averill.................... **200.00**
  Ty Cobb **250.00–750.00**
  Lou Gehrig **250.00–750.00**
  Gabby Hartnett **200.00**
  Mickey Mantle (portrait) **100.00**
  Babe Ruth **250.00–750.00**
  Carl Yastrzemski **100.00**
W467 to W469, Boxers and Wrestlers
1921–1939, Normal Grade: Very Good to Excellent
  Common card **5.00**
  Star card..................... **15.00**
1940–1961, Normal Grade: Excellent to Mint
  Common card **5.00**
  Star card..................... **20.00**
1963 and later, Normal Grade: Near Mint
  Common card **3.00**
  Star card..................... **10.00**

Premier cards
  Cassius Clay.................. **100.00**
  Jack Dempsey............ **25.00–50.00**
  Jack Johnson **100.00**
  Rocky Marciano **100.00**
  John L. Sullivan **100.00**
  Gene Tunney **25.00–50.00**
W468, Football Players
1948–1958, Normal Grade: Near Mint
  Common card **8.00**
  Star card..................... **20.00**
Premier card, Normal Grade: Near Mint, cards found only in 1948 set
  Chuck Bednarik............... **200.00**
  Bob Cifers **175.00**
  Irv Comp **175.00**
  DeWitt Coulter **175.00**
  Clyde LeForce **175.00**
  John Mastrangelo.............. **175.00**
  Walt Schlinkman............... **175.00**
  Herm Wedemeyer.............. **200.00**
W469, Sports Champions, Normal Grade: Excellent to Mint, 1948
  Common card **10.00**
  Star card..................... **25.00**

ART, ORIGINAL

History: The earliest drawings date to prehistoric time. Art is universal. Everyone draws and doodles. Generations of elementary and secondary school art teachers have been unrelenting in their efforts to foster the hidden artistic talents in us all. A surprising amount of material, even that done purely for personal enjoyment, is saved.

    The problem is to separate the good from the

bad, the collectible from the non–collectible. Judgment is subjective. As a result, much of what is preserved should have been destroyed.

Original art is a one–of–a–kind drawing or painting. It is not a copy of something else. It can be done by a youngster or an octogenarian. The definition does not involve the issue of quality, just the act of doing.

Collectible original art is another matter. In order for a piece of original art to be collected, it must have appeal. In order for it to have value, it must be salable on the secondary market and have a viable resale track record (or the potential for one).

Many individuals buy original art simply for the pleasure it brings them. Resale considerations do not enter their mind. These individuals are blessed.

The vast majority of those using this book are concerned about the inherent resale value of original art. As such, there are two key considerations in addition to the traditional concerns with condition, artistic merit, etc.; these are subject and artist recognition.

The modern collecting market is subject driven. Even unaesthetic original art can sell if the subject is a strong one. Just look at the folk art market. The key to value by subject is that the art resemble the object being portrayed as closely as possible.

Included in the following references are several guides that report annual auction prices. The first thing that should be done after acquiring an artist–signed piece of art is to check if the artist has an established resale record. In the vast majority of cases, the answer will be no. Now, there exists one of two possibilities—either the artist is so scarce that his work appears only once every decade or two, or no one cares. The wise understand that in ninety–nine point nine percent of the cases the latter is true.

References: Alan S. Bamberger, *Buy Art Smart: Foolproof Strategies for Buying Any Kind of Art with Confidence*, Wallace–Homestead, 1990; Ann Gilbert, *The Official Identification and Price Guide to American Illustrator Art*, House of Collectibles, 1991; Krexpress, *Art at Auction in America*, Krexpress, 1993; Rosemary and Michael McKittrick, *The Official Price Guide to Fine Art, Second Edition*, House of Collectibles, 1993; Susan Theran, *Fine Art: Identification and Price Guide, Second Edition*, Avon Books, 1992; Jerry Weist, *Original Comic Art: Identification and Price Guide*, Avon Books, 1992.

Periodicals: *Leonard's Annual Price Index of Art Auctions*, Susan Theran and Katheryn Acerbo editors, published annually by Auction Index, 30 Valentine Park, Newton, MA 02165; *Original Art Collector*, 210 Fifth Avenue, Suite 1102, New York, NY 10010.

DRAWINGS

Adams, Neal, 1968, pen and ink on paper, cover artwork for Justice League of America No 66, matted, 15 x 10" **880.00**

Anderson, Murphy, 1965, pen and ink on paper, cover artwork for Showcase No 56, features Doctor Fate and Hourman, matted and framed, 18¼ x 12¼" **4,950.00**

Barks, Carl, c1955, pencil on tissue, model sheet for comic book art, Huey, Louie, and Dewey, inscribed, matted, 7½ x 9½" **1,100.00**

Bernhart, Peter, VA, fraktur, birth and baptismal certificate, 1800, oval center surrounded by stems of branches with flowers and seed pods, 12½ x 7½" **3,500.00**

Breathed, Berk, 1988, Bloom County, india ink on heavy paper, Opus taking first perilous steps, framed, 5 x 16" **1,210.00**

Crumb, Robert, 1972, pen and ink on board, six page story for Fuzzy Bunny in Nut Factory Blues, 12 x 8" **5,500.00**

Ditko, Steve, 1964, pen and ink on paper, page 6 artwork for Spider–Man No 23, 18½ x 12½" **1,100.00**

Eyer, Johann Adam, fraktur, bookplate, dated 1781, watercolor, pen, and ink, blue and yellow peacock perched on flowering tulip tree, 4¼ x 2½" **4,125.00**

Feiffer, Jules, 1960, Munro, blue and black pencil on storyboard sheets, set of 116 drawings, unframed, 3 x 4" each **2,500.00**

Caricature Sketch, grease pencil drawing, eastern Pennsylvania artist, 17½ x 22", $15.00.

Frazetta, Frank, 1970s, pen and ink on paper, nude woman on rock with snake, matted and framed, 3¼ x 5" **2,200.00**

Griffith, Bill, 1978, pen and ink on board, cover art for Yow Comics No 1, sgd, matted and framed, 15 x 11" **3,300.00**

Hanna–Barbera Studio, mid 1960s, pencil on story sheets, Johnny Quest, complete set, Tree Boys episode, unframed, 10 x 12" **880.00**

Herriman, George, 1938, pen and ink on board, Krazy Kat Daily, sgd, 4¼ x 20" **880.00**

Heydrich, Baltzer, Montgomery County, 1845, fraktur, pen, ink, and watercolor on woven paper, altar with stylized flowers in semicircular motif, bird on branch, checkerboard border, inscribed "Baltzer Heydrich . . . 1845 . . . in his 83rd year," framed, 16¼ x 20¼" **7,600.00**

Jay Ward Studio, 1959–1961, colored pencil and conte crayon on animation sheets, 122 drawings of Rocky and His Friends, various sizes **6,600.00**

Jones, Jeff, 1972, pen, ink, and wash on paper, cover art for Wonder Woman No 199, sgd and inscribed, matted and framed, 15 x 10" **3,850.00**

Kubert, Joe, 1959, pen and ink on paper, splash page of Brave and the Bold No. 24, titled "Curse of the Dragon's Moon," matted, 18 x 13" **1,980.00**

Lykens Valley Artist, Taufschein, fraktur, baptismal record for Johann Frederick Lupold, June 6, 1789, watercolor, pen, and ink, framed, 8¼ x 13¼" **2,500.00**

Mauldin, Bill, 1941–45, pen, ink, and pencil on pebble paper, two military men cartoon, sgd, 10 x 8" **1,320.00**

McCay, Winsor, 1921, pen and ink on paper, political cartoon of air power sinking fleet, inscribed, matted, 10½ x 22" **2,750.00**

Moore, Thomas C, 1828, fraktur, pr romantic verse illus, watercolor and ink, framed, 6½" sq and 6½ x 8¾" . . **350.00**

Schaffenberger, Kurt, 1957, pen and ink on paper, sample tryout page of Lois Lane and Superman, mounted with artwork and letter **3,575.00**

Schultz, Charles, 1967, pen and ink on paper, Peanuts Daily Strip, sgd, 5½ x 27" **3,025.00**

Shuster, Joe, graphite pencil on Hotel Stanton stationery, Superman, sgd, matted and framed, 8½ x 5½" **880.00**

Smith, Win, Bosko, 1930, india ink on heavy paper, framed, 19 x 11½" . . . **770.00**

Walt Disney Studio
Alice in Wonderland, Ollie John-

ston, 1951, brown and black pencil on animation sheet, framed, inscribed and sgd, 7½ x 7" **1,320.00**

Alpine Climbers, 1936, red and black pencil on animation sheets, 34 detailed drawings, Mickey landing in eagle's nest, various sizes, unframed **2,530.00**

Mickey Mouse, Floyd Gottfredson, April 20, 1935, india ink and blue pencil on heavy paper, Mickey Mouse Runs His Own Newspaper, framed, 5½ x 26½" **3,190.00**

Moving Day, 1936, red and black pencil on animation sheets, 8 pgs of gag suggestions, Mickey, Minnie, Goofy, and Horace in various story situations, unframed, 8½ x 11" **1,540.00**

Snow White and the Seven Dwarfs, 1937, red pencil on animation sheets, 118 rough drawings of the Queen in studio folder marked "Algar (John) Personal," unframed, various sizes **1,045.00**

Steamboat Willie, 1928, pencil on animation sheet, framed, 6 x 4" . . **2,090.00**

The Dognapper, 1934, red, blue, and black pencil on paper, Officer Donald Duck and Peg–Leg Pete, detailed layout drawing, unframed, 8 x 15½" **1,760.00**

Touchdown Mickey, 1932, red, blue, and black pencil on animation sheet, six pgs of gag suggestions, sgd by artists, unframed, 8 x 10" **1,540.00**

Warner Brothers Studio, In–Studio Gag Drawings, 1940, colored pencil on animation sheet, 85 drawings studio

Portrait, crayon, chalk, and pencil drawing, 9 x 13", 1932, $65.00.

Story Board, pencil, pen, and ink drawing, Pumpernickle Bill, *Allentown Morning Call* comic strip, 10¹/₈ x 4³/₄", $25.00.

caricature drawings, unframed, various sizes **1,540.00**

Whitehead, Paul, 1988, Skunk Dancin, airbrush and tempera on heavy paper, Pepe Le Pew dancing with Felice, framed, sgd, 16¹/₂ x 13"..... **330.00**

PAINTING

American School, 19th C, In the Shade by the Banks of the River/A Hudson River View, oil on board, framed, unsigned, 3¹/₄ x 6¹/₂"............. **770.00**

Beal, Reynolds, American, 1867–1951, Watching the Elephants/A Circus Scene, crayon and colored pencil on paper, framed, sgd and dated, 18 x 23¹/₂"..................... **2,200.00**

Benson, Frank Weston, American, 1862–1951, Camden Hills from North Haven, ME, watercolor and graphite on paper, framed, sgd and dated, 20¹/₂ x 13¹/₂"............. **6,600.00**

Blaney, Dwight, American, 1865–1944, Hollyhocks, watercolor on paperboard, framed, sgd and dated, 13 x 16¹/₄"................. **3,740.00**

Brown, John Appleton, American, 1844–1902, The Sheep Meadow, pastel on brown paperboard, framed, sgd, 14¹/₄ x 19¹/₄"......... **3,025.00**

Cady, Harrison, American, 1877–1970, On the Beach at Pelican Bay, watercolor with graphite and blue pen on paper, framed, sgd and inscribed, 18¹/₂ x 13³/₄"........... **495.00**

Capp, Al, 1950s, watercolor on thin paper, Shmoo sleeping, inscription, matted and framed, 11¹/₂ x 15¹/₂"... **1,210.00**

Chase, Susan Miller, American, 20th C, The Parasol, oil on board, sgd, Newcomb–Macklin frame, 14 x 10"......................... **935.00**

Cross, Roy, American, 20th C, West Indies Trading Sloop Mediator, watercolor and gouache on paperboard, framed, sgd, 7¹/₄ x 12"........... **880.00**

Davis, Charles Harold, American, 1856–1933, The Country Road, Amesbury, oil on board, framed, sgd, 11¹/₂ x 17³/₄"................. **1,210.00**

Davis, Jack, 1957, watercolor on board, James Dean, full length, 13³/₄ x 8"....................... **1,210.00**

Diehl, Arthur Vidal, American, 1870–1929, Oriental street, oil on board, framed, sgd and dated, 19¹/₂ x 28¹/₂" **880.00**

Flannigan, Lucy Agnes, American, c1900, A Leaf from the Grand Tour/The Italian Villa, watercolor on paper, framed, sgd, 30 x 20"........ **525.00**

Goodwin, American, 1864–1929, Sundown, pastel on paperboard, framed, sgd and dated, 15³/₄ x 19³/₄" **475.00**

Gulacy, Paul, 1981, oil on board, cover painting of Bizarre Adventures No 27, Marvel Comics, features Iceman, Phoenix, and Nightcrawler, framed, 29¹/₄ x 19¹/₄" **4,950.00**

Jones, Lawrence A, American, 20th C, The Beach at Jackson Park, Chicago, watercolor and graphite on paper, matted, unframed, sgd and dated, 13¹/₂ x 17³/₄".................. **165.00**

Kaluta, Michael, 1981, watercolor on paper, Vercadian Protector Android No 7 Vacationing on Aguatunisia, matted and framed, 12³/₄ x 12³/₄" ... **2,090.00**

Kelly, Ken, 1975, oil on board, cover painting for Creepy No 66, sgd, 25 x 17" **770.00**

Kronberg, ·Louis, American, 1872–1965, The Ballet/A Fan Design, pastel on blue/gray paper, framed, monogrammed and inscribed, 9 x 17¹/₄"...................... **880.00**

Kuhn, Walt, American, 1877–1949, Amalda, watercolor on paper, framed, sgd and dated, 15³/₄ x 12" .. **4,000.00**

Lansil, Walter Franklin, American, 1846–1925, In the Gulf of Venice, oil on board, framed, sgd and dated "Walter F Lansil 1917," 7 x 8³/₄" ... **300.00**

MacKnight, Dodge, American, 1860–

1950, Lake in the Rockies, watercolor on paper, framed, sgd, 16¼ x 23" **1,430.00**

Margulies, Joseph, American, 1896–1984, On the Beach, Good Harbor, watercolor and graphite on paper, framed, sgd and dated, 14¼ x 20¾" **330.00**

Murphy, Hermann Dudley, American, 1867–1945, Mango trees, oil on board, framed, sgd and monogrammed, 11¾ x 15¾" **525.00**

Patterson, Margaret Jordan, American, 1868–1950
  The Coastal Village, watercolor on paper, framed, sgd, 9½ x 12¾" .. **310.00**
  The Long Ridge, watercolor, gouache, and graphite on paper, framed, sgd and dated, 14 x 16¾" **385.00**

Ripley, Aiden Lassell, American, 1896–1969
  An Italian Harbor, watercolor, graphite, and gouache on paper, framed, 13¼ x 17¾"........... **935.00**
  The Guides' Cabin, watercolor on paper, framed, sgd, 14 x 19¾" ... **1,650.00**

Sample, Paul Starrett, American, 1896–1974, Expedition up River Pinware River Labrador, watercolor and gouache on paper, framed, sgd, 10¼ x 14¼" **1,870.00**

Steacy, Ken, 1991, acrylic on paper, cover painting for King Kong Mini Series, Monster Comic, sgd, matted, 11¾ x 8¾" **3,025.00**

Story, George Henry, American, 1835–1923, The Letter, oil on board, unframed, sgd and dated "G H Story 78," 9⅞ x 8" **1,430.00**

Soyer, Raphael, American, 1899–1987, Meeting with Zosin in Front of Library, watercolor and graphite on paper, framed, sgd, inscription on reverse, 15¾ x 12¼" **935.00**

Stone, Don, American, 20th C, The Winter Pasture, watercolor on paper, framed, sgd, 21 x 14" **1,500.00**

Taylor, Richard, American, 1902–1970, They Look Much Better With Their Clothes On, Don't They?, graphite on paper, sgd, 17 x 13¾" .. **525.00**

Tobey, Mark, American, 1890–1976, Beaver, tempera on paper, framed, sgd and dated, 7½ x 13¾" **1,100.00**

Tuttle Ruel Crompton, American, 18th C, A Walk in the Rain/A Paris Street Scene, watercolor, gouache, and graphite on paperboard, framed, sgd and dated, 17¾ x 13⅜" **275.00**

Turner, Ross Sterling, American, 1847–1915, Le Asuncion, watercolor and gouache on paperboard, framed, sgd, 18½ x 12½" **610.00**

Vess, Charles, 1992, watercolor on paper, April 1985 cover of Web of Spider–Man No 1, mounted on board **3,575.00**

Walker, Robert Hollands, British, 19th/20th C, A Breezy Day on the Mersey, watercolor and gouache on paperboard, framed, sgd, 7½ x 14½" **525.00**

Wrightson, Bernie, 1969, watercolor on paper, captioned "Jason's in the Basement...With Daddy," matted and framed, 11¼ x 8¾" **1,210.00**

Wyeth, Andrew, American, 18th C, A Winter Scene, gouache on paper, framed, sgd and dedicated, 11¼ x 16¾"........................ **8,800.00**

AUTOGRAPHS

History: Autograph collecting is an old established tradition, perhaps dating back to the first signed documents and letters. Letters and documents from the Medieval and Renaissance periods are scarce; hence, they are treasured by individuals when available on the private market. Most are housed in municipal, church, and other institutional archives.

Autograph collecting became fashionable during the 19th century. However, early collectors focused on the signature alone, clipping off the signed portion of a letter or document. Eventually collectors realized that the entire document was valuable.

The advent of movie stars, followed by sports, rock 'n' roll, and television personalities, brought autograph collecting to the popular level. Fans pursue these individuals with autograph books, programs, and photographs. Everything imaginable is used for signatures. Realizing the value of their signatures and the speculation that occurs, modern stars and heroes are less willing to sign material than in the past. In fact, many have hired agents to control the "sale" of their signatures.

The condition and content of letters and documents bear significantly on value. Signatures should be crisp, clear, and located so that they do not detract from the rest of the item. Whenever possible, obtain a notarized statement of authenticity, especially for pieces over $100.

Presentation material, something marked "To _____," is of less value than a non–presentation item. The presentation personalizes the piece and often restricts interest, except to someone with the same name.

The leading auction sources for autographs are Swann Galleries, Sotheby's, and Christie's, all located in New York City.

References: Mary A. Benjamin, *Autographs: A Key To Collecting*, reprint, Dover, 1986; Charles Hamilton, *American Autographs*, University of Oklahoma Press, 1983; Robert W. Pelton, *Collecting Autographs For Fun And Profit*, Betterway Publications, 1987; George Sanders, Helen Sanders, Ralph Roberts, *Collector's Guide To Autographs,* Wallace–Homestead, 1990; George Sanders, Helen Sanders, Ralph Roberts, *The Price Guide To Autographs, 2nd Edition,* Wallace–Homestead, 1991.

Periodical: *The Autograph Collector's Magazine,* P.O. Box 55328, Stockton, CA 95205.

Collectors' Clubs: Manuscript Society, 350 Niagara Street, Burbank, CA 95105; Universal Autograph Collectors Club, P.O. Box 6181, Washington, DC 20044.

REPRODUCTION ALERT: Forgeries abound. Copying machines compound the problem. Further, many signatures of political figures, especially presidents, movie stars, and sports heroes are machine or secretary signed or printed as part of the photograph or document. Photographic reproduction can produce a signature resembling an original. Check all signatures using a good magnifying glass or microscope.

There are autograph mills throughout the country run by people who write to noteworthy individuals requesting their signatures on large blocks of material. They in turn sell this material on the autograph market. Buy an autograph of a living person only after the most careful consideration and examination.

The following abbreviations denote type of autograph material and their sizes.

ADS	Autograph Document Signed
ALS	Autograph Letter Signed
AQS	Autograph Quotation Signed
CS	Card Signed
DS	Document Signed
LS	Letter Signed
PS	Photograph Signed
TLS	Typed Letter Signed

Sizes (approximate):

Folio	12 x 16 inches
4to	8 x 10 inches
8vo	5 x 7 inches
12mo	3 x 5 inches

ENTERTAINMENT

Armstrong, Louis, 10 x 8" glossy sepia photo sgd, signature c1945 in his usual green ink, on verso of photo, six members of his band have sgd in ink. 425.00
Astaire, Fred, 8 x 10" head and shoulder portrait sgd in blue ink 145.00
Bardot, Brigitte, photo, glossy, black and white, bold signature, 8 x 10" . . 35.00
Basie, Count, first day cover sgd honoring Gershwin with thin metal portrait 55.00
Bernstein, Leonard, fine black ink signature on center blank, 1964 first day cover honoring ASCAP 45.00
Boyd, William, (Hopalong Cassidy), "Good Luck from Hoppy" on first day cover honoring Pony Express, canceled St. Joseph, MO, 1940 . . . . 175.00
Burns, George and Gracie Allen, sgd photograph, 8 x 10" matte sepia 250.00
Carson, Johnny, signature double matted with color photo and engraved name plate 22.50
Caruso, Enrico, post card, pencil last name signature and address, 1904, matted with two photos and brass plate 325.00
Diddley, Bo, plain white card, 5 x 3" . . 10.00
Ellington, Duke, celebrated Black American pianist, bandleader and composer, autograph sentiment sgd on gold 3 x 5" card 95.00
Evans, Linda, TV actress' signature double matted with large black and white 18 x 24" photograph 27.50
Field, Totie, document, 1970, 8½ x 11" 40.00
Gluck, Alma, opera, personal card, book plate photo, and obituary, mounted on gray 12 x 16" board . . . 75.00
Godfrey, Arthur, document, 1977, 8½ x 14" 40.00
Gould, Elliot, photo, glossy, black and white, 8 x 10" 12.00
Holly, Buddy, fine pencil signature, January 1959, with color photo 1,350.00
Ladd, Alan, document, 1941, pencil sgd 30.00
Langtry, Lillie, letter, personal stationery. 150.00
Lennon, John, vintage signature matted with two 5 x 7" color photographs and an engraved name plate. 550.00
Mansfield, Jayne, photo, 5 x 7", 1950s 125.00
Melba, Nellie, opera, personal stationery, 3 pgs, photo and news article of her death, 5 x 7" 85.00
Presley, Elvis, sgd document, last page of contract with MGM Studios, 1961, extremely rare form 850.00
Rogers, Ginger, Christmas post card, 1938. . . . . 18.00
The Three Stooges, 10 x 8" black and white sgd photo scene from film. . . . 495.00

HISTORICAL

Astor, John Jacob, document sgd, paid indenture of mortgage, 1830, full ink signature, exceptional 2,000.00
Bradley, Omar N, photo, inscribed and sgd, black and white, 8 x 10" 110.00
Byrd, Richard E., famed explorer, sgd 2" x 3" card 45.00
Calhoun, John C, check, sgd on back . . 100.00

Castro, Fidel, 9″ x 7″ propaganda booklet, approximately 30 pages, 1959, full blue ink signature **1,250.00**

Chase, Salmon, letter, 1 pg, 1868, 5 x 7″ **200.00**

Chauncey, Isaac, letter, Feb 21, 1833 **100.00**

Churchill, Winston, full signature, 1907, matted with black and white photograph **1,250.00**

Clay, Henry, card, bold signature, includes engraving **85.00**

Coolidge, Calvin
Document sgd bank check, 1932 . . . **195.00**
Print, inscribed and sgd, 13½ x 17″ **250.00**

Dearborn, Henry, document, mounted **200.00**

Dix, John A, document, New York pay order, 1833, includes engraved portrait **45.00**

Earhart, Amelia, ½ x 2½″ slip mounted on 1½ x 2½″ piece, typed identification above and below signature **365.00**

Edison, Thomas A., pencil autographed note on 5 x 7″ lined sheet, October 12, 1915, answering message directly below, Edison signature large and clear **425.00**

Eisenhower, Dwight D., large, bold, ink signature on album leaf **175.00**

Ellsworth, Oliver, pay order, June 25, 1777 . . . . **150.00**

Fall, John P, Civil War soldier, autographed letter sgd, Alexandria, VA, 3¼ pages **75.00**

Hale, Edward E, clergy and author, autographed letter sgd, philosophical advice, 2 pages, 1892 . . . . **135.00**

Hoover, Herbert, stationery, dated April 6, 1934, bold signature **100.00**

Howard, Oliver Otis, typed letter, 1 pg, 1892, 8 x 10″ **90.00**

Kennedy, John F, typed letter sgd on 6 x 9″ Congress/House of Representatives stationery, November 25, 1952 **1,950.00**

Kennedy, Robert F., typed letter sgd, Office of Attorney General, June 17, 1964, to US Customs Court Judge, thank you for contribution to RFK Library from American Legion post . . . **450.00**

Lindbergh, Charles A., unpublished original 3½ x 5½″ sgd photo, snapshot of a youthful Lindbergh on deck of ship *Indianapolis* **1,695.00**

McCrady, Edward Jr., Confederate Lt Col, letter, 1892, 8 x 10″ **40.00**

McKaskey, William S., Cavalry Major General, letter sgd, July 1906, HQ Dept of Texas, San Antonio, plain stationery, holograph envelope, 6 pages **75.00**

Mitchell, Billy, huge in "Wm. Mitchell" cut signature, 5 x 2″ from a typed letter **175.00**

MacArthur, Douglas, neatly trimmed magazine bust portrait wearing uniform, mounted on 9½ x 6½″ card, boldly sgd **295.00**

Mussolini, Benito, sepia sgd photo, penned with dark black ink, 1938 . . **695.00**

Parsons, Samuel Holden, document, pay order, dated 1782 . . . . **275.00**

Patridge, William Ordway, American sculptor of Pieta, quotation sgd, "...1915–Character is Destiny, An old Greek motto which is true today...Wm Ordway Patridge" **95.00**

Rockwell, Norman, sgd photo post card, sentiment and full signature. . . **125.00**

Roosevelt, Franklin D., New York Executive mansion card, two color print photos **225.00**

Seton, Ernest Thomas, Boy Scout founder, typed letter, sgd, 1 pg, 1927, 5 x 7″. **50.00**

Stanton, Edwin M., Secretary of War, document, dated July 20, 1863, War Dept stationery **140.00**

Sumner, Charles, note sgd, 1811–74, matted. **75.00**

Taft, Howard, typed letter, August 31, 1925, Supreme Court stationery, framed **250.00**

Twain, Mark, autograph letter and portrait, Hotel Metropole, Vienna, letterhead, 1898, sgd "S.L.Clemens". . **1,895.00**

Van Buren, Martin, document, dated "11th June in The 32nd Year of our Independence," applied state seal . . **200.00**

Washington, Booker T., letter, clipped signature **60.00**

Wise, Henry A., letter, 1 pg, 1843, 8 x 10″ **125.00**

Wright, Orville, typed letter, personal letterhead, 1921 . . . . **800.00**

Wright, Wilbur and Orville, slip sgd by both **1,350.00**

Wyeth, N. C., letter sgd, personal stationery, holograph envelope **695.00**

Wyllys, Samuel, document, dated August 3, 1781 . . . . **45.00**

LITERATURE

Capote, Truman, document, news article, photo on top, black ink signature on photo, 3 x 7″. **75.00**

Doyle, Arthur Conan, letter, May 5, 1904, framed with envelope **175.00**

Glasgow, Ellen, letter, 1901, 1½ pgs, 5 x 7″ **150.00**

Grey, Zane, check, 1928 . . . . **60.00**

Haggard, Henry Rider, English novelist, fragment sheet, "I am glad today of course to find plenty of work on my

hands. Your affec & dutiful svt R
Haggard," 4 x 3½" **50.00**
Longfellow, Henry Wadsworth, letter,
December 3, 1844 . . . .   **475.00**
McManus, Seumas, letter, 1 pg, 5 x 7"   **25.00**
Millay, Edna St. Vincent, book, *The
King's Henchman,* 1927, sgd front . .   **150.00**
O'Neill, Eugene, book, *Mourning Be-
comes Electra,* 1931 . . . .   **150.00**
Sandburg, Carl, book, *Remembrance
Rock,* first edition, black signature . .   **145.00**
Stoddard, Elizabeth, quote, "May
Unfolds Its Leaves, Nature's Eternal
Mystery To Renew. Man Must Be
Less Than Leaf Or Flower, and End?"   **15.00**
Twain, Mark, card, framed with photo   **200.00**
Wells, H. G., English novelist **160.00**

SPORTS

Aaron, Hank, sgd baseball card, 8 x 10"
color photo, and engraved name
plate, double matted. **40.00**
Able, Sid, hockey player, unlined card,
5 x 3". **4.00**
Ali, Muhammed, sgd 8 x 10" color box-
ing pose photograph and engraved
name plate, double matted. **45.00**
Armour, Tom, III, golfer, card sgd. **15.00**
Bench, Johnny, unlined card, 5 x 3" . . .   **7.00**
Bird, Larry, magazine cov, *NBA Hoop,*
full color, sgd, double matted **40.00**
Dempsey, Jack, color post card, knock-
ing out Jess Willard, on verso penned
inscription, sentiment and full signa-
ture **50.00**
Dean, Paul "Dizzy," album leaf, in-
scription, sentiment, and signature in
pencil, matted with two black and
white pictures. **85.00**
Gehrig, Lou, 6 x 9" Pennsylvania Rail-

**Document Signed, Brabender, Hegan,
Smith, Baldwin, and Ermer, 1970 Milwaukee Brewers players, back cover of 1970
Baltimore Orioles Official Scorebook, 8½
x 11", $18.00.**

road menu, ink sentiment and signa-
ture on cov **1,450.00**
Frazier, Joe, limited edition print, No.
105, color, 18 x 24" **95.00**
Henie, Sonja, 7 x 9" black and white
sgd photograph, portrait pose. **95.00**
Namath, Joe, copy of stock certificate,
Broadway Joe's Restaurant, issued,
1969 . . . .   **125.00**
Paige, Satchel, card, 3 x 5" **50.00**
Player, Gary, golfer, card sgd **15.00**
Schmelling, Max, sgd 8 x 10" black and
white boxing pose photograph and
engraved name plate, double matted   **35.00**
Snead, Sam, limited edition print,
"13th at Augusta," Chromiste, artist
Helen Rundell **500.00**
Williams, Ted, sgd 5 x 7" black and
white action photograph, and en-
graved name plate, double matted . .   **80.00**

BIG LITTLE BOOKS

History: Big Little Books, although a trademark of
the Whitman Publishing Co., is a term used to
describe a wealth of children's books published
during the 1930s and continuing to the present
day. The origin of Big Little Books dates to a
number of 1920s series by Whitman among
which were Fairy Tales, Forest Friends, and Boy
Adventure.

The first Big Little Book appeared in 1933. Ten
different page lengths and eight different sizes
were tried by Whitman prior to the 1940s. Whitman and Saalfied Publishing Company dominated the field. However, other publishers did
enter the market. Among them were Engel–Van
Wiseman, Lynn Publishing Co., Goldsmith Publishing Co. and Dell Publishing Co.

Whitman also deserves attention for the various
remarketing efforts it undertook with many of its
titles. It contracted to provide Big Little Book
premiums for Cocomalt, Kool Aid, Pan–Am Gas,
Macy's, Lily–Tulip's Tarzan Ice Cream and
others. Among its series names are Wee Little
Books, Big Big Books, Nickel Books, Penny Books
and Famous Comics.

In the 1950s television characters were introduced into Big Little Book format. Whitman Publishing became part of Western Publishing,
owned by Mattel. Waldman and Son Publishing
Co. under its subsidiary, Moby Books, issued their
first Big Little Book–style book in 1977.

As more research is done and published on Big
Little Books, the factors determining value shift.
Condition always has been a key. Few examples
are in mint condition since the books were used
heavily by the children who owned them. Each
collector strives to obtain copies free from as

many defects (bent edges on cover, missing spine, torn pages, mutilation with crayon or pencil, missing pages, etc.) as possible.

The main character in a book often determines price since it is a collector from another field who vies with the Big Little Book collector for the same work. Dick Tracy, Disney characters, Buck Rogers, Flash Gordon, Charlie Chan, The Green Hornet and Tom Mix are examples. Other cowboy heroes are experiencing renewed popularity.

Until recently, little attention has been directed to the artists who produced the books. Now examples by Alex Raymond and Henry Vallely command top dollar. Other desirable artists are Al Capp, Allen Dean, Alfred Andriola, and Will Gould. Personal taste still is a critical factor at this time.

Little is known about how many copies of each book were printed. Scarcity charts have been prepared, but are constantly being revised. Books tend to hit the market in hoards, with prices fluctuating accordingly. However, the last decade has witnessed a stabilization of prices.

Larry Lowery, in the introduction to his book, has prepared an excellent section on the care and storage of Big Little Books. He also deserves credit for the detailed research he brings to each listing.

References: Larry Lowery, *Lowery's The Collector's Guide To Big Little Books and Similar Books*, privately printed, 1981; James Stuart Thomas, *The Big Little Book Price Guide*, Wallace–Homestead, 1983.

Collectors' Club: Big Little Book Collector's Club of America, PO Box 1242, Danville, CA 94526.

Note: Books are priced in very fine condition. Cover and spine are intact with only slight bending at the corners. All pages are present; only slightest discoloration of pages. Book has a crispness from cover color to inside.

No effort has been made to list the variations and premiums published by Whitman.
Abbreviations:
　　WBLB = Whitman Big Little Book
　　WBELB = Whitman Better Little Book
　　hc = hard cover
　　ms = Movie size, $4^5/8$ x $5^1/4$ x $^7/8$
　　sc = soft cover
　　ss = standard size, $3^5/8$ x $4^1/2$ x $1^1/2$

Better Little Book, Whitman
Andy Panda's Vacation, #1485, 1946, 352 pgs, Walter Lantz Productions **20.00**
Big Chief Wahoo And The Lost Pioneers, #1432, 1942, 432 pgs, Allen Saunders, author, Elmer Woggon, artist **35.00**
Blondie and Baby Dumpling, 1937 . . . **20.00**
Blondie, Cookie and Daisy's Pups, 1943, 352 pgs **20.00**
Brad Turner in Transatlantic Flight,

Scrappy: **Whitman Big Little Book, #1122, 282 pages, $4^3/4$ x $5^1/2$", 1934, $72.00;** *Keep 'Em Flying U.S.A. for America's Defense*: **Whitman Big Little Book, #1420, flip movie, 424 pages, $3^5/8$ x $4^1/2$", 1943, $30.00;** *Men With Wings*: **Whitman Better Little Book, #1475, 234 pages, $3^1/2$ x $4^1/2$", 1938, $35.00;** *Popeye and Queen Olive Oyl*: **Whitman, Big Little Book Classic, #5761, flip movie, 248 pages, $3^1/2$ x $4^1/2$", 1973, $8.00; and** *Two-Gun Montana*: **Whitman Big Little Book, #1104, 424 pages, $3^1/2$ x $4^1/2$", 1936, $26.00.**

1939, Albert B Dale, Robert Jenney artist **22.50**
Buck Jones and the Killers of Crooked Butte, 1940, Gaylord DuBois **20.00**
Buck Rogers, 25th Century A.D. vs The Fiend of Space, 1940, Dick Calkins and Phil Nowlan **30.00**
Bugs Bunny In Risky Business, #1440, 1948, 288 pgs, Warner Bros **15.00**
Calling W–1–X–Y–Z Jimmy Kean and the Radio Spies, 1939, Thorp McClusky **22.50**
Dan Dunn Secret Operative 48 and the Border Smugglers, 1938, Norman Marsh **20.00**
Desert Eagle and the Hidden Fortress, 1941, James O Parsons **16.00**
Detective Higgins of the Racket Squad, #1484, 1938, 432 pgs, Herbert Anderson, Millard Thacksen . . **20.00**
Dick Tracy The Super–Detective, 1939, Chester Gould **35.00**
Donald Duck, Such a Life!, #1404, 1939, 432 pgs, Al Taliaferro **30.00**
Don O'Dare Finds War, 1940, Gaylord DuBois, Erwin L Hess, artist . . . **18.00**
Don Winslow And The Great War Pilot, #1489, 1940, 432 pgs, Lt Frank V Martinek **25.00**

Ellery Queen, Adventure Of Last Man Club, #1406, 1940, 432 pgs, adapted from Ellery Queen **35.00**

Flame Boy and The Indians Secret, #1464, 1938, 300 pgs, Goren Arnold, author, Sekakuku, artist **12.00**

Ghost Avenger, #1426, 1943, 432 pgs, Russell R Winterbotham, author, Henry E Vallely, artist **35.00**

G–Man Breaking the Gambling Ring, 1938, Russell R Winterbotham, Jim Gary, artist **18.00**

*Harold Teen Swinging at the Sugar Bowl,*1939, Carl Ed **18.00**

Inspector Charlie Chan, Villainy On The High Seas, 1942, 432 pgs, Alfred Andriola, artist, adapted from Earl Deer Biggers **45.00**

John Carter of Mars, 1940, Edgar Rice Burroughs, John Coleman Burroughs cover and artist. **35.00**

Kayo and Moon Mullins and the One Man Gang, 1939, Frank Willard . . .   **20.00**

Lone Star Martin of the Texas Rangers, 1939, Peter A Wyckoff, Ted Horn, artist. **20.00**

Mandrake The Magician And The Midnight Monster, #1431, 1939, 432 pgs, Lee Falk **20.00**

Maximo The Amazing Superman, #1436, 1940, 432 pgs, Russell R Winterbotham, author, Henry E Vallely, artist **40.00**

Men With Wings, 1938, Eleanor Packer **25.00**

Perry Winkle and the Rinkeydinks Get a Horse, 1938, Martin Branner **18.00**

Popeye and the Deep Sea Mystery, 1939, Elzie C Segar **25.00**

Porky Pig and Petunia, #1408, 1942, 432 pgs, Leon Schlesinger Productions. **22.00**

Radio Patrol and Big Dan's Mobsters, 1940, Charles Schmidt and Eddie Sullivan **18.00**

Red Barry, Undercover Man, Will Gould, 1939 . . . .   **18.00**

Red Death On The Range, #1449, 1940, 432 pgs, Fred Harman **18.00**

Red Ryder and Little Beaver on Hoofs of Thunder, 1939, Fred Harman . . .   **30.00**

Secret Agent X–9 and the Mad Assassin, 1938, Robert Storm, Alex Raymond, artist **18.00**

Skyroads with Clipper Williams of the Flying Legion, 1938, Dick Calkins and Russell Keaton **18.00**

Smilin Jack Flying High With Downwing, #1412, 1942, 432 pgs, Zack Mosley. **18.00**

Speed Douglas And The Mole Gang, #1455, 1941, 432 pgs, Charles Arthur **30.00**

Tailspin Tommy And The Lost Transport, #1413, 1938, 432 pgs, Hal Forrest, author and artist **35.00**

Terry and The Pirates And The Giant's Vengeance, #1446, 1939, 432 pgs, Milton Caniff **20.00**

The Adventures of Huckleberry Finn, #1422, 1939, 432 pgs. **12.50**

The Green Hornet Returns, #1496, 1941, 432 pgs, adapted from Fran Strinker **30.00**

The Shadow And The Ghost Makers, #1495, 1942, 432 pgs, Maxwell Grant **25.00**

Union Pacific, 1939, Eleanor Packer   **20.00**

Windy Wayne and His Flying Wing, 1942, Russell R Winterbotham, Erwin L Darwin, artist **12.50**

Zip Saunders, King of the Speedway, 1939, Rex Loomis **18.00**

Big Little Book, Whitman

Ace Drummond, 1935, Capt Eddie Rickenbacker. **20.00**

Adventures of Tiny Tim, #767, 1935, 384 pgs, Stanley Link. **18.00**

Air Fighters of America, #1448, 1941, Roy Snell, author, Robert Jenney, artist. **15.00**

Alley Oop and Dinny, #736, 1935, 384 pgs, Vince T Hamlin author and artist. **20.00**

An Hour With You, #774, 1934, 160 pgs **18.00**

Apple Mary and Dennie Foil the Swindlers, #1130, 1936, Martha Orr . . .   **24.00**

Believe It Or Not, #760, 1933, 160 pgs, Robert Ripley **25.00**

Betty Boop in Snow White, #1119, 1934, 160 pgs, Wallace West, $4^{5}/8$ x $5^{1}/4''$ **35.00**

Blaze Brandon with the Foreign Legion, 1938, Gaylor R DuBois. **15.00**

Bob Stone, The Young Detective, 1937, Peter K Maple, Henry E Vallely, cover art **18.00**

Brick Bradford with Brocco the Mod-

Big Little Book type, *Adventures of Tim Tyler,* adapted from the newspaper strip by Lyman Young, Saalfield Publishing, printed color covers, ³/₄" thick, 8 x 3³/₄", 1934, $42.00.

ern Buccaneer, 1938, William Ritt and Clarence Gray............. **25.00**

Bronco Peeler, The Lone Cowboy, #1417, 1937, 432 pgs, Fred Harman...................... **15.00**

Buck Jones and the Two Gun Kid, #1404, 1937, Gaylord DuBois, author, Robert Weisman, artist **30.00**

Buck Rogers and the Depth Men of Jupiter, 1935, Dick Calkins and Phil Nowlan...................... **35.00**

Buffalo Bill Plays A Lone Hand, #1194, 1936, 432 pgs, Buck Wilson......................... **20.00**

Buzz Sawyer and Bomber 13, #1415, 1946, Roy Crane **24.00**

Captain Frank Hawks, Air Ace and the League of Twelve, 1938.......... **20.00**

Chester Gump in the City of Gold, 1935, Sidney Smith **15.00**

Coach Bernie Bierman's Brick Barton & the Winning Eleven, 1938 ...... **32.00**

Dan Dunn, Secret Operative 48, #1116, 1934, 320 pgs, Norman Marsh........................ **20.00**

Danger Trails In Africa, #1151, 432 pgs, Martin Johnson............. **14.00**

David Copperfield, 1934, Eleanor Packer **15.00**

Dick Tracy Solves the Penfield Mystery, 1934, Chester Gould **30.00**

Ella Cinders and the Mysterious House, 1934, Bill Conselman and Charlie Plumb **22.00**

Erik Noble and the Forty–Niners, 1934, Lloyd E Smith, B McNaughton, artist **18.00**

Felix The Cat, #1129, 1936, 432 pgs, adapted from Pat Sullivan **32.50**

Freckles and the Lost Diamond Mine, 1937, Merrill Blosser **14.00**

Gene Autry Cowboy Detective, 1940 **25.00**

Hairbreadth Harry in Department Q T, 1935 .... **15.00**

Inspector Wade Solves the Mystery of the Red Aces, 1937, Lyman Anderson........................ **15.00**

Jack Armstrong And The Ivory Treasure, #1435, 1937, 432 pgs, Leslie N Daniels, Jr, author, Henry E Vallely, artist **30.00**

Jack Swift and His Rocket Ship, 1934, Cliff Farrell and Hal Colson **20.00**

Joe Louis The Brown Bomber, 1936 .. **45.00**

Jungle Jim And The Vampire Woman, #1139, 1937, 432 pgs, Alex Raymond...................... **18.00**

Kay Darcy and the Mystery Hideout, 1937, Irene Ray, Charles Mueller, artist...................... **18.00**

King of the Royal Mounted Gets His Man, 1938, Zane Grey **15.00**

Little Annie Rooney On The Highway

To Adventure, #1406, 1938, 432 pgs, Brandon Walsh, author, Darrell McClure, artist................ **40.00**

Little Big Shot, #1149, 1935, 240 pgs, Warner Bros Pictures, artist **22.50**

Little Men, 1934, Eleanor Packer..... **14.00**

Little Miss Muffet, #1120, 1936, 432 pgs, Fanny Y Cory, author and artist **15.00**

Little Orphan Annie, #703, 1933, 320 pgs, Harold Gray, 3⁷/₈ x 4³/₄" **42.00**

Little Orphan Annie & Mysterious Shoemaker, 1938 .... **20.00**

Mac of the Marines in Africa, 1936, Mark Smith **18.00**

Mickey Mouse The Detective, #1139, 1934, 432 pgs, Floyd Gottfredson, author and artist................ **35.00**

Moby Dick, #710, 1934, 160 pgs, Warner Bros Pictures, 4⁵/₈ x 5¹/₄" ... **16.50**

Moon Mullins and Kayo, #746, 1933, 320 pgs, Frank Willard **20.00**

My District Attorney on the Job, #1408, 1941................. **15.00**

Nancy and Sluggo, #1400, 1946, Ernie Bushmiller **26.00**

Og, Son of Fire, #1115, 1936, 432 pgs, Irving Crump, author and artist **30.00**

Oswald The Lucky Rabbit, #1109, 1934, 160 pgs, Universal Pictures, 4⁵/₈ x 5¹/₄".................... **28.00**

Pat Nelson, Ace of the Test Pilots, #1445, 1937, Dougal Lee........ **15.00**

Pluto the Pup, 1938, Walt Disney Studios **20.00**

Popeye and the Jeep, 1937, Elzie C Segar **23.00**

Prairie Bill and the Covered Wagon, #758, 1934, G A Alkire, author, Hal Arbo, artist.................. **15.00**

Radio Patrol, #1142, 1934, 432 pgs, Charlie Schmidt............... **12.50**

Red Barry, Ace Detective, Hero of the Hour, #1157, 1935, 432 pgs, Will Gould **18.00**

Reg'lar Fellers, 1933, Gerne Byrnes .. **12.00**

Riders of Lone Trails, #1425, 1937, 300 pgs, Steve Saxton **10.00**

Robinson Crusoe, #719, 1934, 360 pgs, 3¹/₂ x 2".................. **16.00**

Secret Agent X–9, 1936, Charles Flanders, Alex Raymond, artist **20.00**

Shooting Sheriffs, #1195, 1936, 432 pgs, Leon Morgan **15.00**

Skeezix At The Military Academy, #1408, 1938, 432 pgs, Frank King **17.50**

Skippy, 1934, Percy Crosby, Sunday reprints...................... **12.00**

Smitty in Going Native, #1477, 1938, Walter Berndt **20.00**

Sombrero Pete, 1936, Morton H Cowen...................... **10.00**

Tailspin Tommy and the Sky Bandits, 1938, Hal Forrest............... **18.00**

Tarzan, New Adventures of, 1935, Edgar Rice Burroughs 22.50

Terry and the Pirates, 1935, Milton Caniff 18.00

Tex Thorne Come Out of the West, 1937, Zane Grey, Allen Dean, artist, Hal Arbo, cover 18.00

The Arizona Kid On The Bandit Trail, #1192, 1936, 432 pgs, Peter K Maple 14.00

The Beasts of Tarzan, #1410, 1938, 432 pgs, Rex Maxon 16.00

The Buccaneer, #1470, 1938, 240 pgs, Paramount Pictures 20.00

The Lone Ranger & the Vanishing Herd, 1936 . . . . 27.50

The Lost Patrol, #753, 1934, 160 pgs, RKO Pictures 40.00

The Spy, #768, 1936, 300 pgs 15.00

The Story of Charlie McCarthy and Edgar Bergen, #1456, 1938, 288 pgs, Eleanor Packer, author, Henry E Vallely, artist 30.00

This Is The Life, #1179, 1935, 240 pgs 21.00

Tim Tyler's Luck: Adventures In Ivory Patrol, #1140, 1937, 432 pgs, Lyman Young 15.00

Treasure Island, #720, 1933, 360 pgs, 3¹/₂ x 4" 18.00

Two–Gun Montana, 1936, Tex Reynolds, Henry Vallely, artist 15.00

Uncle Don's Strange Adventures, 1936, Uncle Don Carney 14.00

Uncle Sam's Sky Defenders, #1461, 1941, Peter A Wyckoff, author, Erwin L Hess, artist. 15.00

Union Pacific, Paramount Pictures, 1939 . . . . 20.00

Wash Tubbs and Captain Easy Hunting for Whales, 1938, Roy Crane . . . 12.00

Westward Ho, #18, 1935, 160 pgs, Republic Pictures, adapted by Edward Finlay, 4¹/₄ x 5¹/₂" 36.00

Wimpy, the Hamburger Eater, #1458, 1938, 432 pgs, Elzie Cresler Segar 25.00

Windy Wayne And His Flying Machine, #1433, 1942, 432 pgs, Russell R Winterbotham 9.75

Little Big Book, Saalfield

Barney Google, #1803, 1935, 160 pgs, Billy de Beck, 6 x 4¹/₂" 21.50

Black Beauty, #31057, 1934, 160 pgs, 4³/₄ x 5¹/₄". 10.00

Burn 'Em Up Barnes, #1091, 1935, 160 pgs, John Rathmell and Colbert Clark, 4³/₄ x 5¹/₄" 12.50

Detective Justice, #1136, 1938, 400 pgs, Ward M Stevens 12.00

It Happened One Night, #1098, 1935, 160 pgs, Columbia Pictures, artists, 4³/₄ x 5¹/₄" 21.00

Just Kids and the Mysterious Stranger, #1324, 1935, Ad Carter 20.00

Kit Carson and the Mystery Riders, #1105, 1935, Charles T Clinton . . . 15.00

Popeye's Ark, #1117, 1936, 160 pgs, Elzie C Segar, author and artist, 4³/₄ x 5¹/₄" 38.50

The Tiger Lady, #1588, 1935, Gertrude Orr 20.00

The West Point Five, #1124, 1937, 168 pgs, Kennedy Lyons, 4³/₄ x 5¹/₄" 9.00

Jumbo Book, Saalfield

Dan of the Lazy L, #1160, 1939, Mark Millis, author, Ralph C Hitchcock, artist 15.00

Joe Palooka's Great Adventure, #1168, 1939, 400 pgs, Ham Fischer 12.50

BILLHEADS

History: A billhead is a printed form used by merchants for the purpose of billing. It replaced the seventeenth–century, general purpose shopman's paper, and by the beginning of the eighteenth century, it was commonplace. Its Golden Age was the last half of the nineteenth century, ca. 1850–1915.

Early billheads evolved from the merchant's trade card. In addition to information about the biller, there was space for the name of purchaser or recipient of services, date, formal agreement ("Bought by..." or "Purchased by..."), a list of goods and services, and amount due. Throughout the eighteenth century and the first half of the nineteenth century, billheads were printed in black ink on white paper. Occasionally a colored paper was used.

As the nineteenth century progressed, the billhead changed from merely an accounting document to a form of publicity for the seller. Billheads became extremely elaborate and image conscious. Engraved vignettes of shops, factories, and products were common. The preoccupation of including buildings in billheads and letterheads continued until the 1930s. Vanity also prompted some individuals to include their own portraits.

Also during the nineteenth century, merchants and manufacturers began utilizing their billhead design as their letterhead. In the middle of the century, German engravers and printers developed the "gaslight style," a form of graphics that captures the play of a lamp on three–dimensional lettering. The style became extremely popular in the United States.

In the 1920s and 30s, the commercial engraver gave way to the graphic designer. Billheads and letterheads became fashion statements, and, as a result, billhead and letterhead style was changed much more frequently.

Billheads, like letterheads, are collectible for a variety of reasons. Paper collectors tend to focus on them as examples of period typography and engraving. Period collectors view them as key accent pieces. Crossover collectors continually search for billheads that relate to the objects or manufacturers within their collecting categories.

Reference: Leslie Cabarga, *Letterheads: One Hundred Years of Design*, Chronicle Books, 1992.

REPRODUCTION ALERT: The photocopy machine has made the reproduction of eighteenth and nineteenth century billheads extremely easy. When handling billheads, closely examine the paper. Make certain that the billhead is on paper that is appropriate to its date.

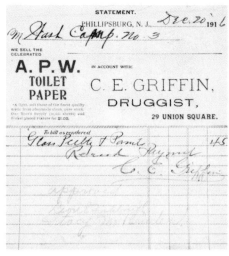

C. E. Griffin, Druggist, 5½ x 6¼", 1916, $4.00.

Adams, Chapman & Co, Commission Merchants, Boston, 1902, Lyman B Brooks Litho, cattle illus, black and white 8.00
Alfred Jones Sons, Wholesale Fish Dealers, 140–142 Broad St, Bangor, ME, dated Aug 20, 1902, engraved factory scene with horsedrawn vehicles and people, Maine coast background with sailing ship, 8 x 7" 18.00
Allen & Wings Coffee & Spice Mills, New Bedford, MA, 1897, black on green 12.00
A S Barnes & Co Publishers, Wholesale Booksellers & Stationers, NY, 1879, black and white 10.00
Atlas Powder Co, 1901 . . . . 15.00
Baldwin Tool Works, Parkensbury, WV, 1917, illus of shovels, spades, and scoops, black and white, color label, used 15.00
Ballard Fish and Oyster Co, Fresh Fish and Oysters, Norfolk, VA, 5½ x 6½" order sheet, mailing envelope, and return envelope, engraved jumping fish over oysters on order sheet 35.00
Brotherhood of Railroad Trainman, PA, 1934, Union Litho, black and white . . 15.00
Buster Brown's Hosiery Mills, Chattanooga, TN, 1921, black and white . . . 10.00
C M Betz, Harness Manufacturers, Carbondale, PA, 1915, black and white . . 10.00
C M Keys & Co, Livestock Comm Merchants, Natl Stock Yards, IL, 1903, great vignette, Woodward & Tiernan, black and white 12.00
Coca–Cola
   Daytona Beach, FL, watermark, slogan "Drink Coca–Cola," woman drinking, bottle, color 15.00
   New York, NY, 1950, logo at top, color 10.00
   Youngstown, OH, water mark, trademark, color 12.00
Consolidated Pump Works, Toledo, OH, 1897, Calvert Litho Co, Detroit, black and white, used 8.00
Cracker & Winsch, Fish of All Kinds, Boston, 1902, blue and white, used 10.00

D Atwood & Co Wholesale & Retail Oyster Dealers, 32 Faneuil Hall Square, Boston, engraved, cream, blue lettering, dated 1902, 7 x 4" 10.00
Dilworths Coffee, Pittsburgh, PA, 1895, black and white, post holes 8.00
Eastman Kodak Co, 1914, monthly statement 10.00
Edgar Newell Co, Ogdensburg, NY, engraved building, 1894 . . . . 6.00
Erie Despach, Fall River Line, MA, March 8, 1887, bill of lading for five bales of cloth shipped, sent to Cohen Bros, Cincinnati, OH, purple ink, 9 x 12½" 15.00
Ezra Clark & Co, Imp & Dealers in Iron Steel, Nails, etc., Hartford, CT, 1854, view of business, black and white, water stain, used 10.00
F W Carpenter, Manuf of Toys, Novelties, Harrison, NY, c1880, black and white 10.00
Fort Scott Foundry & Machine Works, Fort Scott, KS, 1883, black and white, used 8.00
Geo W Gilliatt, Sweet Grass Baskets and Indian Goods, Portland, ME, 1927, used 10.00
G Smith, Commission Merchant, Distributor for Dupont Gunpowder, 1920 . . . 15.00
H Childs & Co, Bessemer Shoes, IL, emb gold, silver, 1897, color, stain 12.00
H Ramey, Self Skimmy Evaporator, Louisville, KY, 1877, black and white, used 7.50
H Somers, Cigars, Quakertown, PA, vignette of granite factory building, black and white 4.00

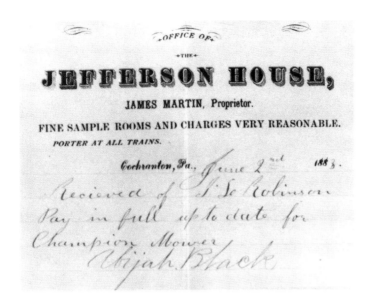

Jefferson House, 4¼ x 5½", 1883, $10.00.

Iver Johnsons Arms & Cycle Works, Fitchburg, MA, 1916, black and white	**10.00**
J J Mitchell, Undertaker & Dealer in Furniture & House Furnishings, Greenville, TN, 1895, for sale of used burial case, black and white, minor stain at folds	**15.00**
Kress Bros Wagon and Truck Manuf, Allegheny, PA, 1895, red and blue, eight fold out pages, extensive bill	**15.00**
Matchless Stove Works, Pittsburgh, PA, 1895, black and white, used	**6.00**
Millerton Iron Co, Salisbury Charcoal Pig Iron, Irondale Dutchess Co, NY, 1886, color	**8.00**
National Sewing Machine Co, Belvedere, IL, Manufacturer of High Grade Bicycles, Wilmanns Bros Litho, 1896, black and white, used	**12.00**
Pepsi Cola, H McCoy Wholesale Grocers, Kinston, NC, red logo, 8½ x 7½", 1920	**17.50**
P L Abbey Co, Manuf Pharmacists, Kalamazoo, MI, 1909, red and black	**10.00**
Polk & Calder Drug Co, Troy, NY, 1902, 8¼ x 14"	**6.50**
Ross's Bottling Guinnesses Stout & Bass's Ale, Sault Ste Marie, MI, 1917, H Gamse & Bro Litho, black and white	**12.00**
S D Elwood, Commercial & Law Stationer, Detroit, MI, 1861, black and white, used	**8.00**
Skinner's Fish and Oyster Market, Danville, VA, white, black lettering and engraved fish and oyster, 5 x 8"	**15.00**
Southbend Iron Works, Oliver Plows, 1893, black on light blue, used	**10.00**

Springfield Grocer Co, Springfield, MO, 1938, color illus of products	**15.00**
S S White Dental Mfg Co, 1904	**4.00**
Studebaker Watch Co, South Bend, black and white	**10.00**
Van Wagenen & Tucker, Hardware and Cutlery, 1850, New York, black and white, minor stains	**8.00**
Warren Bros, Bicycles & Sporting Goods, Birmingham, AL, 1927, black and white, used	**20.00**
W B Mayhen & Co, Maurice River Cove Plant, Oysters, Bivalve, NJ, dated Oct 25, 1926, parchment, engraved oyster, lighthouse, and ship, 5½ x 8"	**25.00**
W J Mathews Wholesale Planter & Shipper of Oysters, Claws and Fish, Assateague, MD, dated June 23, 1916, note paper, engraved hand holding knife and oyster, 6 x 9½"	**20.00**
Wychoff Seamans Benedict, Remington Standard Typewriter, Philadelphia, PA, 1891, red seal with typewriter, creased	**8.00**

BLOTTERS

History: Writing with ink presented several problems. First, some inks were slow to dry. An eighteenth century solution involved sprinkling sand over paper, allowing it to absorb the excess ink, and then removing it. Second, ink accumulated on the pen tip. Bristle, felt, and leather pen wipers were developed to remove excess ink from the steel nib of a fountain pen before the writing process began and to clean the nib once the writing was completed.

Blotters, a piece of blotting paper or a blotting pad, eventually became the principal means of drying wet ink marks. Blotters are made of absorbent unsized paper. The blotting paper is pressed against the ink to absorb any excess. When the blotting paper is saturated, it is discarded.

One of the earliest references to a blotter is found in a 1591 Spanish dictionary. Credit for developing a viable commercial blotting paper is given to a Berkshire, England, paper mill. Initially blotting paper was produced in sheets. Individuals cut it apart and put it on a "rocker," an approach that continued well into the twentieth century. A host of dictionary and literary references indicates that blotter use was prevalent in the eighteenth century.

Perhaps the best known blotter form is the advertising blotter, a second cousin of the trade card. The first advertising blotter appeared in the early 1880s. However, it was Lewis E. Waterman's development of the first reliable fountain pen that led to an advertising blotter explosion.

The advertising blotter was an ideal way to remind a potential customer of a service or product. Although occasionally advertising was printed directly on the unsized blotting paper, most advertising blotters had a slick top surface which was bonded to the blotter and allowed for a much better image.

Most blotters were designed either to fit a standard business or personal envelope. Many merchants included an advertising blotter along with their monthly bill. Calendars were frequently added to make the blotters timely. Series were developed to encourage repeat business.

Virtually every form of product or service can be found on an advertising blotter. Many are examples of the finest graphic design of their period. Further, the artwork of many famous illustrators, from Earl Moran to Norman Rockwell, graced their surfaces.

Blotters also were used to arouse the user's curiosity and to serve important secondary functions. A blotter might contain a recipe, train schedule, or vitamin chart. Blotters with maps and rulers are common. During World War II, patriotic blotters and pin–up blotters helped keep morale high on the home front.

The Golden Age of the blotter was the first half of the twentieth century. As the 1950s progressed, the ballpoint pen increased in popularity, and the need for blotters disappeared. When the Coca–Cola Company printed its last blotter in 1960, it had trouble distributing them. Despite the renewed use among a small group of individuals of the ink fountain pen, there is no evidence that a blotter revival is probable. Like advertising trade cards, the blotter is now a document of the "ancient" past.

Aeronautical Balloons, Daring Cannon Acts	22.00
Arm & Hammer Baking Soda, 1920s, black and white, 4 x 9¼"	10.00
Artcraft Litho Co, Detroit, MI, printed, multicolored	8.00
Badger Soap, You Want The Best, multicolored, attached card	15.00
Brilliant Mazda Lamps, color	15.00
Bromo Quinine, color, creased	8.00
Brown & Bigelow, signed "Paul Webb," 9" l	8.00
Caroid Throat Medicine, 1920s	5.00
Chevrolet Touring Car, two color, corner crease	15.00
Coca–Cola	
Delicious and Refreshing, c1904	45.00
Icy Style Cold Refreshment, c1939	8.00
Santa Claus with children, c1938	8.00
Three girls at fountain, 4 x 8", 1944	6.00
Deluxe Beauty Shop, Grace, 1927, beautiful woman	8.00
Dixon's Eldorado Master Drawing Pencil	5.00
Eagle Pure White Lead, printed, multicolored	6.00
Edison Mazda Lamps, woman reading magazine, color, creases	8.00
Empress, Queen of Pencils, printed, multicolored	10.00
G & J Tires, 1919	10.00
Golden Sun Coffee, color	1.00
Goodrich Rubber Tennis Shoes, children playing ball	10.00
Jersey Cream, 1920s, children illus, 4 x 9"	2.50
Kellogg's Corn Flakes, multicolored	6.00
Kellog's Rice Krispies, color	8.00
Kellogg's Whole Wheat Drumbles	2.00
Mazda, General Electric Co, 1912, full color illus, unused	5.00
Medusa Cement, printed color cover, product use scene and mini monthly calendar, June, 1925, unused, 3½ x 6"	4.00
Morton Salt	5.00
Nash Auto, 1928, 5 x 9"	4.00
National Stoves & Ranges, black printing, yellow ground	10.00

Amoco, red and black, J. C. Leyendecker illus., 1941, $35.00.

Growers Exchange, Norfolk, VA, Elvgren illus., "What a Deal," printed color, 9 x 3⁷/₈", 1940s, $8.00.

Morton's Salt, full color, 3¹/₄ x 6¹/₄", $3.50.

None Such Mince Meat, multicolored factory illus **6.00**
None Such Novelty Mask, multicolored **15.00**
Northwestern Mutual Life **5.00**
Old Grand–Dad Whiskey, product name and whiskey bottles, 3 x 6" **10.00**
Prudential Insurance Co, battleship illus, blue and white **5.00**
Pycnoleum, 1920s **5.00**
Reliance Life **5.00**
Schlitz Beer, woman holding Pilsner glass **4.00**
Smith Brothers Cough Drops, illus of product and Brothers, 4 x 9¹/₂", slight use **8.00**
Spencerian Pens **5.00**
Sundial Shoes, Bonnie Laddie, multicolored **6.50**
Sunoco, Mickey and Minnie Mouse wearing bride and groom outfits, sitting in convertible **25.00**
Tivoli Union Brew Company, Denver, CO **6.00**
Universal Super Strength Milk Bottles, plant photo, white and orange lettering, white ground **7.00**
Up and Up Self Rising Flour, balloon carrying biscuit, color **10.00**
Wayne Oakland Bank, Santa **6.00**
Webster Flour **4.00**

Western Bank Note & Eng Co, Chicago, Lincoln's Gettysburg Speech, engraved to Thomas Johnson, 1892 . . . . **12.00**
Yorktown Cigarettes, 1920s **5.00**

BOOKLETS

History: Are the terms booklet and pamphlet synonymous? For most individuals and all practical purposes, the answer is yes. The distinctions between a booklet and a pamphlet are extremely subtle. Dictionary definitions provide only minimal guidance.

A booklet is a small book, often with paper covers. Its contents are largely informative, rather than opinionated. The number of pages is a factor. While there is no minimum page count, a booklet usually contains in excess of sixteen pages. The vast majority have more than thirty–two.

A pamphlet is a small, thin, unbound printed publication with a paper cover comprised of sheets of paper that are stapled or stitched together. Occasionally, it has no cover at all. Pamphlets frequently range in size from four to sixteen pages, although some with more than sixteen pages can be found. They tend to focus on timely topics of public interest; the points of view expressed are often highly opinionated.

Public perception helps distinguish a booklet from a pamphlet. A booklet has a more permanent quality, something that is meant to be saved and continually referred to. A pamphlet is something to be read once, perhaps twice, and then discarded or passed along to someone else of like persuasion. Booklets frequently are found on library and kitchen shelves, while pamphlets that survived did so because they were put in a drawer to be read when an opportunity presented itself.

When examining booklets and pamphlets from the period 1700 to 1915, the above distinctions can usually be made easily. After World War I, the differences become clouded. Further, the communication revolution after World War II, especially the increased role of television, absorbed many of the roles played by booklets and pamphlets. Their numbers decreased significantly.

The above distinctions are subtle and subjective. Rather than fight about it, most paper collectors simply use the terms interchangeably.

In this first edition of *Warman's Paper*, the two remain as separate categories. This is done as a tribute to the traditionalist paper ephemerists who have built separate booklet and pamphlet collections. However, few modern collectors are continuing this approach. Today most booklets and pamphlets are collected for their subject matter, not type.

Note: Also see "Pamphlets" in the topical section.

The Dutch Boy's Hobby, **child's paint book, 12 pages, with paint, 1926, $10.00.**

Advertising
American Asphalt Paint Co, 8 x 11",
   1931 . . . .   **8.00**
Artistic Footwear For The Dead,
   Bixby's burial shoes, 1917, 8 pgs,
   12¹/₂ x 12¹/₂". **10.00**
Buster Brown Cameras–How to Make
   Photographs, 1917, 12 pgs, 4¹/₄ x 6",
   Ansco Co **6.00**
Dietzgen Co Drawing Instruments,
   1930, 24 pgs, use and care **7.50**
Hartford Trial Range, Hartford Electric
   Light Co, 1930, 12 pgs. **2.75**
Johnson Gasoline, c1920, 4¹/₄ x 5³/₄",
   girl blowing bubbles with pipe illus
   on cov **6.00**
Lydia E. Pinkham Medicine Co, 1929,
   30 pgs, 4¹/₂ x 7" **6.00**
Mark–Rite Articulating Paper, 1910–
   15, unused. **4.00**
Automotive
Leyland Motor Corp, Triumph Herald
   12/50 model, 1950, 8 pgs, 11¹/₂ x 9" **10.00**
Motoring Satisfaction–What Maxwell

Owners Think of Maxwell Cars,
   1910, 32 pgs **15.00**
Pocket Facts About the New '59 Ford **15.00**
Communication, Rates For Telegrams/
   Cables & Money Tranfers, Western
   Union, 1925, 12 pgs **9.50**
Facts
Dr. Peirce's Facts Worth Knowing,
   early 1900s **4.00**
Facts You Should Know About Furs,
   Boston Better Business National As-
   sociation Better Business Bureaus,
   12 pgs, 1936 . . . . **4.00**
Hints of What We Manufacture In
   Graphite, Joseph Dixon Crucible
   Co, Jersey City, NJ, 18 pgs, 1893, 6 x
   3¹/₂" **23.00**
History of the Thing, Hodgman Rub-
   ber Co, NY, 1896, 20 pgs, engraved
   illus **7.50**
The Meat Packing Industry in America,
   Swift & Co, 1937, 108 pgs **4.50**
The Story of Chocolate & Cocoa, Her-
   shey's, 32 pgs, 1926 . . . . **8.00**
Miscellaneous
Battle of Gettysburg, 1895, 56 pgs,
   illus **12.50**
Genealogy, Flanders Family, 1932 . . . **7.50**
Know Your Money, US Secret Service,
   1943, 32 pgs **9.50**
Let's Go To The Movies, Reed Publish-
   ing Co, Number 62, 48 pgs, copy-
   right 1932, 4 x 6" **12.50**
Master Mink Methods, 1918, 43 pgs, E
   J Dailey author and publisher **12.50**
Master Muskrat Methods, 1918, 30
   pgs, E J Dailey author and publisher **12.50**
Payson & Dunton's Penmanship,
   1854, published by Crosby **12.50**
The Art of Ventriloquism, 1930s, 32
   pgs, Johnson Smith & Co Detroit . . . **8.50**
The Berkshire Inn, Barrington, MA,

1920s, 12 pgs, layout of Myantenuck Golf Club 6.50

The Cheapest Way to Cook–90 Cent Gas, Public Service Gas Co, 48 pgs, c1890 . . . . 38.00

The Latest Books, book buyer's guide, 34 pgs, June, 1930, 3$\frac{1}{2}$ x 6" 8.00

The Wedding Album, 1895, 7 x 9", Victorian wedding 6.50

Thirty–ninth Annual Report of Worcester South Agricultural Society, 68 pgs, 1893 . . . . 5.00

Upland Game Propagation, Western Cartridge Co, 59 pgs, 1942 . . . . 4.00

Recipe
Betty Crocker, Let's Eat Outdoors, Recipes & Ideas, 1969, 27 pgs 3.00

Borden's Eagle Brand Book of Recipes, c1920, 32 pgs 15.00

Fleischmann's Recipes, 1924, 48 pgs 6.00

General Foods, A Calendar of Desserts, 1940, 48 pgs 5.00

Mirro Aluminum, Food Surprises From The Mirro Test Kitchen, 16 pgs 8.00

Sewing
Florence Home Needlework, Nonotuck Silk Co, 1887, 96 pgs . . . 15.00

Florence Sewing Machines, 1873, 16 pgs, engraved illus 12.00

Souvenir
Arizona, Grand Canyon Outings, 1917, 20 pgs, 8 x 9", Santa Fe RR . . . 8.50

The Oracle, Chase & Sanborn, fortune telling, 12 pages, 3 x 4", 1897, $45.00.

Chicago–The American Mecca of Commerce & Travel, 1910, 24 pgs 7.50

Grand Canyon National Park, 1927, fold out map 5.50

Great Falls, MT, development and growth of Great Falls/Cascade County, 1919, 52 pgs 13.50

Niagara Falls, 1910, 24 pgs, Wabash RR, 7 x 9" 7.50

The Mountain Lake Sanctuary, Florida, 1940, 24 pgs 6.50

Valley Forge, 1922, 88 pgs, historical sites and fold–out map 7.50

Yellowstone National Park, WY, 1929, 88 pgs 13.50

Yosemite Park, National Park Services, 1933, 62 pgs 10.00

Sports
Gulf Oil Football Manual, 1933, 24 pgs 5.00

Want To Be A Tennis Champion?, 1945, 29 pgs, 7 x 5", Don Budge . . . 9.00

Tour
Clark's Vacation Excursion To Europe & Glasgow Exhibition, S S City of Rome, 1901, 32 pgs 12.00

Famous Guide to New York, 1956, 96 pgs, pictorial and tour guide information, 5 x 7" 8.00

Royal Mail Steam Packet Co, trips to Panama and West Indies, 1923, 32 pgs, 7 x 9" 8.50

Salt Lake City, 7 Wonderful 1–Day Trips, 1930, 8 pgs, 8 x 9" 6.50

Vermont Tours, 1937, 48 pgs 6.50

Travel
Boston, 1928, 64 pgs, 7 x 10", published by Convention Bureau of the Chamber of Commerce 9.00

Burlington Northern Pacific RR, 32 pgs, 8 x 9" 4.50

Cunard Line, Mauretania cruise to Egypt and the Mediterranean, 24 pgs, black and white photos, map, Art Deco design cov, 1931 . . . . 25.00

Hamburg–American Lines, 1927, 20 pgs, illus 11.00

Panama Pacific Line, New York to California, 1923 . . . . 11.00

Royal Blue Line, Boston & New England, 1926, 44 pgs 7.50

San Francisco RR, 1940s, Golden Gate, travel to and from 3.50

World's Fair
Century of Progress, Armor Building, Meat, 1934 . . . . 4.00

New York World's Fair
GM, Futurama exhibit, 1940, 24 pgs 9.50

Making Bread, Northwestern Yeast Co, 1939 . . . . 12.00

Pan–American Expo, 1901, 48 pgs, 5 x 7" 11.50

BOOKS—ANTIQUES AND COLLECTIBLES

History: The first books about antiques appeared at the end of the nineteenth century. By the 1920s, books about antiques were standard fare among publishers. Topics ranged from antique furniture and English Staffordshire to "how–to" books on collecting and going to auctions. Many books from this period, e.g., George and Helen McKearin's *Two Hundred Years of American Blown Glass,* have become classics.

In the 1960s, the antiques and collectibles field witnessed a publishing explosion. The number of books issued yearly increased many fold, and today there are few topics not covered by a specialized book.

Because of the specialized nature of many of these books, titles tend to go out–of–print very rapidly. Many are privately published by the authors or small firms. Many books were published in several printings and editions. Subject collectors strive to include these books in their reference library.

Since most collectors' primary reason for acquiring these books is for the current information that they contain, especially pricing, it is best to acquire the last, not the first, edition, since it most likely contains the most complete information. However, before discarding older editions, carefully consider their value for doing short and long term market analysis.

In the late 1980s, a strong secondary market developed for books about antiques and collectibles. A first edition of Overstreet's comic book price guide sells in the hundreds of dollars. One result is that rather than discount out–of–print books, sellers began to raise the price the moment a book was no longer readily available. Many private sales now include the collector's library divided into numerous small lots as part of the sale.

Many books about antiques and collectibles prior to 1950 had dust jackets. The book should not be considered complete if the jacket has been lost. Also check to make certain that all illustrations are present.

There are a number of dealers who specialize in out–of–print books about antiques and collectibles. You will find their advertisements in the trade magazines and newspapers. Do not hesitate to contact them with your needs. It may take from a few months to several years, but eventually they will find the book or books you are seeking.

References: Allen Ahearn, *Book Collecting: A Comprehensive Guide,* G. P. Putnam's Sons, 1989; Allen and Patricia Ahearn, *Collector Books, The Guide to Values,* G. P. Putnam's Sons, 1991; *American Book Prices Current, Volume 98, 1992* Bancroft–Parkman, Inc., 1993; John Carter (revised by Nicolas Barker), *ABC For Book Collectors, Sixth Edition,* Granada Publishing, 1980; Marjorie M. and Donald L. Hinds, *How To Make Money Buying & Selling Old Books,* published by authors, 1974; *Huxford's Old Book Value Guide, Fifth Edition,* Collector Books, 1993; Jean Peters, ed., *Book Collecting: A Modern Guide,* R. R. Bowker, 1977; Jean Peters, ed., *Collectible Books: Some New Paths,* R. R. Bowker, 1979; Nancy Wright, *Books: Identification and Price Guide,* Avon Books, 1993.

CERAMICS AND POTTERY

Austin, John C., *Chelsea Porcelain at Williamsburg,* Colonial Williamsburg Foundation, 1977, 8½ x 11", 277 pgs, color and black and white illus, dj. . . .   **65.00**

Barber, Edwin A., *Pottery: A Catalogue of American Potteries and Porcelains,* Pennsylvania Museum and School of Industrial Art, 1893, 6 x 9", 43 pgs, color frontispiece, line illus, softcover   **85.00**

Barrett, Richard Carter, *Bennington Pottery And Porcelain,* Bonanza, NY, 1958, 8 x 10", 342 pgs, 462 black and white illus, worn dj **55.00**

Brankston, A. D., *Early Ming Wares Of Chingtechen, Fully Illustrated,* Henri Vetch, Peking, 1938, 5 x 7", silk, color frontispiece, 120 pgs, map, halftone plates, first edition, limited to 650 copies **40.00**

Bushell, Stephen W. and William M. Laffan, *Catalogue Of The Morgan Collection Of Chinese Porcelains,* Metropolitan Museum of Art, NY, 1910, 5 x 7", orig blue wrappers, 195 pgs, 76 halftone plate illus **25.00**

Buten, Harry M., *Wedgwood Rarities,* Buten Museum of Wedgwood, Merion, PA, 1969, 9 x 12", 320 pgs, black and white illus **125.00**

Haines, Flora E., *A Keramic Study. A Chapter In The History Of Half A Dozen Dinner Plates,* Bangor, ME, 1895, 3 x 5", cloth, 127 pgs **35.00**

Hughes, G. Bernard, *English Pottery and Porcelain Figures,* Frederick A. Praeger, NY, 1964, 6 x 9", 224 pgs, 48 black and white plates, dj **25.00**

James, Arthur E., *The Potters And Potteries Of Chester County, Pennsylvania,* West Chester, 1945, 5 x 7", 116 pgs, limited to 600 copies **135.00**

Langenbeck, Karl, *The Chemistry Of Pottery,* Chemical Publ. Co., Easton, PA, 1895, 3 x 5", cloth, 197 pgs, ads, first edition **75.00**

McLaughlin, M. Louise, *China Painting. A Practical Manual For The Use of Amateurs In The Decoration Of Hand*

Porcelain, Clarke, Cincinnati, 1892, 3 x 5", cloth, 103 pgs, ads **35.00**

Mundy, R. G., *English Delft Pottery,* Herbert Jenkins Ltd., London, 1928, 123 pgs, 48 black and white illus **225.00**

Ramsay, John, *American Potters And Pottery,* Clinton, 1939, 5 x 7", 304 pgs, 87 black and white plates, worn dj . . . **85.00**

Schwartz & Wolfe, *A History Of American Art Porcelain,* NY, 1967, 8 x 10", 93 pgs, 7 color, 68 black and white illus, dj **35.00**

Sparkes, John C. L., *A Hand Book To The Practice Of Pottery Painting,* Harper, NY, 1877, printed wrappers, 79 pgs . . **35.00**

FASHION

Beck, S. William, *Gloves, Their Annuals And Associations: A Chapter Of Trade And Social History,* Hamilton, Adams, London, 1883, small 5 x 7", cloth, 263 pgs, owner blind stamp on title **100.00**

Earle, Alice Morse, *Two Centuries of Costume in America,* Macmillian and Company, NY, 1903, two volumes, 6 x 8½", 824 pgs, black and white plates and illus **135.00**

Hope, Thomas, *Costume of the Ancients,* William Miller, London, 1809, 6 x 9½", 54 pgs, 200 engraved plates, full grained leather binding, marbled end papers, elaborate gilt dec on spine . . . **350.00**

Lester, Katherine, *Accessories Of Dress,* Peoria, 1940, 7 x 10½", 587 pgs, 60 black and white plates, 644 black and white illus **100.00**

Liberty & Co, *Liberty's Dresses And Jumpers For Ladies And Frocks For Children,* London, 1932, 5 x 9", 32 pgs, softcover. **30.00**

Parsons, Frank Alvah, *The Psychology Of Dress,* Garden City, 1920, 5 x 7", cloth dull, rubbed, 358 pgs. **35.00**

FOLK ART

Black, Mary and Jean Lipman, *American Folk Painting,* NY, 1966, 9 x 12", 244 pgs, 86 color plates, 146 black and white illus, dj **50.00**

Christensen, Erwin, *Early American Wood Carving,* NY, 1952, 6 x 9", 149 pgs, 5 color and 50 black and white illus, special first edition limited to 1,250 copies, slipcase **50.00**

Doty, *American Folk Art In Ohio Collections,* Akron, 1976, 9 x 8", 10 pgs of text, 11 color and 58 black and white plates, dj **20.00**

Earle, *Scrimshaw, Folk Art Of The Whalers,* Cold Spring Harbor, 1957, 6 x 9", 36 pgs, 8 black and white plates, softcover **15.00**

Fitzgerald, Ken, *Weathervanes and Whirligigs,* NY, 1967, 6 x 9", 186 pgs, line drawings **15.00**

Little, Nina Fletcher, *The Abby Aldrich Rockefeller Folk Art Collection,* Boston/Williamsburg, 1957, 8 x 10", 402 pgs, 165 color plates, boxed **100.00**

Lord, Priscilla and Daniel Foley, *The Folk Arts & Crafts of New England,* Chilton Books, NY, 1965, 9 x 12", 282 pgs, black and white illus, color plates, dj **45.00**

Museum of Modern Art, *American Folk Art–The Art Of The Common Man In America, 1750–1900,* NY, 1932, 7 x 10", 52 pgs, 79 black and white plates, card cov **50.00**

Stoudt, John J.

Early Pennsylvania Arts and Crafts, South Brunswick, 1964, 9 x 12", 364 pgs, 21 color and 344 black and white illus, dj **50.00**

Sunbonnets and Shoofly Pies, A Pennsylvania Dutch Cultural History, Castle, NY, 1973, 10 x 12", 272 pgs **40.00**

Wiltshire, William E., III, *Folk Pottery of the Shenandoah Valley,* E. P. Dutton, NY, 1975, 8½ x 11", 127 pgs, 60 color plates, dj **85.00**

FURNITURE

Bissell, *Antique Furniture In Suffield, Connecticut, 1670–1835,* Suffield, 1956, 7 x 11", 128 pgs, 60 black and white plates, limited to 750 copies . . . **125.00**

Blackie & Son, *The Cabinetmakers Assistant–A Series Of Original Designs For Modern Furniture, With Descriptions And Details Of Construction,* London, 1853, 11 x 15", 123 pgs, 101 engraved plates, quarter leather **375.00**

Blanchard, *How To Restore And Decorate Chairs,* New York, 1952, 8 x 11", 128 pgs, black and white illus, dj **15.00**

Cescinsky, Herbert, *English Furniture From Gothic To Sheraton,* Grand Rapids, 1929, 9 x 12", 438 pgs, 900 black and white illus **150.00**

Curtis Companies Service Bureau, *Permanent Furniture For Better Built Homes,* Clinton, IA, 1923, 3 x 5", color picture wrappers, 48 pgs, illus **15.00**

Eberlein, Harold Donaldson and Roger Wearne Ramsdell, *The Practical Book Of Italian, Spanish and Portuguese Furniture,* Philadelphia, 1927, thick 5 x 7", 254 pgs, first edition **20.00**

Kane, Patricia, *Furniture of New Haven Colony, The Seventeenth Century Style,* New Haven Colony Historical

ANTIQUE FAKES & REPRODUCTIONS

ENLARGED AND REVISED

"A reproduction becomes a fake when it is sold as a genuine antique"

By RUTH WEBB LEE

Lee, Ruth Webb, *Antique Fakes & Reproductions*, Lee Publications, 1950, 317 pages, 5¾ x 8¾", $75.00.

Society, 1973, 7½ x 10½", 93 pgs, black and white illus, softcover **50.00**

Kirk, John T., *American Chairs, Queen Anne and Chippendale*, NY, 1972, 11 x 12", 208 pgs, color frontispiece, 204 black and white illus, dj **250.00**

Lamp, George N., *The Mahogany Book*, Chicago, 1936, 5 x 7", wrappers, 80 pgs, illus, second edition **15.00**

Lea, Zilla Rider, *The Ornamented Chair, Its Development In America 1700–1890*, Rutland, 1966, 8 x 11", 173 pgs, 7 color plates, 290 black and white illus, dj **85.00**

Longnon, Henri and Frances Wilson Huard, *French Provincial Furniture*, Philadelphia, 1927, 5 x 7", 167 pgs, illus, first edition **20.00**

Luther, C. F., *The Hadley Chest*, Hartford, 1935, 8 x 11", 144 pgs, black and white illus, dj, supplemental list **350.00**

Macquoid, P. and H. Edwards, *The Dictionary Of English Furniture*, London and New York, 1924–27, 3 volumes, 11 x 15", 962 pgs, 51 color plates, green cloth cover, gilt titles, first edition **650.00**

Montgomery, Charles F., *American Fur-*

niture, The Federal Period, Viking Press, NY, 1966, 9 x 12", 497 pgs, color and black and white illus, dj, inscribed **350.00**

Sikes, Jane E., *The Furniture Makers of Cincinnati, 1790 to 1849*, 1976, 8½ x 11", 264 pgs, color and black and white illus, dj **125.00**

GLASS

Belknap, E. M., *Milk Glass*, New York, 1949, 7 x 10", 327 pgs, 4 color plates, hundreds of black and white illus, worn dj **50.00**

Chipman, Frank W., *The Romance of Old Sandwich Glass*, Sandwich Publishing Co, 1932, 7 x 10½", 158 pgs, black and white plates, worn and slightly bowed covers **45.00**

Faber, William Frederic, *Stained Glass Windows. An Essay With A Report To The Vestry On Stained Glass Windows For Grace Church, Lockport, New York*, Lockport, NY, 1900, 3 x 5", slight edge chips, 41 pgs **35.00**

Freeman, Larry, *Iridescent Glass*, Century House, Watkins Glen, 1956, 6 x 9", 128 pgs, black and white illus **20.00**

Hartung, Marion T. and Ione Hinshaw, *Patterns and Pinafores, Pressed Glass Toy Dishes*, Wallace–Homestead, Des Moines, 1971, 6 x 9", 102 pgs, black and white illus, dj **25.00**

Heiges, *Henry William Stiegel*, Manheim, 1937, 5 x 7", 80 pgs, 15 black and white plates, dj **25.00**

Hunter, Frederick William, *Stiegel Glass*, Boston, 1914, 7 x 10", 272 pgs, 12 color plates, 159 black and white illus, pictorial covers, limited to 420 copies, inscribed **300.00**

McKearin, G., *Two Hundred Years Of American Blown Glass*, Bonanza, NY, nd, 8 x 11", 382 pgs, 10 color plates, 105 black and white illus, dj **50.00**

Wilson, Kenneth M., *New England Glass and Glassmaking*, Sturbridge, 1972, 8 x 10", 401 pgs, black and white illus, dj **65.00**

MISCELLANEOUS

Cescinsky, Herbert, *The Gentle Art of Faking Furniture*, Chapman & Hall, London, 1931, 8 x 10½", 167 pgs, 292 black and white plates **200.00**

Conningham, Frederic A., *Currier & Ives Prints*, 1970, hardbound **100.00**

Dennis, Lee, *Warman's Antique American Games, 1840–1940*, 1986 . . . . . . **25.00**

Ebert, John and Katherine, *Old American Prints for Collectors*, Charles Scrib-

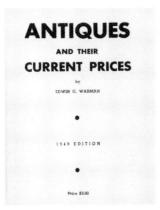

ANTIQUES

AND THEIR

CURRENT PRICES

by

EDWIN G. WARMAN

•

1949 EDITION

•

Price $3.00

Warman, Edwin G., *Antiques And Their Current Prices*, 1949 edition, published by author, 1948, 115 pages, 4⅞ x 6⅝", $50.00.

ner's Sons, NY, 1974, 8 x 10", 277 pgs, color and black and white illus, dj. . . .   **85.00**

Gottesman, Rita Susswein, *The Arts & Crafts In New York, 1726–1804*, 3 volumes, NY, 1938, 1948, 1965, 6 x 9", 1471 pgs, green and red cloth cov. . . .   **250.00**

Hannas, *The English Jigsaw Puzzle 1760 to 1890*, London, 1972, 8 x 10", 164 pgs, color and black and white illus, dj   **50.00**

Hayward, Arthur H., *Colonial Lighting*, Boston, 1923, 6 x 9", 159 pgs, 114 black and white illus, first edition **75.00**

Hughes, Elizabeth and Lester, Marion, *The Big Book of Buttons*, 1981, hardbound.   **275.00**

Luckey, Carl F., *Collector Prints, Old and New*, Books Americana, 1982 . . . . . .   **25.00**

Ness, Zenobia B., *Iowa Artists of the First Hundred Years*, Wallace–Homestead, Des Moines, 1939, 6 x 9½", 253 pgs, color frontispiece, black and white illus **100.00**

Thwing, Leroy, *Flickering Flames, A History of Domestic Lighting Through The Ages*, Charles Tuttle, Rutland, 1958, 6 x 8½", 137 pgs, black and white illus, dj **35.00**

SILVER

Avery, C. Louise, *Early American Silver*, The Century Company, NY, 1930, 6 x 8½", 378 pgs, black and white illus, inscribed **50.00**

Clarke, Herman F., *John Coney, Silversmith 1655–1722*, Houghton Mifflin, Boston, 1932, 8 x 10", 92 pgs, 32 black and white plates, limited to 365 copies   **300.00**

Cutten, George B., *The Silversmiths of*

Utica, Hamilton, 1936, 6 x 10", 67 pgs, five tipped in black and white plates, limited to 257 signed copies . .   **225.00**

Fales, Martha Gandy, *Joseph Richardson and Family, Philadelphia Silversmiths*, Wesleyan University Press, Middletown, 1974, 8½ x 11", 340 pgs, 179 black and white illus, dj. **75.00**

French, Hollis, *Jacob Hurd and His Sons, Nathaniel & Benjamin, Silversmiths 1702–1781*, The Walpole Society, Boston, 1939, 8 x 10", 149 pgs, 28 black and white plates, color frontispiece, limited to 250 copies **400.00**

Gerstell, Vivian S., *Silversmiths of Lancaster, Pennsylvania 1730–1850*, Lancaster County Historical Society, 1972, 6 x 9", 145 pgs, black and white illus **25.00**

Kolter, Jane Bentley, *Early American Silver and Its Makers*, Main Street Press, NY, 1979, 8½ x 11", 160 pgs, black and white illus, dj **35.00**

Ward, Barbara M. and Gerald W. R., *Silver In American Life, Selections from the Mabel Brady Garvan and other Collections at Yale University*, David Godine, Boston, 1979, 8½ x 11", 193 pgs, 196 color and black and white illus, dj **40.00**

TEXTILES

Bath, Virginia C., *Needlework In America–History, Designs and Techniques*, Viking Press, NY, 1979, 8½ x 11", 336 pgs, 22 color illus, numerous black and white illus, dj **40.00**

Bolton, Ethel Stanwood and Eva Johnston Coe, *American Samplers*, Weathervane, NY, 1973, 6 x 9", 416 pgs, 76 black and white plates, dj **40.00**

Bowman, Sara and Michel Molinare, *A Fashion For Extravagance, Art Deco Fabrics and Fashions*, E. P. Dutton, NY, 1985, 8 x 10½", 125 pgs, color and black and white illus, dj **20.00**

Di Brazza, Cora A., *A Guide To Old And New Lace In Italy, Exhibited At Chicago In 1893*, Conkey, Chicago, 1893, 5 x 7", morocco spine labels, 186 pgs   **75.00**

Hall, Eliza Calvert, *A Book Of Handwoven Coverlets*, Boston, 1912, 6 x 9", 279 pgs, 16 color and 48 black and white plates, pictorial cloth covers, first edition. **150.00**

Kent, William Winthrop, *The Hooked Rug*, NY, 1973, 8 x 10", 210 pgs, 172 black and white illus, dj. **50.00**

Little, Frances, *Early American Textiles*, NY, 1931, 6 x 8", 267 pgs, 62 black and white illus, dj **85.00**

Orlofsky, Patsy and Myron, *Quilts In America,* NY, 1974, 8 x 10", 109 color and 205 black and white illus, dj **300.00**
Parnell, Edward Andrew, *Dyeing And Calico–Printing,* London, 1849, 5 x 7", cloth, 288 pgs, ads on end papers, 23 orig fabric samples, first edition **175.00**
Peto, Florence, *Historic Quilts,* NY, 1939, 6 x 9", 210 pgs, 62 black and white plates **125.00**
Pushman Bros, *Arts Panels From The Handlooms Of The Far Orient. As Seen By A Native Rug Weaver,* Chicago, 1911, 5 x 7", 88 pgs, halftone plate illus, color illus **25.00**
Swygert, Mrs. Luther, *Heirlooms From Old Looms, A Catalogue of Coverlets Owned By The Colonial Coverlet Guild Of America And Its Members,* Chicago, 1955, 6 x 10", 406 pgs, second edition **200.00**

BOXES (PACKAGING)

History: The cardboard box and paper labeled tin container achieved popular acceptance during the middle decades of the nineteenth century. They were the result of the nineteenth century transportation revolution; roadways and railroads that allowed for the rapid movement of goods over long distances.

Packaging design was used to promote sales and establish national brand recognition. Few individuals would fail to recognize a Campbell's Soup can from a distance. Most manufacturers followed a program of subtle design change as a means of keeping their packaging "modern."

Advertising characters are one of the hot collecting categories of the 1990s. Advertising characters, e.g., the Morton Salt girl, often appeared on packaging. As a result, packaging with advertising characters currently commands premium prices.

In the 1970s, the principal collectors of packaging used it to supplement a major collecting theme, e.g., a Country general store, or as decorative accents in a room, e.g., the kitchen, bathroom, or laundry room. In the 1990s, packaging is collected primarily for its artwork. Packaging designed by a highly collectible illustrator or which exhibits strong period design characteristics is eagerly sought.

The increased importance of having the original packaging with an object, especially for objects made after 1945, has introduced a new pricing consideration in the packaging area. The original box often adds 25% or more to the value of an object. In some instances, the box is worth more than the object itself. An original box in-

creases the value of a character wrist watch two to three times. The shelf box for Hopalong Cassidy socks is worth ten to fifteen times the price of the socks it originally contained.

A growing interest has developed in the 1990s in old candy boxes, especially those housing candy meant to be sold in retail stores. Prices begin at $10 for the more common examples and can reach over $100 for scarcer examples. Again, surface image and design are the key value components.

References: Al Bergevin, *Food and Drink Containers and Their Prices,* Wallace–Homestead, 1988; Jerry Jankowski, *Shelf Life: Modern Package Design, 1920–1945,* Chronicle Books, 1992; Ralph and Terry Kovel, *Advertising Collectibles Price List,* Crown Publishers, 1986; Robert Opie, *The Art of the Label: Design of the Times,* Chartwell Books, 1987; Robert Opie, *Packaging Source Book,* Chartwell Books, 1989.

Baking Soda, Arm & Hammer Baking Soda, cardboard, unused, 1930s **5.00**
Beauty
  Goldey Hair Rinse, 1940s, 2 x 4½ x 9" **6.00**
  Yardley's Crushed Roses, cardboard, chest shape, rose decoration **15.00**
Bubble Gum
  Beverly Hillbillies, Topps, 1963 . . . . . **75.00**
  Comic Cover Stickers, Topps, 1970 . . **25.00**
  Gilligan's Island, Topps, 1965 . . . . **50.00**
  Hogan's Heroes, Fleer **200.00**
  Make Your Own Name Stickers, Topps **35.00**
  Rat Fink Greeting Cards, Topps, 1965 **50.00**
  Star Trek, Topps, 1979 . . . . **3.00**
  Tarzan, Philadelphia Chewing Gum Co, 1966 . . . . **50.00**
Butter
  Blue River Butter, cows on four sides, blue, green, and yellow **2.50**
  Bossie's Best Brand Butter, pound **2.00**
  Churn Baking Soda, 1920s, woman churning butter, unused **10.00**

National Biscuit Co., "Uneeda Bakers," Royal Lunch, prototype before distribution, 8 x 6 x 6", $35.00.

Cow Butter, Pine Grove Dairy, cows in pasture, 1940s, 2½ x 2½ x 5" 3.00

Enterprise Butter, two cows illus, 1952, 2½ x 2½ x 4½" 3.00

Greer's Moo Girl Creamery Butter, Sutherland Paper Co, Kalamazoo, MI, 1925, 1 lb 3.50

Hill Country Butter, yellow, black, white, stylized floral border. 1.00

Wilson's Clearbrook Butter, yellow, black, white, and red, farm scene, 1 lb 2.00

Candy

Adams Tutti Frutti Gum, cardboard, girl and Louisiana Expo illus 55.00

Beech–Nut Chewing Gum, cardboard, sides and top logo, 6" l 40.00

Big Time OH–Gee Candy 8.00

Boston Wafers Candy, children and wafer illus 20.00

Brach's Candy 40.00

Clark Bar, cardboard, blue, white, and orange, c1940, 9½ x 10 x 1¾" 20.00

Foss Chocolates, cardboard, 4¾ x 7¼"   5.00

Goff's Atlantic City Salt Water Taffy, woman wearing orange swimming suit, Atlantic City scene, 8⅞ x 4⅞ x 2½" 7.50

Hershey Nougat–Almond 10.00

Mary Jane, cardboard, red, white, blue, and yellow, Mary Jane illus on lid, 7 x 10 x 2¼" 25.00

Payday, Salted Nut Roll, Hollywood Brands, Inc, black, red, and blue lettering, yellow background, 8 x 10 x 2" 15.00

Sweet Caporal Candy Cigarettes, 1¾ x 3" 5.00

Whitman Candy, Pickaninny Peppermints, black children, 7" l 12.00

Wrigley's, Spearmint Gum, 1930s, Wrigley man illus, 4 x 6" 50.00

Clothing and Accessories

Buster Brown Shoes. 15.00

Buster Brown Stockings, graphic illus   40.00

Detmer Woolens, store, people wearing woolens on box interior, 21 x 29 x 21". 75.00

Dickens 15 Round End Imitation Collar, cardboard, 3½ x 2" 15.00

Improved Sunnyside Collar, 4 x 4" . . .   15.00

Regal Underwear 15.00

Shirley President Suspenders, 1913, colorful lady and peasant illus 14.00

Food

Armour's Sliced Bacon, cardboard . . .   12.00

Creator's Pop Corn, 1929, cardboard, girl eating popcorn, orange and blue, 7 x 5 x 2" 12.00

Dr Johnson's Educator Crackers 38.00

Edgemont Crackers 12.00

Montgomery Ward Tea, 1913, cardboard, tin lid, 5 lb. 40.00

Mr Delish Popcorn, bellhop illus, 1950s, 2 x 5 x 9". 3.50

Planters Peanuts, 5¢ Salted Peanuts, blue, 5 lb 45.00

St Johnsbury Crackers, 8 x 10½ x 7¾"   25.00

Game, Tiddledy Winks, Milton Bradley, 1939, no contents 20.00

Ink, Well's Different Ink Co, orange and black, 2 x 2 x 2½" 3.00

Snickers Candy Bars, 24 bars, orange, blue, and white, 9 x 7 x 2", $17.50.

Medical

Dewitt's Catarrhal Cream, cardboard, cylindrical, blue and gold	4.50
Dr Charles Flesh Food, cardboard, emb rose floral dec, 3 x 1½"	7.50
Happy Hen White Diarrhea Remedy, 2 x 3¼"	8.00
Jessop's Cough Drops	4.00
Mitchel's Cure–All Corn and Bunion Plasters, cardboard, 2½ x 3½"	15.00

Miscellaneous

Bulldog Jar Rubbers, bulldog in circle, 3³⁄₈ x 3¼ x 1³⁄₈"	2.00
Donald Duck Straws, 1950s	22.00
Eagle Asbestos Stove Lining, cardboard, 2¾ x 3¾"	8.00
Pabst Blue Ribbon Beer Gift Box, 1940s, contains gift set, bank and salt shaker, 2 x 3½ x 4½"	15.00
Pepsi and Pete Safedge Tumblers, cardboard, 8 x 10 x 12", 1940s	900.00
Tower Brand Powdered Rosin, 3¼ x 6½"	5.00

Pet Supplies

Excelsior Bird Food, cardboard, red, black, and yellow, 1 lb.	5.00
Parrot Food, full color parrot illus, 1920s, 3 x 5 x 9"	5.00
Richfield Veterinarian Cures, unused	14.00

Poison, Reynold's Rat Driver Poison, c1900, 3½ x 7" 5.00

Seeds, Nastursham Seeds, full color flower illus, contents, 1916, 1 x 2½ x 3½" 2.00

Soap and Cleaners

Argo Starch, 1930s, unopened	10.00
Armour's Washing Powder	4.00
Bear Cleaner, polar bear illus, 1930s, 2 x 4 x 6"	2.50
Gold Dust Twins, 12 x 20 x 14", unopened.	55.00
Grandpa's Wonder Pine Tar Soap, Beaver Soap Co, Dayton, OH, old man in circle, 2½ x 4¼ x 1½"	12.50
Honor Bright Soap, cardboard, 2½ x 3¼"	5.00
Rub–No–More Cleansing Powder, 5½ x 4½"	20.00
Silver Dust Twins, 7¾ x 5¼"	8.00

Tobacco

Cross–Cut Cigarettes, image of men sawing, slip lid, 3 x 2 x 1"	25.00
Del–Ray Cigar, 1910.	5.50
Eddie Cantor Cigars, Eddie Cantor portrait front and lid interior	80.00
Lucky Joe Tobacco, 1940, cardboard, contains 10 plugs.	25.00
Orphan Boy Tobacco, donkey illus, 1930s, 2½ x 4 x 8"	4.00
Pearson's Red Top Snuff, 1¾ x 2⁵⁄₈" . .	6.00
Prince Albert	8.00
Red Indian Cut Plug Tobacco, cardboard, Indian logo and product name, 5 lb, 14 x 8 x 6"	550.00
Tipperary Tobacco, 1940s, contains six dummy packs, 3 x 5 x 6"	4.00

BROADSIDES

History: What constitutes a broadside? One dictionary definition states that it is "a sizable sheet of paper printed on one side." However, the next definition notes that a broadside can be "a sheet printed on one or both sides and folded." Collectors know from experience that many broadsides are smaller than the traditional 8½" x 11" writing paper.

An easy method to identify a broadside is to think of it as a piece of paper that was meant to be displayed on a bulletin board, fence, or wall to announce a specific event. This makes a broadside timely as well as transitory. Although meant to be discarded, their purpose is to catch one's eye and be read. As a result, broadsides tend to highly graphic, an effect achieved both through the use of type font and illustrations. A sale bill and movie poster are both types of broadsides. The English refer to a large broadside as a broadsheet.

Handbills, a small printed sheet distributed by hand and a favorite among traditional paper ephemera collectors, belongs in the broadside category. A handbill may also be called a flyer, leaflet, or throwaway. The handbill as a form arrived on the scene in the seventeenth century. Its Golden Age was 1850 to 1890 when distribution was so broad that some felt handbills were a public nuisance. In addition to advertising, the handbill often was used as a public expression of private anger. Theaters used handbills as an *ad hoc* poster.

Since large quantities of broadsides survive, a collector must develop a narrow collecting philosophy in order to assemble a meaningful collection in today's market. One collecting focus is by method of printing, e.g., a broadside printed on a letter press versus one done on a lithography press. The most common approach is by subject matter. Popular categories include circus, entertainment, sale, sport, transportation, travel, and war. A few collectors focus chronologically.

Note: Also see "Posters" in the topical section.

Act Concerning...Funds, Boston, 1862	40.00
American Boy, 8½ x 22", offers subscription, attached book coupon . . .	10.00
Arrest of the King's Council of State, Concerning Foreign Commerce, 1785, 11¼ x 7¼"	250.00
Assembly...Fellow Citizens and Countrymen, 1772, 9¼ x 7"	350.00

Grand Strawberry Festival, Mechanicsburg, PA, 5½ x 8½", 1868, $27.50.

Bailey Bros Circus, red, white, and blue, 14 x 41" **25.00**

Battle of Mobile Bay, Farragut, 1864, general orders, 10 x 8" **2,000.00**

Carriers Address of Albion, 1824, grape border, 10 x 15" **40.00**

Cavalry Horses Wanted, Fort Walla Walla, Washington Territory, Sept 15, 1875 .... **175.00**

Champions of Freedom, Greely/Sumner/Seward/Whitter, 14 x 10" .. **150.00**

Columbian Tragedy, Bloody Indian Battle, 1791, 61 x 22" **900.00**

Conditions of Peace Required of the So Called Seceded States, April 24, 1861, 18 x 11" **275.00**

Corbett's Apparatus for Hatching Poultry, 1874, 6 x 9" **35.00**

Death of Andrew Jackson, 1840s, 10 x 15" **75.00**

Decret de la Convention Nationale, 1793, 20 x 16" **250.00**

Don't Unchain The Tiger, July 24, 1863 .... **175.00**

Dr McHenry's Soothing Syrup, To All Who Use..., Stomach Bitters, Oil For Burns, & Popular Liniments, 11 x 14", framed **120.00**

Estate Sale of Slaves, 1858, 18 names and ages, 10 x 8" **600.00**

Free Exhibition & Dollar Sale...JB Burleigh, 1875, 9 x 12" **60.00**

Great India Elephant, 7000 lbs, NY, 1832, 36 x 24" **2,500.00**

Great Secret...Reduced prices, 1858, dry goods, 13 x 10" **25.00**

Indian Exhibition, Penobscot Tribe, 1851, 18 x 12" **375.00**

Indians Take Notice, Ft Smith, AZ, 1893, 11 x 7½" **380.00**

Invitation to Unveiling of Monument in Virginia, 1898 .... **25.00**

Jackson Ticket, three columns of text and portraits, 1828, 22 x 15" **2,000.00**

John Jay for Governor of New York, two columns of text, 1795, 17 x 11" **220.00**

Kansas Prohibition Society, c1890, 5 x 8" **15.00**

Ku Klux Klan, "Native born Protestants of good character," red and white, 9 x 12" **85.00**

Last Week of the Grand Performance of Shakespeare's Comedy...Tempest, 8½ x 20¾" **40.00**

Lee/Jackson Celebration, Virginia, 1914 .... **28.00**

Lee's Tobacco Warehouse, 1880s, 9½ x 12" **38.00**

Massacre at Dartmoor Prison, Boston, 1812, 16 x 9½" **550.00**

Massacre by Cherokees, monument erected, North Carolina, 1897 ..... **35.00**

Maungwudas...Indians, lecture, 1849, 18 x 8" **80.00**

McClellan's Address to Troops, 1862 **200.00**

Miner's Reply to...Toulumne County Water Co, 1855, 13 x 8" **650.00**

Mortgage Sale, Eldorado saloon, New Mexico, 1873, 10 x 7½" **200.00**

Mr England's Patent Self–Acting Car Coupler, endorsed by B & O Railroad, April, 1856, 8½ x 11" **18.00**

Newspaper Advertisement, Will Rogers–Wiley Post crash in Alaska scene, 11 x 16" **185.00**

No Jewing Business, Clothing Sale, 1879, 12 x 4½" **50.00**

North Pacific... Train, St Paul, MN, free land in North Dakota, 1898 .... **35.00**

Oil & Camphene Works, San Francisco, boat and harpooning whalers illus, 6 x 8½" **35.00**

Old Virginia Minstrels & Cake–Walkers, Virginia, 1905, 17 x 5½".. **35.00**

Parliamentary Summons, Oliver Cromwell, London, 1651 .... **200.00**

Proclamation by Gov J Trumbull, Connecticut, 1783, 13½ x 8½" **380.00**

Programme of Exercises, Ohio church, 1871, 8½ x 5½" **10.00**

NOTICE TO BOATMEN.

THE Masters of all Boats carrying Coal upon the *Schuylkill Canal Navigation*, are required hereafter, not to load their Boats to a greater draught of water than

FIVE FEET FOUR INCHES.

Those who by violating this Regulation, ground their Boats in the channels, or upon the Mitre sills, so as to obstruct the navigation, will become liable by law to

A FINE OF TWENTY DOLLARS,

BESIDES THE EXPENSE OF REMOVING THE OBSTRUCTION.

Boatmen are also notified not to crowd *Light Boats* into the Docks, until they are wanted to load, nor to moor them about the Landings, so as to obstruct either the use of the Navigation, or of the Landings.

Ellwood Morris,
Resident Engineer S. N.

ENGINEER'S OFFICE, S. N. }
Waterloo Locks, May 19th, 1849. }

B. BANNAN, PRINTER, POTTSVILLE.

Notice to Boatmen, Schuylkill Canal notice, 1849, $275.00.

Terrific and Thrilling Spectacle, Grand Mammoth Balloon Ascension, A Sight Never Witnessed But Once In A Lifetime, 10½ x 28"	425.00
Testimony of the People Called Quakers, Philadelphia, 1775, 10½ x 6¾"	375.00
Thanksgiving proclamation, lion and unicorn, 1703, 18 x 15"	775.00
The Original Siamese Twins, Chang & Eng, 1853, black and yellow, 6 x 9"	160.00
Torchlight Parade Equipment, red and white, 9 x 14"	200.00
To The Freemen Of Pennsylvania, February 21, 1772, 11½ x 6½"	400.00
Two Headed Girl, Born A Slave, 6 x 10"	85.00
Victory, Clear Track...Springfield, Whig news, 1840, 18 x 12"	350.00
Virginia Instructs Senators and Representatives on Amendments, 1795	1,700.00
Volunteers Wanted, Illinois, February, 1864, nice graphics, 16 x 12"	600.00
White Golden Tonic for Horses, 18 x 24", horse illus	25.00
W W Gavitt's Medical System Regulator, 1880s, 15 x 5½"	15.00

Railroad, California, 1874, passengers warned against playing cards	450.00
Rates of Tools on Santa Cruz Cap Turnpike, 1874, 18 x 12"	350.00
Reward $500, California, 1895, conviction of lynching mob	175.00
Ringling Brothers Circus, c1900, features Kit Carson's Buffalo Ranch Wild West, 10 x 28"	55.00
Runaway, $100 Reward for Negro Man, Maryland, 1853, 10 x 12"	350.00
Sailing News of Alaska Gold Rush, c1899	200.00
Sham Battle, July 4th, 2000 Soldiers, c1890, 30 x 13"	500.00
Shareholders' Meeting at Tremont House, Boston, 1837	15.00
Slias King Dry Goods, Welchville, ME, black and white, horse–drawn express wagon, 14 x 12"	20.00
Splendid Daguerreotype Miniatures, Hayden, 1850s, 10½ x 9"	220.00
Spring Fevers & Malaria, c1880, 5½ x 8¾"	15.00
Stark & Perfect, Dry Goods, Groceries, Ohio, 1859, black and white, 26 x 20"	200.00
Status of Sutro Tunnel Co, Virginia City, NV, 1869, 13½ x 7"	140.00
Steamboat New Hamburgh on Hudson, 1832, 17 x 11"	190.00
Tennessee Proclamation, 1862, civilians obey military, 9 x 11½"	600.00

BUSINESS CARDS

History: The business card traces its origins to the seventeenth century trademan's tradecard. Originally, the "card" was a slip of paper providing a name, location, and trade. The appearance of this information on a "card" occurred in the eighteenth and nineteenth century. Traditionally business cards were printed in black from a copper engraving.

The multi–function tradecard divided into three different components in the eighteenth century—the advertising trade card, product label, and business card. The private business card gained acceptance slowly. It was not until the middle of the twentieth century that the business card achieved universal status. Today it is common for individuals to carry several different business cards, each designed to tout their skills to a specific target group.

A typical business card collection numbers between 5,000 and 10,000 cards. Most are acquired free or through trading. Some collectors refuse to add any card to their collection that they must purchase.

References: Kit Barry, *The Advertising Trade Card, Book 1*, privately printed, 1981; Robert Jay, *The Trade Card in Nineteenth–Century America*, University of Missouri Press, 1987; Avery Pitzak, *Business Cards*, privately printed, 1989; Avery Pitzak, *Business Cards*, privately printed, 1992

(Editor's note: Although this book has the same title as Pitzak's previous book, it is entirely different); Avery N. Pitzak, *Make Your Business Card Incredibly Effective*, privately printed, 1990.

Collectors' Club: American Business Card Club, PO Box 460297, Aurora, CO 80046; Business Card Collectors International, PO Box 466, Hollywood, FL 33022.

Value Note: Most business cards, especially those from the post–1945 period, have no or very limited value. They are something that the owner gives out "for free." Even cards associated with famous business, entertainment, or sport personalities still fall in this category. Do not pay premium prices for any business card from a person who is still alive or who has recently died.

Taylor & Hancock, Mourning Goods, printed, black and white, 3⅝ x 2⅛″, 1890s, $6.00.

Alex Weber, Wines & Liquors, Groceries & Provisions, Toledo, OH, red view of store.	12.00
Atlis Brewing Co, Detroit, MI, multicolored	10.00
Caney & Havana Hack Line, Kansas to Indian Territory, c1892, stagecoach illus, green and red	20.00
Commercial Hotel, Grand Rapids, MI, black and white.	7.50
Comp C G Conn Manufacturer of Band Instruments, Elkhart, IN, Geo Manning, Leader of Band, Hollies, NH, gold gilt	18.00
Daimler Motor Co, Manufacturer of Gasoline Engines for Stationary, Locomotive & Marine Purposes, NY.	10.00
Danville Female Collegiate Institute, List of Teachers, Tuition Cost, 1870s	10.00
Dress Making Mrs J Vincent, Evart, MI . .	6.00
E H Moore, Fancy Pigeons, Milrose, MA, red and black pigeons	10.00
F A Howe, Jr, Contracting Freight Agent, MI, Central RR & Blue Line Chicago, blue printing, white background	10.00
Fairchild & Co, Hats, Caps, and Straw Goods, New Orleans, red bee shape center	15.00

J. R. & F. PARSON,

DEALERS IN

Gents' Furnishing Goods,

AND

TRAVELING BAGS,

No. 414 Walnut Street, Southern Hotel,

St. Louis, Mo.

J. R. & F. Parson, Gents' Furnishing Goods, printed, black and white, 3½ x 2⅛″, 1890s, $4.00.

F G Morse & Co, Commercial Printers & Book Binders	6.00
Frank & Morgan, Lima Sanitary Vacuum Cleaner, large vacuum on horse drawn wagon, printed, black and white, corner crease	8.00
Fr Beck & Co Branch of National Wall Paper Co, Fine Wall Paper & Solid Relief Material, NY, gold name	25.00
George E Goodwin, Practical Apiarist, Collins, MI, bees, queens, black printing, yellow ground	20.00
George Hunzinger & Son, fancy choirs, illus on back	20.00
Geotzmann & Son, Manufacturer of Laundry Soaps, NY	15.00
Gray National Telautograph Co, NY, 1939	5.00
Grubb & Richardson, Poland, China Swine.	8.00
H H Heinrick, Manufacturer of Marine Chronometers, working parts illus on back.	15.00
H H Howe, Collins, MI, Lumber, black and white.	5.00
Horace Stillman Fresh Fish, No 4 Fulton Fish Market, NY, blue printing.	20.00
J A Lowell, Happy New Year, girl	8.00
James Vescelius, Sample Rooms, Pure Wines & Liquors, Milan, MI.	5.00
J O Draper Co Manufacturer Soaps, Pawtucket, RI, blue lettering, printed, color	8.00
Lavern Woody–Victor Radio Trademark	6.00
Milton Bradley Co, Kindergarten material, school aids, Springfield, MA.	15.00
Mrs H B Cooke, special agent for P Centemeri Glove, French rules for putting on glove and prices on back	8.00
N Osborn, Dealer in Expansion Rubber Buckets, Pumps, Woodstock, MI, blue Novelties for the Holidays, Conklin, CT, blue on front	6.00
	5.00
Original Sailor Jack, Tattoo Artist, IL, Pittsburg, PA, designs	10.00

Ornamental Land & Water Fowl, Darien, CT, bird list on back	**6.00**
Pfeiffer Brewing Co, Detroit, MI, multi-colored	**14.50**
Potter & Putnam, Educational Pub, NY . .	**8.00**
Psychometric Readings by Mail, Mrs W G Goffman, Grand Rapids, MI, well known test medium	**20.00**
R W Elliott, Photographer, Knightstown, IN, cupids, camera, photo album, printed, black and white, crease	**15.00**
Silverthaw & Sons Dealers In Diamonds & Watches, New Haven, CT, black with gold lettering, 1880s	**10.00**
Soyer's Worlds Secret Detective Service, NY, World Wide, brown and black, logo	**30.00**
Stephen McCrath, Wines and Ales, Hartford, CT, green	**10.00**
The Newest and Most Sanitary Shop in Providence, man cutting hair, 6 x 3¼"	**10.00**
Union Mills, Dusenberry & Anthony Dealers–Coffee & Spices, Troy, NY, red stamped name	**8.00**
Visit Old Friend Adam Luteman at Home, Toledo, Wines, Beer, Cigars, any parties for Good Hunting Fields call, Best Hunting Dogs, purple stamp	**12.00**

CALENDARS

History: Calendars date back to prehistoric times. With the printing revolution of the nineteenth century, calendars became accessible to everyone. By the end of the nineteenth century, they were one of the most popular forms of advertising giveaways and have remained so through today.

In the 1980s, the "art" or special theme calendar became popular. Moderately expensive, these calendars were designed for the bookstore and gift shop markets. With the exception of a few specific examples, collectors have largely ignored them.

There are classic calendars, such as the Marilyn Monroe "Golden Dream" image, or Chesapeake and Ohio Railroad calendars from the 1940s and 50s featuring Chessie, Peake, and the family.

Value increases between 10% and 20% if all monthly pages are attached. During the past two decades, calendar collectors as a group have diminished. Most calendars are sold in today's market for their subject matter or the birth year of the purchaser.

Artwork from many famous illustrators, e.g., R. Atkinson Fox, Maxfield Parrish, Norman Rockwell, and William Thompson, appears on calendars. These calendars command premium prices in the 1990s market. Price guides devoted to a single illustrator, e.g., Richard J. Perry's *The Maxfield Parrish Identification & Price Guide*

(Starbound Publishing, 1993), often contain a checklist of known calendars by the illustrator.

Since calendars were a favored promotional item, price guides devoted to a specific product, e.g., Allen Petretti's *Petretti's Coca–Cola Collectibles Price Guide, 8th Edition* (Wallace–Homestead, 1992), also contain important calendar checklists. As in the illustrator guides, the prices reflect the value of the calendar to the specialized collector, not to a calendar collector.

References: Douglas Congdon–Martin, *America For Sale: A Collector's Guide to Antique Advertising*, Schiffer Publishing, 1991; Sharon and Bob Huxford, *Huxford's Collectible Advertising: An Illustrated Value Guide*, Collector Books, 1993.

REPRODUCTION ALERT Beware of reproductions of the Marilyn Monroe calendar.

1882, Calendar of the Seasons, Marcus Ward & Co, sgd "Kate Greenaway"	**65.00**
1888, Brown's Iron Bitters, Burren Giles, NY litho	**70.00**
1889, Youth's Companion, opens, calendar on back	**10.00**
1890, Ivory Soap	**65.00**
1894	
Angel, diecut, violet cross, multicolored, sgd "Maud Humphrey"	**75.00**
Hoyt's, lady's, perfumed	**10.00**
1896, Singer Sewing Machines	**37.50**
1897, Berlin Iron Bridge Co, bridges and factory scenes, Kellogg & Bulkeley Co, 14 x 11"	**80.00**
1899	
Clarks ONT	**12.50**
Listers Fertilizers, woman with sheaves of wheat, farm background, full pad, 19 x 29", matted and framed	**125.00**
1900	
Hood's, two girls, full pad	**45.00**
Hoster Brewing Co, young girl, 17 x 23", matted and framed	**1,050.00**
Montgomery Ward, multicolored Montgomery Ward building, 16 x 23", framed	**325.00**
Springfield Breweries Co, calendar months around oval with girl, 21 x 29"	**225.00**
1901	
Colgate, flower illus, miniature	**15.00**
Houghton Co Brewers, dog with game bird in mouth, 17 x 21"	**75.00**
1902, Fertilizer Co, litho scene	**20.00**
1903	
Franco American	**15.00**
Grand Union, young girl and roses, 12½ x 28½"	**150.00**
Grecian Maidens, Raphael Tuck . . .	**18.00**
Hills Cascara Quinine Bromide, little girl, 5 x 10", framed	**50.00**

Melotte Cream Separators, 18 x 23", framed.................... **65.00**

1904

Hoods Sarsaparilla, multicolored, 12" l...................... **35.00**

Plano Harvesting Machinery, little girl with cherries and machinery vignettes, July pad, 21 x 15", framed.................... **340.00**

1905

Christian Herald, diecut, Victorian girls and birds **100.00**

Grand Union Tea Co, diecut, litho, 29 x 10".................... **90.00**

1906

Fleischmann's, horsedrawn wagon, July pad, 14 x 10" **110.00**

Rice Seed Co, cardboard litho, girl, orchid border, December pad, 18 x 12", framed................ **40.00**

The John Beth & Sons Co Choice Groceries & Provisions, 137 N Washington St, Green Bay, WI, 12 x 22" **55.00**

Wales–Goodyear Rubbers, cardboard litho, diecut, women in snow, 10 x 11", framed **150.00**

Youths Companion Minutemen **65.00**

1907, West End Brewing Co, multicolored girl and Victorian scene, full pad, 21 x 26".................. **425.00**

1908

David Stevenson Brewing Co, New York City, color litho, full pad, 20 x 29" **1,600.00**

De Laval Cream Separators, girl hugging a cow, 13 x 20", framed **350.00**

Metropolitan Life Insurance Co, oval center with mother and daughter **60.00**

1909

Bank of Waupun, emb lady **30.00**

Cardul Calendar & Weather Chart, Chattanooga Medicine Co, 13 x 20" **22.00**

1910, Chinese Student Alliance, rope hanger....................... **6.00**

1911

Geo Zett's Bavarian Beer, soldiers returning home, Kaufmann & Strauss, full pad, 18 x 20" **155.00**

Pratts Veterinary Remedies, woman feeding horse, full pad, 16 x 10" .. **225.00**

1912, Fern Brand Chocolates, emb, multicolored................... **6.00**

1913, Dr Daniels' Medicated Dog & Puppy Bread, little girl feeding dogs, 14 x 20", framed **500.00**

1915

Cosgroves Detective Agency, moose hunting scene **10.00**

Hoosier....................... **18.00**

Magic Yeast, paper litho, barefoot

boy carrying yeast and stick, Ketterlinus, Philadelphia, 18 x 10" **225.00**

Packers' Union Animal Matter Fertilizers, two Indians on mountain top, January pad, framed........ **25.00**

1916

Native Meat. . .Oysters, Game In Season, Chicago, full pad, 6 x 15½"...................... **10.00**

Putnam Dyes **40.00**

Weed Tire Chains, four women wearing hats, 30 x 10", framed ... **250.00**

1917, US Ammunition, slain ducks, May pad, 28 x 18", framed **260.00**

1919, Woodrow Wilson............ **10.00**

1922

Sharples Tubular Cream Separators, woman wearing hat, January pad **110.00**

Ulmer Installment Co, Round Oak Stoves & Ranges, Indian couple, full pad, 21 x 11"............... **130.00**

1923, State Bank of Hilbert, Indian maiden Inona, diecut oval mat, 11½ x 15"....................... **20.00**

1924, Pompeian Co, beautiful lady and man......................... **16.00**

1925, Peters Cartridge Co, flying mallard ducks, September pad, 33 x 18", framed **350.00**

1929, Compliments of H. Buch, Butcher and Dealer in Fresh and Smoked Meats, color litho illustration, full pad, 12 x 18¼", $30.00.

1928

Harrisburg Pilot, gypsy girl, 45 x 22"   **90.00**

Hudson Bay Company, multicolored   **70.00**

1929

Absence Makes the Heart Grow Fonder, two Indian maidens, canoe, and moon light scene **45.00**

Farm Equipment Co, Minnesota Binders, DeLavel Separators, Oliver Implements, flapper girl illus, 10 x16" **28.00**

Star Brand Shoes, woman by stained glass window, 26 x 11", framed . .   **140.00**

1930

De Laval Separator Co, Story of John & Mary, sgd Norman Price, orig mailing envelope **150.00**

Strong & Manley Lincoln–Ford–Fordson–General Hardware, Eagle River, WI, full pad **18.00**

1931, Great Northern Railroad, Indian portrait, Yellow Head, July sheet, 15 x 28", matted and framed **120.00**

1932

American Stores, children holding flag, full pad, 31 x 18" **120.00**

General Electric, Solitude, Maxfield Parrish, GE emblem, 9 x 19", orig envelope **310.00**

1933, Keen Kutter, each month with different product **85.00**

1937

Centennial Beer, gentleman holding beer, pointing to advertisement, full pad, 19 x 31", framed **300.00**

C & N W, 12 x 24" **18.00**

1939, Dionne Quintuplets–Five Little Sweethearts, full pad, 16 x 11" **28.00**

1940

A Moonlight Nymph, Laurette Patten, 20 x 46", salesman sample   **25.00**

Columbian Rope **40.00**

Texaco Sky Chief, paper litho **50.00**

1942, Case Farm Machinery, 9½ x 17"   **30.00**

1943, Hercules Powder Co, WWI Anniversary, soldier and dog, 31 x 13"   **150.00**

1944

Dionne Quintuplets–Maytime, 15 x 12" **30.00**

Draped in Silver Fox, salesman's sample, Dilly DeVorss, 16 x 33" . .   **65.00**

Farmers Oil Co, Branch, WI, full pad, 11 x 14¼" **7.00**

Sinclair Gasoline, twelve wildlife photos **20.00**

1945, Double Cola, full pad **110.00**

1946, Good Year Industrial Rubber Goods, full pad, 20½ x 37½" **45.00**

1948

Esquire, Ladies of the Harem, full pad **15.00**

Squirt, pinup girls **27.00**

1949, The Rumford Press, Kodachromes of covered bridges illus, 8½ x 11" **15.00**

1950, Wandering Brook Farm, children and animals **10.00**

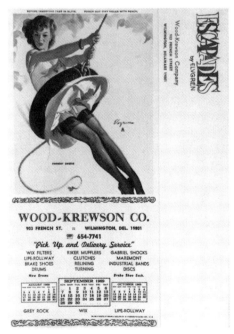

1969, Elvgren pin-up, "Swingin' Sweetie," September, folding punch-out, orig envelope, 4¾ x 10", $15.00.

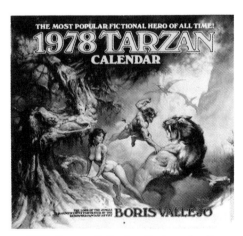

1978, Tarzan, Ballantine Books, color litho, 12 illustrations by Boris Vallejo, orig. cardboard mailer, 13 x 24½", $65.00.

1955, Marilyn Monroe, color photo, red ground, 8 x 14" **125.00**
1956, MacPherson pin–up, "The Lass Round–up," 9½ x 12" **25.00**
1958, National Life Insurance Co, bears illus **10.00**
1959, Paul Webb **35.00**
1960, Dr Pepper, 75th Anniversary . . . **35.00**
1961, TWA, six sheets, 16 x 24" **15.00**
1965, Jayne Mansfield, full color glossy photo, full pad, 9 x 14" **85.00**
1966, North Central Airlines–Wings for Mid–America, scenic view, six sheets, 16 x 33" **12.00**
1969
Curly Horse Ranch, Elvgren, cowgirl illus **46.00**
Union Pacific Railroad Centennial, 19 x 24 . . . . **18.00**
1975
Hummel Figurines, full pad **7.00**
Kewpie **18.00**
Playboy **20.00**
1976, Winchester, Bicentennial, Revolutionary War scenes **59.00**
1980, St Louis Cardinals, Budweiser adv, 15 x 30" **18.00**

CALLING CARDS

History: The personal calling card, also known as a visiting card or carte de visite, reached its zenith during the American Victorian era, circa 1850 to 1915. Cards were carried in calling card cases and dropped into calling card receivers; two three–dimensional objects eagerly sought by calling card collectors.

The style and use of the personal calling card was carefully defined by Victorian era etiquette books. Maud C. Cook's *Modern Etiquette, or Manners and Customs of Polite Society* (1906) noted: "The stress laid by society upon the correct usage of these magic bits of pasteboard will not seem unnecessary when it is remembered that the visiting card, socially defined, means, and is frequently made to take the place of, one's self." Rules were provided involving manner of distribution, how many, proper method to make calls, acceptance of obligatory return visits, manner of dress, attire, appropriate topics of discussion, and length of visit.

Calling cards were sold by printing houses. Sample sheets were available through the mail or at the local stationery shop. While etiquette books recommended plain unadorned cardstock for calling cards, many individuals, especially in smaller communities, opted for something more elaborate. Ornate cards consisting of a base card over which was a diecut floral, fauna, or pastoral scene were common. The name of the individual was hidden under the diecut. Many cards contained sentimental messages.

Formal calling cards consisted of a centered name with address in the lower right. Woman's cards had an "At Home" day printed in the lower left corner. Cards marked with "P.P.C." (*pour prendre congre*) meant that the caller was leaving town for an extended period. Gilt, rounded corners, fancy typeface, and vignettes were simply not permitted. A colored or glazed card was considered the epitome of bad taste.

Cards were not allowed to accumulate. Most were discarded. Some were pasted in family scrapbooks. Others found their way into a candy, cigar, shoe, or other available box and stored in the back of a drawer or closet. The framing of cards was considered a social no–no.

The value of diecut calling cards rests in the theme of the die–cut. Calling cards associated with a famous personality have some value. Hand drawn calling cards, especially those featuring Spenserian script, are collected as art forms, not as calling cards. The vast majority of common, ordinary, everyday calling cards are worth less than $1.00, collected more out of curiosity than anything.

Alice Wyatt, fan shape, multicolored floral **15.00**
Christie Hoover, serrated edge with round corners, chromolithograph of two roses and hand feeding doves, "Life, bear for you its sweetest flower," 1½ x 3", 1890s **12.00**
Clayton Rhynier, engraved, envelope with chromolithograph diecut, "'Mongst, those I most esteem, be sure your place forever is secure," 1½ x 2½", 1890s **12.00**
Enrico Caruso, sgd **75.00**
El West Delight, colorful, 3 x 4", 1933 . . **1.00**
Hattie Wyatt, fan shape, multicolored, floral and landscape scene, "Sweet Remembrance" **15.00**

Engraved Calling Card, diecut calling card mounted on envelope flap, 3⅜ x 2⅜", 1890s, $8.00.

Lithographed, 1880s, $9.00.

Steel Engraved, 3½ x 1⅞", 1870s, $6.00.

J G Harrison & Sons Strawberries, salesman's **22.00**
Jimmy Davis, sgd. **7.00**
Minnie Roff, serrated edge with round corners, chromolithograph doves and flowers, "With Fond Greetings," 1½ x 3", 1890s **12.00**
Mrs Pheobe Maben, multicolored, two frogs and lake scene **10.00**
Sir Harry Lauder **55.00**
Thomas Quincy, Will remain in New Orleans until May, 1832 for the transaction of a General Commission Business, black and white print **50.00**

CATALOGS

History: The purpose of a trade catalog is to sell product. Virtually everything that was manufactured, mined, processed, raised, or salvaged appeared at one time or another in a trade catalog. The variety of forms is endless.

There are basically three types of trade catalogs. Manufacturers' catalogs are supplied to distributors, rarely to the final retail customer. They provide extremely detailed information and illustrations of products. Distributors often issue their own catalogs, incorporating only those specific products from a host of manufacturers that they plan to distribute. Catalogs from distributors are focused toward small merchants and consumers. The consumer catalog is a catalog targeted for the home shopper.

Trade catalogs originated in the 18th century. Benjamin Franklin is credited with issuing the first trade catalog in 1744, offering books for sale to those living in remote areas. Other early catalogs offered the essentials of life, e.g., medicines, as well as garden items, silverware, and jewelry. Catalogs served those craftsmen and merchants who made desirable goods that could be easily shipped over a broad geographical area.

Mail order catalogs arrived upon the American scene about 1872, when A. Montgomery Ward established the first general mail order business in Chicago, Illinois. R. W. Sears and A. C. Roebuck started their business in Minneapolis, Minnesota, about 1886. These first general mail order merchandisers helped to distribute goods across the country, including small towns and rural areas. Rural free delivery and parcel post assured cheap delivery. Low prices along with money back guarantees ensured public buying interest.

The Larkin Company began to issue its famous premium catalogs shortly after the company began in 1875. Larkin's imaginative use of premiums achieved widespread popularity by the 1890s. Housewives everywhere eagerly participated in the program.

A catalog revolution occurred in the 1980s. Sellers found that through market and consumer research, specialized catalogs, and select zip code mailing niche marketing was practical and profitable. Customer lists were sold and swapped. As the decade ended, some mail boxes contained more catalogs than anything else.

Although enjoying its renaissance, the mail order catalog is under fire from newspaper catalog inserts and the home shopping channels on cable television. Macy's recently announced that it was considering launching its own television shopping channel. Add to this the increasing role played by the home computer and the much talked about communication revolution of the 21st century and the printed catalog may well prove to be a twentieth century dinosaur by 2025.

References: Don Fredgant, *American Trade Catalogs: Identification and Value Guide,* Collector Books, 1984; Lawrence B. Romaine, *A Guide To American Trade Catalogs 1744–1900,* Dover Publications, 1960, 1990 reprint.

Agriculture
  Akron Tool Co, Kraus and Akron Sulky Cultivators, c1900, 36 pgs **30.00**
  Dollars In Dynamite, Increase The Farm Size, Drain That Swamp, Break Big Stones, Blast Tree Holes, Dupont Powder Co, Wilmington, DE, 1925, 8 pgs, 3¼ x 6" **12.00**
  Diamond Mill Company, Diamond Grist Mills, Cincinnati, OH, 1869, 16 pgs **65.00**
  Hill Archimedean Lawn–Mower Co, New Charter Oak Lawn Mower, Hartford, CT, 1870, 4 pgs **20.00**
  Munnsville Plow Co, Munnsville, NY, c1900, 36 pgs **35.00**
Ammunition, Western Ammunition Handbook, Western Cartridge Co, East Alton, IL, fully illus, charts, tables of specifications, graphs, ammunition photographs, and Winchester rifles, 1937, 72 pgs **35.00**
Architectural
  Canvas Cottage Co, J W Ormsby, Milwaukee, WI, c1905, 32 pgs **25.00**
  Edwards Manufacturing Co, Sheet Metal Building Material, Cincinnati, OH, 1923, 96 pgs **60.00**
  Modern Plaster Ornament, Architectural Decorating Co, Chicago, IL, 1927, 31 pgs, 9 x 12" **10.00**
  Rutland Fire Clay Company, Success Concrete Building Blocks, Milford, CT, 1921, 76 pgs **75.00**
  Stillman–Paine Co Architectural Ornaments, 1909, 143 pgs. **15.00**
Automotive
  Congdon & Carpenter Co, Automobile Supplies, Providence, RI, c1916, 124 pgs **50.00**
  DeSoto For 1940, 14 pgs **15.00**
  Engines & Transmissions for the '59 Fords, 19 pgs **10.00**
  Frazer Lubricator Co, Frazer Axle Grease, New York, NY, 1915, 2 pgs **25.00**
  Machinery–Tools and Supplies for the

  Auto Glass and Mirror Shop, Net Price Wholesale Catalogue, Number 947, August 1, 1947, Henry G Lange Machine Works, Chicago, IL, fully illus, black and white photographs, 80 pgs, 6 x 9" **12.50**
  Marathon Motor Works, Nashville, TN, Marathon Automobiles, history and pictorial view of the 1913 automobiles, 1912, 32 pgs, 8½ x 12" . . . **143.00**
  The Hatcher Auto Parts Co, Cleveland, OH, illus, auto parts for the manufacturer and repair shop–hand levers, foot brake, universal joints, strainers, transmission gears, clutches, c1917, 44 pgs, 6¾ x 10" **39.00**
Bicycle
  Barnes Cycle Co, Barnes Bicycles–The White Flyer, Syracuse, NY, 1896, 32 pgs **100.00**
  Joe Wiesenfeld Co, Baltimore, MD, bicycle items, 1890–1900, 23 pgs, 3½ x 6" **25.00**
  Keating Wheel Co, Keating Bicycles, Holyoke, MA, 1895, 16 pgs **100.00**
  Western Wheel Works, Crescent Bicycles, Chicago, IL, 1897, 40 pgs **75.00**
Books
  Booklovers Library, Philadelphia, PA, 1903, 18 pgs **30.00**
  Sears Roebuck & Co, Books and Stationery, Chicago, IL, 1908, 36 pgs. . **35.00**

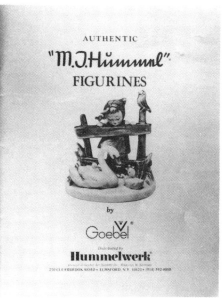

Authentic M. I. Hummel Figurines, Goebel-Hummelwerk, West Germany, 1978, $17.50.

Carriage
Eureka Carriage Co, Rock Falls, IL,
c1890, 40 pgs **100.00**
Murray, Wilber H Mfg Co, World–
Renowned Murray Buggies and
Harness, Cincinnati, OH, 1889, 24
pgs **125.00**
Waynesburg Carriage Co **60.00**
Clothing and Accessories
Brown's Beach Jacket Co, Worcester,
MA, 1940–41, 24 pgs **8.00**
Dunham Bros, shoe, 1917 . . . .   **35.00**
Hamilton Brown Shoe Co, St Louis,
MO, 1913, 96 pgs, $6^{1}/_{2}$ x 9" **23.00**
Hart, Schaffner & Marx, Chicago, IL,
1914, 32 pgs, $5^{1}/_{2}$ x 7" **17.00**
National Cloak & Suit Co, Christmas,
1915 . . . .   **100.00**
Rothmoor Coats, flapper models, 1929   **10.00**
Taylor Bros & Co, Chicago, IL, Fall and
Winter, 1894, 72 pgs **60.00**
Dental
Buffalo Dental Mfg Co, Snow & Lewis
Automatic Pluggers, Buffalo, NY,
1897, 8 pgs **90.00**
Justi, H D , Circular of Dental Special-
ties, Philadelphia, PA, c1880, 40
pgs **165.00**
The S S White Dental Co, Philadel-
phia, PA, 1924, 100 pgs, 7 x $9^{1}/_{2}$" . .   **40.00**

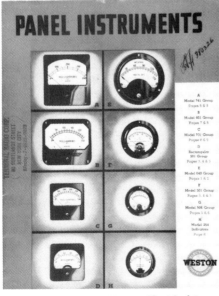

Panel Instruments, Weston Electrical In-
struments Company, black-and-white
product photos, 18 pages, printed red and
black on white cover with real photos,
$8^{1}/_{2}$ x 11", 1930s, $12.00.

Wilmot Castle Co, Rochester, NY,
1926, 16 pgs, 6 x $8^{3}/_{4}$" **23.00**
Farming
American Steel & Wire Co, Chicago,
IL, 1922, 39 pgs **18.00**
Hudson Barn Equipment, 1933, 166
pgs **15.00**
Indiana Silo, Anderson, IN, 1907, 36
pgs **14.00**
Kingman & Co, Inc, Peoria, IL, ND,
CA, 1905, 258 pgs **135.00**
Lena Building Material Co New Book
of Practical Farm Buildings, Lena,
WI, 1919, 96 pgs **20.00**
Newton Giant Incubator, Harrisburg,
VA, ND, CA, 1929, 48 pgs, $8^{1}/_{4}$ x
11" **32.00**
Oliver Chilled Plow Works, South
Bend, IN, 1906, 16 pgs, 5 x $7^{1}/_{2}$" . . .   **26.00**
S L Allen & Co, Philadelphia, PA,
1924, 68 pgs, $5^{3}/_{4}$ x $8^{3}/_{4}$" **24.00**
Firearms
Colt Gun, handguns, rifles, and acces-
sories, 1961, 20 pgs **13.00**
Hopkins & Allen Gun, 1908, 48 pgs . .   **150.00**
Marlin Sporting Firearms, 1969, 24
pgs **10.00**
Winchester, World Standard Guns and
Ammunition, Winchester Repeating
Arms Company, New Haven, CT,
fully illus, drawings and photo-
graphs showing rifles, shotguns and
ammunition, 1933, 62 pgs, 6 x $3^{1}/_{2}$"   **45.00**
Fishing
Heddon Tackle For Everyone, 1968,
68 pgs, 9 x 12" **22.00**
South Bend Co, 1934, 93 pgs, fishing
equipment, 5 x 7" **50.00**
William Mills & Sons, trout and fly–
fishing tackle, 1931, 8 pgs **75.00**
Food
Bell, William G & Co, Wholesale Pro-
vision Dealers, Boston, MA, 1866, 4
pgs **50.00**
Stark Bros Fruits, 1916, 50 pgs **15.00**
Furniture
American Chair Co Tropique Rattan
Furniture, Sheboygan, WI, 1945, 16
pgs, 9 x 12" **15.00**
Crandall–Bennett Porter Co, Oak Din-
ing Room Tables, 1907, 35 pgs **48.00**
Englander Spring Bed Co, Brooklyn,
NY, c1925, 16 pgs **30.00**
Heywood–Wakefield Co, Cane and
Wood Furniture–Catalogue 101–B,
Gardner, MA, 1928, 80 pgs **50.00**
Maddox Table Co, Maddox Tables,
Jamestown, NY, 1922, 55 pgs **50.00**
Peck & Hills Furniture Co, Boston,
MA, 1931, 400 pgs **75.00**
Van Sciver, J B Co, Fashions in Furni-
ture, Camden, NJ, c1920, 28 pgs . . .   **50.00**

Public Service Gas Company, gas stoves and fixtures, printed, color, illustrated, 44 pages, 5½ x 8", c1900, $35.00.

Gardening, The McGregors Bros, Springfield, OH, 1929, 40 pgs, gardening... **17.00**

General Merchandise
Bellas Hess & Co, 1918–19, Fall and Winter, 276 pgs **45.00**
Chicago Mail Order Co, Spring and Summer, 1937, 334 pgs, 8 x 11" ... **15.00**
Direct Separator Co Steam & Oil Separators, 1911, 31 pgs **24.00**
Duplex Mills Co, Springfield, OH, 1920, 24 pgs **9.00**
Fairbanks Co, Railway, Mill, and Contractors Supplies, 1918, 650 pgs ... **33.00**
G E Masters Co, NY/Boston, Summer Travel, 1914, 12 pgs, 8½ x 11" **7.00**
General Merchandise Co, Milwaukee, WI, 1950, 326 pgs, toys, dolls, and giftware **20.00**
Gimble Brothers, Philadelphia, PA, 1928, 62 pgs, 7 x 10" **14.00**
Henion & Hubbell Bathroom Fixtures & Mirrors, 1913, 64 pgs **25.00**
Huntly Mfg Co, Silver Creek, NY, peanut cleaners, shellers, graders, 1927, 44 pgs **10.00**
Kitselman, Muncie, IN, fence materials and supplies, 1938, 64 pgs **14.00**
Marblehead Craft Shop, Marblehead,

MA, 1931, 32 pgs, general merchandise, 6 x 9" **23.00**
Martin Lumber Co, Springfield, MA, 1936, 148 pgs **8.00**
Sears Roebuck Co, Chicago, IL
1905, general catalogue, 658 pgs .. **64.00**
1937–38, Fall and Winter, 970 pgs **40.00**
1941–42, Fall and Winter, 1280 pgs **35.00**
Spiegel, 1944, 630 pgs **12.00**
Household
Columbia Mills, Columbia Guaranteed Window Shades, New York, NY, c1920, 12 pgs.............. **25.00**
Hobart Baking Machines, mixers, beaters, and whips, 1941, 16 pgs .. **10.00**
Horace Turner, Price List of Feathers and Pillows, Detroit, MI, 1890, 20 pgs......................... **40.00**
Hunting, Howe Fur Co, Coopers Mills, ME, 1945, 72 pgs, 8¼ x 10"........ **23.00**
Ice Cream, Thomas Mills & Bros Ice Cream Manufacturers Equipment, 1915, 60 pgs **75.00**
Insulators, Ohio Brass Co, Mansfield, OH, insulators, 1947, 160 pgs....... **12.50**
Interior Decorating
Color In Modern Decoration, Patek Bros Paint Makers Since 1895, 1920, 19 pgs **10.00**

S & H Green Stamp Premiums, NY, sepia covers and product illustrations, 28 pages, 6 x 8¾", 1927, $15.00.

Geo C Mages Co Wholesale Catalog Mouldings, Frames, Mirrors, Cabinet Hardware, Novelties, 1897–98, 160 pgs, 9 x 12" **65.00**

Sherwin–Williams Color Styling Service, 1941, 23 pgs **7.00**

Jewelry

Charig Brothers, Catalogue of Diamonds, Watches, Jewelry, Silverware, New York, NY, c1890, 142 pgs **80.00**

Oskamp Nolting Co, Cincinnati, OH, 1931, 98 pgs, 9 x 11¾" **24.00**

R B Anger & Co Jeweler's, c1925, 26 pgs **6.00**

Keys and Locks, Curtis Key Co, 1941, 80 pgs, keys, locks, key cutting equipment, 8½ x 11½" **12.00**

Lamps and Lighting

Crouse–Hindsco, Syracuse, NY, 1929, 280 pgs, 8 x 10½" **29.00**

Decorators Supply Co, Chicago, IL, 1920s, 96 pgs, glass and glass and metal lighting fixtures, 9¼ x 12¼"   **30.00**

Lincoln Mfg Co, Lighting Fixtures for the Home, Detroit, MI, 1930, 74 pgs   **60.00**

Perkins Marine Lamps & Hardware, 1935, 174 pgs **14.00**

Riddle Decorative Lighting Fitments, 1923, 16 pgs **15.00**

Thurston Supply Co, Anoka, MN, 1935, 68 pgs, 6 x 8¾" **14.00**

Musical Instruments

American Felt Co, Piano and Organ Supplies, New York, NY, 1910, 337 pgs **100.00**

Farrand Organ Co, Detroit, MI, c1910, 28 pgs **45.00**

Niagara Music Co, Buffalo, NY, Special Fall Price List, c1910, 9 pgs. . . .   **20.00**

Optical

Bausch & Lomb Optical Co, Rochester, NY, 1931, 16 pgs **18.00**

DuMaurier Company, Magic Eyes, Elmira, NY, 1934, 36 pgs **35.00**

Willson, T A & Co, Interchangeable Steel Spectacles and Eye Glasses, Reading, PA, 1890, 40 pgs. **150.00**

Outboard Motor Boats

Evinrude Division Outboard Motors Corp, 1929, 32 pgs, 8 x 10¾" **27.00**

Thompson Bros Outboard Motor Boats, Canoes, Motor Boats, 1929, 32 pgs, 8 x 10¾" **20.00**

Photography

Central Camera Co, Chicago, IL, 1938, 128 pgs **8.00**

Defender Photo Supply Co, Rochester, NY, c1925, 48 pgs, 5½ x 7¾" **13.00**

Eastman Kodak Co, Rochester, NY, 1926, 64 pgs **60.00**

Rochester Optical Co, Modern Photography, Rochester, NY, c1893, 24 pgs **25.00**

Plumbing

Bailey–Farrell Mfg Co, Modern Plumbing Fixtures and Sanitary Specialties, Pittsburgh, PA, 1905, 251 pgs **85.00**

Republic Plumbing Supplies, 1928 . . .   **20.00**

Yonkers Plumbing Supply Co, Wrought & Cast Iron Pipe and Fittings, Yonkers, NY, 1923, 452 pgs   **40.00**

Poultry

Hummel's Poultry **10.00**

The Paying Hen, Mann's Green Bone Cutters, F W Mann Co, Milford, MA, Catalogue Number 38, c1900, 24 pgs, fully illus, tinted photographs, 6½ x 9" **20.00**

Pulley

American Pulley Co, Philadelphia, PA, 1927, 120 pgs **10.00**

Klay Universal Gear, Pulley & Wheel Pullers, Scott–Ewing Co, Bluffton, OH, 1927, 32 pgs **10.00**

Radio, Lafayette Radio & Sound Systems, Wholesale Service Co, 1938, 176 pgs   **20.00**

Records

Columbia Records, 1923, 416 pgs . . .   **25.00**

Victor Records, 1922, celebrities illus   **30.00**

School Supplies

Holcomb, JR, School Supplies, Cleveland, OH, 1908, 50 pgs **40.00**

Milton Bradley, school supplies, 1931, 128 pgs **25.00**

Talens School Products Co, San Francisco, CA, 1932, 58 pgs, 6½ x 9¾"   **18.00**

Sewing

Clark's ONT J & P Coats Edgings, 1945, 22 pgs **12.00**

King Sewing Machine Co, Buffalo, NY, 1909, 56 pgs **40.00**

White Sewing Machine Company, Cleveland, OH, 1917, 26 pgs **75.00**

Sporting Goods

American News Company, Sporting and Outing Goods, New York, NY, 1906, 12 pgs **50.00**

Emmons–Hawkins Hardware, Huntington, WV, 1938, 56 pgs, 8½ x 10½" **27.00**

Taxidermy, Chieftain Brand Taxidermy Supplies, 1930, 40 pgs **22.00**

Tools and Machinery

Baker & Co, Findings/Settings, 1920, 62 pgs **33.00**

Boston Gear Works, 1938, 320 pgs. . .   **8.00**

Craftsman & Companion Power Tools & Accessories, 1933, 41 pgs **14.00**

Delta Quality Motor–Driven Tools, 1931, 48 pgs, 8½ x 11" **12.00**

F R Patch Co, belt and power driven planers, 1930s, 8 x 12½" **7.50**

Granite Working Tools, Supplies, Machinery and Hardware, Granite City Tool Co, Barre, VT, St Cloud, MN, Elberton, GA, Catalogue Number 4, February, 1932, fully illus, black and white photographs, 144 pgs, 6 x 9" **12.50**
Union Tool Co, Orange, MA, 1926, 270 pgs, 3 x 5¼" **13.00**
US Air Compressor Co, Cleveland, OH, 1917, 24 pgs **8.00**

Toys

Boucher Playthings Mfg Corp, New York, NY, 1933, 48 pgs **30.00**
Corgi 1979, The Mettoy Playcraft Ltd, Northampton, full color illus and photographs, 48 pgs, 6 x 4" **12.00**
Matchbox Collectors USA Edition 1972, full color illus and photographs, 48 pgs, 5½ x 4" **15.00**

Valves

Jenkin's Brothers Valves and Packing Jenkins Bros Co, NY, black and white artist's illus, c1907, 184 pgs 4 x 6" **15.00**
Halworth Co, NY, valves, fittings, and tools, 1938, 579 pgs **20.00**

Windmills

Flint & Walling Mfg Co, Kendallville, IN, 1891, 24 pgs **150.00**
Jager, Charles J Co, Eclipse Windmills, Boston, MA, c1895, 104 pgs **275.00**
Perkins Wind Mill & Axe Co, Mishawaka, IN, c1885, 8 pgs **65.00**

CEREAL BOXES

History: Packaged, ready–to–eat breakfast cereal arrived on the scene at the dawn of the twentieth century. Hot cooked oatmeal and wheat cereal were a staple of the eighteenth and nineteenth century diet, dispensed by weight in a plain sack at the general store.

During the first decades of the twentieth century, mothers were the principal target of cereal manufacturers. Mothers made the decision of what foods to prepare while doing the grocery shopping. The situation changed dramatically in the early 1930s.

Several cereal manufacturers, including General Mills, Quaker, Post, and Ralston began targeting their cereal advertising toward youngsters. The hook was a free premium that could be obtained by sending in the requisite number of boxtops. Several cereal manufacturers sponsored popular children's radio programs and used this vehicle to tout their free premiums as well. On–pack promotions featuring cut–outs, contests, and games were common.

In the mid–1950s cereal manufacturers intro-

duced sugar-coated cereal. In addition to promoting this cereal on radio, the manufacturers also utilized television. Boxes promoted the characters that appeared on the shows sponsored by the manufacturer. When the use of TV spot advertising began, advertising brand characters were developed to ensure recognition. Arriving on the scene were Tony the Tiger, Sugar Bear, Captain Crunch, and a host of others. For the next fifteen years, America's youngsters were sugar-coated crazy.

In the late 1960s and 1970s, cereal manufacturers developed special promotional brands of cereal, often in conjunction with a popular movie or sports star. Instead of sponsoring an entire television program, cereal manufacturers relied almost exclusively on spot commercials. While most promotional brands were short lived, sales were excellent during the initial promotional period. The 1980s and 1990s have witnessed a major increase in the number of promotional cereal offers. Availability is closely linked to the popularity of the character, person, or event portrayed.

Cereal is packaged about once every three months. Prior to packaging, a market study is done of brand acceptance and premium offers. When a successful sales forecast is achieved, boxes are printed. The amount of cereal prepared for packaging is dependent on the number of boxes printed.

The average retail price of a box of cereal in the 1990s is over two dollars. Much of the cost is reflected in advertising and licensing. Generic boxing and local and regional promotions have reopened the door for smaller cereal manufacturers.

There are a number of key factors in determining the value of a cereal box. The first key is the desirability of the brand name, character, or brand offered on the box. The second is box completeness. Flat (unconstructed boxes) and file copies command a premium of 10% to 25%. Error boxes and withdrawn boxes also are sold at a premium.

Reference: Tom Tumbusch, *Tomart's Price Guide to Radio Premiums and Cereal Box Collectibles*, Wallace–Homestead, 1991.

Periodicals: *Flake*, PO Box 481, Cambridge, MA 02140; *Free Inside*, PO Box 178844, San Diego, CA 92117.

All Bran, 1953, Two Great Treat Recipes, Kellogg's **10.00**
Alpha Bits, Post
  1958, First Happy Box **50.00**
  1970, Archie cutout record on back . . **150.00**
Apple Jacks
  1966, comics on back, Kellogg's **30.00**
  Banana Splits flashlight offer, Kellogg's **100.00**
Banana Frosted Flakes, 1980s, Tony on front, Kellogg's **30.00**

Barbie, 1989, Animal Lovin' Barbie, Ralston **10.00**
Batman, 1989, hologram T–shirt offer, Ralston. **10.00**
Boo Berry, 1970s, monster poster offer, General Mills. **30.00**
Bran Flakes, 1985, Garden Trowel offer, Kellogg's **3.00**
Cap'n Crunch, 1988, Secret Message Writer & Decoder, Quaker **3.00**
Cheerios
   1940s, individual size **14.00**
   1949, Hall of Fun Pop–Out Pictures, Eddie Cantor, General Mills **30.00**
   1956, American Airlines Game Kit offer, General Mills. **20.00**
   1972, Super–Cycle in pack, General Mills. **10.00**
   1976, Bionic Stickers in pack, General Mills. **10.00**
   1978, Star Wars Poster in pack, General Mills **20.00**
Circus Fun, 1980s, clown illus, 3–Ring Circus Puzzle on back, General Mills **10.00**
Cocoa Krispies, Kellogg's
   1973, glow in the dark iron–on patch in pack **10.00**
   1988, Hot Wheels offer **20.00**
Cocoa Pebbles, 1987, Bedrock Biker Race poster in pack, Post. **3.00**
Cocoa Puffs, 1972, Harlem Globe Trotters Trading Cards in pack, General Mills. **20.00**
Cookie Crisp, 1987, Corvette car in pack, Ralston. **10.00**
Corn Chex, 1987, movie ticket discount on front **3.00**
Corn Flakes, Kellogg's
   1920s, sample size **15.00**
   1950s, Superman offer **200.00**
   1952, frying pan set offer. **20.00**
   1957, fire engine offer **20.00**
   1961, Yogi Bear mask offer **50.00**
   1982, Elizabeth Ward, Miss America **10.00**
   1987, Captain Power stamps in pack **10.00**
Corn Pops, 1989, Garfield Water Magic picture, Kellogg's. **10.00**
Count Chocula, 1988, Monster poster offer, General Mills. **10.00**
Crispix, 1988, zoo pass offer, Kellogg's **3.00**
Crispy Critters, 1970, Archies comic book in pack, Post **20.00**
Crunch Berries, 1970s, Quaker. **35.00**
Crystal Oats, Quaker, round **18.00**
Donky Kong Junior, 1984, baseball cards in pack, Ralston. **30.00**
Dunkin' Donuts Cereal, 1988, back to school kit offer, Ralston **10.00**
Frankenberry, 1988, Starburst candy in pack, General Mills **10.00**
Froot Loops, 1970, Mattel Fun on Wheels Contest, Kellogg's. **30.00**

Frosted Flakes, 1987, diving Tony in pack, Kellogg's **10.00**
Frosty O's, 1960s, white bear on unicycle, General Mills. **20.00**
Fruit Islands, 1987, pen and game map in pack, Ralston. **10.00**
Fruity Pebbles, 1972, Post. **50.00**
George Washington Corn Flakes, unopened **60.00**
Ghostbusters, 1989, hologram series, T–shirt offer, Ralston **10.00**
Golden Grahams, 1980s, roller blade offer, General Mills. **3.00**
Grape Nut Flakes, 1957, Black Fury the Horse offer, Post **75.00**
Grape Nuts, 1960s, baseball cards on back, Post **75.00**
Highland Oats. **30.00**
Honey Comb, 1978, Superman Action poster in pack, Post **20.00**
Honey Graham Chex, 1988, Porsche car in pack, Ralston. **3.00**
Honey Nut Cheerios, 1988, Winnie the Pooh offer, General Mills **10.00**
Honey & Nut Corn Flakes, 1980, Dymo label maker offer **3.00**
Honey Smacks, 1970, Banana Splits poster offer, Kellogg's **100.00**
Kaboom, 1987, water monster offer, General Mills. **10.00**
Kix, General Mills
   1949, Tell–A–Vision Shows, cutout on back **20.00**
   1987, personalized pencil offer. **10.00**
Life, 1970s, Quaker. **20.00**
Lucky Charms, 1988, magic tricks in pack, General Mills **3.00**
Mother Hubbard Wheat Cereal. **22.00**
Mother's Oats **20.00**
Mueslix Bran, 1988, Old World Sweepstakes on back, Kellogg's. **3.00**
Natural Bran Flakes, 1988, coupon cutout on back, Post **3.00**
Nerds, Orange 'N Cherry, 1985, Nerds candy in pack, bowl offer, Ralston . . . **20.00**
Nutri Grain, 1989, Kellogg's **3.00**
Oatmeal Raisin Crisp, 1987, Look What We've Done, General Mills. **3.00**
Post Toasties, Post
   1950s, Mighty Mouse offer **75.00**
   1961, Tang bowl and juice glass offer **10.00**
Puffa Puffa Rice, 1971, travel decal in pack, Kellogg's **30.00**
Puffed Rice, 1950s, Bugs Bunny comic book offer, Quaker **100.00**
Puffed Wheat, 1949, Sgt Preston's Yukon Trail model, Quaker **100.00**
Quaker, 1970, Dodge Charger car kit in pack, Quaker. **75.00**
Quaker Muffets Shredded Wheat, 1960s, Authentic Model Civil War Cannon adv on side panel, 3 x 6 x 7" **37.50**

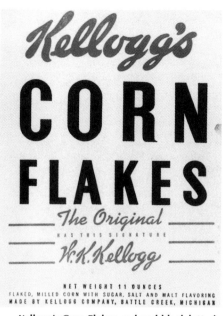

Kellogg's Corn Flakes, red-and-black lettering, white ground, WWII military puzzles on back, 7½ x 10¼ x 2¾", c1945, $27.50.

Quaker Puffed Rice, 1919, 5 oz	**20.00**
Quisp, 1970, Big Slick Gyro car in pack, Quaker	**75.00**
Raisin Bran	
Kellogg's	
1961, Kraft Caramels in pack.	**20.00**
1987, Duck Tales duck track stickers in pack.	**10.00**
Post, 1970, Monkees Mobile car offer	**100.00**
Rice Chex, 1950s, Space Patrol offer, Ralston.	**300.00**
Rice Honeys, 1969, Beatles Yellow Submarine with stickers, Nabisco	**300.00**
Rice Krispies, Kellogg's	
1954, Wild Bill Hickock TV show on back.	**100.00**
1956, flying saucer offer	**50.00**
1964, Pop A Ball offer	**20.00**
1967, self powered tugboat offer.	**20.00**
1988, Chipmunk mask on back, Alvin	**10.00**
Scotch Brand Oats.	**30.00**
Superior Rolled Oats, Sioux City, IA	**16.50**
Shredded Wheat, 1955, baseball ring in pack, Kellogg's	**100.00**
Special K, 1989, Fat to Muscle Diet offer, Kellogg's	**3.00**
Sugar Crisp, Post	
1952, Roy Rogers and Trigger, pop–out card in pack.	**300.00**
1988, Kool–Aid Wacky Warehouse Bank on back.	**3.00**
Sugar Frosted Flakes, Kellogg's	
1956, squirt gun in pack	**30.00**

1967, Apple Jack bowl and mug offer	**20.00**
1981, Tony The Tiger cereal bowl offer	**20.00**
Sugar Jets, 1960s, General Mills	**30.00**
Sugar Pops, Kellogg's	
1969, Hot Wheels coupon	**50.00**
1970, flying saucers and launcher offer.	**20.00**
1974, Soldiers of the Ages in pack. . . .	**20.00**
Sugar Smacks, Kellogg's	
1963, Eager B Beaver.	**50.00**
1971, travel decals in pack, Woody Woodpecker on back	**20.00**
Teenage Mutant Ninja Turtles, 1989, hologram box, T–shirt offer, Ralston	**3.00**
Total Raisin Bran, 1988, General Mills . .	**3.00**
Trix, 1972, Beech–Nut in pack, rocket ship offer, General Mills	**10.00**
Wheat Honeys, 1960s, Disney character offer, Nabisco	**75.00**
Wheaties, General Mills	
1946, Cutout Mask, Pocahontas	**30.00**
1947, Fight For Freedom, Rip the Sabertooth Tiger, General Mills.	**30.00**
1951, Mickey Mouse mask, General Mills.	**50.00**
1954, Yankee Doodle Dandy record	**50.00**
1959, Bowling Champion contest.	**30.00**
1967, Bobby Richardson on back	**20.00**
1977, girl ice skating	**20.00**
1987, Minnesota Twins team photo on front and back	**10.00**
1988, Steve Largent Commemorative	**20.00**
White Swan Oatmeal, 4 oz	**27.50**

CERTIFICATES

History: The dictionary provides a two part definition for certificate. The first states that a certificate is a "document certifying that one has fulfilled the requirements of and may practice in a field." The second says it is a "document evidencing ownership or debt." Implied is that it is highly personal, one of the prime reasons why so few paper collectors collect certificates.

High school and college diplomas, rewards of achievement, and special recognition documents survive in the millions. Their principal value is that of personal or family sentiment; once that is removed, value plummets.

Local and regional collectors are the chief buyers of these documents. Local institution favor is enough to spark their interest. Value increases significantly if the certificate has a vignette based upon a local building or scenic landscape. While often exhibiting the finest engraving and typography of an era, collectors in these categories largely ignore certificates.

Association with an important historical, political, sport, or societal figure changes the picture. Depending on the importance of the personality, these certificates can command in the hundreds of dollars. Another value enhancer is a certificate from a manufacturer of a highly collectible object or object group, e.g., a certificate from Milton Bradley (a major game manufacturer) to an employee.

ALERT: Beware of certificates signed by current entertainment and sport heroes designed for sale to collectors as long term financial investments. These are manufactured and sold in large quantities. One is wise to question if they will retain, let alone increase, their value.

Agriculture, Stockman Protective Association, OK, 1926, farm scene vignette   **6.00**
Appointment, 1936, James Farley, Postmaster General, 10½ x 13½" **26.00**
Baptismal
    1830, handcolored and printed, printed in Leipzig, Germany, 6" sq   **10.00**
    1873, Currier & Ives, 14 x 10" **15.00**
    1925, Aldine May Sittler, PA, printed, pink flowers, white dove, cream to blue–green background, marked "Abingdon Press, New York Cincinnati/No 60," 11½ x 16" **8.00**
Book, Mallott–Hofman Co Wholesale Grocery Co, 1931–33, 32 unissued certificates, eagle vignettes **16.00**
Confirmation
    1877, Samuel W Gerhab, PA, black etching, gold printing, red and gold Bible verses, tortoise shell frame, 8 x 11" **12.00**
    1926, Abingdon Press, New York and Cincinnati, No 80, 11½ x 16" **8.00**
Cradle Roll, 1912, Providence Litho, eight children around end of cradle, 10½ x 13½", used **18.00**
Diploma, Wisconsin School for the Blind, June 4, 1918 . . . .   **5.00**
Education
    Pupils Reading Circle, 1933, printed, butterflies and moth illus **10.00**
    Teacher, 1902–05, Public Schools of OR, Marion County, ornate, school desk, globe, and telescope vignette, 7 x 10" **12.50**
Honor
    1877, George Jones, sixty merits, printed, red and white **20.00**
    1879, card of honor, Diligency, One

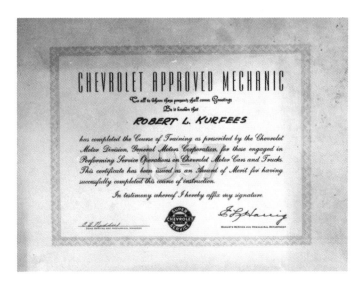

Chevrolet Approved Mechanic, raised ink Keystone logo, 11 x 14", 1957, $35.00.

Department of Police and Excise, Brooklyn, NY, appointment to patrolman, black-and-white engraving, blue city seal, 10½ x 8¾", 1890, $100.00.

Hundred Tokens of Merit, printed, multicolored chromolithograph . . . **15.00**

Marriage
  1892, John Doherty and Mary Green **2.50**
  1898
  E A Strohl and Matilda C Hahn, PA, six vignettes of different stages of married life, Bible verses, multicolored, white ground, marked "No. 105/Published by Ernst Kaufmann, 330 Pearl Street, New York," 12¾" w, 17" l **15.00**
  Ernest Kaufmann, New York, No 105, 13 x 17" **15.00**

Membership
  1882, Members Exchange of St Louis Certificate of Membership, engraved exchange and three buildings, 11¹/₁₂ x 9½" **10.00**
  1898, Association of Descendants of Edward Foulke, Martha Kinsey, commemorates 200th anniversary of landing of Edward and Eleanor Foulke, multicolored emb coat of arms, white ground, framed, 8¼ x 7" **8.00**
  1900s, Merchants Exchange of St Louis Certificate of Membership, waterfront vignette, 11½ x 10" **5.00**

Memorial
  1899, American Flag House & Betsy Ross Memorial Association, numbered and sgd, 11 x 14" **25.00**
  1908, Francis Scott Key Memorial Association, Chas H Weisgerber, #43881, framed, 14½ x 11½" **25.00**
  1926, A Loving Tribute to the Memory

of Rudolph Valentino, photograph of Valentino, multicolored, 7 x 11" **15.00**

Music, card, Theo Presser Co, Philadelphia, green printing, unused **12.00**

Trust, Guarantee National Trust, 1st United Trust, 1965–66 . . . . **4.00**

CHECKS

History: The use of checks is linked to the rise of banking. Banking in medieval Europe was limited because of usury laws. Once Henry VIII legalized the charging of interest, banking expanded across Europe and eventually to the new world. During much of the seventeenth, eighteen, and nineteenth centuries, banks were often speculative ventures. It was not until the arrival of national banking systems that order from chaos was achieved.

A check is a written order directing a bank to pay money as instructed. The difference between it and a bill of exchange payable on demand is that a bank can refuse payment due to lack of sufficient funds in the account of the person writing the check.

Besides their documentation of banking history, the thing that makes pre–1900 checks collectibles are the finely engraved vignettes found on many examples. These checks were prepared by the same manufacturers, e.g., American Bank Note Company, who designed and printed stocks and bonds. In addition, American checks often included embellishments such as elaborate borders and cross hatching.

Often check vignettes were a form of advertising, picturing a company's factory or products. Railroad companies used railroad vignettes, mining companies used mining vignettes. Many vignettes pictured identifiable scenic landmarks.

After 1900, checks became plainer. Gone were the fancy borders and decorative vignettes. A modern check is purely business; hence, it has little appeal to collectors.

Check collectors also collect drafts, promissory notes, and treasury warrants. Although technically not checks, they involve the exchange of funds without the actual handling of money.

When examining a check, pay special attention to the autograph. Checks are an important source of autographs. Checks signed by presidents and famous personalities are readily available in the autograph market.

Many individuals, such as Clark Gable and Pablo Picasso, paid for their purchases, no matter how small, with checks. The reason was simple. Few individuals cashed them. And, why not? The autograph signature was worth more than the check. Several contemporary Hollywood movie and television stars continue this practice.

Finally, crossover collectors eagerly seek checks issued by the manufacturers that made their favorite collectible object. When a check subject corresponds to a major collecting category, value increases several times.

Periodical: *Bank Note Reporter*, 700 East State Street, Iola, WI 54490.

Collectors' Club: American Society of Check Collectors, PO Box 69, Boynton Beach, FL 33425.

1782, June 1, Note from State of Connecticut, 6 pounds, 11 shillings, 3 pence, paid for soldier's service in Continental Army	**40.00**
1792, sgd by General Henry Knox	**35.00**
1812	
Promissory Note, from Noah Dexter for $273 to Bedford Marine Insurance Co, promises to pay premiums within 8 months, partly printed, 4½ x 9½"	**20.00**
Robert Morris, sgd	**10.00**
1816, Office of Pay and Deposit of the	

Bank of Columbia, Washington, March 27, 1816, filled and sgd James Madison	**1,585.00**
1827, sgd by Winfield Scott	**20.00**
1836, sgd by John A Dix, filled out by clerk	**8.00**
1845, Corcoran and Riggs Bank, sgd by Daniel Webster	**28.00**
1846, sgd by Fitzgreen Halleck	**8.00**
1851, sgd by Winfield Scott	**18.00**
1852, Apalachicola, FL, steamship vignette	**25.00**
1853, Illinois Central Railroad, vignettes, 1853	**30.00**
1857, Albany City Bank, drawn to the Treasurer of the State of New York, Canal Fund, deposited by H H Martin	**15.00**
1865	
English, March 21, 12 pounds, eight shillings, blue ink, Charles Dickens	**1,750.00**
P T Barnum, October 17, payable to S H Hurd for $500	**390.00**
Vignette of boat and farmer, two cent bank check stamp, black and white	**7.50**
1870	
Oregon & California Railroad, sgd Holladay	**250.00**
Pay Voucher, May 31, Savage Silver Mine, Comstock Lode, $68 for 17 days work	**30.00**
1871, sgd by Gerrit Smith	**5.00**
1875, Masonic Savings Bank, sgd by Simon Bolivar Buckner, CSA general, revenue stamp on upper left corner	**195.00**
1877, Utah Territory, Wells Fargo Bankers, 1877	**30.00**
1879, sgd by John A Logan	**8.00**
1884	
Henry W Beecher, sgd	**15.00**
I H Hershfield, Helena, MT, vignette, "Pay to order of Fong Foo, San Francisco," slash cancel, 1884	**25.00**
1889	
John Fiske	**10.00**

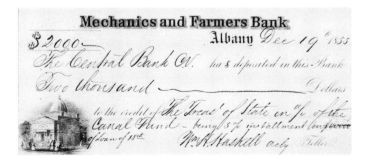

Mechanics and Farmers Bank, Albany, steel engraved, black and white, 7 x 3¼", 1855, $10.00.

The First National Bank, Susquehanna, PA, steel engraved, green and black, 8 x 3", 1899, $7.50.

Susan B Anthony, sgd **25.00**
1900, La Fortuna Mining Co, AZ, cactus vignette **15.00**
1904, Bank of Ouray, CO, Indian vignette **25.00**
1903, Pittsburgh Brewing Co, on German Nat'l Bank, Pittsburgh, red and gold company logo, canceled **3.00**
1906, First National Bank of Liverpool, PA, yellow, sq photograph marked "Old Canal Boat Days, Liverpool, Pennsylvania 1906," boats on Chesapeake and Ohio Canal, unissued . .   **5.00**
1910, The Waycross Coca–Cola Bottling Co, Waycross, GA, 1910, sgd **20.00**
1911, sgd by Admiral R P Hobson **4.00**
1919, Wm Rahr Sons Co, Manitowac, WI, 1919, payable to Busch Brewing Co. **8.00**
1920
George W Carver, sgd **450.00**
Hudson Trust Co, NY, sgd by Enrico Caruso. **45.00**
1934, sgd by Harry Truman, Judge, Jackson County, Kansas City, MO, 3 x 8" **375.00**
1941, sgd by Erroll Flynn **35.00**
1945, First National Bank of Nevada, 1945, filled in and sgd Tyrus R Cobb, cancellation mark. **100.00**
1946, Pepsi–Cola, American State Bank, 10 x 3". **10.00**
1951, sgd by Marilyn Monroe **300.00**
1955, sgd by George Burns **25.00**
1962, sgd by George Lincoln Rockwell, assassinated leader of American Nazi Party **200.00**
1966, sgd by Cary Grant. **25.00**
1968, Carter's Warehouse, Plains Mercantile Co, sgd by Rosalyn S Carter   **20.00**

CHILDREN'S BOOKS

History: William Caxton, a printer in England, is considered to have been the first publisher of children's books. Among his earliest publications was *Aesop's Fables* printed in 1484. Other very early books include John Cotton's *Spiritual Milk for Boston Babies* in 1646, *Orbis Pictis* translated from Latin about 1657, and *The New England Primer* in 1691.

Children's classics had their beginning with *Robinson Crusoe* in 1719, *Gulliver's Travels* in 1726, and Perrault's *Tales of Mother Goose* translated into English in 1729. The well known *A Visit from St. Nicholas* by Clement C. Moore appeared in 1823. Some of the best known children's works were published between 1840 and 1900. A few are Lear's *Book of Nonsense*, Anderson's and Grimm's fairy tales, *Alice in Wonderland, Hans Brinker, Little Women, Tom Sawyer, Treasure Island, Heidi, A Child's Garden of Verses,* and *Little Black Sambo*.

Series books for boys and girls began around the turn of the century. The Statemeyer Syndicate, established about 1906, became especially well known for their series, such as Tom Swift, The Bobbsey Twins, Nancy Drew, Hardy Boys, and many others.

Following the turn of the century, informational books such as Van Loon's *The Story of Mankind* were published. This book received the first Newbery Medal in 1922. This award, given for the year's most distinguished literature for children, was established to honor John Newbery, an English publisher of children's books. Biographies and poetry also became popular.

The most extensive development, however, has been with picture books. Photography and new technologies for reproducing illustrations made picture book publishing a major part of the children's book field. The Caldecott Medal, given for the most distinguished picture book published in the United States, was established in 1938. The award, which honors Randolph Caldecott, an English illustrator from the 1880s, was first given in 1938 to Dorothy Lanthrop for *Animals of the Bible*.

During the late 1800s, novelty children's books appeared. Lother Meggendorfer, Ernest Nister, and Raphael Tuck were the most well known publishers of these fascinating pop–up and mechanical or movable books. The popularity of this type of book has continued to the present. Some of the early movable books are being reproduced, especially by Intervisual Communications, Inc., of California.

Books that tie in with children's television programs, e.g. Sesame Street, and toys, e.g., Cabbage Patch dolls, have become prominent. Modern merchandising methods include multimedia packaging of various combinations of books, toys, puzzles, cassette tapes, videos, etc. There are even books which unfold, becoming a costume to be worn by children.

Most collectors look for books by a certain author or illustrator. Others are interested in books from a certain time period such as the nineteenth century. Accumulating the complete run of a series such as Tom Swift, Nancy Drew, or the Hardy Boys is of interest to some collectors. Subject categories are popular too, and include ethnic books, mechanical books, first editions, award winning books, certain kinds of animals, rag books, Big Little Books, and those with photographic illustrations.

Things to consider when purchasing books are the presence of a dust jacket or box, condition of the book, the edition, quality of illustrations and binding, and the prominence of the author or illustrator. Books should be examined very carefully to make certain that all pages and illustrations are present. Missing pages will reduce the value of a book. Try to buy books in the best condition that you can afford.

References: Barbara Bader, *American Picture Books From Noah's Ark To The Beast Within*, Macmillan, 1976; E. Lee Baumgarten, *Price Guide For Children's & Illustrated Books For The Years 1880–1945, 1991 Edition, Sorted by Artist*, printed by author, 1991; E. Lee Baumgarten, *Price Guide For Children's & Illustrated Books For The Years 1880–1945, 1991 Edition, Sorted by Author*, printed by author, 1993; E. Lee Baumgarten, *Price List for Children's and Illustrated Books For the Years 1880–1940, Sorted by Artist*, published by author, 1993; Margery Fisher, *Who's Who In Children's Books: A Treasury of the Familiar Characters of Childhood*, Holt, Rinehart and Winston, 1975; Virginia Haviland, *Children's Literature, A Guide To Reference Sources*, Library of Congress, 1966, first supplement 1972, second supplement 1977, third supplement 1982; Bettina Hurlimann, *Three Centuries Of Children's Books In Europe*, tr. and ed. by Brian W. Alderson, Worlain ld, 1968; Cornelia L. Meigs, ed., *A Critical History of Children's Literature*, 2nd ed., Macmillan, 1969.

Periodicals: *Book Source Monthly*, PO Box 567, Cazenovia, NY 13035; *Martha's KidLit Newsletter*, PO Box 1488, Ames, IA 50010.

Libraries: Free Library of Philadelphia, PA; Library of Congress, Washington, D.C.; Pierpont Morgan Library, New York, NY; Toronto Public Library, Toronto, Ontario, Canada.

Reprints: A number of replicas of antique period books are now appearing in the market, with most being done by Evergreen Press and Merrimack. A new "Children's Classics" series offers reprints of books with illustrations by Jessie Wilcox Smith, Edmund Dulac, Frederick Richardson, and possibly others.

Note: dj = dust jacket; wraps = paper covers; pgs = pages; unp = unpaged; n.d. = no date; teg = top edges gilt.

Aesop's Fables, Heritage, 1941	**25.00**
Alcott, Louisa M, *An Old Fashioned Girl,* Clara Burd, illus, Winston, 1928, 342, pgs, dj, 1st ed	**30.00**
Alexander, Lloyd, *The Castle of Llyr,* Evaline Ness, illus, Holt, Rinehart & Winston, 1966, 201 pgs, dj, 1st ed, sgd by author	**35.00**
Allen, Betsy, *The Riddle in Red,* Grossett & Dunlap, 1948, 212 pgs, dj, Connie Blair Series	**3.00**
Anderson's Fairy Tales, Grossett and Dunlap, 1940s	**15.00**
Anglund, Joan Walsh, *A Year Is Round,* Harcourt, Brace, World, 1966, unp, dj, 1st ed	**10.00**
Animals on the Farm, Clara Burd, illus, Saalfield, 1936, unp, wraps	**28.00**
Annie & Willie's Prayer Book, Snow, 1885, leather cov	**12.00**
Appleton, Victor	
Don Sturdy in the Land of Giants, Grossett & Dunlap, 1930, 244 pgs, dj	**6.00**
Tom Swift Among the Fire Fighters, Grossett & Dunlap, 1921, 214 pgs	**9.00**
Ardizzone, Edward, *Tim's Last Voyage,* Bodley Head, 1972, unp, dj, 1st ed	**35.00**
Austin, Margot, *Trumpet,* E P Dutton, 1944, dj, 1st ed	**1,650.00**
Bailey, Arthur Scott, *The Tale of Cuffy Bear,* Harry L Smith, illus, Grossett & Dunlap, 1915, 112 pgs, dj	**10.00**
Bancroft, Laura	
Babes In Birdland, R & Britton, 1911, first edition	**150.00**
Sugar–Loaf Mountain, 1906	**125.00**
Bannerman, Helen, *Little Black Sambo,* Platt & Munk, 1932, 12 pgs	**50.00**
Barnyard Babies, Milo Winter, illus, Merrill, 1936, unp, wraps	**18.00**
Bartman, Mark, *Yank in France,* Albert Whitman, 1946, dj	**28.00**
Baum's Snuggle Tales, The Yellow Hen, R & Britton, 916	**50.00**
Bobbsey Twins at Meadowbrook, 1915	**12.00**
Borden, Marion, *Hooray for Lassie,* Carol Marshall, illus, Whitman, 1964, unp, Tell–A–Tale Book	**5.00**
Brandeis, Madeline, *Mitz and Fritz of Germany,* Grossett & Dunlap, 1933, 160 pgs	**4.00**

Animal Pictures, Saalfield Publishing Co., color linenette covers, 7 x 9", 1947, $12.50.

Brice, Tony, *Little Hippo and His Red Bicycle,* Rand McNally, 1943, 42 pgs, dj 32.00

Brown, Margaret Wise, *The Indoor Noisy Book,* Scott, 1942, 44 pgs. . . . 14.00

Burgess, Thornton W
  Lightfoot the Deer, Harrison Cady, illus, Little, Brown, & Co, 1921, 205 pgs, 1st ed 95.00
  Milk and Honey, Nina R Jordan, illus, Whitman, 1927, unp 6.00
  The Adventures of Grandfather Frog, Little, Brown & Co, 1946, 46 pgs, dj. 30.00

Carroll, Lewis, *Alice's Adventures in Wonderland,* Caldwell, The Editha Series, 202 pgs 18.00

Chadwick, Lester, *Baseball Joe, Champion of the League,* Cupples & Leon, 1925, 246 pgs, dj 9.00

Chamberlain, Ethel, *Minnie, the Fish Who Lived In A Shoe,* Graham, 1928, 26 pgs. 24.00

Chapman, Allen
  Fred Fenton the Pitcher, Cupples & Leon, 1913, 206 pgs, dj 7.00
  Ralph on the Midnight Flyer, Grossett & Dunlap, 1923, 248 pgs, dj 9.00

Clarde, J Erskine, *Chatterbox,* J, Esxes & Lauriat, 1896, 412 pgs 16.00

Children In The Wood Stories, Milton Bradley, 1919, 1st ed 20.00

Culbertson, Polly, *The Bear Facts,* Winston, 1948, 28 pgs, dj, 1st ed . . . 20.00

Cyr, Ellen M, *The Children's Second Reader,* Ginn, 1894, 197 pgs 12.00

Curtis, Alice Turner, *Little Maid of Quebec,* Penn Publishing Co, 1936, 224 pgs, dj 8.00

Dawson, Lucy, *Lucy Dawson's Dogs,* Whitman, 1938, unp, wraps. 25.00

De Saint–Exupery, Antoine, *The Little Prince,* Harcourt, Brace & World, 1943, dj 38.00

Disney, Walt, *Pinocchio and His Puppet Show Adventure,* Random House, 1973, unp, 1st ed, Disney's Wonderful World of Reading 8.00

Dixon, Franklin W
  Footprints Under the Window, Grossett & Dunlap, 1933, 214 pgs, Hardy Boys series 4.00
  The Yellow Feather Mystery, Grossett & Dunlap, 1971, 181 pgs, Hardy Boys series 3.00

Drake, Robert L, *The Boy Allies At Jutland,* A L Burt, 1917, 255 pgs, dj, Navy series 6.00

Elliott, Gertrude, illus, *Round the Mulberry Bush,* Harpers, c1941, 36 pgs, 9¼ x 10¼", includes music 18.00

Elson, William H & William S Gray, *Elson–Gray Basic Readers–Book Two,* Scott, Foresman, 1936, 240 pgs 5.00

Engines & Brass Bands, Doubleday, 1933, 1st ed 15.00

Farley, Walter, *The Black Stallion Races,* Random House, 1955, 256 pgs, dj, 1st ed 18.00

Finley, Martha, *Elsie Dinsmore,* Donohue, nd, c1920, 395 pgs 10.00

First of May: A Fairy Tale, Crane, Boston, 1881 . . . . 65.00

Fryer, Jane Eayre, *The Mary Frances Storybook,* Edwin John Prittie, illus, Winston, 1921, 328 pgs 45.00

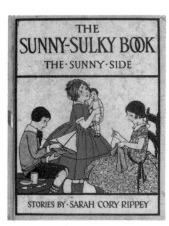

The Sunny-Sulky Book, Sarah Cory Rippey, Rand McNally, multicolor hard covers, black-and-white and color illustrations, two stories, reverse book for second story, 64 pages, 6 x 7¾", 1930 edition, $12.50.

Garis, Howard R
The Curly Tops and Their Playmates,
Cupples & Leon, 1922, 246 pgs . .   3.00
Uncle Wiggily's Airship, Platt &
Munk, 1939, 185 pgs 10.00
Grimm, Jacob and Wilhelm
Grimm's Fairy Tales, Koerner &
Hayes, 1896, full page of litho
plates 30.00
The Golden Bird, MacMillan, c1962,
50 pgs, 9³/₄ x 13¹/₂", 1st ed 38.00
Gruelle, Johnny
Little, Brown & Co Bear, 1920 . . . . .   30.00
Raggedy Ann and Andy and the
Camel With the Wrinkled Knees,
Bobbs–Merrill, 1951, 95 pgs 15.00
Raggedy Ann's Alphabet Book,
Donohue, 1925, 40 pgs, dj 40.00
Sunny Bunny, Algonquin, 1918 . . . .   35.00
Hazlett, Edward E, He's Jake, The Story
of a Submarine Dog, Paul Brown,
illus, Dodd Mead, 1947, 154 pgs, dj   6.00
Hoban, Tana, A, B, See, Greenwillow,
c1892, 32 pgs, 11¹/₄ x 9¹/₂", 1st ed . .   22.00
Hoover, Lathan, The Campfire Boys in
the Brazilian Wilderness, A L Burt,
1929, 255 pgs. 4.00
Hughes, Thomas, Tom Brown's School
Days, Dodd Mead, 1900, 339 pgs . .   10.00
Inchfawn, Fay, Who goes to the Wood,
Diana Thorne, illus, Winston, 1942,
229 pgs. 12.00
Irwin, Ihez Haynes, Marda's Little
Houseboat, Grossett & Dunlap,
1943, 207 pgs. 13.00
James, Will, Sun Up, Tales of the Cow
Camps, Junior Literary Guild, 1931,
342 pgs. 40.00

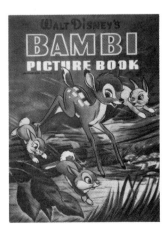

**Walt Disney's Bambi Picture Book, Walt
Disney Productions, 16 pages, 9¹/₂ x 13",
1941, $45.00.**

Jolly Jump–Ups Mother Goose, 1944,
pop–up. 28.00
Keene, Carolyn
Mystery of the Brass Bound Trunk,
Russell H Tandy, illus, Grossett &
Dunlap, 1940, 220 pgs, dj 10.00
The Spider Sapphire Mystery, Gros-
sett & Dunlap, 1968, 176 pgs, dj   3.00
Kubasta, V, Ricky the Rabbit, Bancroft,
1961, 8 pgs, pop–up 20.00
Lang, A, The Yellow Fairy Book, Hurst
& Co 20.00
Lenski, Lois, The Little Farm, Oxford
University Press, 1942, unp, dj, 1st
ed 18.00
Lobel, Arnold, Frog and Toad Together,
Harper & Row, 1972, 64 pgs 8.00
Mayhew, Ralph and Johnston Burooes,
The Pie Party Book, the 5th Bubble
Book, Rhoda Chase, illus, Harper &
Columbia Graphophone Co, 1919,
15 pgs, 3 records. 30.00
Merrill, Marion, The Animated Pinoc-
chio, Citadel Press, 1945, unp, 3
pop–ups 25.00
Merry Matchmakers, Whitman, 1940,
1st ed 20.00
Miller, Olive Beaupre, Nursery Friends
from France, Maud & Miska Pe-
tersham, illus, Book House for Chil-
dren, 1927, 191 pgs 35.00
Milne, A A, Winnie ille pv (Winnie the
Pooh in Latin), Dutton, 1961, 121
pgs, dj 6.00
Miss Bianca in the Antarctic, Little,
Brown & Co, 1971, 1st ed. 25.00
Montgomery, Frances Trego, Billy
Wiskers' Kids, W H Fry, illus,
Saalfield, 1903, 134 pgs, dj 25.00
Mother Goose, Mary Lafetya Russell,
illus, Sam Gabriel, 1911, unp. 15.00
My Farmyard Friends, Linentex, Akron,
OH, 1921, 5¹/₁₂ x 9" 18.00
Nesbit, Wilbur D, The Tumbledown
Town, John Gee, illus, Volland,
1926, unp, Sunny Book 25.00
Newberry, Clare Turlay, Mittens,
Harper, 1936, unp, dj, 1st ed 50.00
Olaf the Glorious, MacMillan, 1929,
1st ed 25.00
Only True Mother Goose, Boston,
1905, 100 pgs, 1st ed 37.50
Packer, Eleanor Lewis, A Day with Our
Gang, Whitman, 1929, unp 18.00
Parish, Peggy, Amelia Bedelia, Harp-
ers, 1963, 6¹/₄ x 8³/₄", dj 35.00
Perkins, Lucy Fitch, The Puritan Twins,
Houghton Mifflin, 1921, 178 pgs . . .   16.00
Perkins, Lucy Fitch, Japanese Twins,
1912. . . . .   4.75
Peter Pan & Wendy, Scribner, 1911,
1st ed 40.00

Petersham, Maud & Miska, *The Story Book of Food,* Winston, 1947, unp ... **7.00**

Pogo Party, Simon & Schuster, 191 pgs, 1st ed **30.00**

Ponsot, Marie, *Chinese Fairy Tales,* Golden, 1960, 156 pgs, 10¼ x 13¾", 1st ed **36.00**

Potter, Beatrix, *The Tale of Peter Rabbit,* Grossett & Dunlap, c1942, 26 pgs, 8¼ x 9½"................. **20.00**

Pyle, Howard, *Otto of the Silver Hand,* Scribner, 1906, 173 pgs **30.00**

Pyle, Katherine, *The Christmas Angel,* Little, Brown, 1900, 136 pgs, 1st ed **40.00**

Schulz, Charles M, *He's Your Dog, Charlie Brown!,* World, 1968, unp, 1st ed **8.00**

Sendak, Maurice, *The Sign On Rosie's Door,* Harper & Row, 1960, 46 pgs, dj, 1st ed **45.00**

Sidney, Margaret, *Five Little Peppers Grown Up,* Mente, illus, D Lathrop, 1892, 527 pgs, 1st ed **75.00**

Snow White & Seven Dwarfs, Disney, NY, 79 pgs, 1st ed **85.00**

Spyri, Johanna, *Heidi,* Frances Brundage, illus, Saalfield, 1924, 307 pgs **18.00**

Stockton, Frank R, *The Bee–man of Orb,* Maurice Sendak, illus, Holt, Rinehart & Winston, 1964, 46 pgs, dj, 1st ed, sgd by illus **100.00**

Sutton, Margaret
 The Name on the Bracelet, Pelagie Doane, illus, Grossett & Dunlap, 1940, 216 pgs, dj **10.00**
 Who Will Play With Me?, Corinne Dillon, illus, Wonder books, 1951, unp **12.00**

Tatham, Julie C, *Cherry Ames Mountaineer Nurse,* Grossett & Dunlap, dj **3.50**

Thorndyke, Helen Louise, *Honey Bunch: Her First Summer on an Island,* Grossett & Dunlap, 1929, 184 pgs...................... **3.00**

Thorne–Thomsen, Gudrun, *East O' the Sun and West O' the Moon,* Frederick Richardson, illus, Row, Peterson, 1912, 218 pgs.................. **20.00**

Trimer, George, illus, *Animal Friends,* No 1537, Merrill, c1949, 12 pgs, 9½ x 13", fuzzy cov **20.00**

Tudor, Tasha, *First Poems of Childhood,* Platt & Munk, 1967, 45 pgs, dj, 1st ed..................... **35.00**

Ungerer, Tomi, *The Mellops Strike Oil,* Harper, 1958, 32 pgs, dj, 1st ed **23.00**

Uttley, Alison, *Little Grey Rabbit's Pancake Day,* Margaret Tempest, illus, Collins, 1967, 63 pgs **25.00**

Watson, Jane Werner, *The True Story of Smokey the Bear,* Feodor Rojan-kovsky, illus, Golden Press, 1955, unp, 1st ed **10.00**

Waugh, Ida, *Holly Berries,* 1881, 40 color prints **30.00**

Wells, Helen, *Vicki Finds the Answer,* Grossett & Dunlap, 1947, dj, Vicki Barr series.................... **5.00**

White, Stewart Edward, *Daniel Boone: Wilderness Scout,* James Daugherty, illus, Garden City, 1922, 274 pgs... **15.00**

Wickes, Frances G, *Beyond the Rainbow Bridge,* Milton Bradley, c1924, 310 pgs, 5¼ x 7½", brown cloth stamped with gold **14.00**

Wiggin, Kate Douglas, *The New Chronicles of Rebecca,* F C Yohn, illus, Houghton Mifflin, 1907, 278 pgs, 1st ed.................... **22.00**

Wilson, E, *The Pirate's Treasure,* P F Volland Co, 1926, 7th ed **15.00**

Winfield, Arthur M, *The Rover Boys Down East,* Grossett & Dunlap, 1911, 288 pgs, dj, 1st ed.......... **10.00**

COLORING BOOKS

History: A number of specialized juvenile magazines, e.g., *St. Nicholas,* originated at the end of the nineteenth century. As an enticement to their young readers, several magazines included paper dolls. This success led to the introduction of pictures to color. By the 1870s, publishers began to package paper dolls and pictures to color as separate publications.

Raphael Tuck and Son's *The Little One's Own Drawing Book* dates from around 1890. By 1900 the company was selling a series of coloring books known as the Little Artist.

The earliest American coloring books are attributed to McLoughlin Bros, a firm actively involved in children's literature, games, and puzzles. McLoughlin paper doll books date to the 1870s. McLoughlin's *The Little Folks Painting Book* has an 1885 copyright. The illustrations are patterned after the work of Kate Greenaway. Full color examples provided guidance in color selection.

Early coloring books were sold as painting books, despite the introduction of wax crayons by Binney and Smith Co. in 1903. It was not until the 1930s that coloring books were labeled for use with either watercolors or crayons.

Until the late 1930s, most coloring books focused on animal, childhood, fairy tale, military, religious, and scenic themes. When the Saalfield Company signed a contract in 1934 to be the exclusive distributor of Shirley Temple material, the focus changed. Character and personality coloring books quickly became standard fare. The Golden Age of character and personality coloring books was the 1940s through the 1960s. Although character and personality licensing continues in the 1990s, the volume is a far cry from that of the Golden Age.

In addition to McLoughlin Bros., Merrill Publishing Company, Saalfield Publishing Company, and Whitman Publishing Company (now part of Mattel's Western Publishing) are the leading American coloring book manufacturers. European manufacturers of note include Ernest Nister (Germany) and Raphael Tuck & Sons (England).

In addition to the standard, large size (approximately 8" x 12") coloring books, paper collectors eagerly seek specialized coloring books designed as advertising premiums. For example, in 1902 George W. Smith & Sons, Baker & Confectioner in White River Junction, Vermont, distributed as a premium *Our Little Artist* a three by five inch, ten page coloring book featuring drawings of animals, flowers, and birds.

Modern coloring books have returned once again to the generic. The few licensed examples focus on highly visible toy products, e.g., a Barbie or G. I. Joe coloring book, or a hoped for blockbuster, e.g. Disney's Little Mermaid. In an effort to enhance sales, many "coloring" books are really activity books, only a portion of which is devoted to pictures to color.

Reference: Dian Zillner, *Collectible Coloring Books*, Schiffer Publishing, 1992.

Addams Family An Activity Book, Saalfield, #4331, 1965	**20.00**
Adventures of Rin Tin Tin, Whitman, #1257, 1955	**15.00**
Alice in Wonderland Paint Book, Whitman, #2167, 1951	**25.00**
Andy Griffith Show Coloring Book, Saalfield, 1963	**25.00**
Andy Panda, Whitman, #681, 1946	**12.00**
Ann Blyth, 1952, unused	**35.00**
Annette, Whitman, #1145, 1964, 128 pages	**12.00**
Annie Oakley, Whitman, 1955, 11 x 14", unused	**18.00**
Around the World in 80 Days, Saalfield, #4828, 1957	**20.00**
Baby Alive Coloring Book, Whitman, #1661, 1976	**8.00**
Baby Huey the Baby Giant Coloring Book, Saalfield, #4536, 1959	**18.00**
Bambi Paint Book, Whitman, #664, 1941	**35.00**
Batman and Robin, Whitman, 1967, unused, 8 x 11"	**15.00**
Bedknobs and Broomsticks Coloring Book, Whitman, #1082, 1971	**15.00**
Beep Beep the Road Runner Paint and Color Book, Whitman, #1133, 1967	**8.00**
Beetle Bailey, Samuel Lowe, #2860, 1961	**15.00**

Ben Casey Coloring Book, Saalfield, #9532, 1963	**15.00**
Bette Davis, Merrill Publishing Co, 1942	**45.00**
Betty Brewer Paint Book, Whitman, 1943	**15.00**
Betty Grable, Whitman, #664, 1947	**25.00**
Beverly Hillbillies, Whitman, 1950–60	**12.00**
Bing Crosby, Saalfield, 1954	**25.00**
Blondie, Dell Publishing, 1954, unused, 8½ x 11"	**20.00**
Bonanza, Saalfield, #1617, 1960	**20.00**
Bonny Braids Coloring Book, Saalfield, #2366, 1951	**20.00**
Bobby Sherman Paint and Color Album, Columbia Pictures, #5160, 1971	**30.00**
Bongo Paint Book, Whitman, #2071, 1948	**25.00**
Boots and her Buddies Coloring Book Saalfield, 1941	**22.00**
Brenda Starr Coloring Book, Saalfield, #9675	**15.00**
Bringing Up Father Paint Book With Jiggs and Maggie, Whitman, #663	**25.00**
Bugs Bunny Porky Pig Paint Book, Whitman, #1152, 1946	**25.00**
Buster Brown	**30.00**
Captain Kangaroo Trace and Color, Whitman, #1413, 1960	**10.00**
Carl Anderson's Henry Paint Book, Whitman, #696, 1951	**20.00**
Ceresota Flour, 1912	**35.00**
Charlie Chaplin, Donohue & Co, 1917, 10 x 17"	**80.00**
Chitty Chitty Bang Bang Coloring Book, #1654, 1968	**10.00**
Cinderella Paint Book, Whitman, #2092, 1950	**25.00**
Circus, Polack Bros Circus, 1954	**15.00**
Daniel Boone Coloring Book, Whitman, #1116, 1961	**15.00**
Deanna Durbin Pictures to Paint, Merrill Publishing Co, #3479, 1940	**40.00**
Debbie Reynolds, Whitman, #1868, 1956	**20.00**
Diana Lynn, Saalfield, #1278, 1954	**20.00**
Dick Tracy, Saalfield, #2536, 1946, 8¼ x 11"	**25.00**
Dick Van Dyke A Coloring Book, Saalfield, #9557, 1963	**22.00**
Different Strokes, Playmore Publishing Inc, #401–3, 1981	**8.00**
Disneyland, Whitman, 1965, 8 x 11"	**20.00**
Doctor Dolittle and His Animals, Watkins–Strathmore Co, 1967	**10.00**
Donald Duck, Whitman, 1946, unused, 7½ x 8½"	**20.00**
Doris Day, Whitman, #1138, 1952	**25.00**
Drowsy Color Book, Whitman, #1041, 1976	**5.00**
Dudley Do–Right Comes to The Rescue A Book to Color, Saalfield, #9571, 1969	**8.00**

Batman Coloring Book, Whitman Publishing, unused, 8 x 11", 1974, $27.50.

Dumbo Cut–Out Coloring Book, Pocket
    Books, Inc, #F5047, 1953 . . . .   25.00
Elizabeth Taylor, Whitman, #1144,
    1954 . . . .   25.00
Esther Williams, Merrill, #1591, 1950 . .   20.00
Eve Arden, 1953, unused 32.50
Fat Albert and The Cosby Kids, Whitman,
    #1066, 1973 . . . .   8.00
Felix the Cat Coloring Book, Saalfield,
    #4655, 1959 . . . .   15.00
Flintstones, Charlton Publications Inc,
    #537, 1971 . . . .   8.00
Gene Autry, Whitman, 1950s 12.00
GI Joe Action Coloring Book, Whitman,
    #1156, 1965 . . . .   10.00
Goodbye, Mr Chips, A Coloring Book,
    Saalfield, #9569, 1969 . . . .   15.00
Grace Kelly, Whitman, 1956, #1752 . . .   40.00
Green Hornet, Watkins–Strathmore,
    1966, unused, 8 x 11" 30.00
Gunsmoke Coloring Book, Whitman,
    #1184, 1958 . . . .   25.00
Hayley Mills In Search of the Castaways,
    Whitman, #1138, 1962 . . . .   10.00
Hardy Boys Coloring Book, Whitman,
    #1167, 1957 . . . .   15.00
Hee Haw Coloring Book, Saalfield,
    #4538, 1970 . . . .   10.00
Hopalong Cassidy, Samuel Lowe Co,
    1951, 48 pages, 5¼ x 5¼" 25.00
Jackie Gleason, Gleason and Ralph
    Kramden driving bus on Madison Ave   50.00
Jane Powell, Whitman, #1133, 1951 . . .   50.00
Joan Carroll Coloring Book, Saalfield,
    1942 . . . .   25.00
John F Kennedy, 1962, unused 25.00
Journey to the Center of the Earth, Whit-
    man, #1137, 1968 . . . .   10.00
Jughead Coloring Book, Western Pub-
    lishing Co, #1045, 1972 . . . .   8.00

Juliet Jones Coloring Book, Saalfield,
    #953, 1954 . . . .   15.00
June Allyson, Whitman, 1952 . . . .   25.00
Lady and the Tramp Coloring Book,
    Whitman, #1183, 1954 . . . .   20.00
Lana Turner Paint Book, Whitman, 1947   40.00
Laraine Day, Saalfield, #2401, 1953 . . .   30.00
Lassie Coloring Book, Whitman, #1039,
    1958 . . . .   15.00
Lennon Sisters, Whitman, 1950–60 . . . .   12.00
Let's Read and Paint, Whitman, 1934 . . .   22.00
Li'l Abner and Daisy Mae Coloring Book,
    Saalfield, #2391, 1942 . . . .   30.00
Little Audrey Coloring Book, Saalfield,
    #9535, 1959 . . . .   15.00
Little Orphan Annie Coloring Book Ju-
    nior Commandos, Saalfield, #300,
    1945 . . . .   30.00
Loretta Young Coloring Book, Saalfield,
    #1108, 1956 . . . .   15.00
Mary Poppins Coloring Book, Whitman,
    #1112, 1966 . . . .   8.00
Mickey Mouse, Avon, 1969 . . . .   1.50
Mickey Rooney, His Own Paint Book,
    Merrill, #3496, 1940 . . . .   25.00
Million Dollar Duck Coloring Book,
    Whitman, #1142, 1971 . . . .   10.00
Mother Goose Paint and Crayon Book,
    Whitman, 1929 . . . .   10.00
My Big Painting & Drawing Book,
    Saalfield, 1916, 10 x 15" 10.00
Old Yeller Coloring Book, Whitman,
    #1199, 1957 . . . .   10.00
One Hundred and One Dalmatians,
    Whitman, #1004, 1960 . . . .   35.00
Peanuts Picture To Color, Saalfield,
    #5331, 1960 . . . .   15.00
Peter Pan Coloring Book, Whitman,
    #2186, 1952 . . . .   20.00
Pinky Lee's Health and Safety Cut–Out
    Coloring Book, Pocket Books, 1955 . .   15.00
Pippi Longstocking, Whitman, G G
    Communications, Inc, #1040, 1975   5.00
Planet of the Apes, Saalfield, 1974, Apjac
    Productions, unused, 8½ x 11" 15.00
Playtime Painting and Drawing, M A
    Donohue and Co, c1900 . . . .   18.00
Presidents of the United States to Color:
    A History In Pictures from Washington
    to Johnson, Saalfield 8.00
Prince Valiant Coloring Book, Saalfield,
    1954 . . . .   15.00
Punky Brewster, Golden Book, Western
    Publishing Co, #1025, 1987 . . . .   4.00
Raggedy Ann and Andy Mini–Coloring
    Book, Hallmark, 1974 . . . .   30.00
Rainbow Brite, I'm A Fit Kid Coloring
    Book, Hallmark Cards, 1983 . . . .   4.00
Red Ryder Paint Book, Whitman,
    #1328, 1952 . . . .   20.00
Rin Tin Tin, Whitman, #1257, 1955,
    partially colored, 8¼ x 11" 15.00

Rita Hayworth Dancing Star, Merrill Publishing Co, #3483, 1942	**45.00**
Rosemary Clooney, Abbott Publishing Co, 1954	**20.00**
Roy Rogers and Dale Evans, 1952, 15 x 11"	**20.00**
Shazam, Whitman, 1975 National Periodical Publications copyright, pinup poster on back cov, 11 x 14"	**12.00**
Siggie's Adventures in Color, c1950s	**8.00**
Skeezix Drawing and Tracing Book, McLoughlin Bros, Inc, #525, 1932	**20.00**
Skipper, Barbie's Little Sister, Whitman, #1115, 1965	**10.00**
Smilin' Jack Coloring Book, Saalfield, #397, 1946	**20.00**
Sonja Henie, Queen of the Ice, Merrill Publishing Co, #3476, 1939	**50.00**
Son of Flubber Coloring Book, Whitman, 1963	**10.00**
Spiderman	**18.00**
Steve Canyon Coloring Book, Saalfield, #123410, 1952	**25.00**
Superman, Whitman, 1966 National Periodical Publications, unused, 8 x 11"	**25.00**
The Black Hole, Whitman, #1002, 1979	**5.00**
The Christmas That Almost Wasn't, Saalfield, #9540, 1970	**5.00**
The Easy Painting Book, McLoughlin Brothers, 1904	**20.00**
The Fantastic Osmonds, Saalfield, 1973	**20.00**
The Rescuers Coloring Book, compliments of General Electric	**10.00**
The Sunshine Family Coloring Book, Whitman, #1003, 1975	**5.00**
The Sword in the Stone, Whitman, #1637, 1963	**10.00**
The Valley of Gwangi, A Coloring Book, Saalfield, #9568, 1969	**8.00**
That Girl, 1970, Marlo Thomas cov, used	**8.00**
Three Little Pigs Cut–Out Coloring Book, Pocket Books, Inc, 1953	**20.00**
Tillie The Toiler Paint Book, Whitman, #662, 1942	**30.00**
Tippee–Toes Coloring Book, Whitman, #1656, 1969	**8.00**
Tom Mix, Whitman, 1935, 96 pages, 11 x 14"	**50.00**
Tom Terrific with Mighty Manfred the Wonder Dog, Treasure Books, #312, 1957	**10.00**
Tonto, Whitman, 1950–60	**12.00**
Tweety Coloring Book, Whitman, #2953, 1955	**10.00**
Uncle Scrooge Coloring Book, Western Publishing Co, 1978	**5.00**
Walt Disney's Coloring Book, Whitman, #1062, 1958	**20.00**
Watergate/Join The Fun/Color The Facts, 1973, 48 pages, 8 x 11"	**25.00**
Wendy The Good Little Witch Coloring Book, Rand McNally and Co, #06416, 1959	**8.00**

The Tiger in the Tank, Humble Oil and Refining Company, multicolor covers, 32 pages, 8½ x 7½", early 1960s, $15.00.

Winnie the Pooh, Whitman, #1058, 1965	**10.00**
Wyatt Earp, Hugh O'Brien cov, unused	**35.00**
Yogi Bear and the Great Green Giant, Modern Promotions, 1976	**8.00**
Young America Coloring Book, Platt and Munk Co, 1928	**8.00**
Zorro Coloring Book, Whitman, #1158, 1958	**20.00**

COMIC STRIPS

History: The ancient origins of the comic strip include the twelfth century Japanese scroll art, church gargoyles of the Middle Ages, and eighteenth century European and American satirical characterizations. Cartoons with a social and editorial message began appearing in American newspapers and magazines during the last decades of the nineteenth century. Palmer Cox's *Brownies,* which began in the 1870s, is just one example.

Most scholars point to the May 5, 1895, appearance of Richard F. Outcault's color panel *At the Circus in Hogan's Alley* in the Sunday *New York Herald* as the dawn of the modern comic strip. The strip introduced the Yellow Kid, the first comic strip collectible character. William Randolph Hearst enticed Outcault to jump to his *New York Journal* from Joseph Pulitzer's *New York Journal* in 1896.

Outcault opened the gate. In late 1897, Rudolph Dirks' *The Katzenjammer Kids* appeared in the *New York Journal.* By 1910, such well known strips as *Foxy Grandpa, Happy Hooligan, Buster Brown, Mutt and Jeff,* and *Toonerville Folks* were launched.

Each decade witnessed the arrival and decline of key comic strips. From the 1920s came *Barney Google, Little Orphan Annie,* and *Moon Mullins.* During the 1929 Depression, Tarzan and Popeye entered the Sunday funnies.

Betty Boop, Blondie, Dick Tracy, Flash Gordon, Li'l Abner, Mickey Mouse, and Snuffy Smith are just a few of the characters introduced in the 1930s. Adventure strips brought characters such as Jack Armstrong, Smilin' Jack and Terry (and the Pirate). Super heroes, among whom were Batman and Superman, arrived in the late 1930s.

World War II produced comic strip heroes as well. Readers followed the adventures of Don Winslow and Steve Canyon. In the 1950s, cowboy heroes such as Hopalong Cassidy, Roy Rogers, and others rode the comic strip pages, challenging the leadership held by Red Ryder. The 1950s also saw the first appearance of Dennis the Menace and the Peanuts gang.

Beginning in the 1960s the Saturday and Sunday morning cartoon shows began challenging the comic strips for attention. Many of the older strips vanished. Some attempted to continue with new artists and writers. However, many readers could tell the difference in style and loyalty waned.

Today's comic strip is much more adult focused. Social commentary, rather than humor, is standard practice. The arrival of *Doonesbury* introduced political commentary to the comic strip page. The funnies of the 1990s simply do not seem as funny as they did in the 1950s and '60s.

References: Ted Hake, *Hake's Guide to Comic Character Collectibles: An Illustrated Price Guide to 100 Years of Comic Strip Characters*, Wallace–Homestead, 1993; Jerry Weist, *Original Comic Art: Identification and Price Guide*, Avon Books, 1992.

1917, features Steve Bunk, 5 pgs.	**30.00**
1927, October 16, *Public Ledger*	**2.50**
1934, Century of Progress, Chicago, sponsored by Reynolds Tobacco, full page.	**15.00**
1935, tabloid size, includes Jiggs and Maggie, Katzenjammer Kids, Nebbs, Mandrake the Magician, Tim Tyler's Luck, Blondie, Count Screwloose, Mortimer, Flash Gordon, Ace Drummond, King of the Royal Mounted, Toots and Casper, Red Barry, Pete the Tramp, Little Annie Rooney, Felix, Skippy, Tillie the Toiler, Little King, Toonerville Folks, 32 pgs.	**80.00**
1936, March 22, *Atlantic City Press,* Silly Symphony, Porky Pig, and Mickey Mouse, full page	**15.00**
1937, March 21, New York American Sunday, 10 pgs, Bringing Up Father, Flash Gordon, Blondie, Barney Google, Bunky, Gags and Gals, and Katzenjammer Kids	**25.00**
1938, Li'l Abner, Polly and Her Pals, Elmer, Just Kids, Thimble Theatre, Katzenjammer Kids, Dixie Duggan, Joe	

Columbus Sunday Dispatch, **Hans & Fritz, full page, color outside page, black-and-white comic inside page, 16³⁄₄ x 23¹⁄₂", January 30, 1916, $35.00.**

The Post, **The Katzenjammer Kids, full page, color outside page, black-and-white inside page, 16³⁄₄ x 23¹⁄₂", August 2, 1914, $35.00.**

Palooka, Toots, Casper, and others, 24
pgs **70.00**
1940–41, Tailspin Tommy, H Forrest, set
of 21 . . . .   **265.00**
1945, Jiggs and Maggie, Prince Valiant,
Katzenjammer Kids, Barney Google,
Henry, Tim Tyler's Luck, Lone Ranger,
The Phantom, Jungle Jim, Little Annie
Rooney, Tillie the Toiler, Skippy,
Blondie, Flash Gordon, Buzz Sawyer,
Little King, and others, 28 pgs **70.00**
1961
Dick Tracy, August 6, C Gould, India
ink, 18 x 27" **550.00**
Yogi Bear, H Isenberg, India ink, 17¼
x 24½" **200.00**
1978, April 2, Donald Duck and Uncle
Scrooge, pen and ink, 16 x 21" **545.00**
1983, July 31, Winnie the Pooh and
Piglet, pen and ink **565.00**

COOKBOOKS

History: When the ruins of Pompeii were
excavated, archaeologists found recipes from 79
A.D. scrawled on fireplace and kitchen walls.
Over 2,000 years ago, Marcus Gavius Apicius, a
Roman, collected and authored a recipe book. R.
Pynson's *The Boke of Cokery*, published in the
1500s, was the first English language cookbook.

The first cookbook published in America was
William Park's *Complete Housewife*, a 1742 reprint of an English cookbook. The first cookbook
written in America was Amelia Simmons'
American Cookery in 1796.

The leading American cookbook writer of the
first half of the nineteenth century was Eliza
Leslie. Mary Randolph's *Virgina Housewife*, published in 1824, was America's first regional cookbook. As in eighteenth century cookbooks, directions and measurements in these early nineteenth
century examples were often unclear.

In the 1880s, cooking schools developed
across America. Their role was to introduce "scientific" cooking to the nation's housewives. Juliet
Corson founded the New York Cooking School in
1874. Schools quickly followed in Boston and
Philadelphia. Cookbooks dating from the end of
the nineteenth century contain exact directions
and standardized measurements.

In the 1890s, Fannie Merritt Farmer became
director of the Boston Cooking School. The first
edition of her *Boston Cooking School Cookbook*
appeared in the late 1890s. Upon Miss Farmer's
death in 1915, the book was taken over by her
sister and upon her death by Wilma Perkins, her
daughter–in–law. The Farmer cookbook remained the popular standard until the appearance of *The Joy of Cooking*.

The key cookbooks are those that have sold

over a million copies. The list includes:
*Settlement Cookbook, Fannie Farmer's Cook-
book, Joy of Cooking, Good Housekeeping,
McCall's Cookbook,* and *Betty Crocker's Cookbook.* The sales record is held by *Better Homes
and Gardens New Cookbook* which sold over
eighteen million copies.

Cookbooks are bought by a variety of different
collectors. Of course, there are cookbook collectors and individuals who want access to the recipes. However, there are far more collectors who
are interested in them for their cover art or advertising sponsorship.

Prices, especially for moderately priced examples, have risen dramatically in the last ten years.
This is reflected in the arrival of a host of cookbook price guides. Much of the pricing is speculative. Remember, cookbooks often had printings in
the hundreds of thousands and millions. Shopping around often results in an example at prices
far below book value.

References: Bob Allen, *A Guide To Collecting
Cookbooks and Advertising Cookbooks,* Collector Books, 1990; Mary–Margaret Barile, *Cookbooks Worth Collecting,* Wallace–Homestead,
1993; Mary–Margaret Barile, *Just Cookbooks!,*
published by author, 1990; Linda J. Dickinson,
Price Guide To Cookbooks and Recipe Leaflets,
Collector Books, 1990, 1993 value update.

Collectors' Club: Cook Book Collectors Club of
America, 231 East James Blvd, St. James, MO
65559.

ABC's of Food Freezing, Ben Hur, 1953,
128 pgs, paperback **3.00**
Alice Bay Cookbook, J Rousseau, 1985,
247 pgs, paperback **4.00**
All About Home Baking, General Foods
Corp, 1935, 144 pgs, yellow and black
plaid cov **7.50**
All About Steam Cooking, C Truax,
1981, 264 pgs, hardbound **7.50**
American Family Cookbook, Juliet
Carson, Chicago, 1898 . . . .   **45.00**
*American Home Cookbook of Ladies of
Detroit,* 1878 . . . .   **45.00**
American Woman's Home, Catharine E
Beecher, Harriet Beecher Stowe, 1869   **75.00**
An Herb and Spice Cookbook, C
Clairborne, 1963, 334 pgs **16.50**
Any One Can Bake, Royal Baking Pow-
der, 1929, 100 pgs **6.50**
Art of Good Cooking, P Peck, 1966, 368
pgs, paperback **10.00**
Aunt Jenny's Favorite Recipes, 1930 . . . .   **4.00**
Baker's Famous Chocolate Recipes,
1928, 63 pgs **6.00**
Baker's Favorite Chocolate Recipes,
1950, 112 pgs **7.00**

How to get the most out of your Sunbeam Mixmaster, black-and-white photo covers, black-and-white illustrations, 42 pages, 1930s, $7.50.

Belgian Relief Cookbook, Reading, PA, 1915, 317 pgs, hardbound, sgd **110.00**
Best From Midwest Kitchens, 1946 . . . . . **5.00**
Better Homes & Gardens Cook Book, c1950, ring binder **30.00**
Bettina's Best Desserts, L Weaver, 1923, 194 pgs, hardbound **20.00**
Betty Crocker, Dinner For Two, 1st ed, 1958, 207 pgs **8.00**
Birds–Eye Cookbook, 1941, 63 pgs, paperback **2.00**
Blueberry Hill Menu Cookbook, E Masteson, 1963 . . . . **12.50**
Bond Bread Cook Book, 1933, 22 pgs . . **15.00**
Boston Cooking School Cookbook, Fannie Farmer, 1912, 648 pgs, hardbound **20.00**
Bread, Rolls, Sweet Dough, P Richards, 1937, 351 pgs **10.00**
Brer Rabbit's Modern Recipes, 49 pgs . . . **15.00**
Brides Book, 1934, soft cov **12.00**
Budget Watchers **8.00**
Buttery Shelf Cookbook, T Tudor **15.00**
Cake Secrets, Ingleheart, 1921 . . . . **15.00**
Cakes & Pastries, J Lambeth, 1938, 115 pgs **10.00**
Calendar of Dinners, Story of Crisco, 1915, 231 pgs **10.00**
Calendar Recipes of Dinners, Crisco, 1923, 231 pgs, hardbound **7.50**
Calumet, Kewpie cov, c1920 . . . . **15.00**
Calumet Reliable Recipes, 1915, Calumet boy on cov **5.00**
Campbell's Great Restaurants Cook Book, paperback **5.00**
Campbell's Main Dishes **8.00**
Canalside Cookery, Brockport Symphony Orchestra, 260 pgs **5.00**
Casserole Cookbook, 1968, 124 pgs **7.50**

Catering For Special Occasions, Fannie Farmer, 1911, 229 pgs **48.00**
Ceresota Flour Cookbook, 1910, boy on cov **4.00**
Chafing Dish Possibilities, Fannie Farmer, 1906 . . . . **8.00**
Chef's Secret Cookbook, Szathemary, 1972, 28 pgs **10.00**
Cheese Making, John W Decker, 1909 . . **30.00**
Chemistry of Cooking, M M Williams, 1885 . . . . **30.00**
Chicago Daily News, 1930s **9.00**
Chinese Cooking with American Meals, 1970, 228 pgs **6.00**
Choice Recipes Cocoa and Chocolate, Baker's, 1916, 64 pgs, paperback **9.50**
Christmas–Time Cookbook, Better Homes & Gardens, 1974, 216 pgs . . . **10.00**
Complete Bean Cookbook, V Bennett, 1969, 298 pgs **8.00**
Complete Pie Cookbook, Farm Journal, Nichols, 1965, 308 pgs, hardbound . . **2.50**
Congressional Club, Bicentennial, 1976, 714 pgs **9.00**
Cookbook for Two, Ida Allen, 1957, 320 pgs **5.00**
Cookery For The Many As Well As For The Upper Ten Thousand, London, 1864 . . . . **125.00**
Cookery From Experience, Mrs Sara T Paul, 1875 . . . . **30.00**
Cookies & More Cookies, L Sumption, 1938 . . . . **5.00**
Cooking For 2, J Hill, 1938 . . . . **5.00**
Cooking with Sour Cream and Buttermilk, Culinary Arts, 1955, 68 pgs, paperback **3.00**
Cook It Right **8.00**

Royal Cook Book, Royal Baking Powder Co., NY, printed color covers, 50 pages, 5 x 8", 1925, $8.00.

Cottolene Shortening, 52 Sunday Dinners, 1915, 192 pgs **8.00**

Country Art of Blueberry Cookery, C Morrison, 1972, 119 pgs **4.00**

Cox's Manual of Gelatine Cookery, 1914, 64 pgs **8.00**

Cross Creek Cookery, Rawlings, 1942 . .   **27.50**

Daily Cookery from Breakfast to Supper, Sproat, 1923 . . . .   **10.00**

Dainty Dishes For Slender Incomes, New York, 1900 . . . .   **25.00**

Dainty Junkets, 1915, 32 pgs, girl waitress on cov **15.00**

Daughter–in–law Cookbook, H Burrnett, 1969, 318 pgs **10.00**

Delightful Cooking With The Three Great Products from Corn, Corn Products Refining Co, NY, 64 pgs, c1920, 5 x 6½" **12.50**

Delineator Cookbook, Delineator Home Institute, 1928, 788 pgs, hardbound . .   **28.00**

Dione Lucas Meat & Poultry Cookbook, 1955, 324 pgs **7.00**

Direction For Cookery, Miss Leslie, Philadelphia, 1863 . . . .   **25.00**

Dishes for Special Occasions, E Blair, 1975, 312 pgs, hardbound **2.50**

Doubleday Cookbook, Volume I, J Anderson, 1975, 780 pgs **3.50**

Duncan Hines Food Odyssey, 1955, 274 pgs, hardbound **5.00**

Easy Gourmet's Dishes, C Adams, 72 pgs, paperback **1.00**

Eating In Bed Cookbook, Byfield, 1962, 132 pgs, hardbound **8.00**

Economy Administration Cookbook, 1913, 696 pgs **45.00**

Eggs & Cheese, Spaghetti & Rice, Good Housekeeping, 1958, 68 pgs, paperback **2.00**

Elena's Famous Mexican and Spanish Recipes, Elena Zelayeta, 4th ed, 1944, 127 pgs **18.00**

Everyday Cookbook & Family Compendium, 316 pgs **15.00**

Fannie Farmer's Chafing Dish Possibilities, Boston, 1899 . . . .   **50.00**

Favorite Recipes of the Movie Stars, 1931, 48 pgs **35.00**

Feeding the Child from Crib to College, Wheatena, 1928, 44 pgs **12.50**

Fish Cookery, 1921, 348 pgs **17.50**

Fleischmann's Recipes, 1910, 26 pgs, paperback **30.00**

Fondue, Chafing Dish & Casserole Cookery, 1969, 290 pgs **6.00**

For Men Only Cookbook, Abdullah, 1937, 205 pgs, hardbound **5.00**

French Household Cooking, Keyzer, 1928 . . . .   **15.00**

Fruit and Their Cookery, H Nelson, 1921   **18.00**

Galloping Gourmet, G Kerr, 1962, 118 pgs **4.00**

General Foods, All About Baking, 1935, 144 pgs **8.00**

Gillette American Cookbook, 1889, 521 pgs **10.00**

Gold Medal Flour Cook Book, Washburn Crosby Co, 1917, 74 pgs, paperback   **14.00**

Good Food & How to Cook It, A Seranne, 1972, 282 pgs **10.00**

Good Housekeeping Book of Meals, 1927, 256 pgs, hardbound **17.00**

Good Things To Eat, D & C Quality Foods **15.00**

Gourmet In Low Calorie Kitchen **8.50**

Grand Union Cookbook, M Compton, 1902, 322 pgs **22.50**

Granite Iron Ware Cookbook, copyright 1887 . . . .   **85.00**

Guide For Nut Cookery, Mrs Almeda Lambert, 1899 . . . .   **145.00**

Healthy Cooking, Mrs E Kellogg, Kellogg Food Co, soft brown cov **7.00**

Heinz Book of Meat Cookery, 1930, 54 pgs, paperback **8.00**

Heinz Book of Salads, 1925, 95 pgs, paperback **10.00**

Hood's Sarsaparilla, Good Pies, 1910, 16 pgs **4.25**

Hotel St Francis Cookbook, G Hirdzler, 1919 . . . .   **20.00**

Housekeeping in Old Virginia, 1965 reprint, slave recipes by Mozis Addams   **35.00**

How I Cooked It, B McDonald, 1949, 256 pgs **6.50**

Ideal Cookery Book–1,349 Recipes, 1891, 402 pgs **22.00**

International Cookbook, Hardin, 1920   **20.00**

It's A Picnic!, N McIntyre, 1969 . . . .   **5.00**

Jell–O Cookbook, 1905–15, bride on cov **45.00**

Jennie Junes' American Cookery Book, Mrs J C Croly, NY, 1870 . . . .   **50.00**

Jewel Stove Cookbook, paperback **4.00**

Jolly Times Junior Recipes, paperback . .   **8.00**

Joy of Eating Natural Foods, 1962, 363 pgs **6.50**

Karo Cook Book, Hewitt, 1909, 47 pgs . .   **8.50**

Kellogg's, 1978 . . . .   **6.00**

Kitchen Sampler, Lakeview Community Church, NY, 1978, paperback **3.50**

Latest Cake Secrets, Swans Down, c1930, 64 pgs **5.50**

Life's Picture Cookbook, 1961, 292 pgs, ring binder **25.00**

Little Red Devil Recipes, Underwood, c1920 . . . .   **4.50**

Lowney's Cook Book, M Howard, 1907, 1st ed **25.00**

Luchow's German Cookbook, J Mitchell, 1952, 224 pgs, hardbound **12.50**

Magic Chef Cooking, American Stove Co, 1935, 196 pgs **7.50**

Majestic Stoves Cookbook, c1900 . . . . .   **12.00**

Malleable Range Cookbook **6.00**

Marjorie Kinnan Rawlings Cookbook, London, 1st ed, 1960, dj **28.00**

Mastering Art of French Cooking, Julia Childs, 1972, 716 pgs **15.00**

Maxwell House Coffee, 1927, 22 pgs . . .   **7.00**

Meal Time Magic, M Mitchell, 1951, 120 pgs, hardbound **2.50**

Mentha–Col Cookbook, mammy on cov   **6.50**

Midwestern Jr League, 1976, 1st ed, tear in dj **8.00**

Miss Parloa's Cookbook, 1881 . . . .   **15.00**

Modern Encyclopedia of Cooking, 1959, 736 pgs **20.00**

Modern Priscilla Cookbook, 1924 . . . . .   **15.00**

Mrs Allen on Cooking Menu Service, 1924, 929 pgs **15.00**

My Grandmother's Cookery Book, S Wolley, 1976, 112 pgs, paperback . . .   **5.00**

National Yeast Co, 1886, 47 pgs, paperback. **5.00**

Nestle Cookbook, Nestle Co, 184 pgs. . .   **3.50**

New Book of Designs For Cake Bakers, H Heug, 1893 . . . .   **30.00**

New Congregational Church Cook Book, LaGrange, IL, 1935 . . . .   **9.00**

New Dr. Price Cookbook **4.00**

Nunsuch Mincemeat, c1915, 28 pgs . . .   **3.00**

Occident Flour, 1936, 24 pgs, paperback   **5.00**

Out of Alaska's Kitchens, 1951, 241 pgs, 8 x 11" **15.00**

Pan–Pacific Cookbook, L McLaren, 1915 . . . .   **35.00**

Pennyslvania Dutch Cook Book of Fine Old Recipes, 1936, 48 pgs, Sunbonnet girl on cov **15.00**

Pepperidge Farm, M Rudkin, 1st ed, orig dj **24.00**

Peter Hunt's Cape Cod Cookbook, 1954, 174 pgs, hardbound **5.00**

Pillsbury Best Cakes, 1960, 65 pgs **7.00**

Pillsbury Family Cookbook, 1963 . . . . . .   **10.00**

Pillsbury Silver Anniversary Bake–Off, 1974, 92 pgs **7.00**

Polish Cookery, M Monatowa, 1958, 314 pgs, hardbound **6.00**

Practical Housekeeping, 1884 . . . .   **15.00**

Principles of Cookery, Anna Barows, Chicago, 1910. . . . .   **20.00**

Quaker Cereal Products and How To Use Them, 56 pgs, 5 x 7" **32.00**

Quick Gourmet Dinners, Rieman, 1972, 141 pgs **6.50**

Rawleigh's Almanac Cookbook, 1915 . .   **16.00**

Recipes for Dainty Dishes, Sunkist Lemon, c1900, 40 pgs, paperback . . .   **4.00**

Recipes for the Sutterley Chafing Dish, H Johnson, 1894, 32 pgs **15.00**

Recipes For Van Camps Pureed Fruits & Vegetables, 1930, 31 pgs **10.00**

Reliable Recipes, Reliable Flour, 1904, 32 pgs, paperback **8.00**

Rocky Mountain Cook Book, Caroline T Norton, Denver, 1903 . . . .   **35.00**

Royal Baking Powder Biscuit Booklet, 1927 . . . .   **4.00**

Royal Cook Book, Royal Baking Powder Co, 1927, 49 pgs **15.00**

Rumford Cookbook, 1909, girl on cov . .   **8.00**

Salads and Sandwiches, Woman's World Magazine, 1924, 48 pgs, hardbound   **5.50**

Savannah Cookbook, 1933 . . . .   **12.50**

Savory Supper, Fashionable Feasts, S Williams, 1985, 335 pgs, hardbound   **12.00**

Seasonings Suggestions, Lea & Perrins, 1920 . . . .   **5.00**

Settlement Cookbook, S Kander, 1949, 623 pgs, hardbound **12.50**

Shumway's Canning Recipes, ...   **4.00**

Sleepy Eye Cookbook, loaf of bread shape. **25.00**

Sourdough Jack's. **8.00**

Standard Cookbook For All Occasions, Marion Lockhart, NY, 1925. . . . .   **15.00**

Sunset Cookbook of Favorite Recipes, San Francisco, 1949, 415 pgs **8.50**

Sunset Kitchen Cabinet Recipes, 1944, dj   **6.00**

Taste of Ireland, 1968, 124 pgs **12.50**

Tempting Good Luck Cookbook, Good Luck Margarine, 1932, 40 pgs, paperback. **4.00**

Tested Recipes for Successful Baking, 6th ed, 38 pgs, paperback **3.00**

The Fish Book Cookbook, published by Woman's World Magazine, Chicago, 1922, 50 pgs, illus **8.00**

The New Banana, United Fruit Co, 1931   **4.00**

The New Cookery, autographed by author, 1922 . . . .   **20.00**

The New England Cook Book, 1936, 48 pgs. **15.00**

The Wilken Family, Home Cooking Album, 1935, 45 pgs. **15.00**

Tested Recipes with Blue Ribbon Malt Extract, color covers and illustrations, 28 pages, 1927, $12.50.

Toll House Recipes, R Wakefield, 1946,
275 pgs **35.00**
Traditional Scots Recipes, J Murray,
1972, 230 pgs, hardbound **5.00**
Tyson Baking Book, Marion, 1916 . . . . .   **15.00**
Universal Cookbooks, 1888, 185 pgs,
Jeanie L Taylor. **15.00**
Wallace Hostess Book, W Fales, Wallace
Silver, 1922, 36 pgs **12.00**
Washington Herald Recipe Book, 1940   **10.00**
Way to a Man's Heart, Settlement Cook-
book, 1930, 624 pgs, hardbound **10.00**
Weight Watchers, 1978, first ed **7.50**
What Shall I Cook Today?, Spry, 1930,
49 pgs **15.00**
*What To Do & What Not To Do In Cook-
ing,* Mrs Lincoln, Boston, 1886 . . . . . .   **55.00**
White House Cookbook, 1902 . . . .   **75.00**
Woman's Favorite Cookbook, 1907 . . . .   **15.00**
Wonder Shredder & Grater, 1931, 32 pgs   **2.75**
Working Wives Cookbook, 1963, 162
pgs. **6.00**
*Young Housekeeper or Thoughts on
Food & Cookery,* Alcott, 1838, 424
pgs. **50.00**

CREDIT COINS AND CARDS

History: Charge coins, the first credit pieces, were
first issued in the 1890s. Charge coins are approximately the size of a quarter or half dollar. Because of their size, they were often carried with
change. This is why they were commonly referred
to as coins.

Charge coins come in various shapes, sizes,
and materials. Most are square, round, or oval but
some are in the shapes of shirts, socks, or hats.
They are made from various materials such as
fiber, German silver, celluloid, steel, and copper.
The issuing store has its name, monogram or initials on the coin. Each coin has a customer identification number. Charge coins were still in use as
late as 1959.

Metal charge plates were in use from the 1930s
to the 1950s. These plates look like military dog
tags. The front of the plate contains the customer's
name, address and account number. The back
has a piece of cardboard that carries the store's
name and customer's signature space.

Paper credit cards were in use in the early
1930s. They were easily damaged, so some companies began laminating them with clear plastic
in the 1940s. Laminated cards were issued until
the 1950s. The plastic cards we know today replaced the laminated cards in the late 1950s.

Specialization is the key to successful collecting. Plan a collection that can be completed.
Completeness tends to increase a collection's
value. When collecting charge coins, stay away

from rusted or damaged pieces. Inferior pieces
attract little interest unless rare.

Metal charge plates have little collector interest. They should remain affordable for years,
which means they'll probably not advance in
value.

The most interest is in credit cards. Scarce and
rare cards, when they can be located, are still
affordable. National credit cards are eagerly
sought. American Express is the most popular.

Paper and laminated paper credit cards are
highly desirable. Despite type, do not compro-
mise standard condition criteria when buying.

Plastic credit cards issued before 1970 are
scarce. Occasionally, you'll find a mint condition
card. Generally, you will have to settle for used.
Plastic cards issued after 1980 should be collected in mint condition.

Reference: Greg Tunks, *Credit Card Collecting
Bonanza, Second Edition* published by author,
1989.

Charge Coin (celluloid)
L. Bamberger & Company **100.00**
Credit Coin (metal)
Abraham & Straus, A & S, hat shaped   **20.00**
Gimbel Bros, lion holding shield, rect   **15.00**
Nathan Snellenberg, NS&Co., irregu-
lar round, white metal **12.50**
Credit Cards (stiff paperboard)
American Express, 1959, red printing,
purplish blue ground **300.00**
Bell System Credit Card, 1964, high
gloss, designed to hold dime **15.00**
Dunhill International Credit Card,
brown on white, "it is a privilege to
extend credit" **10.00**
General Tire, December 31, 1953,
calendar on back **30.00**
Hilton Hotels, 1955. . . . .   **25.00**
Hotel McLure, 1951–52 . . . .   **20.00**
Levy's, 1950s or early 1960s, tan with
brown top, Tuscon, Douglans, and
Warren. **17.50**
Mobilgas, 1951 . . . .   **50.00**
Saks Fifth Avenue **25.00**
Shannon's Furniture, Tulsa, OK, 1939,
black on blue, store drawing **15.00**

**Blotter, Gulf Travel Card adv., 2¼ x 5¾",
$3.50.**

Jigsaw Puzzle, BankAmericard, red, white, and blue, 4 x 5", c1964, $10.00.

Standard Oil, 1956	65.00
The Texas Company (Texaco), 1957, tan and white	40.00
Wallachs, no date, high gloss	17.50
Western Union, 1922, "will accept and send collect messages"	10.00
Zale Jewelry Company, 1954, "43 great stores serving the heart of America"	15.00
Credit Cards (plastic)	
American Express, 1971, green, large centurion profile	20.00
Bank–Americard, 1968, 12 digit account number	10.00
Gulf, car, boat, and plane	12.00
Lit Brothers, blue and white strip	7.50
Mastercharge, early 1970s	10.00
MasterCard, pre–hologram, plain	2.00
Mobil, 1960, full drawing of gas station	20.00
Playboy Club International, gold, Jan. 1979	8.00
Visa, hologram, special design	3.00
Credit Card Ephemera	
Booklet, Diners Club, April 30, 1956, 126 pgs, Hertz advertisement in back with drawing of 1955 Ford, blank memo pgs bound inside to record charge transactions	100.00
Broadside, Gulf Refining Company (Del.), "IMPORTANT NOTICE/REPLACEMENT OF COURTESY CARDS WITH CHARG–A–PLATES," 1932, 12 x 18", text, black ink on white stiff cardboard	35.00

DIECUTS

History: The diecut, known in England as scraps, combined chromolithography printing, the die-cutting process, and embossed relief. Upon their introduction in the 1860s, success was instantaneous.

The diecut originated in Germany and quickly spread to England and America. Prominent manufacturers included Mamelock & Soehne and Zoecke & Mittmeyer in Germany, Raphael Tuck & Sons in England, and Louis Prang in America.

Most printers manufactured diecuts as a sideline. Their principal production was chromolithography printing, much of which was advertising oriented. However, during the peak of the diecut craze, the 1860s and 1870s, many printers devoted a large portion of their effort toward diecuts.

Diecuts were sold separately or in sheets. Diecuts were linked to each other by a narrow tab strip that was removed when the image was sold or used. The tab strip often contained the name of printer or distributor. Occasionally the tab contained a caption or name for the diecut.

Diecuts were used in many different ways. Albums were designed in which diecuts could be saved. Many individuals simply pasted them in existing advertising trade card and family scrapbooks. Diecuts graced envelopes and packaging. Many were used as window and holiday decorations, embellishments on three and four fold scenes, and in framed montages.

References: Alistar Allen and Joan Hoverstadt, *The History of Print Scraps*, New Cavendish Books, 1983; Cynthia Hart, John Grossman, and Priscilla Dunhill, *A Victorian Scrapbook*, Workman Publishing, 1989.

REPRODUCTION ALERT: Diecuts have been reproduced. Many of the modern examples are less brilliant in color and do not have the relief detail of the period pieces. An experienced eye can easily spot their inferiority.

Advertising	
Alox Shoe Laces, figural, shoe, cardboard, 16 x 18", 1930s	8.00
American Tea Co, baby and cat in wicker cradle, 5 x 9"	15.00
Austen's Forest Flower Cologne, boy and girl figure between cologne bottle, Rogers statue shape, 10 x 7", 1880s	125.00
Ayer's Sarsaparilla, man and woman, Rogers Statuary pose, caption "The Deacon: Land sake, Liza, the very sight of that bottle makes me feel like another man," 13 x 7", 1880s	150.00
Bogus Soap, dog, Hughes & Johnson Litho, 7½"	8.00

Budweiser Beer, pr, beer glasses, 8 x
15", 1940s **10.00**
Calumet Baking Powder, figural, can
with boy, double sided, 9½" **15.00**
D R Saunders, Manuf of Straw, Splint,
Rattan & Bamboo Baskets, basket of
chicks, 4½ x 6" **15.00**
Fayette Street Boot and Shoe Store,
vase of flowers, 1880s, 7½ x 5½" . . **25.00**
G A Wrisley & Co, White Velvet Soap,
girl with bar of soap, 8" h **15.00**
Gold Dust Twins, twins in tub **15.00**
Good Native Champagne, Thos Mar-
tindale & Co, pail with dog **10.00**
Harters Iron Tonic, woman painting
picture, 10" h **20.00**
Hartford Millinery Emporium, children
and umbrella, N Ballin, 1883, 10" h **22.00**
H J Baker & Bro Chemical Fertilizers,
NY, 1883, boy in tea cup, 6" h **22.00**
H M Reynolds Shingle Co, Grand
Rapids, MI, figural, house, sample
shingle int., 5" h **8.00**
H O Neill & Co, NY, boy and girl, 8½" **20.00**
Hugh Glenn & Co, Mammoth Dry
Goods, Carpet, Boot and Shoe,
Book and Stationery House, Utica,
NY, trade card, actress photo,
c1885 . . . . **15.00**
Italian Sapone & Hersoms Best Soap,
woman, 7 x 8½" **55.00**
Magic Yeast Cakes, mother cat and kit-
tens, 5½ x 8½". **20.00**

**Advertising Trade Card, Frye Brothers Ci-
gar Manufacturers and Tobacconists, 5 x
8½", $20.00.**

Marseilles White Soap, Lautz Bros,
baby with ball, 8½ x 12" **20.00**
Motor Oil, "In Goes 150–V15D, out
goes sludge," figural, auto, 8" l **15.00**
Royal Yeast Cakes, Dutch girl, 8½" h **20.00**
San–Curo Ointment Cures, Cuts,
Burns, hand with bandage, 7 x 8" . . **25.00**
Shipman & Tygert, Undertakers and
Furniture Dealers, Vernon, NY,
woman behind fan, 7 x 9½" **65.00**
Stevenson & Co, Useful Presents for
the Holidays **15.00**
The Great Atlantic & Pacific Tea Co,
beautiful woman, 5½ x 8" **20.00**
The Wright, Russell & Bay Co, Toledo,
OH, scalloped edge, 5 x 8" **15.00**
Wheaties Breakfast Food, stand–up,
Uncle Sam, cereal box illus, 6½" h **15.00**
White Velvet Soap, girl with soap, 8" h **10.00**
Wool Soap, Swift & Co, My Mamma
Used Wool Soap, 1896 . . . . **20.00**
Angel
Child, 6¼" h **25.00**
Gold, emb, 1880s, 4 x 4". **10.00**
With tree, blue clothes, store adv on
back. **65.00**
Artist Pallet, bird, nest, and flowers illus,
7 x 10½" **15.00**
Baby, wrapped in pink bow, double bow
folds out, Int Art Pub, 3½ x 4" **10.00**
Basket of Flowers, emb, c1885, 5 x 3". . . **10.00**
Basket with babies, pr, one with white
babies, other with black babies with
watermelon, 9" h. **125.00**
Blacks
Little Boy, standing on boxes on chair,
"Little Jim Finds the Watermelon,"
5" h **15.00**
Man, caricature, wearing top hat rid-
ing ostrich, 1880s, mounted, 6½ x
5". **75.00**
Mother and Child, "But His Mother
Suddenly Comes In" **15.00**
Bowl of Fruit, leaf shape bowl, "Happy
Christmas To You," 7 x 4½", 1880s . . **25.00**
Butterfly, glitter trim, early 20th C, Ger-
man **50.00**
Carnations, emb **8.00**
Cat, 6½ x 12". **30.00**
Cherub and Flowers, early 20th C **35.00**
Chick
Chick with hat, 6 x 9". **20.00**
Open book, and floral, emb, c1900,
3½ x 4" **10.00**
Children
Playing on gate, "As Happy as a
King," emb, 7 x 9½" **20.00**
Sitting in boat, swan in water along
boat, 12 x 6". **25.00**
Couple
"A Gift of Love," hand folds out, 4½ x
6" **12.00**

Oval with couple center, cutout edge, emb, 4¹/₂ x 6¹/₂" **12.00**
Sitting in boat with dog, Sackett, Withedom & Betzig Litho, 7¹/₂ x 10" **15.00**
Wearing early clothing, compliments of C R Mabley, 6 x 12" **20.00**

Duck
Carrying egg on back, standup, "Happy Easter," 1920s **9.00**
Pulling Easter basket, movable rabbit, 1920s, 7 x 5" **7.50**

Easter
Child in egg, fence with violets, two layer, stand–up, emb, 5¹/₂ x 7".... **35.00**
Four part, wall hanging, cupid with phone, cross, butterfly with boy's head, egg shape with flowers...... **20.00**

Easter Egg
Floral motif, c1895, 3³/₄ x 2³/₄" **10.00**
Rabbits and violets, 6 x 7¹/₂" **25.00**

Egg with bunnies and eggs and flowers, "Compliments of Sister Isie, Washington DC," August Gast & Co, NY, 1880s......................... **55.00**
Fan, early 20th C.................... **50.00**
Father Christmas, pr, German, c1910, 3¹/₂ x 5" **8.00**

Girl
Christmas girl, garland of roses, glitter dec, 6¹/₂" **15.00**
Girl with cat and dog, 9" h......... **15.00**
Pretty girl surrounded by oak leaves, emb, 8¹/₂ x 11"................ **25.00**
With basket of kittens, 6¹/₂" h **10.00**
With cows, compliments James Nicholson, Terre Haute, IN, 8¹/₂ x 1".... **15.00**
With parasol, compliments M D Madigan, Chicago, 8 x 8¹/₂"....... **20.00**
With fence, 11" **25.00**

Goats, emb, good color and detail, 6 x 9¹/₄"........................... **12.00**
Hot Air Balloon, c1880, view of gondola and people, 4¹/₂ x 2", mounted **45.00**
Jumbo the Elephant, glossy, 7¹/₂ x 5¹/₂", 1880s......................... **50.00**
Little Girl, riding pony, "The First Ride," compliments of James Nicholson, Terre Haute, IN, 9¹/₂ x 10¹/₂"...... **35.00**
Man with white horse, emb, 7 x 8" **15.00**
Place Card, Dutch girl, 3³/₄" easel back.. **8.00**
Rabbit and Chick, driving auto, emb, standup, Tuck & Sons, c1905 .... **27.50**
Rabbit and Egg, expands to four rabbits, one emerging from egg, Nister, c1890, 9 x 3" expanded.................. **20.00**
Rooster, 7 x 11" **25.00**
Sailing Ship, life rafts on sides, US flag, intricate, 10 x 13", 1880s........... **65.00**

Santa
Blowing horn, emb **12.00**
Feather beard, Norcross, 1940s, 8 x 11"............................ **12.00**

Holding large doll, wearing green suit, emb, repaired legs **6.00**
Paper costume and boots, 1920, German **75.00**
Walking, brown suit, emb **18.00**
With girl, playing violin, red suit, emb, 6¹/₂" h........................ **20.00**
Ship, detailed, American flag, 12 x 10".. **25.00**
Soldiers, digging trench, emb, 4¹/₂ x 6¹/₂" **8.00**
Swan, bird scene **8.00**
Tamborine, "Merry Christmas," Meilink, Small & Co, Toledo, OH, woman, 9¹/₂" **10.00**
Woman and child, garden scene, cutting roses, 5 x 6¹/₂" **10.00**

DIME NOVELS

History: The dime novel originated in 1860 when Erastus Beadle, an Otesgo County, New York, printer, published a book of popular song lyrics that he sold for a dime. If the concept worked for song lyrics, it could work for novels. *Malaeska: The Indian Wife of the White Hunter*, Beadle's first dime novel and inspired by James Fenimore Cooper's *The Last of the Mohicans*, sold 300,000 copies the first year. For the next thirty years, Beadle produced two dime novels a month.

The dime novel, often thirty–two pages in length, drew largely upon American history for its stories. The American west was a favorite topic. While real life individuals such as Buffalo Bill and Wild Bill Hickok appeared in its pages, the stories were pure fiction. An ample supply of fictional heroes, e.g., Deadeye Dick and Fred Fearnot, was also present. Whether real or fictional, the basic theme of each story was action and adventure. The novels played well to America's sense of self–reliance and achievement.

Beadle's success with historical based stories through his Beadle's Pocket Library enabled him to launch his Pluck and Luck series, stories with a "blood and thunder" focus. Ann S. Stephens produced over two hundred titles in the series. When Beadle died in 1893, Frank Tousey took over the Pluck and Luck series. The price was dropped to a nickel. Wild West Weekly and Secret Service, two new series, were begun.

One of Tousey's contributions to the dime novel was elaborate, full color, pictorial, wrap around covers. This enhanced the dime novel's appeal, especially to the younger generation. New series, e.g., All Around Weekly and Work and Win, continued to emerge.

Beadle's success spawned a number of imitators. Among these were Irwin P. Beadle's American Novels, Nickel Library's Border Boys Library, and Wide Awake Library. In the 1880s, John R. Coryell created Nick Carter and Gilbert Pattern Frank Merriwell, the all American hero. Total sales of dime novels during the nineteenth century is believed to have exceeded 125 million copies.

American readers were tiring of the dime novels by 1900. The concept continued until 1915, the advent of World War I. Eventually Big Little Books and comic books would fill the dime novel void.

Periodical: *Dime Novel Round–Up*, 87 School Street, Fall River, MA 02720.

Badger, Joseph E Jr, Beadle & Co, NY
  Little Thunderbolt, 1873, 100 pgs **30.00**
  Red Dan the Ranger, 1872, 102 pgs . . **22.00**
  The Mad Ranger, 1871, 99 pgs **25.00**
  The Partisan Spy, 1871, 100 pgs **45.00**
Bowen, James L, *The Frontier Scouts*,
  Beadle & Co, NY, 1865, 44 pgs **40.00**
Burns, Tom, *Danger Signal Dave–The Dashing Boy Engineer of the West*, Frank Tousey, NY, #42, 1910, 29 pgs **15.00**
Bushnell, W H, *Old Cheyenne*, The American Library Co, NY, 1885, 24
  pgs **22.00**
Carew, *The Leaping Panther*, George Munro & Co, NY, 1870, 99 pgs **35.00**
Clark, C Dunning, Beadle & Co, NY, 4 x 6¼"
  Mohawk Nat, A Tale of the Great North Woods, 1868, 98 pgs. **18.00**
  Star Eyes, 1865, 97 pgs **35.00**
  The Red Outlaw, 1870, 98 pgs **35.00**
  The Scout of the Mohawk Valley, 1866, 98 pgs **38.00**
  The Witch of Cherry Valley, 1871, 102 pgs **16.00**
  The Young Ranger's Bride, 1870, 98 pgs **35.00**
Cobb, Weldon J Jr, George Munro & Co, NY
  Cowboys and Skinners, 1866, 100 pgs **28.00**
  Lightfoot The Scout, 1864, 95 pgs **30.00**
Coomes, O, *The Boy Ranger*, Beadle & Adams, NY, 1884, 90 pgs **25.00**
Cowan, J F, *Hardskull, The Avenger*, George Munro & Co, NY, 1867, 100
  pgs **25.00**
Donovan, Dick, *The Man–Hunter*, Arthur Westbrook, OH, 147 pgs **10.00**
Ellis, Edward, Beadle & Adams, NY
  Kent the Ranger, 1886, 96 pgs. **18.00**
  The Forest Spy, 1861, 98 pgs. **20.00**
  The Wood Rangers, 1865, 100 pgs . . . **60.00**
Ewing, Edwin E, *The Black Wolf*, Beadle & Adams, NY, 1876, 100 pgs **25.00**
Gardner, Lewis J, George Munro & Co NY
  Keen–Eye, the Ranger, 1884, 97 pgs. . **25.00**
  The Wabash Rangers, 1875, 90 pgs . . **35.00**
Gerstacker, Friedrich, Beadle & Co, NY
  Red John, the Bush Rangers, 375, 1871, 100 pgs **36.00**

New Buffalo Bill Weekly, Buffalo Bill's Barbecue, color litho cover, 32 pages, 8 x 11", October 6, 1917, $20.00.

  The Bush Ranger, #74, 1871, 99 pgs **35.00**
  War Axe, #83, 1871, 96 pgs **45.00**
Griswold, Miner A, George Munro & Co, NY
  Old Nick, the Wolf Slayer, 1871, 100 pgs **28.00**
  The Lost Hunter, 1875, 100 pgs **25.00**
Grover, G Clabon, *The Little Trumpeter*, Amalgamated Press, London, 1933, 64
  pgs **8.00**
Hall, Samuel S, *Bald Head's Pards*, Beadle & Adams, NY, 1889, 37 pgs. **15.00**
Hazelton, Harry, *The Schuylkill Rangers*, Beadle & Co, NY, 1865, 96 pgs **20.00**
Hynes, Captain A, *Old Ben Woolley*, George Munro & Co, NY, 1866, 100
  pgs **35.00**
Ingraham, Col Prentiss, Beadle & Adams, NY
  Buffalo Bill Baffled, 1892, 30 pgs **28.00**
  Emerald Ed of Devil's Acre, 1892, 29 pgs **15.00**
Judson, Colonel, *Luliona, The Seminole*, #54, Beadle & Co, NY, 1869, 85 pgs **45.00**
Lewis, Julius Warren, *Daredeath Dick, The King of the Cowboys*, Beadle & Adams, NY, 1890, 28 pgs **15.00**
Manning, William H, *Border Bullet, The Prairie Sharpshooter*, Beadle & Adams, NY, 1888, 31 pgs. **12.00**
Meserve, Arthur L, George Munro & Co, NY
  The Old Kentucky Scouts, 1874, 100 pgs **25.00**
  The Rough Ranger, 1870, 96 pgs. **22.00**
  Walking Bear, 1870, 96 pgs **30.00**
Nunnes, Joseph A
  Rube The Ranger, Frederic A Brady, NY, 1869, 100 pgs. **170.00**

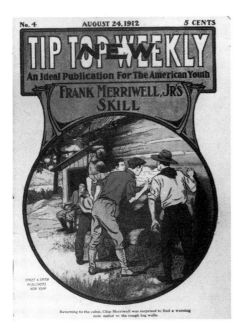

Tip Top Weekly, Frank Merriwell Jr's Skill, **32 pages, 8 x 11", August 24, 1912, $9.00.**

The Green Mountain Boys, Irwin P
Beadle, NY, 1865, 95 pgs **55.00**
Rathborne, Harry St G, *Roaring Ralph
Rockwood, the Reckless Ranger,* Bea-
dle & Adams, NY, 1884, 30 pgs **18.00**
Robinson, Dr G W, *Fighting Nat,* Beadle
& Co, NY, 1868, 100 pgs **25.00**
Robinson, Dr J H, *Scotto the Scout: A
Romance of the North and South,* Bea-
dle & Co, NY, 1871, 55 pgs **55.00**
Senarens, Lu, *The Pioneer Hunters of
Kentucky,* George Munro & Co, NY,
1874, 99 pgs **35.00**
St John, Percy B, *Reckless Rob,* Robert
Dewitt, NY, 1869, 100 pgs **25.00**
Urner, Nathan D, Street & Smith, NY
The Queen of the Canons, 1892, 31
pgs **22.00**
The Thunderbolt of the Border, 1891,
31 pgs **28.00**
Victor, Mrs Metta V, *The Wrecker's
Daughter,* Beadle & Adams, NY, 1882,
100 pgs **15.00**
Vincent, Lewis, *The Phantom of the
Woods,* George Munro & Co, NY, 93
pgs **22.00**
Whittaker, Frederick, Beadle & Adams,
NY
Black Nick, The Hermit of the Hills,
1879, 98 pgs **15.00**
Double–Death, 1901, 27 pgs **22.00**

Willet, Edward, Beadle & Co, NY
The Border Avengers, 1869, 100 pgs   **28.00**
The Shawnees' Decoy, 1870, 99 pgs   **35.00**
The Texas Avengers, 1874, 98 pgs . . .   **42.00**

DIRECTORIES

History: For the purpose of this category, a directory is defined as an alphabetical list, usually of
names and addresses. It may be the membership
list of an organization or a list of manufacturers of
a specific product. Size is not important. Some
directories may be only a few loose leaf pages,
others large hardcover tomes.

Directories are valuable research tools. Collectors use city, county, and regional directories to
establish the location and longevity of manufacturers. Often these directories provide detailed information about the principal corporate structure
of the business being researched.

Business directories, especially when they relate to the manufacturers of a specific object or
collecting category, e.g., the Furniture Dealers'
zone reference books of the late 1920s and
1930s, are eagerly sought by collectors. These
directories help us understand the extent of manufacturing during a specific time period and serve
to identify major and secondary companies. In
many cases, they contain advertising that often
contains brief histories of the advertiser.

Organizations of all types, from churches to
social clubs, published membership lists. It is
common for these directories to include other
useful information as well, e.g., annual reports,
history of the organization, and photographs of
officers, members, social functions, and buildings.

Since the principal emphasis and value of most
directories is local, directories are usually difficult
to sell outside the region to which they apply.
Prices are modest, usually under $20.00.

American Warehouses & Forwarding
Companies 1921–22 In Principle Cit-
ies, 116 pgs **7.00**
Camp Papago Park, Prisoner of War
Camp, Phoenix, AZ, telephone, early
1940s **12.00**
City, New Bedford, MA, No 8, 1856 . . . .   **20.00**
Doan's Directory of the United States
Cities Census Division, 1910–11, 32
pgs, lists census figures for most cities
and illus ads for products **15.00**
Fond du Lac Labor Review, Union Direc-
tory & Buyer's Guide, 1924, illus **10.00**
Gazetteer & Business Directory, Onon-
daga County, NY, 1868, 435 pgs **69.00**
Gehrig Hotel Directory & Tourist
Guide...US & Canada, 1927, 256 pgs,
60 pgs black and white road maps . . .   **10.00**

Directory and Bulletin of a Decade of Pastoral Work in Plainfield Reformed Charge, black-and-white photo illustrations and advertisements, 44 pages, 5 x 6¾", 1913, $4.00.

Hartford and East Hartford, 781 pgs, 1897	**50.00**
New York's Montgomery & Fulton Counties, 1869–70, 312 pgs	**15.00**
Plant Production Directory, Industry's Buying Guide, Spring, 1944, 12 x 11"	**18.00**
Pocket Congressional Directory, January 1953, 83rd Congress	**10.00**
Rail Fan's Directory, lists collectors in US and Canada, 156 pgs, 1964	**5.00**
Reedsburg, WI, telephone, 1943	**6.00**
R L Polk & Co Marinette Nemoniminee Directory 1907–1908, 614 pgs	**18.00**
Salesman's Monitor; A Directory to the Dry Goods Trade of the US, 230 pgs, 1880	**22.00**
Oceanliner	
Cunard Line, *RMS Aquitania,* sailing from Chamborg, Saturday, June 20, 1925, 28 pgs, 5 x 8" book with double fold insert lists passengers	**35.00**
White Star Line, *SS Olympic,* sailing from New York, Friday, July 1, 1932, 12 pgs, 5 x 8" book with passenger list.	**20.00**
Sullivan's Chicago Law Directory 1936–37, 696 pgs	**8.00**
Taunton, MA, 1861, telephone	**18.00**
The Mercantile Agency Reference Book– Containing Ratings of Merchants,	

Manufacturers & Traders Generally, R G Dun & Co, 1933–34	**25.00**
Traction Fan's Directory, model trolley, 200 pgs, 1962	**4.00**

DOCUMENTS

History: The dictionary definition of a document that applies to this category is "an original or official paper relied upon as the basis, proof, or support of something." While these original or official papers may be hand written, the vast majority are printed forms with blanks to be completed by the user.

If one uses the broadest definition possible, bill heads, certificates, checks, letters, letterheads, licenses, and even photographs are documents. However, the paper collecting market has reached a point of sophistication where these and other similar "documents" are separate collecting categories. In *Warman's Paper* the document category consists of business, e.g., bills of lading, receipts, and waybills, and governmental, e.g., commissions and deeds, material. Emphasis is on printed form material.

Paper collectors prefer documents from the eighteenth and nineteenth century. In addition to collecting them for their historical importance, they are also collected for the engraved vignettes. Documents with a historical flavor are favored over documents that merely record daily business and governmental activities.

Documents are an important source of autographs. However, all signatures should be authenticated. Many presidential and military documents, especially those after 1825, are secretarial–signed. In some cases, signatures are engraved, added to the document during the printing process.

American collectors prefer American documents. Foreign documents, even with attractive vignettes and some historical content, are difficult to sell in the American market.

The vast majority of documents, e.g., a collection of deeds for a piece of land, have no or very little value. Less than one out of a hundred documents has strong collectibility. Age is perhaps the least important value factor. Content, historical importance, signatories, and displayability are the keys.

BUSINESS DOCUMENTS

Bill of Sale	
Bentley Auto, 1926	**2.00**
Black Raven Coal and Coke Co, 1906, ornate, raven logo	**6.50**
Fresno Agricultural Works, Fresno, CA, 1902, engraved.	**5.00**
H J Thompson Inc, June 4, 1906	**10.00**

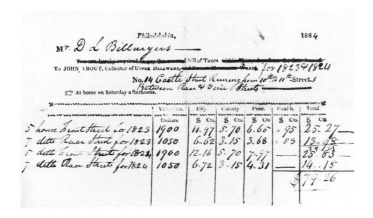

Business Document, receipt, Durham Pepsi-Cola Bottling Company, printed, black and white and red and white, double dot logo, 3³/₈ x 5⁵/₈", 1950s, $4.00.

Bond, Selma, Marion & Memphis Railroad, $1,000, sgd by N B Forrest **500.00**
Check
   Coca–Cola Bottling Co, Newark, OH, 1949, canceled, Art Deco logo **10.00**
   Sedalia, S P Johns & Sons, 1909, ornate, canceled **5.00**
   Sonoma Vineyards, L M Martinia Grape Products, Kingsburg, CA, 1939, canceled **8.50**
Draft, South Sea Bubble Company, sgd by Philip Yorke, April 4, 1722 . . . . **400.00**
Letter, William Waldorf Astor, Financier, Jan 2, 1916 . . . . **100.00**
Pay Slip, Savage Mine, VA, 1868 . . . . . . **22.50**
Receipt
   A E Miller, Manufacturers & Jobbers of Confectionery, Brattleboro, VT **10.00**
   Earle & Lynde, Wholesale & Retail

Dealers, Flower Meal Grain, Hay, Feed, Brattleboro, VT **10.00**
Hygeia Bottling Works, Pensacola, FL, Bottlers of Soda Water & Coca–Cola **10.00**
Myers Cox Co, Dubuque, IA, 1918, notification to customers that receipts will not be sent **5.00**
Saint Nicholas Hotel, Springfield, IL, dated 1857, hotel illus, receipt for room and board, 7 x 8" **20.00**
The Independent Newspaper, Salmon Falls, 1901, receipt for one year subscription **6.50**
Stock Certificate
   ABC Brewing Corporation, 1934, green, ornamental engraving **10.00**
   Austin Hotel Company, 1932, brown border, eagle vignette **3.50**
   Babcock & Wilcox Company, Nuclear Plant Designers, 1959–71, green border, two men and logo vignette **4.00**
   Holiday Mining Co, General Land Office, CO, 1884 . . . . **35.00**
   Jewish Colonial Trust Ltd, 1901 . . . . . . **50.00**
   Lincoln Printing Company, 1962–65, engraved Abe Lincoln vignette **6.00**
   Northampton Brewing Corporation, 1934, orange, engraved **20.00**
   San Antonio Land & Irrigation Co, 1911, pioneer in electric street cars **100.00**

GOVERNMENT DOCUMENTS, FEDERAL

Bond, Confederate, $1,000, Jeff Davis picture, attached coupons **45.00**
Booklet
   US Official Postal Guide, Sept, 1880, 60 pgs, "Speaking Telephones by National Bell Telephone Co" adv . . **25.00**
   US Patent Law; Instructions To Obtain Letters Patent For New Inventions, Munn & Co, New York City, 108 pgs, 1870 . . . . **9.00**

Government, local, tax bill, Philadelphia, PA, 6¹/₂ x 4", dated 1824, $20.00.

Check

General C C Washburn, Vicksburg, state bank Madison, WI, Jan 20, 1879 . . . .   50.00

18th Precinct State House, July 1863 to William Parliman, sgd by Mayor Opdyke 40.00

Clothing Record, John Pearce Co E 68 Regt of PA, Aug 11, 1862 on one side, William Pike Co on other, marked in red "Deserted Sept 1, 1862 at Philadelphia" 30.00

Company Orders

Civil War, Confederate, Nov 30, 1862, H–Qtrs, 8th Confederate Reg, Camp Wheeling. 95.00

Civil War, General, details and actions, dated 1862, 4½ x 7", set of 4   10.00

Ninth Co, Eighth Regt New Hampshire Militia, soldier ordered to go to Richard Melvin's Tavern armed and equipped for military duty, sgd by Regimental Sgt James L Webster, 4 x 8". 30.00

Court Marshall, Headquarters Dept of the East, New York City, Feb 20, 1865, Spl Order 44, Court Marshall in Burlington VT, By Command of Maj Gen Dix, two attached travel expenses. . . .   12.00

Customs Certificate, Benjamin Lincoln, Boston, 1804, emb seal, 5 x 9½". 55.00

Eviction Notice, November 4, 1864, military order to evict negroes from sheds, 1 pg, Headquarters U S Forces, Natchez, MS to Lt Col Mitchell, Provost Marshall of Freedmen from Capt T C Prescott 75.00

Honorable Discharge, Vicksburg Muster–Out Roll, Aug 1, 1863, Lt Joseph Treadway, 23rd WI Volunteers, sgd by officers 30.00

Letter

Henry Adams, July 8, 1875, two pages 250.00

Herbert Hoover, June 28, 1943, Herbert Hoover letterhead, letter of thanks 125.00

John F Kennedy, Congressman, MA, August 29, 1949, House of Representatives letterhead, to T W Alexander 750.00

Ordinance, 46th Penn Infantry, War Dept, Washington DC, June 13, 1865, to Lt Col E L Whitman 16.00

Pay and Allowance, Civil War officer, 1864, 11 x 17". 15.00

Pay Receipt

1780, to Rev War Officer, sgd by Oliver Wolcott Jr 27.00

1783, April, Rev War General, Gen Jedidiah, Huntington, CT, 6 x 5" . . .   33.00

Promissory Note, to Franklin D Roosevelt for $700, February 1, 1927, 3½ x 8½". 400.00

Receipt Form, Theodore Roosevelt, Governor of NY, 1900 . . . . 175.00

Requisition, 1st Regt NY Dragons, "nr Strausburg VA 27 Oct 1864," list of supplies 20.00

Telegram, military

Gen L P Walker, Huntsville, penciled to Gen Ruggles at Corinth, March 12, 1862 . . . .   60.00

General S Cooper, Richmond, to General Beauregard, Goldsboro, May 3, 1864 . . . .   50.00

Treasury Certificate, Revolutionary War, MA, dated Jan 1, 1780, payable to John Bradford 400.00

GOVERNMENT DOCUMENTS, LOCAL AND STATE

Agreement, Ulster Co, NY, saw mill built by two men, hand–written, 4 pgs, 1813 . . . .   16.00

Bill of Sale, State of Missouri, 1847, grant for negro boy a slave for life, dark ink, 6¾ x 7½". 75.00

Certificate

Certificate of Organization of Oak Park Republican Committeemen's Organization, State of Illinois, Office of Secretary of State, March 5, 1937, engraved, 8½ x 14" 25.00

Inspection, bark Carolina of NY, inspected for hiding slaves, sgd by Inspector Gibson, 4½ x 7". 75.00

Deed, Pike County, IL 1856, attached receipt, emb seals, dated July 9, 1856 . .   18.00

Document and Promissory Note, requesting Sheriff of Plymouth Co, Abington, MA to seize property of David Blake, 1823. . . . .   18.00

Land Grant

Georgia, July 1832, sgd by Wilson Lumkin, orig seal, 2 pgs 50.00

Miami River, Cincinnati, OH, 1827, sgd by John Quincy Adams 350.00

Land Indenture, Greenland, NH, Jan 9, 1786 . . . . 150.00

Legal, Whitley County, KY, 1857, summmons for court appearance, 3½ x 7". 18.00

Letter, Office of the Minority Leader, House of Representatives, Dec 30, 1949, sgd Joseph W Martin, Jr 9.00

Order, State of South Carolina, 1788, ordering Benjamin Port to answer summons, emb state seal 375.00

Receipt

Education for Freedom, April 1865, Memphis, TN, rent for school house to meet the necessities of the colored people for school rooms, paid amount specified $100, sgd by Capt Walker. 40.00

Slave, 1847, payment for bringing slave from one state to another, sgd by Justice, docketed, 5 x 7" **45.00**

State Tax, State of Louisiana, Parish of Orleans, dated Dec 14, 1897, 6 x 7¹/₂" **9.00**

Ship's Manifest

Harvard arriving at Philadelphia, blue paper, masted ship illus, dated August 10, 1859, 6 x 8" **15.00**

Virginia, lists merchandise from Port to NY, September 10, 1832, 8 x 13" . . **23.00**

Summons, Whitley County, KY, 1857, summons for court appearance, 3¹/₂ x 7" **18.00**

EROTICA

History: Erotica deals with objects of an artistic or literary nature that have an erotic theme or quality. The principal role of erotic objects is to arouse sexual desire. Erotic objects can be explicit or implicit.

Society and the courts have offered a wide variety of opinions on what constitutes artistic and literary merit in respect to erotica. While opinions differ, the simple truth is that erotica sells, and sells well, in the paper collectibles market. In fact, the more sexually explicit an object is, the better it sells. Although you rarely see erotica openly displayed at shows, the "under the table" market is strong.

Tijuana Bibles or Eight–Pagers are among the more commonly found material. These eight page pamphlets, usually measuring three inches by four and one–half inches, are extremely explicit, sexually oriented cartoons. They appeared upon the scene in the post–World War I era and disappeared by the early 1950s. Many of the issues spoofed the leading cartoon, entertainment, gangster, and political figures of the era. Series of eight and ten were common. Among the more popular are the adventures of the Fuller Brush man and a trip to the 1939–40 New York World's Fair.

Nude and sexually explicit cabinet cards, post cards, and stereo views exist in large numbers. Many date from the last half of the nineteenth century. By the 1930s, they were replaced by "racy" black and white photographs. Much of this material is European in origin.

Novels and booklets, often illustrated with graphics and/or photographs, constitute an important category within the antiquarian book community. Many book auctions hold specialized sales devoted exclusively to erotic material.

Oriental erotica, especially from Japan and India, is among the most desirable material. Most drawings are works of art. Scrolls, prints, and books are plentiful. Hand drawn examples command premium prices.

Do not confuse "girlie" and "pin–up" material with erotica. While the former may produce some of the same desires as erotica, it is tame by comparison. Although it can be suggestive, most erotic objects leave nothing to the imagination.

Album, ten 2¹/₂ x 4" glossy black and white photos of model in various stages of undress down to just stockings, posed with iron and/or ironing board, 1940s. **40.00**

Book, *Erotic Art of Japan,* 274 pgs, forty color plates, hardbound **8.00**

Cookbook

Cooking in the Nude–For Playful Gourmets, 1987, 64 pgs **3.00**

Cooking in the Nude–For Red Hot Lover, 1987, 64 pgs **3.00**

Drawing, Frank Frazetta, 1957, pencil on paper, full length nude woman, standing, sgd, matted, 16¹/₂ x 10¹/₂" **1,100.00**

Flip Booklet, *Hotsy Totsy In Her Original Fanny Dance,* 2¹/₄ x 3", 1930s. . . **25.00**

Magazine

Real Boudoir Tales, Vol 1, #31, 1930s, 24 pgs, Lida cov art **30.00**

Real French Capers, Vol 1, #34, 1930s, 24 pgs, Greenwood cov art **25.00**

Sex Science Illustrated, July, 1955 . . **10.00**

Paperback Book

Bingham, Carson, *The Gang Girls,* Monarch, 372 . . . . **10.00**

Cargo, Francis, *Perversity,* Berkley, G–33 . . . . **4.00**

Drago, Sinclair, *Women to Love,* Novel Library, 16 . . . . **6.00**

Farmer, Philip Jose, *Fire and the Night,* Regency, 118 . . . . **6.00**

Leem, Hannah, *Yaller Gal,* Handi–Book, 84 . . . . **5.00**

Woodford, Jack, *The Abortive Hussy,* Avon, 146 . . . . **4.00**

Paperdoll, Cherie, pull tab to remove dress, bra, etc., 1940s **5.00**

Cigar Label, reclining nude, stock, red, gold, and green, 8 x 5³/₄", $30.00.

Tijuana Bible, 8 pager, *She Saw The Director With The Office Boy's Help,* yellow-and-black covers, 4³/₈ x 3", $10.00.

Photograph, nude female stripper, James J Kriegsmann photographer, 9¹/₄ x 7¹/₂" **20.00**
Playing Cards, Ladies Home Companion, male nudes, sepia, orig box, unopened, 1972 . . . .   **10.00**
Program, Olsen and Johnson's New Hellzapoppin, burlesque, 1939 . . . .   **10.00**
Pulp Magazine
  Bedtime Stories, Winter, Vol 1, #1, 1932, 72 pgs, subtitled "For Grownups Only," 7 x 10" **25.00**
  Men Call Her Tramp, December, 1950, 128 pgs **8.00**
  Real Bedtime Tales, Vol 1, #1, September, 1934, 6³/₄ x 10" **50.00**
  Real Telling Tales, Vol 1, #1, September, 1934, 64 pgs, 6³/₄ x 10" . .   **60.00**
  Spicy Adventure Stories, Vol 1, #1, June, 1935, Culture Publications, 128 pgs, 7 x 10" **55.00**
  Spicy Detective Stories, Vol 1, #1, January, 1935, Culture Publications, 128 pgs, 7 x 10" **55.00**
Stereoview
  Female nude, bare breasted **45.00**
  Man hugging woman, nude, printed in France, divided back **15.00**
  Peek–a–Boo, 1820s **15.00**
Tobacco Card, risque woman on couch, G & A, Navy Long Cut, 3³/₄ x 2¹/₄" **4.00**

FAMILY LETTERS

History: It is hard for a person living in the 1990s to remember when hand written and typed letters were the principal form of communication. Nowadays, it is so easy to pick up the telephone in lieu of writing. Further, the electronic revolution has produced computer bulletin boards and E–mail, all of which leave no printed records behind.

A surprisingly large number of personal letters were saved. First, they chronicled a personal relationship or a family's history. Second, readers frequently enjoyed reading them over and over again and sharing them with other family members and friends. Third, in some cases, they were the last communication received from an individual who died far from home.

The value key to any family letter or group of letters is content. Letters that discuss highly personal family matters tend to have little value unless associated with a prominent individual. Letters that offer opinions on the happenings of the day, e.g., politics or foreign policy, are highly prized.

Military letters, whether from the Civil War or World War II, that discuss only day to day life are worth less than letters which comment on specific battles, offer opinions about commanders and strategy, and discuss equipment. Given the censorship practiced by the military during the twentieth century, high content military letters are scarce.

When examining a collection of family letters, check the stationery, envelope, and postmark cancellation. Some letterheads are highly collectible. Envelopes, especially those that match the stationery and feature an engraving, are sought by specialized collectors. A postmark from a discontinued post office is a treasure to a postmark collector. Forget the stamps. The chances of them having value are extremely remote.

A surprisingly large number of family letters contain drawings and other miscellaneous notations. Depending on quality, they add value. Always open and examine each letter in a large group. You never know if something additional (and collectible) was inserted.

Discretion is important. When a letter is extremely personal, i.e., expressing sentiments that should not be shared with the general public, destroy it. Little is served by putting the letter into the marketplace.

1833, February 4, Benjamin Callum to Joseph Farley, Brookline, NH, notifying him of son's death **18.00**
1853, January 27, William Leahluz to his uncle, blue lined paper, 3 pgs **50.00**
1862
  January 27, Edward M Aldrich, Hatteras Inlet, RI, 5th Reg, Co D, Burnside Expedition, patriotic letterhead with red, white, and blue design, pencil script, describes conditions, trial, and death of soldier, 3¹/₂ pgs, 4 x 5" **100.00**
  April 1, Lt Stephen Colby, certifying typhoid death of Civil War soldier Thomas Dunlap, 15th, NH, 1 pg . . .   **35.00**
  May 12, Civil War soldier writes to

wife from camp near West Point, VA, details of life, injury, and Union Army prisoners, 1½ pgs **75.00**

September 20, Civil War, Concord, NH, O H Marston to wife Sarah, one page, ink, emb paper **35.00**

1863, October 23, from soldier in Union Hospital at Camp Dennison, OH, describes condition, discourse on friendship and love **40.00**

1864

February 9, Alexander Dimitry to Capt John N Egan, Confederate States of America Post Office Dept letterhead, regretting seeing him at his office, 1¼ pgs **115.00**

August 27, Chaplin John W Adams, 2nd HN Vols, from Chesapeake Hospital, to colonel, describes the sick, wounded, and those coming, sends regrets over colonel's malaria, urging him to recover to lead Old 2nd to victory. **75.00**

1880, Adjutant General's Office, Washington, DC, discharge of war clerk having been revoked, sgd by Chief Clerk, 1 pg **15.00**

1883, W H Barger, Dry Goods, Clothing, Boots & Shoes letterhead, describes shipping and problems in sale, 1 pg, 8 x 10″ **15.00**

1884, War Dept, Washington, to Major Gibson, Fort Leavenworth, KS, concerns discharging a messenger for Major H G Thomas, sgd by Gibson, 2 pgs, 8 x 10″ **25.00**

1885, mining camp, Nicolia, ID Territory, payment on account and asks for two nude pictures, prices of mirrors, and to send one barrel of whiskey, 1 pg, 5 x 8″ **40.00**

1897, Buffalo, WY, to a man, congratulates him for being named Supt of the Low Boy Mine, 3 pgs **20.00**

1898

A H Mayne, Mining Broker, to a man, Ames, CO, complaining Golden Gate Mill is not running to capacity, will stay a few months but will leave later, 1 pg. **25.00**

Canon City, CO, man to a friend, seeking work and apologizes for many misspellings, 3 pgs and Alfred Packer story, 5 x 8″. **75.00**

Pastor, Seattle, WA, to Northern Pacific RR, bought clergyman's ticket but became sick and could not travel and complains of mistreatment by ticket agent, 2 pgs, 8 x 10″ **25.00**

Spanish American War, May 4, husband writes to wife, 3 pages, red, white, and blue American flag upper left corner **16.50**

1901

May 15, Frank L Baum to Kendall family, sending thanks for gift of flowers, 3 pgs **300.00**

October 12, Carrie M Pierce, Honolulu, HI, to Mrs Piper, 4 pgs **5.00**

1902, from Gold Mine, SD, to a man, asks about taxes on mine claims and kept sober for some time, 1 pg. **20.00**

1905, January 11, sailor writing to brother, two pages. **15.00**

1917, letterhead Willy's Overland Automobile, Marietta Motor Car Company dealership salesman H D Davidson to prospective costumer Mr Rich, good deal on car purchase asking to keep price confidential, 2 pgs **25.00**

1918, salesman to individual, Mr. Thielens, General Sales Manager Studebacker Co, Southbend, IN, see Studebacker wagons at several customers' homes, pasted poster stamp of multicolored Studebaker Surrey, black and white Studebacker letterhead, 1 pg **20.00**

1920, Mr McCormick to friends, inviting them to join in business enterprise, West Continent Oil Corp letterhead, 1 pg and inserts. **15.00**

1921, son to mother regarding need to repay loan, United Motors Club Corp, Winston Salem, NC, printed color automotive scene, 2 pgs **35.00**

1927, Mr Henderson to wife, starts letter with "Dearest Nigger," describing how hard he is working in tobacco company, handwritten, 2 pgs **35.00**

1929, executive Mr Thompson of South Gate Molasses Co, engraved letterhead, to company in Roanoke, VA, information they requested will be delayed **12.00**

1930, Mr Stephenson to Mr Andrews of Roanoke, VA, Ria–Patterson Milling Co, Coffeeville, KS letterhead with multicolored farm scene, quoting product prices **20.00**

1941, Knox Gelatine Co, Johnstown, NY letterhead with black children illus, General Mangager Jim Knox, asking salesmen to set standards high and make quota for April **25.00**

1945, August 9, Herbert Hoover to Stanford University, appreciates friendly greeting, personal stationery, 1 pg. . . . **75.00**

1956, Mrs Charles Dean from paternal grandmother, sorrow over loss of grandson James Dean, envelope postmarked Fairmount, IN **225.00**

FANS

History: Today, people tend to think of fans as fragile, frivolous accessories wielded by women, yet the origin of the fan was no doubt highly practical. Early man may have used it to winnow his grain, shoo flies, and cool his brow. This simple tool eventually became a symbol of power: ancient lore maintains that Emperor Hsien Yan (ca. 2967 B.C.) used fans and the tomb of Egypt's Tutankhamen (1350 B.C.) yielded two ostrich feather fans with gold mounts. Fans also began to assume religious significance and were used to whisk flies from altars. Early Christians recognized the practicality of this and included a flabellum, or fixed fly–whisk, in their early services. Meanwhile, the Chinese and Japanese continued to use fans in their courts, often incorporating materials such as ivory, gold, and jade.

Until the seventh century A.D., fans were non–folding. Then, according to Japanese legend, Emperor Jen–ji noticed the logic of a bat's folded wings and applied his insight to a new fan design. Later, European traders returned from the East with samples of these wonders. By the sixteenth century sophisticated Italian women had appropriated the fan, which soon became *de rigueur* throughout Europe. Now primarily feminine fashion accessories, their styles changed to complement the ever–changing dress styles.

The popularity of fans led to experimentation in their production and merchandising. They also became popular as a way for artists to test their skills—a fan leaf's curved, folding surface offered challenges in perspective.

World War I was the end of slower eras. The 1920s raced at a frantic pace. The modern woman set aside her ubiquitous fan, freeing both her hands to drive her roadster or carry her political banner. Fans became more an advertising tool than a fashion statement.

Fan Terminology:
Brise—fan with no leaf, but made of rigid, overlapping sticks held together at base by a rivet and at the other end by a ribbon.
Cockade—pleated fan opening to form complete circle.
Folding fan—fan with flexible, pleated leaf mounted on sticks
Frontage—shape of folding fans, c1890–1935, with center of leaf longer than guards.
Guard—the outermost sticks, usually the height of the fan.
Leaf or mount—flexible, pleated material which unites the upper parts of a folding fan's sticks.
Loop—often "u" shaped finger holder attached to rivet at base of fan; rare before 1830.
Pique–point—decorative small gold or silver points or pins set flush with surface, sticks, or guards.
Rivet—pin about which sticks of a folding fan pivot.
Sticks—rigid framework of a folding fan.
Studs—exposed end of rivet, sometimes shaped as decorative paste "gem."
Washer—small disk to prevent friction between end of rivet and fan.

References: Nancy Armstrong, *A Collector's History of Fans*, Clarkson N. Potter, 1974; Nancy Armstrong, *Fans: A Collector's Guide*, Souvenir Press, 1984; Anna G. Bennett, *Unfolding Beauty*, Thames and Hudson, 1988; Susan Mayor, *A Collector's Guide to Fans*, Wellfleet Books, 1990; McIver Percival, *The Fan Book*, T. Fisher Unwin Ltd., London, 1920; G. W. Woolliscroft Rhead, *The History of the Fan*, Kegan Paul, Trench, Trubner & Co., London, 1910.

Collectors' Club: FANA (Fan Association of North America), 505 Peachtree Road, Orlando, FL 32804.

Advertising
Borden's Condensed Milk Co, diecut, cardboard, full color illus, wood handle, c1910 . . . . **35.00**
Buster Brown, Brown's 5–Star Shoes, cardboard, Buster Brown and Tige illus, wood handle, c1910, 7 x 8" . . **35.00**
Chevrolet, "It's Wise To Choose A Six," cardboard, diecut, full color illus of woman driving car, c1930 . . **30.00**
Clark's Pharmacy, Cillicothe, MO, Nature's Remedy and Tums, little boy holding lollipop, full color **25.00**
Coca–Cola, cardboard, hand holding bottle, logo on back, wood handle, 1956, 12 x 8" **28.00**
Croft Ale **30.00**
Dr Pepper, cardboard, six pack of soda illus, red and green **50.00**
Emerson's Drugs, girl playing tennis, soda fountain giveaway **35.00**
Gold Dust & Fairy Soap, cardboard,

Anna Held Cigars, adv., folding, $85.00.

Gold Dust twins overlooking 1904 World's Fair, 12 x 8" **70.00**

Hillcrest Dress Shop, flapper, 1925, 11" **15.00**

Hormel Dairy Brand Ham, diecut, farm girl illus **25.00**

J J Evans Mfg, San Francisco, CA, hand shape, 3½ x 2" **2.00**

Levering Coffee **12.00**

Lucky Strike Cigarettes, paper, leaf shape, Frank Sinatra illus, 1940s . . .   **38.00**

Maple Leaf Rubbers Wpg, Victorian woman illus **15.00**

Millar's Coffee, full color Indian illus   **25.00**

Moxie
Doctor with girl on knee sitting on Moxie box, full color, 1924, 7 x 8"   **40.00**
Girl and soda jerk **38.00**
Laura Walker illus, full color, 1920s, 6 x 8" **30.00**
Muriel Ostriche illus, full color, 1916, 6 x 8" **50.00**

Pepsi–Cola, Pepsi Pete, 1930s **75.00**

Piedmont Cigarettes, cardboard, wood handle, 7 x 10½" **325.00**

Putnam Dye, cardboard, color litho of General Putnam. **20.00**

Red Dot Cigars, cardboard **65.00**

Character and Personalities
Dionne quintuplets, chromolithograph handscreen, titled "School Days," lists important events of their early lives, Palmerton Sanitary Dairy adv on reverse, 1940, 14¾" h **28.00**
Smokey Bear, cardboard, full color, Smokey and other animals in forest scene, wood handle, 1950s, 7 x 8"   **15.00**

Folding
1760, paper with water color scene of man on horseback and two other men, twenty wood sticks, subtle flo-

Gilmore's Funeral Directors, adv., 9 x 13½", 1940s, $22.00.

ral motif painted on top half of guard, 18" w opened **175.00**

1854–1865, double paper, litho, hand colored harem scene, reverse with central cartouche of two women wearing 18th C rural costume, man bearing basket of flowers, fourteen bone sticks with pierced dec with silver foil, mirror on right guard, orig box, 19" w opened **125.00**

Mid 19th C, double paper, pastoral scene of shepherds and shepherdess, reverse with three women and one man on rural estate scene, eighteen mother–of–pearl sticks, center sticks with relief carved bucolic scene, red paste stud, 19¾" w opened. **200.00**

1860, double paper, litho, gouache painted and gilded scene of couples walking, eating, and watching puppet show on castle grounds, reverse with three medallions of Oriental scenes, ornate stylized gold floral and architectural motifs on deep blue shiny paper, fourteen japanned papier mâché sticks with oil paint, center sticks with three women and two men with slightly raised faces, gilt stud, orig box, 20½" w opened   **140.00**

Political
Franklin Roosevelt, cardboard, litho bust illus, Boyd School, Washington, DC adv on reverse, 7½ x 10½"   **20.00**
For The Cause Of Liberty, heart shape, Washington, Lincoln, and Wilson photos, red, white, and blue **30.00**
Wilson and Hughes, jugate photos and eagle, Woman's Sufferage endorsement on reverse, 1916 . . . .   **40.00**
Social Cause, Prohibition Ledger of the Woman's Temperance Union, state of New York, 1930, chromolithograph handscreen, suburban children and German shepherd standing on front lawn, 12" h **28.00**

Souvenir
Booker T Washington, salutes Washington for starting Tuskegee Institute and for being elected to the Hall of Fame, New York University in 1945, Smith's Grocery adv on reverse, 10" w opened **40.00**
Col Charles A Lindbergh, 1927, cardboard handscreen, photos of Lindbergh and *Spirit of St Louis*, commemorative poem, and hardware store adv, 11¼" h, 8" w **65.00**
Columbian Expo, Chicago, 1893, angelic herald wrapped in red and white striped skirt and starred blue sash standing on pedestal, exhibit

building background, lagoons and other buildings scene on both sides, sixteen wood sticks, 26" w opened **130.00**
Philadelphia Centennial, 1876, eagle with US flag and 1776–1876, reverse of Independence Hall, stamped "Registered June 8, 1875," thirty wood sticks, 20" w opened . . **150.00**
Presidents of the United States from Washington to Coolidge, 1925, cardboard handscreen, sepia tone photos, presidents term around photo of US Capitol, National Bank adv on reverse, 10⁹/₁₆" h **40.00**
Valentine, paper, folding, girl illus, "With All My Love, My Valentine," 8" **20.00**
World War II, 1944, blonde WAC, Pledge of Allegiance printed below, pull out sides with tank and battleship, reverse commemorates 20th anniversary of a dance school, 10½" w opened **15.00**

GAMES

History: Mass production of board games did not take place until after the Civil War. Firms like McLoughlin Brothers, Milton Bradley, and Selchow and Righter were active in the 1860s, followed by Parker Brothers in 1883. Parker Brothers bought out the rights to the W. & S. B. Ives Co., which had produced some very early games in the 1840s, including the "first" American board game, The Mansion of Happiness. All except McLoughlin Brothers are giants in the game industry today.

McLoughlin Brother's games are a challenge to find. Not only does the company no longer exist (Milton Bradley bought them out in 1920), but the lithography on their games was the best of its era. Most board games are collected because of the bright, colorful lithography on their box covers. In addition to spectacular covers, the large McLoughlin games often had lead playing pieces and fancy block spinners, thus making them even more desirable.

Before the advent of television, the board game was a staple of home evening entertainment. Parker Brothers issued its first monopoly game in 1933. Many board games from the 1930s and 40s focused on radio personalities, e.g., Fibber McGee or The Quiz Kids.

In the late 1940s, television became popular. The game industry responded. The Golden Age of the TV board game was between 1955 and 1968. Movies, e.g., James Bond, also lead to the creation of games, but never to the extent of the television programs. Principal post–1945 game manufacturers include Milton Bradley, Hasbro,

Ideal, Lowell, Parker Brothers, Remco, Selchow & Righter, Transogram, and Whitman.

Common games like Anagrams, Authors, Jackstraws, Lotto, Tiddledy Winks, and Peter Coddles do not command high prices, nor do the games of Flinch, Pit, and Rook, which still are being produced. Games, with the exception of those just stated, generally are rising in price. However, it is worth noting that certain games dealing with good graphics on popular subject matter, e.g. trains, planes, baseball, Christmas and others, often bring higher prices because they are also sought by collectors in those particular fields.

Condition is everything when buying. Do not buy games that have been taped or that have price tags stickered on the face of their covers. Also, beware of buying games at outdoor flea markets where weather elements can cause fading and warping.

References: Avedon and Sutton–Smith, *The Study of Games*, Wiley & Son, 1971; R. C. Bell, *The Board Game Book*, The Knapp Press, 1979; Lee Dennis, *Warman's Antique American Games, 1840–1940*, Wallace–Homestead, 1991; Walter Gibson, *Family Games America Plays*, Doubleday, 1970; Caroline Goodfellow, *A Collector's Guide To Games and Puzzles*, The Apple Press, 1991; Jefferson Graham, *Come on Down!!!, The TV Game Show Book*, Abbeville Press, 1988; Brian Love, *Great Board Games, 1895–1935*, Macmillan Publishing, 1979; Brian Love, *Play The Game: Over 40 Games From The Golden Age Of Board Games*, Reed Books, 1978; Rick Polizzi and Fred Schaefer, *Spin Again: Board Games from the Fifties and Sixties*, Chronicle Books, 1991; Harry L. Rinker, *Collector's Guide To Toys, Games, and Puzzles*, Wallace–Homestead, 1991; Bruce Whitehill, *Games: American Boxed Games and Their Makers, 1822–1992*, Wallace–Homestead, 1992.

Collectors' Club: American Game Collectors Association, 49 Brooks Avenue, Lewiston, ME 04240.

Museum: Washington Dolls' House and Toy Museum, Washington, D.C.

Abbott & Costello Who's On First?, Selchow & Righter, 1978 . . . . **10.00**
Across The Channel, Wolverine Supply, 1926 . . . . **85.00**
Admiral Byrd's South Pole Game, Merchandisers, Inc, 1939 . . . . **120.00**
Adventure In Science, Jacmar Mfg Co, 1950 . . . . **30.00**
Air Empire, Avalon Hill, 1961 . . . . **25.00**
Alee–Oop, Royal Toy Co, 1937 . . . . **50.00**
Alien, Kenner, 1979 . . . . **45.00**
All Star Baseball, 1962 . . . . **45.00**

American Boy Game, Milton Bradley, c1920 .... **125.00**

Animal Crackers, Milton Bradley, c1970 **7.00**

Around The World In 80 Days Game, Transogram, 1957 .... **40.00**

Babe Ruth's Baseball Game, Milton Bradley, 1926 .... **500.00**

Balloonio, Frederick H Beach, Beachcraft, 1937 .... **40.00**

Banana Tree, Marx, 1977 .... **15.00**

Basilinda, E I Horsman, 1890 .... **175.00**

Bat Masterson, Lowell, 1958 .... **75.00**

Battle Game, Parker Brothers, c1890 ... **200.00**

Beat Inflation, Avalon Hill, 1961 .... **25.00**

Beetle Bailey, 1963 .... **30.00**

Behind The 8 Ball Game, Selchow & Righter, 1969 .... **30.00**

Big Apple, Rosebud Art Co, Inc, 1938 ... **50.00**

Billionaire, Parker Brothers, 1973 ...... **20.00**

Bingo, Rosebud Art Co, Inc, c1925 ..... **25.00**

Black Beauty, Stoll & Edwards, 1921 ... **65.00**

Blackout, Milton Bradley, 1939 .... **75.00**

Blockade, Corey Games, 1941 .... **60.00**

Blow Football Game, 1912 .... **50.00**

Bobbsey Twins, Milton Bradley, 1957 .. **45.00**

Bottoms Up, The Embossing Co, 1934 .. **35.00**

Bradley's Telegraph Game, Milton Bradley, c1900 .... **145.00**

Break The Bank, Bettye–B Co, 1955 .... **60.00**

Bringing Up Father, Embee Distributing, 1920 .... **75.00**

Brownie Horseshoe Game, M H Miller Co, c1900 .... **50.00**

Buffalo Hunt Game, 1914 .... **100.00**

Bulls and Bears, Parker Brothers, 1936 .. **125.00**

Cabbage Patch Kids, Parker Brothers, 1984 .... **10.00**

Cabin Boy, Milton Bradley, 1910 ...... **100.00**

Call My Bluff, Milton Bradley, 1965 .... **20.00**

Camelot, Parker Brothers, 1930 .... **45.00**

Captain Caveman And The Teen Angels, Milton Bradley, 1981 .... **10.00**

Capture The Fort, Valley Novelty Works, c1914 .... **75.00**

Cargoes, Selchow & Righter, 1934 ..... **75.00**

Cats & Mice, Cantaloupe, Lost Diamond Games, McLoughlin Brothers **350.00**

Centipede, Milton Bradley, 1983 ...... **10.00**

Chasing Villa, Smith, Kline & French, 1920 .... **110.00**

Chutes & Ladders, Milton Bradley, 1956 **15.00**

Clue, Parker Brothers, 1986 .... **50.00**

Coastal Defense Game, Baldwin Mfg Co **85.00**

Combat, Ideal, 1963 .... **60.00**

Construction Game, Wilder Mfg Co, 1925 .... **100.00**

Country Farm Game, Parker Brothers ... **75.00**

Crow Hunt, Parker Brothers, c1904 .... **60.00**

Curly Locks Game, 1910 .... **100.00**

Dark Shadows Game, Whitman, 1968 .. **65.00**

Davy Crockett Adventure Game, Gardner, 1956 .... **75.00**

Dealer's Choice, Parker Brothers, 1972 **22.00**

Deputy Dawg TV Lotto, 1961 .... **35.00**

Diamond Heart, McLoughlin Brothers, 1902 .... **185.00**

Diplomacy, Avalon Hill, 1976 .... **25.00**

Discretion, Volume Sprayer Mfg Co, 1942 .... **45.00**

Disney Queen Of Hearts, Golden **15.00**

Dispatcher, Avalon Hill, 1958 .... **35.00**

Diver Dan, Milton Bradley **15.00**

Dog Sweepstakes, Stoll & Eisen, 1935 .. **75.00**

Donald Duck's Own Game, Walt Disney, c1930 .... **40.00**

Donkey Party Game, Saalfield Publishing, 1950 .... **25.00**

Dracula Mystery Game, Hasbro, c1960 **75.00**

Dragnet, Transogram, 1955 .... **60.00**

Dreamland Wonder Resort Game, Parker Brothers, 1914 .... **250.00**

Drummer Boy Game, 1914 .... **100.00**

Eagle Bombsight, Toy Creations, c1940 **40.00**

Election, Fireside Game Co, 1896 ...... **35.00**

Electro Gameset, Knapp Electric & Novelty Co, 1930 .... **45.00**

Emenee Chocolate Factory, 1966 ...... **10.00**

Emily Post Popularity Game, Selchow & Righter, 1970 .... **20.00**

Escape From The Death Star, Parker Brothers, 1977 .... **35.00**

Ethan Allen's All–Star Baseball, Cadaco Ltd, 1941 .... **50.00**

Fairyland Game, Milton Bradley, c1880 **95.00**

Family Affair, Whitman, 1967 .... **40.00**

Famous Authors, Parker Brothers, 1943 **15.00**

Fangface, Parker Brothers, 1979 .... **8.00**

Fantastic Voyage Game, Milton Bradley, 1968 .... **25.00**

Fat Albert, Milton Bradley, 1973 .... **25.00**

Felix The Cat Dandy Candy Game, 1957 **15.00**

Boxed, Jungle Hunt, Rosebud Art Co., 56 pieces, 15¹⁄₂ x 13 x 1¹⁄₂″, 1940s, $15.00.

Fig Mill, Willis G Young, 1916 . . . . **40.00**

Finance And Fortune, Parker Brothers, 1936 . . . . **50.00**

Fire Department, Milton Bradley, c1930 **80.00**

Fishbait, Ideal, 1965 . . . . **60.00**

Flapper Fortunes, The Embossing Co, 1929 . . . . **30.00**

Flash, J Pressman & Co, c1940 . . . . **40.00**

Flight To Paris, Milton Bradley, 1927 . . . **250.00**

Flintstone's Hoppy The Hopperoo Game, Transogram, 1964 . . . . **75.00**

Flip It, Deluxe Game Corp, 1940 . . . . . . **30.00**

Floating Satellite Target Game **25.00**

Flying Nun Game, Milton Bradley, 1968 **30.00**

Fooinstein, Coleco **25.00**

Formula One Car Race Game, Parker Brothers, 1968. . . . . **65.00**

Fortune Telling & Baseball Game, 1889 **140.00**

Fox and Geese, McLoughlin Brothers, 1903 . . . . **350.00**

Fox Hunt, E S Lowe, Inc, c1930. . . . . **35.00**

Frenzy **35.00**

Frog He Would A Wooing Go, Mc-Loughlin Brothers, 1898 . . . . **750.00**

F–Troop, Ideal, 1965 . . . . **75.00**

Fugitive, Ideal, 1966 . . . . **150.00**

Fu Manchu's Hidden Hoard, Ideal, 1967 **55.00**

Funky Phantom Game, Milton Bradley, 1971 . . . . **15.00**

Gang Busters Game, Lynco, 1938. . . . . . **250.00**

Garfield, Parker Brothers, 1981. . . . . **6.00**

Garrison's Gorillas, Ideal, 1967 . . . . **75.00**

General Headquarters, All–Fair, c1940 **75.00**

Gentle Ben Animal Hunt Game, Mattel, 1967 . . . . **25.00**

George of the Jungle Game, Parker Brothers, 1968. . . . . **65.00**

Get The Balls Baseball Game, 1930 . . . . **30.00**

Ghosts, Milton Bradley, 1985 . . . . **6.00**

Gilligan's Island, T Cohn Inc, 1965. . . . . **200.00**

Go Bang, J H Singer, c1898. . . . . **60.00**

Go To The Head Of The Class, Milton Bradley, 1938 . . . . **50.00**

Godfather, Family Games, 1971. . . . . . . **10.00**

Going To The Fire Game, 1914. . . . . **150.00**

Gold Hunters, Parker Brothers, c1900 . . **175.00**

Gomer Pyle Game, Transogram, c1960 **60.00**

Good Old Aunt, McLoughlin Brothers, 1892 . . . . **250.00**

Good Things to Eat Lotto, Sam'l Gabriel Sons & Co, c1940 . . . . **25.00**

Goofy's Mad Maze, Whitman, c1970. . . **10.00**

Goosy Goosy Gander, McLoughlin Brothers, 1896. . . . . **500.00**

Great Grape Ape Game, Milton Bradley, 1975 . . . . **25.00**

Greyhound Racing Game, Rex Manufacturing, 1938. **25.00**

Grizzly Adams Game, House of Games, 1978 . . . . **50.00**

Gulf Strike, 1983 . . . . **25.00**

Gumby **15.00**

Gunsmoke Game, Lowell, c1950. . . . . . **65.00**

Gym Horseshoes, Wolverine Supply & Mfg Co, 1930. . . . . **45.00**

Hair Bear Bunch, Milton Bradley **10.00**

Hangman, Milton Bradley, 1976 . . . . . . **8.00**

Happy Days, Parker Brothers, 1976 . . . . **25.00**

Hardy Boys Mystery Game, Milton Bradley, 1968 . . . . **25.00**

Hare and Hounds, Selchow & Righter, 1890 . . . . **250.00**

Hashimoto, Transogram, 1963 . . . . **45.00**

Haunted Mansion, Lakeside, c1970 . . . . **50.00**

Hawaii Five–O, Remco **25.00**

Hector Heathcote, Transogram, 1963 . . **85.00**

Hel–Lo Telephone Game, J C Singer, 1898 . . . . **150.00**

Hi–Ho! Cherry–O, Whitman, 1975 . . . . **10.00**

Hickety Pickety, Parker Brothers, 1924 **75.00**

Hidden Authors, Clark & Sowdon. **20.00**

Hide N Seek, Ideal, 1967 . . . . **15.00**

Hippety Hop, Corey Games, c1947 . . . . **40.00**

Hit The Beach, Milton Bradley, 1965 . . . **60.00**

Hock Shop. **20.00**

Hocus Pocus, Transogram, c1960 . . . . . **45.00**

Hold That Tiger, J Pressman & Co **85.00**

Hold Your Horses, Klauber Novelty, c1930 . . . . **20.00**

Hollywood Squares, Ideal, 1974. . . . . . . **10.00**

Home Game, Pressman, c1950 . . . . **50.00**

Honeymooners Game, TSR, 1986 . . . . . **12.00**

Hornet, Samuel Lowe Co, 1941 . . . . **45.00**

Hot Spot, Parker Brothers, 1961 . . . . **20.00**

House Party, Whitman, 1968 . . . . **15.00**

How To Succeed In Business Without Really Trying, Milton Bradley, 1963 . . **15.00**

Huckleberry Hound, Milton Bradley, 1981 . . . . **10.00**

Non-Boxed, American Football Game, Intercollegiate Football, Inc., 9¹⁄₈ x 9¹⁄₄", copyright 1935, $35.00.

Hullabaloo, Remco, 1965 . . . .   **85.00**
Humpty Dumpty Game, Lowell, c1950   **10.00**
Hunting The Rabbit, Clark & Sowdon,
  c1895 . . . .   **115.00**
I Dream Of Jeannie Game, Milton Brad-
  ley, 1965 . . . .   **55.00**
I'm George Gobel, And Here's The
  Game, Schaper, 1955 . . . .   **60.00**
Improved Geographical Game, Parker
  Brothers, 1890s **100.00**
Incredible Hulk Smash Up Action Game,
  Ideal **15.00**
Indiana Jones Raiders Of The Lost Ark,
  Kenner, 1981 . . . .   **35.00**
International Yacht Race, McLoughlin
  Brothers **175.00**
Ipcress File, Milton Bradley, 1966 . . . . . .   **70.00**
Jack and Jill, Milton Bradley, 1909 . . . . .   **75.00**
Jack And The Beanstalk, National
  Games, Inc **45.00**
Jack The Ripper **45.00**
James Bond 007 Goldfinger Game, Mil-
  ton Bradley, 1966 . . . .   **85.00**
Jan Murray's Charge Account **40.00**
Jeane Dixon's Game Of Destiny, Milton
  Bradley, 1968 . . . .   **12.00**
Jeopardy, Milton Bradley, 1964 . . . .   **15.00**
Jerome Park Steeple Chase, McLoughlin
  Bros **175.00**
Jetsons Fun Pad Game, Milton Bradley,
  1963 . . . .   **75.00**
John Drake Secret Agent, Milton Bradley,
  1966 . . . .   **45.00**
Johnny Get Your Gun, Parker Brothers,
  1928 . . . .   **75.00**
Jolly Pirates, Russell Mfg Co, 1938 . . . . .   **35.00**
Jonny Quest Game, Transogram, 1964 . .   **100.00**
Jumbo Jet, Jumbo, 1963 . . . .   **10.00**
Jungle Hunt, Rosebud Art Co Inc, c1940   **50.00**
Junior Bingo–Matic, Transogram, 1968   **10.00**
Junior Executive, Whitman, 1963 . . . . . .   **15.00**
Justice, Lowell, 1954 . . . .   **45.00**
Kar–Zoom, Whitman, 1964 . . . .   **20.00**
Kentucky Jones, T Cohn Inc, 1964 . . . . .   **40.00**
King Kong Game, Ideal, 1966 . . . .   **15.00**
Kings, Akro Agate Co, 1931 . . . .   **95.00**
Ko–Ko The Clown, All–Fair, 1940 . . . . .   **30.00**
Kukla & Ollie, Parker Brothers, 1962 . .   **45.00**
Land And Sea War Games, Samuel Lowe
  Co, 1941 . . . .   **65.00**
Laramie, Lowell, 1960 . . . .   **75.00**
Last Straw, Schaper, 1966 . . . .   **10.00**
Leap Frog Game, McLoughlin Brothers,
  1900 . . . .   **275.00**
Leave It To Beaver Ambush Game, 1959   **65.00**
Lee At Havana, Chaffee & Selchow,
  1899 . . . .   **90.00**
Legend Of The Lone Ranger **10.00**
Letters, E I Horsman, 1878 . . . .   **45.00**
Library Of Games, American Toy Works,
  1938 . . . .   **25.00**

Life Of The Party, Rosebud Art Co, Inc,
  c1940 . . . .   **50.00**
Linus the Lionhearted Uproarious Game,
  Transogram, 1965 . . . .   **85.00**
Little Bo–Beep Game, 1914 . . . .   **100.00**
Little Colonel, Selchow & Righter, c1936   **100.00**
Little House On The Prairie, 1978 . . . . . .   **25.00**
Little Nemo Game, 1914 . . . .   **100.00**
Little Orphan Annie Game, Milton Brad-
  ley, 1927 . . . .   **250.00**
Looney Tunes Game, Milton Bradley,
  1968 . . . .   **75.00**
Los Angeles Dodgers Baseball Game,
  Ed–U–Cards Mfg Co, 1964 . . . .   **50.00**
Lost In Space Game, Milton Bradley,
  1965 . . . .   **75.00**
Lucky Break, Gabriel, 1975 . . . .   **20.00**
MacDonald's Game, Milton Bradley,
  1975 . . . .   **20.00**
Macy's Pirate Treasure Hunt, Einson–
  Freeman, 1942 . . . .   **35.00**
Mad Magazine Game, Parker Brothers,
  1979 . . . .   **25.00**
Magnet Jack Straws, E I Horsman, 1891   **45.00**
Magnificent Race, Parker Brothers,
  c1970 . . . .   **6.00**
Major League Baseball, Cadaco, 1965 . .   **20.00**
Man Hunt, Parker Brothers, 1937 . . . . . .   **125.00**
Mansion of Happiness, D P Ives & Co,
  1864 . . . .   **300.00**
Marble Head, Milton Bradley **10.00**
Mary Hartman Mary Hartman, Reiss
  Games, c1976 . . . .   **35.00**
Mary Poppins Carousel Game, Parker
  Brothers, 1964 . . . .   **25.00**
Match 'em, All–Fair, 1926 . . . .   **20.00**
McHale's Navy Game, Transogram,
  1962 . . . .   **50.00**
Meet the Missus, Fitzpatrick Bros, paper
  gameboard, cards, orig envelope **15.00**
Melvin The Moon Man, Remco, c1960   **85.00**
Mental Whoopee, Simon & Schuster,
  1936 . . . .   **15.00**
Merry Milkman, Hasbro, 1955 . . . .   **120.00**
Mickey Mantle's Big League Baseball,
  Gardner, c1955 . . . .   **100.00**
Mickey Mouse, Parker Brothers, 1976 . .   **10.00**
Mid Life Crisis, Gameworks Inc, 1982 . .   **7.00**
Mighty Hercules Game, Hasbro, 1963 . .   **100.00**
Milton The Monster, Milton Bradley,
  1966 . . . .   **45.00**
Mind Over Matter, Transogram, 1968 . .   **15.00**
Miss Muffet Game, 1914 . . . .   **100.00**
Mission Impossible, Ideal, 1967 . . . .   **85.00**
Mister Ed Game, Parker Brothers, 1962   **50.00**
Modern Game Assortment, J Pressman,
  c1930 . . . .   **40.00**
Monkees Game, Transogram, 1968 . . . .   **50.00**
Monopoly, Parker Brothers, 1935 . . . . . .   **75.00**
Monster Game, Ideal, 1977 . . . .   **75.00**
Moon Mullins, Milton Bradley, 1927 . . .   **65.00**

Mork and Mindy, Milton Bradley, 1978	**10.00**
Mother Hubbard Game, 1914	**100.00**
Movie Inn, Willis G Young, 1917	**75.00**
Mr. Bug Goes To Town, Milton Bradley, 1955	**125.00**
Mr. Novak, Transogram	**25.00**
Mr. Ree, Selchow & Righter, 1957	**45.00**
Muppet Show, Parker Brothers, 1977 ...	**15.00**
My Fair Lady, Standard Toycraft, Inc, 1962	**40.00**
Mystery Date, Milton Bradley, 1966....	**60.00**
Mystic Skull The Game Of Voodoo, Ideal, 1965	**50.00**
Name That Tune, Milton Bradley, 1959	**30.00**
National Derby Horse Race, Whitman, 1938	**35.00**
Navigator, Whitman, 1938..........	**75.00**
Nebula, Nebula Inc, 1976...........	**6.00**
Nellie Bly, J H Singer, c1898.........	**90.00**
New Adventures of Pinocchio, Lowell, 1961	**45.00**
New Frontier, Colorful Products, Inc, 1962	**50.00**
Newlywed Game 1st Edition, Hasbro, 1967	**14.00**
Nine Men Morris, Milton Bradley, c1930	**45.00**
North Pole Game, Milton Bradley, 1907	**75.00**
Number Please TV Quiz, Parker Brothers, 1961	**25.00**
Numble, Selchow & Righter, 1968	**20.00**
Object Lotto, Samuel Gabriel Sons & Co, c1940	**25.00**
Ocean To Ocean Flight Game, Wilder Mfg Co, 1927...................	**95.00**
Off To See The Wizard, 1968	**15.00**
Oh Magoo Game	**20.00**
Old Mother Goose, Chaffee & Selchow, c1898	**175.00**
Oldtimers, Frederick H Beach, Beachcraft, 1940.................	**20.00**
One Two Button Your Shoe, Master Toy Co, c1940	**25.00**
On Guard, Parker Brothers, 1967	**10.00**
Opportunity Hour, American Toy Works, c1940	**35.00**
Orbit, Parker Brothers, 1959	**55.00**
Ouija, William Fuld, 1920	**25.00**
Our Union, Fireside Game Co, 1896 ...	**40.00**
Outdoor Survival, Avalon Hill, 1972 ...	**10.00**
Pac Man, Milton Bradley, 1980	**6.00**
Panama Canal G, Parker Brothers, c1910	**225.00**
Parcheesi, H B Chaffee, c1880	**150.00**
Park And Shop Game, Milton Bradley, 1960	**35.00**
Partridge Family, Milton Bradley, 1974	**15.00**
Password, Milton Bradley, 1963	**16.00**
Pebbles Flintstone Game, Transogram, 1962	**35.00**
Peg At My Heart, Willis G Young, 1914	**35.00**
Peggy, Parker Brothers, 1923	**55.00**
People Trivia Game, Parker Brothers, 1984	**11.00**

Perry Mason Case Of The Missing Suspect Game, Transogram, 1959	**30.00**
Peter Coddle's Trip To New York, Milton Bradley, 1900s	**15.00**
Peter Pan, Selchow & Righter, 1927	**200.00**
Peter Rabbit Game, Milton Bradley, 1910	**95.00**
Pinafore, Fuller, Upham & Co, 1879....	**75.00**
Pink Panther Game, Warren Paper Products, 1977	**50.00**
Pirate and Traveller, Milton Bradley, 1953	**35.00**
Planet Of The Apes Game, Milton Bradley, 1974	**12.00**
Pony Express, Stoll & Edwards, 1926 ...	**55.00**
Pop Yer Top!, Milton Bradley, 1968	**20.00**
Poppin Hoppies Game, Ideal, 1968	**12.00**
Price Is Right Game, 1958............	**30.00**
Princess In The Tower, Parker Brothers, 1890s.........................	**150.00**
Psychology Of The Hand, Baker & Bennett Co, 1919...................	**30.00**
P T Boat 109 Game, Ideal, 1963	**50.00**
Puss In The Corner, Parker Brothers, 1895	**100.00**
Pyramids, Knapp Electric & Novelty Co, c1930	**20.00**
Race For The Cup Game, 1914........	**100.00**
Radio Amateur Hour Game, Milton Bradley, c1930	**125.00**
Raggedy Ann Game, Milton Bradley, 1974	**15.00**
Rawhide, Lowe, 1959...............	**85.00**
Red Ryder Target Game, Whitman, 1939	**95.00**
Rich Uncle, Parker Brothers, 1946	**50.00**
Ricochet Rabbit Game, Ideal, 1965	**75.00**
Ripley's Believe It Or Not, Milton Bradley, 1984	**90.00**
Rip Van Winkle, Clark & Sowdon, c1890	**125.00**
Riverboat Game, Parker Brothers, c1950	**35.00**
Robin Hood, Harett–Gilmar, Inc, 1955	**50.00**
Roll And Score Poker, Lowe, 1977	**7.00**
Round Up, Milton Bradley	**75.00**
Runaway Sheep, R Bliss Mfg Co, 1892 ..	**275.00**
Sailor Boy Game, 1910..............	**100.00**
Scoop, Parker Brothers, c1950	**20.00**
Scrabble, Selchow & Righter, 1953.....	**12.00**
Scruples, Milton Bradley, 1986........	**10.00**
Seven Seas, Cadaco–Ellis, 1960	**50.00**
Show–Biz, Lowell..................	**65.00**
Silly Carnival, Whitman, 1969	**12.00**
Sinking Of The Titanic, Ideal, 1976.....	**45.00**
Ski–Hi New York To Paris, Cutler & Saleeby, 1927	**200.00**
Skirmish, Milton Bradley, 1975........	**35.00**
Skyscraper, Parker Brothers, 1937	**100.00**
Smurf Game, Milton Bradley, 1984	**7.00**
Snagglepuss Fun At The Picnic Game, Transogram, 1961...............	**60.00**
Snakes In The Grass, Kohner, c1960....	**15.00**
Snow White And The Seven Dwarfs, Milton Bradley, 1938	**75.00**

Snug Harbor, Milton Bradley, c1930 . . .   **85.00**
Solid Gold Music Trivia, Ideal, 1984 . . .   **10.00**
Space Age Game, Parker Brothers, 1953   **75.00**
Spider And Fly Game, Milton Bradley,
          c1925 . . . .   **50.00**
Spin It, Milton Bradley, c1910. . . . .   **25.00**
Spot Cash, Milton Bradley, 1959. . . . . . .   **15.00**
Stagecoach West Game, Transogram,
          1961 . . . .   **100.00**
Star Ride, Einson–Freeman Publishing
          Corp, 1934 . . . .   **25.00**
Star Trek Game, Ideal, c1960 . . . .   **75.00**
Steps Of Toyland, Parker Brothers, 1954   **35.00**
Stock Market, Avalon Hill, 1970. . . . . . .   **12.00**
Stop and Go, All–Fair, 1928 . . . .   **150.00**
Strategic Command, Transogram, c1950   **45.00**
Sunken Treasure, Parker Brothers, 1948   **15.00**
Supercar To The Rescue Game, Milton
          Bradley, 1962 . . . .   **60.00**
Superman Speed Game, Milton Bradley   **50.00**
Swayze Game, Milton Bradley, 1954 . . .   **35.00**
Sword In The Stone Game, Parker Broth-
          ers, c1960 . . . .   **15.00**
Taffy's Party Game, Transogram, c1960   **15.00**
Tarzan To The Rescue, Milton Bradley,
          1976 . . . .   **15.00**
Telegrams, Whitman, 1941. . . . .   **70.00**
Tennessee Tuxedo, Transogram, 1963 . .   **125.00**
Them Bones Game, Mego. **30.00**
This Is Your Life, Lowell, 1954 . . . .   **25.00**
Three   Little   Pigs   Game,   Einson–
          Freeman, 1933 . . . .   **95.00**
Three Men In A Tub, Milton Bradley,
          1935 . . . .   **65.00**
Through The Clouds, Milton Bradley,
          1931 . . . .   **125.00**
Ticker, Glow Products Co, 1929. . . . . . .   **75.00**
Time Machine, American Toy Mfg, 1961   **115.00**
Toboggan   Slide,   Hamilton–Myers,
          c1890 . . . .   **385.00**
Tom & Jerry, Selchow & Righter **30.00**
Top Cop, Cadaco–Ellis, 1961 . . . .   **65.00**
Touchdown, Cadaco Ltd, 1937. . . . .   **110.00**
Tournament, Mayhew & Baker, 1858. . .   **300.00**
Traffic Game, Matchbox, 1968. . . . .   **55.00**
Trailer Trails, Offset Gravure Corp, 1937   **60.00**
Trapped, Bettye–B Co, 1956. . . . .   **75.00**
Trick Track Game, Transogram. **50.00**
Trip To Washington, Milton Bradley,
          1884 . . . .   **75.00**
Trust Me, Parker Brothers, 1981 . . . .   **8.00**
Twilight Zone Game, Ideal, c1960 . . . . .   **75.00**
Uncle Sam's Mail, McLoughlin Brothers,
          1893 . . . .   **350.00**
Underdog, Milton Bradley, 1964 . . . . . .   **150.00**
Vanderbilt Cup Race, Bowers & Hard,
          1906 . . . .   **400.00**
Voice Of The Mummy, Milton Bradley,
          c1960 . . . .   **35.00**
Walking The Tightrope, Milton Bradley,
          c1920 . . . .   **70.00**
Walt Disney's Game Parade, c1930 . . . .   **50.00**

Wanted Dead or Alive, Lowell, 1959 . . .   **75.00**
Watermelon   Patch,   Craig   Hopkins,
          c1940 . . . .   **45.00**
What Shall I Be, Selchow & Righter,
          1966 . . . .   **15.00**
Whattzit?, Milton Bradley, 1987 . . . .   **50.00**
Whippet Race, J Pressman & Co, c1940   **35.00**
Who's On First, Abbott & Costello,
          Selchow & Righter. **25.00**
Winnie The Pooh Game, Parker Broth-
          ers, 1933 . . . .   **125.00**
Yacht Race, Parker Brothers, 1961 . . . . .   **100.00**
Yankee Doodle, Cadaco–Ellis, 1940 . . .   **50.00**
Yogi Bear Break A Plate Game, Transo-
          gram, c1960 . . . .   **80.00**
You Don't Say!, Milton Bradley **15.00**
Yours For A Song, Lowell, 1962 . . . .   **35.00**
Zip Code Game, Lowell, 1964 . . . .   **55.00**
Zoo Hoo, Lubbers & Bell, 1924. . . . .   **75.00**

GREETING CARDS

History: Greeting cards date back to antiquity.
Archaeologists have discovered new year greetings as far back as the sixth century B.C. The
modern greeting card originated in the middle of
the fifteenth century in the Rhine Valley of medieval Germany. Master E. S., unknown except for
his initials, did the woodcut engraving for a hand
colored card. Printed new year greetings gained
in popularity during the seventeenth and eighteenth centuries.

Queen Victoria's interest in holiday and special
occasion cards helped establish the sending of
greeting cards as a regular event. In 1843 Henry
Cole, an Englishman, sent out a Christmas card
designed by John Colcott Horsely. This is the earliest Christmas card known. It was not until the
1870s that Christmas cards achieved widespread
popular usage.

Greeting cards from firms such as De La Rue,
Raphael Tuck & Sons, and Marcus Ward were
heavily exported to the United States at the end of
the nineteenth century. De La Rue was responsible for a major greeting card design advance in
the 1880s—cards having illustrations that
matched the event. Previously cards used generic
floral, fauna, juvenile, and landscape scenes.

Louis Prang, a color lithography printer, was
one of the first American manufacturers of greeting cards. When cheap, shoddy domestic and
foreign imports flooded the market in the 1890s,
Prang quit in disgust.

The post–World War II era witnessed the
growth of a number of card manufacturers who
eventually would dominate the industry. The Hall
Brothers (Joyce C., Rollie, and William), Kansas
City post card distributors and publishers, began
printing "French fold" greeting cards in 1910.
Fred Winslow Rust established Rust Craft Com-

pany. Cincinnati's Gibson Art Co. entered the greeting card field. Arthur D. and Jane Norcross formed a mutual partnership in 1915.

Although greeting cards are collected primarily by event or occasion, a growing number of collectors seek specialized types. Mechanical action greeting cards are extremely popular. Die–cut cards are sold at a slight premium. Licensed character and personality cards are sold largely to crossover collectors.

Holiday and specialized collectors still represent the principal buyers of greeting cards in the 1990s. Greeting card collectors do exist, but are unorganized. Opportunities abound in this category.

References: Ernest Dudley Chase, *The Romance of Greeting Cards*, Rust Craft, 1954; Helaine Fendelman and Jeri Schwartz, *The Official Price Guide to Holiday Collectibles*, House of Collectibles, 1991; Ellen Stern, *The Very Best From Hallmark: Greeting Cards Through The Years*, Harry Abrams, 1988.

Wife's Birthday, printed color cover with Scottie dog, Greetings, Inc., bi-fold, 4¾ x 6", 1948, $7.50.

Birthday
Blondie, full color Dagwood illus, Hallmark, 1939 . . . .   **15.00**
Children illus, 19th C **4.00**
Floral design, blue fringe, c1880 . . . . .   **20.00**
Chanukah, emb paper, gilted dec, box, mid 20th C **10.00**
Christmas
A Merry Christmas and Happy New Year, children playing under Christmas tree, c1870 . . . .   **5.00**
A Merry Christmas To You All, family strolling through snowy woodland, c1880 . . . .   **8.00**
Best Wishes, cherub holding dove, raised message, ribbon on top, c1900 . . . .   **1.50**
Birds and flowers, blue fringed, c1880   **35.00**
Clint Eastwood, 1959 . . . .   **20.00**
Hail, Day of Joy, angel kneeling, dove on finger, L Prang and Co, 1870s . . .   **15.00**
Mechanical, bird and birdhouse, litho, late 19th C **25.00**
Merry Christmas and Happy New Year, children playing in snow, church background, c1860 . . . .   **5.00**
Nativity Scene, fold–out, c1820 . . . . .   **8.00**
Santa Claus, fold–out **12.00**
Victorian, message surrounded by paper lace, c1800 . . . .   **12.00**
Wishing You a Merry Christmas, fireplace scene, cat and kittens looking up chimney, L Prang and Co **25.00**
With a Thousand Good Wishes, May Christmas Bring Happiness and Sweet Content, country church yard

and women wearing colonial dress, c1900 . . . .   **1.50**
With Best Christmas Wishes, girl holding flowers, Raphael Tuck and Sons, late 1800s **15.00**
Easter
Angel, diecut, easel type, Maud Humphrey **95.00**
Birds, Bible verses, late 19th C **4.00**
Floral Cross, German, 19th C **5.00**
Floral, religious, Tuck **15.00**
Girl climbing out of egg shell, fringed, German, 19th C **12.00**
Joyous Easter, angel in oval, daisies and emb decoration, c1910 . . . . . .   **2.00**
Loving Wishes for Easter, cherub on emb ground, crucifix motif, emb flowers on edges, 1890–1900 . . . . .   **3.00**
New Year
Girl holding bird, palm tree, 19th C . .   **5.00**
Here Comes the New Year with Lots of Good Cheer, child with Christmas tree and toys, c1870 . . . .   **15.00**
Wishing You a Happy New Year, girl on front, man on back, fringed, tasseled cord, L Prang and Co, c1884   **25.00**
Thanksgiving
Family seated at table, mid 20th C . . .   **3.00**
Happy Thanksgiving, turkey dec, mid 20th C **5.00**
Turkey, feather tail, 1930s **8.00**

ILLUSTRATORS

History: Modern illustrators trace their origins to medieval manuscript illuminators and the satrical cartoonists of the seventeenth and eighteenth centuries. However, it was the mass market printing revolution of the late nineteenth century that provided the opportunity for the professional illustrator.

Many of the illustrators listed in this category provided illustrations for books. Concentrating solely on this medium, however, ignores the important role their art played in calendars, magazines, prints, games, puzzles, and a host of advertising and promotional products.

Illustrator art breaks down into three major categories: (1) original art, (2) first strike prints sold as art works, and (3) commercially produced art. While the first two categories are limited, the third is not. Often images were produced in the hundreds of thousands and millions.

Magazines, more than any other medium, were responsible for introducing the illustrator to the general public. Norman Rockwell covers for *Boy's Life* and *The Saturday Evening Post* are classics. Magazine covers remain one of the easiest and most inexpensive means of collecting illustrator art.

Throughout much of the twentieth century, the artistic community looked down its nose at the commercial illustrators. A reversal in attitude that began in the 1970s was in full swing by the 1980s. Groups of collectors began to collect the work of their favorite commercial illustrator. They also began biographical research of commercial artists whose principal efforts graced magazine covers, post cards, and lesser known books. Their efforts are reflected in the references listed below.

Illustrator material is hot and promises to get even hotter. Remember, it is craze oriented. An illustrator can be "hot" today and "cool" tomorrow. Individuals such as Maxfield Parrish already have experienced several collecting crazes. Stress displayability when buying any example.

References: General: E. Lee Baumgarten, *Price Guide for Children's & Illustrated Books for the Years 1880–1945: Sorted by Artist*, published by author, 1993; Anne Gilbert, *The Official Identification and Price Guide to American Illustrator Art*, House of Collectibles, 1991.

R. Atkinson Fox: Rita C. Mortenson, *R. Atkinson Fox: His Life and Work, Revised*, L–W Book Sales, 1991; Rita C. Mortenson, *R. Atkinson Fox, Book Two*, L–W Book Sales, 1992.

Harrison Fisher: Joseph Mashburn, *The Super Rare Postcards of Harrison Fisher*, World Comm, 1992.

Kate Greenaway: Ina Taylor, *The Art of Kate Greenaway*, Pelican Publishing, 1991.

Bessie Pease Gutmann: Victor Christie, *Bessie Pease Gutmann: Her Life and Works*, Wallace–Homestead, 1990.

Maud Humphrey: Karen Choppa and Paul Humphrey, *Maud Humphrey: Her Permanent Imprint on American Illustration*, Schiffer Publishing, 1993.

Leyendecker: Denis C. Jackson, *The Price & Identification Guide to J. C. & F. X. Leyendecker, Second Edition*, published by author, 1992.

Rose O'Neill: John Axe, *Kewpies: Dolls and Art of Rose O'Neill and Joseph L. Kallus*, Hobby House Press, 1987; Janet Banneck, *The Antique Postcards of Rose O'Neill*, Greater Chicago Publications, 1992; Lois Holiday Holman, *Rose O'Neill Kewpies and Other Works*, published by author, 1983; Denis C. Jackson, *The Price & Identification Guide to Rose O'Neill*, published by author, 1988.

Maxfield Parrish: Denis C. Jackson, *The Price & Identification Guide to Maxfield Parrish, Eighth Edition*, published by author, 1992; Stephanie Lane, *Maxfield Parrish: A Price Guide*, L–W Book Sales, 1993; William R. Holland and Douglas Congdon–Martin, *The Collectible Maxfield Parrish*, Schiffer Publishing, 1993; Coy Ludwig, *Maxfield Parrish*, Schiffer Publishing, 1973, 1993 reprint; Richard J. Perry, *The Maxfield Parrish Identification & Price Guide*, Starbound Publishing, 1993.

Cole Phillips: Denis C. Jackson, *The Price & Identification Guide to Cole Phillips*, published by author, 1986.

Norman Rockwell: Mary Moline, *Norman Rockwell Collectibles Value Guide, Sixth Edition*, Green Valley World, 1988; Denis C. Jackson, *The Norman Rockwell Identification and Value Guide To: Magazines, Posters, Calendars, Books, Second Edition*, published by author, 1985.

Jessie Wilcox Smith: Edward D. Nudelman, *Jessie Wilcox Smith: A Bibliography*, Pelican Publishing, 1989; Edward D. Nudelman, *Jessie Wilcox Smith: American Illustrator*, Pelican Publishing, 1992.

Alberto Vargas and George Petty: Denis C. Jackson, *The Price & Identification Guide to Alberto Vargas & George Petty, Second Edition*, published by author, 1987.

Periodical: *The Illustrator Collector's News*, PO Box 1958, Sequim, WA 98382.

Collectors' Clubs: R. Atkinson Fox Society, 1511 West 4th Avenue, Hutchinson, KS 67501; Rockwell Society of America, 597 Saw Mill River Road, Ardsley, NY 10502.

Museums: Norman Rockwell Museum, Philadelphia, PA; The Norman Rockwell Museum at Stockbridge, Stockbridge, MA; Society of Illustrators Museum of American Illustration, New York, NY.

Armstrong, Rolf
Calendar
1944, Beauty Parade, six pgs, 9 x
13".......................... **75.00**
1948, Sure Enough, full pad, 16 x
33".......................... **80.00**
1958, So Nice, strawberry blonde
woman wearing pink sunsuit,
"Season's Greetings" pad cover **20.00**
Becker, Charlotte, calendar, 1958,
baby with teddy bear, Everett Ice
Cream Co adv, 26 x 14"......... **45.00**
Bradley, Will
Book, *The Wonderbox Stories,* au-
thor and illus............... **135.00**
Magazine, bound volume, May to
October, 1916, two full page and
two partial page illus, contains
Wonderbox Stories........... **30.00**
Magazine Cover
Inland Printer, Thanksgiving,
1894, black illus on green back-
ground, matted............ **50.00**
St Nicholas, December, 1913, The
Wonderbox story illus........ **15.00**
Brehm, Worth, poster, "We'll Get 'Em
This Afternoon Boy–Don't Worry!,"
old man and boy sitting on log,
DuPont Powder Company adv,
1919, 17 x 25⁵/₈"............... **550.00**
Bull, Charles Livingston, calendar,
1917, two turkeys, Hercules Powder
adv, 12 x 29¹/₄"............... **550.00**
Christy, Earl, post card, University Girl,
Columbia College, Raphael Tuck... **15.00**
Clapsaddle, Ellen H
Calendar, 1902, two fairies, scal-
loped edges, Victorian........ **35.00**
Post Card, Valentine greeting,

"Woman's sphere is in the
Home," girl threading needle.... **50.00**
Colby, V, post card, dogs and cats,
1906...................... **25.00**
Cox, Palmer
Almanac, G Green Woodbury,
Brownies illus, 1890.......... **20.00**
Book
Brownies Around the World, 1894 **60.00**
Brownies At Home, Century Co,
c1893, 144 pgs............. **100.00**
Booklet, 1893, 15 pgs, advertising
upcoming articles for *Ladie's
Home Journal,* 4¹/₂ x 6"........ **10.00**
Card Game, Game of Brownies **15.00**
Children's Book, *Jack the Giant,*
Frank Millers Crown Shoe Dress-
ing, loose cov................ **15.00**
Comic Sheet, 1907.............. **25.00**
Sheet Music, *Dance of the Brownies* **25.00**
DeLand, Eugene, poster, "Before Sun-
set Buy A US Government Bond of
the 2nd Liberty Loan of 1917,"
Statue of Liberty, stars and stripes
background, 20¹/₂ x 31"......... **140.00**
Devorss, calendar, 1938, woman
wearing bathing suit, full pad, 9 x 14" **40.00**
Getty, F E, poster, woman holding rifle,
Remington Arms Company adv,
1901, 10¹/₂ x 16"............... **225.00**
Fangel, Maud
Magazine Cover, *Life,* June 24, 1909 **18.00**
Print, salesman's sample, "All
Tuckered Out," full color, 7¹/₂ x
5³/₄"...................... **15.00**
Fisher, Harrison
Book, *The Fifth String*........... **10.00**
Post Card, "Dumb Luck," woman
and horse.................. **150.00**

**Armstrong, Rolf, sheet music, "I'm For-
ever Thinking of You," sgd., A. J. Stasney
Music Co. Pub., full color litho, 9¹/₄ x
12¹/₄", 1919, $35.00.**

**Fisher, Harrison, magazine, *Saturday Eve-
ning Post,* sepia and black wash cover,
sgd., 44 pages, 11¹/₄ x 14¹/₄", November
27, 1909, $45.00.**

Flagg, James Montgomery
Post Card, Jack Dempsey–Jess Willard fight, 1919 . . . .   **6.00**
Poster
Boys and Girls! You Can Help Your Uncle Sam Win The War, Save Your Quarters, Buy War Savings Stamps, Uncle Sam, boy, and girl illus, 37 x 24½", framed **140.00**
I Want You For The US Army, 27 x 40" **275.00**
Fox, R A, print, Promenade, orig frame   **60.00**
Frost, A B
Calendar, 1901, "Fresh Meat for the Outfit" top illus, bottom illus "Winter Fun on the Farm," 14⅜ x 27⅛" **700.00**
Magazine Tear Sheet, Collier's, August 5, 1905, "Waiting At The Seventh Tee For The Younger Generation" **10.00**
Fuller, Arthur, calendar, 1920, "A Surprise Party," Hercules Powder Co adv, 13 x 30" **125.00**
Greiner, Magnus, post card, "Contemplation," two Dutch children playing house, divided back **15.00**
Humphrey, Maud
Book Illustration, The Three Bears, 1892, 14 x 18", matted **40.00**
Post Card, girl wearing straw hat, bird, 1909 . . . .   **8.00**
Puzzle, Parker Brothers, c1925, 15 pcs **30.00**
Humphrey, Walter Beach, calendar, 1932, "Stowaways," Hercules Powder Co adv, 13 x 30" **175.00**
Kettering, Charles, magazine cover, Time, January 9, 1933 . . . .   **10.00**
Leyendecker, J C
Magazine, cov illus
SEP, August 31, 1907 . . . .   **25.00**
Success, March, 1907 . . . .   **45.00**
Magazine Cover, Success, July, 1906, man and woman in row boat, 10 x 14" **22.50**
Post Card, Chesterfield adv **45.00**
Leyendecker, F X
Book, The City of Delight, Millier, 1908 . . . .   **42.00**
Magazine
Leslie's, September 2, 1915 . . . . .   **35.00**
S.E.P., October 28, 1899 . . . .   **40.00**
Magazine Cover, Life, Birds of a Feather, February 10, 1921 . . . . . .   **35.00**
Magazine Cover
Collier's, July 5, 1902 . . . .   **50.00**
Country Gentleman, November 7, 1914 . . . .   **40.00**
Life, June 2, 1921 . . . .   **65.00**
Saturday Evening Post, April 30, 1910 . . . .   **35.00**

Woman's Home Companion, October, 1918 . . . .   **50.00**
Magazine Tear Sheet, Palmolive adv, Saturday Evening Post, August, 1920 . . . .   **15.00**
Lundgren, calendar, 1897, "Saving His Scalp," The Knapp Co, Lith, NY, 14¾ x 29" **550.00**
Moran, Earl
Calendar
1933, woman wearing orange bathing suit, full pad, 10 x 17"   **65.00**
1941, Out in Front, majorette, full pad, 11 x 22" **70.00**
Post Card, Sheer Nonsense, pinup girl, undivided back, printed color, 1940s **8.00**
Mucha, Alphonse
Advertisement, Whitman's Sampler, "Salamagundi" illus, 8½ x 11½"   **35.00**
Book, Scene Painting and Bulletin Art, 1927, tan cov, emb "Salon des Cent" image on cov, blue, red, brown, black, and white image, 8 x 10½" **30.00**
Magazine Cover, Literary Digest, December 4, 1909 . . . .   **40.00**
Post Card, Warner Corset adv **500.00**
Noseworthy, Florence, post card
Boy and girl with sled, gold border . .   **8.00**
Children picking grapes, gold border   **15.00**
O'Neill, Rose
Book
Lady in White Veil, 1909 . . . .   **40.00**
The Loves of Edum, author and illus, 1904 . . . .   **85.00**
Magazine, Puck, November 16, 1898, full color illus on back cover titled "When Alice Made Candy," one quarter page illus int **35.00**
Magazine Advertisement, Jell–O, five girls with Jell–O dessert illus, 1921 . . . .   **15.00**
Magazine Cover
Outlook, October 21, 1914, Kellogg's adv **15.00**
Woman's Home Companion, January, 1924 . . . .   **30.00**
Magazine Tear Sheet, Puck, 1905, color page titled "By de Fiah," 14 x 18" mat **35.00**
Post Card
Christmas, Kewpies **25.00**
I'd Like to Travel with You, Kewpie with suitcase **30.00**
Sign, cardboard, Santa Claus Kewpie, 1913, 11½" h **65.00**
Osthaus, Edmond H, calendar, hunting dog, DuPont Powder Co adv, 1908, 19¾ x 30¼" **550.00**
Outcault, Ricard F
Book, Me & My Bubble, 1903 . . . . .   **245.00**

Calendar, 1907, Buster Brown, printed, color **25.00**

Post Card

A Smooth Bit of Road, Buster Brown **20.00**

Don't Be an April Fool, 1907 . . . . **18.00**

One Good Turn Deserves Another, J Ottmann, 1905 . . . . **8.00**

Valentine Series, Raphael Tuck . . **12.00**

Parrish, Maxfield

Advertisement, Jell–O, 1923, 9½ x 6½" **45.00**

Book

Arabian Nights, Scribner, 1909 . . **200.00**

Emerald Storybook, Duffield, 1924 . . . . **75.00**

Golden Treasury of Songs & Lyrics, Duffield, 1926 . . . . **150.00**

Italian Villas & Their Gardens, Century & Co, 1st Edition, 1905 **250.00**

King Albert's Book, 1914 . . . . **95.00**

Maxfield Parrish: The Early Years, Paul Skeeters, 1973, dj **250.00**

Poems of Childhood, Scribner, 1904, 1st ed. **175.00**

The Golden Age, 1899, Kenneth Grahame, 22 Parrish illus **160.00**

The Golden Treasury of Songs & Lyrics, 1911 . . . . **180.00**

Booklet, 1939 World's Fair, New Hampshire exhibit, 5 x 6" **75.00**

Box, candy, Crane's Chocolates, Cleveland, New York City, Kansas City, stork illus **200.00**

Calendar

1908, "Jason and the Talking Oak," 9 x 11" **120.00**

1923, Cadmus Sowing the Dragon's Teeth **130.00**

1928, "Contentment," Edison/Mazda, framed, full pad **475.00**

1930, "Ecstasy," Edison/Mazda adv, cropped and framed **675.00**

1932, "Solitude," Edison/Mazda adv, small, complete **450.00**

1934, "Moon Light," cropped image, Edison/Mazda **295.00**

1956, "Autumn Afternoon," full pad, 17 x 10" **125.00**

Calendar Print

Canyon, 12 x 16" **150.00**

Golden Hours, Edison/Mazda adv, 15 x 21" **575.00**

Cigar Label, Old King Cole, 1920s . . **250.00**

Greeting Card, Twilight Hour **17.50**

Magazine

Collier's, Pirate with Sword, June, 1909 . . . . **95.00**

Lady's Home Journal, Sweet Nothings, April, 1921 . . . . **135.00**

Life, December, 1922 . . . . **100.00**

Magazine Advertisement

Community Plate, *Good Housekeeping,* December, 1918 . . . . **35.00**

Jell–O, "Polly Put The Kettle On," *House & Garden,* 1923, 8½ x 12" **75.00**

Magazine Cover

Collier's

Harvest illus, September 23, 1905 **65.00**

Jack Frost **135.00**

Summer, July 27, 1905 . . . . **32.50**

Ladies' Home Journal, July, 1896 **100.00**

Menu

Broadmoor Hotel, 21 x 14½" **270.00**

St Regis Hotel, NY, The King Cole Bar and Lounge, 1919 . . . . **30.00**

Playing Cards

In the Mountain, Brown & Bigelow **165.00**

New Moon, MIB **150.00**

Print

Autumn, 1905, 14 x 18" **190.00**

Canyon, 12 x 15" **200.00**

Circe's Palace, 1908, 15½ x 12½" **110.00**

Cleopatra, 12 x 13¾" **375.00**

Daybreak, 33½ x 21½", orig frame **375.00**

Dinkey Bird, 11 x 16" **235.00**

Early Autumn, 16 x 13" **125.00**

Evening Shadows, summer scene, 14½ x 18½", Brown and Bigelow **390.00**

Falls by Moonlight, 11 x 8" **100.00**

Parrish, Maxfield, cigar label, Old King Cole, red, blue, and green, gold ground, 6 x 10", $250.00.

Garden of Allah, 12 x 21" **195.00**
Hilltop, 12 x 20" **350.00**
King's Entrance, Knave of Hearts   **85.00**
Lantern Bearers **210.00**
Moonlight, 12 x 15" **200.00**
Night Is Fled, Edison/Mazda adv,
  1918, 17 x 14" **900.00**
Peaceful Valley, 1955, 16 x 12" . .   **180.00**
Sleeping Giant, 7 x 9" **100.00**
Stars, 20 x 12" **500.00**
Three Wise Men, 9¼ x 6" **50.00**
When Day Is Dawning, 1954, 13 x
  17", orig frame. **200.00**
Program, Cohan & Harris Theatre,
  1920s **130.00**
Puzzle
  Daybreak, 1970s **20.00**
  Queen's Page, orig box. **100.00**
  The Broadmoor, 1940s **75.00**
  The Prince, orig box **100.00**
  The Prince and The Princess, orig
    box **100.00**
Recipe Booklet, Jell-O, 1924, color
  illus, 6½ x 4¼" **65.00**
Stationery, 1920s **100.00**
Petty, calendar, 1940, Petty girl, Old
  Gold Cigarettes adv for each month   **85.00**
Phillips, Coles
  Advertising Trade Card, Blue Moon
    Silk Stockings, attached silk sam-
    ples **10.00**
  Magazine Advertisement
    Community Plate, "Flapper Girl,"
      full page, color, 1923 . . . .   **10.00**
    Overland, *Ladie's Home Journal,*
      July, 1916, double pg, color . . .   **20.00**
  Magazine Cover, *Life,* December 12,
    1912 . . . .   **25.00**
Price, Norman
  Calendar, 1919, "Bagged In
    France," Hercules Powder Com-
    pany adv, 13 x 29⅝" **125.00**
  Magazine Cover, *St Nicholas,* De-
    cember, 1911, Victorian Santa
    with reindeer. **10.00**
Remington, Frederic
  Calendar, 1891, "Shoot Or You Will
    Lose Them," Winchester adv,
    14⅝ x 24⅛" **600.00**
  Magazine Tear Sheet, *Collier's,* Sep-
    tember 23, 1905, "A Halt in the
    Wilderness," 2 pgs **20.00**
  Post Card, "Evening on a Canadian,"
    two men and dog in canoe, 1905   **60.00**
Rockwell, Norman
  Book
    My Adventures as an Illustrator,
      Rockwell, 1960. . . . .   **20.00**
    *Norman Rockwell Collectibles
      Value Guide,* Mary Moline,
      Rumbleseat Press, 1978, 150
      pgs. **8.00**

Rockwell, Norman, magazine, *Saturday Evening Post,* red and gray color wash cover, sgd., 128 pages, 11 x 14", December 2, 1922, $135.00.

  The Secret Play, Barbour, 1916 . .   **100.00**
  Tom Sawyer, Heritage Press, 1936   **20.00**
  Calendar
    1920, Painting the Kite, De Laval
      adv **325.00**
    1941, boy and dog, Hercules Pow-
      der Company adv, 13 x 30¼" . . .   **175.00**
    1946, John Morrell & Co, Tom
      Sawyer.   **60.00**
    1948, Boy Scouts, Men of Tomor-
      row. **75.00**
  Catalog
    Montgomery Ward, 1925 . . . .   **35.00**
    Sears, Roebuck & Co, 1932 . . . . . .   **65.00**
    Top Value Stamp Catalog, 1967 . . .   **30.00**
    Winchester Western Sporting Arms,
      1966. . . . .   **35.00**
  Lithograph
    Jester, 21 x 17", #119, sgd **1,200.00**
    Weighing In, 23½ x 13", #14/100,
      sgd **700.00**
  Magazine, illus cov
    American Artist, 1976. . . . .   **20.00**
    Country Gentleman, October 6,
      1917 . . . .   **60.00**
    Leslie's, March 30, 1918. . . . .   **50.00**
    Life, June 1, 1945 . . . .   **60.00**
    Literary Digest, August 17, 1918   **40.00**
    SEP, January 29, 1921, cover and
      full pg ads **35.00**
  Magazine Cover
    Life, November 22, 1917. . . . .   **40.00**
    Literary Digest, May 8, 1920 . . . . . .   **25.00**
    Saturday Evening Post, July 31,
      1920. . . . .   **65.00**
  Magazine Tear Sheet
    Advertisement, Jell-O, *Country
      Gentleman,* 1922. . . . .   **20.00**

Article, Rockwell story, *Good Housekeeping,* February, 1929   **8.00**

Illustration, *Boy's Life,* January, 1914 ....   **25.00**

Poster

  Freedom of Speech, WWII, 1943   **35.00**

  Maxwell House Coffee, 1931–32   **325.00**

Print, "A Christmas Minuet," *Ladie's Home Journal,* 1932, subscriber's gift, 5$\frac{1}{4}$ x 7"..................   **25.00**

Sheet Music

  Family Sing–a–long with Mitch, 1962 ....   **15.00**

  Little French Mother, Goodbye, 1919 ....   **45.00**

  Over There, 1918 ....   **45.00**

  Over Yonder Where the Lillies Grow, 1918................   **85.00**

Rosseau, poster, "Quail Shooting In England," man hunting, two dogs, Marlin Fire Arms adv, 17 x 20$\frac{1}{4}$" ...   **550.00**

Sager, Xavier, post card, "Love is in your eyes," couple **15.00**

Schmucker, S L S, post card, St Patricks Day greeting, emb **25.00**

Schoonover, Frank E, poster, Colt's The Arm of Law and Order, cowboy on horse, 19$\frac{5}{8}$ x 33" **1,600.00**

Smith, Jessie Wilcox

  Book

    Jessie Wilcox Smith Baby Book, Just's Food Co, 1901, emb cov   **60.00**

    The Princess & The Goblin, 1920, eight book plates...........   **40.00**

  Magazine, *Good Housekeeping*

    1922, July, illus cov **20.00**

    1932, May, little girl aviator on cov **12.00**

  Magazine Cover, *McClure's,* August, 1904 ....   **20.00**

  Magazine Tear Sheet, *Ladie's Home Journal,* October, 1913, Goldilocks eating porridge, full color **10.00**

  Post Card, "The Lily Pool" **20.00**

  Poster, The Secret of Ideal Heating, American Radiators & Ideal Boilers, 20 x 30" **300.00**

  Print

    "The Lovers Quarrel," little girl in forest with teddy bears, 10$\frac{1}{2}$ x 16"......................   **15.00**

    Two girls playing patty cake, 9 x 18$\frac{1}{2}$".....................   **50.00**

Surch, Ruth, post card, Christmas.....   **6.00**

Thiele, Arthur, post card

  Cats and teddy bear with phonograph.......................   **30.00**

  Chickens at party **20.00**

  "You Make Me Laugh"..........   **8.00**

Underwood, Clarence

  Magazine Cover, *McClure's,* November, 1913 ....   **7.00**

"*An hour slipped by, but still the mayor did not come*"

Smith, Jessie Wilcox, print, "An Hour Slipped By," Child's Garden of Verses, color, $30.00.

Post Card, "Pleasant Reflections," woman wearing hat, looking into mirror **15.00**

Varga

  Calendar Yearbook, 1945 ....   **125.00**

  Datebook, 1945, Esquire, Susan Heyward cov, 5 x 7" **125.00**

  Magazine Cover, Theatre, January, 1925 ....   **60.00**

  Playing Cards, complete deck of 54 cards **65.00**

Wheelan, Nister, post card, "For My Valentine" **15.00**

Wyeth, N C

  Book, *Treasure Island,* 1947.......   **45.00**

  Calendar

    1910, "Over Yonder," three men and two dogs, Ballistite and Empire adv, 15 x 26" **550.00**

    1933, three men holding leashed hunting dogs and guns, Hercules Powder Company adv, 13 x 27$\frac{3}{4}$".....................   **125.00**

LABELS

History: This category deals with product labels. While examples are known from the eighteenth and early nineteenth centuries, the principal focus of label collectors begins in the mid–nineteenth century and extends to the present. The starting date corresponds closely to the development of chromolithography. While serious collectors will purchase a black printed text label, the vast majority of collectors buy labels because of their colorful images.

Collectors like labels that can be removed from the product and stored flat in drawers or albums. They do not consider the cut out front of a package a label. A label must be applied.

Within the past decade, label collectors have widened their collecting range considerably. Can, luggage, and wine labels have found a home among cigar and fruit crate label collectors. A number of topical label books have been published. More are on the way.

The fruit crate label is typical. The first fruit crate label was created by California fruit growers about 1880. The labels became very colorful and covered many subjects. Most depict the type of fruit held in the box. With the advent of cardboard boxes in the 1940s, fruit crate art ended. Shortly thereafter, their labels became collectible.

Many of the labels sold in the market today were never used on products. They were discovered in large hoards in warehouses. Those controlling the hoards are releasing material into the market a little at a time in order to keep prices high. Even this policy will eventually flood the market.

Further, a few dealers are attempting to promote several label groups, e.g., cigar labels, as works of art, charging "art prices" for them. While excellent examples of American lithography, few in the art community see them as an art form. Serious questions need to be raised about the resale value of many of these high ticket pieces.

References: Joe Davidson, *The Art of the Cigar Label*, Wellfleet Press, 1989; Joe Davidson, *Fruit Crate Art*, Wellfleet Press, 1990; Jerry Chicone, Jr., *Florida's Classic Crates*, published by author, 1985; David Craig, *Luggage Labels: Mementos from the Golden Age of Travel*, Chronicle Books, 1988; Lynn Johnson and Michael O'Leary, *En Route: Label Art from the Golden Age of Air Travel*, Chronicle Books, 1993; Gordon T. McClelland and Jay T. Last, *Fruit Box Labels, A Collector's Guide,* Hillcrest Press, 1983; Robert Opie, *The Art of the Label: Designs of the Times,* Chartwell Books, 1987; John Salkin and Laurie Gordon, *Orange Crate Art, The Story of Labels That Launched a Golden Era,* Warner Books, 1976.

Collectors' Clubs: Citrus Label Society, 131 Miramonte Drive, Fullerton, CA 92365; International Seal, Label & Cigar Band Society, 8915 East Bellevue Street, Tuscon, AZ 85715.

BOTTLE

Ammonia, Buffalo, buffalo and flowers, red, white, and blue.	.50
Beer	
Chief, Indian chief, pine trees, deer, and lake	.50
Lone Star, 1940s	.50
Old Craft Brew, four brewery workers making beer, gilt dec	.50
Old Style, stagecoach, Indians, tepee, train, airplane, and car.	.50
Catsup	
Farmer's Pride	.25
Red Medal Brand Tomato Catsup, maltese cross	.50
Wilson Brand Catsup, red tomato, 2 x 3¼"	.25
Ink, Winslows Indelible Ink, gold and blue, printed, color	8.00
Olive Oil, Pastore Olive Oil, Indian chief with raised hands, bead work border, 7 x 10"	1.00
Soda	
Black Hawk Lime Rickey, Indian chief	.50
Myopia Club, diamond shape, Indian chief profile, gilt dec	.50
Orang–O–3, three oranges and leaves	.25
Palm Springs, silver Art Deco design, black and gold background, dated 1935	.50
Smile, "It Must Be Cloudy," oval, orange headed figure	.25
Twin Lights, shore scene, two light houses, gilt dec	.25
Whiskey	
Air Port, red tri–motor airplane, c1940	.75
Apricot Brandy, two apricots, gilt dec, 5 x 3¼"	1.50
Bellows Club Bourbon, green, black, and cream	.75
Crown Prince, crown, 2½ x 3½".	.50

Bottle, Ritz Lemon Soda, yellow and black, 3½ x 4¼", $4.00.

Hickory Whiskey, Portland, OR, gilt, black, red, and white 1.00
Hunter Bourbon, hunter and dog 1.50
Little Bourbon Whiskey, white dec, black background 1.00
More's Malt Whiskey, 5 x 3½" 1.00
Old Crown, distillery scene, 3½ x 4½" .75
Rocking Chair, Mr Boston and rocking chair, 3¼ x 5" 1.50
Waterfill and Frazier, emb, gilt, red and black background, 4 x 5¼" 1.00

BEAUTY

Annette Hair Preparation for Grey Hair, white silhouette of lady, green flowers .25
Fairy Cream, emb, gilt dec, florals 1.00
Hair Tonic, Victorian lady, beveled corners 1.00
Kooling Balm, emb, gilt dec 1.75
Little Fairies, fairies, florals, and butterflies 75
Mentholated Cream, emb, gilt, floral and leaf dec 50
Odor Roses, rose branch, with hazel, 3¼ x 4½" 75
Shave Rite, blue striped dec 25
Superior Bay Rum, green bay leaf, gilt border, 2 x 3" 50
Talcum Powder, beautiful women, black ground 1.50
Violet Ammonia, purple flowers, white background, York, PA 75
Violet Toilet Water, oval, gilt, multicolored violets, 5½ x 4" 75
Violet Witch Hazel, purple flowers, white background, 3 x 4" 50
Wisk Shaving Cream, man's face, black, blue, and silver 25

CAN

Asparagus, Isaacs, forest, stream, and mountains scene, asparagus on plate 1.00
Black Eyed Peas, Old Black Joe, black man and cabin 1.00
Cocoa, Elkay Cocoa, emb, cup of cocoa, dark blue, gold, and white 10.00
Coffee
    Marvel Coffee, coffee cup and falls, yellow, orange, gold, and blue, 1 lb 12.00
    Pecan Valley Coffee, pecan cluster and trees 1.00
    Zodiac, aqua background 1.00
Corn
    Arcadia Beauty, two ears of corn, emb, white background 1.00
    Blue Hill, white corn, house and river scene 3.00
    Butterfly, Golden Sweet Corn, bowl of corn 1.00

Cloth of Gold, Golden Bantam Corn, red bird, gilt 3.00
Danas Jardiniere Sweet Corn, jardiniere on stand with plant 2.00
Delta Brand Sugar Corn, country scene, Art Nouveau design 2.00
Electric Sweet Corn, gilt dec 2.00
Good Buy Corn, yellow, white, green, and brown 3.00
Great Northern Country Gentleman Corn, Indian illus, aqua, 1910 . . . . . 16.00
Newark Sweet Corn, two ears of white corn 1.00
Og–Na, Indian chief, peace pipe, tomahawk, and white corn, white background, emb and gilt dec, 1920s 1.00
Rowley's Golden Sweet Corn 50
Sun Bird Sugar Corn, bird, red, green, white, and yellow 15.00
William Byrd Shoe Peg Corn, man, red, white, green, and blue 7.50
Cranberry Sauce, Ocean Spray Cape Cod Cranberry Sauce, aqua, red, and white 15.00
Evaporated Milk
    Chippewa Evaporated Milk, Indian chief, arrows, and moccasins 2.00
    Country Maid, milk maid, carrying milk pail, blue and red background 2.00
    Marvel, two tan cows 50
    Roseco Evaporated Milk, cow, milking stool, and bucket, red rose 2.00
Green Beans
    Butterfly Golden Wax Beans, butterfly illus 4.00
    Maryland Chief, Extra Small Whole Green Beans, blue and red 25
    Mi–Boy, laughing boy and green beans 2.00
    Newark Green Beans, two floral bowls of green beans 1.00
    Premier, Old Fashioned French Green Beans, women, pale blue and green .25
    Winsom, emb, gilt 1.00
Kidney Beans
    Electric, gilt dec 2.00
    Rowley's, two bowls of kidney beans .75
Lima Beans
    Dubon, two bowls of lima beans, blue background 50
    Ellendale, forest, stream, mountains, and limas in pods 1.00
    Farmers Pride, grandfather and little girl with doll 1.00
    Forest City, autumn leaves, 1920s 2.00
    Great A & P, lima vines, pods, and yellow flowers, gilt background . . . 1.00
    Preston, limas, pods, leaves, black and red background 1.00
Mixed Fruit, Memory, two grannies, one bowl of mixed fruit 1.00

Can, My Choice Salmon, red and blue, 4¹⁄₈ x 9³⁄₄", $8.00.

Cigar, Fifty Little Orphans, red and blue, 8¹⁄₂ x 6", $12.00.

Oysters, High Tide Cove Oysters, ship
scene, red, white, pink, and green, 10
oz. 8.00

Peaches

Del Monte Sliced Yellow Cling
Peaches, sliced peaches in bowl . . .   1.00

Mt Hamilton Sliced White Cling
Peaches, Mt Hamilton Observatory,
horse, and carriage 2.00

Ole Skipper, mariner at ships wheel . .   2.00

Peas

Butterfly Sweet Peas, emb, bowl of
peas and butterfly 1.00

Hart Sifted Early June Peas, white, red,
green, and gold, 11 oz 3.00

Isaacs Brand, lake and woods scene,
sailboat, ten, and peas and pods . . .   1.50

June Peas, crystal bowl of peas, red
roses and leaves. 2.00

Little Joe, whistling black boy going
fishing, crowder peas. 1.00

Marcella Peas, girl and roses, aqua,
white, red, and gold. 6.00

Rowley's, hand pouring can of peas
into bowl, white background. 1.00

Squaw, Indian mother and papoose . .   1.00

Templar, knight in armor, riding horse   2.00

Wauneca Sweet Wrinkled Peas, In-
dian, red, white, and blue 15.00

West Shore, glass bowl, palm trees,
and homes 2.00

Pizza Sauce, Claudia, two ladies. 1.00

Pork & Beans

Fancy Beans & Pork, flowers, bowl,
and boat, gold and blue 15.00

Forest City, beans in bowl, 1920s 2.00

Three P's Pork & Beans, red, blue, and
green 15.00

Powder Sugar, Roseco, Angel Cake Pow-
der Sugar, rose, gold, and blue 12.00

Pumpkin

Butterfly Golden Pumpkin, pumpkin
and butterfly 50

Cloth of Gold, red bird and golden
pumpkin 2.00

Electric Golden Pumpkin, gilt dec. . . .   3.00

Red Beets

Maryland Chief, two Indian chief's . . .   1.00

Silver Lake, sailboat on lake, train, and
beets in bowl 3.00

Winsom, bowl of diced beets, gilt dec   1.00

Salmon

Marvel, fish 2.00

Tube City Red Alaska Salmon, fish,
white, red, and blue. 7.00

Strawberries

Forest City, berries in glass bowl,
1920s. 2.00

Home Grown Brand Strawberries, berries and flowers 3.00
Succotash
Cloth of Gold, red bird, bowl of succotash.   1.00
Rowley's, fancy succotash, white background 50
Sweet Potato
Forest City, two sweet potatoes, 1920s   2.00
Kirk Sweet Potato. 70.00
Syrup
Dixie Maid Syrup, girl pouring syrup on waffles 50
Longwood Plantation's Syrup, smiling black lady, wearing red bandanna   1.00
Southern Plantation, syrup, emb, black workers 50
Uncle Remus Syrup, 1924. . . . .   8.00
Tomato
Ashland Brand Tomatoes, red tomato, green leaves. 3.00
Bare Foot Boy Tomatoes, boy, aqua, blue, white, and red. 12.00
Bridgeton Tomato Pulp, girl wearing bonnet, red, white, and green, 10 oz   12.00
Defender Tomato, yacht at sea scene   1.00
Westwood Tomatoes, golfer, gold trim, 4¼ x 11", printed color, emb   8.00

CIGAR

Big B Grand, honey bee, yellow background, 2¼ x 5¼". 25
Booker T Washington, litho, raised, multicolored 175.00
Buzzer, ornate butterfly, cigar body 3.00
Castle Hall, castle, soft colors 1.00
Emilia Garcia, lady in pink, standing on globe, ships in bay 2.00
J A C, tobacco leaves 25
Jewelo, romantic gentleman and lady. . .   1.00
La Boda, wedding ceremony. 2.00

Fruit Crate, Kentucky Cardinal Apples, red and blue on cream, 9½ x 11½", 1910, $50.00.

La Mareva, woman wearing blue hat . . .   1.00
La Miretta, lady and plantation scene . . .   3.00
La Venga, eagle, outstretched wings. 50
Mareys La Rubia, pretty women, gold trim, printed, color, emb 2.00
Old Well, stone well 2.00
Our Kitties, white cat, blue ribbon, 5½ x 2½" 35
Peg, black high toe shoe 1.00
Prima Lucia, woman wearing decolette gown 3.00
Red Tips, horse's head in horseshoe, white background 1.00
Rolamo, man with beard, wearing red jacket. 1.00
Rosa Moro, brunette lady, two lions 1.00
Senora Cubana, woman wearing black lace mantilla 2.00
Sunny Boy, father and son, 2¼ x 6½" 25
Uncle Jake's Nickel Seegar, comical man with beard and cat, 1925. . . . .   3.00
Western Bee, four beehives, bees, and bundle of cigars 2.00

FRUIT CRATE

Apple
Cascade, smiling boy holding partially eaten apple, blue background 50
Lakeview, yellow and red apples, orchard, blue background 1.00
Pete's Best, laughing boy, red apple, yellow background 1.00
Webster, spider web, navy background 2.00
Asparagus
Mo–Chief, asparagus bundle, scenic background, Fresno, CA 2.00
Red Rooster, crowing rooster, yellow, red, and navy background 1.00
Spring Time Magic, elves celebrating asparagus harvest 1.00
Carrot, DOE, doe's head, bunch of carrots 1.00
Cherry
Exposition, black bing cherries, red background 15
San Ardo, red cherries cluster, farm scene, blue background 25
Grape
American Beauty, big red rose, dark green ground 2.00
Corsair, handsome galleon sailing on rough seas, clouds and sky ground   .25
Domingo, yellow grapes, country scene 50
Mirador, ranch scene, red grapes, Uncle Sam's hat 1.00
Moose, very dignified brown moose, yellow lettering, green ground. 25
Old Mission, Spanish Mission scene, mission bells, green grapes, 1920s   .50

Tobacco, Big John Plug Cut, blue and red, 4½ x 9½", $35.00.

Pride of Dinuba, lady wearing yellow flowing gown, holding bunches of grapes, blue and red background .. .50

Reliance, three kinds grapes, yellow background.................... .25

Rooseville Belle, 1930s lady, big bell, pink rose, purple grapes, scenic ground...................... .50

Grapefruit, Dixie boy, black child eating half grapefruit 2.00

Lemon

Arboleda, scenic, Goleta........... 1.00

Cub, cute brown bear cub eating lemons, red ground, Upland, CA. . . 4.00

El Merito, lemons, blue, green, and yellow background, Santa Paula . . . 1.00

Exposition, certificate of Alaska Yukon Pacific Exposition, Seattle, 1909, diploma for grand prize won for lemon exhibit, black ground, Santa Barbara, CA 2.00

Kaweah maid, Indian girl wearing turquoise beads, brown background, Lemon Cove 3.00

Lemonade, three large lemons and leaves, orchard background, Ivanhoe 1.00

Meteor, meteor streaking through evening sky, San Fernando, CA....... 3.00

Ocean Spray, glass lemonade, red roses in blue vase, Santa Paula 5.00

Sunside, two lemons and leaves, orange and brown background, Santa Paula 1.00

Tom Cat, huge black and white cat lying on red cushion, orange ground, Orosi, CA 35.00

Orange

Airship, old four prop commercial plane, royal blue ground, Fillmore, CA 10.00

Altissimo, pink, aqua and blue mountains, dated 1918, Placentia 1.00

Big J, red and yellow letter J, blue seal, San Francisco.................. 1.00

Bronco, cowboy swinging lariat, riding galloping brown horse, western desert scene, Redlands 2.00

Cambria, brown eagle, two torches, blue background, brown border, Placentia 1.00

Coed, smiling girl graduate, purple ground, Claremont, CA 2.50

Esperanza, pretty senorita wearing lace mantilla, holding fancy lace fan, carnation in hair, blue ground, Placentia, CA................. 1.00

Hill Choice, orchard scene, orange with leaves and blossoms, aqua background, Porterville.......... 1.00

Lochinvar, brave Lochinvar and fair damsel, black horse, red ground, East Highlands, CA 6.00

Mammy, black lady eating an orange, yellow ground, Florida 2.50

Miracle, genie holding tray with three oranges, dated 1928, Placentia 4.00

Nimble, orchard scene, aqua background, Santa Paula............. 1.00

Orbit, meteor in shape of orange, streaking through starry evening sky, royal blue ground, Exeter, CA 2.50

Pala Brave, Indian chief wearing headdress, maroon background, Placentia...................... 3.00

Royal Knight, brave knight in armor on horseback, castle, yellow background, Redlands 2.00

Scotch Lassie Jean, Scottish lassie wearing kilts, castle, thistle, blue, green, and black ground, Strathmore, CA 2.50

Shamrock, shamrock in sky over orange groves, Placentia.......... 1.00

Unicorn, galloping buckskin and white pinto unicorn, blue ground, East Highlands, CA 10.00

Pear

Blue Parrot, green and blue parrot on flowering branch .... .75

Camel, camel and his master, sunrise desert scene **2.00**
Duckwall, wood duck standing by brick wall **2.00**
Lady of the Lake, lady in green gown standing by lake, holding pear **2.00**
Maltese Cross, maltese cross, white background, gilt dec **1.00**
Oh Yes–We Grow The Best, two yellow pears, blue background . . . . . .   **.50**
Old Orchard, two young girls in orchard **1.00**
Pirate's Cove, lake and country scene   **.50**
Round Robin, saucy wide–eyed robin, blue ground **3.00**
Summit, snowy mountains, forest scene **2.00**
Triton, red Neptune holding trident and apple and pear, scenic background **1.00**
Westside, orchard and mountain scene, palm tree and big pear **2.00**
Plum, Valley Home, purple plums, aqua background **1.00**
Prune, Wellman, nude Mercury standing on world **1.00**
Tomato
Big Chief, Indian chief and tomatoes   **.25**
Green Feather, green feather, black background . . . .   **.25**
Sun Prince, tomato background . . . . .   **.25**
Yam
Jack Rabbit, gray rabbit on red triangle, aqua background, green border . . .   **2.00**
Sunset Packers, two yams, deco look design . . . .   **.50**
Treasure, pirates treasure chest, four large yams **1.00**

HOUSEHOLD

Dixie Broom, black man seated on Bench, playing banjo **1.00**
Furniture Oil for Oiling Walnut, C Schrock & Co, Philadelphia, black and white **10.00**
Indian Queen Broom, Indian lady in forest, tepees . . . .   **.50**
Skysweep Broom, bi–plane, dated 1931   **.50**
Winner Broom, lady holding torch . . . . .   **.50**

MEDICINE

Alkaline and Antiseptic Tablets, two corners with design . . . .   **.25**
Blumers I Tonic, eye, Chicago . . . .   **.25**
Dr B D Eldridge's Forest Leaf Compound, Indian maiden illus, gold trim, black and white **10.00**
Dr Blumers Automatic, comical . . . .   **.25**
Essence Jam Ginger, floral, blue and white . . . .   **.50**

Farrier's Liniment, horse and man, black printing, green ground, folded, unused   **8.00**
Lydia Pinkham, Vegetable Compound . .   **5.00**
Nature's Cure For Diseases of the Kidneys, Blood and Urinary Organs, blacks with baskets on heads, 9 x 6" . .   **15.00**
Poison Oak Remedy . . . .   **.25**
Skiddo Skitoes Safe Sure Protection Against Mosquitoes, blue and white . .   **.50**
Seidlitz Powders, four corners with faces, black and white . . . .   **.75**

TOBACCO

Arline, lady wearing low cut dress, garden background, 7 x 14" **37.50**
Belle of Virginia, beautiful lady holding fan, multicolored, 7 x 14" **20.00**
Cora, child seated by giant flower blooms, 7 x 14" **37.50**
Diadem, beautiful lady warrior holding spear, 11 x 11" **36.00**
Gypsy, pretty lady wearing gypsy dress, woodland background, 11 x 11" **18.00**
International, clipper ship, Liberty ladies and topless nude, 7 x 14" **45.00**
Juno, crowned lady sitting on throne and peacock, 7 x 14" **45.00**
La Plata, Liberty and two Indians, 11 x 11" **27.00**
Octaroon, beautiful lady, 7 x 14" **55.00**
Old Sport, dog wearing business suit, reading paper and drinking, 11 x 11"   **60.00**
Red Bird, red bird on branch, lagoon background, 7 x 14" **27.00**
Sailor's Hope, lady on dock, wearing nautical dress, clipper ship, 7 x 14" . . .   **50.00**
Welcome Nugget, gold miner holding up giant nugget, 11 x 11" **65.00**
Winner, horse racers jumping through stirrup, 11 x 11" **65.00**

TRAVEL

Albright, bicyclist riding in park, 4 x 4" . .   **10.00**
American Airlines, color **6.00**
Barbizon Plaza Hotel, black, white, and silver, 1930s **4.00**
Bellevue Hotel, Stratford, red and white, 1930s **4.00**
Brown Palace Hotel, hotel view, brown and tan **3.50**
Carlton Hotel, Cairo, red, green, and brown **12.00**
City of Denver, color **3.00**
Great Northern, color **2.00**
Hotel De Coronado, 1930s **4.00**
Hotel Mount Everest, Darjecting, India, blue and red **15.00**
Netherland Plaza, silver, white, and black **4.00**
North Coast Limited, sheet of eight **8.00**

Travel, baggage label, Hotel Royal, Bangkok, black on orange, 1920s, $6.00.

Northwest Airlines, color	**6.00**
Salt Lake City, UT, beehive, color	**5.00**
St Francis Hotel, emb, yellow, blue, pink, and gold.	**5.00**
Trans Canada, gold, red, and white	**2.50**
Yellowstone Park, bear, white, red, and blue	**3.00**

LEDGERS AND JOURNALS (DAY BOOKS)

History: A ledger is a book containing accounts to which debits and credits are posted from books of original entry. A journal is a record of current transactions, e.g., a book of original entry in double–entry bookkeeping.

Hand written eighteenth and early nineteenth century journals and ledgers provide important insights into the day-to-day operations of businesses and households. Principal collector interest focuses on craftsmen journals and ledgers and the business accounting records of major manufacturers. General store and other mercantile business are viewed as less desirable, but still collectible. Household ledgers and journals hold little interest for collectors, but are purchased by university reference libraries.

Paper fakers go to great lengths to acquire journals and ledgers. What they want is the aged, period paper. They cut out the blank pages and use them for their handiwork. The end and fly leaves from eighteenth and early nineteenth century books, the larger the size the better, also fall victim to their need for period paper.

The collecting of paper for its own sake was extremely popular from the 1920s through the 1950s. Cut apart journals and ledgers were one of the principal sources of supply. Many paper collectors focused on watermarked examples. A surprisingly large number of eighteenth and nineteenth century ledgers and journals used high quality, watermarked paper.

Journals and ledgers increase in value the more that is known about them. Always attempt to identify the location from which the journal or ledger originated. It generally will bring its greatest value at its point of origin.

A number of greedy paper dealers have begun the practice of cutting journals and ledgers apart and selling the pages separately. This is especially true for manufacturing and transportation related journals and ledgers. Condemn this practice when you encounter it. Cutting journals and ledgers apart totally destroys their research value.

Note: Also see "Billheads" in the topical section.

Account Book

Financier Nathan Appleton, Lowell, MA, 1821–29, entries from Portsmouth, Boston, marble and leather board cov, over 160 pgs, 8 x 6½"	**100.00**
Joseph Parker, Chelmsford, MA, January 1762 to December 1805, 180 pgs, farm work and crops with prices, leather bound, 180 pgs, 6 x 8"	**85.00**
Revolutionary War, July to November 1776, lists discharges of soldiers, death of two soldiers, cash paid to each soldier, and rum for officers, 20 pgs, 4 x 7"	**300.00**
Transportations to Poughkeepsie, Mr Richard Davis's Store, 1765–69, pork, beef, flax seed, butter, flour, and other grains, contracts for supplies for troops, hard cover, 16 pgs	**200.00**

General Store

1843–44, "Samuel M Shaeffer, Shaefferstown, Lebanon County" written inside cov, worn cover and spine, 12½ x 4"	**50.00**
1861–64, lists wood and sumac, tools and hauling services, and transactions, bound, 94 pgs	**100.00**

Log Book

Bark *Otranto,* New Bedford, January 17, 1847 to April 30, 1849, whale stamps and ship stamps.	**3,080.00**
Draco, South Atlantic Ocean Voyage, July 1, 1875 to June 9, 1878, whale stamps, whale oil record, provisions lists	**1,400.00**

Receipt Book

American Express, New England Division, Thompson & Co, June–August, 1864, 24 pgs, cover with broadside style advertisement and train vignette.	**50.00**
Pacific Express, 1881, St Louis, MO, 50 receipts, 17 used, 4 x 9"	**125.00**
Schoolmaster's Tuition Book, Troy, NY, Andrew Hemphill's, 1811–47, list payments from students, over 100 pgs, leather cov, 4 x 6½"	**50.00**

Tax Record Book, 1851, New Bedford and surrounding towns, indexed alphabetically, several people listed as "at sea," cloth and leather board cov, 297 pgs, 14½ x 12½" **225.00**

LETTERHEADS

History: One of the first steps a new business takes is to obtain a printed business card, letterhead, and billhead. These help establish an air of legitimacy to the operation. Often letterheads and billheads were printed from the same plate, the principal reason why letterhead collectors also tend to be billhead collectors.

The ability to produce a letterhead required two key technological advances—paper and printing. By the early 1500s, the art of paper making was well known in England, Germany, Holland, and France. Early paper utilized plant fibers. In 1851, a chemical method was discovered to make paper from wood pulp. Paper became inexpensive and commonplace. The letter press was well established in Europe by the end of the sixteenth century.

One final step was necessary before the letterhead could evolve—an inexpensive mail system. It was not until early in the sixteenth century that a series of regular mail routes was established in Europe. Costs remained high.

In eighteenth century America, it was the recipient, not the sender, who paid for the delivery charge based on distance and number of sheets. Postal reform in the mid–nineteenth century, with cost based on weight, not sheets, paved the way for the use of an envelope and the development of the letterhead.

The letterhead traces its origins to the engraved merchant's trade card of the seventeenth and eighteenth centuries. The backs of these cards were used for brief correspondence, receipts, and other business documents. As the need for more formal receipts developed, the trade card became a large billhead.

When the postal service introduced a mail class system, merchants began to send printed advertising circulars to their best clients. Many early examples are printed on company letterhead.

The development of the typewriter expedited the use of formal business letterhead. Letterhead followed the same design evolution as billheads. The Golden Age was the 1890s, a time of extravagant design. Following World War I, a feeling developed that the Victorian design excess was tasteless. Graphic artists, rather than engravers and printers, became the principal designers of letterheads. Visual appeal now rested in the arrangement of type and color rather than in graphics.

Will the electronics revolution eliminate the need for the printed letterhead? Many individuals now use a computer generated letterhead, changing it whenever the whim dictates. All too often, it is crafted by an amateur rather than a skilled designer. The future is very uncertain.

Reference: Leslie Cabarga, *Letterheads: One Hundred Years of Great Design*, Chronicle Books, 1992.

Agency, Central Railroad and Banking, Georgia, 1849, black and white, used **9.00**

A J Weidener, Lamps, Chandeliers, Champion Lamps, Philadelphia, 1866, black and white, used **15.00**

Altamont Stock Farm, Champion Shropshire Sheep, Millbrook, NY, 1902, green printing, yellow ground **10.00**

American Herb Co, Indian Herbs, Washington, DC, 1911, red and white **12.00**

Arctic Fire Insurance Co, iceberg and sailing ship vignette **8.50**

Aviation, WWII, air base illus, includes printed envelope **4.00**

Baker & Lackwood Mfg Co, Awnings, Tents, Kansas City, MO, 1908, Dunston Litho, illus, black and white, creased **5.00**

Bankettsaal and Gabenlemphel, NY, Charles Magnus, color. **20.00**

Boone Hardware Co, NC, color, corner creased, used. **15.00**

Case Power Farming Machinery, 1929, color, staple cut, used **18.00**

C Emrich, Stoves, Ranges, Hollow Ware, Columbus, OH, 1913, black and white, used **7.50**

Chas Rippe Manuf Awnings, Tents, Tarpaulins, Wagon Covers, St Louis, 1881, illus adv over horse, wagon, tent, blue and black, folds **15.00**

Chicago, Burlington & Quincy Railroad Co, Boston, 1879, map, black and white **25.00**

Chicago Vaudeville, Newspaper, Progressive Circuit, Burlesque of a Higher Class, 1913, black and white. **12.00**

Church Arm Recreation Hut or Tent, service with British Expeditionary Force, July 30, 1918, letter to girl friend, red and black, 8 x 10" **8.00**

Davis & Yonger, Horses & Mules, Oklahoma City, OH, 1919, Hommer, Wilson, Walker & Co Litho, black and white, used **7.00**

Dempster Mill Mfg Co, Farm & Franch, Windmills, Beatrice, NE, 1908, illus, black and white, creased, used **5.00**

Dr Kennedy & Kergan, Detroit, 1906, illus, blue, crease. **15.00**

JAMES B. GODWIN
610 S. MAIN STREET
SUFFOLK VIRGINIA

DEALER FOR
NANSEMOND AND
ISLE OF WIGHT COUNTIES

Willys Light, advertising letter for Willys Auto-Lite generator, 8½ x 11", c1900, $10.00.

D S Erb & Co, Keystone Cigar Factory, Boyertown, PA, 1893, C Jourgensen, NY, 6 x 9", black and white, used **8.00**

Eagle Scale & Mfg Co, Harrisville, MO, 1911, two tone sepia, used **7.50**

E B Estes & Sons Wooden Clothespins, NY, 1915, Brooks Banknote Co, Springfield, MA, used **18.00**

Eureka Digger Co, Implements, Post Hole Diggers, Chicago, IL, 1909, green and white, used **10.00**

Fairbanks–Morse Products, 1925, illus of farm pumps, two color, used **12.00**

Filene's, Boston, Sept 4, 1914, letter from V Pres E J Frost, regarding public relations matter **6.00**

Fire Association of Philadelphia, dated 1892, pump and fire hose logo **6.50**

Floto–Johnson Cycle Co, Steubenville, OH, 1928, black and white, used **20.00**

Gendron Wheel Co, Toledo, OH, 1918, children's bicycles, carts illus, black and white, used **18.00**

Grand Union Hotel, NY, 1881, Fay & Cow, black and white, minor folds, used **10.00**

Green's Nursery Co, Rochester, NY, black and white................. **7.50**

Hershey Chocolate Co, Gies & Co, black and white, used **10.00**

H I Heinze Co, Jan 1915, plant illus on back, printed by Eastern Bank Note Co, black and white.............. **20.00**

Hunt Circus, illus, color **12.00**

Iver Johnsons' Arms & Cycles Works, Fitchburg, MA, 1915, black and white **10.00**

John P Lovell & Sons, Manuf & Wholesale Dealers In Fire Arms, Boston, 1879, black and white, used **12.00**

J Stevens Arms Co, Chicopee Falls, MA, 1916, black and white, used **12.00**

Keystone Plow Co, New Castle, PA, 1894, blue illus, used **10.00**

Laften & Taylor Gun and Locksmith, Jacksonville, FL, 1927, orange illus, rough condition................. **10.00**

Lyons, McKee, 1891, engraved, 1 page typed letter..................... **4.00**

Mackinac House, Mackinac, MI, 1884, black and white, used **10.00**

Mack International Motor Truck Corp, Fire Engine Div, 1948, 300th Anniversary of Volunteer Fireman, color, minor folds....................... **25.00**

Michigan Hotels, Wayne, Detroit, The Grand, Mackinaw Island, Arlington, Petosky, 1890s, G H Dunston Litho, black and white, used **10.00**

Oneida Truck Mfg Co, c1910, vehicle illus, unused **5.00**

Packard & Co, Jobbers of Hardware, Greenville, PA, 1884, J A Warner Litho, black and white, used......... **8.00**

P D Bechwith, Round Oak Stoves, Dowagic, MI, 1912, Gies & Co, black and white, used **10.00**

Speer Hardware Co, Fort Smith, AK, 1903, great illus, Stephens Litho, used, black and white, torn corner **10.00**

Standard Oil Co, New York........... **7.50**

The Baxter Stove Co, Mansfield, OH, 1887, G H Dunston Litho, black on orange........................ **8.00**

The Champion Blower & Forge Co, Lancaster, PA, 1891, Craig Finley & Co Litho, black and white............ **6.00**

The El Reno Mill & Elevator Co, El Reno, OK, 1909, Western Litho Co, black and white, used **7.00**

The Marlin Firearms Co, New Haven, CT, 1914, black and white **10.00**

The Miami Cycle Mfg Co, High Grade Bicycles, Middletown, OH, 1918, black and white, used **15.00**

The Star Tontine Assoc, 1891, black and white **7.50**

The Thomas Manuf Co, Thomas Rakes & Tedders, Lawn Mowers, Springfield, 1892, Winters Litho, half sheet, black and white...................... **8.00**

The Wick China Co, 1891, engraved, 1 page typed letter **4.00**

Turnbill Motor Truck and Wagon Co, Defiance, OH, engraving of factory, illus of truck, orig envelope, Nov 1917   **15.00**

United States Cigar Co, York, PA, 1933, two color **8.00**

United States Fireman, Charles Magnus, illus, color, opens **75.00**

White Star Line, US and Royal Mail Steamers, Chicago, 1887, black and white, edge nicks **10.00**

Winchester Repeating Arms Co, New Haven, CT
    1916, color crest, black and white, used **15.00**
    1929, non pictorial, black and white, staple hole, used **10.00**

Worcester Wire Novelty Co, Rat Traps & Baskets, Canton, OH, letterhead and attached flyer, black and white, used   **15.00**

Wright Steam Engine Works, Newburgh, NY, 1882, black and white **15.00**

W T Grant Co, 1914, letter from Portland Maine store manager, tennis shoes selling for 25¢ a pair **8.00**

Zone Oil Co, Cleveland, OH, 1890s. . . .   **7.50**

LICENSES

History: A license is a document that implies permission from a competent authority for a person to engage in a particular occupation or in an activity that is otherwise unlawful. In most cases, it is a printed document.

Licenses document the level of restrictions imposed on private actions. The vast majority result from local, regional, state, or the federal governments. Few individuals stop to think how often licensing issues enter their lives. Everyone knows you need a license to drive a vehicle. Most municipalities require pets to be licensed. Businesses are subject to a wide variety of licensing fees. Few in the antiques and collectibles field are unaware of the need for a sales tax license and the growing trend not to reciprocate between states.

Only a handful of licenses have value to collectors, e.g., chauffeur, fishing, and hunting licenses. The vast majority have no value.

Value rests largely with the crossover collector. The owner of a 1925 automobile will buy an example of a 1925 driver's license as a curiosity piece. Collectors of dog memorabilia will buy an early paper dog license. Barber shop collectors will buy barber shop licenses. As demonstrated, the principal value of a license rests in its subject matter.

As with other paper items, if the license is associated with a famous personality or manufacturer, its value increases. A Walt Disney licensing agreement does have value to a Disney collector. Beware of assigning too much value to this association. An increase of 25% to 50% is usually all that is warranted.

Antlerless Deer, 1937, Warren County, white, black letters **5.00**

Archery, 1952, Pennsylvania, issued to Warren Rex Shoff, Pittsburgh, 3$\frac{1}{2}$ x 6$\frac{1}{4}$" **5.00**

Entertainment, 1919, City of Providence, RI, order that *Star Spangled Banner* shall be played at every performance   **15.00**

Fishing
    1922, Pennsylvania, issued to Wilson Heffelfinger, white, black printing, 5$\frac{1}{2}$ x 7" **300.00**
    1960, pink, black printing, 2$\frac{1}{2}$ x 4". . .   **4.00**
    1976, red, white, and blue, Liberty Bell illus, 2$\frac{1}{2}$ x 3" **10.00**

Hunting
    Junior Hunter, 1963, waterproof tagboard, blue, black letters and numbers **6.00**
    Resident
        1913, paper, Philadelphia County, white, black letters, 6$\frac{3}{4}$ x 10$\frac{1}{4}$". .   **20.00**
        1943, cardboard, tan, black letters, 3$\frac{1}{2}$ x 4$\frac{1}{2}$" **5.00**
        1962–69, waterproof tagboard, 3$\frac{1}{2}$ x 6$\frac{1}{4}$", various colors and printing   **3.00**
        1970–80, waterproof tagboard, 3$\frac{1}{2}$ x 6$\frac{1}{4}$", various colors and printing   **2.00**

Liquor, Railroad Car, New York State Railroad, early 1960s, 8 x 11" **9.50**

Marriage
    1946, August 24, Paul W Swavely and Shirley E Kerr, First Brethren Church, Montgomery County, Pottstown, PA **8.00**
    1954, September 25, William Yeakel to Julia Lazor, Old Zionsville United Church of Christ, Zionsville, PA, Lehigh County **6.00**

Muzzleloading, 1974, Pennsylvania, issued to Clark B Spencer, Boyertown, pink, black letters and numbers, 3$\frac{1}{2}$ x 4$\frac{3}{4}$" **5.00**

Trapping, non–resident, 1951, white, stamped year in black ink, red letters and numbers **10.00**

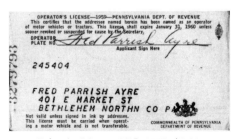

Driver's, PA, 4 x 2$\frac{1}{8}$", 1959, $2.00.

Trapper & Firearm Hunter, 1962, New
Jersey, display holder **10.00**

LITTLE GOLDEN BOOKS

History: Simon & Schuster published the first Little Golden Books in September, 1942. They were conceived and created by the Artists & Writers Guild Inc., which was an arm of the Western Printing and Lithographing Company. The initial twelve, forty–two page titles, priced at 25¢ each, sold over 1.5 million books within five months of publication. By the end of WWII, thirty–nine million Little Golden Books were sold.

A Disney series was begun in 1944, and Big and Giant Golden Books followed that same year. In 1949, the first Goldencraft editions were introduced. Instead of side–stapled cardboard, these books had cloth covers and were sewn so that they could hold up under school and library use. In 1958 Giant Little Golden Books were introduced, most combining three previously published titles together in one book.

1958 also marks Simon & Schuster selling Little Golden Books to Western Printing and Lithographing Company and Pocket Books. The books then appeared under the Golden Press imprint. Eventually Western bought out Pocket Books' interest in Little Golden Books. Now known as Western Publishing Company, Inc., it is the parent company of Golden Press, Inc.

In 1986, Western celebrated the one–billionth Little Golden Book by issuing special commemorative editions of some of its most popular titles, such as *Poky Little Puppy,* and *Cinderella.* In 1992, Golden Press celebrated the 50th birthday of Little Golden Books.

Books published in the forties, fifties, and sixties are in the most demand at this time. Books from this period were assigned individual numbers usually found on the front cover of the book except for the earliest titles where one must check the title against the numbered list on back of the book.

Although the publisher tried to adhere to a policy of one number for each title during the first thirty years, old numbers were assigned to new titles as old titles were eliminated. Also, when an earlier book was re–edited and/or re–illustrated, it was given a new number.

Most of the first thirty–six books had blue paper spines and a dust jacket. Subsequent books were issued with a golden–brown mottled spine. This was replaced in 1950 by a shiny golden spine.

Early books had 42 pages. In the late 1940s, the format was gradually changed to 28 pages. Early 42 and 28 page books had no price on the cover. Later the price of 25¢ appeared on the front cover, then 29¢, followed by 39¢. In the mid–fifties, the number of pages was changed to 24. In the early fifties, books were produced with two lines that formed a bar across the top of the front cover. This bar was eliminated in the early sixties.

Look for books in good or better condition. Covers should be bright with the spine paper intact. Rubbing, ink and crayon markings, or torn pages lessen the value of the book. Pencil markings are fairly easy to remove, unless extensive. Stroke gently in one direction with an art gum eraser. Do not rub back and forth.

References: Barber Bader, *American Picture Books from Noah's Ark to the Beast Within,* Macmillan, 1972; Rebecca Greason, *Tomart's Price Guide to Golden Book Collectibles,* Wallace–Homestead, 1991; Dolores B. Jones, *Bibliography of the Little Golden Book,* Greenwood Press, 1987; Steve Santi, *Collecting Little Golden Books,* Books Americana, 1989.

Periodical: *Pokey Gazette,* 19626 Ricardo Avenue, Haywood, CA 94541.

Note: Prices are based on the first printing of a book in mint condition. Printing is determined by looking at the lower right hand corner of the back page. The letter found there indicates the printing of that particular title and edition. "A" is the first printing and so forth. Occasionally the letter is hidden under the spine or was placed in the upper right hand corner, so look closely. Early titles will have their printings indicated in the front of the book.

Any dust jacket, puzzles, stencils, cutouts, stamps, tissues, tape, or pages should be intact and present as issued. If not, the book suffers a drastic reduction in value–up to 80 percent less than the listed price. Books that are badly worn, incomplete, or badly torn are worth little. Sometimes they are useful as temporary fillers for gaps in a collection.

2, *Bedtime Stories,* illus Gustaf Tenggren,
1942, 42 pgs **15.00**
5, *Prayers for Children,* illus Eloise Wilkin and Rachel Dixon, 1942, 42 pgs . .   **15.00**
8, *The Poky Little Puppy,* Janette Sebring Lowrey, illus Gustaf Tenggren, 1942,
dj **45.00**
13, *The Golden Book of Birds,* Hazel Lockwood, illus Fedor Rojankovsky,
1943, dj **22.00**
17, *Hansel and Gretel,* Brothers Grimm,
illus Erika Weihs, 1943, 42 pgs **12.00**
23, *The Shy Little Kitten,* Cathleen Schurr, illus Gustaf Tenggren, 1946, dj   **40.00**
24, *The New House In The Forest,* Lucy Sprague Mitchell, illus Eloise Wilkin,
1946, dj **45.00**
33, *Let's Go Shopping,* Lenora Combes,
1948 . . . .   **10.00**
41, *The New Baby,* Ruth and Harold Shane, illus Eloise Wilkin, 1948 . . . . .   **12.00**

49, *Mr. Noah and His Family,* Jane Werner, illus Alice and Martin Provensen, 1948 .... **14.00**

57, *Little Black Sambo,* Helen Bannerman, illus Gustaf Tenggren, 1948 **40.00**

67, *The Jolly Barnyard,* Annie North Bedford, illus Tibor Gergely, 1950, puzzle edition, with puzzle in back cov **60.00**

74, *The Little Golden Funny Book,* illus J P Miller, 1950 .... **8.00**

82, *Pets for Peter,* Jane Werner, illus Aurelius Battaglia, 1950 .... **8.00**

93, *Brave Cowboy Bill,* illus Richard Scarry, 1950 .... **10.00**

102, *Ukele and Her New Doll,* puzzle back cov, 1951 .... **15.00**

119, *A Day at the Playground,* Miriam Schlein, illus Eloise Wilkin, 1951 .... **15.00**

121, *Howdy Doody and Clarabell,* Edward Kean, illus Art Seiden, 1951 .... **12.00**

129, *Tex and His Toys,* Elsa Ruth Nast, illus Corinne Malvern, 1952, with Texcell Tape **35.00**

136, *Bugs Bunny Gets a Job,* Annie North Bedford, illus Warner Bros, 1952 .... **8.00**

142, *Frosty the Snowman,* Annie North Bedford, illus Corinne Malvern, 1951 **5.00**

147, *Hopalong Cassidy and the Bar–20 Cowboy,* Elizabeth Beecher, illus Sahula Dycke, 1952 .... **18.00**

149, *Indian Indian,* Charlotte Zolotow, illus Leonard Weisgard, 1952 .... **10.00**

159, *The Tin Woodman of Oz,* Peter Archer, illus Harry McNaught, 1952.. **20.00**

169, *Rabbit and His Friends,* written and illus Richard Scarry, 1953 .... **3.00**

174, *Bible Stories of Boys and Girls,* Jane Werner, illus Rachel Taft Dixon, 1953 **3.00**

183, *Bugs Bunny at the Easter Party,* Kathryn Hitte, 1953............... **8.00**

194, *The Twelve Dancing Princesses,* illus Sheilah Beckett, 1954 .... **6.50**

203, *Little Lulu and Her Magic Tricks,* written and illus Marge Henderson Buell, 1954, with orig Kleenex **50.00**

208, *Tiger's Adventure,* William P. Gottlieb, 1954, photos **7.00**

213, *Dale Evans and the Lost Gold Mine,* Monica Hill, illus Mel Crawford, 1955 **12.00**

223, *It's Howdy Doody Time,* Edward Kean, illus Art Seiden, 1955 .... **18.00**

227, *The Twins,* Ruth and Harold Shane, illus Eloise Wilkin, 1955 .... **22.00**

231, *Roy Rogers and the Mountain Lion,* Ann McGovern, illus Mel Crawford, 1955 .... **12.00**

233, *My Puppy,* Patsy Scarry, illus Eloise Wilkin, 1955 .... **6.00**

238, *5 Pennies to Spend,* Miriam Young, illus Corinne Malvern, 1955 .... **8.00**

243, *Numbers,* Gertrude Crampton, illus Violet La Mont, 1955............. **5.00**

251, *Cars,* Kathryn Jackson, illus William J Dugan, 1956 .... **5.00**

254, *Buffalo Bill, Jr.,* Gladys Wyatt, illus H. Milton Greene, 1956 .... **7.00**

258, *Heidi,* Corinne Malvern and Johanna Sypri, 1954, 24 pgs **5.00**

266, *Winky Dink,* Ann McGovern, illus Richard Scarry, 1956.............. **12.00**

277, *Lassie and the Daring Rescue,* Charles Spain Verral, illus Joseph E Dreany, 1956 .... **6.00**

285, *How To Tell Time,* Jane Werner Watson, illus Eleanor Dart, 1957, with clock face and hands, "Gruen" on face **15.00**

290, *Circus Boy,* Irwin Shapiro, illus Joan Walsh Anglund, 1957 .... **14.00**

305, *The White Bunny and His Magic Nose,* Lily Duplaix, illus Feodor Rojankovsky, 1957 .... **12.00**

318, *Cheyenne,* Charles Spain Verral, illus Al Schmidt, 1958 .... **12.00**

325, *Play Ball!,* Charles Spain Verral, illus Gerald McCann, 1958......... **6.00**

328, *Tales of Wells Fargo,* Leon Lazarus, illus John Leone, 1958.............. **15.00**

340, *My Baby Sister,* Patsy Scarry, illus Sharon Koester, 1958 .... **5.00**

356, *Steve Canyon,* written and illus Milton Caniff, 1959.................. **8.00**

360, *Party in Shariland,* Ann McGovern, illus Doris and Marion Henderson, 1959 .... **12.00**

372, *Woody Woodpecker Drawing Fun for Beginners,* Carl Buettner, illus Harvey Eisenberg and Norman McGary, 1959 .... **12.00**

384, *Baby Listens,* Esther Wilkin, illus Eloise Wilkin, 1960............... **6.00**

395, *Yogi Bear,* S. Quentin Hyatt, illus M. Kawaguchi and Bob Barritt, 1960 **10.00**

399, *Doctor Dan at the Circus,* Pauline

***Cheyenne*, #318, Charles Spain Verral, Al Schmidt illus., Simon and Schuster, NY, 24 pages, 1958, $12.00.**

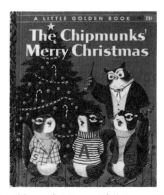

The Chipmunks' Merry Christmas, #375, David Corwin, Richard Scarry illus., Golden Press, NY, 24 pages, 1959, $6.00.

Uncle Remus, #D6, Joel Chandler Harris, retold by Marion Palmer, Bob Grant illus., Simon and Schuster, NY, 42 pages, 1947, $10.00.

Wilkins, illus Katherine Sampson, 1960, orig Johnson & Johnson Band–Aids 40.00

408, *Rocky and His Friends,* Ann McGovern, illus Ben DeNunez and Al White, 1960 . . . . 12.00

418, *My Dolly and Me,* Patricia Scarry, illus Eloise Wilkin, 1960 . . . . 20.00

432, *Dennis the Menace Waits for Santa Claus,* Carl Memling, illus Al White, Norm McGary, Bill Lorencz, 1962 . . . 10.00

443, *Puff the Blue Kitten,* written and illus Pierre Probst, 1961. . . . . 14.00

451, *Ten Little Animals,* Carl Memling, illus Feodor Rojankovsky, 1961 . . . . . 4.00

465, *My Little Golden Animal Book,* Elizabeth MacPherson, illus Moritz Kennel, 1962 . . . . 5.00

476, *Little Lulu,* Gina Ingoglia Weiner, illus Woody Kimbrell and Al White, 1962 . . . . 10.00

483, *Mister Ed The Talking Horse,* Barbara Shook Hazen, illus Mel Crawford, 1962 . . . . 12.00

500, *The Jetsons,* Carl Memling, illus Al White and Hawley Pratt, 1962 . . . . . . 18.00

537, *Beany Goes To Sea,* Monica Hill, illus Hawley Pratt and Bill Lorencz, 1963 . . . . 20.00

546, *Fireball XL5,* Barbara Shook Hazen, illus Hawley Pratt and Al White, 1964 18.00

552, *We Like Kindergarten,* Clara Cassidy, illus Eloise Wilkin, 1964 . . . . 4.00

556, *Peter Potamus,* Carl Memling, illus Hawley Pratt and Bill Lorencz, c1964 9.00

569, *Little Mommy,* written and illus Sharon Kane, c1967 . . . . 8.00

A2, *Circus Time,* Marion Conger, illus Tibor Gergely, c1955, with wheel. . . . 10.00

A6, *Trucks,* Kathryn Jackson, illus Ray Quigley, 1955, punch–out trucks 35.00

A17, *Stop and Go,* Loyta Higgins, illus Joan Walsh Anglund, c1957, with wheel. 15.00

A34, *Little Red Riding Hood,* illus Sharon Koester, c1959, with paper dolls, uncut 45.00

A44, *ABC Around the House (Wheel Book),* Kathleen N Daly, illus Violet La Mont, 1957 . . . . 6.00

D2, *The Cold Blooded Penguin,* Robert Edmunds, illus Walt Disney Productions, c1944, dj 40.00

D11, *Johnny Appleseed,* Walt Disney Studios, illus Ted Parmalee, 1949 . . . . 10.00

D21, *Grandpa Bunny,* Jane Werner, illus Walt Disney Studios, c1951 . . . . 14.00

D34, *Donald Duck and the Witch,* Annie North, illus Dick Kelsey, 1953. . . . . . . 10.00

D48, *Robin Hood,* Annie North Bedford, illus Walt Disney Studios, 1955 . . . . . 10.00

D50, *Jiminy Cricket Fire Fighter,* Annie North Bedford, illus Samuel Armstrong, 1956 . . . . 14.00

D65, *Old Yeller,* Irwin Shapiro, illus Edwin Schmidt and E Joseph Daly, 1957 . . . . 10.00

D71, *Sleeping Beauty & The Fairies,* Annie North, 1958, 24 pgs 10.00

D83, *Goliath II,* written and illus Bill Peet, 1959 . . . . 14.00

D95, *Swiss Family Robinson,* Jean Lewis, illus Paul Granger, c1961 . . . . 6.00

D126, *Robin Hood,* Walt Disney Studios, 1973 . . . . 4.00

LOBBY CARDS

History: A lobby card is a movie poster, printed on heavy stock, and measuring approximately eleven by fourteen inches. It normally contains the title of the film, a list of stars, and a scene from the film. Lobby cards were displayed in the lobby or outside bulletin boards of a movie theater to promote upcoming or current attractions.

Lobby cards generally were issued in sets. Sets of 4, 8, 10, and 12 cards are known. Eight card sets are the most common. A typical set of eight cards included one title card and seven scene cards. Exceptions abound. In the 1930s and 1940s, Paramount issued sets without a title card. A "close up" card replaced the title card, making Paramount sets from the era highly desirable.

A title card is a lobby card that graphically illustrates the title of the movie and its stars. It is the most desirable card in a set. Usually its premium value is about 25%. However, in a few cases, such as the title card for *Casablanca*, it may be equivalent to the movie's one sheet movie poster.

A jumbo lobby card measures fourteen by seventeen inches. Normally it is printed on a better quality poster board, i.e., one that has a bright, glossy surface. The same value keys that apply to standard size lobby cards also apply to jumbo cards.

The key value component is the image on the card. This means that cards within the same set often have a different collector value. An image with strong sex appeal, important scenes from the movie, and key characters, e.g., the monster in a horror movie, increases the value of a card. Close up shots are more favored than distant shots.

Lobby cards from sound films have stronger market appeal than those from silent films. Silent film lobby cards sell in the $10.00 to $35.00 range. Cards dating from the late 1930s through the early 1950s currently enjoy the strongest collector interest.

Lobby card value is often pegged to the value of the film's one sheet movie poster. A general rule is that a lobby card is worth 10% to 25% of the retail price of the one sheet.

A close cousin to the lobby card is the window card. Window cards are found in two standard sizes, fourteen by twenty–two inches and twenty–two inches by twenty–eight inches. These heavy, cardboard posters have a blank section in which the show date, times, and location can be written. Once the movie was shown, theater owners often cut away the blank portion. This reduced the size to fourteen by seventeen inches, the same size as a jumbo lobby card. Check the edges of any fourteen by seventeen inch "jumbo lobby card" to make certain it is not a trimmed down window card.

References: Richard De Thuin, *The Official Identification and Price Guide to Movie Memorabilia*, House of Collectibles, 1990; Jon R. Warren, *Warren's Movie Poster Price Guide, 1993 Edition*, American Collectors Exchange, 1992.

Abbott and Costello Meet The Invisible Man, 1951, Universal Pictures, Bud Abbott and Lou Costello	20.00
A Child Is Born, 1940, Warner Brothers	18.00
Across The Pacific, 1942, Warner Brothers, Humphrey Bogart, Sidney Greenstreet, Mary Astor	18.00
Across 110th Street, United Artists, set of 8	10.00
Adventures of Martin Eden, 1942, Columbia Pictures.	15.00
A Farewell To Arms, 1963, Rock Hudson	24.00
Alias The Badman, 1932, Ken Maynard	125.00
Alien, 1979, set of 8	75.00
Always In My Heart, 1942, Warner Brothers, Kay Francis and Walter Huston	25.00
American Guerrilla In The Philippines, 1950, Twentieth Century–Fox, Tyrone Power	28.00
Andy Hardy's Private Secretary, 1941, Metro–Goldwyn–Mayer, Mickey Rooney	12.00
Arabesque, 1966, Gregory Peck and Sophia Loren, complete set	34.00
Armored Command, 1961, complete set	24.00
Barbarian & Geisha, John Wayne, 11 x 14"	25.00
Batman, 1989, set of 8	30.00
Bar C Mystery, Dorothy Phillips, black and white	30.00
Belles on Their Toes, 1952, 11 x 14" . .	15.00
Ben Hur, 1959, Metro–Goldwyn–Mayer, Charlton Heston and Jack Hawkins	8.00
Berlin Express, RKO Radio Pictures, 1948, set of 8	50.00
Black Tuesday, 1955, United Artists, Edward G Robinson	8.00
Blade Runner, 1982, set of 8	45.00
Blood of Dracula, 1957, American International	10.00
Body and Soul, 1947, United Artists, John Garfield	25.00
Border Cafe, 1937, RKO Radio Pictures	25.00
Carrie, 1976, set of 8	25.00
Charlie Chan At Monte Carlo, 1937, Twentieth Century–Fox	45.00
Chatterbox, 1942, Republic Pictures, Joe E Brown and Judy Canova.	10.00
Check Your Guns, Eddie Dean, 11 x 14"	15.00
Circus of Horrors, 1960, American International	6.00
Clockwork Orange, 1972, set of 8	150.00
Colorado Sunset, 1939, Republic Pictures, Gene Autry	25.00
Curse Corpse	22.00
Day the Earth Stood Still	300.00

A Very Special Favor, Rock Hudson, Leslie Caron, Charles Boyer, full color, 11 x 14", $25.00.

Dimension 5, 1966, set	24.00
Don't Fence Me In, 1945, Republic Pictures, Roy Rogers	10.00
Dracula, Prince of Darkness, 1966, Twentieth Century–Fox, Christopher Lee, black and white	5.00
Earth vs The Flying Saucers, 1956, Columbia Pictures, Hugh Marlowe and June Taylor	15.00
Easy Payments, 1920s	70.00
Empire Strikes Back, 1980, set of 8	45.00
Eve's Secret, Betty Compson and Jack Holt	20.00
Experience, Paramount Pictures, Richard Barthelmess	50.00
Fallen Sparrow, 1943, RKO Radio Pictures, John Garfield and Maureen O'Hara	25.00
Finger of Guilt, 1956, RKO Radio Pictures, set of 8	12.00
Flight Command, 1941, Metro–Goldwyn–Mayer, Robert Taylor . . .	15.00
Frenzy, 1972, set of 8	30.00
Funeral In Berlin, 1967, Michael Caine and Eva Renzl, set	30.00
Gateway, 1938, Don Ameche, 11 x 14"	125.00
Going My Way, 1944, 11 x 14"	50.00
Goodbye Mr Chips, 1939, 11 x 14" . . .	85.00
Guns of the Night, Bill Elliott and Slim Summerville	18.00
Hail to the Rangers, Charles Starrett color photo, Columbia picture, 1943	18.00
Havoc, 1925, Madge Bellamy	90.00
Hell On Frisco Bay, 1956, Warner Brothers, Alan Ladd and Edward G Robinson	12.00
High Society, Bing Crosby, Grace Kelly, and Frank Sinatra	25.00
His Majesty, The American, 1919, Douglas Fairbanks	125.00
Horror of Beach	22.00

Hot Millions, 1968, Peter Ustinov, Bob Newhart, and Maggie Smith, complete set	20.00
Hush, Clara Kimball Young, color photo	25.00
I'll See You In My Dreams, Doris Day, 11 x 14"	25.00
Intrigue, George Raft	20.00
Jaws, 1975, set of 8	75.00
Just Around The Corner, Paramount Pictures	5.00
Keeper of the Bees, Gene Stratton–Porter	5.00
Kentuckian, Oliver Hardy and Vera Ralston	30.00
Kidnapper, Peter Lorre	150.00
Lady Godiva, 1955, Maureen O'Hara and George Nader, set of 8	25.00
Little Miss Broadway, Shirley Temple, 11 x 14", set	1,500.00
Lola, 1971, Charles Bronson, set	22.00
M*A*S*H, Donald Sutherland photo . .	5.00
Marked Trails, Bob Steele and Hoot Gibson	18.00
Men of the Night, 1934	35.00
Miss Tatlock's Millions, 1948, Robert Stack and Dorothy Wood, framed . .	40.00
News Parade, Sally Phipps and Nick Stuart	20.00
Night Patrol, Rich Talmadge, set of 8 . .	130.00
Not As A Stranger, 1955, United Artists, set of 8	45.00
Octopussy, 1983, set of 8	35.00
Parade of Comedy, 1964	25.00
Phantom From Space, 1953, United Artists, set of 8	12.00
Play Misty For Me, 1971, Universal Pictures, Clint Eastwood, Jessica Walter, and Donna Mills	6.00
Psycho, 1960, set of 8	400.00

Arizona Whirlwind, Ken Maynard, Hoot Gibson, and Bob Steele, The Trail Blazers, Monogram Pictures, color photo, 11 x 14", 1944, $20.00.

Raiders of the Lost Ark, 1981, set of 8 . . **50.00**
Rainmaker, 1956, 11 x 14". **10.00**
Range Law, Johnny Mack Brown, 11 x
14" **25.00**
Rawhide Rangers, Universal, Johnny
Mack Brown **15.00**
Reap Wild Wind, octopus scene **15.00**
Robocop, 1987, set of 8 . . . . **30.00**
Room At The Top, 1959, L Harvey and
S Signoret **18.00**
Rough Riders, West of the Law **40.00**
Rupert of Hentzau, 1920s. **100.00**
Shampoo, 1975, Warren Beatty,
Goldie Hawn, and Julie Christie, set **38.00**
Shine On Harvest Moon, Roy Rogers,
Mary Hart, and Lulu Belle. **32.00**
Sisters, Lillian Gish and Dorothy Gish,
set of 8. . . . . **500.00**
Soft Cushions, Douglas MacLean. **18.00**
Sonny, Richard Barthelmess, color
photo **25.00**
Spy Who Loved Me, 1977, set of 8 . . . . **40.00**
Tank Battalion, 1958, Edward G Robin-
son, set of 6 . . . . **35.00**
Target, RKO Radio Pictures, 1952, Tim
Holt. **18.00**
Teenage Monster **20.00**
Telefon, 1977, Charles Bronson and
Lee Remick, complete set. **20.00**
Terminator, 1984, set of 8 . . . . **35.00**
The Cross and The Switchblade, 1970,
Pat Boone and Erik Estrada, com-
plete set. **24.00**
The Exorcist, 1973, set of 8. . . . . **40.00**
The Fighting 69th, James Cagney and
Pat O'Brien **22.00**
The Galloping Dude, 1920s, Franklyne
Farnum **40.00**
The Gorilla Ship, 1932, Ralph Ince and
Vera Reynolds **35.00**
The Hindenburg, 1975, George C Scott
and Anne Bancroft, set **35.00**
The Lucky Horseshoe, 1925, Tom Mix **175.00**
The Kansan, 1943, R Dix and J Wyatt **20.00**
The Long Gray Line, Columbia Pic-
tures, 1955, set of 8. . . . . **25.00**
The Midnight Watch, 1930s. **25.00**
The Moon Is Blue, 1960, William
Holden, set of 8. . . . . **35.00**
The Ole Swimming Hole, Charles Ray,
color photo **25.00**
The Spoilers, John Wayne and Marlene
Dietrich **90.00**
The Woman Condemned, 1934,
Mischa Auer and Lola Lane, set of 6 **70.00**
Timbuktu, 1959, Victor Mature and
Yvonne De Carlo, set of 7 . . . . **24.00**
Virginia City, 1940, Errol Flynn,
Humphrey Bogart, and Miriam Hop-
kins. **160.00**
Warming Up, Richard Dix **14.00**

We're No Angels, Humphrey Bogart
and Aldo Ray **10.00**
We're Not Married, 1952, Fred Allen,
Victor Moore, and Marilyn Monroe **30.00**
Winter Meeting, Bette Davis **25.00**
Yogi Bear, 1964. . . . . **20.00**
Young Frankenstein, 1974, set of 8 . . . . **35.00**

MAGAZINE COVERS

History: Magazine cover design attracted some of America's leading illustrators. Maxfield Parrish, Erte, Leyendecker, and Norman Rockwell were dominant forces in the 20th century. In the mid–1930s, photographic covers gradually replaced the illustrated covers. One of the leaders in the industry was *Life,* which emphasized photojournalism.

Magazine covers are frequently collected by artist signed covers, subject matter, or historical events. Artist signed covers feature a commercially printed artist signature on the cover, or the artist is identified inside as "Cover by..." Most collected covers are in full color and show significant design elements.

Black memorabilia is often reflected in magazine covers and tear sheets. It is frequently collected for the positive effect it has on African–Americans. However, sometimes it is a reflection of the times in which it was printed and may represent subjects in an unfavorable light.

Many of America's leading artists also illustrated magazine advertising. The ads made advertising characters such as the Campbell Kids, the Dutch Girl, and Snap, Crackle and Pop world famous.

A good cover should show the artist's signature, have the mailing label nonexistent or in a place that does not detract from the design element, and have edges that are crisp, but not trimmed.

References: David K. Henkel, *Magazines: Identification and Price Guide,* Avon Books, 1993; Denis C. Jackson, *The Masters Price & Identification Guide to Old Magazines,* published by author, 1985; Denis C. Jackson, *Men's Girlie Magazines: The Only Price Guide!: Newstanders, Third Edition,* The Illustrator Collector's News, 1991; Patricia Kery, *Great Magazine Covers of The World,* Abbeville Press, 1982; Frank Zawacki, *Famous Faces: Price Guide and Catalog for Magazine Collectors,* Wallace–Homestead, 1985 (Although the prices in this book are badly dated, its listing are accurate. It is an important reference tool for any library.) **Note**: See "Illustrators" in topical section for books devoted to specific illustrators.

Periodical: *PCM (Paper Collector's Marketplace),* PO Box 128, Scandinavia, WI 54977.

Note: Prices of covers and complete magazines have remained stable the last few years, but those of tear sheets have declined as more and more magazines have glutted the market. While only a short time ago magazines were thrown away when attics and garages were cleaned, now they are offered for sale. The public has been educated by seeing many magazine tear sheets being offered for sale at flea markets and mall shows. Dealers prefer to purchase complete magazines and glean their profit from the contents.

As more and more magazines are destroyed for the tear sheets, complete magazines rise in value as the supply decreases. If a magazine is in mint condition, it should be left intact. We do **NOT** encourage removing illustrations from complete magazines. Only the complete magazine can act as a tool to interpret that specific historical time period. Editorial and advertising together define the spirit of the era.

ARTIST SIGNED

Armstrong, Rolf	25.00
Atwell, Mabel Lucie, Pictorial Review, November 1913	35.00
Benito, Herbert	10.00
Bevans, Torre	
Children	15.00
McCall's, 1920–21	18.00
Pictorial Review, April 1920	18.00
Woman	8.00
Boileau, Phillip	45.00
Campbell, The Prudential, 1937, children fishing	18.00
Cassandre, A M	35.00
Christy, Howard Chandler	12.00
Coffin, Haskell	12.00
Crane, S W	6.00
Dillion, Corrine Boyd	6.00
Drayton, Grace	30.00
Eastman, Ruth	
Look	5.00
The Designer, August 1913	18.00
Erte, Harper's Bazaar	65.00
Fisher, Harrison, Ladies' Home Journal, December 1913	40.00
Flagg, James M, Liberty, December 21, 1918	10.00
Gibson, C. D.	
Collier's, 1905	3.00
Greer, Blanche, Woman's Home Companion, June 1907	20.00
Gunn, Archie, Truth, June 20, 1896	35.00
Gutmann, Bessie Pease	45.00
Harris, Collier's, fishing motif, 1937	6.00
Hays, Mary A, McCall's, May 1915	5.00
Hoff, Guy, The Woman's Magazine, December 1918	15.00
Hunter, Frances Tipton, S.E.P., April 12, 1941	15.00

King, Hamilton, Coca–Cola girl	15.00
Leyendecker, F X	
Literary Digest, soldiers, March 9, 1918	18.00
Saturday Evening Post, Christmas, December 7, 1901	15.00
S.E.P.	
1911, April 29, girl seated at piano	18.00
1913, June 21, bride and groom	17.00
Linson, Corwin Knapp	6.00
Marsh, Lucille Patterson	15.00
Mayer, My, Truth, August 15, 1896	25.00
McClelland, Barclay	6.00
McMein, Neysa, McCalls, 1930	12.00
Mucha, Alphonse	
Century	100.00
Literary Digest	40.00
O'Neill, Rose	
Ladies' Home Journal, Kewpies, December 1910	35.00
Metropolitan, February 1900	20.00
The Designer, August 1911	35.00
The Pictorial Review, January 1914	35.00
Woman's Home Companion, January 1924	20.00
Outcault, Truth, February 15, 1896	15.00
Parkhurst, McCall's, December 1916	15.00
Parrish, Maxfield	
Collier's, July 8, 1905	60.00
Ladies' Home Journal, December 1912	70.00
Thanksgiving, November 17, 1906	45.00
Tramp's Thanksgiving, November 18, 1905	70.00
Penfield, Edward, Harper's Weekly, December 1898	35.00
Phillip, Cole, McCall's, June 1918	15.00

***Fortune*, A. Petruccelli cover illus., sgd., blue and purple, 11 x 14″, February 1935, $40.00.**

Ralph, Lester	**6.00**
Robinson, Robert	**8.00**
Rockwell, Norman	
Boys' Life, 1951	**20.00**
Leslie's, woman on telephone, March 22, 1919	**35.00**
Smith, James Calvert, McCall's, November 1921	**8.00**
Smith, Jessie Wilcox, Good Houskeeping	**20.00**
Stanlaws, Penny	**8.00**
Twelvetrees, Charles	
Capper's Farmer, 1930s	**12.00**
Collier's, 1930s	**12.00**
Pictorial Review	
Large format	**30.00**
Small format	**10.00**
Suffrage, January 1921	**25.00**
Usobal, McCall's, March 1921	**8.00**
Vargas	**50.00**
Williamson, J., Saturday Evening Post, October 27, 1962	**2.00**
Wireman, H. E., Woman's Home Companion, December 1915	**12.00**
Wood, Lawson, monkey image	**10.00**

BLACK

Armstrong, Louis	**18.00**
Black images, Saturday Evening Post	**20.00**
Clay, Cassius	**10.00**
Davis, Jr, Sammy	**9.00**
King, Martin Luther	**15.00**
Slave Auction, Life, 1956	**15.00**

GENERAL

American Home, artist sgd	**6.00**
American Magazine, May 1918, woman bidding farewell to soldiers, J Knowles, Cream of Wheat ad on reverse	**18.00**
Asia, Art Deco design	**10.00**
Collier's, general, 1906	**4.00**
Delineator, general	
Large format	**30.00**
Small format	**12.00**
Designer, general	
Large format	**30.00**
Small format	**12.00**
Flair, general	**3.00**
Fortune, general	**12.00**
House Beautiful, artist sgd	**2.00**
House and Garden	
Art Deco design	**3.00**
General	**3.00**
Junior Home, artist sgd	**6.00**
Le Rire, general	**6.00**
Le Sourire, general	**8.00**
Leslie's	
Artist sgd	**12.00**
General	**4.00**
Liberty, August 2, 1941, woman golfer	**15.00**

Scribner's Magazine, unsigned, August 1907, $10.00.

Life	
General	**3.00**
Political	**5.00**
VIP	**8.00**
War	**5.00**
Literary Digest, general	**3.00**
Look, general	**3.00**
McCall's	
Cream of Wheat	
Large format	**28.00**
Small format	**12.00**
General	
1920s	**12.00**
1930s	**8.00**
McClure's, general	**8.00**
Modern Priscilla, general	**2.00**
Needlecraft	
Cream of Wheat	**18.00**
General	**3.00**
Pictoral Review	
Large format, pre 1920	**40.00**
Small format	**12.00**
Popular Science	
Prior to 1930	**10.00**
After 1930, non-photographic	**4.00**
Saturday Evening Post	
Prior to 1930	**8.00**
1930-1950	**5.00**
Truth, general	**20.00**
Vanity Fair, general	**20.00**
Woman's Home Companion, general	**15.00**
Woman's World, general	**8.00**

MAGAZINES

History: In the early 1700s general magazines were a major means of information for the reader. Literary magazines, such as *Harper's,* became popular in the nineteenth century. By 1900, the first photo–journal magazines appeared. *Life,* the prime example, was started by Henry Luce in 1932.

Magazines created for women featured "how to" articles about cooking, sewing, decorating, and child care. Many were entirely devoted to fashion and living a fashionable life, such as *Harper's Bazaar* and *Vogue.* Men's magazines were directed at masculine skills of the time, such as hunting, fishing, and woodworking, supplemented with appropriate "girlie" titles.

A rule of thumb for pricing general magazines without popular artist–designed covers: the more you would enjoy displaying a copy on your coffee table, the more elite the publication; and, the more the advertising or editorial content relates to today's collectibles, the higher the price. *Life* magazine went into millions of homes each week, *Harper's Bazaar* and *Vogue* did not. Elite families had a greater tendency to discard last month's publication while middle–class families found the art on the *Saturday Evening Post* and *Collier's* irresistible and saved them. The greater the supply, the lower the price.

Juvenile and literary magazines are a tough sell. A juvenile will sell if it has a cover or article illustrated by a famous illustrator or includes an insert, e.g., paper dolls, of interest to a crossover collector.

References: David K. Henkel, *Magazines: Identification and Price Guide,* Avon Books, 1993; David K. Henkel, *The Official Identification and Price Guide to Rock and Roll: Magazines, Posters, and Memorabilia,* House of Collectibles, 1992: Marjorie M. and Donald L. Hinds, *Magazine Magic,* The Messenger Book Press, 1972; Denis C. Jackson, *The Masters Price & Identification Guide to Old Magazines,* published by author, 1985; Denis C. Jackson, *Men's Girlie Magazines: The Only Price Guide!: Newstanders, Third Edition,* The Illustrator Collector's News, 1991.

Note: Most magazines have little or no value. Do not be deceived by the list that follows. The individual copy retail prices below may be considerably higher than what would be offered for an entire collection filling your basement or garage.

Bulk prices for common magazines such as *Life, Collier's,* and *Saturday Evening Post* are generally from fifty cents to one dollar per issue. Dealers have to sort, protect with plastic covering, discard ones that have items clipped from the interior, or have marred covers, and they make no money on those which they never sell. The end result is that a lower price is paid for magazines purchased in bulk.

BOUND ISSUES

American Magazine, July–December 1940, Rockwell cov illus	**7.50**
Arizona Highways, January 1981 to December 1982	**14.50**
Godey's Lady's Book, bound yearly	**50.00**
Harper's, thirteen volumes, 1867–1877	**10.00**
National Geographic, 1937, two volumes	**15.50**
Peterson's, bound yearly	**40.00**
Popular Science, 1926, twelve issues . . .	**60.00**
QST Radio, 1957	**15.00**
Scribner's, 1932–36, ten volumes	**40.00**
St Nicholas, 1900–1909, twenty–three volumes	**150.00**
The Century Illustrated Monthly, two volumes, May 1886–April 1888, ex–library, cov wear	**24.00**
The Survey, three volumes	**12.00**
Youth's Companion, bound year, 1908	**125.00**

CONSECUTIVE RUNS, SOLD AS LOTS

American Rifleman, 1925 through 1980, six hundred sixty issues	**750.00**
Capper Farmers, 1930 through 1940s, seventy issues	**165.00**
Detective, 1930s, one hundred sixteen issues	**135.00**
Farmer's, 1917, twenty issues	**52.00**
Farm Journal, 1920s, eight issues	**35.00**
Field and Stream, 1931 through 1944, one hundred fifty–six issues	**1,000.00**
National Geographic, 1920 through 1930s, sixty–four issues	**95.00**
Outdoor Life, 1931 through 1952, two hundred fifty issues	**1,250.00**
Playboy, 1971, three issues	**5.00**
Popular Mechanics, 1940s, forty issues	**42.00**
Popular Science	
1940s, sixty–five issues	**68.00**
1950s, one hundred issues	**70.00**
Romance, 1940s and 1950s, forty–two issues	**50.00**
Southern California Alumni Review, 1943–44, four issues	**3.00**
Successful Farming, 1920 through 1930s, twenty–five issues	**95.00**
The Larkin Idea, 1914 to 1915, five issues	**75.00**
True Confessions, 1946–57, twelve issues	**15.00**
True Love, 1939–51, ten issues	**12.00**
True Story, 1930s, thirty–four issues . .	**45.00**
Yank Army Weekly, 1945, twenty issues	**18.00**

SINGLE ISSUES

All Hands, September, 1945, Navy magazine, End of War edition, atomic photos	**18.00**
American Magazine	
1926, December, Earl C Christy cov . .	**10.00**
1932, July, tennis player cov	**4.00**
American Artist, April, 1960	**5.00**
American Boy	
Prior to 1929	**8.00**
Prior to 1940	**5.00**

American Golfer, December, 1932	**18.00**		Business Week		
American Home	**2.00**		Prior to 1940	**5.00**
American Motorist, 1916	**8.50**		Prior to 1960	**3.00**
American Photography, 1932	**8.00**		After 1960	**2.00**

American Golfer, December, 1932 . . . . **18.00**
American Home **2.00**
American Motorist, 1916 . . . . **8.50**
American Photography, 1932 . . . . **8.00**
Antiques, October, 1931 . . . . **7.50**
Argosy **2.00**
Arizona Highways
    Prior to 1930 . . . . **12.00**
    Prior to 1940 . . . . **8.00**
    Prior to 1960 . . . . **3.00**
    After 1960 . . . . **2.00**
Architectural Record, #7, 1932 . . . . **18.00**
Art and Beauty, 1926 . . . . **8.00**
Asia, Art Deco cov. **25.00**
Atlantic Monthly
    1868 . . . . **2.00**
    1907, November, anniversary edition **18.00**
    1911–1914 . . . . **4.00**
    1915–1927 . . . . **2.00**
    1928–1935 . . . . **1.50**
Automobile Digest, September 1925 . . . **4.00**
Barbie Talk, Barbie Fan Club Magazine,
    Mattel Inc. publisher, 1970, January–
    February, Vol 2, No. 1, 24 pgs, arti-
    cles, products, games, and puzzles,
    8½ x 11" **18.00**
Barnum & Bailey Circus, 1909, 30 pgs . . **20.00**
Better Homes and Gardens, prior to 1935 **1.50**
Better Photo, 1913 . . . . **2.50**
Black Cat Magazine
    Cat's head cov **8.00**
    Full figure of dressed cat on cov **25.00**
Bonanza, Vol #1, 1965. . . . . **25.00**
Boys' Life, 1916, Rockwell cov **35.00**
Boy's World **1.00**
Breed's Gazette, April, 1885 . . . . **6.50**
Building Age National Builder, 1920s. . . **8.00**
Burr–McIntosh, March, 1907, C Hobart
    cov **15.00**

Business Week
    Prior to 1940 . . . . **5.00**
    Prior to 1960 . . . . **3.00**
    After 1960 . . . . **2.00**
California '71 Earthquake, JEK publisher,
    Hollywood, CA, 80 pgs, "Killer
    Quake," black and white photos of be-
    fore and after, 9 x 12" **15.00**
Canal Record, published by Isthmian Ca-
    nal Commission to all Employees,
    Wednesday, May 6, 1908, Vol. 1, No.
    36, 8 pgs, Ancon Canal Zone, facts
    and figures of canal progress, 9 x 12" **18.00**
Capper's Farmer
    Prior to 1930 . . . . **3.00**
    Twelvetrees cov. **12.00**
Carpenter Magazine, 1916, 60 pgs **5.00**
Century
    1882–1893 . . . . **3.00**
    1917–1926 . . . . **1.00**
    Mucha cov. **100.00**
Charlie, June 1971, John Lennon article **4.00**
Children's Play Mate, September, 1953 **8.00**
Child's Life, 1930 . . . . **5.00**
Coast Magazine, Seattle, 1900–1912 . . . **10.00**
Collier's
    December 11, 1940, Vernon Grant
      cov. **4.00**
    June 9, 1938 . . . . **7.00**
    May 5, 1906, San Francisco Earth-
      quake. **75.00**
Connoisseur, October, 1907. . . . . **12.00**
Coronet, prior to 1950. . . . . **3.00**
Cosmopolitan, 1907 . . . . **5.00**
Country Gentleman, 1914, Leyendecker
    cov. **20.00**
Country Home . . . . **.75**
Country Life. **1.00**
Country Music, Country Song Roundup,

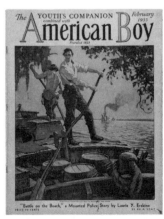

American Boy, printed color cover illus. by Henning, 50 pages, 10½ x 14", February 1933, $10.00.

Collier's, Fred Turner cover illus., sgd., orange and black color wash, 30 pages, 10½ x 14", October 28, 1922, $6.00.

February, 1966, 34 pgs, black and
white photos, country music stars articles, 9 x 12" **8.00**

Delineator
1902 .... **20.00**
1918–1920 .... **25.00**
1921–1935 .... **15.00**

Demorist Fashion, September, 1876. ... **10.00**

Designer
Large format **18.00**
Small format **12.00**
1900–04, color fashion plates. **20.00**

Des Moines Register Sunday Magazines,
early 1940s **5.00**

Ebony, 1958 .... **5.00**

ERA, June, 1931, photographer and cine-
matographer **15.00**

Esquire
1934, September................ **18.00**
1941, Christmas, Petty Girl Revue,
306 pgs **52.00**
1951, April, Printer's Devil Gatefold
by Al Moore.................. **15.00**
1957, January **2.00**

Etudes, 1940s **4.00**

Everyday Science and Mechanics, February, 1934, full color cov art and article
of *The Invisible Man,* 64 pgs, 8½ x
11½" **25.00**

Farm & Fireside, November 1920, Frederic Stanley cov **4.00**

Farm Implement News, 1892 .... **30.00**

Farm Journal, April, 1936 .... **1.50**

Farm Mechanics, mid 1920s.......... **8.00**

Farmer's Wife
Mueller, Benson cov, August, 1925 .. **10.00**
Prior to 1950 .... **2.00**
Others **1.00**

Field and Stream **3.00**

Flair, diecut hole in cov.............. **4.00**

Fortune
Cigar band page inside **50.00**
Prior to 1935 .... **15.00**
Prior to 1940 .... **12.00**
Prior to 1950 .... **10.00**
Prior to 1960 .... **8.00**

Gentelman's Magazine, 1732, early life
in Carolinas **25.00**

Girl's Companion
Prior to 1940 .... **3.00**
After 1940 .... **1.00**

Godey's Lady Book
1856 .... **150.00**
1861 .... **50.00**

Golf Illustrated, September, 1934 ...... **10.00**

Good Housekeeping, prior to 1955 ... **2.00**

Hammond Times, 1940, July, Walt Disney cov **17.50**

Harper's Bazaar
Erte cov **50.00**
Illustrated cov **10.00**
Photographic cov **5.00**

Harper's Monthly
1873–1896 .... **8.00**
1902–1906 .... **6.00**
1910–1917 .... **5.00**
1919–1925 .... **4.00**
1930–1935 .... **2.00**

Harper's Weekly
1873–1898 .... **12.00**
December 1900 .... **15.00**

Harvest World, 1931............... **2.50**

Highway Traveler, Greyhound, 1936 ... **2.50**

Hit Parader, January, 1944, Rita Hay-
worth cov **7.00**

Hobbies, August 1942............. **2.00**

Holiday, 1950 .... **1.00**

Hollywood Dream Girl, 1955, 1st issue,
13 pgs of Marilyn Monroe photos **30.00**

Home Needlework, 1910 .... **12.00**

Hot Rod
Prior to 1960 .... **2.00**
After 1960 .... **1.00**

Hounds & Hunting, 1922 .... **4.00**

House Beautiful, July 1933 .... **5.00**

House and Garden
Art Deco design................ **10.00**
Other **6.00**

House Beautiful
Illustrator cov.................. **12.00**
Photographic cov **4.00**

Household Magazine, November 1927,
Norman Rockwell Sun–Maid Raisin
back cov **8.00**

Jack & Jill, 1960, Howdy Doody cov. ... **12.00**

Judge
Drayton cov................... **30.00**
Others **5.00**
Teddy Roosevelt **20.00**

Junior Home **1.00**

Ladies' Home Journal
1939, June, New York World's Fair
issue....................... **18.00**
1973, July, color Marilyn Monroe
photo on cov **15.00**

Leica & Ziess, 1938................ **10.00**

Le Rire **3.00**

Le Souire **3.00**

Leslie's, prior to 1920 .... **4.00**

Liberty, June 23, 1928, Leslie Thrasher
poker game cov................ **7.00**

Life
Lee Harvey Oswald cov, February 21,
1964 .... **20.00**
Peter Max cov, September 5, 1969 ... **15.00**
Photographic cov, 1936–1972
Baseball Stars................. **25.00**
Beatles..................... **25.00**
Chaplin, Charlie **10.00**
Garbo, Greta **20.00**
Manson, Charles **15.00**
Monroe, Marilyn **35.00**
November 23, 1936–first **110.00**
Political figures **4.00**

Wayne, John **10.00**
World War II **8.00**
Illustrated cov, small format, 1883–
1936
Artist signed covs **20.00**
Other **8.00**
Space Walk, June 18, 1969, sixteen
color pgs **15.00**
Literary Digest
1920–1926 . . . .   **1.00**
1927–1932 . . . .   **.75**
1935 . . . .   **.50**
Important 20th century authors **5.00**
Mucha cov.   **40.00**
Norman Rockwell cov, June 24, 1922   **3.00**
Living Church, 1924 . . . .   **1.00**
Look
James Dean cov, October 16, 1956,
inside story **18.00**
Jinx Falkenberg tennis cov. **4.00**
John F Kennedy memorial issue, No-
vember 17, 1964 . . . .   **20.00**
Lunatickle, Vol 1, #1 . . . .   **12.00**
Mad Monsters, 1961, 1st issue **15.00**
Mattel Barbie Magazine, November–
December, 1963 . . . .   **10.00**
McCall's
1919–1925 . . . .   **8.00**
1930–1940 . . . .   **10.00**
McClure's **8.00**
Mechanics Arts, 1989 . . . .   **2.50**
Mechanics Illustrated **1.00**
Metropolitan Magazine, July 1907 . . . . .   **10.00**
Modern Priscilla, March 1930 . . . .   **3.00**
Modern Screen, 1956, March, Doris Day   **15.00**
Motion Picture, August 1939, Gary Coo-
per cov **6.00**
Motor, January, 1927 . . . .   **50.00**
Motorcycling & Bicycling, 1920 . . . .   **25.00**
Move Classic, January 1933, Kay Francis
cov **6.00**
Movie Makers, June, 1939, 350 pgs, The
Amateur Cinema League, filming of
fair, multicolored Art Deco design of
New York World's Fair sgd by N Culin,
black and white photos, 9 x 12" **65.00**
Movie Star Parade, January, 1947 . . . . . .   **22.00**
National Geographic, June, 1926 . . . . . .   **3.00**
National Observer, December, 1968 . . .   **1.00**
Nature Magazine, March 1925 . . . .   **5.00**
Naturo–Post, German, health magazine,
1904 . . . .   **2.50**
Needlecraft
1927 . . . .   **3.00**
Rockwell Norman ads **4.00**
New England Home, 1898 . . . .   **20.00**
New Idea Woman's Magazine, 1902 . . .   **20.00**
Newsweek
Hitler cov **12.00**
Mae West cov **9.00**
New Yorker, 1948 . . . .   **2.50**
Outdoor Life, 1932 . . . .   **12.00**

**The Mentor, features Henry Ford collec-
tor, black-and-white illustrations, 71
pages, 8½ x 11½", June 1929, $15.00.**

Pennsylvania Packet, Philadelphia, July
19, 1773, John Dunlap publication,
western expansion to Mississippi and
"Slaves for sale" ads **40.00**
People's Home Journal, prior to 1920 . . .   **8.00**
Physical Culture, 1917 . . . .   **2.00**
Pictorial Review
Large format **25.00**
Milwaukee Sentinel, 1946, Donald
Duck and Disney characters on cov   **12.00**
Small format **4.00**
Photoplay, March 1941, Ginger Rogers
cov **4.00**
Playboy
Beatles, interview issue **30.00**
December, 1962 . . . .   **8.00**
Volume 1, No. 1, Marilyn Monroe . .   **2,500.00**
Popular Homecraft, May 1931 . . . .   **4.00**
Popular Mechanics, 1952 . . . .   **1.50**
Popular Science
Prior to 1930 . . . .   **6.00**
After 1930 . . . .   **1.00**
Popular Songs, 1930s **2.00**
Prairie Farmer, February, 1867 . . . .   **4.00**
Private Lives of Movie Stars, Arco Pub-
lishing Co, 1945, 50 pgs, 8½ x 11" . . .   **20.00**
Puck
1871–1873, St Louis **15.00**
1898–1916, New York **12.00**
Radford's American Builder, 1920s **6.00**
Reader's Digest
Prior to 1930 . . . .   **2.00**
After 1930 . . . .   **1.00**
Redbook, April, 1925 . . . .   **5.00**
Rolling Stone, 1974, June 20, James
Dean cov, 6 page article **17.50**
Saturday Evening Post
1916, May 20, first Rockwell cov **150.00**

1922, New Year's Eve, Leyendecker cov........................ **30.00**

1923

Pearl Harbor **10.00**

Rockwell cov.................. **25.00**

1936, Springtime, Norman Rockwell **12.50**

1938, Christmas, Leyendecker **15.00**

1952, Norman Rockwell........... **8.00**

1964, December 12, Johnny Unitas on cov........................ **12.00**

Science and Invention, May, 1925, full color cov art and article, *The Lost World,* 104 pgs, 8½ x 11½" **30.00**

Scientific American, June, 1933 .... **3.50**

Screen Romances, January 1944, Frank Sinatra........................ **4.00**

Screen Stories, December, 1952, Lana Turner **4.00**

Scribner's Monthly, An Illustrated Magazine for the People, 1874–77, 15 issues **45.00**

S.E.P.

1920, January 3, Leyendecker cov, Edison Mazda ad by Maxfield Parrish........................ **25.00**

1921, January 29, Norman Rockwell cov........................ **35.00**

Shooter News, Shooter–For Shooters, six issues, 1951.................... **9.00**

Silver Screen

1940, September, Paulette Goddard cov........................ **6.00**

1945, December, Judy Garland cov .. **4.00**

1953, April, Ava Gardner **15.00**

1970, October, Elvis and Johnny Cash **10.00**

Small Home Builders Year Book, World's Fair Edition, 82 pgs, 1939 ... **20.00**

Spinning Wheel, July, 1960 .... **30.00**

Sport, Stan Musial cov, 1950.......... **30.00**

Sports Illustrated

Baseball Cards, first issue, August 16, 1954 .... **300.00**

Swimsuit issue................... **4.00**

Stage and Screen, 1926.............. **4.50**

St Nicholas, 1928 .... **7.00**

Sunbathing for Health, December, 1951 **2.50**

The Camera, 1930................. **8.00**

The Theater Magazine

Prior to 1910 .... **20.00**

Strong Art Deco covs, 1920s........ **18.00**

Time

1939 .... **1.00**

1940, Mickey Rooney **10.00**

1969, August 8, John Wayne cov, 4 page article "John Wayne the Last Hero" **17.50**

Tip Top Weekly, 1904.............. **9.00**

Tobacco World, 1902............... **8.00**

Town and Country, July, 1948, Dali cov, poppy, cornflower, and wheat **35.00**

Travel, 1915, Santa cov, Murad **25.00**

Trump, Vol 1, #1 .... **12.00**

True............................ **.50**

Truth **8.00**

T. V. Guide

Bond, James Bond cov............. **30.00**

Captain Video cov, February 22, 1952 **50.00**

Dark Shadows cov................. **30.00**

Elvis cov......................... **30.00**

Monkees cov **30.00**

Doc Savage **30.00**

Pre–national, NYC TeleVision Guide, No. 1 .... **200.00**

NYC–TeleVision Guide, 1948–1953 **40.00**

Marilyn Monroe, March 18, 1950, first cov........................ **500.00**

Superman **30.00**

UNCLE **30.00**

Others, early **5.00**

After 1970 .... **1.00**

TV Star Parade, 1961, August, Michael Landon **10.00**

US Camera, New York World's Fair, 1939, No. 5, 80 pgs, Underwood & Underwood official fair photographers, black and white and color photos, 11¾ x 12½" **115.00**

Vanity Fair....................... **4.00**

Vogue

Illustrated cov **10.00**

Photographic cov **5.00**

Wild West Weekly, 1915 .... **7.00**

Woman's Home Companion

1907, June, N. C. Wyeth ad......... **12.00**

1909–1912 .... **9.00**

1915 .... **30.00**

1916 .... **25.00**

1917, Betty Bonnett.............. **25.00**

1925 .... **20.00**

Woman's World, February, 1936 ...... **5.00**

Working Craftsman, The, winter, 1977.. **4.00**

World Today, The, 1909............. **4.00**

MAGAZINE TEAR SHEETS

History: Magazine interior advertising design attracted some of America's leading illustrators including Maxfield Parrish, Erte, Leyendecker, and Norman Rockwell just to name a few. Illustrated advertising reigned supreme until the late 1950s when it was challenged and eventually replaced by advertisements featuring photographs of the product.

While illustrators frequently signed their magazine cover illustrations, advertising illustration often went unsigned. Collectors learn to identify specific artists by their drawing styles. Add a slight premium if an illustrator signature appears.

The key value component for tear sheets is subject matter. As a result, ninety–nine percent plus are purchased by crossover collectors. Except for illustrator collectors, crossover collectors care little if the tear sheet features a drawing or photograph. The most desirable tear sheets are in full color and show significant design elements.

Tear sheets are an excellent resource for examples of advertising characters, e.g., the Campbell Kids, the Dutch Girl, and Snap, Crackle and Pop. Advertisements that promote a premium are eagerly sought by collectors of that premium. Ethnic stereotype advertising also attracts a strong following.

References: Richard De Thuin, *The Official Identification and Price Guide To Movie Memorabilia*, House of Collectibles, 1990; David K. Henkel, *Magazines: Identification and Price Guide*, Avon Books, 1993; Denis C. Jackson, *The Masters Price & Identification Guide to Old Magazines*, published by author, 1985; Denis C. Jackson, *Men's Girlie Magazines: The Only Price Guide!: Newstanders, Third Edition*, The Illustrator Collector's News, 1991; Patricia Kery, *Great Magazine Covers of The World*, Abbeville Press, 1982; Frank Zawacki, *Famous Faces: Price Guide and Catalog for Magazine Collectors*, Wallace-Homestead, 1985 (Although the prices in this book are badly dated, its listing are accurate. It is an important reference tool for any library). **Note:** See "Illustrators" in topical section for books devoted to specific illustrators.

Periodical: *PCM (Paper Collector's Marketplace)*, PO Box 128, Scandinavia, WI 54977.

Note: In the late 1980s, the price of magazine tear sheets stabilized. Most examples sold for less than $5.00. This affordability attracted increased number of crossover collectors, the result of which has been a significant increase in prices. Another reason behind recent price increase is the use of magazine tear sheets by decorators as a moderately priced, framed picture.

There is little question that the real value of most magazines in the 1990s market is their advertising tear sheets. Thus, a dilemma—should one cut apart a complete magazine or not? A seller concerned only about immediate profit will quickly answer yes. It is our opinion that if a magazine is in mint condition, it should be left intact. We do NOT encourage removing illustrations from complete magazines. Only the complete magazine can act as a tool to interpret that specific historical time period. Editorial and advertising together define the spirit of the era.

When buying matted and framed tear sheets, keep in mind that the greatest part of the value rests in the matting and framing. More likely than not, the tear sheet is worth less than $10.00.

ADVERTISEMENTS

American Tobacco Co, Tuxedo Smoking
Tobacco, black and white photos of
Dick Rudolph and Hank Gowdy, "Star

Batters of the Boston Nationals, World's Champions both smoke Tuxedo," 1915 .... **45.00**
Atwater Kent Radio, full color page, one dial receiver..................... **12.00**
Bon Ami, children illus............. **2.00**
Catalin Corporation, color photo of Catalin stylized radio and clock, 1940 ... **18.00**
Campbell's Soups, color, children, Grace Drayton................... **12.00**
Coca–Cola, color illus, early 1900s **22.00**
Cream of Wheat Cereal.............. **8.00**
Dr. Pepper, early.................. **10.00**
Dutch Cleanser, color, large format **5.00**
Edelweiss–A Case of Good Judgement– Peter Schoenhofen Brewing Co, half page........................ **5.00**
Fisk Tires, *Saturday Evening Post*, May 1, 1926, baseball theme **10.00**
Ford Motor Co, "Stamped and Delivered 5¢," black and white illus, plane being loaded with mail, 1929 .... **18.00**
Gainsborough Powder Puffs, "Where Faces are Fortunes," Art Deco multicolored woman with large powder puff, Nell Patterson, sgd, 1924 ..... **15.00**
Jell–O, full color, Rose O'Neill illus **10.00**
Johnson's Wax, two women sitting at table and maid holding product, c1920 **1.25**
Jos Schlitz Brewing Co, *Fortune*, June, 1937, one page, color scene of people enjoying product, large inset of 1930s bottle, 11 x 14" **8.00**
Hamm's Beer..................... **4.00**
IBM
1934, "Build with Facts," artist sketch of people building bridge and skyscraper...................... **12.00**
1950, typewriter, "Just Touch And Go Lightly," full color photo, hands on IBM typewriter................ **10.00**
Keen Kutter, black and white photo of seven pocket knives and two razors on display, full page, *S.E.P.*, 1915 ...... **18.00**
Kellogg's Cereal, children illus, Leyendecker artist **8.00**
Libbey Owens Ford, safety glass, "Stop that man before he costs you money," black and white photo, policeman on motorcycle, *Fortune Magazine*, 1934 **9.00**
Lionel and Ives Trains **12.00**
National Enamel and Stamping Co, Royal Graniteware, color kitchen, stone, and graniteware set on bottom illus, full page, 1925 .... **20.00**
Nipper, *McCall's, Paper Dolls*, January, 1925, "Nipper goes Sharp–shooting in Africa," sepia and black Nipper, African guide, and five animals, 11 x 14" **20.00**
Palmolive, Keep That School Complexion, *Delineator*, September 1921, golf theme **3.00**

Advertisement, Ralston Purina, *Ladies' Home Journal*, unsigned, 9½ x 14½", March 1919, $30.00.

Parker Fountain Pens, listed Parker points, three pens illus, c1920. . . . . . .   6.00

Pennzoil, "More Than Six Days in the Air," black and white with yellow wash, airplane being refueled in mid air, inset gas station sketch, 1929 . . . .   18.00

Pepsi Cola
  1941, color bottles of Pepsi, Joan Blondell and Dick Powell drinking Pepsi, ½ pg 12.00
  1946, August 5, *Time,* black and white, Root Day cartoon, street vendor selling product, 9 x 12" 12.50
  1957, September–February, "Timeout for Pepsi–The right Refreshment," full page, color bowling alley scene, 11 x 14" 8.00

Plaskon, full color photograph of molded color radios, electric clocks, and appliances, 1940. . . . .   15.00

Rawlings Sporting Goods Co, black and white photos of Stan Musial, Mickey Mantle, Bob Pettit, and Earl Buchotz, gloves and ball, ½ pg, 1958 . . . .   6.00

Rice Krispies, "Snap, Crackle, and Pop," full page, color cereal dish photo, bottom right inset Vernon Grant cartoon, 11 x 14" 15.00

Seven–Up. 2.00
Sterling Engine Co, "The New Models for 1935," multicolored Donald Doulgas painting of yacht, 1935 . . . .   15.00
Waterman's, multicolored, sixteen pens with prices, c1930. . . . .   10.00

ARTICLES

Black History story 2.00
Camels of Winston Salem, *Fortune,* January, 1931, black and white photos, map of tobacco industry, and article, matted 65.00
Circus, *National Geographic,* October, 1931, 53 pgs illus story with 16 color pgs. 9.50
Phillip Morris & Company, *Fortune,* March, 1936, pgs 106–112, article and photos. 18.00
Rose O'Neill, illus story. 3.00
Seven Stages of Childhood, Jessie Wilcox Smith 15.00
The Beer Business, *Fortune,* May, 1932, two page color sketches of Bergner and Engel Brewery, Philadelphia, 11 x 14". 12.00

ILLUSTRATORS

Armstrong, Rolf. 12.00
Atikins, Alan 6.00
Bayer, Herbert.   6.00
Benito, Edwardo 20.00
Cassandre, A M 20.00
Christy, F Earl 15.00
Coffin, Haskell 12.00
Crane, S W 8.00
Davis, Marguerite 6.00
Dohanos, Stevan. 4.00
Duncan, Fredrick 8.00
Eastman, Ruth 6.00
Eric 15.00
Fancher, Louis.   6.00
Flagg, James Montgomery, black and white illus 3.00
Free, Maurice 4.00
Giusti. 3.00
Gunn, Archie. 8.50
Hays, Mar A. 6.00
Hoff, Guy 9.00
King, Hamilton 9.00
Leyendecker 6.50
Lustig. 3.00
McClelland, Barclay 9.00
O'Neill, Rose, Kewpie. 25.00
Parrish, Maxfield 15.00
Penfield, Edward. 30.00
Phillip, Coles, color illus 25.00
Reid, Robert 4.00
Rockwell, Norman, black and white. . . .   6.00
Sandberg, Valentine 8.00

Smith, Jessie Wilcox, *Ladies' Home Journal,* October 1913, Goldilocks eating porridge...................... **30.00**

Vargas

Black and white................... **3.00**

Centerfold or pin–up............. **20.00**

Willenborg, Lee.................... **2.00**

Wilson, John F.................... **5.00**

Wistehuff, Revere **3.00**

Wood, Lawson, monkey image........ **8.00**

MANUALS AND INSTRUCTION BOOKLETS

History: Repair and instruction manuals and instruction booklets have been a fact of life since the nineteenth century. A cookbook is really nothing more than an instruction manual. However, this category focuses primarily on manuals and instruction booklets pertaining to objects with mechanical moving parts. A surprisingly large number of these technical manuals survive.

Innate American curiosity to understand how things work coupled with a thriftiness geared to the adage of "why buy a new one when you can repair the old one" provide the justification for printing manuals and instruction books. Although the language and skill required often exceeded that of the manual owner, manuals and instruction booklets were saved and/or acquired for virtually every mechanical apparatus purchased.

Collectors of any mechanical object are continually searching for the repair manual and instruction booklet that relates to their specific object. One of the most active areas for this type of material is among collectors of antique and classic cars. The problem is that most collectors are manual specific. They are unwilling to buy a manual unless it relates to their specific model.

Most buyers want the manual or instruction booklet for the information it contains, not for display purposes. As a result, condition is not as critical a factor as it is for other material whose principal function is that of display. On the other hand, completeness is essential. Missing or heavily soiled pages rapidly decrease value.

Military manuals are one area where values are strong. Drill and tactic manuals are as eagerly sought as equipment manuals. While age is important, World War II and Korean War manuals appear most in demand.

Air–Way Electric Appliance Corp Sanitary System, Air–Way vacuum cleaner, 1929, 40 pgs **10.00**

Air–Way Operating Manual, 1929, 39 pgs............................ **8.00**

Basic Photography, 1941–43 .... **10.00**

Black & Decker Portable Electric Saw Handbook, 1940, 9 x 10¾"........ **7.00**

Browning Aircraft Machine Gun....... **8.00**

Buick, owner's, 1950 .... **10.00**

Cadets Gunnery Outline–The Machine Gun.......................... **8.00**

Carpentry, 1941–43 .... **5.00**

Chrysler, owner's, 1936 .... **18.00**

DeSoto, owner's, 1948 .... **8.00**

Dodge 1962 Lancer Operating Instructions, 1963.................... **5.00**

Drawing the Figure, Russell Tredell, 10 x 14"......................... **7.00**

Driver's Manual Dodge Trucks, Series–B–I–D........................ **6.00**

Driver's Manual–US Army, 1941 ...... **4.00**

Driver Selection & Training, 1941–43 .. **10.00**

Figures From Life, Robert Duflos and Walter Foster, 10 x 14" **7.00**

Fleishers Knitting and Crocheting Manual, 1902, 48 pgs................ **8.00**

Ford Model "A" Instruction Book, 1930 **10.00**

Ford Truck Shop Manual, Vol 1, 1970 .. **18.00**

Fundamentals of Elementary Flight Maneuvers, Civil Aeronautics Administration, 82 pgs, 1943 .... **5.00**

Handbook of Light Gymnastics, Lucy B Hunt, 1887, 92 pgs **50.00**

Handbook for Owners of Military ¼–Ton Trucks, 1963 .... **4.00**

How To Beautify Your Home, Proctor & Gamble, 62 pgs, 1942............. **10.00**

How Canedo Draws the Figure, c1960, Foster, 10 x 14" **7.00**

How To Invest, Wall Street Investigator, 1923, 16 pgs **6.50**

How To Make More Money With Poultry, The Poultryman's Manual, Park Pollard Co, 1940, 64 pgs, 8½ x 12"... **4.00**

Basic Field Manual, Soldier's Handbook, EM 21-100, U. S. Government Printing Office, black-and-white photos and illustrations, 264 pages, 4½ x 6¾", 1941, $20.00.

How To Operate Lionel. **9.00**
How to Ride & Train the Saddle Horse . .   **6.00**
How To Use Hand Tools, Jamestown, NY, 1957, 36 pgs, 5^1/$_2$ x 7^1/$_4$". **8.00**
Imperial Airways Instructions For Passengers on Their Silver Wing, 1930, 8 pgs   **20.00**
Installation & Maintenance of Telegraph Printer Equipment, 1941–43. . . . .   **5.00**
Instruction Book for White Gasoline Cars, 1915–17, 30 pgs, 5^1/$_4$ x 8" **15.00**
Instruction, Eastman's No. 2 Eureka Camera, c1899, 18 pgs **20.00**
Instructions for Gilbert HO Trains, 1955   **10.00**
Introductory Mail Course in Horsemanship, Jesse Beery, 1913. . . . .   **6.00**
It's Easy to Fix Your Bike, 1958, 36 pgs, 8^1/$_2$ x 11" **6.50**
Jeep 4WD Model 6–230/F4–134 Owner's Manual, 1962 . . . .   **4.00**
Jeep Tornado 230 Engine Service Manual **4.00**
Jeep Utilities Vehicles Service Manual, 1961 . . . .   **5.00**
Keuffel & Esser Co, A Self Teaching Manual, 1938, 90 pgs, 5^1/$_4$ x 8". **22.00**
Little Orphan Annie Secret Society, 1937, 8 pgs, 6 x 8^1/$_2$" **55.00**
Manual of Instructions for Use with Gilbert Puzzle Parties, 1919, 9 pgs. **7.00**
Manual of the Principal Instruments Used In American Engineering & Surveying, 1910, 470 pgs, 4^1/$_2$ x 6^3/$_4$" **47.00**
Mechanical Engineers Handbook, Baumeister, McGraw Hill, 1964, 6th ed. **15.00**
M Heminway & Sons Silk, Watertown, CT, 1917, 72 pgs, 5^1/$_2$ x 7^3/$_4$" **14.00**
Military Protective Construction, 1941– 43 . . . .   **8.00**
One Hundred and One Uses For Diamond Crystal Salt, Diamond Crystal Salt Co, St Clair, MI, 20 pgs, 1925, 3^1/$_2$ x 6". **7.50**
Operating the Simplex Ironer, 24 pgs . . .   **8.00**
Operator's Manual–1947 Ford Heavy Duty Truck. **10.00**
Outdoor Sports Manual, Popular Mechanics, 1948 . . . .   **10.00**
Overland Whippet–Operation and Care, Model 96, 1926, 36 pgs. **50.00**
Palmer's Manual of Cage Birds, 1879, 32 pgs, beige and black pict wraps, Palmer Toiletries adv. **18.00**
Radio Orphan Annie's Secret Society, 1937 . . . .   **30.00**
Recognition Pictorial Manual, Bureau of Aeronautics, Navy Department, Washington, DC, June 1943, 80 pgs, 6 x 10" **45.00**
Scale Model Aircraft Construction Procedure, Robert W Hambrook, 1942, Federal Security Agency, 20 pgs **7.00**

Scripture Manual, Ordinance of Baptism, Samuel Wilson, 1772, 4th ed, 32 pgs, 4^1/$_2$ x 6^1/$_2$". **22.50**
Self Instructor For The American Mandolinharp, 1900, 12 pgs, 10^3/$_4$ x 8^3/$_4$" **24.00**
Service and Parts, Graflex, photography, c1948, 60 pgs **15.00**
Shell Petroleum, Olympic Edition, 1936, 48 pgs, 3^1/$_4$ x 6^1/$_4$" **15.00**
Signal Corps Field Manual, 1941–43 . . .   **8.00**
Speer Manual For Reloading Ammunition, 1967, 382 pgs **10.00**
Studebaker
  1924, Standard Six Owner's Manual   **15.00**
  1945, owner's **10.00**
Templar Motor Cars Corporation, Instruction for Care and Operation of Templar Cars, 1925, 16 pgs. **70.00**
The Amateur Mechanic's Manual & Catalogue of Scroll Saws & Lathes, Rochester, NY, 1881, 32 pgs, 6 x 9^1/$_4$" **47.00**
The Army Baker, 1941–43 . . . .   **8.00**
Things To Do With Plastic Wood, 1930, 48 pgs, Addison–Leslie Co, Canton, MA. **6.50**
Vega & Monza Service & Overhaul Manual Supplement **25.00**
Volkswagen, owner's 1965. . . . .   **6.00**
Washington Instructions for Launderall, 1947, 16 pgs **6.00**
33 Rope Ties & Chain Releases, American Magic Corp, 1915, 40 pgs. **6.00**
66 Chevrolet Owner's Guide **5.00**

MANUSCRIPTS

History: A manuscript is a written or typewritten document. Technically it contains no printing, although a hand written letter on printed letterhead is considered a manuscript.

The key to understanding this category is to remember several key distinctions made by autograph collectors. An ALS is an authograph letter signed; a TLS is a typed letter signed. Although typed material is counted as manuscript, collectors assign a premium to hand written material.

The photocopying machine has complicated the issue. If an original typed draft of a movie script is a manuscript, what is a photocopy? Does it deserve to same degree of collectibility as the original? Where does an old fashion "carbon" copy fit? The answer to these questions differs from collector to collector. Clearly photocopies do not deserve the same value as an original, even though they are exact copies. "Carbon" copies are treated with a bit more respect, although valued downward from the typed original.

A large amount of hand written manuscript material survives. Most is worthless. No one wants another individual's high school or college notes. Content and originality are the key. A magnificant hand written copy of a group of mid–nineteenth century poetry is nothing more than a copy, collectible perhaps for its hand, but certainly not for its originality or content.

Drafts of literary works, ranging from novels to movie manuscripts, speeches, and reports are among the most collectible types of manuscripts. Collectors and dealers no longer hesitate to contact the executors of the estate of a famous author, politician, teacher, or scientist in hopes of acquiring manuscript material.

Collectors' Club: The Manuscript Society, 350 North Niagara Street, Burbank, CA 91505.

Note: Also see "Family Letters" in the topical section.

1714, June 2, order for Pierre Gruyn to pay amount to King of France, Louis XIV, handwritten, 1 pg, 12 x 16".... **950.00**

1754, February 18, extract of Council Meeting, Williamsburg, VA, list those present and order of business, handwritten in ink, 1 pg, 8 x 7½" ... **650.00**

1759, October 9, King of England, George II approving payment for French and Indian War provisions for May 7–June 17, 1¾ pgs, 12 x 16" **1,800.00**

1762, deposition, Honourable William Lord Viscount Barrington of the Kingdom of Ireland, three emb revenue stamps on each page, 81 pgs, handwritten **175.00**

1763, payment, received of Daniel Stafford, 6¾ x 2½" **50.00**

1765, will of James Harris, White Clay Creek, Virginia land matters, handwritten, 1 pg, 11½ x 7⅝" **75.00**

1766, June 28, act appointing commissioners for supplying barracks and supplies, Governor William Franklin, NJ, 2 pgs, 12½ x 16"......... **435.00**

1768, January 4, King's warrant, handwritten, mounted in plastic, 2 pgs... **675.00**

1776, June 14, CT, encourage and facilitate enlistment of troops, 2 pgs, 12 x 16"..................... **100.00**

1777, April 29, pay order to Azariah Brown, sgd by Oliver Ellsworth, 1 pg, 5 x 7"..................... **75.00**

1777, September 26, order from Col Jonathan Foy to Massachusetts military Lieutenant Josephet Bancroft to draft half of his men with six days' provisions, 1 pg, 7¼ x 3½"....... **585.00**

1779, act to enable owners and possessors to erect a dam across Maple Island Creek, Newark, NJ, Essex County, sgd by Governor William Livingston, 7 pgs.............. **285.00**

1780, Revolutionary War pay order for war expenses, 5 x 8" **15.00**

1780, February 1, account of clothing issued to Col Wessons' 9th Massachusetts Regt, list items delivered to named officers, penned, 10 x 7".... **75.00**

1781, Revolutionary War pay order for war expenses **20.00**

1786, October 13, transfer of deed, 1 pg **165.00**

1788, March 3, Roger Sherman to John Lawrence, payment due of forty shillings, 1 pg **375.00**

1791, July 1, Bill of Reed & Forde, skins and prices for twenty otter and three bear skins, hand written **65.00**

1793, February 16, French text on Dunkirk Invasion, orig silk sewn left margin, 28 pgs, 12 x 16"......... **300.00**

1793, July 30, itemized receipt for making clothing from skins, sgd by Susanna Conkle, hand written **60.00**

1794, September 21, New York City land deed, sold by Thomas and Elizabeth Storm to Gerard Rutgers, part of Indian purchase, 1 pg, 12 x 16" .. **250.00**

1794, September, lease for ten plantation parcels of land, to Wade Hampton by Robert Waring, 1 pg, 12 x 16" **150.00**

1796, March 20, French text, Count du Moustier statement of intentions towards people of France, 17 pgs, 12 x 16", neatly penned............ **400.00**

1804, March, 8¼ x 13", recommendation of committee to "adopt some economical plan for support of poor" **25.00**

1804, November 6–April 7, 1805, log, schooner *Sally*, daily entries, missing cover, 28 pgs, 13¼ x 8¼"......... **200.00**

1805, March 16, recommendation for appointing Nathaniel Cook as Justice, sgd by William Henry Harrison and others, ¾ pgs, 8 x 10"........ **675.00**

1805, April 22, notice to Turnpike Company for inspection, 1 pg...... **235.00**

1808, bill of sale for black man sold by Joshua Owings to Joseph Boswell, Fayette County, KY, 1 pg, 5 x 7".... **125.00**

1809, August 28, bill of sale for black woman sold by James Fishbach to Dr Joseph Boswell for $250, 1 pg, 5 x 7" **125.00**

1816, 9 x 16", details payment of $17,000 to US Soldiers for War of 1812, ruled lines, laid paper..... **35.00**

1823, musical score, titled "Love's Last Words," 1 pg, written on both sides, water marked paper, hand written, 11¾ x 8⅞" **75.00**

1829, November 20, New York Debating Society, neatly penned, 2½ pgs **50.00**

1831, March 2–July 28, log, Captain John Phillips, ship *Thomas Scattergood*, Philadelphia, lists daily events, 44 pgs, 9 x 6½"................ **175.00**

1833, July 28, bill of sale for black woman by Richard H Clarke to Rachel Clarke for $5, Washington, DC, 1 pg, 12 x 16"............. **150.00**

1836, November to March 1838, log, *US Dolphin*, A E Watson, USN, daily events and descriptions of voyage, 75 pgs, 12 x 16"............... **500.00**

1838, July, sgd and sworn statement of Amos P Gallaway, states he will not sell liquor to slaves and will not permit gambling on premises, 1 pg, 8 x 10"......................... **150.00**

1839, emancipation affidavit, affirming black man was previously manumitted, cream paper, 4 x 7½"....... **55.00**

1840, September 9, Orville Browning asking for continuance of trial for sick defendant, 1 pg, 8 x 10"....... **135.00**

1845, September 29, Queen Victoria of England, accepting Alexander J Bergen as consul, seal, hand written, 1 pg..................... **100.00**

1847, receipt for payment for bringing slave boy to North Carolina, sgd by Justice and docketed, handwritten in ink, 5 x 7".................... **45.00**

1847, February 19, H Stanton to Major DD Tompkins, 1 pg, 5 x 7"........ **35.00**

1850, February 23, M F Maury, text titled "The Atmosphere Is A Vast Machine," observations of environment, 40 pgs.................. **550.00**

1852, August 30, bill of sale for black servant to Joseph Walsh from Ellen Lucas, 1 pg, 5 x 7"........... **150.00**

1853, May 31, monthly return of public animals, wagons, horses, and horse equipment, chart form, 1 pg, 12 x 16"..................... **250.00**

1853, November 29, bill of sale for black woman and child sold to Francis Hilton from Levi Pumphrey for $100, 1 pg, 12 x 16"........... **150.00**

1856, February 25, act for incorporation of Exit Fire Arms Co, NJ, 25 pgs, 12 x 16"..................... **75.00**

1859, ministerial record, D M Gilbert, entries from December 4 to May 10, 1863 at Staunton, VA and June 7, 1863 to June 27, 1871 at Savannah, GA, lists church activities, sermons, meetings, list of members, etc., neatly written, leather bound notebook, 150 pgs, 5½ x 8¼"........ **125.00**

1860, October 19, promissory note to William Little, sgd on front and back docket by Gist, Confederate General, 1 pg, 5 x 7".............. **650.00**

1861, diary, Captain Francis Josselyn's, daily entries of naval activities, tan leather cov, pencil and ink, 73 pgs.. **500.00**

1876, July 3, quatrain of verse by John Greenleaf Whittier, 1 pg, 8 x 5".... **250.00**

1885, November 1–October 21, 1889, diary, William Langdon, daily entries, brown ink, lined sheets, 184 pgs....................... **150.00**

1899, ten line poem to Leon Mead from Eugene Field, orig envelope, 2 pg, 5 x 7"..................... **550.00**

1898, typescript account of Civil War soldier's experiences with the army, 23 pgs, 5 x 7".................. **50.00**

1904, Grover Cleveland draft of press statement on death of Ruth Cleveland, lined paper, penned in dark ink, 1 pg, 10 x 8"............. **400.00**

1916, June 8, poem by Robert Bridges, in memory of military hero Sudan, titled "Lord Kitchener," 1 pgs, 8 x 10"........................ **575.00**

1930, Arthur Conan Doyle, text for article titled "Notes from a Strange Mailbag," revisions and editorial mark, autographed, 25 pgs, 8 x 10"........................ **7,500.00**

1930, January 25, to pay for opening of 12th Street from Broadway to the Bowery...................... **50.00**

1931, play, *The Dump*, Everett Shinn, typed carbon copy, 39 pgs........ **25.00**

1932, May 23, debate between journalist Lincoln Steffens and John Beardsley, typewritten, 35 pgs..... **40.00**

1945, May 1, radio broadcast, "The Fuehrer has nominated me as his successor," Karl Donitz to German people, typed, 1 pg............. **200.00**

Undated

Legal petition for James K Polk's client to the court for granting divorce, handwritten, 2 pgs, 12½ x 7½"....................... **475.00**

Short story by Pearl S Buck, titled "Enough for a Lifetime," holograph additions and corrections, 23 pgs, 8 x 10"............... **250.00**

Sir Henry R Bishop, words and music for song captioned "Indian Air, and No 6 National Melodies," browned paper, 3 pgs, 12 x 16".. **350.00**

U S Army Provost Marshal Prisoner record book, Manchester, VA, civilian and military arrests for misbehavior, 26 pgs, 12 x 16"...... **110.00**

Washington Irving, text from *Mahomet and His Successors*, includes several revisions and cross-outs, number upper right 548, mounted on matching paper, 1 pg, 5 x 7".................. **700.00**

MAPS

History: Maps provide one of the best ways to study the growth of a country or region. From the sixteenth to the early twentieth century, maps were both informative and decorative. Engravers provided ornamental detailing which often took the form of bird's eye views, city maps, and ornate calligraphy and scrolling. Many maps were hand colored to enhance their beauty.

Maps generally were published in plate books. Many of the maps available today result from these books being cut apart and their sheets sold separately.

In the last quarter of the nineteenth century, representatives from firms in Philadelphia, Chicago, and elsewhere traveled the United States preparing county atlases, often with a sheet for each township and a sheet for each major city or town. Although mass produced, they are eagerly sought by collectors. Individual sheets sell for between $35 and $100. The atlases themselves can usually be purchased in the $200 to $400 range. Individual sheets should be viewed solely as decorative and not as investment material.

In the late 1970s, gasoline companies and affiliated stations ceased the practice of giving away free road maps. Even the Automobile Association of America carefully monitors map requests from individual members. Having to pay for a modern map has rekindled an interest among collectors in older automobile roadway maps.

Gasoline company map collectors are focusing on maps from the 1930s to the early 1950s. The first appearance of an Interstate Highway on a road map was in 1952. Examples that sold for 50¢ a year or two ago now command between $3.00 and $5.00. Many of these maps were heavily used and are separated at the folds. Collectors want near mint examples. Any damage immediately makes the map landfill material.

Collectors' Clubs: The Association of Map Memorabilia Collectors, 8 Amherst Road, Pelham, MA 01002; The Chicago Map Society, 60 West Walton Street, Chicago, IL 60610.

Alaska, geological map of Chitna River
  Valley and surrounding areas, 29 x
  53", 1939 . . . .   **15.00**
America
  Hondius, Amsterdam, 1631, based
    on Mercator's maps, engraved,
    14¾ x 19" **925.00**
  Merian, Frankfurt, second quarter
    17th C, engraved, 11 x 14" **350.00**
Baron Munchausen (Jack Pearl) Presents His Olde Mappe of Radio Land
  As It Lies, 1935, folder, 19 x 14" **12.00**
Biblical, Manual of Biblical Geography, c1887, 25 full page colored

maps, small maps, diagrams, fold–
  out panorama of Jerusalem, loose
  cover **30.00**
Chicago and A Century of Progress
  Road Map, 1934, folder **15.00**
English Colonies and Canada, Amsterdam, Visscher, c1680, engraved,
  18½ x 23½" **1,600.00**
German
  Originalkarte Des Aquatorialen Ost–
    Africa, 1881, hand colored, 16 x
    19" **15.00**
  Phanologische Karte Von Mittel
    Europa, 1881, hand colored, 14 x
    17" **12.00**
Map of Los Angeles, The Earth's Garden   Spot/Population   800,000,
  c1920, folder, Bekins Moving and
  Storage adv **8.50**
Map of Louisiana, Mississippi, and Alabama, Philadelphia, A Finley, 1827,
  colored, 18¾ x 25" **115.00**
Netherlands, 1880, 12½ x 14" **8.00**
New York City Street Map, 1922, fold–
  out, 8½ x 17" opened **9.00**
Oregon Territory, D F Robinson, 1828,
  shows Oregon territory and California as "unexplored region," left half
  of double page map, soiled. **15.00**
Philadelphia, Augusburg, Scull, and
  Heap, 1777, engraved, includes
  street plan and surrounding villages,
  18 x 23½" **1,150.00**

Ashland Flying Octanes Road Map, Kentucky and Tennessee, 1950s, $12.50.

Esso Road Map, Delaware, Maryland, Virginia, and West Virginia, red, blue, and green, 4 x 8¼" folded, 24 x 33" open, 1961, $8.00.

United States
  Arrowsmith, London, 1795, engraved, 48 x 56" **1,625.00**
  Bouchon, Paris, 1825, engraved, 16 x 21" **200.00**
  Virginiae Partis Australis, et Floridae Partis Orinetalis, Amsterdam, Blaeu, c1640, Chesapeake Bay to northeastern Florida, Indians and ships at sea cartouche, colored outlines, 18½ x 23" **375.00**
  West Indies, from Mitchells Geography, c1852, hand colored **18.00**
  Wisconsin Fun Map, Wisconsin Conservation Dept, 1936, 24 x 28" **8.00**
  World, Vander Leyden, Holland, c1720, engraved, Europe and Eastern Asia, distorted North and South America, 20 x 26" **1,000.00**

MATCHCOVERS

History: The book match was invented by Joshua Pusey, a Philadelphia lawyer, who also was a chemist in his spare time. In 1892, Pusey put 10 cardboard matches into a cover of plain white board. Two hundred were sold to the Mendelson Opera Company who, in turn, hand-printed messages on the front.

The first machine-made matchbook was made by the Binghamton Match Company, Binghamton, New York, for the Piso Company of Warren, Pennsylvania. The only surviving cover is now owned by the Diamond Match Company.

Few covers survive from the late 1890s–1930s period. The modern craze for collecting matchcovers was started by a set of ten covers issued for the Century of Progress exhibit at the 1933 Chicago World's Fair.

The Golden Age of matchcovers was the mid–1940s through the early 1960s when the covers were a popular advertising medium. Principal manufacturers included Atlas Match, Brown and Bigelow, Crown Match, Diamond Match, Lion Match, Ohio Match and Universal Match.

The arrival of throw–away lighters, such as BIC, brought an end to the matchcover era. Manufacturing costs for a matchbook today can range from below a cent to seven or eight cents for a special diecut cover. As a result, matchcovers no longer are an attractive "free" give–away item.

Because of this, many of the older, more desirable covers are seeing a marked increase in value. Collectors have also turned to the small pocket type boxes as a way to enhance and build their collections.

Matchcovers generally had large production runs; very few are considered rare. Most collectors remove the matches, flatten the covers, and mount them in albums by category. They prefer the covers be unused.

Trading is the principal means of exchange among collectors, usually on a one for one basis. At flea markets and shows, matchcovers frequently are seen marked for $1.00 to $5.00 for categories such as beer covers or pin–up art (girlie) covers. These purchasers are best advised to join one of the collector clubs and get involved in swapping.

Pricing in Bill Retskin's recently published *The Matchcover Collector's Price Guide* suggests a significant movement upward in the value of matchcovers. Collectors and dealers are warned to keep these prices in perspective. For every high value cover there are dozens of covers whose value remains minimal.

References: Yosh Kashiwabara, *Matchbook Art,* Chronicle Books, 1989; Bill Retskin, *The Matchcover Collector's Price Guide,* World Comm, 1993; Bill Retskin, *The Matchcover Collectors Resource Book and Price Guide,* published by author, 1988; H. Thomas Steele, Jim Heimann, Rod Dyer, *Close Cover Before Striking, The Golden Age of Matchbook Art,* Abbeville Press, 1987.

Periodicals: *The Front Striker Bulletin,* 3417 Clayborne Avenue, Alexandria, VA 22306–1410; *The Match Hunter,* 740 Poplar, Boulder, CO 80304.

Collectors' Clubs: Rathkamp Matchcover Society, 1359 Surrey Road, Vandalia, OH 43577;

Trans–Canada Matchcover Club, Box 219, Caledonia, Ontario, Canada NOA–1A0. There are over 30 regional clubs throughout the United States and Canada.

Abbott's Bitters, Tones the Stomach	3.00
ABC Coach Lines, Fort Wayne, IN	2.00
Air Force One	5.00
Albert Sheetz Mission Candies/Ice Cream, diamond quality	2.00
Anheuser–Busch, horses and wagon, stock cov	6.00
Antique Automobile, Drive Carefully, St Cesaire, Quebec	1.50
Apollo Flight 8	5.00
Arizona State Fair, November 5–14, 1965	1.50
Arthur Feilchenfeld Hats, Caps, Gloves, black and white photo, diamond quality	2.50
Athens Athletic Club, Oakland, CA, diamond quality	2.00
Bank of Goochland, Goochland, VA . . .	2.00
Belfast Old Fashioned Mug Root Beer, mug on front	3.00
Big Boy Cola & Mission Orange Juice, 1950s.	4.75
Big Joe Sells Best Because It Is Best, diamond quality	2.00
Blackstone Hotel, Chicago, IL, diamond quality	1.50
Blue Pig Barbecue, "Open Until 12 O'Clock," diamond quality.	2.50
Bob's Tavern, Brewster, NE.	2.00
Boy Scouts, Seattle Area Boy Scout Council, Troop 15, July, 1953	4.00
Brass Rail, San Diego, CA, diamond quality	3.00

Amusement Park, West View Park, Pittsburgh, PA, orange and blue on white, roller coaster and clown illus, 1½ x 3¾", 1930s, $8.00.

Bromo–Seltzer, girls, stock cov, diamond quality	1.75
Champion Spark Plugs	1.25
Charlie Lindbergh, photo on front.	500.00
Charlie Low's Forebidden City, Chinatown, San Francisco night club, 1940	8.50
Chevrolet, 1952	3.00
Christmas, Season's Greetings Knothole	2.00
Chuckles Candy at Walgreen's, diamond quality	2.00
City Club Beer	2.50
Clark's Teaberry Gum	1.25
Classic Car Series, Ohio Match Co, 1977	2.25
Cleo Cola for Goodness Sake on front, bottle on back	2.00
Colleges and Universities, assorted institutions	2.50
Credit Unions, assorted sizes	3.00
Crescent Park, Riverside, diamond quality.	2.00
Country Clubs, assorted cities	3.50
Davenport Hotel, Spokane, USA, diamond quality	2.00
Davis Cafe, Vallejo, CA, telephone, 1858	2.50
Delta Airlines, 50th Year, 1929–79	2.50
Disneyland Hotel	3.00
Drink Coca–Cola, 1930s	5.00
Dwight D Eisenhower, Five Star General	15.00
Earl & Tal's Restaurant, Standardsville, VA	2.00
Ehlers Coffee, 1930s	1.50
Emerson Hotel, Baltimore, MD, Central Location, diamond quality	2.25
E S Shuck Hotel, 400 Rooms, 300 Baths, diamond quality	2.25
Feuer's Restaurant, Chicago, IL, "We Never Close," diamond quality.	2.00
First State Bank, Paint Rock, TX	2.50
Flock's Pale Lager, "It Stands on Top" . .	2.00
Ford, automobile, color photo, 1973 . . .	4.50
General Douglas MacArthur, I Shall Return	100.00
G H Nollen, South Side Druggist, Newton, IA, stock cov, diamond quality. . .	2.00
Gimbels, Philadelphia, 1842–1945	5.00
Golden Gate International Expo, San Francisco, CA, 1939, Court of the Moons Gardens	2.50
Griffith's Sinclair Station, Danielsville, GA	2.00
Gruen Veri–Thin Match, 1930s	3.00
Highlander Pilsner Beer, FL, bright colors and design	3.00
Horse, Diamond Match Co	2.00
Hotel Jamestown, 300 Rooms, 250 Baths, diamond quality	2.75
Hygrade Frankfurters and Honey Brand Ham, diamond quality	2.25
Iris Coffee, 1930s.	1.75
Jack Dempsey's Restaurant, NY, building and insert photo of Dempsey, c1940	4.50

J F G Coffee, 1930s **1.50**
J L Oliver, Wicomico, VA **2.00**
Joe DiMaggio, New York Yankees, Joe in
  batting pose, c1939 . . . .   **12.50**
Joe Louis and Max Schmeling, champi-
  onship fight **25.00**
John Canella, New York Giants **2.50**
Krasdale Coffee, 1930s **1.50**
Lake Manahoac Motel, Washington, VA   **2.00**
Lone Star Beer, stock cov. **2.50**
Los Angeles county's Olive View Sanato-
  rium, 1930s **4.00**
Lou's Diner, Mill Plain, CT, Phone 3–
  9400 . . . .   **3.00**
Lovingston   Hotel   &   Restaurant,
  Lovingston, VA **2.25**
Mammoth Cave Hotel, 1930s **3.00**
Marriage of Charles & Diana, 29th July,
  1981 . . . .   **3.00**
Martin A Burke, Chicago Black Hawks . .   **4.00**
Matson Line, San Francisco, Los Angeles,
  Hawaii Oceanic Line **2.75**
Mayor La Guardia, Vote City Fusion,
  photo **3.00**
Medford Cafe, Mystic 6010, "Always at
  your Service," diamond quality **2.25**
Monument Lodge, Yorktown, VA **2.50**
Motel Washington, Fairfax, VA **3.00**
Murray's   Restaurants,   "All   Women
  Cooks & Bakers" **3.00**
Muskogee, OK, Free State Fair, 1939 . . .   **3.50**
National Airlines, face and sun **2.50**
New York World's Fair
  Anacin adv, 1939 . . . .   **3.50**
  Brazilian Coffee adv, 1939 . . . .   **3.00**
  Chrysler Motors Building. **2.00**
  Hall of Marine Transportation **1.50**
  RCA Building.   **1.50**
  Star Olive Oil adv, 1939 . . . .   **2.00**
Old Master Coffee, 1930s **1.75**
Olmsted Grill, Washington, DC, Sea
  Food, Steaks, Chops, diamond quality   **2.25**
Philadelphia A's Schedule, elephant with
  A's logo, 1940 . . . .   **10.00**
Phoenix Sportsmen's Association, "It Is
  Your Right To Own and Bear Arms" . .   **3.50**
Piper Cub, "Easy to Fly" and "Easy to
  Buy," airplane views, free catalog ad,
  1930s **7.50**
Playboy Club, Atlanta **2.00**
Playland At The Beach, San Francisco . .   **3.50**
Pontiac Motor Division, "Look and
  Live!" **3.50**
Presidential Helicopter, "Marine One"   **10.00**
Presidential Yacht, *Patricia* **10.00**
President Kennedy, White House on
  front. **5.00**
Pull for Willkie **28.00**
PullQuick, The Eat Shop & The Kenesaw
  Cafe **8.00**
Racquel Welch, color photo **15.00**
Revelation Tooth Powder, The Smoker's

Dentifrice–Removes Tobacco Stains,
  1930s **6.00**
RMS 19th Convention, Miami Beach, FL,
  Aug 24–30, 1959 . . . .   **2.50**
Roosevelt, photo, "United Behind the
  President" **15.00**
San Diego Zoo, Atlas Four Color, c1970   **1.00**
Scheidt's Valley Forge Special Beer **2.75**
Shanghai Cafe, Chop Suey, San Fran-
  cisco, CA **2.00**
Shurfire Coffee, 1930s **1.50**
Spiro T Agnew for Governor on Nov 8 . .   **6.00**
Stoeckle Select Beer, Stoeckle Brewery   **6.00**
Superior Match Co, RMS 14th Conven-
  tion, September 9–11, 1954 . . . .   **2.00**
Suwannee Hotel, St Petersburg, FL, hotel
  on back **3.00**
Taft Hotel, NY, New York World's Fair
  ad and logo, 1940 . . . .   **3.00**
Taxi Cabs, assorted companies **4.00**
Telephone Companies, assorted themes
  and sizes **5.50**
Texas Centennial, Dallas, 1936, Live-
  stock Building **2.50**
The Waldorf Astoria, New York City, dia-
  mond quality **2.50**
Thompson's Restaurants, Pure Food, dia-
  mond quality **1.25**
Tobacco Shop, 1950s **3.00**
Tupelo Hotel, Wewahitchka, FL **3.00**
TWA Airline **5.00**
Ty Cobb, baseball player. **4.00**
US Athletic Clubs, assorted sizes. **3.50**
Van   Ness   Automobile   Products,
  "Everything for the Auto," diamond
  quality **2.50**
Vote for Governor Brown, photo. **2.00**
Vote Rockefeller, March 10th on front, R
  for President on back, photo **6.00**
Washington Redskins, picture on back . .   **2.00**
Wrigley's Chewing Gum. **3.00**

MENUS

History: "What is for supper" is a question as old
as the human race. Who started the first restaurant? No one knows. Some ancient, no doubt.
Blend question with the institution and the need
for a menu arises.

Menus are collected for a variety of reasons.
Food historians view them as valuable documents
of America's forever changing eating habits. It
was a common practice to have a printed menu
for a public or private banquet during the Victorian era and first decades of the twentieth century.
Specialized food collectors find these menus fascinating. Oyster collectors are constantly searching for banquet menus featuring oysters or whose
cover has an oyster theme.

Transportation collectors eagerly seek menus

associated with their favorite form of conveyance. Large oceanliners printed a menu for every meal. Passengers saved them as trip mementos. In addition to recording what was served, transportation menus often pictured the company logo, the vehicle, or scene from the journey on the cover.

Advertising and specialized collectors seek menus for the cover art, rather than the interior contents. Beer and soda manufacturers provided menu covers to bars and restaurants that served their product. They were frequently changed to promote a new product or company image. These menus tend to be pricey, the price point aimed at the specialized collector rather than the menu collector.

Local collectors treasure menus from local restaurants, especially lunch counters and diners. Their nostalgic appeal is extremely high. Many are stock menu covers with mimeographed menu inserts. A public or private banquet menu increases in value when sold in the community in which the banquet was held.

Institutional and organizational collectors exist. Little is written about their collecting, a fact they relish since lack of attention keeps prices low. Business and fraternal organization banquet menus also sell well.

There are collectors for material from nationally and internationally known restaurants. Again, their number is small. A general rule is that the more well known the restaurant, the more money one of its menus will bring.

Printed banquet menus from the pre–1915 period bring the highest prices. These have long been a favorite of the paper ephemera traditionalist. Typography and cover illustrations are the prime reasons that they are collected.

A major problem with most menus is that they are undated. A collector will accept a date being written on a menu if it is done in an inconspicuous location. Knowing the date of the menu adds a premium of 25 percent.

Menus survive in large quantities. Prices remain modest unless focused on the specialized crossover collector. Prices in excess of $5.00 to $10.00 are enough to discourage most collectors. Further, collectors want menus in near mint condition or better. If a menu is badly soiled, bent, missing pages, or torn, value virtually disappears.

Reference: Karl D. Spence, *Oceanliner Collectibles*, published by author, 1992.

Alaska Huskie Jack, *SS Alaska*, 1949, 5½
x 8½" **12.00**
Aleck's Cafe Broiler, Salt Lake City, UT   **5.00**
Amtrak, Good Morning, single card, 7 x
11" **1.50**
Andrea Doria. **15.00**
Banquet To The Western Michigan Press,
Reed City, 1883, folder, Robinson Engraving Co, black and white **15.00**

Beck's Sea Food Specialist On The Potomac **5.00**
Burlington Northern, April 1970, breakfast, folder, 5 x 7" **4.00**
California Zephyr Lines, 1968, Cable Car Room, cocktail menu, folder **4.00**
Chicago & North Western Railway, 1958, luncheon, Mt Rushmore on cov, issued for "Sam Campbell Alaska Tour" **4.50**
Cosulich Lines, 1929. . . . . **8.00**
Down Under Restaurant, Rockefeller Center, 1942, red, white, and blue cov, 4 pgs, 7 x 11" **10.00**
Empress of Canada I, Canadian Pacific Line, Easter, 1924, tassel dec **16.00**
Farewell Dinner, *RMS Franconia,* Sept 1936 . . . . **5.00**
Fletcher Family 4th Reunion, Lowell, MA, dinner, August 25, 86 . . . . **10.00**
Hotel Peabody, Memphis **8.00**
Hurricane Cove, Catalina Island, CA, 1950s, 10 pgs, 10 x 12" **17.50**
Johnson Line **10.00**
Lafayette French Line, 1937 . . . . **5.00**
Lancastria, Cunard Line, luncheon, 1939, color sailing ship on cov **15.00**
Lehigh Valley, Black Diamond Express, dinner, 1927, chef and train on cov . . **35.00**
Lehigh Valley Railroad, dinner, 1950–60, tugboat photo on cov **5.00**
Liberte, December 10, 1956, 9 x 11½", 4 pgs, silver gray cov **75.00**
Lond Boar's Head Coffee House, c1820, wall type **200.00**
Mocambo Night Club, green, red, and white, 10½ x 14½" **25.00**
Mattson Line **7.00**
Metropolitan Hotel, c1874, 4 pgs **35.00**

Schlitz Brewing Company blank, Milwaukee, WI, 7½ x 10¼", 1950s, $6.00.

Mrs Gray's Inn, Wilshire at Westwood Blvd	10.00
New York Central, The James Whitcomb Riley, dinner, locomotive illus	6.00
Norddeutscher Lloyd Bremen, ocean liner, dinner, 1900–10	3.00
NYC, Thrift Grill, folder, 1955	3.50
Portland Commercial Club, dinner, May 19, 1911, gold New Jersey and Oregon seals on cov, 6 x 9"	12.00
Queen Elizabeth	20.00
RMS Samaria, Cunard Line, 1953	5.00
Santa Fe, Super Chief, luncheon, folder, 1971	4.00
Scythia, Cunard Line, 1949	5.00
Sevilla Biltmore, Havana, Cuba, 1930	5.00
Simon's Drive In, Los Angeles	8.00
SS City of Omaha, Christmas, 1940	5.00
SS Lurline, March 1960, L Macouillard cov art	15.00
SS Oakwood, American Export Lines, Christmas, 1939	5.00
The Mount Washington Hotel, dinner, July 22, 1910	5.00
Third Annual Reunion, 83rd Old Settlers, 1905, Excelsior Springs, advertising, 4½ x 6½", printed, emb, color	10.00
Union Pacific, City of Los Angeles, dome liner, breakfast, 1971	2.50
United States Hotel, Saratoga Springs, NY, 1882, 7 x 10"	12.00

NEWSPAPERS

History: America's first successful newspaper was *The Boston Newsletter,* founded in 1704. The newspaper industry grew rapidly, experiencing its golden age in the early twentieth century. Within the last decade, many great evening papers have ceased publication, and many local papers have been purchased by the large chains.

Newspapers are collected first for their story content and second for the advertising. Volume One, Number One of any newspaper brings a premium because of its crossover value. Beware of assigning too much value to age alone. Eighteenth and nineteenth century newspapers with weak story content and advertising are frequently framed and used for decorative purposes.

Collecting headline edition newspapers has become popular during the last twenty years, largely because of the decorative value of the headlines. Also, individuals like to collect newspapers related to the great events which they have witnessed or which have been romanticized through the movies, television, and other media, especially those reporting events, the Old West, and the gangster era.

Saving the last edition of a newspaper has become a national fad. If the volume of sales of the last issue equaled that of a daily issues, most of these papers would still be publishing. While there are collectors for the "first" of something, there are very few collectors for the "last" of something. It is doubtful that most of these "final" issues will have any long term value.

All newspapers must be complete with a minimal amount of chipping and cracking. The post–1880 newsprint is made of wood pulp and deteriorates quickly without proper care. Pre–1880 newsprint was composed of cotton and rag fiber and has survived much better than its wood pulp counterpart.

Front pages only of twentieth century newspapers command about 60 percent of the value for the entire issue, since the primary use for these papers is display. Pre–twentieth century issues are collectible only if complete, as banner headlines were rarely used. These papers tend to run between four and eight pages.

Major city issues are preferable, although any newspaper providing a dramatic headline is collectible. Banner headlines, those extending completely across the paper, are most desirable. Also desirable are those from the city in which the event happened and command a substantial premium over the prices listed. Complete series collections carry a premium as well, such as all twentieth century election reports, etc.

Twentieth century newspapers are easily stored. Issues should be placed flat in polyethylene bags, or acid free folders that are slightly larger than the paper, and kept from high humidity and direct sunlight.

Although not as commonly found, newspapers from the seventeenth through the nineteenth century are highly collectible, particularly those from the Revolutionary War, War of 1812, Civil War, and those reporting Indian and "desperado" events.

Two of the most commonly reprinted papers are the *ULSTER COUNTY GAZETTE,* of January 4, 1800, dealing with Washington's death and the *N.Y. HERALD,* of April 15, 1865, dealing with Lincoln's death. If you have either of these papers, chances are you have a reprint.

Reference: Harold Evans, *Front Page History,* Salem House, 1984; Robert F. Karolevitz, *From Quill To Computer: The Story of America's Community Newspapers,* National Newspaper Foundation, 1985; Jim Lyons, *Collecting American Newspapers,* published by author, 1989.

Periodicals: *Collectible Newspapers,* PO Box 19134, Lansing, MI 48901; *PCM (Paper Collector's Marketplace),* PO Box 128, Scandinavia, WI 54977.

HEADLINE

| 1801, March 2, The House Of Representatives Votes For Thomas Jefferson For President, Connecticut Courant | **85.00** |

1811, September 21, Niles Weekly Register, article on affair of Little Belt, event leading to War of 1812 . . . . **10.00**

1836, April 23, The Fall of the Alamo, The New Yorker **100.00**

1858, September 13, Lincoln/Douglas Debates–Lincoln Stands on the Old Whig Platform, Illinois State Journal . . **95.00**

1859, November 5, Harper's Ferry **15.00**

1860, Lincoln/Douglas Election **42.00**

1862

Emancipation of the Slaves–Proclamation by the President of the United States, Chicago Tribune **200.00**

The Monitor vs the Merrimac "Exciting News–Big Naval Fight–A Terrible Fight between the Monitor and the Merrimac" **70.00**

The Second Battle of Manassas, Charleston Mercury **60.00**

1863, Battle of Gettysburg **175.00**

1864, November 11, Abraham Lincoln Re–Elected by an overwhelming majority, The Liberator **75.00**

1865

End of Civil War **200.00**

Fall of Richmond **125.00**

Funeral of Abraham Lincoln in NY, New York Times **95.00**

Further Particulars of the Assassination of President Lincoln, Daily American Flag **80.00**

Important Arrival of General Grant in Washington, New York Herald **25.00**

Killing of Booth, Leslie's Illustrated . . . **75.00**

The Crowning Glory–Surrender of Lee and His Whole Army! The Story Told–Official, Essex County Mercury **48.00**

The National Bereavement Proclamations of the Governors **100.00**

1868, Grant/Seymour Election **12.00**

1871, October 28, Great Chicago Fire, Leslie's Illustrated **150.00**

1872, Grant/Greeley Election **12.00**

1876

Bull's Braves, Sitting Bull Interviewed, Chicago Times, July 15 . . . . **30.00**

Custer's Last Stand **250.00**

Hayes/Tilden **8.00**

1880, Garfield/Hancock Election **8.00**

1881

Billy the Kid Killed, July 20, New York Tribune **115.00**

Garfield Assassinated **40.00**

Gunfight at OK Corral **400.00**

1882, April 5, Jesse James Killed, Chicago Tribune **500.00**

1884, Cleveland/Hancock Election **8.00**

1885, July 23, Ulysses S. Grant Dies **70.00**

1886, October 28, Statue Of Liberty Dedicated **45.00**

1888, Harrison/Cleveland Election **10.00**

1889, Johnstown Flood **30.00**

1892

Cleveland/Harrison Election **8.00**

Lizzie Borden Crime and Trial **15.00**

1896, McKinley/Bryan Election **12.00**

1898

Spanish American War Begins **35.00**

The Maine Is Sunk, February 15 . . . . . **40.00**

1900

James Jeffries Defeats Jack Corbett to Retain Heavyweight Boxing Title, May 11 . . . . **22.00**

McKinley/Bryan Election **8.00**

1901

September 6, McKinley Is Shot **40.00**

September 14, McKinley Dies **35.00**

1903, December 17, Wright Brothers Fly **220.00**

1904, Roosevelt/Parker Election **10.00**

1906, San Francisco Earthquake

Chicago Daily News **110.00**

San Francisco paper **200.00**

1908, Taft/Bryan Election **8.00**

1909, September 6, Peary Discovers The North Pole **15.00**

1912

Titanic Sunk, April 15 . . . . **175.00**

Wilson/Roosevelt/Taft Election **10.00**

1914, World War I Begins **40.00**

1915

Allies Battering the Dardanelles, Chicago Sunday Herald **12.00**

Lusitania Sunk, May 7 . . . . **115.00**

Torpedo Wrecks Big Liner Lusitania/ Many boats Rush to Save Passengers, Cunard Liner Which Left New York Last Saturday Falls Victim to Torpedo and is Beached off the Coast of Ireland, Chicago Daily News **80.00**

1916, Wilson/Hughes Election **9.50**

1917, April 2, Wilson Calls For Declaration Of War **38.00**

1918, November 11, Armistice Signed . . **50.00**

1919, June 28, Peace Treaty Signed **15.00**

1920

Harding/Cox Election **5.00**

Prohibition Takes Effect **22.00**

1921, August 3, Black Sox Acquitted by jury, Nashville Tennessean **25.00**

1923, August 3, President Harding Dies of Stroke Executive Passes Without Warning, San Francisco Journal **50.00**

1924

Coolidge/Davis Election **5.00**

Woodrow Wilson Dies, February 3 . . . **20.00**

1925, Scopes "Monkey" Trial Verdict . . **22.00**

1926, September 23, Tunney Defeats Jack Dempsey **22.00**

1927

Babe Ruth's 60th Homerun, Galveston Daily News **82.00**

Headline, *La Porte Argus Bulletin,* "Night of Horror," one column headline describes Titanic sinking in graphic terms, full page column with continuing story, 16 pages, 16 x 24½", April 17, 1912, $200.00.

Lindbergh Flies The Atlantic, May 21	35.00
1917 Detroit and Sox Scandal, Nashville Banner........................	9.00
1928, Hoover/Smith Election.........	5.00
1929	
Byrd Flies To The South Pole, November 29........................	10.00
Capone Sentenced To Prison, May 17	35.00
Ruth's Wife Dies In Fire, Nashville Tennessean	11.00
Stock Market Crashes, October 28 ...	65.00
St. Valentine's Day Massacre, February 14........................	65.00
1929, Byrd Flies To South Pole........	15.00
1931, October 17, Al Capone Sentenced For 11 Years On Tax Evasion........	22.00
1932	
March 1, Lindbergh Baby Kidnapped	18.00
November 8, Franklin D. Roosevelt Elected......................	15.00
1933	
January 30, Hitler Made Chancellor Of Germany	12.00
December 5, Prohibition Repealed...	23.00
1934	
May 23, Bonnie & Clyde Killed......	70.00

July 22, Dillinger Shot & Killed......	35.00
1936	
First Hall of Famers, The Morning Post	16.00
King Edward VIII Renounces The Crown, December 10...........	17.00
Roosevelt/Landon Election.........	15.00
1937	
May 6, Hindenburg Crashes In Flames	40.00
July 2, Amelia Earhart Vanishes In Round The World Flight.........	14.00
1938, March 11, Nazis Seize Austria ...	9.00
1939, Sept 1, Cincinnati Post, Undeclared War On Nazis Bomb Warsaw........................	15.00
1940, Roosevelt/Wilkie Election.......	8.00
1941	
Hitler Wars On Russia, June 21......	10.00
Japan Attacks Pearl Harbor, December 7........................	42.00
Lou Gehrig's Death, The Morning Post, December 8	31.00
Pearl Harbor Attack, San Francisco Chronicle, December 8..........	55.00
United States Declares War, December 11........................	17.00
1500 Killed In Hawaii Raid; Two US	

Warships Down–EXTRA!, Milwaukee Journal, December 8 . . . .   **35.00**
1943, September 8, Italy Surrenders **9.00**
1944
Allied Armies Land In France, June 5   **18.00**
D–Day **20.00**
Roosevelt Wins 4th Term, November 7 . . . .   **10.00**
1945
First Atomic Bomb Dropped On Japan, August 6 . . . .   **24.00**
Japan Surrenders–War Over, August 14 . . . .   **25.00**
President Roosevelt Is Dead, four column photo of Roosevelt with black border, April 13 . . . .   **16.00**
War In Europe Ends, May 7 . . . .   **24.00**
1948
Babe Ruth's Death **100.00**
Truman/Dewey Election **8.00**
1950, US Enters Korean War **12.00**
1951, April 10, Truman Relieves MacArthur Of His Command **8.00**
1952, Eisenhower/Stevenson Election . .   **8.00**
1953, July 26, Truce Signed Ending The Korean War **11.00**
1954, May 17, Court Bans School Segregation **10.00**
1956, Eisenhower/Stevenson Election . .   **5.00**
1957, October 4, Soviets Launch Sputnik   **14.00**
1958, June 30, Alaska Joins The Union . .   **17.00**
1959, March 12, Hawaii Joins The Union   **18.00**
1960, Kennedy/Nixon Election **15.00**
1961, Roger Maris Hits 61st home Run, Breaks Ruth's Record **85.00**
1962
John Glenn Orbits The Earth, February 20 . . . .   **15.00**
Marilyn Monroe's Death **30.00**
1963, John F Kennedy Assassination, November 22 . . . .   **50.00**
1964, Johnson/Goldwater Election **5.00**
1967, Superbowl I **12.00**
1968
Martin Luther King Slain, April 5 . . . . .   **15.00**
Robert Kennedy Assassination **18.00**
1969, July 20, Man Walks On The Moon   **20.00**
1972, Nixon/McGovern Election **5.00**
1973, Vietnam Peace Pacts Signed **10.00**
1976, Carter/Ford Election **5.00**
1977, August 17, Elvis Dies, Los Angeles Times **27.00**
1980
John Lennon's Death, New York title   **18.00**
Reagan/Carter Election **4.00**
1986, January 28, Challenger Explodes   **5.00**

NON–HEADLINE

London Gazette, quarto format of news of the world, early English language,

Headline, *The Indianapolis Star*, "President Shot By Assassin," 15 x 24", November 23, 1963, $20.00.

printed during reign of King George I, 1725 . . . .   **28.00**
Salem Gazette, Nov 6, 1783, Federal City, US Congress passed resolution, and half pay pension for Revolutionary War Officers **55.00**

FACSIMILE

Godey's Lady's Book, 1868, monthly issues **18.00**
Good Words, May, 1891 edition, Isbister and Co, London, pictorial wrappers . .   **35.00**
Harper's Weekly, 1858, full year bound, orig cloth binding **475.00**
News of the World, Sunday, October 16, 1966, London, 24 pgs, 5$^7/8$ x 4$^1/16$" **12.00**
San Francisco Chronicle, 1865–1965–A Portfolio of Historic Chronicle Front Pages, 1965 . . . .   **5.00**
The Daily Mail, November 20, 1962, 16 pgs, 5 x 3$^1/4$" **5.00**
The Daily Telegraph, September 21, 1947, London, 36 pgs, 5$^1/2$ x 4" **8.00**
The Massachusetts Centinel, 1789 . . . . .   **50.00**
The Observer, Sunday, January 13, 1963, London, 36 pgs **16.00**
The Times, April 11, 1967, London, 32 pgs **8.00**

NON–SPORT TRADING CARDS

History: The birthplace of the modern bubble gum (trading) card is the tobacco insert cards of the late nineteenth century. From 1885 to 1894 there were over 500 sets issued, with only about 25 devoted to sports. Trading cards lost their popularity in the decade following World War I. However, in 1933 "Indian Gum" issued a product containing a stick of bubble gum and a card in a waxed paper package—a revolution had begun.

Goudey Gum and National Chicle controlled the market until the arrival of Gum, Inc., in 1936. Gum, Inc., issued The Lone Ranger and Superman sets in 1940. From 1943 to 1947 the market in cards was again quiet. In 1948 Bowman entered the picture. A year later Topps Chewing Gum produced some non–sports cards. A war between Bowman and Topps ensued until 1956 when Topps bought Bowman.

Although Topps enjoyed a dominant position in the baseball card market, it had continual rivals in the non–sports field. Frank Fleer Company, Leaf Brands, and Philadelphia Chewing Gum provided competition in the 1960s. Fleer and Donruss Chewing Gum provide the modern day assault.

In the 1990s, the non–sport trading card is experiencing a revival, a revival based on the baseball card and comic book shop markets. Comic and special issue trading cards are hot. Dozens of new issues are arriving on the scene each month. *Comic Values Monthly* (Attic Books, Ltd., 15 Danbury Road, Ridgefield, CT 06877) reports regularly on these new issues.

Although every collector is tempted by the individual cards, the goal is to assemble a complete set. If you have the funds available, buy complete sets from the start. The price of sets tends to be less than the sum of individual cards. Any set should contain a sample of the wrapper plus any stickers that belong to the set.

Because of the availability of these cards, make certain the sets you buy are in mint condition. You can buy boxes of gum packages. With Topps, you are 100 percent certain you will get at least one full set from a box. Donruss and Fleer average 85 percent.

Collectors should store cards in plastic sleeves. Place the wrapper first and then the cards in numerical order.

References: Christopher Benjamin, *The Sport Americana Price Guide to Non–Sports Cards, 1930–1960, No. 2*, Edgewater Book Co., 1993; Christopher Benjamin, *The Sport Americana Price Guide to Non–Sports Cards, Part Two: 1961–1992, No. 4*, Edgewater Book Co., 1993; J.

R. Burdick, ed., *The American Card Catalog: The Standard Guide on All Collected Cards and Their Values*, reprinted by Nostalgia Press, 1988; John Neuner, *Checklist & Prices of U. S. Non-Sport Wrappers*, privately published, 1992; Robert Reed, *Collector's Guide To Trading Cards: Identification & Values*, Collector Books, 1993.

Periodicals: *Collect*, Tuff Stuff Publications, 2309 Hungary Road, Richmond, VA 23228; *Non-Sport Network*, 19 Lores Plaza, #160, New Milford, CT 06776; *The Non–Sport Update*, Roxanne Toser Non–Sport Enterprises, Inc., PO Box 5858, Harrisburg, PA 17110; *The Wrapper*, 7 Simpson Street, Apt. A, Geneva, IL 60134.

Baltimore Chewing Gum Company,	
Flags of the Nations, 50 cards	**275.00**
Blatz Gum	
Chicago World's Fair, 32 cards, printed back	**175.00**
Screen Stars, 20 cards, 3½ x 5½"	**110.00**
Bowman	
America Salutes The FBI, 36 cards, 2¹/₁₆ x 2½"	**150.00**
Firefighters, 64 cards	**275.00**
Frontier Days, 1953, 128 cards	**200.00**
Jets, Rockets, Spacemen, 1951, 108 cards	**875.00**
Television and Radio Stars of The National Broadcasting Company, 1953, 96 cards	**275.00**
US Presidents, 36 cards	**55.00**
Wild West, 1949, 180 cards	**750.00**
Donruss	
Addams Family, 1964, 66 cards	**60.00**
All–Pro Skateboard	
1977, 44 cards	**5.00**
1978, 44 sticker cards	**6.00**
Bionic Woman, 1976, 44 cards	**3.50**
BMX, 1984, 59 cards	**5.00**
Choppers and Hot Bikes, 1972, 66 cards	**25.00**
Combat, Series I, 1964, 66 cards	**55.00**

Frontier Days, Bowman, No. 14, "Look! The Stagecoach!", multicolor, 3¾ x 2½", 1953, excellent condition, $2.50.

U. S. Presidents, Bowman, No. 34, Franklin D. Roosevelt, and No. 11, Martin Van Buren, 2½ x 3¾", 1952, excellent condition, price each, $2.00.

Dallas, 1981, 56 cards	5.00
Disneyland, 1965, 66 cards, puzzle back	45.00
Dukes Of Hazzard, 1980, 66 cards	3.50
Elvis Presley, 1978, 66 cards	35.50
Flying Nun, 1968, 66 cards	55.00
Freddie & The Dreamers, 1965, 66 cards	40.00
Green Hornet, 1966, 44 cards	50.00
Idiot Cards, 1961, 66 cards.	75.00
King Kong, 1965, 55 cards	50.00
Kiss, 1st, 1978, 66 cards	35.00
Magnum PI, 1983, 66 cards	3.50
Monkees, 1966, 44 cards	38.00
Osmonds, 1973, 66 cards.	30.00
Rock Stars, 1979, 66 cards	2.50
Fleer	
Casper, 1960, 66 cards	175.00
Drag Nationals, 1972, 70 cards	16.00
Dragon's Lair, 1984, 63 stickers, 30 rub–off games.	10.00
Gomer Pyle, 1965, 66 cards	10.00
Gong Show, 1979, 66 cards, 10 stickers	5.00
Goofy Gags, 1963, 55 cards	15.00
Here's Bo, 1981, 72 cards, 12 posters	5.00
Mad, 1983, 128 stickers	15.00
My Kookie Klassmates, 1968, 20 cards, nine autograph stamp sheets	15.00
Spins and Needles, 1960, 80 cards	175.00
Three Stooges	
1959, 96 cards.	650.00
1966, 66 cards.	80.00
Yule Laff, 1960, 66 cards	55.00
Goudey Gum	
Action Gum, 1938–39, 96 cards . . .	750.00
Auto License Plates, 1937, 36 cards	150.00
First Column Defenders, 1940, 24 cards	350.00

Indian Gum, 1930s, 216 cards	**1,150.00**
Sea Raiders, 1933, 48 card, 2⅜ x 2⅞".	**850.00**
Sky Birds, 1941, 24 cards, 2⁵⁄₁₆ x 2⅞".	**175.00**
Gum, Inc	
Bring 'Em Back Alive, 1938, 100 cards	**250.00**
Film Funnies, 24 cards	**500.00**
G–Men & Heroes of the Law, 168 cards	**4,250.00**
History of Aviation, 1936, 10 cards	**150.00**
Horrors of War, 1938, 288 cards . . .	**4,500.00**
Movie Stars, 1939–42, 19 cards. . . .	**175.00**
Pirate's Picture Bubble Gum, 72 cards, 2⁷⁄₁₆ x 3⅛"	**850.00**
Superman, 1940, 48 cards, 2⅜ x 2⅞".	**1,100.00**
War Gum, 1941–42, 132 cards	**1,100.00**
Wild West Series, 49 cards, 2½ x 3⅛".	**350.00**
International Chewing Gum Company, 1938, Don't Let It Happen Over Here, 24 cards	**750.00**
Leaf	
Foney Ads, 1960, 72 cards	**75.00**
Garrisons' Gorillas, 1967, 72 cards	**50.00**
Good Guys & Bad Guys, 1966, 72 cards	**50.00**
Pirate Cards, 1948, 49 cards	**225.00**
Star Trek, 1967, 72 cards	**550.00**
National Chicle Company	
Dare Devils, 24 cards	**275.00**
Sky Birds, 1933–1934, 108 cards, 2⁵⁄₁₆ x 2⅞".	**2,225.00**
Novelty Gum	
Action Pictures, 1934, 24 cards	**275.00**
League of Nations, 50 cards	**475.00**
Philadelphia Chewing Gum Co	
Blackstone's Magic Tricks, 1953, 24 folders.	**60.00**
Daktari, 1967, 66 cards	**20.00**
Dark Shadows, Series II, 1969, 66 cards, green	**80.00**
Green Berets, 1966, 66 cards	**40.00**
Happy Horoscopes, 1972, 72 cards	**20.00**
James Bond	
1965, 66 cards.	**55.00**
1966, 66 cards.	**60.00**
Tarzan, 1966, 66 cards	**40.00**
Wild West Series, #46	**4.00**
Picture Pack Gum, Aeroplane Series, 1930s, 25 cards	**175.00**
Shelby Gum	
Fighting Planes, 1930s, 24 cards . . .	**175.00**
Hollywood Screen Stars, 40 cards . .	**650.00**
Humpty Dumpty Up–To–Date, 24 cards	**225.00**
Topps	
Alf, 1987, 22 cards, 18 stickers	**8.00**
Alien, 1979, 84 cards, 22 stickers. . .	**6.00**

Angry Stickers, 1967, 88 cards	150.00
Astronauts, 1963, 55 cards	50.00
A–Team, 1983, 66 cards, 12 stickers	3.50
Batman Movie, Series #1, 1989, 132 cards, 22 stickers.	30.00
Batman Returns, 1992, 88 cards, 10 stadium club cards	5.00
Batman, Series 4, Riddler back series, 1966, 38 cards.	200.00
Battlestar Galactica, 1978, 132 cards, 22 stickers.	10.00
Bay City Rollers, 1975, 66 cards. . . .	20.00
Beverly Hillbillies, 1963, 66 cards . .	80.00
Beverly Hills 90210, 1991, 88 cards, 11 stickers.	10.00
Bobby Sherman "Getting Together," 1971, 55 cards	450.00
Brady Bunch, 1970, 88 cards	150.00
Buck Rogers, 1979, 88 cards, 22 stickers	5.00
Casey & Kildare, 1962, 110 cards . .	95.00
Charlie's Angels, Series I, 1977, 55 cards	6.00
Civil War News, 1962, 88 cards. . . .	175.00
Close Encounters, 1978, 66 cards, 11 stickers.	3.50
Comic Cover, 1970, 44 stickers	75.00
Crazy Cards, 1961, 66 cards.	60.00
Cyndi Lauper, 1985, 66 cards.	3.00
Daniel Boone, 1965, 55 cards	25.00
Davy Crockett, 1956, 80 cards, orange backs	125.00
DC Comic Book Foldees, 1966, 44 cards	150.00
Desert Storm, Operation Desert Storm, 1991, 88 cards, 22 stickers, brown shield front.	32.00
Desert Storm Victory, 1991, 88 cards, 11 stickers.	15.00
Dick Tracy, 1990, 88 cards, 11 stickers	16.00
Empire Strikes Back, Series I, 1980 . .	5.00
E T The Extra–Terrestrial, 1982, 87 cards, 12 stickers.	12.50
Evel Knievel, 1974, 60 cards	35.00
Famous Americans, 1963, 80 cards	260.00
Fighting Marines, 1953, 96 cards . . .	350.00
Flag Midgee, 1963, 99 cards	40.00
Flags of the World, 1956, 80 cards . .	110.00
Flags of the World–Parade, 1949, 100 cards	100.00
Flip–O–Vision, 1949, 50 cards	425.00
Flipper, 1966, 30 cards.	400.00
Funny Valentines, 1959, 66 cards . .	55.00
Good Times, 1975, 55 cards, 21 stickers	8.00
Goofy Series Post Cards, 1957, 60 cards	45.00
Grease, Series I, 1978, 66 cards, 11 stickers	3.00
Green Hornet, 1966, 44 stickers. . . .	225.00
Happy Days, 1976, 44 cards, 11 stickers	4.00
Hit Stars, 1958, 88 cards.	350.00
Hook, 1991, 99 cards, 11 stickers . .	12.50
Howard The Duck, 1986, 75 cards, 22 stickers	12.00
Incredible Hulk, 1979, 88 cards, 22 stickers	20.00
Johnson vs. Goldwater, 1964, 66 cards	45.00
Little Shop of Horrors, 1986, 44 stickers	8.00
Look 'N See, 1952, 135 cards.	550.00
Lost In Space, 1966, 55 cards	160.00
King Kong, 1965, 55 cards	20.00
Kookie Plaks, 1965, 88 cards	60.00
Marvel Comics, 1979, 33 cards	25.00
Marvel Super Heroes Stickers, 1976, 40 stickers, 9 puzzle cards	100.00
Masters of the Universe, 1984, 88 cards, 21 stickers.	12.00
Nintendo, 1989, 33 sticker/tip cards, 60 game cards.	9.00
Rails and Sails, 1955, 200 cards	500.00
Rambo, 1985, 66 cards, 22 stickers	8.00
Return of the Jedi, Series 1, 1983, 132 cards, 33 stickers	25.00
Robin Hood, 1957, 60 cards	100.00
Robin Hood Prince of Thieves, 1991, 88 cards, 9 stickers	15.00
Roger Rabbit, 1988, 132 cards, 22 stickers	25.00
Scoop, 1954, 156 cards	950.00
Simpsons, 1990, 88 cards, 22 stickers	8.00
Star Trek, The Motion Picture, 1979, 88 cards, 22 stickers	35.00
Star Trek, 1976, 88 cards, 22 stickers	220.00
Star Wars, Series 1, 1977, 66 cards, 11 stickers, blue	30.00
Superman, 1966, 66 cards, black and white photos	180.00
Superman in the Jungle, 1968, 66 cards, test set.	700.00
Teenage Mutant Ninja Turtles–Cartoon, 1989, 88 cards, 11 stickers	15.00
Terminator 2, 1991, 44 stickers	5.00
The Rocketeer, 1991, 99 cards, 11 stickers	15.00
Toxic Crusaders, 1991, 88 cards, 8 holograms.	12.50
TV Westerns, 1958, 71 cards	175.00
Wacky Packages, 1990, 55 stickers	12.00
X–Ray Round Up, 1952, 200 cards	375.00
Zorro, 1958, 88 cards.	175.00
Upper Deck, Looney Tunes Comic Ball, 1990, 297 cards	25.00
Wolverine Gum Company, Believe It Or Not, 1937, 48 cards.	750.00

PAMPHLETS

History: Are the terms pamphlet and booklet synonymous? For most individuals and all practical purposes, the answer is yes. The distinctions between a pamphlet and a booklet are extremely subtle. Dictionary definitions provide only minimal guidance.

A pamphlet is a small, thin, unbound printed publication with a paper cover comprised of sheets of paper that are stapled or stitched together. Occasionally, it has no cover at all. The number of pages is a factor. Pamphlets frequently range in size from four to sixteen pages, although some with more than sixteen pages can be found. They tend to focus on timely topics of public interest; points of view expressed are often highly opinionated.

A booklet is a small book, often with paper covers. Its contents are largely informative, rather than opinionated. While there is no minimum page count, a booklet usually contains in excess of sixteen pages. The vast majority have more than thirty–two.

Public perception helps distinguish a pamphlet from a booklet. A pamphlet is something that is meant to be read once, perhaps twice, and then discarded or passed along to someone else of like persuasion. A booklet has a more permanent quality, something to be saved and continually referred to. Pamphlets that survived did so because they were put in a drawer to be read when an opportunity presented itself. Booklets frequently found a home on library and kitchen shelves.

When examining pamphlets and booklets from the period 1700 to 1915, the above distinctions can usually be made easily. After World War I, the differences become clouded. Further, the communication revolution after World War II, especially the increased role of television, absorbed many of the roles played by pamphlets and booklets. Their numbers decreased significantly.

The above distinctions are subtle and subjective. Rather than fight about it, most paper collectors simply use the terms interchangeably.

In this first edition of *Warman's Paper*, the two remain as separate categories. This is done as a tribute to the traditionalist paper ephemerists who have built separate pamphlet and booklet collections. However, few modern collectors are continuing this approach. Today most pamphlets and booklets are collected for their subject matter, not type.

Note: Also see "Booklets" in the topical section.

A Friend In Need, Arm & Hammer Baking Soda, 1933, 28 pages, blue cov . . .   **4.00**

Baccardi Party Book, 1969, 22 pgs, M Eckley **1.00**
Baker's Coconut, Cut Up Cakes, 1956 . .   **3.00**
Bake with Bundt, LFP Church, 1970, 20 pgs **2.00**
Ball Canning, 1933 . . . .   **5.00**
Best Wartime Recipes, Royal Baking Powder, 1917 . . . .   **2.00**
Betty Crocker, Frankly Fancy Foods, 1959, 26 pgs **5.00**
Biscuits & Cakes, Reliable Flour, 1911, 62 pgs **5.00**
Bon Ami, The Chick That Never Grew Up **10.00**
Book of Breads, Ithaca, NY, Brewer, 1929 . . . .   **2.00**
Cake and Food Decorating, Wilton, 1956, 16 pgs **1.00**
Cake Secrets, Inglehearts, purple cov . . .   **2.25**
Campbell's Cooking with a Purpose for Girl Scouts, c1975, 15 pgs. **1.50**
Certo, Certo Recipes For Making Jams & Jellies, 1937, 31 pgs. **4.00**
Cheese and Ways to Serve It, M Dahnke, 1931, 46 pgs **3.00**
Chiquita Bananas, Chiquita Banana Presents 18 Recipes, 1951, 18 pgs **6.00**
Chocolate Cooker, General Foods, 1929, 36 pgs **6.50**
Cookery Notebook, Mechanics Inst **5.00**
Cooking with a Velvet Touch, Carnation, c1960, 48 pgs **4.00**
Cook's Digest, Nov 1940, 70 pgs **2.00**
Cottolene Shortening, Cottolene Recipes, 1905. . . . .   **15.00**
Cox's Gelatin, Cox's Delicious Recipes, 1933, 30 pgs **4.00**
Deep Sea Recipes, c1930 . . . .   **2.50**
Discover Gold, Galliano, 1972, 24 pgs   **1.00**

POLSKA FEDERACJA CAMPINGU

Polish Campgrounds, foldout map, full color, 24 x 29", 1971, $10.00.

Easy to Make Pickles and Relishes, Cornell, 11 pgs 2.00
Eggs Summer–Side Up, American Egg Board, 1973, 31 pgs 2.00
Fleischmann's Yeast, recipes, 1910, 26 pgs........................... 30.00
Food Triumphs with New Minute Tapioca, General Foods, 1934, 47 pgs.... 4.00
French Dressings for Your Favorite Salads, Kraft, 1957, 22 pgs 2.00
Fun Filled Butter Cookies, Pillsbury, 49 pgs........................... 3.00
Gambling Games Exposed by Gilbert Vitale, Rochester, NY, 1930–40 ..... 60.00
Gold Medal Sandwich Book, 35 pgs.... 2.50
Good Things To Eat, M Anderson, 1940, 15 pgs 3.00
Good Things To Eat–Tested Recipes, Arm & Hammer Baking Soda, 1936, 116th edition, 32 pgs.............. 10.00
Gorton, Codfish Recipes, 1906........ 4.00
Guide to Better Foods, Westinghouse, 1930, 40 pgs 1.50
Hanford's Balsam, Noah's Ark Primer... 12.00
Hershey's, Hershey's Favorite Recipes, 1970, 32 pgs 4.00
Highland Brand Evaporated Cream, diecut, can shape 20.00
Housekeeping, Robinson, 1980, 1st ed 20.00
How Phyllis Grew Thin, L Pinkam, 32 pgs.............................. 3.50
How to Barbecue, Test Institute, NY, 15 pgs.............................. 1.00
It's All in Knowing How, Arm & Hammer, 1935, 37 pgs 2.00
Jell–O, 1917, 20 pgs 9.00
Jell–O Girl Gives A Party, Rose O'Neill illus 25.00
Johnston's Fluid Beef, Wm M Shoemaker, Proprietor 9.00
Keep on the Sunny Side of Life, Kellogg, 1933, 32 pgs 5.00
Knox Dainty Desserts For Dainty People, 1915, 41 pgs 12.00
Knox's Gelatine, 1896, recipes, black boy illus........................ 25.00
Knox Gelatine Desserts, Salads, Candies & Frozen Dishes, 1933, 75 pgs 9.00
Ladies' Aid Society, Lancaster, NY, 1932–35 .... 3.00
La Rosa Macaroni, 101 Ways To Prepare Macaroni, 1929, 31 pgs........... 4.00
Meals Planning Guide, 1943, 67 pgs, Santa cov....................... 2.00
Meg's Macaroni Co, Delicious Ways To Make Pennsylvania Dutch Bott Boi, Pot Pie, 1960s, 40 pgs 4.00
Mexican Cookbook, Sunset, 1971, 96 pgs.............................. 4.00
Montgomery Ward, Farm–Dairy Equipment, 1934, 15 pgs 8.00

Mr Ham Goes To Town, Morrell, 1939, 14 pgs 1.50
National Macaroni Mfg, Ass'n, Thrift Recipes, 1931, 16 pgs............. 6.00
New Calumet Baking Book, Parker, 1931, 31 pgs 3.00
New England Mince Meat, diecut, pie shape........................ 9.00
New Orlean's Coffee, Fairy Tales, c1899 23.00
Proven Recipes–Three Great Products from Corn, 66 pgs, Indian cov 4.00
Prunes for Epicures, 1933 .... 2.00
Recipes to Stretch Your Sugar Ration, Arm & Hammer, 1942............ 5.00
Reynolds Wrap
  Casual Cooking, 1954, 15 pgs....... 5.00
  New Holiday Know–How For Use With Reynolds Wrap, 1957, 16 pgs 6.00
  The Way Mama Cooked It, 1981, 31 pgs......................... 4.00
Riches of New Jersey, 1952, 32 pgs 4.00
Royal, Desserts With Ginger Rogers, 1940 .... 6.00
Rumford Southern Recipes, M Wilson, 1894, 65 pgs 7.00
Sealtest Food Advisor, 1939, 15 pgs, New York World's Fair 4.50
Sharples Separator.................. 10.00
Sunkist
  Sunkist Recipes For Everday, 1933, 35 pgs........................ 3.00
  Sunkist Recipes, Oranges–Lemons, 1916, 64 pgs 4.00
Swans Down Shortening, New Swans Down Desserts & Hot Breads, 1945 .. 2.00
Sweet Ending, Dream Whip, 1974, 27 pgs.............................. 1.50
Tasty Dishes, 1898, 48 pgs 1.50
The Railroad Workers and The War, 1941, 15 pgs, Wm Z Foster, 5 x 7".... 20.00
Three Meals a Day, Metro Life, 16 pgs .. 2.00
Veterinary 1st Aid Hints, G. C. Hanford Mfg Co, horse cov, 1935 .... 10.00
Walter Baker & Co, Baker's Best Chocolate Recipes, 1932............... 8.00
Wheatena, 1906 .... 3.00

PAPERBACK BOOKS

History: Paperback volumes have existed since the fifteenth century. Mass–market paperback books, most popular with collectors, date from the post 1938 period. The number of mass market publishers in the 1938–50 period was much greater than today. These books exist in a variety of formats, from the standard size paperback and its shorter predecessor to odd sizes like 64 page short novels for 10¢ and 5¼" x 7½" volumes known as digests. Some books came in a dust jacket; some were boxed.

The Golden Age for paperback books was from 1939 to the late 1950s, a period generally characterized by a lurid and colorful graphic style of cover art and title lettering not unlike that of the pulp magazines. A lot of early paperback publishers had been or were publishers of pulps and merely moved their graphic style and many of their authors to paperbacks.

Most collections are assembled around one or more unifying themes. Some common themes are: author (Edgar Rice Burroughs, Dashiell Hammett, Louis L'Amour, Raymond Chandler, Zane Grey, William Irish, Cornell Woolrich, etc.); fictional genre (mysteries, science fiction, westerns, etc.); publisher (early Avon, Dell and Popular Library are most popular); cover artist (Frank Frazetta, R. C. M. Heade, Rudolph Belarski, Roy Krenkel, Vaughn Bode, etc.); and books with uniquely appealing graphic design (Dell mapbacks and Ace double novels).

Because quantity lots of paperbacks still turn up, many collectors are cautious as they assemble their collections. Books in the highest condition grades remain uncommon. Many current dealers try to charge upper level prices for books in lesser condition, arguing that top condition is just too scarce. This argument is not valid, just self–serving.

Paperback books should be in fine or better condition. Many titles are commonly found in unsatisfactory condition. Learn to ignore them. Unique items, such as paperbacks in dust jackets or in boxes, are highly desirable.

References: Kenneth Davis, *Two–Bit Culture: The Paperbacking of America*, Houghton Mifflin, 1984; Kevin Hancer, *The Paperback Price Guide, Third Edition*, Wallace–Homestead, 1989; Piet Schreuders, *Paperbacks USA, A Graphic History, 1939–1959*, Blue Dolphin, 1981; Jon Warren, *The Official Price Guide to Paperbacks,* House of Collectibles, 1991.

Periodical: *Paperback Parade*, PO Box 209, Brooklyn, NY 11228.

Museum: University of Minnesota's Hess Collection of Popular Literature, Minneapolis, MN.

Note: The prices given are for books in fine condition. Divide by 3 to get the price for books in good condition; increase price by 50 percent for books in near mint condition.

Adams, Cleve, *And Sudden Death*, Prize Mystery, 5	**6.00**
Addams, Charles, *Drawn and Quartered*, Pocket Book, 1964	**4.00**
Anderson, Poul	
Brain Wave, Ballantine Books, 1954	**6.00**
Golden Slaves, Avon, T–388	**4.00**
Andrews, Robert Hardy, *Great Day In*	

The Morning, Ace Books, 1957, D–206	**3.75**
Anthony, Piers and Robert E Margroff, *The Ring*, Ace Books, 1968, A–19	**2.50**
Avallane, Michael, *The Coffin Things*, Lancer, 74–942	**5.00**
Baldwin, Faith, *Men are Such Fools*, Dell, 138	**5.00**
Barry, Joe, *The Third Degree*, Prize Mystery, 12	**6.00**
Bartlett and Lay, *Twelve O'Clock High*, Bantam, 743	**4.00**
Blackstone, Harry, *Blackstone's Tricks Anyone Can Do* , Permabook, 15	**7.50**
Bliss, Tip, *The Broadway Butterfly Murders*, Checkerbook, 2	**15.00**
Bloch, Robert, *Firebug*, Regency, 101.	**8.00**
Boltar, Russell, *Woman's Doctor*, Ace Books, 1956	**6.00**
Bosworth, Allan R, *Border Roundup*, Bantam Books, 1947	**3.00**
Boyington, Gregory, *Baa Baa Black Sheep*, Dell, F88	**2.00**
Brackett, Leigh, *Rio Bravo*, Bantam, 1893, tie–in with John Wayne movie	**8.00**
Bradbury, Ray, *The Autumn People*, Ballantine, EC, comic reprints with Frazetta cov	**8.00**
Brönte, Emily, *Wuthering Heights*, Quick Reader, 122	**8.00**
Burroughs, Edgar Rice, *Tarzan and the Lost Empire*, Ace, F–169	**4.00**
Busch, Harold, *U–Boats at War*, Ballantine, 120	**4.00**
Campbell, John W., *Who Goes There?*, Dell, D–150	**3.00**
Capp, Al, *Li'l Abner*, Ballantine, 350K, tie–in with movie	**4.00**
Carr, J. D., *The Four False Weapons*, Berkley, G–91	**4.00**
Carter, Nick, *Death has Green Eyes*, Vital Book, 3	**6.00**
Cavanaugh and Weir, *Dell Book of Jokes*, Dell, 89	**24.00**
Cellini, Benvenuto, *The Autobiography of Cellini*, Boni Book	**4.00**
Chidsey, Donald Barr, *Panama Passage*, Perma Book, P248	**2.00**
Christian, Paula, *Edge of Twilight*, Crest, 267	**7.00**
Christie, Agatha, *Murder At The Vicarage*, Dell, 1961, R–106	**3.00**
Cochran, Hamilton, *Windward Passage*, Ace Books, 1957	**3.75**
Cushman, Dan, *Tall Wyoming*, Dell, 1957, 1–140	**3.00**
Davenport, Basil (ed.), *Tales to be Told in the Dark*, Ballantine, 380	**3.00**
Davidson, David, *The Steeper Cliff*, Bantam Books, 1950, 801	**3.00**
Dean, Dudley, *The Diehards*, Gold Medal, 1956, 584	**5.00**

deCamp, L. Sprague (ed.), *The Spell of Seven,* Pyramid, R–1192, Virgil Finlay cov............................... 5.00

Dickson, Carter, *The Peacock Feather Murders,* Berkley, 1963, F–861 ..... 3.75

DiMaggio, Joe, *Lucky to Be a Yankee,* Bantam, 506 .... 4.00

Disney, Walt, *Our Friend the Atom,* Dell, LB117 .... 1.50

Donovan, B., *Eichman–Man of Slaughter,* Avon, T–464 .... 2.00

Duncan, David, *Beyond Eden,* Ballantine Books, 1955 .... 6.00

Edmonds, Walter, *The Wedding Journey,* Dell, 10¢, 6 .... 5.00

Finney, Jack, *The Body Snatchers,* Dell, 42 .... 10.00

Fisher, Clay, *War Bonnet,* Ballantine, 11 4.00

Flora, Fletcher, *Skulldoggery,* Belmont Books, 1967, B50–738 .... 3.00

Ford, Leslie, *Old Lover's Ghost,* Bantam Books, 1947, 114 .... 3.75

Fox, Gardner F., *Woman of Kali,* Gold Medal, 438 .... 4.00

Fox, Norman, A., *Broken Wagon,* Ballantine Books, 1954.............. 4.00

Gaddis, Peggy
  Dr. Prescott's Secret, Beacon, B302 .. 6.00
  Intruders In Eden, Belmont Books, 1966, B50–711 .... 2.50
  Rehearsal For A Wedding, Belmont Books, 1966, B50–673 .... 2.50

Gaines, William (ed.), *The Brothers Mad,* Ballantine, 267K 4.00

Galus, Henry, *Unwed Mothers,* Monarch, 524, Robert Maguire cov 5.00

Gunsmoke (Horseshoe Combine), Leslie Ernenwein, Signet Books, The New American Library, NY, 143 pages, 4¼ x 7⅛", 1949, $3.75.

Goodis, David
  Cassidy's Girl, Gold Medal, 1955, 544   17.50
  The Wounded And The Slain, Gold Medal, 1955, 530 .... 50.00

Grey, Zane, *Nevada,* Bantam, 3 .... 3.50

Grove, Walt, *The Wings of Eagles,* Gold Medal, 649, tie–in with John Wayne movie 5.00

Gruber, Frank, *The Buffalo Box,* Bantam Books, 1946 .... 3.00

Guild, Leo, *The Loves of Liberace,* Avon, T–118 .... 8.00

Hamilton, Donald
  Death of A Citizen, Gold Medal, 1963, K–1334 .... 4.00
  The Removers, Gold Medal, 1963, K–1336 .... 2.00

Hammett, Dashiell, *Hammett Homicides,* Bestseller, B81............. 10.00

Harmon, Jim, *The Great Radio Heroes,* Ace A Series, Ace Books, 1968 ...... 2.00

Hatlo, Jimmy, *They'll Do It Every Time,* Avon, 366 .... 5.00

Haycox, Ernest, *Long Storm,* Bantam Books, 1950, 788 .... 3.00

Heinlein, Robert A., *Beyond This Horizon,* Signet, 1891................ 4.00

Hershfield, Harry, *Book of Jokes,* Avon, 65 .... 10.00

Holmes, J R, *This Is Guam,* Pacific Press, 1953, 240 pages 6.50

Hopson, William, *Hell's Horseman,* News Stand Library, 1950, 126...... 6.00

Horner, Lance, *Rogue Roman,* Gold Medal, T1978, cov by Frazetta 3.00

Get Smart Once Again!, William Johnston, Tempo Books, Grosset & Dunlap, NY, 154 pages, 4¼ x 7", 1966, $2.50.

Howard, Mark, *A Time For Passion,* Dell, 1960, B–171 . . . . **3.00**

Howard, Robert E., *Almuric,* Ace, F–305 **6.00**

Howe, Cliff (ed.), *Lovers and Libertines,* Ace, D–271 . . . . **4.00**

Hubbard, L. Ron, *Return to Tomorrow,* Ace, S–66 . . . . **6.00**

Hunter, John, *West of Justice,* Ballantine Books, 1954 . . . . **4.00**

Hynd, Alan, *We are the Public Enemies,* Gold Medal, 101 . . . . **6.00**

Irish, William, *Bluebeard's Seventh Wife,* Popular Library, 473 . . . . **10.00**

Jacobs, Bruce (ed.), *Baseball Stars of 1955,* Lion Library, LL12 . . . . **5.00**

Joe DiMaggio's Baseball for Everyone, #719, Signet **50.00**

Jones, Raymond, *The Deviates,* Beacon, 242 . . . . **8.00**

Kane, Frank
Juke Box King, Dell, 1959, B–137. . . . **4.00**
Syndicate Girl, Dell, 1958, B–123 . . . **3.75**

Kerr, Jean, *Please Don't Eat the Daisies,* Crest, S263 . . . . **2.00**

Kipling, Rudyard, *Captain Courageous,* Bantam Books, 1946 . . . . **3.00**

Kline, Otis Adelbert, *Maza of the Moon,* Ace, F–321, Frazetta cov. **5.00**

Kurtzman, Harvey
Help!, Gold Medal, K1485 . . . . **3.00**
The Mad Reader, Ballantine Books, 1954 . . . . **10.00**

Lafferty, R. A., *Space Chantey,* Ace H–56, Vaughn Bode cov **4.00**

L'Amour, Louis, *Hondo,* Gold Medal, 347, tie–in with John Wayne movie . . **8.00**

Lehman, Paul Evan, *Range Justice,* Star Books, 8 . . . . **5.00**

Lindsay, Phillip, *Sir Rusty Sword,* Harlequin, 225 . . . . **10.00**

Links, Marty, *Bobby Sox,* Popular Library, 678 . . . . **3.00**

Lovecraft, H. P., *Weird Shadow over Innmouth,* Bart House, 4 . . . . **25.00**

Lyon, Dana, *I'll Be Glad When You're Dead,* Quick Reader, 132 . . . . **5.00**

Manfred, Frederick, *Lord Grizzly,* Cardinal, C192. . . . . **4.00**

Marlowe, Stephen, *Killers Are My Meat,* Gold Medal, 1957, 693 . . . . **6.00**

Martin and Miller, *The Story of Walt Disney,* Dell, D266. . . . . **3.00**

Miller, Henry, *Quiet Days In Clichy,* 1965, Grove Press **15.00**

Mooney, Booth, *Here Is My Body,* Gold Medal, 1958, 781 . . . . **5.00**

Moravia, Alberto, *The Wayward Wife,* Ace A Series, Ace Books, 1968, photo cov. **2.00**

Murphy, Audie, *To Hell and Back,* Perma Book, M4029. . . . . **2.00**

Neumann, Alfred, *Strange Conquest,* Ballantine Books, 1954 . . . . **3.75**

Old Scout, An, *Buffalo Bill's Leap for Life,* Gold Star, IL7–33, dime novel reprint. **4.00**

Orwell, George, *Animal Farm,* Signet, 1289 . . . . **5.00**

Ozaki, Milton K, *Case Of The Deadly Kiss,* Gold Medal, 1957 . . . . **6.00**

Palmer, Al, *Sugar Puss On Dorchester Street,* News Stand Library, 1949, 84 **9.00**

Patch, Virgil Franklin, *Man The Beast And The Wild, Wild Women,* Dell, 1962, R–129 . . . . **2.50**

Patten, Lewis B
Gunsmoke Empire, Gold Medal, 1955, 526 . . . . **5.00**
White Warrior, Gold Medal, 1956, 602 . . . . **5.00**

Pendleton, Chris, *Too Soon Tomorrow,* Dell, 1961, K–108. . . . . **2.00**

Prather, Richard S
Joker In The Deck, Gold Medal, 1964, K–1376 . . . . **5.00**
Strip For Murder, Gold Medal, 1964, K–1381 . . . . **2.50**

Prescott, John B, *Treasure Of The Black Hills,* Dell, 1961, B–225 . . . . **2.50**

Rabe, Peter
Mission For Vengeance, Gold Medal, 1958, S–773 . . . . **7.50**
Stop This Man!, Gold Medal, 1964, K–1403 . . . . **3.00**

Raddall, Thomas, *Roger Sudden,* Harlequin, 141 . . . . **9.00**

Ransom, Stephen, *Death Checks In,* Mystery Novel Classic, 1945, 77 . . . . . **3.75**

Reisner, Mary, *The Hunted,* Belmont Books, 1967, B50–742 . . . . **3.00**

Renin, Paul, *Flame,* 1951, Kaywin Publishing **4.00**

Robertson, Frank C., *Red Rustlers,* Reader's Choice Library, 24 . . . . **4.00**

Robinson, Ray (ed.), *Baseball Stars of 1961,* Pyramid, G–605 . . . . **2.50**

Runyon, Charles
Color Him Dead, Gold Medal, 1963, K–1320 . . . . **4.00**
The Death Cycle, Gold Medal, 1963, S–1268 . . . . **4.00**

Scholz, Jackson, *Fighting Coach* Comet, 25 . . . . **2.50**

Scotland, Jay, *Traitor's Legion,* Ace, G–532, Jay Scotland is a pseudonym for John Jakes **5.00**

Scott, Tarn, *Don't Let Her Die,* Gold Medal, 1957, 668 . . . . **6.00**

Siegel, Jerry, *High Camp Superheroes,* Belmont, B50–695, comic book reprints from the co–creator of Superman **4.00**

Silverberg, Robert, *Regan's Planet*, Pyramid, F–986 . . . .   **3.00**
Sinclair, Gordon, *Bright Path to Adventure*, Harlequin, 288 . . . .   **9.00**
Snyder, Leonard, *The Velvet Whip*, Berkley Books, 1955, 326. . . . .   **3.75**
Sperry, Armstrong, *Wagons Westward*, Comet, 1 . . . .   **2.50**
Stern, Bill, *Bill Stern's Favorite Boxing Stories*, Pocket Books, 416 . . . .   **3.00**
Stoker, Bram, *Dracula*, Perma Book, M4088, tie–in with Christopher Lee movie **5.00**
Striker, Fran, *The Lone Ranger and the Secret of Thunder Mountain*, Bantam, 14 . . . .   **60.00**
Thomas, T. T., *I, James Dean*, Popular Library, W400 . . . .   **6.00**
Tiempo, E. K., *Cry Slaughter*, Avon, T–179 . . . .   **2.00**
Tully, Jim, *The Bruiser*, Bantam. **2.00**
TV Super Stars, Lackmann, 1979, biography **10.00**
Uris, Leon, *Battle Cry*, Bantam, F1996 . .   **3.00**
Vagts, Alfred, *Hitler's Second Army*, Penguin, S214 . . . .   **3.00**
Williams, Charles, *Talk Of The Town*, Dell, 1958, A–164 . . . .   **4.00**
Woolrich, Cornell, *The Black Curtain*, Dell, 208 . . . .   **6.00**
Wright, W., *Life and Loves of Lana Turner*, Wisdom House, 104. . . . .   **2.00**
Yerby, Frank, *Captain Rebel*, Cardinal, C249 . . . .   **2.00**

PAPER DOLLS

History: The origin of the paper doll rests with the jumping jacks (pantins) of Europe. By the nineteenth century, famous dancers, opera stars, Jenny Lind, and many general subjects were available in boxed or diecut sheet form. Raphael Tuck and Sons in England began to produce ornate dolls in series form in the 1880s.

The advertising industry turned to paper dolls to sell products. Early magazines, such as *Ladies' Home Journal*, *Good Housekeeping*, and *McCall's*, used paper doll inserts. Children's publications, like *Jack and Jill*, picked up the practice.

The paper doll books first appeared in the 1920s. The cardboard covered books made paper dolls available to the mass market. Leading companies were Lowe, Merrill, Saalfield, and Whitman. The 1940s saw the advent of the celebrity paper doll books. Celebrities were drawn from screen and radio, followed later by television personalities. A few comic strip characters, such as Brenda Starr, also made it to paper doll fame.

The growth of television in the 1950s saw a reduction in the number of paper doll books produced. The modern books are either politically or celebrity oriented.

Most paper dolls are collected in uncut books, sheets, or boxed sets. Cut sets are priced at 50% of an uncut set if all dolls, clothing, and accessories are present.

Many paper doll books have been reprinted. An identical reprint is just slightly lower in value. If the dolls have been redrawn, the price is reduced significantly.

Barbara Ferguson's *The Paper Doll* has an excellent section on the care and storage of paper dolls.

References: Marian B. Howard, *Those Fascinating Paper Dolls: An Illustrated Handbook For Collectors*, Dover, 1981; Denis C. Jackson, *The Price & Identification Guide to Old Magazine Paperdolls*, published by author, 1988; Martha K. Krebs, *Advertising Paper Dolls: A Guide For Collectors*, two volumes, privately printed, 1975; Mary Young, *A Collector's Guide to Magazine Paper Dolls*, Collector Books, 1990; Mary Young, *Tomart's Price Guide to Lowe and Whitman Paper Dolls*, Tomart Publications, 1993.

Collectors' Club: United Federation of Doll Clubs, PO Box 14146, Parkville, MO 64152.

Periodicals: *Celebrity Doll Journal*, 5 Court Place, Puyallup, WA 98372; *Doll Reader*, PO Box 467, Mount Morris, IL 61054; *Midwest Paper Dolls & Toys Quarterly*, PO Box 131, Galesburg, KS 66740; *Paper Doll News*, PO Box 807, Vivian, LA 71082; The Original Paper Doll Artist Guild, PO Box 176, Skandia, MI 49885.

Museums: Children's Museum, Indianapolis, IN; Detroit Children's Museum, Detroit, MI; Kent State University Library, Kent, OH; Museum of the City of New York, New York, NY; Newark Museum, Newark, NJ; The Margaret Woodbury Strong Museum, Rochester, NY.

Notes: Prices are based on uncut, mint, original paper dolls in book or uncut sheet form. It is not unusual for two different titles to have the same number in a single company.

Advertising
Buster Brown, 12" h, Navy suit, outfits, and two hats. **175.00**
Barbours Irish Flax Threads, set of 3 . . . .   **10.00**
Carnation Ice Cream, 1955, punch out doll, four outfits **12.50**
McLaughlin's Coffee **8.00**
Palmolive, Dionne Quintuplets, uncut . .   **65.00**
Ann Blythe, Merrill, 1953, book, mermaid and assorted outfits **25.00**
Ann Sothern, Saalfield, #4407, 1956, two dolls, outfits **35.00**
Annette, Whitman, 1958, book, two dolls, outfits **15.00**

Annie Oakley, Whitman, book, three
   dolls, outfits, uncut **45.00**
Baby Betsy, book, 1967, one doll, outfits,
   uncut **8.00**
Baby Brother, Saalfield, #1736, book,
   baby, wading pool, uncut **10.00**
Baby Dears, Saalfield, #4418, 1957,
   book, three dolls, uncut **18.00**
Baby Doll, 1957, Samuel Lowe, uncut . .   **12.00**
Babykins, Whitman, 1970, book, two
   dolls **10.00**
Baby Sandy, Merrill, 1941, uncut **22.00**
Baby Sparkle Plenty, Saalfield, #1510,
   1948, book **50.00**
Betsy McCall, 1960s **15.00**
Bride and Groom, Merrill, 1949, book,
   six dolls, gowns **20.00**
Candy Stripers, Saalfield, 1973 . . . .   **8.00**
Career Girls, Samuel Lowe, 1942, uncut   **15.00**
Carmen Maranda, Saalfield, #1558,
   1952, two dolls, outfits **12.00**
Carol Lynley, Whitman, #2089, 1960,
   book, one doll, uncut **50.00**
Children Of America, Saalfield, #2335,
   1941, book **10.00**
Claudette Colbert, Saalfield, #2503,
   1945 . . . .   **18.00**
Connie Francis, Whitman, #1956, 1965,
   book, folder, outfits **22.00**
Dolls of Other Lands, Watkins, 1968, six
   dolls, outfits **12.00**
Dolly Dingle's World Flight In Italy,
   1932, Italian doll **18.00**
Donna Reed, Saalfield, #4412, 1959,
   two dolls, outfits, folder **12.00**
Doris Day, Whitman, 1952, book, dolls
   and outfits, folder. **30.00**
Dude Ranch, Samuel Lowe, 1943, uncut   **20.00**
Dutch Treat, Saalfield, 1961, uncut **12.00**

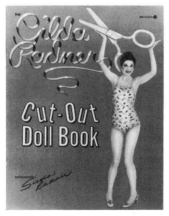

Book, *Gilda Radner Cut-Out Doll Book,*
Avon Books, color, 14 pages, uncut, 8½ x
11", 1975, $17.50.

Magazine Page, The Lettie Lane Paper
Family, Sheila Young, *Ladies' Home Journal,* uncut, 10½ x 15", 1909, $30.00.

Eve Arden, Saalfield, #4310, 1953, book   **25.00**
First Date, Merrill, 1944, uncut **18.00**
Flying Marvels, 1945, Captain Marvel,
   Captain Junior, and Mary **5.00**
Ginger Paper Doll, Golden Book, one
   doll, outfits, uncut **30.00**
Girls In The War, Samuel Lowe, 1943,
   uncut **20.00**
Hayley Mills In Summer Magic, Whit-
   man, 1963, book, one doll, outfits,
   folder with handle, uncut **45.00**
Hansel and Gretel Push Out Book, Whit-
   man, 1954 . . . .   **15.00**
Happy Birthday, Merrill, 1939, uncut . . .   **25.00**
Harry The Soldier, Lowe, #1074, 1941,
   book **8.00**
Hedy Lamarr, Merrill, 1942, two dolls,
   five outfits **4.00**
Janet Leigh, Abbott, #1805, 1958, book   **50.00**
Judy Garland, Whitman, 1955, uncut . . .   **85.00**
Julia, Saalfield, 1968, uncut **18.00**
June Allyson, Whitman, 1950, book, two
   dolls, outfits **25.00**
June Bride, Stephens Company, 1946,
   book, uncut **18.00**
Junior Miss, Saalfield, 1942, book, uncut   **20.00**
Karen Goes To College, Merrill, 1955,
   uncut **8.00**
Lennon Sisters, Whitman, #1979, 1957,
   book **45.00**
Little Ballerina, Whitman, 1969, book,
   four dolls, outfits, uncut. **12.00**
Little Cousins, Samuel Lowe, 1940,
   uncut **15.00**
Little Kitten To Dress, Samuel Lowe,
   1942, uncut **12.00**

Newspaper, Brenda Starr Reporter, Dale Messick, Sunday color comics, orig. doll with clothes, 14 x 9½", 1950, $14.00.

Little Lulu, Whitman, 1960, book	30.00
Little Miss America, #2358, Saalfield, book, fifteen dolls, uncut	50.00
Majorette Paper Dolls, #2760, 1957, book	6.00
Molly Dolly, Samuel Lowe, 1962, uncut	18.00
Mother and Daughter, 1950s, mother wearing green suit, daughter wearing blue suit	18.00
Movie Starlets, Whitman, #960, book, five dolls, six pages of outfits	100.00
Nanny and the Professor, Artcraft, #4283, 1970–71, book	20.00
Nora Drake–Radio Star, Lowe, 1952, book, two dolls, outfits, uncut	25.00
Paper Dolls Around the World, Saalfield, 1964, seven dolls, 9" h	12.00
Partridge Family, Saalfield, 1971, uncut	40.00
Pat Crowley, Whitman, 1955, book, two dolls, eight pages of outfits, uncut	60.00
Patchy Annie, Saalfield, 1962, uncut	4.00
Patty Duke, Whitman, 1964, two dolls, folder	15.00
Polly Pal, Samuel Lowe, 1976, uncut	3.50
Raggedy Ann, Whitman, 1970	18.00
Ranch Family, Merrill, 1957, uncut	15.00
Ricky Nelson, Whitman, 1959, book, two dolls, six pages of outfits, uncut	65.00
Rita Hayworth, Merrill, 1942, book, two dolls, outfits, uncut	65.00
Sabrina and the Archies, Whitman, 1971 copyright Archie Music Corp, book, uncut	25.00
School Friends, Merrill, 1955–60, book, three dolls, Linda, Bobbie, and Diane, cowgirl suit and dresses, uncut	15.00
Schoolmates, Saalfield, 1947, uncut	15.00
Shari Lewis, Saalfield, 1958, uncut	20.00
Shirley Temple, Saalfield, 1934, book, four dolls, outfits	50.00

Square Dance, Saalfield, 1950, five dolls, six pages of outfits, uncut	18.00
Susan Book, Merrill, 1950, book, three dolls, outfits	15.00
Trudy In Her Teens, Merrill, 1943, uncut	15.00
Tuesday Weld, Saalfield, 1960	18.00
Twiggy, Whitman, 1967, book, one doll, outfits, uncut	30.00
Two Marys, Merrill, 1950, uncut	8.00
Vera Miles, Whitman, 1957, book	20.00
Wedding Party, Saalfield, #2721, 1951, book	15.00
World's Fair Paper Doll Book, Peter and Wendy Dress Up, Singer, 10 x 14", two pages of characters on heavy stock, five pages of costumes, 1964–65	30.00

PAPER SOLDIERS

History: Paper soldiers arrived upon the scene in the early nineteenth century. All that is needed to create a toy soldier is a sketch, paint, cutting device, and mounting block. Many of the earliest soldiers were homemade.

In the late nineteenth century, a number of American manufacturer's of children's books, card games, and board games became interested in the toy soldier genre. Milton Bradley, McLoughlin Bros., and Parker Brothers produced large numbers of sets. The typical soldier figure was a lithograph image glued to cardboard and nailed or slotted into a wooden stand. The average size was approximately six inches in height.

Paper toy soldier interest was strong during the Spanish American War and World War I. In the 1920s and 1930s, few paper toy soldier sets were manufactured. World War II changed everything;

paper was one of the few materials available to toy manufacturers, which lead to a paper toy soldier revival. The period from 1940 to 1950 is known as the second Golden Age of paper toy soldier collecting.

The variety of paper toy soldier products increased significantly during the 1940 to 1950 period. Punchout sets, paper doll books, construction sets, battle sets, and target sets challenged the traditional boxed paper soldier set.

Collectors allow a broad definition of what constitutes a paper soldier. In addition to soldiers printed on paper, soldiers printed on cardboard and lithograph paper applied to wood are also included in this category. Among the principal manufacturers of this latter material were Concord Toy Company, Handi-Kraft, Lowe, Merrill, J. Pressman and Co., and Whitman.

Several manufacturers offered cutout and punchout paper military soldier related premiums during the war. One example is the 1944 Kellogg's Pep cereal offer of punchout paper military airplanes.

References: Richard O'Brien, *Collecting Toy Soldiers: An Identification and Value Guide, No. 2*, Books Americana, 1992; Richard O'Brien, *Collecting Toys: An Identification and Value Guide, 6th Edition*, Books Americana, 1993; Blair Whitton, *Paper Toys of the World*, Hobby House Press, 1986.

Periodicals: *Old Toy Soldier Newsletter*, 209 North Lombard, Oak Park, IL 60302; *Toy Soldier Review*, 127 74th Street, North Bergen, NJ 07047.

Collectors' Club: Toy Soldier Collectors of America, 6924 Stone's Throw Circle, #3802, St. Petersburg, FL 33710.

All-Nu Paper Soldiers, 5" h, c1942	
Charging with rifle	3.50
Flag Bearer, WWI helmet	5.00
General MacArthur	8.00
Marching, slope arms, WWI helmet	4.50
Nurse	4.50
Officer kneeling, holding binoculars	4.50
Ski trooper	6.00
Three soldiers leaving boat, holding rifles	6.00
Throwing grenade, WWI helmet	3.00
Built-Rite, No 1 Toy Soldiers, WWI helmet, 1930s	2.25
Concord Toy Co, nine 3½" press-out soldiers, wood cannon and ammunition, boxed set	60.00
J Pressman and Co, NY, Soldier Set, No. 1551, five 4½" h cardboard soldiers, marbles, c1940	40.00
Marks, Mickey Mouse Soldier set, 1930s	175.00
McLoughlin, 5 to 6" h, 1898–1910	
Artillerymen and cannon	6.00
Boy Scout, holding rifles, c1915	6.00

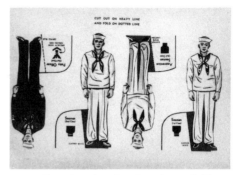

Cardboard, printed color, four 3½" h Navy officers with insignia, 6¾ x 5", 1940s, $9.00.

Doughboy, c1915	1.00
Flag Bearer, c1915	5.00
Sailor in blue	5.00
Set, Playtime Soldiers on Parade, 175 pcs, copyright 1937	95.00
Spanish–American War Infantry	4.00
Milton Bradley	
Bradley's Cavalry–50, 6" h, set	125.00
Bradley's Infantry, twenty five 6" soldiers, 1900–10	110.00
Cavalry, individual, 6" h	2.50
Highlander, 6" h, c1915	4.00
Sharp–Shooters, eleven 6" cavalry figures and two pistols	100.00
Soldiers Five with Pistol, No 4518, 1920s	80.00
Parker Brothers, 1900–1920	
Cavalry, red, 1900–1920	4.00
Doughboy, charging, 6" h	2.50
Infantry, red, 6" h, 1900–1920	2.50
Set, The Battle Game, thirty soldiers, pistol, and ammunition, Boer War scene	170.00
Post Toasties Premium, uncut piece, 1930s	20.00
Samuel Gabriel Sons & Co, NY	
Cavalry, boxed set	55.00
Soldier	
Cardboard, wood stands	2.00
Paper	1.00
Rocking Horse Cavalry	30.00
USA Band and Infantry, boxed set	55.00
Whitman, 100 Soldiers Punch–Out Book, No 999, 1943	55.00

PAPER TOYS

History: Paper toys is a vast category. It includes paper and folding educational card games, boxed board games, blocks, puzzles, peep shows, panoramas, toy books with movement, paper soldiers, paper dolls, cardboard doll houses, theater groups including circuses, construction sets, optical toys, and a host of other categories. In *Warman's Paper* it serves as a catchall category.

Paper is broadly interpreted. Cardboard is considered paper. A wooden toy with applied lithograph paper is considered a paper, not a wooden toy. If the principal decorative motif of an object involves paper, it is considered a paper toy.

Paper toys are one of the few areas where American collectors (1) do not assign a premium to American made products and (2) eagerly seek and buy foreign examples. Form and age are much more important than country of origin. It is important when buying a paper toy from outside the United States to make certain that you have an understanding about the toy's scarcity in its country of origin. Unknowledgeable collectors often pay premium prices in America for a foreign toy only to discover later that it is readily available and inexpensive in its country of origin.

Original packaging is extremely important with respect to paper toys. Often it is highly graphic and contains information about the manufacturer and assembly instructions not found on the toys themselves. Many paper toys are cut, punched, or pressed out. A premium is assigned when these toys are encountered in uncut, unpunched, or unpressed out condition.

One highly specialized collecting field within the paper toy category is Sunday "Art Supplements" from the 1895 to 1905 period. Subjects ranged from Armies and Navies of the world to cut–out celebrity dolls. Almost every Sunday newspaper offered these premiums.

World War II was the Golden Age of the paper toy in America. Wartime necessities limited the use of certain raw materials. Even Lionel felt the shortage. Paper was the one material readily available to the toy industry. It issued a die–cut cardboard paper train during the war. Most toys made during this period have a military or patriotic theme.

Collectors have identified hundreds of American companies that have manufactured paper toys. Among the leaders are Milton Bradley, Built–Rite, McLoughlin Bros., Merrill, Lowe, Parker Brothers, Saalfield, and Whitman.

References: Richard O'Brien, *Collecting Toys: Identification & Value Guide*, 6th Edition, Books Americana, 1993; Blair Whitton, *Paper Toys of the World*, Hobby House Press, 1986.

Note: Also see "Games," "Paper Dolls," "Paper Soldiers," and "Puzzles" in the topical section.

Activity Book
  Bewitched, Treasure Books, 1965, 64 pgs, 8 x 11". **15.00**
  Howdy Doody Dot–To–Dot. **20.00**
  Lone Ranger Sticker Fun/Dot–To–Dot

  Activity Book, Whitman, 1952 copyright, 10½ x 12". **45.00**
My Fair Lady Sticker Book, Ottenheimer, Inc, 1965, 8½ x 11" **5.00**
101 Dalmatians Sticker Book, Panini, c1985, 32 pgs, 9 x 10½" **18.00**
Star Wars Luke Skywalker's Activity Book, Random House, 1979 Black Falcon, Ltd copyright, 32 pgs, 8 x 8" **15.00**
Airplane, Fleers Double Bubble Gum, red, white, and blue paper, brass weight attached to nose, wings with "Fleers Double Bubble Gum Won't Stick To Lips or Face, Pure and Wholesome," tail with "Blows Big Bubbles," design details, c1930, 6½" l **30.00**
Artistic Toy Novelty Series, Raphael Tuck & Sons, orig box
  Driving to Pasture, No 123, six stand–up children, animals, and fowl, c1920 . . . . **55.00**
  Rocking Horse, No 120, self standing rocking horses with dressed figures or animals, set of 6, c1920. . . . . **30.00**
  See Yourself, No 130, three merry mirror groups, c1910 . . . . **60.00**
Big Top Circus, General Electric Premium, 60 pcs, envelope with blue and red printing and refrigerator, 1950, 15¼ x 16½" **65.00**
Blocks, Mother Goose Nested Blocks, McLoughlin Brothers, 1911, set of 7 . . **75.00**
Book
  Bobby Bear, Whitman Publishing Company, 1935, 7⅝ x 14½ x 2½" opened. **40.00**
  Little Red Riding Hood, Dean and Son, London, c1860, fold–out, eight three tier scenes, 10 x 7⅛". **90.00**
  The Little Showman's Series No 2, Summer, McLoughlin Brothers, New York City, copyright 1884, three tier fold–outs, 13½ x 10½ x 13½" **80.00**
  The Pop–Up Dick Tracy, Capture of Boris Arson, Blue Ribbon Press, Pleasure Books, Inc, Chicago, 1935, 9¼ x 15¾ x 2½" opened. **85.00**
  The Pop–Up Mother Goose, Blue Ribbon Press, New York City, copyright 1934, 6½ x 15¾ x 9¼" **60.00**
  The Pop–Up Tim Tyler in the Jungle, Blue Ribbon Press, Pleasure Books, Chicago, IL, 1935, three double page pop–ups, 6¼ x 15¾ x 9¼". . . **65.00**
  Visions of St. Nick in Action, In Action Book Publication, Phillips Publishers, Inc, 1950, opens to form five point star, 7 x 14½" **60.00**
Card Game
  Addams Family, complete, 1965 . . . . **30.00**
  Archie Bunker Card Game, 1972 . . . . **25.00**

Model, Fun in the Toy Cupboard, Block-Litho Ltd., Richmond, VA, punch-out, unused, 9¼ x 12¾", 1960s, $65.00.

Feronica's Hierogryphical Riddles, 24 hand colored cards, four page folder, marked "Made in Germany," c1860, cards 3⅝ x 2¼" ... 80.00
Popeye, orig box, Whitman, 1937 ... 40.00
Colorform Set
  Flintstones, 1972, orig box 20.00
  Raggedy Ann Colorforms Dress–Up Kit, 8" h diecut full color cardboard doll, orig box, Colorforms, Bobbs–Merrill, 1967 copyright 30.00
  Superman Colorforms Adventure Set, several figures, street illus on cardboard background with Magic Telephone Booth, orig box, unused, copyright 1978 DC Comics Inc 25.00
  Winnie The Pooh, instruction sheet, orig box, complete, 1964 copyright 50.00
Construction Set
  Build It With Scissors, A Modern Put–Together Book, six building projects, Samuel Gabriel Sons & Company, New York City, 1929 .... 60.00
  Merry–go–round, Micky Maus Karussell, J F Schreiber, Germany, c1954, uncut sheet 85.00
  Robinson Crusoe Meets Friday, A & E Dickens, London, c1925, one of six scenes, uncut 14 x 14¾" sheet 65.00
  Ships Aloft, A Construction Book For Future Flyers, Harper & Brothers, New York City, 1936 .... 60.00
Doll House
  Garage Set, with car, No 115, Built–Rite 65.00
  Modern Doll House, No 35, Built–Rite 75.00
  Five Room Suburban Doll House, No 115, Built–Rite 85.00
  The Fold–Away Doll House, stiff card-

board folder unfolds to three int. rooms, eleven furniture pcs, Garden City Books, 1949 copyright 50.00
  Three Room, furnished, No36F, Built–Rite 85.00
Doll House Furniture, Built–Rite
  Bedroom Furniture, No 47 .... 45.00
  Five Room Set, No 459 .... 35.00
  Living Room, No 45 .... 55.00
  Farm Set, No 57M, 8 pcs 45.00
Flip Book, *Donald & Pluto,* Merrimack Publishing Company, New York City, 1930s......................... 25.00
Game, Popeye Toss Game, 8¼" h diecut cardboard figure on wood block, three cardboard rings, orig box, Rosebud Art Co, 1935 copyright 75.00
Game of Chance, Merry–go–round, cut-out horses and riders, Raphael Tuck & Sons, c1925, 6¼" h, 9" d 40.00
Gun
  Buster Brown Shoes, red, white, and blue cardboard sheet, unpunched pistol, 9 x 9½", 1940s 50.00
  Hopalong Cassidy, Buzza Cardozo, Hollywood, 7" l scissored stiff paper, c1950 .... 50.00
Gyrating Shadow Lantern, McLoughlin Brothers, New York City, late 1890, shadow box with silhouette figures int., semi–transparent sides, powered by two candles, 13½ x 11" 75.00
Kite, Flash Gordon Super–Flyer Kite, orig package, unused, 1950s 25.00
Magic Slate
  Beatles, 8½ x 13½", Merit......... 200.00
  Mickey Mouse, 2½ x 4" stiff black cardboard pad, light blue paper cov, white plastic sheet, holds orange wood stylus 100.00
Military
  Ambulance, All–Nu Paper Soldiers, c1942 .... 4.50
  Army Outpost, No 22, Built–Rite 50.00
  Army Plane Hangar, No 7, Built–Rite 45.00
  Army Raider's Victory Unit, truck, tank, AA gun, jeep, semi–tract truck, and twenty soldiers, 28 pcs, Built–Rite.................... 75.00
  Fort and Soldier Set, fort, soldiers, two sandbag foxholes, and fiberboard pistol, Built–Rite 125.00
  Jeep with three men, All–Nu Paper Soldiers, c1942 .... 4.50
  Tank with three men, All–Nu Paper Soldiers, c1942 .... 6.00
  Toy Army Tents, Sail–Me Co, Chicago, set of six different tents, orig box, 1931 .... 80.00
  Toy Trench, No 2, Built–Rite........ 35.00
Paint Book
  Blondie with Dagwood, Baby Dump-

ling and Daisy Paint Book, Whitman, 605, 1940 copyright, 142 pgs, 8½ x 11½", partially used **25.00**
Bugs Bunny, Whitman, 1944, 8½ x 11", unused **12.00**
Lone Ranger, 1940 . . . .   **40.00**
Looney Tunes–Merry Melodies Paint Book, Whitman, 661, 143, 128 pgs, 8½ x 11" **25.00**
Roy Rogers, Whitman, 1158, 48 pgs, copyright, 1948, 11 x 15", unused   **60.00**
Paint By Number Set
Maverick, cardboard scenes, oil paints, orig box with Gardner photo, unused **125.00**
Roy Rogers, four 8 x 10 cards, oil paints, orig box, Craft Master, 1954 Roy Enterprises copyright, partially used **75.00**
Paint Set, Popeye, five 4 x 4¾" picture sheets, 18 water color tablets mounted on inset board, orig box, Milton Bradley, 1934 copyright **125.00**
Panorama
Autumn Sports, McLoughlin Brothers, c1890, 8 x 12" closed, accordion style, twelve panels, children gathering nuts, picking apples, rolling hoops, playing marbles, and enjoying archery **110.00**
Coronation Procession Panorama, Raphael Tuck & Sons, Ltd, 1953, accordion style, four panels, 10" h . . .   **40.00**
The Wild West Show, McLoughlin Brothers, 1890, 10 x 12½ x 1¾", reel type, features Buffalo Bill and frontier life scenes **75.00**
Paper Doll
Army Nurse and Doctor, Merrill, No 3425, 1942 . . . .   **50.00**
Belle of Newport, Raphael Tuck, c1895, boxed set **85.00**
Dennison's Crepe and Tissue Paper Doll Outfit, Dennison, c1915, boxed set **30.00**
Fanny Gray, Crosby, Nichols & Company, Boston, MA, 1854, boxed set   **65.00**
Fluffy Ruffles, J Ottmann Litho Company, New York City, 1907 copyright, 10½" doll, uncut clothing **70.00**
Polly Pitcher & Her Playmates, Jacobs & Company, 1918 copyright, portfolio, 14 x 9". **85.00**
The Bridal Party, Raphael Tuck, c1895, boxed set **80.00**
Petite Napoleonic Coach, Fisher Body Craftman's Guild, cutout, complete, 1930 . . . .   **85.00**
Phenakistiscope, seven 9" disks, short shaft with handle, discs published by Ackermann & Co, London, c1855. . . .   **110.00**

Pop Gun, Sunbeam Bread, figural revolver with paper foldout, printed, blue and orange, 7 x 3½", 1940s, $15.00.

Pop Gun, G Man, cardboard, red, black, and gray, Lesher's, Perkasie, PA adv, 7" l. **5.00**
Punch–Out Book, Dr Kildare, Golden Furniture, 1962 . . . .   **20.00**
Railroad Accessory Set, No 111, Built–Rite **25.00**
Railroad and Station Set, No 375, Built–Rite **35.00**
Service Station, No 17, Built–Rite. **70.00**
Steamboat, Mississippi, five page folder containing parts, J F Schreiber, Germany, c1950, unassembled **35.00**
Steam Locomotive, four page folder containing parts, J F Schreiber, Germany, c1950, unassembled **35.00**
Theater, Great Theater for Children, 16 x 28" stage, matching side scenes, 44 characters, 24 accessory pieces, marked "AK," Germany, missing play book **40.00**
Train Accessory Set, No 178, Built–Rite   **35.00**
Train Set, Borden's Train, punch out, 1950s, 16 x 16" **125.00**
View Master Reel, three reel set with story book
Arabian Nights, FT–50, A, B, and C, SAW. **11.00**
Beverly Hillbillies, B–570, SAW. **25.00**
Bobby the Bunny, 830, A, B, and C, SAW. **9.00**
Bonanza, B4711, B4712, and B4713, titled "A Pink Cloud From Old Cathay," 1964 copyright **50.00**
Colorado Ski Country, A–331, GAF . .   **6.00**
Cowboy Stars, 950, 955, and 960, SAW. **10.00**
Dale Evans/Queen Of The West, 944 A, B, and C, orig envelope **35.00**
Fairy Tales III, FT–7, 8, and 9, SAW . .   **10.00**
Grand Canyon River Expedition, A–372, GAF. **4.00**
Green Hornet, titled "Programmed For Death," orig envelope, copyright 1966 Greenway Productions Inc. . .   **25.00**
In Darkest Africa, B–095, SAW. **20.00**

Mash, J–11, GAF	**10.00**
Old–Time Cars, B–795, GAF	**10.00**
Pinnochio, orig envelope, 1957 copyright	**40.00**
The Old South, A–856, GAF	**8.00**
US Spaceport, Kennedy Space Center, Fl, J–79, VMI	**4.00**
Walt Disney Productions Presents The Love Bug, B–501, GAF, 1968	**3.00**
Whistle, Cracker Jack	**10.00**

PHOTOGRAPHS

History: The earliest attempts to project images involved the camera obscura, a device known to the Greeks and Romans. The Scientific Revolution of the seventeenth century, especially in chemistry, paved the way for capturing images on plate and film.

In 1830, J. M. Daguerre of France patented a process consisting of covering a copper plate with silver salts, sandwiching the plate between glass for protection, and exposing the plate to light and mercury vapors to imprint the image. The process produced Daguerreotypes.

Fox Talbot of Britain patented the method for making paper negatives and prints (calotypes) in 1841. Frederick Scott Archer introduced the wet collodion process in 1851. Dr. Maddox developed dry plates in 1871. When George Eastman produced roll film in 1888, the photographic industry reached maturity.

Cartes de visite, or calling card, photographs were patented in France in 1854, flourished from 1857 to 1910, and survived into the 1920s. The most common cartes de visite was a 2¼" x 3¼" head and shoulder portrait printed on albumen paper and mounted on a card 2½" x 4". Multi–lens cameras were used by the photographer to produce four to eight exposures on a single glass negative plate. A contact print was made from this plate that would yield four to eight identical photographs on one piece of photographic paper. The photographs would be cut apart and mounted on cards. These cards were put in albums or simply handed out when visiting, similar to today's business cards.

In 1866, the cabinet card was introduced in England and shortly thereafter in the United States. Its production was similar to that of a carte de visite, but could utilize several styles of photographic processes. A cabinet card measured 4" x 5" and was mounted on a card 4½" x 6½". Portraits in cabinet size were more appealing because of the larger facial detail and the fact that images could be retouched. By the 1880s, the cabinet card was as popular as the cartes de visite, and by the 1890s was produced almost exclusively. Cabinet cards flourished until shortly after the turn of the century.

A vintage print is a positive image developed from the original negative by the photographer or under the photographer's supervision at the time the negative is made. A non–vintage print is a print made from an original negative at a later date. It is quite common for a photographer to make prints from the same negative over several decades. Changes between the original printing and subsequent prints usually can be identified. Limited edition prints must be clearly labeled.

Most photographic listings focus only on professionally produced images—but not *Warman's Paper.* One of the fun discoveries by collectors of the 1990s is the wealth of information available in amateur photographs. Subject matter is the key. Snapshots of people and scenic places remain worthless. However, a photograph showing a person playing with a toy, riding a bicycle, working in an office, or standing by the family automobile have assumed value. Value remains relatively modest, usually only a dollar or two. Before discarding any collection of family photographs, examine them carefully for any examples with strong subject content.

References: Stuart Bennett, *How To Buy Photographs,* Salem House, 1987; William C. Darrah, *Cartes de Visite in Nineteenth Century Photography,* published by author, 1981; O. Henry Mace, *Collector's Guide To Early Photographs,* Wallace–Homestead, 1990; Lou W. McCulloch, *Card Photographs, A Guide to Their History And Value,* Schiffer Publishing, 1981; Floyd and Marion Rinhart, *American Miniature Case Art,* A. S. Barnes and Co., 1969; Susan Theran and Kathyrn Acerbo (ed.), *Leonard's Annual Price Index of Prints, Posters, and Photographs, Volume I,* Auction Index, 1992; Susan Theran, *Prints, Posters, and Photographs: Identification and Price Guide,* Avon Books, 1993; John Waldsmith, *Stereoviews, An Illustrated History and Price Guide,* Wallace–Homestead, 1991.

Collectors' Clubs: American Photographic Historical Society, 520 W. 44th St., New York, NY 10036; National Stereoscopic Association, PO Box 14801, Columbus, OH 43214.

Museums: International Museum of Photography, George Eastman House, Rochester, NY; Smithsonian Institution, Washington, DC; University of Texas at Austin, Austin, TX.

REPRODUCTION ALERT: Excellent reproductions of Lincoln as well as other Civil War era figures on cartes de visite and cabinet cards have been made.

CABINET CARDS

Acrobat, Victorelli & Young Eldon, Cincinnati, OH	**18.00**
Arizona Scenes Series, Mission int. view, Buehman, Tucson	**15.00**

Cabinet Card, young girl wearing first holy communion dress, photo by Sol Young, NY, oval mat, 5 x 8", 1909, $12.00.

Bandsman, Eugene, OR, wearing uniform, holding large brass instrument, 1892 . . . . **20.00**
Bartlett Family, Wild West team, holding rifles. **55.00**
Blacks
   Black Boy, fancy dress, large bow **10.00**
   Man, well dressed, studio pose, Hunt Paducah, KY Photographer, c1880 **18.00**
   Woman, Alabama **12.00**
Cat. **8.00**
Children
   Baby in wicker carriage. **10.00**
   Boy on crutches, World's Fair Photo View Co **20.00**
   Boy on tricycle, metal wheels, trimmed. **10.00**
   Boy sitting at Wherlock piano, c1880 **10.00**
   Girl with "Hamiltons Studios" on skirt, flag on hat **20.00**
   Circus Performer **12.00**
Civil War
   Avery, General, seated pose, sepia tone **18.00**
   Young boy, wearing uniform, playing drum, tent background **25.00**
Corbett, Jim, boxer stance, Newsboy, New York City **12.00**
Doctor with instruments **15.00**
Dreyfus, Captain and Mrs Alfred Dreyfus, parlor photo before his conviction, black and white, 1899 . . . . . . **15.00**
Ducks, babies **8.00**

Emerson, Ralph Waldo, poet. **15.00**
Family, sitting on studio lawn **2.00**
Fielding, Maggie, actress. **8.00**
Fox, Della, wearing fancy hat, Morrison, Haymarket Theater, Chicago, 1895 . . **8.00**
GAR Veteran, wearing uniform, holding sword. **15.00**
Graduate, woman wearing white dress, flowers, diploma, and fan, Rensselaer, c1880, 4 x 6" **7.50**
Harpist, girl, wearing fancy dress, Obermuller and Son, 888 Bowery, New York City **8.00**
Indian
   Group photo **45.00**
   Sitting Bull **65.00**
Irving, Sir Henry, actor **7.00**
Langtry, Lillie. **20.00**
Longfellow, Henry Wadsworth, poet . . . **15.00**
McKinley and his wife. **8.00**
Military
   General, soldiers, and older boys, c1880, 5 x 6" **15.00**
   Man wearing full uniform with sword, marked "J M Fuller, Richfield Springs NY and U S Naval Academy, MD," c1880 . . . . **15.00**
Oriental Boy, wearing kimono, full pose **6.00**
Patti, Adelina, portrait, wearing feathered hat, N Sarony, copyright 1882 . . . . **20.00**
Photographer with camera **150.00**
Portrait of Twins **1.00**
Queen Victoria, three quarter length pose, holding crochet hook and material **17.00**
Sports
   Amateur baseball player **15.00**
   Fisherman holding rod **7.00**
   Roller Skater, portrait. **4.00**
Sutherland Family, seven sisters, displaying their long hair, hairgrower adv on back, Morris, Pittsburgh **20.00**
Woman
   Posing with bicycle, 1885–90. . . . . . . **18.00**
   Sulky driver, holding buggy whip, 1892 . . . . **28.00**
   Three women, holding six flags, Gates of Charleston, WV **7.00**
   Wearing large cross around neck, Taber, San Francisco, CA. **3.00**

CARTES DE VISITE

Actor with pistol and sword, full pose, Koenig. **8.00**
Albino Girl, portrait, Charles Eisenmann photographer, NY **17.00**
Alvord, General Benjamin, trimmed top and bottom margin **30.00**
Astor, Colonel J J, NY, JH Bufford, Pub, Boston **15.00**

Asylum for the insane, Jacksonville, IL,
  c1869 .... **9.00**
Bernadette, kneeling holding cross **8.00**
Bishop Potter, Sarony **9.00**
Black
  Baby, hand tinted, Nashville, TN **12.00**
  Policeman, holding billy club, J J
    Ghegan, Newark, c1870 .... **200.00**
Blacksmith, man wearing apron, anvil,
  c1870 .... **12.00**
Burnhardt, Sarah **20.00**
Children
  Baby in elaborate carriage, Defsaur,
    NY **2.00**
  Boy with American Flag **12.00**
  Girl holding doll, fancy dress and high
    top shoes, 1870s **15.00**
  Girl holding China head doll **6.00**
Civil War
  Battle Scene.................... **35.00**
  Davis, Jefferson, confederate president **17.00**
  Soldiers, Union **25.00**
Court House, Corinth, MS **20.00**
Dog, wearing hat and spectacles, read-
  ing newspaper.................. **7.00**
Doctor operating on patient **25.00**
Dunn, Phoebe, fat lady, 17 years old,
  437 pounds, 1866 .... **12.00**
Everett, Edward, statesman **10.00**
Egyptian Woman, water jug on head ... **12.00**
English Military Officer **6.00**
Factory, int. view with workers **15.00**
Fairy Wedding, midget bride, groom,
  and attendants, Brady, c1880 .... **15.00**
Foreign Soldier, information on back,
  1864 .... **5.00**
Fraternal, man wearing Masonic uniform **8.00**
Greeley, Horace, journalist, Sarony, NY **15.00**
Hancock, General, 1824–1886 .... **12.00**
Indian
  Geronimo **65.00**
  Group, full dress **35.00**
Kalamazoo, MI, main street view, Schuy-
  ler C Baldwin photographer **15.00**
Ku Klux Klan, member wearing costume,
  c1878 .... **40.00**
Lawrence, Fannie Casseopia, redeemed
  five year old slave child **20.00**
Leonard, Henry, Basil, OH, survived
  snowstorm on straw pile, 1868..... **10.00**
Lincoln, Robert Todd, C M Bell photog-
  rapher, Washington, DC **5.00**
Longfellow's Children, art drawn, black
  and white..................... **8.00**
Mardi Gras, New Orleans, 1881 .... **12.00**
Midget, group of three, black and white **10.00**
Minnie Ha–Ha, Upton photo **18.00**
Mountain Man, Kentucky rifle, pistol,
  and Sheffield Bowie knife **35.00**
Musician, holding instrument **7.00**
President
  Garfield, James, bust pose **9.00**

Johnson, Andrew, Brady Gallery..... **35.00**
Lincoln, Abe **15.00**
Priest, wearing religious garb **4.00**
Prince of Wales and family **8.00**
Schenck, Major General Robert C, Chas
  Magnus, NY, "Peter E Blow, Co K, 153
  Regt NYSV Alexandria, Va" inscribed
  on back **25.00**
Sumner, Charles, Whitehurst **10.00**
Spanish–American War Soldier, full
  pose, wearing hat, holding rifle...... **7.00**
Sports
  Ice Skater, portrait **5.00**
  Mountain Climber................ **3.00**
  Professional baseball player or team.. **30.00**
Stuffed Owl on branch **3.00**
The Domestic Blockade, 1863, Thomas
  Nast........................ **12.00**
Thumb, General Tom, Mr. & Mrs., wear-
  ing wedding costumes, pub by EHT
  Anthony from Brady negative, 1863 .. **10.00**
Wedding, bride and groom photo...... **3.00**
Woman
  Wearing Danish costume, hand tinted,
    Hansen Schou & Weller photogra-
    pher........................ **8.00**
  Wearing mourning dress, leaning on
    stool, hand tinted, L S & P Co, 579
    Broadway, NY **6.00**

PROFESSIONAL AND SNAPSHOT

Baseball Team, Agosta, OH ball team,
  black and white.................. **20.00**
Blacks
  Two Men, posed with liquor bottles,
    1920s....................... **8.00**
  Woman, well dressed, 1911 .... **8.00**
Brass Band, black and white
  Men with instruments **10.00**
  Young Guards Brigade Band, Suttons
    Bay, MI **8.00**
Dog in Buggy..................... **8.00**
Boy, two boys with bicycles in cornfield **6.00**
Calvin Coolidge, with owners of
  Lakeside Inn, FL, 7 x 11" **15.00**
Children Roller Skating, black and white **8.00**
Chinese Children, studio portrait, one
  holding flower, other holding ABC
  Book of Birds, San Francisco, orig
  stand–up mount, c1925, 6 x 4"..... **27.50**
Christmas Tree, decorated, dolls and toys
  beneath, 10 x 12"................ **40.00**
Church Scene, ext. view with well
  dressed men, women, and children,
  mounted, c1890, 9 x 11".......... **22.50**
Circus Wagon, pulled by ponies, black
  and white..................... **15.00**
Delivery Truck, J Batthof, Folcroft, PA,
  1928, 3½ x 4½" **8.00**
Disaster
  Destruction caused by crazed maniac,

Snapshot, Armistice Day Celebration, parade float, black and white, 8 x 10", 1931, $30.00.

dead horses, Bath, MI, May 18, 1927	20.00
Train wreck at bridge, PA Lines, 8 x 10"	10.00
Donut Shop, "Sip and Bite Donut Shop," ext. view, 7 x 9"	25.00
Elephant and Trainer, The Stadler Photographing Co, Chicago	20.00
Farm Machinery, thresher and wagons	6.00
Feed Sack, Blatchfords Calf Meal adv and calf, black and white	10.00
Frank Graf, playing accordion	8.00

Girl
Girls in Horse–Drawn Cart, 4¼ x 6½"	8.00
Sitting on Chair, holding doll, Prof Ehrlich photographer, NY, 1893	20.00
Two Girls by Organ, 6 x 8"	10.00
With Doll, 5 x 7"	10.00
With Puppy	6.00
Grocery Store, int. view, 5 x 7"	20.00
Harbor of Vladivastok, Siberia, ships and ship building, Sept 8, 1902, 8 x 11½"	20.00

Hawaiian Girl
Hula Dancer, standing in front of grass shack, black and white, Honolulu Photo Supply, c1910, 6 x 8"	35.00
Playing Ukelele, wearing grass skirt, c1910, 6 x 8"	40.00
Holts Landing, log crane railroad cars, St P RR, black and white	12.00
Hotel Store Front, Merchants Hotel, EK Smith Paper Twines, New England, 4½ x 6½"	15.00
Horsedrawn Ice Harvesting Sled, black and white	25.00
Logging Camp Cooks, one holding large horn, black and white	8.00

Lorena Trickey, Champion Relay Rider, Cheyenne, WY	6.00

Man
Washing Clothes, Fairbanks Gold Dust box and log train	10.00
With Motorcycle, 1943	8.00
Working in Shingle Mill, black and white, Boyne Falls, MI, 1912	8.00
Mexican Revolutionist, standing beside smiling woman	8.00
Natural Bridge of Virginia, Burrows, hand tinted, framed, 18½ x 15"	45.00
Office, int. view, 7 x 9"	15.00
Parade, small bark house on wagon, decorated with flags, children looking out, 4½ x 8"	8.00
Paradise Valley Campground, Rainier National Park, Tatoosh Range background, cars, black and white	8.00
Radio Studio, int. view, close up of equipment, man at mike, and engineer, black and white, 1920s, 11 x 7"	18.00
Red Cross Soldier	6.00
Saw Dust Pile, Cheboygan, MI, largest in world	8.00
Seed Store, int. view with Ferry Seed Co display racks and sales people, 1920, 5 x 7"	10.00
Silver Shop, int. view, 6 x 8"	25.00
Steamer, De Grasse, San Francisco, 1930s, 6 x 9"	12.50

Store
Ext. view, AJ Metge, Dry Goods, Notions, Candy, 8 x 10"	20.00
Int. view, seed store, c1920, 5 x 7"	18.00
Supermarket, int. view, 1950s, 8 x 10"	15.00
Tailor Shop, ext. view, bicycle in front	10.00

Snapshot, child on metal riding toy, black and white, 2³/₄ x 4¹/₂", 1920s, $6.00.

Underwood Bi–Plane, German, wrecked, newspaper photo, WWI, 5 x 7¹/₂"	**8.00**
USA Aviation Corps, 1918, 5¹/₄ x 6³/₄" . .	**20.00**
Ventriloquist with dummy, black and white	**35.00**
Watkins Wagon, horse drawn, winter scene, salesman's suitcase opened showing products, blanket marked "Prince for Watkins," black and white	**150.00**
Wedding, bride and bride's maid, bride's veil spread on floor, 1930, 9¹/₂ x 7" . . .	**18.00**

Woman
Seated, holding guitar, unusual dress and hat, Unionville, MO photographer, 1880s	**22.00**
Sitting on motorcycle, sepia tones, c1920, 5 x 7"	**35.00**
With brooms, mop, pail, standing in front of church or school	**10.00**

PLAYING CARDS

History: The first use of playing cards dates to twelfth century China. By 1400, playing cards were in use throughout Europe. French cards were known specifically for their ornate designs. The first American cards were published by Jazaniah Ford, Milton, Massachusetts in the late 1700s. United States innovations include upper corner indexes, classic joker, standard size, and slick finish for shuffling. Bicycle Brand was introduced in 1885 by the U.S. Playing Card Company of Cincinnati.

Card designs have been drawn or printed in every conceivable size and on a variety of surfaces. Miniature playing cards appealed to children. Novelty decks came in round, crooked, and diecut shapes. Numerous card games, besides the standard four suit deck, were created for adults and children.

Always purchase complete decks in very good condition. Do research to identify the exact number of cards needed. An American straight deck has 52 cards and usually a joker; pinochle requires 48 cards; tarot decks use 78. In addition to decks, uncut sheets and single cards, if very early, are sought by collectors.

Many collectors focus on topics. Examples are politics, trains, World's Fairs, animals, airlines, advertising, etc. Most collectors of travel–souvenir cards prefer a photographic scene on the face.

The most valuable playing card decks are unusual either in respect to publisher, size, shape, or subject. Prices for decks of late nineteenth and twentieth centuries cards have shown modest increases over the past decade.

References: Phil Bollhagen (comp.), *The Great Book of Railroad Playing Cards*, published by author, 1991; Trev Davis and Fred Chan, *Airline Playing Cards: Illustrated Reference Guide, 2nd Edition*, published by authors, 1987; Everett Grist, *Advertising Playing Cards*, Collector Books, 1992; Gene Hochman, *Encyclopedia of American Playing Cards*, six parts, privately printed, 1976 to 1982; Sylvia Mann, *Collecting Playing Cards*, Crown, 1966; H. T. Morley, *Old and Curious Playing Cards: Their History and Types from Many Countries and Periods*, Wellfleet Press, 1989; Roger Tilley, *Playing Cards*, Octopus, London, 1973.

Collectors' Clubs: Chicago Playing Card Collectors, Inc., 1559 West Platt Blvd., Chicago, IL 60626; 52 Plus Joker, 204 Gorham Avenue, Hamden, CT 06154; Playing Card Collectors Assn., Inc., PO Box 554, Bristol, WI 53104.

Museum: Playing Card Museum, Cincinnati, OH.

Advertising
Alexander Schroeder Hardwood Lumber, 5401 Lawndale, Houston, TX, building illus	**7.50**
American Fletcher National Bank, vertically printing on black background	**5.00**
Avis, Avis Features GM Cars, white vertical lettering, red vertical triangles	**5.00**
Ben Hur Life Insurance, yellow, building illus	**10.00**
Castle Steel Distributors, black castle logo, orange background, white border	**7.00**
Champion Spark Plugs, red and black logos, repeated gold world graphics, white border	**8.00**
Chatfield & Woods, gold edges	**8.00**
Chicago Tribune, black newspaper	

Cigar Label, Trump Cigars, man holding hand of cards, tan and black, 10 x 6", $35.00.

building, white background, gold and red edge 8.00

Chocolate Cream Coffee, gold product on blue background, gold and white border 4.00

Clavecin, Catel & Farcey, c1960. . . . .   15.00

Clysmic Table Water, orig box 18.00

Coca–Cola, stewardess and Coke bottle with wings, 1943 . . . .   50.00

Dubuque Packing Plant, South San Francisco Plant, red graphics, white background, gold and red border . .   5.00

Elgin Coal & Ice, black, white, and gold, eagle illus 3.50

Frank's Kutlery Kuts, USPC, c1900, orig box 30.00

Hertz Rent A Car, dark green, multicolored spherical illus, stars, yellow lettering 8.00

Imperial Washable Wallpapers, white, silver, and dark blue 5.00

Inland Rubber Corp, white, red oval with lettering, red border 8.00

Johnnie Walker Black Label Scotch, yellow logo, black background 8.00

Kellogg's Frosties, Tony the Tiger eating cereal, 1978–80 . . . .   10.00

Kool Milds, cigarette pack 12.00

Lemke Milk Products, Wausau, WI, white, blue and gold border. 3.50

Marlboro Cigarettes, black, red, and white logo 9.00

Maull's Barbecue Sauce, red bottle, white background, red and gold border 8.00

National Food Company, cow illus, yellow background 5.00

North West Paper Co, Canadian Mountie standing by horse, mountains background 5.00

Oil/Service Station, c1910 . . . .   35.00

Phoenix Coffee, coffee can, red and gold border 15.00

Pillsbury Plus, cake box design 10.00

Rock Island Sash & Door Works, Rock Island, IL, green, black, and gold design 5.00

Southwestern Timber Company, gold, white Texas outline, green trees . . .   3.50

United Founders Life Insurance Company, blue, white illus and lettering   7.50

Walter Bledsoe & Company Coal, multicolored lighthouse and ocean illus 6.50

Wrentham Implement Co, Inc, Wrentham, MA, chef holding chicken on platter 15.00

Airlines

American Airlines, DH–4 . . . .   10.00

American President Lines, white stylized eagle and four stars, orange background, gold bands with lettering 10.00

Braniff International, white center line, vertical lettering, orange background 12.00

Capital Airlines, white logo center, red, blue, and black lettering, black background, gold edge 15.00

Delta Air Lines, Los Angeles, woman wearing white gown 10.00

Ozark Air Lines, Up There With The Biggest, white logo, forest green background, white border 8.00

Pan American, white logo, light blue background, white border 10.00

Piedmont Airlines, red vertical printing, white background, light blue logo and border 15.00

TWA, red letters and airplane 15.00

Western Airlines, boxed 15.00

Country

Austria, La Provence, Paitnik, 1960, 53 cards 22.00

France, Bataille De Nancy, Grimaud, 500th Anniversary, 1977, 54 cards   12.00

Italy, World Bridge, Modiano, 1953, 54 cards 28.00

United States, Braille, USPC, 54 cards, case **20.00**
Victoria, British Hong Kong, 54 cards **12.00**

Hotels and Casinos
El Mirador Hotel, Palm Springs, CA, multicolored photo of exterior **6.50**
Golden Nugget Gambling Hall, multi-colored photo of exterior, neon lights **6.50**
Hotel Fremont and Casino, Las Vegas, NV, red and white, diamond design **5.00**
Hotel Westward Ho, Phoenix, AZ, blue, building photo, gold and white border **10.00**
Palace Club, Reno, NV, red and white, diamond design **5.00**
Schiaparelli, black, red lace, white and black rose **10.00**
Thunderbird Hotel & Casino, Las Vegas, dark blue and white, diamond design **5.00**

Liquor
Black Velvet, woman wearing black gown, bottle, and glass illus **10.00**
Early Times Kentucky Straight Bourbon Whiskey, bottle illus **7.50**
Johnnie Walker Black Label Scotch, black, gold design **8.00**
Squires Distilled London Dry Gin, white, gold and black design **7.50**
100 Pipers Scotch, Seagram, four Scottish men with bagpipes, red back ground, gold dec, white lettering . . . **10.00**
Pinup, unopened, MIB, 1950s **18.00**

Railroad
Alaska Railroad **12.00**
B & O Railroad, Sleep Like A Kitten, two decks **35.00**
Cheasepeake & Ohio Railroad, Chessie cat, two decks, boxed **30.00**
Southern Railroad, red plush box **15.00**

Souvenir
Adventureland, Des Moines, IA **5.00**
Chicago, Sears Tower, aerial view . . . **7.50**
Knott's Berry Farm, multicolored train and people scene **5.00**
Lookout Mountain, TN, Rock City, photos **6.50**
Mount Rushmore, SD, photo, yellow border **12.50**
Pro Football Hall of Fame, Canton, OH **7.50**
Roadside America, Shartlesville, PA, multicolored **7.50**
Sea World, blue, black, and white, 1978 Sea World Inc **7.50**
Smithsonian Institute, National Air & Space Museum, Montgolfier Balloon, 1783 first sustained aerial flight, hot air balloon **10.00**
Wild Animal Park, San Diego, animals, yellow border **6.50**

Salesman's Sample, printed color, printed obverse only, 2¼ x 3½", 1930s, $1.00.

World's Fair
Chicago Century of Progress, 1933, 54 different views **14.00**
Columbian Exposition, 1892, 52 card, blue, landing of Columbus **65.00**
New York World's Fair
1934, complimentary gift from Markwell Staplers, orig box **35.00**
1939, 48 cards, trick deck **50.00**
1964, full color exhibit illus, 52 cards **30.00**
Pan American Exposition, 1901, multicolored design, orig box **35.00**

POST CARDS

History: The Golden Age of post cards dates from 1898 to 1918. While there are cards printed earlier, they are collected for their postal history. Post cards prior to 1898 are called "pioneer" cards.

European publishers, especially in England and Germany, produced the vast majority of cards during the golden age. The major post card publishers are Raphael Tuck (England), Paul Finkenrath of Berlin (PFB–German), Whitney, Detroit Publishing Co., and John Winsch (United States). However, many American publishers had their stock produced in Europe, hence, "Made in Bavaria" imprints. While some Tuck cards are high priced, many are still available in the 50¢ and $1.00 boxes.

Styles changed rapidly, and manufacturers responded to every need. The linen post card which gained popularity in the 1940s was quickly replaced by the chrome cards of the post–1950 period.

Concentrate on one subject area, publisher, or illustrator. Collect cards in mint condition, when possible.

The more common the holiday, the larger the city, the more popular the tourist attraction, the easier it will be to find post cards about these subjects because of the millions of cards that still remain. The smaller runs of "real" photo post cards are the most desirable of the scenic cards. Photographic cards of families and individuals, unless they show occupations, unusual toys, dolls, or teddy bears, have little value.

Stamps and cancellation marks may affect the value of cards, but rarely. Consult a philatelic guide.

Post cards fall into two main categories: view cards and topics. View cards are easiest to sell in their local geographic region. European view cards, while very interesting, are difficult to sell in America.

Although the most popular collecting period is 1898–1918, the increasing costs of post cards from this era have turned collectors' interest to post cards from the 1920s, 1930s, and 1940s. The main interest in the 1920–1930 period is cards with an Art Deco motif. The cards collected from the 1940s are "linens" which feature a textured "linen–like" paper surface.

Cards from the 1950–1970 period are called chromes because of their shiny surface paper. Advertising post cards from this chrome era are rapidly gaining popularity.

References: Many of the best books are out–of–print. However, they are available through libraries. Ask your library to utilize the inter–library loan system.

Diane Allmen, *The Official Price Guide Postcards*, House of Collectibles, 1990; Janet Banneck, *The Antique Postcards of Rose O'Neill*, Greater Chicago Publications, 1992; John Margolies, *Palaces of Dreams: Movie Theater Postcards*, Bulfinch Press, 1993; Joseph Mashburn, *The Postcard Price Guide: A Comprehensive Listing*, WorldComm, 1992; Joseph Mashburn, *The Super Rare Postcards of Harrison Fisher*, WorldComm, 1992; Frederic and Mary Megson, *American Advertising Postcards—Set and Series: 1890–1920,* published by authors, 1985; Frederic and Mary Megson, *American Exposition Postcards, 1870–1920: A Catalog and Price Guide*, The Postcard Lovers, 1992; Ron Menchine, *A Picture Postcard History of Baseball*, Almar Press Book Publishers, 1992; Jones Publishing, *Post Card Collector Annual*, Jones Publishing; Cynthia Rubin and Morgan Williams, *Larger Than Life: The American Tall–Tale Postcard, 1905–1915*, Abbeville Press, 1990; Doro-

thy B. Ryan, *Picture Postcards In The United States, 1893–1918*, Clarkson N. Potter, 1982, paperback edition; Jack H. Smith, *Postcard Companion: The Collector's Reference*, Wallace–Homestead, 1989; Robert Ward, *Investment Guide to North American Real Photo Postcards*, Antique Paper Guild, 1991; Jane Wood, *The Collector's Guide To Post Cards*, L–W Promotions, 1984, 1993 value update.

Periodicals: *Barr's Postcard News*, 70 S. 6th Street, Lansing, IA 52151; *Postcard Collector*, Joe Jones Publishing, 121 North Main Street, Iola, WI 54945.

Special Note: An up–to–date listing of books about and featuring post cards can be obtained from Gotham Book Mart & Gallery, Inc., 41 West 47th Street, New York, NY 10036.

Collectors' Clubs: *Barr's Postcard News* and the *Postcard Collector* publish lists of over fifty regional clubs in the United States and Canada.

Note: The following prices are for cards in excellent to mint condition—no sign of edge wear, no creases, not trimmed, no writing on the picture side of the card, no tears, and no dirt. Each defect would reduce the price given by 10 percent.

ADVERTISING

Atles Beer, truck dec, multicolored, divided back	30.00
Buffalo Sled Co, Gliderole, The Roller Sled, multicolored, divided back	12.00
Bulova Watch, government postal back	6.00
Campbell's Soup, horizontal format	30.00
Clough & Warren Instruments, Adrian, MI, black and white, divided back	6.00
Coca–Cola, Duster girl in car	450.00
Conrad Seipp Brewing Co, Chicago, bottle, automobile, and logo	80.00
Do–Wah–Jack	10.00
DuPont Gun, birds	30.00
Edsel, endorsed by Kim Novak	8.00
Elgin Watch Co	6.00
Heinz Ocean Pier, Atlantic City, Sun Parlor	8.00
Indian Motorcycles, Springfield, MA factory, motorcycle, and logo, 1930s	35.00
Johns Service, Funeral Parlors, Inc, hearse, Curt Teich, 1942	20.00
Livermore & Knight Publishing	10.00
Michelin Tire Company, features Michelin man	30.00
Parker Gun	200.00
Pontiac for 1947	8.00
Rockford Watch, calendar series	15.00
Seed Company, good images	6.00
Sleepy Eye Indian, flour adv, set of 9	1,000.00
Warner Corset, Mucha	500.00
Waverly Cycle, Mucha	5,000.00
Yellow Kid, calendars, Outcault	100.00
Zeno Gum, mechanical	25.00

Advertising, Zeno Chewing Gum, tinted black and white photo, Battery Park, NY, undivided back, 5½ x 3½", c1905, $25.00.

ZENO Means Good CHEWING GUM　　BATTERY PARK, NEW YORK.

ARTIST SIGNED

Armstrong, Rolf, beautiful woman	20.00
Atwell, Mabel Lucie	
Comic, regular.	6.00
Raphael Tuck, early.	12.00
Barber, Court, woman.	8.00
Basch, Arpad, Art Nouveau design	125.00
Boileau, Philip	
Raphael Tuck.	100.00
Reinthal Neuman	15.00
Boulanger, Maurice, large cat image . . .	25.00
Brown, Ken, Beware of Geeks Bearing	
Gifts.	2.00
Browne, Tom	
Advertising	15.00
American Baseball series, green background	9.00
Brundage, Frances	
Children	10.00
Greeting, divided back	12.00
Raphael Tuck, chromolithograph, early.	30.00
Brunelleschi, Art Nouveau design.	200.00
Busi, Art Deco design	8.00
Caldecott, early	8.00
Carr, Gene, St Patrick's greeting	8.00
Carmichael, comic	3.00
Chiostri, Art Deco design	20.00
Clapsaddle, Ellen Hattie	
Children	15.00
Floral, sleds, crosses	2.00
Mechanical	
Halloween.	100.00
Valentine.	45.00
Corbella, Art Deco design.	10.00
Corbett, Bertha, sunbonnet babies	15.00
Curtis, E, children	3.00
Daniell, Eva, Art Nouveau design, Raphael Tuck.	85.00
Dixon, Dorothy, children	10.00

Dwiggins, Clare Victor	
Halloween.	15.00
Mirror	8.00
Valentine, Zodiac, Raphael Tuck	12.00
Fisher, Harrison.	12.00
Gassaway, K, children.	6.00
Gibson, Charles Dana, sepia.	6.00
Golay, Mary, flowers.	1.50
Greenaway, Kate, sgd	350.00
Greiner, M	
Blacks	12.00
Children	5.00
Molly and Her Teddy.	12.00
Griggs, H B	8.00
Gunn, Archie.	3.00
Gutmann, Bessie Pease	10.00
Hays, Margaret	8.00
Humphrey, Maud, sgd	70.00
Innes, John, western theme	3.00
Johnson, J, children	4.00
Kirchner, Raphael	
Santa	200.00
Woman playing with marionettes, stippled gold background and dec	120.00
Klein, Catherine	
Alphabet	9.00
Floral	2.00
Koehler, Mela, early	65.00
Mauzan, Art Deco design	15.00
May, Phil, English comic series	8.00
McCay, Winsor, Little Nemo.	25.00
Mucha, Alphonse	
Art Nouveau design, months of the year	200.00
Murals, Slavic period.	75.00
Woman, full card design	600.00
O'Neill, Rose	
Kewpies.	35.00
Gross Publishing Company	125.00
Pickings from Puck−acks	100.00

Comic, MWM General Comic Series, color litho, 5½ x 3½", $2.00.

Rock Island Railroad	60.00
Suffrage, National Woman Suffrage . .	300.00
Opper, Frederick, comic	8.00
Outcault, Richard Felton	
Buster Brown	20.00
Rockford Watch calendars	25.00
Patella, woman	15.00
Pease, Bessie Collins, Falling Out, two little girls, one holding umbrella, other holding doll, Gutmann & Gutmann, 1907	25.00
Pepin, Maurice, glamour design	15.00
Phillips, Cole, adv	30.00
Remington, Frederic, general	35.00
Robinson, Robert, young boy pitching ball, Edward Gross	35.00
Rockwell, Norman, Fisk Tires adv	20.00
Russell, Charles, camp scene, two men, horses, and bear illus, 1907	15.00
Sager, Xavier, woman and Uncle Sam . .	25.00
Sandford, M Dix, Seaside Coons series, Raphael Tuck	10.00
Schmucker, Samuel	
Butterfly series	150.00
Childhood Days series	200.00
National Girls series	125.00
Shinn, Cobb	5.00
Smith, Jessie Wilcox, The Lily Pool, Reinthal & Newman	20.00
Sowerby, Millicent, Wet, girl holding umbrella, 1911	10.00
Studdy, Bonzo Dog	12.00
Thiele, Arthur	
Black, riding bike	45.00
Cat, action scene	15.00
Pig with large head	25.00
Thompson, Nyla	5.00
Underwood, Clarence	15.00
Wain, Louis	
Cat, A Rose Between Two Thorns	40.00
Frog	35.00
Wall, Bernhardt, sunbonnets	15.00
Wellman, Walter, Suffragette series	30.00
Zimmerman, H G	10.00

GREETING

April Fools, American comic	3.00
Birthday	
Floral	.10
Children	.50
Christmas, Santa	
Black face, Coontown series	100.00
German, highly embossed	15.00
Hold to light type	100.00
Tuck, blue suit, multicolored	12.00
Easter	
Animals, dressed	5.00
Chick	2.00
Children	4.50
Cross	.25
Fourth of July	
Children	5.00
Uncle Sam	8.00
Ground Hog Day, Loundsbury Publishing	250.00
Halloween	
Bats, witch on pumpkins, multicolored, divided back, Gibson	12.00
Children, artist sgd	8.00
Winsch Publishing	45.00
Woman bobbing for apples, Jack–O–Lantern border, emb, artist sgd E C Banks, 1909	12.00
Hanukkah Greeting from Cleveland, skyline with menorah, Nu–Vista Prints, 1989	25.00
Labor Day, Nash Publishing	95.00
Leap Year	5.00
Mother's Day, early	5.00
New Year	
Beautiful girls, multicolored, 1907 . . .	8.00
Bells	.25
Beautiful woman, Winsch Publishing	15.00
Father Time	4.00
St. Patrick's Day, children	4.50
Thanksgiving, children	3.50
Valentines	
Beautiful woman, Winsch Publishing	15.00
Hearts, comic	1.00
Mechanical, wheel turns as faces change, multicolored, divided back	6.00

MISCELLANEOUS

Bathing beauties, H King	12.00
Bear, busy bears, Austen	12.00
Black, jitterbug couple, C T Jitterbug Comics series, Curt Teich, 1938	25.00
Exaggerated Hats, Acme	8.00
Fairy Tales, Lorna Steele	10.00
Floral Alphabet Series, artist sgd, C Klein	20.00
Halley's Comet, celestial map, copyright 1910, J W Donaldson, St Paul	35.00
Horse, realistic image	12.00
Indians	8.00

Ocean Liner
  Carconia II, Cunard Line, green, port
    side **5.00**
  Philadelphia, American Line, color,
    New York harbor scene **15.00**
  President Wilson, American President
    Lines, color, Oriental harbor scene **15.00**
  SS Baltic Steamship **5.00**
Psychedelic Peace Sign, 23½ x 25½",
  Gemini Rising Co, 1971, red, hot pink
  and blue design **45.00**
Patriotic, Give Us Independence, multi-
  colored, divided back **20.00**
Portland Rose Festival **4.00**
Portola Festival
  Poster style...................... **15.00**
  Views............................ **3.00**
Priest of Pallas **10.00**
Suffrage
  Cargill **12.00**
  Clapsaddle **50.00**
  Kewpie **125.00**
  Parades **10.00**
Sunbonnet design, Thursday, H I Rob-
  bins, Boston..................... **20.00**

PHOTOGRAPHIC

Alaska, dog sled scene **10.00**
Auctioneer Col Casey, selling a
  $3,400.00 Case Steam Tractor, SD,
  c1910 .... **55.00**
Baptist Church, Evans, IL............. **10.00**
Baseball Players, St Petersburg, FL, 1944,
  identified **30.00**
California, Main Street
  Red Bluff **15.00**
  Roseville **18.00**
Christmas, children under trees. **10.00**
Circus Performer, identified and close–
  up **15.00**
Cook of the North Pole, whistle stop

view, Dr Cook, Discoverer of the
  North Pole, Litchfield, IL, 1909 ...... **30.00**
Dodgeville Motor Co, WI, 1930s **25.00**
Highwood Ice Cream Parlor, Highwood,
  IL, soda fountain foreground, 1920s .. **65.00**
Ku Klux Klan, four hooded members and
  flag decked automobile, dated plate
  on car 1928 .... **150.00**
Lindbergh at Fargo, ND, airplane and
  people **25.00**
Loyal Order of the Moose Brass Band,
  detailed studio view of large band,
  c1910 .... **15.00**
Marriage, 1898–1918............... **10.00**
Military people with flags **5.00**
Motorcycle Repair Shop, ext. view, men
  and motorcycles **30.00**
Ocala, FL, street scene **12.00**
Occupation, American **15.00**
Ostrich cart, CA................... **10.00**
Pool Hall, int. view, Oxley **35.00**
Portraits, family................... **1.00**
Potlach, ID, multiple view........... **30.00**
Ringling Bros Circus Band, Al Sweet's
  Concert Band, 1909 season, promo-
  tion by Conn's Brand Instrument Fac-
  tory, detailed view of band **65.00**
Railroad
  Depot scene **8.00**
  Depots with trains **12.00**
Shop Exteriors, identified **6.00**
Shop Interiors, identified location...... **25.00**
Stuttgart Harvest, rice, AR **10.00**
Telephone Operators, int. view of four
  women sitting at switchboards, stand-
  ing supervisor, A J Kingsbury, Antigo,
  WI, 1908 .... **50.00**
Texas Co, Lockport, IL, tanks. **10.00**
Viking Ski Club, Arbor Vitae, WI, foot of
  ski jump with flag draped coffin, G A
  Lau............................ **15.00**
Wheaton College, IL **10.00**
Winter Park, El Cortez, FL **10.00**

**Photographic, Lehigh
University Library,
Bethlehem, PA, black
and white, 5½ x 3½",
1905, $4.50.**

Souvenir, Elephant Landmark at South Atlantic City, color litho, 5³/₈ x 3¹/₂", $2.00.

POLITICAL

Andrew Johnson, portrait, Presidents of the United States series, Raphael Tuck & Sons, artist sgd, L P Spinner	20.00
Birthplace of President Coolidge, Plymouth, VT, black and white, divided back.	10.00

Campaign
1900	100.00
1904	65.00
1908	35.00
Harry Truman, campaign card	25.00
John F Kennedy, Assassination Scene, chrome view, Texas Postcard & Novelty Co, 1960s	4.00
McKinley's death	6.00
Nazi, purple zeppelin hand stamp, Berlin cancel with spread eagle and swastika, imprinted Hitler stamp, unused . .	30.00
Roosevelt's African Tour	3.00
Russo–Japanese War.	20.00
The Nation's Choice, Taft and Sherman, H M Rose Co, 1908	15.00
Theodore Roosevelt, giving speech from Ah–Wa–Go Hotel, Oswego, NY, black and white, divided back.	20.00
William Howard Taft, cartoon type.	12.00
William Jennings Bryan, colored, Bryan with shock of corn, 1908, 3⁵/₈ x 5¹/₂". .	15.00
Woodrow Wilson, portrait, "Hail to Our President"	100.00

WORLD'S FAIRS AND EXPOSITIONS

Alaska–Yukon Pacific Exposition, 1909	10.00
California Midwinter, 1894.	250.00
Columbian Exposition, Chicago, 1893 . .	25.00
Cotton States Exposition, 1895	200.00
Hudson–Fulton.	10.00

Jamestown Exposition, 1907
Mechanical, dressed bear, 144 outfits.	350.00

"The Handclasp of Centuries," Theodore Roosevelt	15.00
Lewis and Clark Exposition, 1905, The Inside Inn	100.00

Louisiana Purchase Exposition, St Louis, 1904
Eggshell paper	10.00
Hold to light type, int. view of inn . .	125.00
New York World's Fair, 1939, Trylon and Perisphere, gold, orange, and indigo, 3¹/₈ x 5"	4.00
New York World's Fair, 1964	12.00

Pan–American Exposition, Buffalo, 1901
Black and white.	6.00
Color	10.00
Trans–Mississippi, Omaha, 1898, adv	125.00

POSTERS

History: The poster was an extremely effective and critical means of mass communication, especially in the period before 1920. Enormous quantities were produced, helped in part by the propaganda role posters played in World War I.

Print runs of two million were not unknown. Posters were not meant to be saved. Once they served their purpose, they were usually destroyed. The paradox of high production and low survival is one of the fascinating aspects of poster history.

The posters of the late nineteenth and early twentieth century represent the pinnacle of American lithography printing. The advertising posters of firms such as Strobridge or Courier are true classics. Philadelphia was one center for the poster industry.

Europe pioneered in posters with high artistic and aesthetic content. Many major artists of the twentieth century designed posters. Poster art still plays a key role throughout Europe today.

Posters are collected either for their subject or historical value, e.g., movie, railroad, minstrel, etc., or for their aesthetic appeal. Modern art historians have recognized the poster as one of the most creative art forms of our times.

Often a popular film would be re–released several times over a period of years. Most re–releases can be identified by looking at the lower right corner in the white border area. A re–release will usually be indicated with an "R" and a diagonal slash mark with the year of the newest release. Therefore, a "R/47" would indicate a 1947 issue.

References: John Barnicoat, *A Concise History of Posters*, Harry Abrams, 1976; Tony Fusco, *The Official Identification and Price Guide To Posters, First Edition*, House of Collectibles, 1990; George Theofiles, *American Posters of World War I: A Price and Collector's Guide*, Dafram House Publishers; Walton Rawls, *Wake Up, America!: World War I and The American Poster*, Abbeville Press, 1988; Stephen Rebello and Richard Allen, *Reel Art: Great Posters From The Golden Age of The Silver Screen*, Abbeville Press, 1988; Susan Theran and Katheryn Acerbo (eds.), *Leonard's Annual Price Index of Prints, Posters & Photographs, Volume I*, Auction Index, 1992; Susan Theran, *Prints, Posters, and Photographs: Identification and Price Guide*, Avon Books, 1993; Jon Warren, *Warren's Movie Poster Price Guide, 1993 Edition*, American Collector's Exchange, 1992; Bruce Wright, *Yesterday's Tomorrows: The Golden Age of Science Fiction Movie Posters, 1950–1964*, Taylor Publishing, 1993.

Advertising
   Arrow Shirts With Starched Cuffs, J C Leyendecker, man in smoking jacket reads book, c1916, 21 x 11" **150.00**
   Be Refreshed with Healthful Delicious Doublemint Gum, Otis Shephard, twins with sleek car, c1937, 11 x 42" **200.00**
   Camomille Liqueur, yellow bottle, blue background, c1890, 32 x 51" **225.00**
   Chesterfield Cigarettes, cardboard ... **18.00**
   Coca–Cola–Yes, Harold Sundblum, bathing beauty, 1946, 11 x 27" **150.00**
   Dunlopillo Mattresses, blue, orange, brown, yellow, gray, and black, 30 x 44" **275.00**
   Hilton–The Starched Collar For Fall– Tooke Brothers, Ltd, adv for celluloid collars, autumn leaves background, c1915, 11 x 21" **50.00**
   Kodak, monotone photo of young lady in beret, jacket, and necktie, self framed, c1920, 17 x 26" **200.00**
   Kool Cigarette, paper, full color Willie the Penguin portrait, wearing military outfit, 12 x 18" **45.00**

   Maxon's Polish, Belgian, boot polish adv, brunette poses with horse, green, red, brown, blue, and black, c1950, 14 x 20" **75.00**
   Mission Orange Soda, Everybody's Choice, 1940–50, paper, 20 x 26¼" **50.00**
   Sloan's Liniment For All Mankind!, red, black, green, yellow, blue, speckled white, and brown, 30 x 46" **150.00**
   Tuttle's Horse Elixir, black, yellow, and red, 30 x 46" **150.00**
   US Cream Separator, Vermont Farm Machine Co, Bellows Falls, VT, W N Dunklee, Agent, 12¼ x 17" **35.00**
   Use Virginia Dare Double Strength Extracts, smiling housewife making cookies, c1925, 21 x 28" **175.00**
   Welch's Wine Coolers–Wouldn't This Hit The Spot Right Now? Taste It ... You'll Love It, Says Eddie Cantor, 1952, 11 x 21" **100.00**
   Wide Angle Tillyer Lenses, Norman Rockwell, window card, color, 1929, 18 x 23" **165.00**
Automobiles
   Mercedes Benz, showroom poster, brown, blue, black, red, and yellow, white ground, futuristic racing car against ghostly logo, 1955, 23 x 33" **975.00**
   Pontiac Big Six–Big Car Quality Typified by Smart, Luxurious Fisher Bodies, Hyden, showroom poster, enlargement of 1929 Saturday Evening Post double page adv, 38 x 26" **225.00**
   The New Oakland All American Six, showroom poster, color enlargement of Saturday Evening Post adv, 1929, 26 x 38" **225.00**
   The Pierce Arrow, J Sheridan, placard, color, 8 x 10" **80.00**
Aviation
   American Airlines
      Aloha Hawaii, E. McKnight Kauffer, 1953, 27 x 41" **275.00**
      American Airlines–East Coast, E McKnight Kauffer, 1948, seaman carving sailing ship, 30 x 30" **250.00**
      Los Angeles–American Airlines, Fred Ludikens, DC7 flies over LA nightscape, c1954, 30 x 39" **350.00**
   Lufthansa Airlines, c1955, 25 x 39" ... **150.00**
   Northwest Airlines, Two Down and One to Go, 1943, 24 x 36" **265.00**
   TWA
      Along The Way of TWA–California Yosemite National Park, deep tint color photo panorama view of park, c1947, 35 x 28" **125.00**
      Las Vegas–Fly TWA, David, showgirl, montage of roulette wheels, cards, etc, airliner flying in background, c1960, 25 x 40" **225.00**

Health and Fitness
Aquatics . . . Swimming Is A Life–
Saver–Learn to Be at Home in the
Water, 1920. . . . .   **20.00**
Good Posture For Health & Country–
Fitness For Victory, Samuel Higby
Camp Institute for Better Posture,
full color illus, 24½ x 18" **65.00**
Healthy & Happy, full color illus,
c1940, 21 x 17". **18.00**
Setting Up Exercises . . . Set Up Boys &
Girls In Health–Spirits–Mental
Alertness, 1921 . . . .   **24.00**
The Peak of Health Means Beauty–
Strength–Success, woman silhou-
ette on mountain top, National
Child Welfare Assoc, 1928, 14½ x
23". **35.00**
Movie
Annie Get Your Gun, 1950, 14 x 36"   **60.00**
Arson, Inc, Lippert Productions, 1949,
22 x 28" **30.00**
Avenging Rider, Tim Holt, 1942, 27 x
40". **100.00**
Barbarian & Geisha, John Wayne, 14 x
36". **40.00**
Beach Blanket Bingo, Frankie Avalon,
22 x 22" **20.00**

**Movie, comedy, *All Hands on Deck,* Pat
Boone, Buddy Hackett, Barbara Eden,
20th Century Fox, 1961, $20.00.**

Big Jake, John Wayne **30.00**
Black Fury, Paul Muni, 1935, 23 x 43"   **175.00**
Black Trail, Johnny Mack Brown, 27 x
41". **35.00**
Bus Stop, Marilyn Monroe, 27 x 41" . .   **550.00**
Cahill, John Wayne, 27 x 41" **25.00**
Call of the Wild, 1953, 41 x 81" **185.00**
Castle on Hudson, J Garfield and A
Sheridan, 14 x 36" **125.00**
Cincinnati Kid, 1965, 22 x 28" **40.00**
Circus World, John Wayne **45.00**
Curse of Werewolf, 1961, 81 x 80" . . .   **125.00**
Deep Blue Sea, Vivien Leigh, 27 x 41"   **45.00**
Dial M for Murder, 1954, 63 x 47" . . .   **100.00**
Dirty Dozen, Lee Marvin, 27 x 41" . . .   **15.00**
Empire Strikes Back, Mark Hamill, 27
x 41". **25.00**
Facts of Life, Bob Hope and Lucille
Ball, 14 x 36" **65.00**
Fantasia, 1950, litho in USA, 57 x 40"   **150.00**
Fish Hooky, 1952, Little Rascals, 41 x
27". **135.00**
Gentlemen Prefer Blondes, 1953, 22 x
28". **275.00**
Godzilla, 1956, Paul Anthony Enter-
prises, 27 x 41". **195.00**
Gone With The Wind, 1943, purple,
black, and white, 27 x 41". **800.00**
Harlow, Carol Baker, 27 x 41". **10.00**
I Thank A Fool, Susan Hayward, 14 x
36". **25.00**
In The Good Old Summer Time, 1949,
41 x 81" **225.00**
King Kong, 1956, 27 x 41". **680.00**
Life with Father, 1947, 14 x 36". **85.00**
Little Miss Broadway, 1938, Shirley
Temple, 27 x 41". **1,100.00**
Mame, Lucille Ball, 27 x 41" **25.00**
Mummy's Curse, Lon Chaney Jr, 14 x
36". **40.00**
Niagara, Marilyn Monroe, 22 x 28". . .   **575.00**
Rage of Paris, 1938, 27 x 41". **100.00**
Raiders of The Seven Seas, United Art-
ist, 1953, 27 x 41" **30.00**
Red Badge of Courage, 1951, 41 x 81"   **90.00**
Return of Vampire, Bela Lugosi, 14 x
36". **175.00**
Riders of Deadline, Hopalong Cassidy,
27 x 41" **40.00**
River of No Return, 1954, Marilyn
Monroe, 22 x 28". **100.00**
Room Service, Marx Bros, 22 x 28" . . .   **500.00**
Rooster Cogburn, John Wayne **40.00**
Saratoga Trunk, 1945, 14 x 36" **70.00**
Shine On Harvest Moon, Ann Sheri-
dan, 1943, 27 x 40". **100.00**
Snake Pit, 1948, 14 x 36". **85.00**
Speedway, Elvis Presley and Nancy Si-
natra, 27 x 41" **100.00**
State Fair, 1962, 22 x 28". **10.00**
Stick to your Guns, 1941, Hopalong
Cassidy, 27 x 41" **100.00**

Movie, horror, *Frogs,* Ray Milland, Sam Elliott, American International, 1972, $25.00.

Streetcar Named Desire, Marlon
  Brando and Vivien Leigh, 22 x 28" **100.00**
The High and The Mighty, John
  Wayne, 27 x 41" **75.00**
The Sound of Fury, United Artist,
  1950, 14 x 36" **25.00**
Till the Clouds Roll By, 1946, 27 x 41" **100.00**
To Have and Have Not, Humphrey
  Bogart, 22 x 28" **225.00**
Tom Mix Circus & Wild West, 28 x 42" **200.00**
Winning Team, Ronald Reagan and
  Doris Day, 14 x 36" **200.00**
You Only Live Twice, 1967, 14 x 36" **150.00**
Oceanliner
Panama Pacific Liner New York–
  California, gleaming white liner go-
  ing through Panama Canal, orig
  frame with brass plaque, c1920, 27
  x 23" **250.00**
Red Star Line, Antwerpen–New York–
  Canada, star behind large ship, 20 x
  26" **200.00**
S. S. Washington, Worden Wood, ship
  in choppy water at sunset, 1933, 24
  x 30" **175.00**
The *Queen of Bermuda* Entering Hamilton Harbor, Adolph Treidler,

silkscreened design, multicolored,
  1947, 30 x 39" **275.00**
Publishing
Football & Love: A Story of the Yale–
  Princeton Game of '94, 1895 novel
  by Burr W McIntosh, blue, yellow,
  brown, green, and black, 12 x 12".. **85.00**
Harper's, February 1896, Edward
  Penfield, courting couple walking
  beside woods at dusk, 11 x 20" **200.00**
Inland Printer, January 1897, J C
  Leyendecker, allegory of angels
  blowing trumpets in heavens,
  rearing Pegasi, 10 x 17" **325.00**
Lippincott's, April 1897, J J Gould,
  finely dressed gentleman walking
  under umbrella with young ladies,
  13 x 16" **300.00**
Prang & Co's Holiday Publications,
  Louis J Rhead, litho, maiden among
  brightly colored books and folios,
  holding string tied booklet, rich violet, green, deep blue, deep red, and
  brown, background of holly,
  berries, and mottled yellow, 1896,
  17 x 23" **650.00**
Romance and Tragedy of Pioneer Life,
  broadsheet adv book, vignettes of
  American exploration, c1875, 25 x
  36" **200.00**
Railroad
British Railways, The Night Ferry,
  woodcut design by A. N.
  Wolstenholme, sleeping cars on
  ferry between London and Paris, 25
  x 40" **280.00**
The New Haven Railroad, Ski, Saucha
  Maurer, brown, blue, red, green,
  and orange, 28 x 42" **245.00**
Wheeling & Lake Erie Railroad Excur-
  sions to the Great Forepaugh and
  Wild West Shows, illus both sides,
  1889, 11 x 29" **115.00**
Sports
Evening Standard–Best of All For
  Sport, Anon, c1950, 20 x 30"...... **75.00**
Fidass Sporting Goods, F Romoli,
  1962 Italian soccer player, 29 x 52" **300.00**
George Brett, 7–Up adv, 19 x 25".... **10.00**
Willie Mays, Coca–Cola adv, 18 x 24" **10.00**
York Streamlined Barbell and Body
  Building System, 1950s, red and
  blue, 14 x 22" **15.00**
Theater
Bringing Up Father, McManus, col-
  ored litho, 1915, 41 x 81" **425.00**
Carter Beats The Devil, Otis Litho,
  1920s, window card, color, 14 x 22" **75.00**
Claudine, French Opera, 1910, full
  color, 26 x 35" **275.00**
Dangers of a Great City, Anon, c1900,
  color litho, 21 x 28" **150.00**

E Demas, cabaret comedian, French
stone litho, c1900, 23 x 36"....... **165.00**
George–The Supreme Master of Mag-
ic, 1929, Otis Litho, magician floating cards over approving Buddha,
20 x 27" **150.00**
Human Hearts–An Idyl of the Arkansas Hills, c1905, Miner Litho,
face of young child with blonde
hair, looking up, silhouettes of pink
and red hearts ski, 21 x 28" **165.00**
Magic City, Leo Rudge, 1913, colored,
47 x 63" **375.00**
Slaves of the Mine, Enquirer Co, Cincinnati, American melodrama,
c1890, 29 x 42" **225.00**
The Missouri Girl Sadie Raymond as
Daisy, Donaldson Litho, c1905, star
in country attire, bright red back-
ground, 28 x 42" **175.00**
Three Penny Opera, Paul Davis, 1976,
two panels, 41 x 81"............ **275.00**
World War I
America's Tribute to Britain, Fred G
Cooper, woodcut design, 20 x 30" **350.00**
Americans All!, Howard Chandler
Christy, Miss Liberty paying honor
to Honor Roll of ethnic names,
Chartex back, 28 x 40".......... **225.00**
Civilians–The Jewish Welfare Board–
United War Campaign–Week of
November 11, 1918, soldier illus,
blue and brown, beige background,
22 x 33" **95.00**
Enlist in the Navy, Follow the Boys in
Blue for Home and Country, 29 x
21"........................... **85.00**
Feed a Fighter, litho image of ex-
hausted soldier having cup of cof-
fee, 20 x 29".................. **90.00**
Hey Fellows! Your Money Brings the
Book We Need, Sheridan, brilliant
colors, 20 x 30" **80.00**
See Him Through–Help Us To Help
The Boys, National Catholic Wars
Council Knights of Columbus,
United War Campaign, Nov 11,
1918, Knight in military uniform
and soldiers going to war illus, 20 x
32"........................... **35.00**
That Liberty Shall Not Perish From the
Earth, Joseph Pennell, Chartex
backed, 20 x 30" **230.00**
The Hun–His Mark/Blot It Out, bloody
handprint on white ground, 20 x 30" **50.00**
The Road to France/The Road to Ber-
lin, James Montgomery Flagg, black
and white, 18 x 24" **125.00**
The Salvation Army Lassie, Keep Her
on the Job, 30 x 40" **120.00**
World War II
Bits of Careless Talk, Stevan Dohanos,

bold, brutish Nazi hand putting
pieces together to figure out Allied
secrets, 20 x 28"............... **145.00**
Guard Our Shores, US Army Coast Artillery recruiting poster, dark blue,
orange, red, blue–green, and black,
25 x 38" **175.00**
Hasten the Homecoming–Buy Victory
Bonds, full color Norman Rockwell
illus, 1945, 29 x 20"............ **37.00**
I'm Counting On You!, L Helguera
portrait of Uncle Sam, finger to lips,
bright blue background, 22 x 28" .. **80.00**
Lock Up These Papers/The Enemy is
Vigilant, Office of War Information,
stark bold letters in red, yellow, and
black, 22 x 28"................ **70.00**
Remember Dec 7th!, tattered American flag flies at half mast, grim background of fire and smoke, 28 x 40" **185.00**
United We Are Strong, United We
Will Win, Koerner, allied cannons
blast into fiery sky, 20 x 28"....... **70.00**
Victory–Now You Can Invest In It!
Victory Loan, full color illus, 1945,
25 x 18½" **30.00**

PRINTS

History: Prints serve many purposes. They can be
a reproduction of an artist's paintings, drawings,
or designs. Prints themselves often are an original
art form. Finally, prints can be developed for mass
appeal as opposed to aesthetic statement. Much
of the production of Currier & Ives fits this latter
category. Currier & Ives concentrated on genre,
urban, patriotic, and nostalgia scenes.

Prints are beginning to attract a wide following.
This is partially because prices have not matched
the rapid rise in oil and other paintings.

References: Frederic A. Conningham and Colin
Simkin, *Currier & Ives Prints, Revised Edition,*
Crown Publishers, 1970; Victor J. W. Christie,
Bessie Pease Gutmann: Her Life and Works, Wal-
lace–Homestead, 1990; William P. Carl,
*Currier's Price Guide to American and European
Prints at Auction, Second Edition,* Currier Publi-
cations, 1991; Peter Hastings Falk, *Print Price
Index 93,* Sound View Press, 1992; Denis C. Jack-
son, *The Price & Identification Guide to J. C.
Leyendecker & F. X. Leyendecker,* published by
author, 1983; Denis C. Jackson, *The Price & Iden-
tification Guide To: Maxfield Parrish, Eighth Edi-
tion,* printed by author, 1992; M. June Keagy and
Joan M. Rhoden, *More Wonderful Yard–Long
Prints,* published by authors, 1992; William D.
Keagy et al., *Those Wonderful Yard–Long Prints
& More,* published by authors, 1989; Robert Kipp,
*Currier's Price Guide to Currier & Ives Prints,
Second Edition,* Currier Publications, 1991; Craig

McClain, *Currier & Ives: An Illustrated Value Guide,* Wallace–Homestead, 1987; Rita C. Mortenson, *R. Atkinson Fox, His Life and Work,* Revised (1991) and *R. Atkinson Fox, Vol. 2,* (1992) L–W Book Sales; Richard J. Perry, *The Maxfield Parrish Identification and Price Guide,* Starbound Publishing, 1993; Ruth M. Pollard, *The Official Price Guide To Collector Prints, 7th Edition,* House Of Collectibles, 1986; Susan Theran and Katheryn Acerbo (eds.), *Leonard's Annual Price Index of Prints, Posters & Photographs, Volume I,* Auction Index, 1992; Susan Theran, *Prints, Posters, and Photographs: Identification and Price Guide,* Avon Books, 1993.

Collectors' Clubs: American Historical Print Collectors Society, Inc., PO Box 1532, Fairfield, CT 06430; Prang–Mark Society, PO Box 306, Watkins Glen, NY 14891.

Periodical: *The Illustrator Collector's News,* PO Box 1958, Sequim, WA 98392.

REPRODUCTION ALERT: Reproductions are a problem, especially Currier & Ives prints. Check the dimensions before buying any print.

Note: Also see "Illustrators" in topical section.

Audubon
  Bien, Julius
    Blue Jays, Plate 231, full size **1,700.00**
    Flycatchers, Plate 54, half page .. **300.00**
    Purple Martin, Plate 45, full size .. **1,500.00**
    Towhee Bunting, Plate 195, half
      page **300.00**
    Yellow–throated Warbler, Plate
      79, full size **350.00**
  James, John, after, hand colored etching, engraving, and aquatint by R Havell & Son, London, watermark of J Whatman Turkey Mill
    American Redstart, Plate 40 ..... **1,650.00**
    Audubon's Warbler, Plate 395 ... **1,100.00**
    Bonaparte's Flycatcher, Plate 5.. **990.00**
    Fox Colored Sparrow, Plate 108 .. **1,540.00**
    Havell's Tern, Plate 409 .... **2,420.00**
    Pine–creeping Warbler, Plate 140 **880.00**
    Roscoe's Yellow Throat, Plate 24 **1,320.00**
    Rice Bird, Plate LIV, 1936, full
      sheet, 39³⁄₄ x 26¹⁄₈" **770.00**
    Swamp Sparrow, Plate 64....... **1,100.00**
    Wood Ibis, Plate CCXVI, 1834, full
      margins, 38¹⁄₈ x 25¹⁄₄" **6,600.00**
Benton, Thomas Hart, 1889–1975, Jessie and Jake, litho, sgd in pencil lower right and "Benton" in pencil lower right, annotated "To Kitsie . . ." in pencil lower left, wove paper, framed, 13³⁄₈ x 9 1⁵⁄₁₆" **1,100.00**
Bontecou, Lee, c1931, untitled, black and brown etching and aquatint, lower right pencil signature, dated

1967, numbered 133/144, 26 x 17¹⁄₈"...................... **300.00**
Calder, Alexander, American, 1898–1976, Spider's Nest, color litho, sgd in pencil lower right, numbered 25/95, 29¹⁄₂ x 43¹⁄₄" **500.00**
Church, Frederick Stuart, 1842–1923, Dissertation On A Roast Pig, etching, "F. S. Church/NY 83," titled in pencil on mat, matted and framed **50.00**
Currier and Ives
  American Whalers Crushed in the Ice–205, small folio **1,000.00**
  Black Eyed Susan–551, small folio **150.00**
  Maple Sugaring, Early Spring in the Northern Woods–3975, small folio **600.00**
  The Express Train, hand colored litho, touches of gum arabic, 1870, red pencil inscription in lower left margin corner, slight soiling, 10 x 14" sheet size **1,760.00**
  The Midnight Race on the Mississippi–4116, large folio **3,500.00**
  Winter In The Country, The Old Grist Mill, after the painting of George H Durrie, hand colored litho, 1864, framed, 22¹⁄₈ x 30" sheet size **6,600.00**
Dow, Arthur Wesley, 1857–1922, Sunset Bayberry Hill, color woodblock, sgd and dated in pencil lower left and lower right, title on inner mat, framed, 4 x 6⁷⁄₈" sight size..... **2,970.00**
Erbit, Jules, nude on rock holding shell to ear, untitled, 15 x 20" **18.00**
Fangel, Maud Tousey, child and teddy bear, 8 x 10", framed. **20.00**
Gag, Wanda, 1893–1946, Blacksmith's Shop, litho, sgd in pencil lower right, wove paper, framed, 11¹⁄₂ x 13³⁄₄" **385.00**
Gifford, Robert Swain, 1840–1905, Coal Dock, New Bedford, MA, etching, sgd in plate lower right, 6³⁄₄ x 4³⁄₄", matted and framed **70.00**
Gutman, Tea For Two, 11 x 14", framed **30.00**
Hintermeister, Hy, Grandma Gets the Brass Ring, 12 x 16¹⁄₂". **12.00**
Homer, Winslow, 1836–1910, The Army Of The Potomac–A Sharp–Shooter On Picket Duty, engraving done for Harper's Weekly, Nov 15, 1862, sgd "Homer" in illustration lower right, titled lower center, faded, several repaired tears, 9 x 13¹⁄₂", matted and framed......... **20.00**
Icart, Louis, French, 1888–1950
  Arrival, woman entering doorway .. **700.00**
  Cat, paw in fishbowl. **750.00**
  Dear Friends................... **1,100.00**

Down Among the Coal Mines—"Chutes Loading the Canal-Boats on the Lehigh Canal" and "Weighing the Cargoes in the Weigh-Lock on the Lehigh Canal," black and white, published in *Harper's Weekly*, full page, 10⁷/₈ x 15³/₄", February 22, 1873, $18.00.

Girl in Crinoline, color aquatint, 1937, 23¼ x 19½" **1,800.00**
Jardinare, woman lying by urn **1,000.00**
Mother and Child, soldier in background **2,000.00**
Venetian Nights **900.00**
Woman, departure scene, stepping into coach with coachman **700.00**
Kelly, Ellsworth, Yellow, color litho, numbered 39/75, printed on white Rives paper, 23¼ x 15¼" **400.00**
Kent, Rockwell, Climbing The Bars, 1928, transfer printed, tan paper, stamped "Oct 11, 1929" on verse, printed by George Miller, framed, 11 x 8" **275.00**
Kernan, J F, Dog Gone, 12 x 13" **12.00**
Kingman, Doug, twentieth C, Spirit of July 4th 1976, litho, titled on reverse, numbered 451/500, matted and framed, 20½ x 31¾" **100.00**
Liebermann, Max, German, 1847—1935, Girl With Dachshund, transfer

litho, sgd in pencil lower right, 13¼ x 7½" **550.00**
Lindenmuth, Tod, American, 1885–1976, Dory Fisherman, color woodblock, sgd in pencil lower right, titled in pencil lower left, metal frame, 11¼ x 14" **550.00**
Moran, Thomas, The White Squadron, 1891, after Edward Moran, etching, sgd in pencil lower right, also sgd lower left Edward Moran, 22¾ x 32⁵/₈" **400.00**
Parrish, Maxfield
Above the Balcony, knaves and maidens in garden **35.00**
Circe's Palace, maiden standing on porch **70.00**
His Christmas Dinner, tramp having dinner **50.00**
Pandora's Box, maiden sitting by large box **70.00**
Sea Nymphs, 1914, 12 x 14" **45.00**
Stars, House of Art, nude sitting on rock, large size **525.00**
Rembrandt Van Rijn, Dutch, 1606—69
A Peasant In A High Cap Standing Leaning On A Stick, etching, 1939, Basan impression, 3¼ x 1³/₄", unframed **2,000.00**
Man Standing In Oriental Costume and Plumed Fur Cap, etching, 1632, 18th C impression, 4¼ x 3" **400.00**
Peter and John At The Gate Of The Temple, etching, 1659, impression of Nowell–Usticke's fifth or sixth state, 7⅛ x 8³/₈" **450.00**
Rembrandt's Mother In Oriental Headdress, 1631, etching, impression of Nowell–Usticke's fourth state, 5³/₄ x 5" **300.00**
Remington, Frederic Sackrider, 1861–1909,
The Retreat, 1889, litho, plate sgd and dated, matted and framed, 20¼ x 35½" **75.00**
The Smoke Signal, litho, matted and framed, 22¼ x 33¼" **275.00**
Victory Dance, litho, matted and framed, 19¼ x 20½" **125.00**
Ripley, Aiden Lassell, 1896–1969, Partridge Eating Grapes, drypoint, cream wove paper, framed, 6⁹/₁₆ x 8⁷/₁₆" **110.00**
Smith, Granville, A Popular Wave, four young women swimming in sea, c1900, 20 x 13½" **24.00**
Thorne, Diane, Russians, etching, matted, 6 x 7³/₄" **55.00**
Tittle, Walter Ernest, 1883–1960, Golfer, drypoint, framed, 11¾ x 9³/₄" **315.00**

View of Mauch Chunk

View of Mauch Chunk, black and white, Sinclair's Lith., 8¹⁄₄ x 6″ sheet size, $20.00.

Wengenroth, Stow, 1906–1977, Summer Shadows Wiscasset Maine, litho, wove paper, annotated "Ed/85" lower left, framed, extensive foxing in margins, mount staining, 8³⁄₈ x 15³⁄₈″ **360.00**

Whistler, James Abbott McNeill, The Little Pool, 1961, etching, 3¹⁄₂ x 4⁵⁄₈″   **500.00**

PREMIUMS

History: A premium is an object given free or at a reduced value with the purchase of a product or service. Premiums divide into two groups: (1) point of purchase (you obtain your premium when you make the purchase) or (2) proof of purchase (you sent proof of purchase, often box labels or seals, to a distribution point which then sends the premium to you).

Premiums are generational. The sixty–something and seventy–something generations think of radio premiums, the fifty–something, forty–something, and the older thirty–something generations identify with cereal and radio premiums. The twenty–something and modern–somethings collect fast food premiums.

A relatively small number of premiums were made of paper. Collectors place a premium on three–dimensional premiums. However, many of these premiums arrived in paper containers and envelopes and contained paper instruction sheets. In the 1990s, a premium is considered complete only if it has its original packaging and all the units that came with it.

Ovaltine's offer of a "Little Orphan Annie" music sheet was one of the earliest radio premiums. Jack Armstrong, Lone Ranger, and Tom Mix premiums soon followed. By the middle of the 1930s every child eagerly awaited the phrase "Now, an important word from our sponsor," pad in hand,

ready to write down the address of the latest premium offer. Thousands of radio premiums were offered in the 1930s, 40s, and 50s.

Cereal manufacturers found that the simple fact that a premium was included in the box, even if it was unrelated to a specific radio or television show, was enough of an incentive to buy the product. Cereal premiums flourished in the post–1945 period. Although television premiums were offered, they never matched in numbers those offered over the radio.

The arrival of the fast food restaurant and eventual competition between chains led to the use of premiums to attract customers. Many premiums were tied in with television shows and movies. Although not a premium, fast food packaging has attracted the interest of collectors.

Not all premiums originated via radio, television, cereal boxes, or fast food chains. Local merchants used a variety of paper premiums to attract customers. A collection of paper pop guns would number in the hundreds of examples. Cracker Jack issued a number of paper premiums.

Few premiums contain a date. Fortunately, a number of reference books do exist to help establish the date when a premium was issued. Exact dating adds a 10% premium to value.

References: Ken Clee and Suzan Hufferd, *A Collector's Guide to Fast–Food Restaurant Kid's Meal Promotions (Other Than McDonald's)*, published by authors, 1991; Gary Henriques & Audre DuVall, *McCollecting: The Illustrated Price Guide to McDonald's Collectibles*, Piedmont Publishing, 1992; Tom Tumbusch, *Tomart's Price Guide to Radio Premiums and Cereal Box Collectibles*, Wallace–Homestead, 1991; Meredith Williams, *Tomart's Price Guide to McDonald Happy Meal Collectibles*, Tomart Publications, 1992.

Collectors' Clubs: Box Top Bonanza, 3403 46th Street, Moline, IL 61265; Flake, PO Box 481,

Cambridge, MA 02140; Free Inside, PO Box 178844, San Diego, CA 92117.

Periodical: *Collecting Tips Newsletter: Tips for Collecting McDonald's Restaurant Memorabilia,* PO Box 633, Joplin, MO 64802.

Album
  Photo
    Eddie Cantor, Chase & Sanborn, 1932 .... **5.00**
    Howdy Doody, Poll–Parrot Shoes **55.00**
    Stamp, Captain Midnight, 8 pgs, Skelly Oil, 1939 .... **20.00**
Big Little Book
  Buck Rogers in the 25th Century, Cocomalt, 1933 .... **40.00**
  Story of Skippy, Phillips Dental Magnesia, 1934 .... **40.00**
Blotter
  Donald Duck, Donald driving car, Sunoco, 1942 .... **12.00**
  Mickey Mouse, Mickey driving car, Sunoco, 1940 .... **15.00**
Book
  Bachelor's Children, 26 pgs, photos and stories, hard cov, 5 x 7¼", Old Dutch Cleanser, 1939 .... **15.00**
  Dick Daring, 68 pgs, magic tricks, Quaker Oats, 1933 .... **30.00**
  Kellogg's Funny Jungleland Book, 1932, movable flaps change faces on animals **12.00**
  Mother Goose, As Told by Kellogg's Singing Lady, 1932–34 .... **35.00**
  Tarzan of the Apes, Hal Foster artist, Sears, 1935 .... **25.00**
  They Got Me Covered, Bob Hope, Pepsodent, 1941, illus envelope ... **18.00**
Booklet
  Dari–Rich Chocolate Drinks, 24 pgs, 1938 .... **8.00**
  Death Valley Days, 15 pgs, Borax, 1934 .... **30.00**
  Dizzy Dean, *How to Pitch,* Post Cereal **12.00**
  Tom Mix, 8 pgs, illus, National Chicle Gum, 1934 .... **18.00**
Card Game, Bobby Benson, 32 cards, instruction book with 32 pgs, Hecker–H–O, 1934 .... **18.00**
Catalog
  Buck Rogers, Popsicle Pete Radio News Premiums, 1939–41 .... **35.00**
  Space Patrol.................... **80.00**
Certificate
  Counter–Spy Junior Agents Club, 6 x 8½", Pepsi–Cola, c1950 .... **25.00**
  Dick Tracy, used for pasting promotional stickers, Quaker Oats, 1938 **30.00**
  Junior Justice Society of America, membership.................. **30.00**
  Tom Corbett, Space Cadet, Space Academy, Kellogg's, 1953........ **35.00**

Christmas Card
  Captain Marvel, 1941 .... **30.00**
  Howdy Doody, Mars Candy, set **45.00**
Coloring Book, Howdy Doody, Poll–Parrot Shoes **50.00**
Comic Book, Lone Ranger, 16 pgs, Cheerios, 1954 .... **15.00**
Cookbook
  Aunt Jenny's Favorite Recipes, Spry .. **8.00**
  One Man's Family, Twentieth Anniversary Souvenir Cookbook, Standard, 1952.................... **20.00**
Decoder, Tom Corbett, Space Cadet, cardboard, Kellogg's **60.00**
Figure, Amos 'N Andy, Amos driving cab, Pepsodent, 1931 .... **18.00**
Gun, Cisco Kid, paper, Tip–Top Bread .. **18.00**
Gun and Helmet Set, Buck Rogers, paper, Cocomalt, 1933–35........... **225.00**
Handbook
  Space Patrol, *Space Patrol Handbook,* marked "For Official Use Only by Members of the Space Patrol"..... **80.00**
  The Secret Three, Three Minute Oats Cereal **35.00**
Hat, Howdy Doody, Wonder Bread **50.00**
Helmet, Buck Rogers, stiff paper, multicolored, Cocomalt, c1933 .... **175.00**
Iron–On Transfer, Captain Midnight's Secret Squadron, 4" d, orig envelope, Ovaltine, c9148 .... **110.00**
Manual
  Bobby Benson Code Book, 24 pgs, Hecker–H–O, 1935 .... **75.00**
  Buck Rogers, *Solar Scout Manual,* Cream of Wheat, 1935–36 .... **170.00**
  Captain Frank Hawks, Air Hawks, 1936–37 .... **18.00**
  Cisco Kid, cattle brands, 8 pgs, Tip–Top Bread, 1953 .... **75.00**

Ceresota Flour, coloring and story book, *The Adventures of Ceresota,* Marshall Whitlatch, Alice Sargent Johnson illus., pub. by Northwestern Consolidated Milling Co., color litho covers and illustrations, 44 pages, 8 x 6", 1912, $50.00.

Lone Wolf, 32 pgs, secret signs and signals, Wrigley Gum, 1932 ...... **100.00**

Melvin Purvis, *Law and Order Patrol Secret Operator's Manual,* 28 pgs, Post Toasties Corn Flake's, 1937 ... **40.00**

Orphan Annie, 12 pgs, secret signs and signals, Ovaltine, 1934 .... **40.00**

Secret Squadron, Captain Midnight, membership, 12 pgs, Ovaltine, 1940 .... **110.00**

Straight Arrow, *Secrets of Indian Lore and Know–How,,* Nabisco **30.00**

The Life of Tom Mix and the Ralston Straight Shooters Manual, Ralston, 1933 .... **50.00**

Map

Amos 'N Andy, aerial view of Weber City, Pepsodent, 1935 .... **30.00**

Captain Midnight, Chuck's Treasure Map, Skelly, 1939 .... **70.00**

Capt Silvers Sea Chart, 20 x 26″, Western Hemisphere, Blue Network Inc, Radio City, NY, 1942........... **25.00**

Renfrew of the Mounted, Map of Wonder Valley, Wonder Bread, 1936–40 .... **85.00**

Uncle Don, Terry, Ted, and Major Campbell, Bond Bread **50.00**

Mask

Ed Winn, Texaco, 1934........... **50.00**

Howdy Doody, Wheaties **15.00**

Lone Ranger, Wheaties, 1951–56.... **20.00**

Membership Card

Batman Club Card, movie serial **65.00**

Buck Rogers Rocket Rangers, 1944–50 .... **15.00**

Captain Battle Boy's Brigade, 1941–42 .... **60.00**

Captain Video **30.00**

Roy Rogers Riders Club, Post Cereal, 1952 .... **30.00**

Secretary Hawkins, oath on back, Ralston, 1932 .... **40.00**

Shield G–Man, Pep Comics, 1942 ... **60.00**

Skippy, Mystic Circle Club, Phillips Dental Magnesia, 1934 .... **25.00**

Spy Smasher, Victory Battalion Membership Card **35.00**

Paint By Number Set, Roy Rogers, Post Cereal, 1953–55 .... **50.00**

Photo

Amos 'N Andy, cast **15.00**

Buck Rogers and Wilma, Cocomalt, 1933–35 .... **55.00**

Captain Midnight, Skelly, 1939...... **25.00**

Chandu The Magician, Chandu wearing costume, Beech–Nut **50.00**

Dizzy Dean, 8 x 10″, Post Cereal..... **12.00**

Hopalong Cassidy, 8½ x 11″, color, Bond Bread, 1950–53 .... **15.00**

Jack Armstrong, Wheaties, 1934..... **18.00**

Jimmie Allen, Richfield Oil, 1934 .... **18.00**

Renfrew of the Mounted, Wonder Bread, 1936–40................ **8.00**

Rin Tin Tin, cast, Nabisco, 1954–56.. **15.00**

Roy Rogers, Roy and Trigger, color, Post Cereal, 1952............... **8.00**

Sgt Preston, 8½ x 11″, Quaker Cereal, 1949 .... **15.00**

Spy Smasher **35.00**

Post Card

Cisco Kid, Tip–Top **10.00**

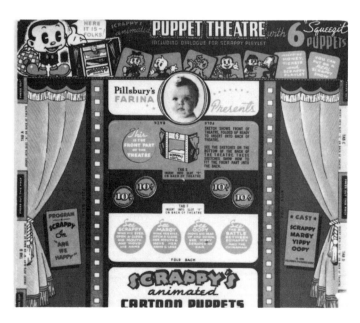

Pillsbury's Farina, Scrappy's Animated Cartoon Puppets, punch-out, 11 x 12″ closed, 1936, $115.00.

Roy Rogers, Quaker Oats Contest,
1948 . . . .   **10.00**
Poster
Hopalong Cassidy, Hoppy and Top-
per, Spunny Spread, 1950–53 . . . . .   **20.00**
Sgt Preston and King, contest winner,
Quaker Cereal, 1950 . . . .   **400.00**
Puppet, Super Circus, Mary Hartline and
Cliffy the Clown. **100.00**
Puzzle
Amos 'N Andy, 1931 . . . .   **50.00**
Death Valley Days, 20 Mule Team,
1933 . . . .   **18.00**
Orphan Annie, Tucker County Horse
Race, 9 x 12½", orig instruction
sheet and mailing box, Ovaltine,
c1933 . . . .   **70.00**
Ruler, Black Flame of the Amazon, card-
board, 10" l, Mayrose Meats **55.00**
Scrapbook, One Man's Family, Barbour
Family, Standard, 1946 . . . .   **10.00**
Sheet Music
Amos 'N Andy, *Check 'N Double
Check,* 1931 . . . .   **10.00**
Orphan Annie, Ovaltine, 1930 . . . . . .   **30.00**
Stationery, Buck Rogers, Flight Com-
mander, Cream of Wheat, 1935–36 . .   **60.00**
Transfer Book, Bobby Benson, H–O
Oats Company, 1932–35 . . . .   **55.00**

PROGRAMS

History: A program is a printed sheet, pamphlet,
or booklet, often with extensive explanatory notes
and advertising, for an entertainment or similar
performance. It usually contains the order of performance and the cast of characters. Programs
cover a wide range of events, from a high school
commencement to a sporting event.

Only a few programs are highly collectible.
Most have limited appeal, mementos for individuals whose names appear within or as a record of
a local or regional event. Typography collectors
acquire examples to document period typefaces
and layout.

Sports programs are the "hot" programs of the
1990s—all sports, not just baseball. Premium
programs are those associated with a major event
within the sport, e.g., an all star game or championship series. Value is localized. Programs sell
best in the city in which the team is located.

The 1980s and 90s also have seen renewed
interest in movie programs. Many 1930s, 40s, and
50s feature films included with their release a
program booklet that theater patrons could buy.
These often contained production photographs.

For whatever reason, theater patrons love to
save theater programs. *Playbill,* the popular program used by New York theaters, is an excellent
example. The market for theater programs is very

limited. Most university and private theater archives own a complete run. However, before discarding any collection you might encounter,
check for signatures. Theater programs were a
quick paper source for autograph seekers.

Always check the cover art of a program. A
number of famous illustrators, e.g., Maxfield Parrish, lent their talents to the design of program
covers. Most illustrations are unsigned, another
reason why it is important to learn an illustrator's
style.

Often the real value of the program rests with
the supplemental material printed inside. Printed
material can range from an institutional or business history to a summation of a speaker's remarks. Do not overlook the photographic illustrations. Since most programs contain the date of the
performance or event, the photographs become
important research documents.

References: Roderick A. Malloy, *Malloy's Sports
Collectibles Value Guide,* Wallace–Homestead,
1993; Richard De Thuin, *The Official Identification and Price Guide to Movie Memorabilia,*
House of Collectibles, 1990.

Periodicals: *Big Reel,* PO Box 83, Madison, NC
27025; *Movie Collector's World,* PO Box 309,
Fraser, MI 48026; *Nostalgia World,* PO Box 231,
North Haven, CT 06473.

Collectors' Club: Hollywood Studio Collectors
Club, 3960 Laurel Canyon Blvd., Suite 450, Studio City, CA 91604.

Amusement Park, Coney Island, Brighton
Theatre, 1913, 12 pgs, litho beach
scene on cov **45.00**
Circus
King Bros–Cristani, 1952 . . . .   **25.00**
Ringling Bros & Barnum & Bailey Cir-
cus, 1953 . . . .   **12.00**
Concert
An Evening With Procol Harem, 1973,
8 pgs, 8½ x 11" **25.00**
Jackson 5, 20 pgs, 10 x 13" **25.00**
The Doors, Saturday, May 11, 1967,
Cobo Arena, Detroit, MI, 4 pgs, 8½
x 11" **100.00**
The Who 1981, 24 glossy pgs, 9½ x
11½" **18.00**
Corporate Event
Annual Christmas Dinner, Bank of
California, Fairmont Hotel, Decem-
ber 15, 1927 . . . .   **8.00**
Consolidated Fireworks Co, employee
picnic, 1900 . . . .   **24.00**
Entertainment
Ed Sullivan & His Toast of the Town
Revue, 1955 . . . .   **15.00**
Johnny Mathis, c1970, color photos
on cover, 10 x 13" **10.00**
Movie
Ben Hur, MGM, 1926 . . . .   **30.00**

Gone With The Wind, 1939 . . . .   **95.00**
White Shadows in the South Seas,
    MGM, 1928 . . . .   **35.00**
Ocean Liner, Cunard Line, 1928 . . . . . .   **7.00**
Presentation
    Eastern States Horse Show, West
        Springfield, MA, 1963, Arthur
        Godfrey on horse Goldie photo, 92
        pgs **6.00**
    Ice Capades, 1949 . . . .   **20.00**
    Ice Follies, 1949, 16 pgs, 8 x 11″ **6.50**
    Mansfield Municipal Airport Dedica-
        tion and Sky Show, 1946, July 20–
        21, red, white, and blue cov **15.00**
    Miss America Pageant
        1943 . . . .   **18.00**
        1973 . . . .   **10.00**
    Royal Lipizzan Stallion Show, First
        National Tour, 1970 . . . .   **5.00**
    Tournament of Roses Parade, Pasa-
        dena, CA, 1962 . . . .   **8.00**
Sports
    Army–Navy 1955 Official Program,
        Philadelphia, November 26, 1955   **8.00**
    All–American Football Conference,
        Chicago Rockets vs. San Francisco
        Forty–Niners, 1946 . . . .   **75.00**
    Calumet All–Stars vs. Chicago Bears,
        1935 . . . .   **100.00**
    Chicago White Sox World Series,
        1959 . . . .   **125.00**
    First Annual College All–Stars vs. Chi-
        cago Bears Football Game, 1934 . . .   **200.00**
    George Washington Centennial Inau-
        gural, 1789–1889, engraved front
        cov, compliments "James H Hart
        Co, Brooklyn," 4 pgs **14.00**
    D W Griffith Presents the Colossal

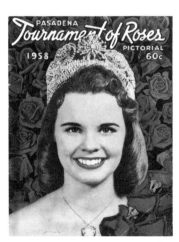

**Pasadena Tournament of Roses, black-
and-white and color photographs, 28
pages, 8¼ x 11″, 1958, $20.00.**

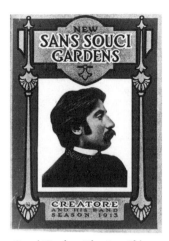

**Sans Souci Gardens Theatre, Chicago, 26
pages, 5¼ x 7½″, 1913, $6.50.**

Spectacle Intolerance, Lillian Gish,
    Constacle Talmadge **10.00**
Harlem Globetrotters, 1959 . . . .   **20.00**
Los Angeles Olympics, 1932, August
    4, 12 pgs, 8 x 11″ **35.00**
New York Giants Football Game, De-
    cember 19, 1943, Giants and
    Redskins **30.00**
Official Program Miami Beach Dog
    Racing, February 22, 1946 . . . .   **4.00**
New York Hippodrome Souvenir
    Book, Spring, 1914, Revival of Gil-
    bert and Sullivan masterpiece HMS
    Pinafore, sailing ships illus, 9 x 12″   **30.00**
Second Annual Armed Forces Benefit
    Game, Chicago Bears vs. Washing-
    ton Redskins **75.00**
US Olympic Team Weightlifting
    Trials, 1948, 24 pgs, 8 x 11″ **35.00**

PULP MAGAZINES

History: The pulp magazine was the direct de-
scendant of the dime novel and the ancestor of
the paperback book, coming into popularity in
the early twentieth century and lasting into the
early 1950s. The early pulps were dimensionally
a little smaller than the average magazine. They
derived their collective name from the fact that
they were printed on cheap, pulpwood paper.
Most had untrimmed edges.

Pulp magazines generally were aimed at a
male audience and devoted to so-called "cheap"
genres such as western, mystery, science fiction,
jungle adventure, sport, air war and combat,
horror, and girlie themes. "Nothing was too
cheap that could not be exploited," wrote the
early pulp writer Frank Gruber.

A main attraction of pulp magazines is some of the most lurid and colorful cover art ever produced. These covers were created to entice the buyer. Many are totally outrageous. The covers promised (and sometimes delivered) an interior filled with excitement, adventure, and enchantment.

Pulp magazines reached their peak of general public popularity in the 1930s, the "golden age" of this collectible in most collectors' eyes.

World War II paper shortages caused the demise of many titles and several publishers. The emergence of the popular mass market paperback a few years later finished the job. After early 1953, very few pulps existed in their original format. Those that did survive changed to a handier, digest–size format.

There was a considerable renewal of interest in the pulps in the 1960s. Some of the most popular characters, e.g., Doc Savage and The Shadow, were revived and reprinted in paperback form.

Pulp collections can be limited to certain themes or as unlimited and varied as a collector's interest. Many collectors specialize in certain titles (e.g., *Weird Tales*), certain genres (science fiction and horror being the most popular), special characters (Doc Savage, The Shadow, The Spider, Wu Fang, G-8, Tarzan, etc.), or special authors (H. P. Lovecraft, Robert E. Howard, Edgar Rice Burroughs, Dashiell Hammett, etc.).

A typical collecting problem for many novice collectors is the unknowledgeable dealer who, knowingly or unknowingly, prices common issues far above any retail price that could possibly be realized from a serious collector. Much of the overpricing results because the general dealer has no experience with pulps and their actual prices among collectors. New pulp collectors are advised to find an established pulp dealer early in their collecting career to avoid overpaying for the core portion of their collection.

References: Tony Goodstone, *The Pulps*, Chelsea House, 1980; Frank Gruber, *The Pulp Jungle*, Sherbourne Press, 1967; Kenneth Jones, *The Shudder Pulps*, FAX Collectors Editions, 1975; McKinstry and Weinberg, *The Hero Pulp Index*, Opar Press, 1971; Robert Sampson, *Yesterday's Faces: Glory Figures, Vol. 1*, Bowling Green University Press, 1983; Robert Sampson, *Yesterday's Faces: Strange Days, Vol. 2*, Bowling Green University Press, 1984; Lee Server, *Danger Is My Business: An Illustrated History of the Fabulous Pulp Magazines*, Chronicle Books, 1993; Don and Maggie Thompson, *The Official Price Guide To Science Fiction And Fantasy Collectibles, Third Edition*, House of Collectibles, 1989.

Periodicals: *Echoes*, 504 E Morris St, Seymour, TX 76380; *Golden Perils*, 5 Milliken Mills Road, Scarboro, ME 04074; *Pulp Review*, 4704 Colonel Elwell Court, Upper Marlboro, MD 20772. *Pulp Vault*, 6942 North Oleander Avenue, Chicago, IL 60631.

Museum: The Hess Collection of Popular Literature, University of Minnesota, Minneapolis, MN.

Ace High, March 3, 1937	**4.00**
Ace Sports Monthly, April, 1936, Vol 1, #4, Magazine Publishers Inc, 128 pgs	**15.00**
Action Stories, February, 1926	**3.50**
Air Stories, 1920s	**8.00**
All–Story Weekly, October 21, 1916 . . .	**10.00**
All Western, July, 1932	**4.00**
Amazing Vol 1, No 1, April, 1926	**30.00**
Vol 3, No 5, August, 1928, first Buck Rogers story	**40.00**
Amazing Detective, 1941	**3.00**
Amazing Stories, September, 1943, Ziff–Davis Publishing Co, 208 pgs, 7 x 10"	**30.00**
American Angler, Vol 1, No 1, October, 1881	**8.00**
American Horse Breeder, Christmas, 1902	**20.00**
American Rifleman, March, 1920	**10.00**
Argosy, August 22, 1936, part one of "Don Peon"	**5.00**
Astounding, March, 1930	**50.00**
Avenger, Vol 1, No 1, September, 1939	**8.50**
Aviation Novel Magazine, No 1, April, 1929	**18.00**
Avon Science Fiction and Fantasy Reader, Vol 1, No 1, January, 1953 . . .	**8.00**
Big Baseball Stories, November, 1948, Vol 1, #3, Interstate Publishing Corp, 96 pgs, 7 x 10"	**18.00**
Bill Barnes, c1935	**5.00**
Black Book Detective, June, 1938.	**10.00**
Black Mask, September, 1949.	**4.00**
Blue Book, August, 1916.	**12.00**
Blue Ribbon, July, 1937	**2.50**
Buffalo Bill Weekly, September, 1916 . .	**2.50**
Candid Confessions, Vol 1, No 1, 1937	**8.50**
Captain Future/Man of Tomorrow, 1944, Better Publications Inc, 130 pgs, 7 x 10".	**25.00**
Collegiate Wit, November, 1923, Edna Leedom, Ziegfield Follies	**10.00**
Complete War Novel, Vol 1, No 1, September, 1942.	**10.00**
Cosmos Science Fiction and Fantasy, Vol 1, No 1, September, 1943	**3.00**
Crack Detective, January, 1945	**5.00**
Crime Busters, January, 1931	**5.00**
Crime Confessions, Vol 1, No 1, 1939 . .	**7.50**
Crime File, Vol 1, No 1, 1936	**10.00**
Crime Suspense Stories, July, 1951	**20.00**
Dan Dunn, No 2, November, 1936	**27.00**
Dare–Devil, March, 1936, Popular Publications Inc, 112 pgs, 7 x 10"	**25.00**
Detective, Vol 1, No 1, 1941	**7.50**
Detective Book, No 1, April, 1930	**18.00**

.44 Western Magazine, **color covers, Popular Publication, Inc., Vol. 3, No. 1, 112 pages, 7 x 10", Nov-Dec 1938, $3.50.**

Detective Digest, Vol 1, No 1, 1937	6.50
Detective Fiction Weekly, August 3, 1940	6.00
Detective Novel, Spring, 1942	4.00
Detective Short Stories, November, 1942	4.50
Detective Story, June, 1946.	2.00
Detective Tales, January, 1936	8.00
Dime Detective, Vol 1, No 1, January 15, 1925	8.00
Dime Mystery, June, 1936, popular Publications, 128 pgs, 7 x 10"	50.00
Doc Savage	
April, 1936, Canadian edition.	10.00
July, 1936	20.00
Doctor Death, Vol 1, No 1, February, 1935	200.00
Double Action, January, 1937	2.50
Dynamic Science Fiction, Vol 1, No 1, December, 1952	8.00
Ellery Queen's Mystery, Vol 1, No 1, Fall, 1941	35.00
Exciting Western, May, 1947	4.00
Famous Detective Cases, Vol 1, No 1, 9135	7.50
Famous Fantastic Mysteries	
Vol 1, No 2, November, 1939	12.00
Vol 7, No 1, December, 1945	5.00
Famous Monsters of Filmland, No 2, 1958	40.00
Fantastic Adventures, Vol 1, No 1, September, 1939.	18.00
Fantastic Digest, Vol 1, No 1, Summer, 1952	6.00
Fantastic Novels, Vol 1, No 1, September, 1940.	12.00
Fantastic Story Quarterly, Summer, 1950	2.00
Fantastic Universe, April, 1956.	2.50

Fantasy, Vol 1, No 2, November, 1950. .	2.50
Fate, Vol 1, No 1, Spring, 1948	5.00
15 Mystery Stories, June, 1950	3.00
Flying Aces, November, 1932.	6.00
Foreign Legion Adventures, Vol 1, No 1, August, 1940.	30.00
Four Track News, September, 1896	4.00
Frontier Stories, Fall, 1946	5.00
Front Page Detective, 1940s	4.00
Future Science Fiction, #28, 1955, contains "Cornzan the Mighty"	2.00
Galaxy, Vol 1, No 1, 1950	4.00
G–Men Detective, January, 1940	6.00
Golden Fleece, Vol 1, No 1, October, 1938	12.00
Guilty Detective Story Magazine, March, 1960	1.25
Headline Detective, October, 1940	3.00
Horn's Railroad Gazette, June 7, 1849 . .	12.50
Hopalong Cassidy, Winter, 1951	25.00
Horror Stories, December, 1935, Popular Publications, 128 pgs, 7 x 10"	50.00
Ideal Love, March, 1948	1.00
Imagination, February, 1953.	2.00
Infinity, February, 1956.	1.25
Inside Detective, October, 1941	3.00
International Detective, November, 1888	20.00
Ka–Zar, Vol 1, No 2, January, 1937	35.00
Lone Ranger, Vol 1, No 1, April, 1937 . .	60.00
Love Affairs, December, 1928	3.00
Mammoth Mystery, June, 1947.	3.00
Marvel Science Stories, Vol 1, No 1, August, 1938	12.00
Masked Rider, May, 1945	3.50
Modern Romances, January, 1939	2.50
Mystery, Vol 1, No 1, March, 1943.	5.50
Mystery Book, Vol 9, No 2, Winter, 1950	2.00

Five-Novels Monthly, **color covers, Dell Publishing Co., Inc., #236485, 162 pages, 6½ x 9½", August 1938, $8.00.**

Mystery League, Ellery Queen, Vol 1, No
1, 1933 . . . .   **25.00**
National Police Gazette, October 1,
1887 . . . .   **6.00**
New Detective, Vol 19, No 2, 1953 . . . .   **2.00**
New Science Fiction Stories, Vol 1, No 1,
1953 . . . .   **4.00**
New Western, September, 1949 . . . .   **1.50**
Nick Carter, Vol 7, No 4, June, 1936 . . . .   **25.00**
Official Detective, July, 1938 . . . .   **1.25**
Old Sleuth Weekly, January, 1910 . . . . .   **5.00**
Operator 5, January–February, 1938 . . .   **20.00**
Other World, June, 1951 . . . .   **1.50**
Out of This World Adventures, Vol 1, No
2, December, 1950, Avon Periodicals
Inc, 130 pgs, 7 x 9¹/₂" **50.00**
Pete Rice, September, 1954 . . . .   **15.00**
Phantom Detective, November, 1939 . .   **6.50**
Photo Detective, Vol 1, No 1, 1937 . . . .   **5.00**
Picture Crimes, Vol 1, No 1, 1937 . . . . . .   **7.50**
Pioneer Western, #1, 1950 . . . .   **7.00**
Planet Stories, 1944, Love Romances
Publishing Co, 128 pgs, 7 x 10" **10.00**
Popular Radio, Vol 1, No 1, 1922 . . . . . .   **5.00**
Popular Western, April, 1947 . . . .   **1.50**
Private Detective Stories, October, 1944   **2.00**
Public Enemy, December, 1935 . . . .   **25.00**
Radio News, September, 1928 . . . .   **6.00**
Radio World, July, 1921 . . . .   **4.00**
Range Riders, Fall, 1940 . . . .   **3.50**
Real Love, September 15, 1930 . . . .   **3.50**
Real Police Story, Vol 1, No 1, 1937 . . . .   **9.00**
Real Western, December, 1936 . . . .   **4.00**
Red Star Mystery, June, 1940 . . . .   **30.00**
Rio Kid, August, 1942 . . . .   **6.50**
Rocket, Vol 1, No 1, April, 1953 . . . .   **5.00**
Saint Detective Magazine, September,
1957 . . . .   **2.50**

Weird Tales, **fantasy, horror, and super-
natural, printed multicolor covers, 96
pages, 6¹/₂ x 9³/₄", March 1950, $10.00.**

Science Fiction, Vol 1, No 1, 1939 . . . . .   **10.00**
Science Fiction Adventures, November,
1952 . . . .   **2.50**
Science Fiction Plus, March, 1953 . . . . .   **12.00**
Scientific Detective, Vol 1, No 1, Janu-
ary, 1930 . . . .   **20.00**
Secret Agent X, Vol 1, No 1, March, 1935   **18.50**
Secret Service Operator 5, Vol 1, No 1,
April, 1934 . . . .   **75.00**
Shock, Vol 1, No 1, March, 1948 . . . . . .   **6.50**
Short Wave & Television, January, 1938   **4.00**
Six Gun, Vol 1, No 1, December, 1937,
missing two pgs **2.00**
Sky Aces, 1928–41 . . . .   **6.00**
Sky Birds, December, 1929 . . . .   **5.00**
Sky Fighters, September, 1932 . . . .   **15.00**
Smashing Detective, February, 1950 . . .   **3.00**
Smashing Novels, Vol 1, No 4, Decem-
ber, 1936 . . . .   **2.50**
Space Science Fiction, August, 1952 . . .   **1.00**
Spaceway, December, 1953 . . . .   **3.50**
Sparkling Love Stories, #1, 1950 . . . . . .   **7.00**
Speed Mystery, February, 1933 . . . .   **25.00**
Spicy Adventure Stories, June, 1935,
Culture Publications, 128 pgs, 7 x 10"   **50.00**
Spicy Detective Stories, December,
1934, Culture Publications, 128 pgs, 7
x 10" **50.00**
Startling Stories
November, 1939 . . . .   **4.00**
Summer, 1945 . . . .   **2.50**
Vol 1, No 1, January, 1939 . . . .   **15.00**
Star Western, October, 1934 . . . .   **3.75**
Stirring Science, Vol 1, No 1, February,
1941 . . . .   **40.00**
Strange Tales, Vol 1, No 3, January, 1932   **22.00**
Super Detective, December, 1949 . . . . .   **1.50**
Super Science Fiction, April, 1957 . . . . .   **2.50**
Super Science Stories, April, 1944 . . . . .   **1.75**
Suspense, February, 1951 . . . .   **4.00**
Sweetheart, January, 24, 1928 . . . .   **2.00**
Tailspin Tommy, Vol 1, No 1, October,
1936 . . . .   **38.00**
Ten Detective Aces, May, 1949, Ace Pe-
riodicals, 96 pgs, 7 x 10" **20.00**
Ten Story Fantasy, #1, 1951 . . . .   **10.00**
Ten Story Mystery, Vol 1, No 1, Decem-
ber, 1942 . . . .   **5.00**
The Avenger, January, 1942, Street &
Smith Publications, 114 pgs, 6¹/₂ x
9¹/₄" **18.00**
The Lone Eagle/Fighting Ace, August,
1940, Better Publications, 112 pgs, 7 x
10" **20.00**
The Shadow, December, 1943 . . . .   **8.00**
The Spider, October, 1941, Popular Pub-
lications, 112 pgs, 7 x 10" **70.00**
Thrilling Adventures, August, 1936 . . . .   **5.00**
Thrilling Detective, June, 1946 . . . .   **2.50**
Thrilling Western, October, 1948 . . . . . .   **1.50**
Thrilling Wonder Stories, June, 1942 . . .   **3.00**
Triple Detective, Summer, 1948 . . . .   **3.00**

Triple X, October, 1932	**4.00**
True Confessions, November, 1938	**1.25**
Undercover Detective, Vol 1, No 1, December, 1938	**12.00**
Unknown Worlds, Vol 6, No 5, February, 1943	**18.00**
War Birds, September, 1935	**10.00**
Weird Tales, July, 1935	**30.00**
Western Aces, November, 1938	**1.75**
Western Action, August, 1938	**2.50**
Western Novel & Short Story, February, 1946	**4.00**
Western Short Stories, Vol 2, No 2, September, 1938	**4.00**
Western Trails, June, 1937	**3.50**
Western Yarns, Vol 1, No 2, March, 1938	**4.50**
Wonder Story Annual, #1, 1950	**4.00**
Worlds Beyond, December, 1950	**4.00**

PUNCHBOARDS

History: Punchboards are self-contained games of chance made of pressed paper containing holes with coded tickets inside each hole. For an agreed amount, the player uses a "punch" to extract the ticket of his or her choice. Prizes are awarded to the winning ticket. Punch prices can be 1¢, 2¢, 3¢, 5¢, 10¢, 20¢, 50¢, $1.00 or more.

Not all tickets were numbered. Fruit symbols were used extensively as well as animals. Some punchboards had no printing at all, just colored tickets. Other ticket themes included dice, cards, dominoes, words, etc. One early board had Mack Sennet bathing beauties.

Punchboards come in an endless variety of styles. Names reflected the themes of the boards. Barrel of Winners, Break the Bank, Baseball, More Smokes, Lucky Lulu and Take It Off were just a few.

At first punchboards were used to award cash. As legal attempts to outlaw gambling arose, prizes were switched to candy, cigars, cigarettes, jewelry, radios, clocks, cameras, sporting goods, toys, beer, chocolate, etc.

The golden age of punchboards was the 1920s to the 1950s. Attention was focused on the keyed punchboard in the film "The Flim Flam Man." This negative publicity hurt the punchboard industry.

Punchboards which are unpunched are collectible. A punched board has little value unless it is an extremely rare design. Like most advertising items, price is determined by graphics, illustrator, and subject matter.

The majority of punchboards sell in the $10.00 to $40.00 range. The high end of the range is represented by boards such as Golden Gate Bridge at $85.00 and Baseball Classic at $100.00.

Museum: Amusement Sales, 390 "K" Street, Salt Lake City, UT 84103.

Baseball Bucks, round, 10"	**15.00**
Bell Pots, slot symbols, $1.00 punch. . . .	**30.00**
Big Bills, 25¢ punch	**18.00**
Big Game, fruit symbols	**10.00**
Block Buster, double jackpot, cash payout, 5¢ per punch	**18.00**
California or Bust, 11 x 12"	**25.00**
Canasta, 5¢ punch, removable score card	**50.00**
Charlie Ten Spots	**10.00**
Chocolate Cherries, 12 x 13".	**10.00**
Cross Country Winner, seals, cash pay . .	**20.00**
Delicious Cherries.	**10.00**
Dime Joe, cash pay, 10¢ punch	**15.00**
Dixie Queen Cigarettes, ten color tickets	**8.00**
Dollar Game, cash board	**5.00**
Forty Sawbucks, counter insert	**25.00**
Full of Tens, cash pay, 25¢ per punch. . .	**15.00**
Gas with a Punch, old pump and car . . .	**15.00**
Glades Chocolates, set of 3	**25.00**
Good As Gold, colorful, seals	**20.00**
Hearts Desire, heart shape, 10 x 10"	**25.00**
Hi Yo Silver, cash board, 25¢ per punch	**15.00**
Hit a Buck	**6.00**
Joe's Special Prize, cash board with name, 25¢ per punch	**18.00**
Junior Kitty, kitten picture, cash pay	**30.00**
Lucky Coins, 12½ x 18"	**20.00**
Lulu Belle	**8.00**

**Card, Ole Man Santa Claus, cardboard, single sheet, red and black, 5 x 6¼",
$7.50.**

Knee High, cash girlie board	**15.00**
Musical Cigarettes.	**12.00**
National Winner	**20.00**
Nickel Fins, 1,000 holes with seals	**15.00**
Odd Pennies Cigarettes.	**15.00**
Off We Go!, 5¢, play for packs of cigarettes, 10 x 12½"	**15.00**
Pass–Hit & Crap, dice tickets, 50¢ punch	**25.00**
Pep and Beauty, 2¢, green, 10 x 9½" . . .	**15.00**
Pick a Cherry, cash pay, cherry seals. . . .	**20.00**
Planters Peanuts, 5¢ punch, peanut logo	**30.00**
Prize Pots, red head girl, 50¢ punch	**65.00**
Put and Take, candy bars.	**10.00**
Section Play, 25¢ cash board	**10.00**
Shirley Temple, Miss Charming doll, unused.	**10.00**
Six Fine Prizes, fruit symbols and seals . .	**15.00**
Spend Your Pennies Here, 2¢ a Chance to Receive Cigarettes, c1920, 14 x 7½"	**30.00**
Sports Push Cards, baseball, football, basketball	**5.00**
Sunshine Special	**15.00**
Take It Easy, colorful, nude	**50.00**
Ten Big Sawbucks, 20¢ cash board.	**20.00**
Tip Top Charley.	**15.00**
Turkey Dinners, turkey illus, 10 x 12" . . .	**15.00**
Win a Buck	**5.00**
Worth Going For, 50¢ punch, girlie board	**20.00**
Yankee Trader	**20.00**
Your Pick, money seals, 10¢ per punch	**30.00**

PUZZLES, JIGSAW

History: The jigsaw puzzle originated in the mid–18th century in Europe. John Silsbury, a London map maker, was selling dissected map jigsaw puzzles by the early 1760s. The first jigsaw puzzles in America were English and European imports and aimed primarily at children.

Prior to the Civil War, several manufacturers, e.g., Samuel L. Hill, W. and S. B. Ives, and McLoughlin Brothers, included puzzle offerings as part of their line. However, it was the post–Civil War period that saw the jigsaw puzzle gain a strong foothold among the children of America.

In the late 1890s and first decade of the twentieth century, puzzles designed specifically for adults first appeared. Both forms have existed side by side ever since. Adult puzzlers were responsible for two twentieth century puzzle crazes: 1908–09 and 1932–33.

Prior to the mid–1920s the vast majority of jigsaw puzzles were cut using wood for the adult market and composition material for the children's market. In the 1920s the diecut, cardboard jigsaw puzzle evolved. By the time of the puzzle craze of 1932–33, it was the dominant puzzle medium.

Jigsaw puzzle interest has cycled between peaks and valleys several times since 1933. Mini–revivals occurred during World War II and in the mid–1960s when Springbok entered the American market.

Puzzles are often difficult to date. Anne Williams' *Jigsaw Puzzles: An Illustrated History and Price Guide* is an extremely helpful source. Some puzzles, such as Milton Bradley's Smashed Up Locomotive, were produced for decades. The most popular prints were kept in inventory or reproduced as needed, often by several different manufacturers. Thus, the date when a puzzle was made is often years later than the date or copyright on the print or box. Avoid puzzles whose manufacturer cannot be determined, unless the puzzle has especially attractive graphics or craftsmanship.

The number of jigsaw puzzle collectors has grown dramatically in the past decade. Current collectors appear to be concentrating their efforts on wooden and die–cut, cardboard puzzles made before 1945, a few specialty areas, e.g., advertising and World War II, and turn of the century juvenile puzzles. Die–cut cardboard puzzles in excess of five hundred pieces remain primarily garage sale items. However, some collector interest exists for early Springbok puzzles.

References: Linda Hannas, *The Jigsaw Book*, Dial Press, 1981; Harry L. Rinker, *Collector's Guide To Toys, Games and Puzzles*, Wallace–Homestead, 1991; Francene and Louis Sabin, *The One, The Only, The Original Jigsaw Puzzle Book*, Henry Regnery Co., 1977; Anne D. Williams, *Jigsaw Puzzles: An Illustrated History and Price Guide*, Wallace–Homestead, 1990.

Collectors' Club: American Game Collectors Association, 49 Brooks Avenue, Lewiston, ME 04240.

Value Notes: Prices are for puzzles whose surface is free of dirt and blemishes, have their original box, and *NO* missing pieces. Since most collectors buy puzzles to assemble and for their surface image, even one piece missing greatly reduces value. One missing piece lowers value up to 50%; three or more missing pieces means the puzzle is a junker. A missing box lowers value 25%.

The only way condition can be determined is to see the puzzle assembled. Collectors have learned that this is the only way to trust most dealers when they say the puzzle is complete. An unassembled puzzle with no guarantee of completeness is valued between 5% and 15% of a ''complete'' puzzle's price.

Twentieth century die–cut cardboard puzzles from the post–1930 period are plentiful. Those with nondescript scenes, e.g., birch trees, cottage in the woods, etc., are valued complete in the $1.00 to $5.00 range.

Handcut wooden puzzles for adults normally sell in the 10¢ to 15¢ per piece range. Price depends on subject matter, number of pieces, and quality of cut. Par and other custom cut and designed puzzles are sold at a premium.

Note: When known, the name of the artist or puzzle illustrator appears in bold face.

WOOD

Artist or Illustrator Identified

A–1 Puzzle Club, Impressionist Landscape by **August Renoir** (untitled, 1882 painting), woman strolling along road of tree–shaded landscape, 24 x 20", 600 pcs, c1910 .... 65.00

Bliss, R. W., Wallaston, MA, The Arab Raiding Party, **A. D. Schreyer** print of armed horsemen riding at dusk, 12 x 9", 153 pcs, black and orange box, early twentieth C 25.00

Milton Bradley Co., Premier Jigsaw Puzzles, 500 pcs, Why the Guests Were Late, country scene of snowbound coach being rescued, **Talbert Wright**, 19 x 12", 37 figural pcs, original box .. 50.00

Fretts, Alden L., The Yankee Cut–ups, Home Memories, English thatched roof cottage and garden scene, **Thompson**, 23 x 16", 676 pcs, 24 figural pcs, c1930s 45.00

Gleason, H. A., Cheerio Jig Saw Puzzles, Mine's the Largest, 1940s style pin–up girl with ten gallon hat, **Holt Armstrong**, 16 x 12", 326 pcs, 7 figural pcs, original box 45.00

Hanks Puzzle Shop, Conway, NH, A Colonial Sweetheart, portrait of Dutch colonial woman with vase of flowers, **J. Van Vredand**, 16 x 20", 538 pcs, original box 50.00

Houser, Glad, The Rug Merchant, Near Eastern woman displaying rug to elderly gentleman buyer, **Balesio Roman Tivol**, 8 x 6", 100 pcs, original box, c1920 .... 18.00

Kingsbridge by Atlantic, The Arrival (A Hunting Morn), hunters pause in Tudor town, **L. Cury Cox**, 15 x 11", 400 pcs, original box, 1960s 20.00

Leisure Hour Puzzle Co., Paul Revere's Ride, F. M. Stone, 16 x 19", 589 pcs, original box 50.00

Miller's Pharmacy, cut for Fessenden's Library, Venetian Revelers, harbor scene at sunset, **Moran**, 13 x 10", 251 pcs, c1930s 30.00

Parker Brothers, Pastime Picture Puzzle, 183 pcs, Master of the House, **H. M. Brett**, portrait of family with infant at table, 13 x 9", 19 figural pcs, c1920s .. 25.00

Just Plain Bill, Kolynos Dental Cream giveaway, radio premium, 150 pcs., orig. envelope, 12 x 9", $30.00.

Shenandoah Community Workers (Virginia), Audubon Bird Picture Puzzles, set of 3: Chickadee (**Allen Brooks**), Scarlet Tanager (**R. Bruce Hersfall**), and Belted Kingfisher (**R. Bruce Hersfall**), each print shows male and female of species and is encased in its own tray, each puzzle 6 x 8", approx 30 pcs per puzzle, late 1930s, original box 45.00

Straus, Joseph K.
282 pcs, White Clipper, three–masted square rigger under full sail, 16 x 12", **D. Sherring**, original box, 1940s....................... 20.00

482 pcs, Guardians of Liberty, World War II scene of battleship and planes passing Statue of Liberty, **T. J. Slaughter**, 16 x 20", original box, mid–1940s 25.00

Unknown Cutter
80 pcs, The Birth of Our Country, Ben Franklin, colonial hearthside scene, **Hy Hintermeister**, 13 x 9", c1920 .. 20.00

200 pieces, Old Glory Forever, John Van Arsdale's exploit at Fort George, November 25, 1783, **Clyde G. DeLand**, 14 x 10" 25.00

Victory Artistic Wood Jigsaw Puzzle, English, 500 pcs, Calvi, Mediterranean harbor scene, **M. Buzle**, 20″ x 15″, original box **35.00**

West, W. Frank, Newport, RI, Picture Puzzles, In a Japanese Store, 1920s print of two American women perusing wares at Japanese bazaar, **Ethel Pennewill Brown**, 11 x 9″, 130 pcs, original box, c1930s **25.00**

Artist or Illustrator Unknown

Milton Bradley Co., Premier Jigsaw Puzzles, 168 pcs, Port of Heart's Desire, 1920s kneeling mother holding daughter, 8 x 10″, original box **20.00**

Glencraft/Glendex, Fishing Pier, harbor scene of New England fishing boats, 22 x 15″, 720 pcs, c1960s **35.00**

Hassett, Waman S., Pine Tree Puzzle, In Old Kentucky, Daniel Boone–style deerslayer sighting his prey, 12 x 16″, 410 pcs, original box **30.00**

Hodges, William, Mt. Desert, ME, Acadia National Park, photograph of ocean surf on rocky Maine coast, 11 x 8″, 334 pcs, original box, c1970s **20.00**

Macy's Jigsaw Puzzle, On a Canal in Venice, canal boat at sunset in Venice, 10 x 12″, 253 pcs, wooden slice–top box, 1930s. **30.00**

Madmar, Interlox Puzzle, Spoils of War, Prussian officers enjoying leisurely evening of music and relaxation in European parlor, 20 x 16″, 755 pcs, original box. **50.00**

Parker Brothers, Pastime Picture Puzzle
  200 pcs, Chess Players, drawing room scene of gentlemen at game table, 14″ x 10″, 17 figural pcs, original box, late 1930s **25.00**
  350 pcs, A Shady Pathway, lake country scene with shepherd and sheep, 17 x 11″, 36 figural pcs, original box, dated March 28, 1931 . . . .   **30.00**
  482 pcs, Coolidge's Birthplace, misty landscape of President's farm amidst fields and mountains, 21 x 16″, 48 figural pcs, original box, dated January 28, 1932. . . . .   **55.00**
  523 pcs, Landscape with Mountains (untitled), American western scene of fertile valley with sandstone butts and snow–capped mountains in background, 23 x 16″, 60 figural pcs, c1930s **45.00**

Picture Puzzle Exchange, Boston, The First Note of the Bell, colonial Philadelphia scene of christening of Liberty Bell, 14 x 10″, 196 pcs, original box, 1916 . . . .   **30.00**

Pixie Picture Puzzle, Melrose, MA, Halting at the Inn, huntsmen enjoying

quaff outside Tudor Tavern, 10 x 8″, 175 pcs, original box **25.00**

Tuck's Famous Zig–Zag Picture Puzzle, English, The Band of the Household Cavalry Passing the King at Buckingham Palace, 13 x 9″, 150 pcs, 17 figural pcs, original box **25.00**

Unknown cutters
  64 pcs, Wing and Wing (untitled), lead sloop sailing with the wind, 9 x 10″, c1940s. **15.00**
  101 pcs, The Heart of Nature, landscape scene of stream coursing through mountainous countryside, 7 x 9″, dated March 12, 1933 . . . .   **20.00**
  300 pcs, Dined Well But Not Wisely, English, Pears' print of English "diners" discovering a buddy who has had one too many, 12 x 18″, c1910   **45.00**
  323 pcs, My Little Girl, elderly host introducing marriageable–age daughter to young huntsman, 14 x 10″. **30.00**
  495 pcs, Sulgrave Manor, The Ancestral Home of George Washington, 20 x 16″ **40.00**

CARDBOARD

Advertising

Burgess Battery Co., "Sparkalong Burgess," young cowboy jumps wooden fence riding animal that is part horse and part zebra, $5^7/_8$ x 4″, glassine envelope rubber stamped with distributor   **15.00**

Campfire or Angelus Marshmallows, No. 1 in series of four, "Fishing Boats," boats tied up at wharf, 48 pcs, $9^3/_4$ x $6^3/_4$″, paper envelope **10.00**

Chase & Sanborn, Chase & Sanborn's Puzzle Picture, Picking Coffee Berries, one of series of four, 63 pcs, 8 x 6″, cardboard box, $3^1/_4$ x $2^1/_2$ x 1″, c1910   **20.00**

Chevrolet, boxed set of 2 puzzles, "Superior Chevrolet Utility Coupe" and "Superior Chevrolet 5 Passenger Touring," 12 pcs each puzzle, each puzzle $6^1/_2$ x $4^1/_2$″, box with picture of Superior Chevrolet 5–Passenger Sedan, 1923–24 . . . .   **150.00**

Cocomalt, R. B. Davis Co., "The Windmill Jig–Saw Puzzle", windmill and harbor at low tide, 65 pcs, 10 x $6^1/_2$″, paper envelope **10.00**

College Inn Food Products Co., Hotel Sherman, Chicago, No. 1 of series of four, At Anchor, two–masted sailing ships moored beside each other in harbor, paper envelope, $7^1/_8$ x $9^1/_2$″, early 1933 . . . .   **15.00**

Curtis Candy Company, "Singing in the Rain" Jig Saw Puzzle, double sided, front shows boy and girl under umbrella, reverse shows one cent candies produced by Curtis, 5⅝ x 7½", paper envelope **25.00**

Dearborn Truck Company, Chicago, IL, "For Every Job the Dearborn Truck," shows stake body truck, 30 pieces, 10½" x 7", paper envelope **45.00**

Dunlop Tire & Rubber Corporation, Dunlop Circular Picture Puzzle, approx. 600 pcs, outer border is Dunlop tire, center is picture looking up through the hole on a tee at group of golfers, one of which is removing Dunlop golf ball from hole, 19" d, cardboard box, 10½ x 7½ x 1½", c1970 . .   **30.00**

Goodrich Tire, Akron, OH, The Goodrich Silver Fleet at Niagara Falls, approx. 50 pcs, 9¾ x 7½", paper envelope, 10 x 8", no adv on envelope except Stock No. 4091–GT **30.00**

Green Spring Dairy, Baltimore, MD, shows processing machinery in dairy, 10¾ x 9", envelope missing **20.00**

Greyhound Jig Saw Puzzle Cartoon Map of the United States, over 300 pcs, 250 four color illus on map plus historical data, 20 x 13½", cardboard box, 8½ x 6¼ x 1½" **25.00**

Heinz 57 Varieties, shows children playing store with all 57 products displayed on shelf, 10⅛ x 12", paper envelope **35.00**

International Salt Co., A Family Reunion, approx. 125 pcs, central figure of young boy holding puppy, puppy's mother in front of dog house on left, **Alfred Gulloy**, 12 x 9", paper envelope, 12⅜ x 9½", c1933 . . . .   **15.00**

Jack and Jill Jell, Special Offer, 5 Boxes of Jack & Jill Jell and a 100 piece The Fisher Bros. Co. Picture Puzzle, No. 17, "Modern Beauty," two 1930s beauties, 10¼ x 8", paper envelope . .   **15.00**

Lambert Pharmacal Co., Listerine, three children in bathroom gargling with Listerine, dog taking part, **Frances, Tipton Hunter**, 13¾ x 10¾", paper envelope, premium from radio show Phillips Lord, The Country Doctor. . . .   **30.00**

McKesson & Robbins, McKesson's "Our Gang" Jig–Saw Puzzle, drugstore and soda fountain scene, chamfered corners, 14 x 10¾", paper envelope with guide picture, 11 x 14". **85.00**

R. J. Mrizek Co., makers of Mrizek's Bohemian Rye Bread, Chicago, "Washington's Childhood Home," 7 x 8⅝", paper envelope **15.00**

Pacific Coast Borax Co., "Hauling 20 Mule Team Borax Out Of Death Valley," 20 mule head figural pieces,

10¾ x 8¼", 1933, paper envelope with newsprint cartoon insert **30.00**

Penick & Ford, Vermont Maid Syrup, 2 Jig–saw Puzzles, "Home" and "Ready For The Pasture," 49 pcs per puzzle, each puzzle 7⅜ x 9¼", green letter on paper envelope, envelope notes "New Series" **17.50**

Pennzoil, winter scene of snowball fight behind freezing snowman, 16 pcs, line cut, 5¾ x 8", paper envelope. **15.00**

Phillips Petroleum Company, double sided puzzle, Alaska and Hawaii, central map of each state surrounded by scenes from state, 15 x 11", 1973, can   **10.00**

Plee–Zing Palm Oil Soap, Free Jig–Saw Puzzle with 4 Bars, ocean liner entering New York harbor, 9⅞ x 7¾", paper envelope **20.00**

RCA Victor, "All that the Victrola gives to others it will give to you," seated couple in front of record player surrounded by miniature musicians, folk singers, and opera singers, RCA logo in lower right, 8⅞ x 8", dated 1932, paper envelope **75.00**

Richfield Golden Gasoline/Richlube Motor Oil, "Goofy Golf" Jig–Saw Puzzle, No. 2 in a series of six, "In Hawaii– And How!," 49 pcs, 7 x 9", paper envelope, front of envelope contains golf lesson by Alex Morrison **25.00**

C. F. Sauer Co., Richmond, VA, Sauer's Vanilla and Duke's Home Made Mayonnaise, Sauer's Gardens, colored picture of garden setting, blue border, 8 x 10¼", paper envelope, 8½ x 10½", c1933 . . . .   **20.00**

Shultz's Pretzels, Hanover, PA, winter scene featuring stone arch bridge, adv. information printed on puzzle, 3 x 6", paper envelope **10.00**

Standard Oil Company of Ohio, Radio Jig Saw Puzzle, No. 3, A Bully Time in Spain, 252 pcs, double sided, obverse shows Lena fighting bull in Spanish bullring, reverse with head and shoulder portrait of Gene and Glenn, 14½ x 11", advertising sheet with guide picture, cardboard box, 6¾ x 8¼", c1933   **15.00**

Swift & Company, "Milking Time at a Brookfield Dairy Farm," central scene of dancing cows above information oval on "Brooksie" the famous white cow and her pals, pieces within puzzle spell out "SWIFT & CO.," 12 x 12", box **45.00**

Sunshine Lone Star Sugar Wafers, child pushing wheelbarrow filled with children, 40 pcs, 9¼ x 7", **Twelvetrees**, 1932, paper envelope with guide picture **25.00**

John Wanamaker, New York, 40 pcs, double sided, obverse shows **E. J. Meeker** etching of Grace Church and Wanamaker's New York City store, reverse is twenty-five line description of Wanamaker's store entitled "THE GREAT STORES OF THE WORLD," orig packaging missing, c1933 ...... 65.00

Wausau Insurance Company, The Famous Wausau Depot, unopened can measuring 4" d and 5⁷/₁₆" h, guide picture on can..................... 15.00

Weinberger's Cut Rate Drugs, Co-Operation, 15 pcs, baking scene of young Dutch boy and girl in kitchen, 3¹/₄ x 4³/₄, paper envelope labeled "WEINBERGER'S Gift Picture Puzzle for Boys and Girls," c1933 .... 25.00

Adult

Depression Era Jigsaw Craze, 1932–33
American News Company, Miss America Puzzle Series, No. 4 of four known, "In Blossom Time," over 300 pcs, 13¹/₄ x 10", 1933 .... 12.00

Einson–Freeman
Every Week Jig–Saw Puzzle Series No. 17, "Abraham Lincoln," **Ray Morgan**, 10⁵/₈ x 14¹/₂", box 17.50
"Mystery–Jig" Puzzle, No. 2 in series of four, "By Whose Hand," approx. 300 pcs, 19⁷/₈ x 14", booklet enclosed, 1933 cardboard box................... 25.00

Movie Cut–Ups, Peabody, MA, Movie Cut–Up No. 7, "Bitter Tea of General Yen," over 225 pcs, 9⁷/₈ x 13¹/₈", box 30.00

University Distributing Company, Jig of the Week Puzzle, No. 23, "Hunters," 13¹/₈ x 10¹/₈, insert, box...... 12.00

Viking Manufacturing Company, Picture Puzzle Weekly
Series A–4, "Lions at Sunset", 13⁷/₈" x 10", box................... 12.00
Series D–1, "The Olde Kentucky Home", Blacks surround banjo player, white woman listens in background, 14¹/₂ x 10⁵/₈", box .. 20.00

1930s
Ballyhoo Magazine, Ballyhoo, "No Nudes is Bad Nudes," 333 pcs, 10¹/₂ x 15¹/₂", 1930s, cardboard box 30.00

Milton Bradley, The Dover Jig Picture Puzzle, No. 4728, "The Circus," over 300 pcs, 1930s, guide picture on box 10.00

Piccadilly Jig Picture Puzzle, No. 81, "On the Loire," over 200 pcs, 1930s, box with blue and white ground 5.00

J. R. Brundage, Empire Jig Picture Puzzle, "A Canadian Landscape," over 400 pcs, box features sketch of Empire State building........... 4.00

Consolidated Paper Box
Big Star, No. 1010, "School Patrol," over 250 pcs, approx 10 x 13¹/₂", late 1930s, guide picture on blue tone box................... 3.00
Big 10 Perfect Picture Puzzle, No. 1010, "Millstream in Winter," over 250 pcs, approx 13¹/₂ x 10", late 1930s, box.............. 2.00
Perfect Picture Puzzle, No. 25, "Dawn's Early Light No. 305," over 375 pcs, approx 15¹/₂ x 19¹/₂", small guide picture on box with puzzle pieces theme, orange ground 5.00
Perfect Picture Puzzle, No. 2016, "No. 211 Cool and Silence," over 450 pcs, small guide picture on box...................... 3.00

E. E. Fairchild Corporation, No. 647, Finesse Picture Puzzle, "Gypsy Love Call," over 250 pcs, approx 11 x 14", guide picture on box 5.00

Gebhart Folding Box Co., Dayton, OH, Wonder Picture Puzzle, "The Cascade," over 300 pcs, box...... 4.00

Harter Publishing Company, Cleveland, OH, No. H–131, Series III, No. 4, "Fishin' and Wishin'," over 200 pcs, approx 15 x 11", green tone box..................... 3.00

Lutz & Sheinkman, Merry Mood Jig Saw (Type) Puzzle, "After the Hunt," **R. Jlinek**, over 400 pcs, approx 18¹/₂ x 14¹/₂", box measures 4³/₈ x 10³/₈ x 2³/₈" 12.00

Oxford Specialty Co., Boston, MA, "Budge:Sports," diecut cardboard, 17 x 17", cardboard box contains instructions for four players to race to assemble their quarters first 22.50

Regent Specialties, Inc., De Luxe Picture Puzzle, "Snow Capped Peaks," approx 400 pieces, approx 20 x 16", 1930s, box measures 4³/₄ x 9³/₄ x 2¹/₂" 10.00

The Reynolds & Reynolds Co., Dayton, OH, The American Individual Picture Puzzle, "19B A Bit of French Tapestry," over 350 pcs, orange tone box..................... 4.00

A. Schoenhut Co., Philadelphia, PA, "Schoenhut" Picture Puzzle, "Let's Go," over 200 pcs, 10 x 22", box... 15.00

Simkins Paper Box Mfg. Co., Philadelphia, PA, Simco Jig Puzzle, "The Landing," over 300 pieces, approx 16 x 12", box marked "Par 4 Hours" 5.00

Tichnor Brothers, Inc., Cambridge, MA, See American First, No. 39, "Natural Bridge, Va.," over 300 pcs, box **8.00**

Upson Company, Tuco Picture Puzzle "Quietude," over 200 pcs, approx 16 x 12", gold stripes on red ground box **4.00**

"The Last Roundup," over 300 pcs, approx 20 x 16", horizontal maroon bands across box lid, guide picture covers approx one–half lid **6.00**

Whitman Publishing Co., Guild Picture Puzzle, No. 2900, Series RR, "Millpond," 304 pcs, approx 18 x 15½", guide picture on box **2.00**

Post 1940

Consolidated Paper Box

Perfect Picture Puzzle, "Mountain Warfare," over 375 pcs, approx 19½ x 15½", c1943, eight stars on box **15.00**

Perfect Picture Puzzle, No. 250–29, "Proof Positive," boy photographing dog holding fishing float, over 375 pcs, approx 19½ x 15½", c1950s **3.00**

Dell Publishing Co., All–American Picture Puzzle, No. 2, "Wings in the Night", aerial combat over enemy harbor, approx 280 pieces, 1942, guide picture on box **17.50**

Janus Games, Inc., The Janus Mystery Jigsaw Puzzle, No. 1 of four, "The Case of the Snoring Skinflint" by Henry Slesar, over 500 pcs, approx 22 x 15", 1973, story on back of cardboard box **12.00**

Jaymar Specialty Company, Hobby Jig Saws, "Grizzly Bear," over 300 pcs, approx 14 x 22", small guide picture on box, green ground in treasure chest motif **5.00**

J. Pressman & Co., Inc., Victory Picture Puzzle, No. 20, "Flying Fortresses Bombing Enemy Base," over 375 pieces, approx. 19¼ x 15¼", c1945, guide picture on box **20.00**

Children

Pre–1915: General

Milton Bradley Company, Smashed Up Locomotive, 9 x 7", wood box . .   **250.00**

Seymour Lyman, New York, Tally Ho Puzzle, 30 sliced pcs, 28½ x 13¼", box lithography of stage coach crash **250.00**

J. Ottmann Lithography Company,

Dissected Circus, sliced pcs, 18½ x 12¾" **75.00**

McLoughlin Brothers, New York, NY Locomotive Picture Puzzle, puzzle pictures engine at station, 24¾ x 18", 1887 . . . .   **225.00**

The Young Blue Jackets, set of two, United States Cruiser *Columbia*, 18 pcs, 10" x 6", and United States Cruiser *San Francisco*, 15 pcs, 9 x 6½", box lithography shows three sailors around naval gun **250.00**

Peter G. Thomson, Cincinnati, OH, "The Blow Up Steam Boat, *Queen City* going up Ohio River," sliced format, 28 pcs, 16¼ x 12¼", box with guide picture **275.00**

1915–1945: General

Milton Bradley Co., 4341, Wee Willie Winkie, double sided puzzle, 30 pcs, 7¼ x 10", one guide picture on box **20.00**

Consolidated Paper Box Co., Big 4 Circus Puzzles Jig–Saw Type, three puzzle set, Set No. 1, each puzzle approx 9⅜ x 7¼" **15.00**

E. E. Fairchild Corporation, All–Fair Puzzle, No. 680, Children of American History Picture Puzzle, two puzzle set, Series 3, each puzzle 9½ x 6¾" **8.00**

Madmar Quality Company, Utica, NY, Madmar Dissected Map Puzzle, Junior Series, No. 773, California, guide picture on box **25.00**

Saalfield Publishing Co., No. 567, Kitty–Cat Picture Puzzle Box, six puzzle set, **Fern Biesel Peat**, each puzzle approx 7⅞ x 9⅞", guide picture for one puzzle on box lid **45.00**

Post–1945: General

Cadco–Ellis, Jingo: The Jigsaw Bingo Game, the first player to fit 5 pieces vertically, horizontally, or diagonally into his Jingo Board wins the round, 1941, box measures 13¼ x 10 x 1" **35.00**

Consolidated Paper Box Company, No. 41, 2 Perfect Jig Saw Type Interlocking Children's Puzzles, No. 5, boy stopping girl from crossing street and boy and grandfather in rowboat (**Hintermeister**), each puzzle 7⅛ x 9¼", box shows boy and girl waving puzzle boxes **7.50**

Jaymar, Bedtime Story Picture Puzzle, "Puss In Boots," guide picture on box **5.00**

Sifo Company, St. Paul, MN, Sammy Sun– tells the Days and Months, frame tray clock with months and numbers in outer circle and days of week in inner circle, central sun ... **10.00**

Volland, birthday card, B101, "Happy Birthday– and I'm Not Telling," verse beneath semi–circle with home, bird, and tree branch motif, 6 x 5", envelope **10.00**

Whitman Publishing Co.

2991, Little Golden Picture Puzzle, Tottle, 6⅛ x 7½", guide picture on box, 1946 copyright **10.00**

Sound A Round Talking Puzzle Master Unit, durable frame holds talking record and sturdy large piece puzzle, self adjusting magic tone arm, hard cover story book, "Choo–Choo at the Zoo," box measures 15½ x 11 x 2¼" **15.00**

Comic Characters

Built Rite, Sta–N–Place Inlaid Puzzle, frame tray, No. 1129, Blondie, Dagwood and children rush out door while Blondie watches, 13½ x 10⅝", early 1960s **15.00**

E. E. Fairchild Corporation

1600–2, frame tray, Little Roquefort and Percy Puss, A Terry–Toon Puzzle, Percy holds Roquefort in hand, 11 x 8½" **8.00**

1652, Weird–ohs Picture Puzzle, Freddy Flameout: The Way Out Jet Jockey, one of series of four, 108 pcs, approx 15 x 10½", guide picture on box **15.00**

Jaymar, frame tray, Rudolph the Red–Nose Reindeer, Rudolph leads sled, 11 x 14", 1950 copyright **15.00**

Saalfield Publishing Co.

No. 910, Just Kids Picture Puzzles, four puzzle set, each puzzle approx 9¾ x 8", guide picture for one of puzzles on front of box ... **40.00**

7042, frame tray, Artcraft, Diver Dan, Dan in bottom of sea surrounded by three fish, mermaid in background, 10½ x 14", 1957 copyright **20.00**

Whitman Publishing Co., 4457, frame tray Hanna–Barbera Top Cat, Top Cat sits in trash can sipping milk from bottle on porch while policeman looks on, 11⅜ x 14⅜", 1961 copyright **15.00**

Movie

Milton Bradley, 4691–1, James Bond 007 Jigsaw Puzzle, Thunderball, No. 1, "Spectre's Surprise," over 600 pcs, approx 24 x 14", portion of puzzle pictured on box cover **25.00**

Jaymar, frame tray, Walt Disney's 101 Dalmatians, couple and maid ad-

miring newborn puppy, 12¾ x 9¾" **12.00**

Squarecut Puzzle Co., New York City, Movie Squarecut Puzzle, "Keeper of the Flame," more than 500 pcs, 22 x 16¾", two sections, small guide picture on box................... **60.00**

Whitman Publishing Co., 2975, frame tray, Walt Disney Cinderella Picture Puzzle, Cinderella carrying wood to kitchen stove, 14⅞ x 11½", 1950 copyright, wrapper with guide picture on front with puzzle piece lines and unmarked picture on back suitable for framing **17.50**

Radio

Whitman Publishing Company

2628, frame tray, Little Beaver Picture Puzzle, drawing of Little Beaver fishing, 11⅜ x 14⅞", 1954 copyright.................. **15.00**

No. 3932, Edgar Bergen's Charlie McCarthy Picture Puzzles, two puzzle set, approx 7¼ x 10", 1938 copyright **35.00**

Television

Built Rite, Sta–N–Place Inlaid Puzzle, frame tray, No. 1229, Jungle Jim, chimp rubs Jungle Jim's hair, 10¾ x 13½", 1956 copyright **20.00**

Milton Bradley, 4318, Dr. Kildare Jigsaw Puzzle, No. 2, "We are going to call him Jimmy," over 600 pieces, includes 14 x 12" color portrait for framing, guide picture on box, 1962 copyright.................... **17.50**

HG Toys, No. 465–02, Happy Days Featuring "The Fonz," 150 pcs, approx 14 x 10", guide photograph on box......................... **5.00**

Jaymar, No. 2060, Mr. I. Magination, 414 pcs, 19¼ x 14", 1951 copyright, guide picture on box........ **15.00**

Saalfield, frame tray, Authorized Edition, "Would You Believe?", Don Adams in Get Smart, Adams lighting match around boxes of TNT, 10½ x 14", 1965 copyright **30.00**

Whitman Publishing Co.

Series 302, Authorized Jr. Jigsaw Puzzle, Hugh O'Brian As Wyatt Earp, 63 pcs, guide picture on box **15.00**

4427, frame tray, Tales of Wells Fargo, photograph of hero drawing gun as he enters saloon, 11¼ x 14½", 1958 copyright........ **17.50**

4427, frame tray, Wagon Train, drawing of wagon master and scout hunting buffalo, 11⅜ x 14½", 1961 copyright **12.50**

4454, Walt Disney's Babes In

Toyland, couple sharing drink, large Queen of Hearts card in background, 11¼ x 14⅜", 1961 copyright **12.00**

JIGSAW PUZZLE EPHEMERA

Advertising Tear Sheet
  Miss America, Vol. 5, No. 6, April 1947, Page 8, Noxzema jigsaw puzzle theme ad **3.00**
  Playboy, May 1981, back cov features Crown Royal jigsaw puzzle ad **4.00**
Broadside
  Einson–Freeman, Problem Jig–Saw Puzzle, Princess and Peasant Problem, cardboard, 12¾ x 15½" **25.00**
  University Distributing Company, Jig of the Week, No. 22, Boyhood of Sir Walter Raleigh, paper, 14 x 10¾" . .   **15.00**
Catalogs
  Madmar Quality Company, Utica, NY, "Madmar Puzzles For All Ages," 6 x 9⅛", 16 pgs, no date (mid–1930s)   **25.00**
  Parker Brothers Autumn List 1913 Famous Pastime Puzzles, double sided sheet, 9 x 15½", fold marks (folded twice in thirds) **15.00**
Comic Book
  Archie's Madhouse, Vol. 1, No. 1, September 1959, Archie Comic

Sheet Music, *Juggling A Jig-Saw*, pink, black, and white covers, Donaldson-Douglas & Gumble Music Publishers, 9⅛ x 12", 1933, $8.00.

Publications, jigsaw puzzle theme cov, very good cond. **60.00**
Detective Comics, No. 367, September 1967, DC (National Periodical Publications), Batman jigsaw puzzle theme cov, 12¢, very good cond . . .   **10.00**
Jigsaw: Man of A Thousand Parts, Vol. 1, No. 1, September 1966, Funday Funnies, Inc., Harvey Thriller, 12¢, fine cond **10.00**
Magazine
  Ellery Queen's Mystery Magazine, Vol. 51, No. 6, June 1968, jigsaw puzzle theme cov **5.00**
  Future, No. 10, May 1979, space station jigsaw puzzle theme cov **5.00**
  Life, Vol. 17, No. 2, July 10, 1944, Nimitz of the Pacific, contains article on Par puzzles **7.50**
  Popular Home Craft, Vol. 3, No. 3, September–October 1932, cov show individual cutting jigsaw, **Raymond Baker**, also contains articles entitled "Jigsaw Puzzles—How to Make 'em" and "Jigsaw Dust Blower" **15.00**

PUZZLES, MECHANICAL

History: Slocum and Botermans define the mechanical puzzle as "a self–contained object, comprised of one or more parts, which involved a problem for one person to solve by manipulating using logic, reasoning, insight, luck, and/or dexterity." Mechanical puzzles have solid pieces that must be manipulated by one's hands to find a solution. Although some are made into a picture (the standard definition for a jigsaw puzzle) most are not.

Collectors divide mechanical puzzles into put–together puzzles, take–apart puzzles, interlocking solid puzzles, disentanglement puzzles, sequential movement puzzles, puzzle vessels, dexterity puzzles, vanish puzzles, impossible objects puzzles, and folding puzzles. Paper, except as a container, is not the material of choice for most of these categories. Put–together puzzles are the exception.

Put–together puzzles are the oldest and largest class of mechanical puzzles. Included in this group are checkerboard puzzles, cross puzzles, head and tail puzzles, letter dissections, Sam Loyd's trick mule and similar type puzzles, Question du Lapin puzzles, sliced or dissected puzzles, and tangrams. All are found in paper.

In 1880, Henry Luers obtained a U.S. patent for a Sectional Checkerboard consisting of fifteen different shaped pieces that had to be assembled to make a complete checkerboard. More than fifty different manufacturers followed suit, offering over thirty different 8 x 7 checkerboard solutions.

A cross puzzle is nothing more than a dissected cross. The puzzle was extremely popular in the nineteenth century. The difficulty of the puzzle is increased by dividing the cross into a larger and larger number of pieces.

In order to solve a head and tail puzzle, you have to match the corners and sides of pieces. E. L. Thurston patented the first puzzle of this type in 1893. This was a popular form of advertising premium, the Calumet Baking Powder Company of Chicago being among the best known.

Letter dissections were another favorite advertising premium. The goal is to make the appropriate letter, often the first letter of the company's brand. The two most popular letters were "H" and "T." The oldest letter "T" puzzle known was issued by Seeman Brothers White Rose Ceylon Tea in 1903.

Sam Loyd's trick mule involved cutting the puzzle parts along a dotted line and arranging the three resulting pieces to form an identifiable object. P. T. Barnum sold millions of copies of a version of this puzzle known as "P.T. Barnum's Trick Mules."

A Question du Lapin puzzle is a silhouette puzzle by which one must correctly stack the silhouette pieces on top of one another to form the shape of an object. The pieces were generally octagonally cut so each piece could be placed eight different ways. The idea was originated by Watilliaux in Paris around 1900.

Sliced or dissected puzzles were known to the ancient Greeks. They were popular in eighteenth century Japan and nineteenth century China. When the final solution of a sliced or dissected puzzles is a picture, it generally is classified as a jigsaw puzzle. When the object is to put the units together to make a specific outline or figure, it is classified as a mechanical puzzle. Most collectors confine their definition of a sliced or dissected mechanical puzzle to objects that turn into geometric forms.

When the principal goal of a sliced or dissected puzzle is to form the outline of a figure, it is called a tangram. Most tangram sets contain seven pieces. Solutions number in the hundreds. Tans (a tangram piece) can form a triangle, trapezoid, parallelogram, letters, numbers, and a wide range of building, floral, fauna, and other objects. A tangram craze swept through Europe and America in the early nineteenth century. In America, the tangram was known as the "Chinese Puzzle." McLoughlin Brothers published many different versions.

Many mechanical puzzles are sold in cardboard boxes or paper envelopes. Although the puzzles are not made of paper, a magnificent packaging collection focusing just on mechanical puzzles could be assembled.

Reference: Carla van Splunteren and Tony Burrett, *Jerry Slocum–Jack Botermans Puzzles Old &*

New: How to Make and Solve Them, University of Washington Press, 1986.

Checkerboard puzzle
  Checkerboard Puzzle Co., Detroit, MI, Wrobbell's Checkerboard Puzzle, manufactured by The Western Paper Box Co., Detroit, 14 pcs, puzzle measures 8 x 8", orig cardboard box, 8¼ x 8¼ x 78", orig selling price 15¢ **15.00**
  D & S Novelty Company, Harrisburg, PA, The Great Nut–House Puzzle, 14 pcs, puzzle measures 3⅜ x 3⅜", double fold cardboard with punch-out puzzle, open measures 4⁷/₁₆ x 10⅛", orig selling price 10¢ **2.00**
  J. W. Fose Printing Co., Niagara Falls, NY, Checker Board Puzzle, 14 pcs, puzzle measures 6⅝ x 5⅝", orig cardboard box, 5⅝ x 4⅞ x ¾", orig selling price 15¢ **12.50**
Head and tail puzzle
  A–Treat Bottle Co., Allentown, PA, A–Treat Mystery Puzzle, 9 pcs, A–Treat bottles on different colored grounds, puzzle measures 7⁹/₁₆ x 7⁹/₁₆", different advertising on the back of each piece, paper envelope, 3⅛ x 5½" **10.00**
  Norton Company, Worcester, MA, Norton Abrasive Puzzle, 9 pcs, portions of grinding wheel on different colored grounds, puzzle measures 6⅛ x 6⅛", advertising letter on reverse making puzzle easy to assemble, paper envelope 3⅛ x 5½" **15.00**
Letter dissection puzzle
  Royal Typewriter Company, New York, NY, The "R" Puzzle, 7 pcs, Royal logo on the front of pieces, paper envelope, 4½ x 3" **20.00**
  B. Wise and C Kipp, distributors, letters "H" (6 pcs) and "T" (4 pcs) in same package, plain black pcs, paper envelope, 6½ x 3⅝", orig selling price 10¢ **7.50**
  Mueller's Spaghetti, 1933, titled "Shift–A–Square," blue and white card with squares, 6 x 6" **18.00**
Sam Loyd's trick mule puzzle type
  The Magic Shop (location unknown), The Williard–Johnson (sic.) Prize Fight Puzzle, "four strips of cardboard, each 3 inches by 1½ inches, show Willard and Johnson in various absurd postures. The solution of the puzzle lies in arranging the strips that show, *in the completed picture,* Willard the heavy–weight champion," instruction sheet provides solution, copyright 1915, paper enve-

Fourmost Puzzle, National Distillers Products Corp., NY, 4 pcs., orig. envelope, 4½" sq. assembled, $8.00.

lope 4¼ x 2⅝", orig selling price
10¢ **100.00**
Sliced or dissected puzzle
  William Ayres & Sons, Philadelphia,
  dealer imprint for Peerless Vehicle
  & Imp. Co., Stockton and Lodi, CA,
  5A Horse Blanket Puzzle, 9 pcs, engraving of rider holding bridle of
  blanketed horse on larger pieces,
  puzzle measures 6¼ x 6¼", cardboard box, 3¹⁄₁₆ x 3¹⁄₁₆ x ³⁄₁₆" **20.00**
  Dickinson's Brands, 8 pcs, title piece
  and seven individual product pcs
  (Globe Scratch Feed, Snowball Popcorn, Crescent chick feed,
  Evergreen Lawn Grass seed, Santa
  Claus Popcorn, Dickinson's Lawn
  Seed, and Yankee Popcorn), color-

ful lithograph sketches, puzzle measures 9½ x 4¾", paper envelope,
  6⁷⁄₁₆ x 3⅝" **45.00**
  Pratt Food Co., Philadelphia, PA,
  dealer rubber stamp for W. D.
  Wilder, Laurenceville, NY, Pratt's
  Cut Up Puzzle (2 Puzzles in One),
  10 pcs, front image shows group of
  animals laughing and making sarcastic remarks to a gentleman attempting to get them to eat "Imitation Food," light green ground
  (another version has a dark yellow
  ground) back contains series of slogan advertisements, puzzle measures 9 x 6¼", paper envelope, 6⅛ x
  4⅝" **25.00**

RECORD JACKETS

History: Record collectors cringe when you tell
them that in many cases the record jacket is more
valuable than the record. For decades, just the
opposite has been true. Record collectors have
visions of millions upon millions of records being
discarded; and, they should.

The arrival of the CD and ready availability of
enhanced period recordings means that anyone
interested in the music has easy access, even to
the most obscure pieces. Recent announcements
project the next step in record sales will involve a
store putting a blank CD disk or tape into a recorder attached to a computer, accessing a central data bank, and making instant records. Times
have changed. They really, really have.

Period design collectors and interior decorators
have discovered the record jacket as an aesthetic
and decorative treasure. Many, especially those
from the psychedelic era, are works of art, some-

Wrobbell's Checkerboard Puzzle, Checkerboard Puzzle Co., Western Paper Box Co., Detroit, red-and-black puzzle pieces, blue-and-white printed box, 8¼ x 8½", $12.00.

thing that can be framed and hung on a wall. Personality collectors want image, not records. A record album cover has far more displayability than a black vinyl disk.

The collecting of record jackets with or without the records has just begun. It is a trend that promises to accelerate as the 1990s progress. The pricing in Marino and Furfero's *The Official Price Guide to Frank Sinatra Records and CDs* depends heavily on jacket image. If not, the prices are way out of line.

Further support for the idea that the pictorial aspect of records is becoming increasingly important can be seen in the rising values for picture records from companies such as Vogue. The record is not even a factor when considering the infamous Beatles' butcher cover.

References: L. R. Docks, *1900–1965 American Premium Record Guide, 4th Edition*, Books Americana, 1992; Anthony J. Gribin and Matthew Schiff, *Doo–Wop: The Forgotten Third of Rock 'n' Roll*, Krause Publications, 1992; Fred Heggeness, *Country Western Price Guide*, FH Publishing, 1990; Vito R. Marino and Anthony C. Furfero, *The Official Price Guide to Frank Sinatra Records and CDs*, House of Collectibles, 1993; Jerry Osborne, *The Official Price Guide To Movie/TV Soundtracks and Original Cast Albums*, House of Collectibles, 1991; Jerry Osborne, *The Official Price Guide to Records, Tenth Edition*, House of Collectibles, 1993; Neal Umphred, *Goldmine's Price Guide to Collectible Jazz Albums, 1949–1969*, Krause Publications, 1992; Neal Umphred, *Goldmine's Price Guide to Collectible Record Albums, 1949–1989, Second Edition*, Krause Publications, 1991; Neal Umphred, *Goldmine's Rock 'n' Roll 45 RPM Record Price Guide*, Krause Publications, 1990.

Collectors' Clubs: Association For Recorded Sound Collectors, PO Box 10162, Silver Spring, MD 20914; International Association of Jazz Record Collectors, Box 10208, Oakland, CA 94610.

Periodicals: *Discoveries*, PO Box 255, Port Townsend, WA 98368; *Goldmine*, Krause Publications, 700 East State Street, Iola, WI 54990.

Andy Williams, LP, sgd, Columbia, c1970	28.00
Anna Moffo, LP, sgd	35.00
Anthony Newley, "Stop the World," orig Broadway cast, sgd and inscribed	55.00
Barbra Streisand, LP, sgd, Funny Girl, Columbia, 1968	225.00
Barry Morell, LP, sgd	15.00
Beatles, Abbey Road, Apple, 1969	100.00
Bill Monroe, LP, sgd	40.00
Brigit Nilsson, LP, sgd	28.00
Cassius Clay, The Champ Sings, Columbia, 1964	25.00
Charlie Pride, sgd, RCA	10.00

Cher, Liberty, 1981	8.00
Chet Atkins, LP, sgd, RCA, 1960s	35.00
Chubby Checker, Lp, Parkway, 1960–66	25.00
Dave Clark Five, Try Too Hard, Epic, 1966	20.00
Dean Martin, LP, sgd and inscribed on back, Favorites, Capitol	45.00
Del Shannon, Runaway, Big Top, 1961	50.00
Diahann Carroll, LP, sgd	18.00
Elizabeth Schwarzkopf, sgd	38.00
Elvis Presley, Elvis, RCA, 1973	50.00
Fleetwood Mac, Hot Rocks	50.00
Frankie Laine, LP, sgd, Capitol	50.00
Frank Sinatra, LP, sgd, Columbia	100.00
Grandpa Jones, LP, sgd	35.00
Hank Snow, LP, sgd, RCA	40.00
Hank Williams, 78 rpm, MGM, sgd, 1952	175.00
Harry Belafonte, LP, sgd, RCA, 1960s	38.00
Herb Alpert, LP, sgd, A & M, 1960s	60.00
Johnnie Burnette, Dreamin, Liberty, 1960	30.00
Judy Garland, MGM #E3149, 33⅓ rpm, collage on front	25.00
Julie London, Julie, Liberty, 1966	10.00
Kay Starr, Sons for Stags, Capitol	30.00
Lana Cantrell, LP, sgd, RCA, 1967–69	15.00
Leontyne Price, LP, double album, sgd	150.00
Marilyn Monroe, Some Like It Hot, Ascot, 1964	75.00
Marty Robbins, Rock'n Roll'n Robbins, Columbia, 1956	150.00
Mitch Miller, LP, sgd, Columbia	35.00
Montserrat Caballe, LP, sgd and inscribed	45.00
Nat King Cole, Capitol, 1958–68	35.00
Peggy Lee, LP, sgd, Capitol, 1964–68	40.00
Perry Como, LP, sgd, RCA, c1964	38.00
Ray Charles, LP, sgd	25.00
Regine Crespin, LP, sgd	15.00
Richard Tucker, LP, sgd	50.00
Sammy Davis Jr, LP, sgd, 20th Fox, 1964	55.00

The Best of the Doors, Jim Morrison photo cover, $8.00.

Sherrill Milnes, sgd and inscribed **22.00**
Susan Hayward and John Gavin, *Back Street* soundtrack, 33⅓ rpm, portraits on front **15.00**
Tex Ritter, 78 rpm, sgd, double album, 1946 . . . . **135.00**
Tito Gobbi, sgd **38.00**
Tony Bennett, LP, sgd, Columbia, 1970s **40.00**
Walt Disney's Fantasia, Leopold Stokowski, Buena Vista Records, 33 rpm, 1957 . . . . **15.00**
Zinka Milanov, LP, sgd **55.00**

REWARDS OF MERIT

History: Awards of merit played an important role in American nineteenth century education and religions. These miniature cards were used to record accomplishments and good deeds and served as a permanent reminder to the receiver of a job well done.

The earliest rewards of merit were handwritten. By the early nineteenth century printed examples appeared. Most were printed with black ink and featured a fanciful border and one or more vignettes in addition to the text. Color appeared in the 1850s.

Religious rewards of merit stressed "diligence and good behavior." Merit points could be earned at church and school. Twenty–five and fifty merit award cards are common.

Education awards of merit were given for "Correctness in Recitation," "Correct Deportment," and "Neatness in Writing." They were inscribed and signed by the teacher and addressed to a specific student. Rewards of merit often served a double purpose. Many educational rewards of merit were used as bookmarks. They are commonly found in old Bibles and books.

American greeting card printers quickly jumped aboard the reward of merit bandwagon. Rewards of merit appeared with general greetings, e.g., "Think of me." Diecut forms replaced the more traditional rectangle.

The reward of merit experienced its Golden Age in America. English schools used rewards of merit, but they were almost always issued by the administration rather than the individual teacher. Their themes are less inventive, primarily instructional. Most were given for punctuality and regular attendance, not academic merit.

Reference: Lar and Sue Hothem, *School Collectibles of the Past*, Hothem House, 1993.

1820–40, wove paper, hand drawn stylized vining plant with flowers and birds, green, brown, blue, and faded red, initials "F Z," framed, 12¾ x 16⅞" **1,600.00**

1827, hand drawn bird in floral bush, one stylized tulip and one daisy above heart reserve, sgd "Anna/1827/Tier," 4¼ x 3¼" **350.00**
1852, Bank of Industry, five honors, hand colored children, rounded corners, printed by A C Beaman, used **18.50**
1862, hp, school house, list of students on back, used **6.00**
1865, Reward of Merit, children reading, light cardboard, pencil date, 2¹/₁₆ x 3⅜" **5.00**
1866, Reward of Merit, ornate design, two boys, one with books over shoulder, marked "Gibson & Co The Southern District of Ohio," 2¾ x 4", used . . **12.50**
1870s, Reward of Merit
    Bird motif, color, used **15.00**
    Little boy at window, 3 x 5", used **18.00**
    Little Tommy Tucker, used **10.00**
1872, A Testimonial of Approbration, printed, black and white, 8½ x 10¼" **12.00**
1874, "Happy Days," Reward of Merit, two women, used, artist sgd Gibson, 3³/₁₆ x 4½" **12.00**
1876
    Excelsior, Fifty Merits, white and blue, gold gilt, used **10.00**
    Toledo Public Schools, Grade 1, blue and red, used **8.00**
1877, "Time Is Money," Reward of Merit, girl and swan, artist sgd Gibson, 3½ x 5⅛" **12.00**
1879, One Hundred Merits, green, red, and white, used **20.00**
1880, Reward of Merit
    Issued by the Massachusetts Society For The Prevention of Cruelty to Animals, color litho scene on front, poem on back, 3 x 5⅛" **35.00**
    Multicolored, flowers, 4", unused **3.50**
1880s, Presentation, fan shape, blue owl and frog, John Gibson, 3¹/₁₆ x 5⅛". . . . **30.00**
1885, Reward of Merit, little girl wearing sunbonnet hat holding doll and basket, 4½ x 3", unused **6.50**
1886, floral front, hand written on back "Promotion Card, Lizzie Carrell is promoted to seventh grade, Whitwell Schools," sgd "Geo M Clary, June 4, 1886," 4½ x 2½" **12.50**
1892, fruit motif, used **10.00**
1893, Excelsior, Fifty Merits, printed, color, castle illus, copyright 1876, used **8.00**
Unknown Date
    Class Merit, head of class in standing, used **8.00**
    Cupid writing on rock, flowers, hand colored, used **8.00**
    Flower motif **6.00**
    Girl standing by arbor, used **10.00**

REWARD OF MERIT

To ____ BY ____ TEACHER

Color Litho, pasted on cardboard backing, sgd. by teacher, 7½ x 9½", $15.00.

Mother and Children reading, Presented by Teacher, used **8.00**
Roman Ships, chromolithograph, red, used **8.00**
Young Gibson Tots, raised flowers, colored flower border, The Gibson Art Co, 3½ x 5" **12.00**

SCRAPBOOKS

History: From the Victorian era through the 1960s, almost everyone kept a scrapbook. Most scrapbooks were personal, filled with newspaper clippings, invitations and announcements, and photographs related to one's immediate and extended family and community. "Pretty" things and objects of curiosity also worked their way into the scrapbook.

Making scrapbooks was a popular school assignment from elementary to high school. Popular events, local history, and numerous scientific topics were documented in scrapbook form. School related scrapbooks can easily be identified by the grade marking and teacher's comments that almost always appear in them.

Children and adults also kept subject scrapbooks. Young boys created scrapbooks around sports, the military, and vehicles. Young girls favored animals, dolls, and clothing. Adult scrapbooks ranged from clipping a popular column or cartoon from the local paper to assembling a collection of favorite recipes.

Stationery stores, five and dime stores, and most drugstores with a general line of merchandise sold scrapbooks. Most had a fancy full color cover and inexpensive, wood pulp paper inside. Many individuals did not bother to buy a scrapbook. Instead they utilized an old trade catalog, account journal or ledger, or magazine.

Most material was pasted in scrapbooks with white paste or rubber cement. Occasionally scotch tape was used. Most discolored the object and page and came loose. Short term, rather than long term preservation was the goal of the maker.

Victorian scrapbooks are valued because they often contain a wealth of advertising trade cards, diecuts, greeting cards, post cards, and programs. Exercise care in removing materials since the backs of many of these objects contain information that should not be damaged or lost. In fact, consider not removing the material at all. An intact scrapbook is an invaluable tool to the social historian.

Albums, a form of scrapbook, were developed for a number of specific paper topics, e.g., diecuts, matchcovers, post cards, and tobacco cards. In the case of tobacco cards, special series albums were designed. Until recently, collectors paid little attention to these albums, often removing their contents and discarding them. Collectors now realize that the albums themselves are critical to achieving a full understanding of their collecting category.

References: Alistair Allen and Joan Hoverstadt, *The History of Printed Scraps*, New Cavendish Books, 1983; Cynthia Hart, John Grossman, and Priscilla Dunhill, *A Victorian Scrapbook*, Workman Publishing, 1989.

Advertising, contains trade and advertising cards, album cards, pictures, 66 pgs, 5½ x 9". **35.00**
Baseball, Big Ted and Gus Bell newspaper articles and complete newspapers, 4 x 5" Cincinnati Baseball Club photos of each player, assembled by Ted Kluszewski, 1953 . . . . **25.00**
Celebrity
   Amelita Galli–Curci, 85 articles relating to career. **100.00**
   Bee Gees, 34 pgs, 9 x 12" **15.00**
   Carson Robinson, 65 press cuttings, photos, and other material, 1940s. . **130.00**
   Claudio Arrau, photos, post cards, letters, and news articles **300.00**
   Eydie Gorme, news articles, photos, and other material of her and Steve Lawrence. **100.00**
   Hillbilly and Western Stars, photos, 52 pgs, 1952. . . . . **15.00**
   Liberace, photos, letters, and other material **375.00**
   Loretta Young, items on both sides of pages, 61 pgs **50.00**
   Ray Conniff, photos, news articles, worn **150.00**
   Shirley Temple, Saalfield, 1937 copyright, 11 x 15". **25.00**

Scrapbook, printed color paper covers, tape binding, 72 pages, 11 x 15½", 1930s, $12.00.

Vaughn Monroe, photos, news and
    magazine articles. **325.00**
Children's
    Magazine prints, yellow linen, 1915. .   **8.00**
    Valentine cards with mechanicals,
      early 1940s **40.00**
Cigarette Cards
    Adolf Hitler, September, 1935, 132
      pgs, mounted photos of Nazi Ger-
      many **65.00**
    Fancy Dress Ball Costumes **50.00**

Scrapbook, emb cardboard covers, 104 heavy paper pages, 12¼ x 14½", 1950s, $8.00.

German Military, Sturm cigarettes,
    1813–15, 240 cards, German text   **125.00**
    Reign of King Geo V, 50 cards, orig
      album **50.00**
Fish, post card, articles, labels, photos,
    and chromo card, 82 pgs, gold emb
    cover, E A Housman, 7 x 10½" **250.00**
Greeting Cards
    Cardboard cov, multicolored butter-
      flies dec, 1950s **5.00**
    Celluloid cov with center mulicolored
      medallion of Gibson girl type por-
      trait, 1910–20 . . . . **25.00**
Indian Territory, 1875–1880, photos of
    Main Street, Ochilata, Southern Hotel,
    National Supply of Kansas, and hard-
    ware store, 5 x 7" **35.00**
Jumbo, 1930s, newspaper and magazine
    clippings of movie stars and other ce-
    lebrities, glued on both sides of pages,
    over 100 pgs **45.00**
Magazine, three *Puck* magazines, 1892   **7.50**
Matchbook Covers, 1940s **10.00**
Miscellaneous, 1939, 167 color cards,
    aviation, famous people, flags, autos,
    world's fairs, etc **16.00**
New York Theater Clippings, 1887–
    1918, 40 pgs, James J Corbett, Maud
    Adams, Mary Pickford **20.00**
Photographs, 1901–41, vacations, ships,
    autos, fly fishing, Buffalo Exposition,
    Pres McKinley, about 300 glued pho-
    tos **50.00**
Shriners, 1912, trip of Caravan of LuLu
    Temple on Pennsylvania RR, photo
    post cards, photos, and tickets. **40.00**
Travel
    England trip on *Queen Mary,* June 5,
      1935, post cards of Maiden voyage,
      England, and Tuck cards **100.00**
    Europe, 1930–31, photos, menus, bil-
      lheads, booklets, steamships, 50 pgs   **20.00**
    State, 50 pgs, post cards with map of
      state, capitol, state bird, and flower,
      stamp with state flag on each page,
      corner mounts **50.00**
    World Cruise, *SS Devonian,* 1911, 76
      pgs, includes passenger list, deck
      plan, photos, menus, Europe memo-
      rabilia **125.00**
Unused, black cardboard cov and pages,
    green script written on cov **5.00**
Victorian
    117 trade cards, album cards, and
      prints **95.00**
    315 trade cards, diecuts, and valen-
      tines **185.00**
    319 trade cards and calling cards, 160
      die cuts **280.00**
White Mountain, 1945, 56 pgs, red and
    silver cov **14.00**

SHEET MUSIC

History: Sheet music, especially piano scores, dates to the early nineteenth century. Early music sheets contain some of the finest examples of American lithography. Music sheets were often bound in volumes and accompanied a young lady when she was married.

Covers of sheet music chronicle the social, political, and other trends of any historical period. The golden age of the illustrated cover dates from 1885 to 1952. Leading artists such as James Montgomery Flagg lent their talents in the sheet music area. The cover frequently sold the song.

Once radio and talking pictures became popular, covers featured the stars. A song sheet might be issued in as many as six different cover versions depending on who was featured. When piano playing lost popularity in the 1950s, the market for sheet music declined. Further, song sheets failed to maintain their high quality of design. There is little collector interest for sheet music issued after 1960.

Center your collection on a theme—show tunes, songs of World War I, Sousa marches, Black material, songs of a lyricist or composer—the list is endless. Be alert to dealers who assign a high value to a subject theme sheet based upon the premise that the specialized collector will pay anything to buy something they want. Learn the value of a sheet to the sheet music collector and buy accordingly.

Be careful stacking sheets on top of one another. Cover inks tend to bleed. The most ideal solution is to place acid free paper between each cover and sheet. Unfortunately, people used tape to repair tears in old sheet music. This discolors and detracts from value. Seek professional help in removing tape from rarer sheets.

The vast majority of sheet music is worth between $1.00 and $3.00, provided it is in near mint condition. Despite this, many dealers are now asking on average between $5.00 and $10.00 per sheet for mundane titles. Part of the reason for this discrepancy in pricing is the crossover influence of subject collectors. These collectors have little patience with the hunt. Not realizing how easy it is to find copies, they pay high prices and fuel the unrealistic expectations of the general dealer.

Further complicating the picture is the inaccurate, highly manipulative pricing in the Guiheen and Pafik guide. The book has been roundly criticized, and rightly so, within the sheet music collecting community.

References: Debbie Dillon, *Collectors' Guide To Sheet Music*, L–W Promotions, 1988, 1993 value update; Anna Guiheen and Marie–Reine Pafik, *The Sheet Music Reference & Price Guide*, Collector Books, 1992.

Collectors' Clubs: National Sheet Music Society, 1597 Fair Park Avenue, Los Angeles, CA 90041; New York Sheet Music Society, PO Box 1214, Great Neck, NY 11023; Remember That Song, 5821 North 67th Ave., Suite 103–306, Glendale, AZ 85301; The Sheet Music Exchange, PO Box 69, Quicksburg, VA 22847.

After The War Is Over, 1917	**5.00**
All Shook Up, Elvis Presley	**15.00**
Alone, Marx Bros cov, 1935	**10.00**
Always and Always, Joan Crawford cov, 1937	**6.00**
A New Star Shines in Heaven, Jean Harlow, 1938	**15.00**
Angel Eyes, Nat King Cole	**5.00**
Animal Crackers In My Soup, Shirley Temple, 1935	**18.00**
April Showers, Al Jolson	**10.00**
As Time Goes By, Humphrey Bogart and Ingrid Bergman cov	**12.00**
As Years Go By, Hepburn, Henreid, and Walker cov, 1947	**5.00**
A Signal From Mars, E T Paull, multicolored	**35.00**
Babes in Toyland	**10.00**
Barney Google, 1923	**15.00**
Beyond The Blue Horizon, 1930	**6.00**
Bible Tells Me So, 1940, Roy Rogers and Dale Evans	**4.00**
Banjo, Lee & Walker, Philadelphia, 1863, 11 x 13"	**55.00**
Bicycle Girl, Lena Hulett, 1896	**45.00**
Boy Scout March, Buck & Lowney, St Louis, MO, full color cov, 1912, 11 x 13"	**95.00**
Boys In Blue, Anthony L Maresch, Schiebert Music Litho	**8.00**
Buffalo Bills Farewell, M Witmark & Sons, 1908, 10 x 14"	**150.00**
By A Wishing Well, Sonja Henie and Richard Greene, 1938	**8.00**
Camp Custer, March–One–Step, Chas Roat Music, Battle Creek, MI, 1907, 10 x 14"	**85.00**
Cape May Mount Vernon Polka, Lee & Walker, 1855, 10 x 13"	**90.00**
Clicqout Club Fox Trot March, banjo playing eskimos, 1926	**5.00**
Come on Pappa, Eddie Cantor cov	**20.00**
Comin' on the Six–Fifteen, Roy West & Range Riders, 1945	**5.00**
Cycling Maid, National Music Co, Chicago, 1895, 10 x 14"	**45.00**
Cycling March, Bruce Priddy, 1896, 11 x 14"	**45.00**
Down Among The Sheltering Palms, 1914	**5.00**
Elaine, Pearl White, 1915, 10 x 14"	**75.00**
Everybody Shimmies Now, Mae West, 1918, 9 x 12"	**35.00**

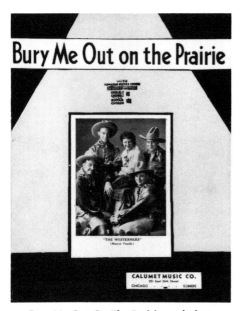

Bury Me Out On The Prairie, real photo of "The Westerners" (The Massey family), 9 x 12", 1935, $6.00.

False Faces, Thomas Ince, 1919, 9 x 12" **40.00**

For Me and My Gal, Judy Garland **8.00**

Funny Charlie Chaplin, James Ellis, Acme Music Pub, 1915, black and white **10.00**

Gathering Sea Shells From the Seashore, Morgan Litho, Cleveland, 1877, 10 x 13" **65.00**

Give Me Liberty or Give Me Love, Claudette Colbert cov, 1933 . . . . **5.00**

Going My Way, Bing Crosby, Burke and Van Heusen, New York, 1944 . . **18.00**

Gold Dust Twins Rag, multicolored, framed **250.00**

Good Bye Boys, Al Jolson, 1913, 10 x 14" **38.00**

Good–Bye France, Irving Berlin, 1918 **10.00**

Good Ship Lollipop, Shirley Temple . . **12.00**

Greeting To Cape May, Lee & Walker, 1879, 11 x 14" **75.00**

Hand Me Down My Walkin Cane, Calumet Music, 1935 . . . . **12.00**

Heartbreak Hotel, Elvis Presley **20.00**

High and Mighty, 1954 . . . . **8.00**

Hi–Yo Silver, Lone Ranger, 1938, 9 x 12" **65.00**

I Got Stung, Elvis Presley **20.00**

I'll Never Change Dear, Stoney & Wilma Lee Cooper, 1944 . . . . **5.00**

I'll Sing You A Thousand Love Songs,

Clark Gable and Marion Davies cov, 1936 . . . . **12.00**

I'll Tell The World, Mary Pickford, 1919, 9 x 12" **45.00**

I Met Her On The Ferris Wheel, National Music Co, Chicago, 1893, black and white litho of Columbian Expo wheel, 10 x 14" **75.00**

I'm Gonna Getcha, I Betcha, Red River Dave, 1947 . . . . **10.00**

I Love You California, 1913 . . . . **7.00**

In My Harem, Irving Berlin, 1913 . . . . . **8.00**

It's V V V For Victory, Rex Music Publishing, Seattle, 1942, 9 x 12" **38.00**

Jolly Girl From Gay Paree, Howley, Haviland & Co, New York, 1897, 10 x 14" **40.00**

Just A Lonely Hobo, Cole, Autry cov, 1932 . . . . **20.00**

Laugh Clown Laugh, Lon Chaney, 1928, 9 x 12" **30.00**

Lay Him Low Dirge, dedicated in memory to Gen'l Philip Kearny, 1863, 10 x 13" **50.00**

Let's Talk About You, Eddy Morgan, 1943 . . . . **5.00**

Lincoln Centennial March, E T Paull, New York, 1909, 11 x 14" **65.00**

Little Nemo, Won't You Be My Valentine, 1908, 11 x 14" **75.00**

Little Orphan Annie **15.00**

Lonely Renfro Valley Rose, Cliff Japhet & Western Aces, 1945 . . . . **5.00**

Love Me Tender, Elvis Presley **15.00**

March of The Boers to Ladysmith, Sol Bloom, Chicago, 1900, 10 x 13" **50.00**

Masquerade March Two Step, E T Paull, 1907, 10 x 14" **45.00**

Melody Time, Blue Shadows on the Trail, Disney, 1948, 9 x 12" **30.00**

Mickey Mouse's Birthday Party, Irving Berlin Music Publishers, 1936, 9 x 12" **75.00**

Midnight Flyer March, E T Paull, 1903, 9 x 12" **50.00**

Mona Lisa, Nat King Cole **5.00**

Money Can't Buy Back Your Mother, Jimmie Ritter, 1946 . . . . **5.00**

Mother O'Mine, 1903, Rudyard Kipling **10.00**

Muzzle the Back Seat Driver & Drive Wherever You May, McDermott, 1928 . . . . **12.00**

My Buddy, Al Jolson, c1922 . . . . **10.00**

My Cousin Caruso, Gus Edwards Music, New York, 1909, 11 x 14" **45.00**

My Man, 1921, Fanny Brice cov **25.00**

My Prairie Songbird, 1909, Indian girl cov **3.00**

Nothing More To Say, Big Slim, 1946 **5.00**

Oh Come My Love, Tex Atchison, 1946 . . . . **10.00**

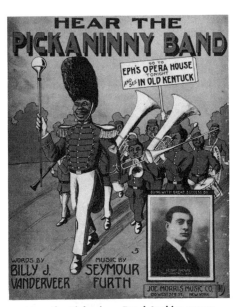

Hear the Pickaninny Band, Jenkins cover illus., sgd., Joe Morris Music Co., 11 x 13", c1911, $60.00.

Oh How I Hate To Get Up In The Morning, Irving Berlin, 1914	7.00
Oh Susanna, 1923, 9 x 12"	45.00
On the Atchinson, Topeka & Santa Fe, 1945, Judy Garland cov	22.50
Our Little Girl, Shirley Temple	30.00
Over The Rainbow, Judy Garland	15.00
Pacers Two Step, Anna Stafford Henry, F A Mills, New York, 1897, 11 x 14"	50.00
Paul Revere's Ride, E T Paull, black and white	30.00
Ping Pong, Samuel Fox, Fox Music Co, Cleveland, 1902, 11 x 14"	60.00
Political, President–Vice President, J Church, Cincinnati	65.00
Popeye The Sailor Man, Irving Berlin, 1931, 9 x 12"	75.00
Respectfully Dedicated to Rudolph Valentino, 1932, brown and white, 9 x 12"	22.00
Rockaway–Or On Old Long Island's Sea Girt Shore, Geo P Reed, Boston, 1860, 10 x 14"	65.00
Roses In The Rain, Frank Sinatra	5.00
Rosey's Scorcher, George Rosey, 1897, 11 x 14"	70.00
Rum & Coca–Cola, Andrews Sisters, 1944	13.00
Sally's In The Movies Now, Coleen Moore, 1925, 9 x 12'	45.00
Salvation Lassie of Mine, 1919	20.00
Saratoga Schottisch, Horace Waters, New York, 1851, 13 x 10"	85.00

Scorcher, Popular Bicycle Song, Willis Woodward, 1897, 11 x 14"	95.00
Shoo–Shoo Baby, Andrews Sisters cov 1943	5.00
Silver Sleigh Bells, 1906, E T Paull color illus	30.00
Skating Polka, Root & Cady, Chicago, 1861, 13 x 10"	110.00
Skating Rink Girl, W Woodward & Co, New York, 1907, 11 x 14"	45.00
Somebody Stole My Gal	5.00
Some Sunday Morning, Errol Flynn and Alexis Smith, 1945	5.00
Song Of The South, Disney, 1946	10.00
Stein Song, Rudy Vallee	5.00
Tales My Mother Told To Me, 1911	17.50
Texas–Where The Mockin Bird Is Singin, Passenger Department, Texas & Pacific Railway, 1898, 11 x 14"	110.00
That Sinatra Swing, Frank Sinatra, 1944	10.00
The Band Played Nearer My God To Thee As The Ship Went Down, Morris Music Co, New York, 1912, 10½ x 14"	60.00
The Banjo Pickers, Frederic Groton, Carl Fisher Inc, 1929, green illus, white background	20.00
The Baseball, Johann C. Schmid, 1915, published by United States Music Co, blue on yellow	50.00
The Bus Stop Song, Marilyn Monroe, 1956	35.00
Theda Bara I've Lost You, 1916, 10 x 13", blue portrait	30.00
The Dying Drummer, Thomas Manahan & Mrs Parkhurst, 1864, 10 x 14"	35.00
The Flying Fortress, Gene Autry, 1944	10.00
The Grandpappy Polka, Johnny Giacoma, Gordon Jennings, 1947	5.00
The Illinois Waltz, Red Thompson Prairie Pioneers, 1948	5.00
The Light Ahead, Gertrude Lawrence, Lanny Ross, 1944	10.00
The Light of Western Stars, Zeke Williams, 1945	5.00
The Little Ford Rambled Right Along, C R Foster, 1914, 11 x 14"	50.00
The Mary Pickford Waltz, Art Craft Pictures, 1917	10.00
The Midnight Fire Alarm, E T Paull, minor wear	25.00
Then I'll Come Back to You, 1917, soldier and girl on cov	3.00
The Trolley Song, Judy Garland, 1944	35.00
They Were All Out of Step But Jim, 1928, Berlin	3.00
Three Little Words, 1930, Amos and Andy cov	15.00
Toot Toot Tootsie, Al Jolson, 1922	10.00
Union Soldier's Battle Song, Oliver Ditson & Co, Boston, 1864, 10 x 13"	35.00

Vassar Girl Waltzes, 1904, 8 pgs, Lewis and Clark	25.00
We Are Marching On To Victory, Horace Waters Publishing, New York, 1865, 10 x 13"	60.00
When I Lost You, Irving Berlin, 1912 . .	4.00
When It's Circus Day Back Home, c1917	8.00
When My Ship Comes Sailing Home, 1913	6.00
When The Kaiser Does The Goose Step, WWI	15.00
When You Wish Upon A Star, Pinocchio.	15.00
Whistle While You Work, 1937, Snow White and Seven Dwarfs cov	17.50
White Christmas, Irving Berlin, 1924 . .	7.00
Why Can't You?, Al Jolson cov	5.00
Walk The Straight and Narrow Way, Harpo & Bobby Cook, 1946	5.00
We Shall Meet Again, Amanda Snow, WLS Chicago, 1943	5.00
When I Die Make My Home in the Valley, Marty Licklider & Missouri Fox Hunters, 1946	5.00
When I Dream About the Wabash, Roy Rogers, 1945.	10.00
You, The Great Ziegfeld, 1936	5.00
You'll Never Understand, Patsy Montana, Jenny Lou Carson, 1945.	5.00
You're The Cream In My Coffee, 1928	5.00

My Pal Harry, black-and-white photo cover, Francis, Day & Hunter Ltd., 10 x 12¼", 1926, $4.00.

Your Melody of Love, June Barr, 1945	**5.00**
You Waited Too Long, Gene Autry cov, 1940	**12.00**

I'll Love You (All Over Again), F. Earl Christy illus., sgd., A. J. Stasny Music Co. Pub., full color litho, 9 x 12", 1920, $35.00.

STEREOGRAPHS

History: Stereographs, also known as stereo views, stereo view cards, or stereoscope cards, were first issued in the United States on glass and paper in 1854. From the late 1850s through the 1930s, the stereograph was an important visual record of every major event, famous person, comic situation, and natural scene. It was the popular news and entertainment medium until replaced by movies, picture magazines, and radio.

The major early publishers were Anthony (1859–1873), Kilburn (1865–1907), Langeheim (1854–1861), and Weller (1861–1875). By the 1880–1910 period, the market was controlled by large firms among which were Davis (Kilburn), Griffith & Griffith, International View Company, Keystone, Stereo Travel, Underwood & Underwood, Universal Photo Art, and H.C. White.

Value is determined by condition, subject, photographer (if famous), rarity, and age—prior to 1870 or after 1935. A revenue stamp on the back indicates an age of 1864–66, when a federal war tax was imposed. Litho printed cards have very little value.

Collect images that are of good grade or above, except for extremely rare images. Very good condition means some wear on the mount and a little dirt on the photo. Folds, marks on the photo, or badly worn mounts reduce values by at least 50%. Faded or light photos also reduce value.

Do not try to clean cards or straighten them. Cards were made curved to heighten the stereo effect, an improvement made in 1880.

With common cards, it pays to shop around to get the best price; for rarer cards, it pays to buy them when you see them since values are increasing annually. Dealers who are members of the National Stereoscopic Association are very protective of their reputation and offer a good starting point for the novice collector.

Use your public library to thoroughly study the subject matter you are collecting; it is a key element to assembling a meaningful collection.

References: William C. Darrah, *Stereo Views, A History Of Stereographs in America And Their Collection,* published by author, 1964; William C. Darrah, *The World of Stereographs,* published by author, 1977 (Out–of–print, but copies available from N. S. A. Book Service); John Waldsmith, *Stereo Views: An Illustrated History and Price Guide,* Wallace–Homestead, 1991.

Collectors' Club: National Stereoscopic Association, PO Box 14801, Columbus, OH 43214.

Note: Prices given are for very good condition, i.e., some wear and slight soiling. For excellent condition add 25%, and for mint perfect image and mount, double the price. Reverse the process for fair, i.e., moderate soiling, some damage to mount, minor glue marks, some foxing (brown spots) and poor folded mount, very dirty and damage to tone or both images.

Actress, J Gurney & Son, 1870s	**10.00**
Admiral Faraqutt, Anthony, Prominent Portrait series	**45.00**
Airplane, Keystone #V18921, twin seat fighter	**9.00**
Air Mail Plane, Keystone #29446, Cleveland	**25.00**
Alaska Gold Rush	
Keystone #21100, panning for gold . .	**12.00**
U & U #10655, looking into glory hole	**15.00**
Annie Cary, singer, J Gurney & Son	**15.00**
Apache Indians, J C Burge, bathing scene	**100.00**
Atlantic City, H C White, #476, bathers on beach scene	**5.00**
Automobile, U & U, 1903, early auto in Los Angeles	**18.00**
Aviators, Keystone #26408, six men who first circled earth	**15.00**
Babe Ruth, Keystone #32590, baseball player	**225.00**
Balloon, Anthony #4114, Prof Lowe's flight from 6th Ave, New York City . . .	**100.00**
Battleship, *USS Brooklyn,* Griffith #2535, 1902	**8.00**
Bicycle Bum, Graves, #4551–58, "Weary Willie," four card set	**20.00**

Bicycle, Thorne, early 1870s, big two wheeler	**40.00**
Biplane, Keystone #32785, five flying over Chicago field museum	**10.00**
Bird, Hurst's 2nd series, #7, birds perched in tree	**4.00**
Blackfeet, Indian, Keystone #V23181 . .	**8.00**
Blacks	
Boy and Mule, Kilburn #14317	**3.00**
Gambling	**12.00**
Happiest Coon, Whiting #961	**8.00**
Picking Cotton, Keystone #9506, "We done all dis a' morning"	**6.00**
Swimming, Singley #10209, "One never came up"	**12.00**
Blacksmith, Keystone #18206, blacksmith and tools	**5.00**
Booker T Washington, Keystone #V11960, with Andrew Carnegie	**60.00**
Boxer Rebellion, U & U, 1901, set of 72 cards	**175.00**
Boy, "The Attack," carving roast, ivory mounted, hand tinted	**4.00**
Bronx Zoo, Keystone #V21232, walrus	**3.00**
Brownies and Santa, Universal #4679, sleigh foreground	**20.00**
Buffalo Bill, American Scenery #1399, on horseback in New York	**50.00**
California Mid–Winter, Kilburn #9474– 2894, 1894	**12.00**
Century of Progress, Chicago, 1933, Keystone #32993, Lief Ericksen	**15.00**
Charles Lindbergh	
Sitting in plane with wife, Keystone #18920	**45.00**
Standing next to Spirit of St Louis, Keystone #30262T	**30.00**
Chicago Fire, Lovejoy & Foster, 1871, ruins	**10.00**
Chief Black Hawk, Keystone #23095 . . .	**8.00**
Children with Tree, Griffith #16833, Christmas dinner	**17.00**
Circus	
U & U, Chicago	**20.00**
Windsor & Whipple, Olean, NY, people with elephant	**35.00**
Clara Barton, Keystone #28002, American Red Cross founder	**50.00**
Columbian Exposition, Chicago, 1894, Kilburn, ferris wheel	**10.00**
Comet, Keystone #16645, Morehouse's	**9.50**
Cowboy, Keystone #12465, KScm7.00	
Crow Indian, F J Hayes #865, burial ground	**20.00**
Crystal Palace, ext. view, yellow mount	**25.00**
Crystal Springs Cave, Keystone #33516, int. view	**5.00**
Czar of Russia, U & U, President of France	**10.00**
Dancer, Keystone #33959, Bali, Dutch Indies	**2.00**
Death Valley, Keystone #32666, pool . .	**10.00**

Centennial Views, Phila., New Excelsior Series, Horticultural Hall From South East, orange ground, 7 x 3³/₈", $7.50.

Doll

Doll's Maypole, Webster & Albee #160 .... **20.00**

Girl asleep with cat and doll, U & U #6952 .... **9.00**

Playing Doctor, U & U #6922 ...... **15.00**

Sunday School Class, Graves #4362 **20.00**

Egypt, U & U, set of 100 cards **225.00**

Engine on Chestnut Hill Railroad **20.00**

Esquimau Indians, Griffith #11873, St Louis Fair **8.00**

Farming, Kilburn #1796, 1870s, hay ... **7.00**

Fire Engine, early 1870s, close view of pumpers **40.00**

Fireman, G K Proctor, horse drawn mid–distance hook–ladder **35.00**

Fishing

Bass, Ingersoll #3159, string of bass .. **6.00**

Halibut, Keystone #22520, commercial fishing **5.00**

Trout, Kilburn #115, 1870, a day's catch **5.00**

Galveston Flood, Graves, 1900, ruins... **6.00**

Garden of the Gods, Rodeo McKenney, Pike's Peak...................... **5.00**

General Custer, Taylor #2438, dog and camp scene **550.00**

Gene Sarazen, Keystone #32436, golfer **35.00**

Glacier Park, Forsyth, set of 30 cards ... **150.00**

Gold Hill, Houseworth #743, city overview...................... **75.00**

Going with Stream, U & U, hugging couple **6.00**

Graf Zeppelin, Keystone #32277, hanger in Lakehurst, NJ **35.00**

Grand Teton, Wm H Jackson, #503 .... **20.00**

Great Oregon Cave, Keystone #9586, man in front of cave............. **6.00**

Grocery Store, Keystone #18209, int. view...................... **15.00**

Gypsies, in front of tent **18.00**

Hawaii

Hula Girls, Keystone #10156 .... **9.00**

Waikiki Beach, Keystone #10162 ... **10.00**

Hoosac Tunnel, Ward #808, completion **15.00**

Hopi Indian, U & U **9.00**

Hunting

Deer, Keystone #26396, hunters and kill **4.00**

Moose, Keystone, #9452, 1899, big game kill **5.00**

Wildcat, Keystone #12264, man shooting sleeping wildcat **6.00**

Indian Girl, Keystone #23118, common view...................... **4.00**

Industry, Keystone #33143, employees leaving Ford plant **2.00**

International Exhibition 1876, Centennial Photographic Co, Philadelphia .. **22.00**

Jamestown Exposition, 1907, Keystone #14219, life saving demonstration ... **5.00**

Johnstown Flood, Baker, ruins **10.00**

Lewis & Clark Centennial, Portland, 1905, Watson Fine Art #34, building **9.00**

Lighthouse, Keystone #29207, common view...................... **4.00**

Lou Gehrig, Keystone #32597, baseball player **225.00**

Louisiana Purchase Exposition, St Louis, 1904

Education & Manufacturing buildings, White, #8491 .... **8.00**

Missouri Fruit Exhibit, Whiting #620 **10.00**

Luray Caverns, U & U **8.00**

Luther Burbank, Keystone #16746, with cactus **5.00**

Mammoth Cave, Waldack, 1866, #8, early magnesium light view........ **15.00**

Man, U & U, 1897, sneaking in after drinking, two card set **7.50**

Mark Twain, Evans & Soule........... **325.00**

Marriage, Keystone #2346–7, before and after wedding, cuddling and reading **7.00**

Mars, Keystone #16767T, the planet ... **6.00**

Michelin Bomber, Keystone #18920 ... **15.00**

Milkman, Keystone #P–26392, horse drawn wagon................... **10.00**

Mill Creek Flood, 1874, house **4.00**

Mining, Easter, Anthony #474, working a gold chute................... **45.00**

Minot Ledge Lighthouse, Williams **15.00**

Lehigh Valley Views, Mauch Chunk and Vicinity, No. 175, Coal Pockets, Loading Canal Boats, photographed and published by M. A. Kleckner, Bethlehem, PA, yellow ground, 7 x 3⅜", $10.00.

Moon
Beer Bros 1866, photo by Rutherford   **15.00**
Kilburn #2630, full moon **6.00**
Native Cane Grinders in Sunny FL, group of smiling blacks with sugar cane musical instruments, c1900 . . . .   **25.00**
New York City, Anthony #3938, typical street view **20.00**
New York Sanitary Fair, Anthony #1689–2864, fountain view **15.00**
Niagara Falls
Falls, Anthony #3731 . . . .   **4.00**
Ice Bridge, Barker **2.00**
Tourists, U & U **2.00**
Nieuport, Keystone #19049 . . . .   **9.00**
Opera Singer, James Cremer, studio pose in costume **12.00**
Opium Den, two tier bed, opium pipe . .   **60.00**
Pan American Exposition, Buffalo, 1901, Kilburn, President McKinley **8.00**
Piute Squaw, Soule #1312 . . . .   **50.00**
Planetarium, Keystone #32688, Adler's Chicago **10.00**
Portland Fire, 1866, Soule #469, ruins . .   **8.00**
President
Abraham Lincoln, Anthony #2948, funeral **50.00**
Calvin Coolidge, Keystone #28004, sitting at desk **20.00**
Harding, addressing boy scouts **18.00**
Henry Ford, Keystone #28023 . . . . . .   **40.00**
Prison, Pach, view of cabinets of rifles . .   **15.00**
Pueblo Indians, Continental Stereo Co, eating bread **55.00**
Quakake Station **20.00**
Queen Victoria, U & U 1897, having breakfast with Princesses **35.00**
Rogers Statuaries Group **8.00**
Rumors, H C White, 5576–5578, quickest way to spread news: "Tell a graph, tell a phone, tell a woman," three card set **20.00**
Sailboat, Anthony #22, early view **18.00**
San Francisco Earthquake Scene
Keystone #13264, Market St **5.00**
U & U #8180, California St **15.00**

Santa, Keystone #11434, coming down chimney with toys **12.00**
Seth Kingman, California Trapper **100.00**
Sioux Indian, F J Hayes #1742 . . . .   **50.00**
Sneaking–In, U & U, 1807, man caught by wife after night on town **6.00**
Steamship, *Yukon,* Keystone #24704, stern wheeler being loaded in Alaska   **30.00**
St Pierre Eruption, Kilburn #14941, ruins **3.00**
Summit Station **20.00**
The French Cook, Keystone #12312–22   **35.00**
Thomas Edison, Keystone #V28007, working in lab **95.00**
Thousand Islands, St Lawrence River, La Rue Island, A C McIntyre artist, 1870–80 . . . .   **15.00**
Tom Thumb Wedding, 1863, Anthony Brady photographer **45.00**
Toy Train, Keystone P–21329, boy playing with Lionel trains **25.00**
Train Wreck, Dole **50.00**
Unexpected, Weller #353, couple necking **4.00**
US Close Up Centennial, Centennial Photo Co, 1876
Corliss Engine **12.00**
Monorail **65.00**
Statue of Liberty **85.00**
Wall Street & Trinity Church, color litho, c1910 . . . .   **7.50**
Watkin's Glen, NY, titled "Artist's Dream" **2.25**
Wedding, White, #5510–19, scenes of getting ready, wedding, reception, and alone in bedroom **40.00**
West Michigan State Fair, 1908, Keystone #21507 . . . .   **12.00**
Whale, Nickerson, beached whale **45.00**
Wolpi Indian, U & U **10.00**
Woman Drinking, R Y Young 1901, two cards **16.00**
Worcester, MA Flood, Lawrence, 1876, damage **5.00**
World Peace Jubilee, Boston, Pollock, 1872, Coliseum int. view **8.00**

Wright Bros, Keystone #V96103, flight
in Ft Meyers **85.00**
Yellowstone National Park
Universal **4.00**
Wm H Jackson, #422 . . . .   **15.00**
Yosemite, U & U, set of 30 cards **125.00**
Zoo, London Stereo Company, animals
in London Zoo **10.00**

STOCK AND BOND CERTIFICATES

History: The use of stock to raise capital and spread the risk in a business venture dates back to England. Several American colonies were founded as joint venture stock companies. The New York Stock Exchange on Wall Street in New York City traces its roots to the late eighteenth century.

Stock certificates with attractive vignettes date to the beginning of the nineteenth century. As engraving and printing techniques developed, so did the elaborateness of the stock and bond certificates. Important engraving houses emerged among which were the American Bank Note Company and Rawdon, Wright & Hatch.

Some of the factors that affect price are (1) date [with pre-1900 more popular and pre-1850 most desirable], (2) autographs of important persons [Vanderfeller, Rockefeller, J. P. Morgan, Wells and Fargo, etc.], (3) number issued [most bonds have number issued in text], and (4) attractiveness of the vignette.

Stocks and bonds are collected for a variety of reasons, among which are the graphic illustrations and the history of romantic times in America, including gold and silver mining, railroad history, and early automobile pioneers.

Reference: Bill Yatchman, *The Stock & Bond Collectors' Price Guide,* published by author, 1985.

Periodical: *Bank Note Reporter,* 700 East State Street, Iola, WI 54990.

Collectors' Club: Bond and Share Society, 26 Broadway, New York, NY 10004.

BOND

Arlington Gas Co, NJ, $1,000, state seal
vignette, coupons, issued, 1880 . . . . .   **20.00**
Atchison, Topeka & Santa Fe RR, $1,000,
blue, two railroad station int. vi-
gnettes, issued **18.00**
Broadway Surface RR, New York City,
$1,000, gray, eagle and flag vignette,
issued, 1885 . . . .   **35.00**
Central New York & Western RR,

$1,000, old train vignette, fancy bor-
ders, green, pages of coupons, issued
and canceled, 1892 . . . .   **75.00**
City of Fort Wayne, Paul Baer Field Avia-
tion, $1,000, high wing radial engine
plane vignette, brown border, cou-
pons, issued, 1929 . . . .   **45.00**
Consolidated Edison Co, NY, $1,000,
blue, tower, Brooklyn Bridge, and
New York City background vignette,
issued, 1949 . . . .   **7.50**
Consolidated Railway Company,
$10,000, horse drawn trolley and
street scene, brown printing, unissued,
1905 . . . .   **25.00**
Delaware & Hudson Railroad Company,
$1,000, two women and farm scene
vignette, 1963 . . . .   **5.00**
Erie Railroad Company, $1,000, man,
woman, and logo vignette, red border,
1945 . . . .   **8.00**
Ford International Capital Corporations,
$1,000, blue, black, and white, 1968   **12.00**
General Motors Corp, $1,000, stream-
lined car, truck, locomotive, three
heads, and factory building vignette,
coupons, issued, 1954 . . . .   **15.00**
Gulf Mobile & Ohio, $1,000, diesel lo-
comotive, vignette, orange border,
1957 . . . .   **6.00**
Indiana Central Railway Company,
$1,000, train vignette, ornate border,
1852 . . . .   **175.00**
Lehigh Valley RR, steam locomotive in
switch yard vignette, issued **25.00**
Pennsylvania Canal Company, $1,000,
canal and surrounding area vignette,
two first issue revenue stamps, issued
and canceled, 1870 . . . .   **85.00**
Southern Bell Telephone & Telegraph,
$1,000, person speaking on telephone
and city and rural landscapes vignette,
coupons, issued, 1947 . . . .   **15.00**
Sovereign Gold Mining, $5,000, Cana-
dian, peach borders, coupons, issued
and canceled, 1903 . . . .   **15.00**
United Air Lines, $100 share, olive,
1970s **6.00**
USA City of Providence, RI, $1,000, In-
dians landing of pilgrims vignette **8.00**
Wisconsin Interurban System, orange,
state seal vignette, coupons, issued but
not canceled, 1917 . . . .   **45.00**

STOCK

Academy Motor Sales & Service, Inc, ea-
gle vignette, unissued **12.00**
Alaska Treadwell Gold Mining Com-
pany, blue, two miners and mountains
vignette, ornate, 1931 . . . .   **15.00**

Black Canyon Gold Mining Company, 500 shares capital stock, ornate black-and-white steel engraving, official seal in green, 11 x 8¼", 1907, $35.00.

American Express Co, issued and canceled, 1860s, bulldog vignette, sgd Henry Wells and William Fargo **750.00**

American Antimony Company, UT Territory, eagle on beehive flanked by Indian village and locomotive vignette and young girl vignette, 1883 . . . . **75.00**

Atwood Grapefruit Company, grapefruit, color, 1941–51 . . . . **10.00**

Baltimore, Ohio Railroad Co, engine and cars vignette, 1893 . . . . **25.00**

Bandoro Mining Co, State of Colorado, 1892 . . . . **30.00**

Banner Oil Co, AZ, oil well vignette **6.00**

Ben–Hur Motor Car, brown certificate, car and chariot vignette, issued, not canceled, 1917 . . . . **125.00**

Burlington, Chicago, Quincy Railroad Co, State of Illinois, train vignette **20.00**

Chicago Cotton Manufacturing Co, brown center, factory vignette, ornate design, unissued, 1870 . . . . **10.00**

Chollar Gould & Savage Mining Co, CA, 1941, ornate design, canceled **6.50**

Cienequita Securities Corp, miners and buildings vignette, 1909 . . . . **6.00**

Colt Manufacturing Co, CT **15.00**

Commerical Farms Co, Davidson Co, deer vignette, unissued, 1922 . . . . **6.00**

Confederate States of America Loan, February 20, 1863, engraved soldier in field **35.00**

Continental Motors Corp, orange certificate, car engine vignette, issued **15.00**

Cunard Steam Ship Co, Ltd **7.50**

Fairview Golden Boulder Mining Co, NV, brown certificate, gold nugget vignette, unissued, 1900 . . . . **12.00**

Four Seasons Nursing Centers of America, Inc, four cherubs vignette, 1970s **2.50**

Fruit of the Loom Inc, fractional share of common stock, script, green, black, and white, 1938 . . . . **5.00**

Gambrinus Brewing Co, Columbus, OH, king savoring glass of beer vignette, issued, 1909–13 . . . . **25.00**

General Public Utilities Corp, green certificate, man and generator wheel vignette, issued **3.00**

Gila River Mining Company, five eagle, horseman, and pelicans vignette, unissued **12.00**

Gray Manufacturing Co, State of CT, telephone vignette **10.00**

Gulf Mobile & Ohio Railroad Company, green, locomotive and women vignette, 1943 . . . . **5.00**

Hale Nouross Mining Co, Virginia Mining District Nevada, San Francisco, miner vignette **12.00**

H J Heinz, Co, red, issued **4.00**

Hornell Airways, Inc, vignette of two women and sun rising over mountains, issued and canceled, 1920s **75.00**

Humauma Oil Co, CA, ornate design, woman and bear, 1911 . . . . **22.50**

Ishpeming Livery Co, Ltd, MI, 1903, horse vignette, unused **6.00**

Jantzen Knitting Mills, engraved, woman diving into water vignette, issued, 1930s **35.00**

Kaiser–Frazer Corp, blue certificate, issued, 1940s **6.00**

Lehigh Valley Railroad Co, State of PA, man with beard and train vignettes, 1899 . . . . **20.00**

Elizabeth Iron Company, 40 shares captial stock, black and white, orange seal and stamp, 9½ x 5½", 1868, $40.00.

Lincoln Motor Company, orange certificate, issued, 1920s, sgd by W C Leland   20.00

Lincoln Printing Company, engraved Abe Lincoln vignette, 1962–65......   5.00

Narragansett Electric Co, Providence, RI, sailing ship vignette, 1877..........   25.00

Nashville, Chattanooga & St Louis RR, pink certificate, trains at railroad station vignette, issued..............   10.00

Northampton Brewery Corp, PA, orange certificate, engraved, woman, ship, and city skyline vignette, issued, 1930s........................   15.00

North Butte Mining Co, miners working in mine vignette, 1911.............   7.00

Old Colony Railroad Corporation, two train vignettes, red seal, 1848 ....   50.00

Ottaquechee Woolen Co, VT, unissued, 1870s........................   4.50

Pacific Railroad, MO, green certificate, train and mountains vignette, issued but not canceled, 1875 ....   75.00

Palmer Union Oil Co of Santa Barbara, CA, oil wells vignette, ornate design, canceled, 1928, 7½ x 11"..........   12.50

Panther Creek Mining Company, spread eagle vignette with two miners on top, green seal, unissued 8.00

Penn National Bank & Trust Co, Reading, PA, gray certificate, colonial man vignette, issued but not canceled, 1930   15.00

Pioneer steamship Co, Lake County, OH, ship vignette, 1914 ....   25.00

Pittsburgh, McKeesport & Youghiogheny RR, train vignette, sgd by Cornelius Vanderbilt for Lake Shore & Michigan Southern RR which guaranteed stock, purple, issued 250.00

Pittsburgh Tin Plate & Steel Corp, eagle over city vignette, canceled, 1920 ...   15.00

Providence, Boston Railroad, Co, boats, factories, and train vignette, 1883 ....   25.00

Purissima Hills Oil Co, marked "Incorporated Laws of Territory of Arizona,

February 1908," ornate oil well vignette, canceled, 1911 ....   22.50

Reading Fair Co, cows, horse, wagons, and farm buildings vignette, 1883....   25.00

Rio Grande Southern RR, CO, rust certificate, engraved, train coming out of mountain pass vignette, issued, 1890s   250.00

Santa Clara Valley Mill & Lumber Co, CA, lumber mill vignette, unissued, 1873 ....   15.00

Sentinel Radio Corp, green certificate, goddess and two radio towers vignette, issued, 1956..............   5.00

Submarine Signal Co, green certificate, ship on ocean vignette, issued, 1940   15.00

The Real Estate Association, Petaluma, CA, 1876, small size, black and white Issued, 1890s...................   25.00

Unissued 4.00

Thomas B Jeffery Co, CA, eagle vignette, issued and canceled, c1910 ....   125.00

Tuolumne County Water Co, mining methods vignette, 1854–62 ....   75.00

Utica & Mohawk Valley Railway, engraved, street car vignette, unissued, c1900 ....   25.00

Vallejo City Water Co, CA, early Vallejo city area vignette, unissued, 1868....   15.00

Verde Mines Milling Co, State of AZ, 1929 ....   6.00

Woolworth, F W & Co, vignette of eagle over two hemispheres, brown.......   3.00

Wyadot Copper Co, State of MI, Boston, MA........................   6.00

TICKETS

History: Collectors in more and more collecting categories are discovering what paper ephemera traditionalists have known for a long time—tickets are important social documents. Transportation, sports, and World's Fair collectors are just a few of the collecting groups where tickets are becoming a major emphasis.

Paper ephemera traditionalists' ticket interests have focused on admission tickets and toll/turnpike tickets. Admission tickets are a security document, serve as a record of an event, and, through typography, capture the flavor of the moment. In other words, tickets, especially those from the eighteenth, nineteenth, and early twentieth centuries, can have a personality all their own. Variety abounds. Age, decoration, and subject determine value.

Sports tickets and ticket stubs are one of the hottest paper categories in the sports memorabilia market. A stub is all that is needed for collectibility. Value rests in the importance of the game or match. All star and world series game tickets are worth more than one for a regular season game. Entertainment tickets, especially those associated with major rock 'n' roll concerts, also are experiencing strong sales. Collectors need to be concerned about unsold hoards. The reason so many Woodstock tickets still exist is that (1) all ticket security broke down early in the concert and (2) a stash of unsold tickets has worked its way into the market.

Toll or turnpike tickets were the first category of transportation tickets to be collected. Most people are unaware that many eighteenth and nineteenth century bridges and roads were built by private turnpike companies who charged a toll to recover construction and maintenance costs. Early tickets were usually printed in sheets and had to be cut apart. In order to prevent reuse, different colored tickets were printed and changed from day to day. Canal, ocean liner, railroad, railway (trolley), and steamship tickets are eagerly collected. Airline tickets lag behind.

Interest is growing in admission tickets to amusement parks and special events such as World's Fairs. Many of these tickets were sold in book form. Ticket books are sold at a slight discount, which has prompted some dealers to separate them and offer the tickets individually to get more money. Do not support this practice when you encounter it.

References: Stanley L. Baker, *Railroad Collectibles: An Illustrated Value Guide, 4th Edition*, Collector Books, 1990, 1993 value update; Richard Friz, *The Official Price Guide to World's Fair Memorabilia*, House of Collectibles, 1989; Roderick A. Malloy, *Malloy's Sports Collectibles Value Guide*, Wallace–Homestead, 1993; M. Donald Raycraft and R. Craig Raycraft, *Value Guide to Baseball Collectibles*, Collector Books, 1992.

Aviation
   Fall River Line, first class, New York to Fall River, 1882 . . . . **3.00**
   International Aviation Meet, Long Island, 1911, unused **22.00**
Baseball
   Baseball Circus, Indianapolis, black player illus, unused **55.00**
   Baseball O.S.U. vs. Kenyon, Benson Athletic Field, 1895–1900, May 2, game called at 3:15 PM, Admission 50 cents, light green, black print, $2^{1}/_{4} \times 3^{3}/_{4}$" **15.00**
   Harvard Baseball Association, 1880s, logo on front and back, green and black, $4^{1}/_{2} \times 1^{1}/_{2}$" **30.00**
Bowling, 32nd International Tournament, Detroit, MI, 1932, 5 x 3" **6.00**
Boxing, Jack Dempsey vs Tom Gibbons World's Heavyweight Championship fight, July 4, 1923, O'Toole County American Legion, Shelby, MT, Ringside, three part ticket, $7 \times 2^{3}/_{4}$" . . . **50.00**
Bus, Wasworth Transfer Co, one bus fare **3.00**
Circus
   Cole Bros Circus, Beatty and Maynard pictorial, 1938, unused **20.00**
   King Bros Circus, colorful, 1930s, unused **17.00**
   Von Bros Circus **4.00**
Lottery
   Kansas State Lottery, 1894, multicolored **8.00**
   New York State, Medical Science Lot-

Blue & Gray Championship Football Game, Montgomery, AL, 5¼ x 2⅛″, December 26, 1964, $8.00.

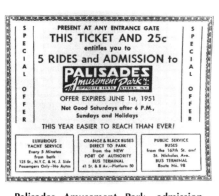

Palisades Amusement Park, admission and five rides, double folded, orange and blue, 4 x 9", expires June 1, 1951, $7.50.

tery Promotion, 1915, orange and
white 8.00
Music
  Cab Calloway & His Cotton Club Or-
    chestra, 1935 . . . .   12.00
  Elvis Presley, San Antonio Convention
    Center Concert, Oct 8, 1974,
    unused 50.00
  Grand Negro Jubilee Concert, c1890,

Southland Nightingales–Company
  of Negro Jubilee Singers 28.00
Pass
  Chicago Rapid Transit Co, 1933,
    weekly 2.00
  Gary Railways Co, Sunday, 1935 . . . .   2.50
  Mt Vernon Transit, 1946 . . . .   4.00
  Sturgeon Bay Transit, 1946 . . . .   5.00
  Two Rivers Transit, 1946 . . . .   4.00
Political, Democratic National Conven-
  tion, 1960, unused 12.00
Railroad
  Baltimore and Ohio, 1930s 3.00
  Boston and Main, 190s 2.00
  Cheasapeake and Ohio, 1920s 3.75
  Fort Smith & Western, 1920s 3.75
  Long Island Railroad, Hempstead can-
    cel, printed, black and white 12.00
  Northern Pacific, 1940s 2.25
  Pennsylvania, 1940s 1.75
  R L & N F Railroad, 1860s 50.00
  Susquehanna & New York, 1918 . . . .   6.00
  Union Pacific, 1920s 3.50
  Wisconsin Central, 1910 . . . .   3.50
Theater, School Matinee Diamond The-
  ater, A Call To Arms, orange and black   5.00
World's Fair
  Centennial Exposition, Philadelphia,
    1876, admission 20.00

World's Heavyweight Championship Fight, Dempsey vs. Gibbons, Shelby, MT, $50.00 ringside, red, black, yellow, and white, 7 x 2¾", July 4, 1923, $50.00.

YMCA Easter Breakfast, printed color, emb. diecut cross, orig. envelope, 6 x 3½", 1919, $10.00.

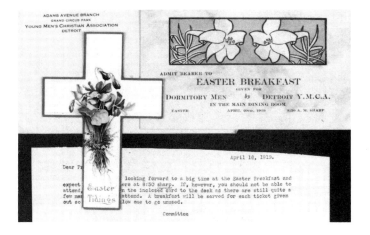

Columbian Exposition, Chicago, 1893
 General Admission, 5¢, 2 x 1" **27.50**
 Set of Java Village tickets, 50¢, 75¢,
 and $1.00 orange, $1.50, $2.00,
 $2.25, and $2.50 blue, and
 $3.00, $4.00, and $5.00 green . . **125.00**

TOBACCO CARDS

History: J. R. Burdick is responsible for the basic catalog by which all series trading cards are collected. The numbering system he assigned to each set is still used by collectors today. No paper collector should be without a copy of his *The American Card Catalog: The Standard Guide on All Collected Cards and Their Values*. It is available as a reprint from Nostalgia Press, PO Box 293, Franklin Square, NY 11010.

Burdick was fascinated by insert cards. An insert card is a single card from a series that is packed in a product. The desire to complete the set caused the individual to keep buying the product. The concept of insert cards was introduced in the 1870s and enjoyed widespread acceptance by 1885. Although employed by a wide variety of companies, including coffee, candy, chewing gum, and other food product manufacturers, the biggest user of the concept was the tobacco industry.

In 1880, the cigarette, especially the paper wrapped type, played only a minor role in the tobacco industry. Little cigars, cigarettes with a tobacco leaf wrapping, had a small following. In 1885, the shell and slide cigarette box was introduced. Ten cigarettes sold for a nickel. Insert cards were added to boost sales. It worked—sales soared. Automatic machines had to be developed to replace hand rollers to produce sufficient quantity of cigarettes to meet the demand.

Burdick divided tobacco insert cards into: nineteenth century American cards; twentieth century American cards; United States cards issued abroad; Canadian cards; and Central and South American cards. The twentieth century American cards are known as the "T" series; the most famous is the T204 set that contains the Honus Wagner card.

Tobacco insert cards fluctuate around a standard size of 1½" x 2¾". Larger cards tend to measure 2¼" x 4". The number of cards in each set varied. Sets of 25, 50, and 100 were popular in the nineteenth century.

Allen & Ginter, Duke, Goodwin, Kimball, Kinney, and P. Lorillard constitute the major users of tobacco insert card promotions in the nineteenth and early twentieth century. Most manufacturers sold a variety of brands. Allen & Ginter's brands included Virginia Brights, Richmond Gem, Richmond Straight Cut No. 2, Bower, The Pet, Little

Beauties, Dixie, Old Rip, Opera Puffs, Dubec, Dixie Dainties, Napoleon, Louisiana Perique, Old Dominion, and more. Card sets appeared in a variety of different brands.

In the first decades of the twentieth century, a craze developed for Turkish cigarettes. Brands such as Hassan, Mecca, Fatima, and Turkish Trophies arrived on the scene. These cigarettes were distributed worldwide and so were their insert cards.

Not all tobacco cards were plain picture cards. Novelty cards included Turkish Trophies jigsaw puzzle cards consisting of over two hundred views and subjects; Egyptian Oasis jumping novelties; and Fatima's movie booklets. Lucky Strike Bridge Tallies and Bridge Placecards are other popular novelty items among collectors.

In addition to individual cards, the tobacco companies issued souvenir albums. Albums with a complete set of cards could be obtained by accumulating the appropriate number of redeemable coupons. Other enterprising manufacturers developed albums to hold the individual cards.

Tobacco card collecting is international. It is especially strong in England where Murray Cards (International) (51 Watford Way, Hendron Central, London, England NW4 3JH) is one of the leading dealers and auctioneers. The company also offers an extensive list of books devoted to cigarette and other cards, many of which include exhaustive catalog listings.

References: J. R. Burdick, *The American Card Catalog: The Standard Guide on All Collected Cards And Their Values*, 1967, 1988 Nostalgia Press reprint; Murray Cards International, *Cigarette Card Values: 1992 Catalogue of Cigarette and Other Trade Cards*, Murray Cards (International), 1992.

REPRODUCTION ALERT: Be alert for cigarette card reprints. The English firm of Brooke Bond has reprinted a number of its early sets for the sole purpose of sale to collectors. Other commercial reprints, some dangerously close to the period sets, have appeared. Check carefully before buying.

Actresses, Lorillard's Climax Plug, ten
 sample views, 5 x 3¼" **7.00**
Advertising, Du Maurier Cigarettes, 1931 **4.00**
Air Raid Precautions, Churchman's Ciga-
 rettes, 1938, set of 48 . . . . **8.00**
Alice in Wonderland, Carreras Ciga-
 rettes, 1930, set of 48, round corners **25.00**
Animals at the Zoo, Ardath Tobacco Co,
 1924 . . . . **1.50**
Auto Racing
 Alfa–Romeo, Player Cigarettes, 1936 **5.00**
 Blue Bird, State Express Cigarettes,
 1935 . . . . **5.50**
 Freddie Dixon, Ardath Tobacco Co,
 1936–39, black and white photo . . **5.00**

Jaguar XK 120C, Wills, Imperial Tobacco, 1981................... **1.50**
Motor Racing, Turf Cigarettes, 1925 .. **7.50**
Richard Seaman, Churchman's Cigarettes, 1939 .... **3.00**
Thunderbolt, Ardath Tobacco Co, Ltd, 1935 .... **5.00**

Aviation
Air Raid Precautions, Churchman's Cigarettes, 1938, set of 48 .... **55.00**
Famous Airmen and Airwomen, Carreras Cigarettes, set of 50, 1³/₈ x 2⁵/₈" **240.00**
Fighting and Civil Aircraft, Ardath Tobacco Co, 1936, set of 25, printed in blue and gray shades **150.00**
Flying, Senior Service Cigarettes, 1938, set of 48, photo cards....... **90.00**
International Airlines, Player Cigarettes, set of 50, 1936, 1³/₈ x 2⁵/₈"... **75.00**
Ballerina, on couch, titled "Just So," 4 x 2¹/₂" **4.00**

Baseball
Fatima Cigarettes, major league teams, 1913, 5³/₄ x 2¹/₂"
  Boston, American League **30.00**
  Cincinnati, National League **20.00**
  Detroit, American League **45.00**
  Philadelphia, National League **20.00**
  Pittsburgh, National League **20.00**
  St Louis, American League........ **75.00**
Fez Cigarettes, 5³/₄ x 8", 1911
  5, Sam Crawford **25.00**
  8, Fred Clarke **20.00**
  23, Nap Lajoie **25.00**
  27, Christy Mathewson **30.00**
  39, Rube Waddell **35.00**
  42, Cy Young.................. **25.00**
  80, Chief Bender **22.00**

Billiards
Billiards, Turf Cigarettes, 1925, man playing pool, several men looking on......................... **7.50**
Joe Davis, Top Flight Cigarettes, 1959 **2.50**
Melbourne Inman, Churchman's Cigarettes, 1928, caricature image **9.00**
Birds & Their Young, Player Cigarettes, 1937, set of 50 .... **8.00**

Boxing
Mecca Cigarettes, early 1900s
  Joe Coburn.................... **1.50**
  Johnny Frayne **1.00**
  Terry McGovern **1.75**
Turkey Red Cigarettes, 5³/₄ x 8", early 1900s
  Johnny Coulon................. **25.00**
  Stanley Ketchel **38.00**
  William Papke................. **40.00**
Captain Dreyfus, Odgen Cigarettes, c1900, photo, 1¹/₂ x 2¹/₂".......... **12.50**
Children of All Nations, Ogden's Cigarettes, 1924, set of 50............. **20.00**

Chinese Scenes, United Kingdom Tobacco Co, 1933, set of 24 .... **8.00**
Christmas Greeting Card, Churchman's Cigarettes, 1938 .... **1.50**
Dogs, Player Cigarettes
Artist drawing, Arthur Wardle, pair of different breeds on each card, set of 25, 2¹/₂ x 3" **120.00**
Scenic background, full color, set of 50, 1³/₈ x 2⁵/₈", 1925............. **210.00**
Domino Cards, International Tobacco Co, 1938, set of 28............... **8.00**
Famous Buildings & Monuments, Series B, International Tobacco Co, 1934 ... **2.00**

Fire Fighting
Emergency Heavy Pump Unit, Wills Cigarettes, 1938................ **2.00**
Fire Fighting, Imperial Tobacco Co, 1³/₈ x 2⁵/₈", brown.............. **5.00**
Horsedrawn Steamer with Search Lights, Henley Cigarettes......... **15.00**
Hose Laying Lorry, Churchman's Cigarettes, 1938 .... **2.00**
Metropolitan Fire Brigade, Ogden's Cigarettes, c1901, 2¹/₂ x 1³/₈", black and white.................... **17.50**
Motor Fire Engine, Transport Then & Now, 1940.................... **2.00**
The Stirrup Hand Pump, Will's Cigarettes, 1938 .... **2.00**

Flower
Flower Culture in Pots, Will's Cigarettes, 1925, set of 50........... **12.00**
Garden Flowers, Will's Cigarettes, 1902, set of 50 .... **15.00**
Orchid, Carreras Cigarettes, 1925, set of 24........................ **10.00**
Football, Football Fixture Cards, The Casket Tobacco & Cigarette Co, 1909 **100.00**

Golf
Archie Compston, Churchman's Cigarettes, 1928, caricature illus **10.00**
Championship Golf Courses, Player

ROYAL AIR FORCE HEAVY BOMBER

Cigarette Card, Wings Cigarettes, Series B Heavy Bomber, #33, 2¹/₂ x 1³/₄", 1940s, $5.00.

Cigarettes, 1936, set of 25, 2¹/₂ x
3¹/₄", green, red, and yellow **600.00**
Famous Golfers, J Millhoff & Co, Ltd,
1927, set of 27, sepia tone photos .. **975.00**
Golf, Player Cigarettes, 1939, set of
25, 2¹/₂ x 3¹/₄", full color.......... **900.00**
Percy Aliss, Ardath Tobacco Co, 1935   **7.50**
Hot Air Balloon
Gordon Bennet Cup Balloon Race,
Turf Cigarettes, 1925 .... **5.00**
Over London In a Balloon, Ogden's
Cigarettes, 1900–04 .... **15.00**
Household Hints, Will's Cigarettes,
1927, set of 50.................. **8.00**
Jesse Owens, "Kings of Speed," Church-
man's Cigarettes, 1939, sepia photo,
1³/₈ x 2⁵/₈".................... **7.50**
Kings Coronation, Churchman's Ciga-
rettes, 1937, set of 50............. **8.00**
Military
History of Naval Uniforms, Carreras
Cigarettes, 1937, set of 50, 1³/₈ x
2⁵/₈", full color **225.00**
Life on Board A Man of War In 1805
and 1905, Imperial Tobacco Co, set
of 50, 1³/₈ x 2⁵/₈", full color....... **450.00**
Propelled Weapons, Mills Cigarettes,
1953, set of 25, full color, 1³/₈ x 2⁵/₈" **15.00**
World of Firearms, Will's Cigarettes,
1982, set of 36, 1³/₄ x 2³/₄" **30.00**
Movie, A & M Wix Tobacco Co, 1940
A Day At The Races, Marx Bros, 4 x
2³/₄" **10.00**
Dodge City, Errol Flynn and Olivia De
Haviland, 3 x 2¹/₂" **5.00**
Jezebel, Bette Davis and Henry Fonda,
black and white, 4 x 2³/₄"........ **5.00**
Singing Fool, Al Jolson, 3 x 2¹/₂" **10.00**
Way Out West, Laurel and Hardy,
black and white, 3 x 2¹/₂"........ **11.00**
Oceanliner
Celebrated Ships, Will's Cigarettes,
1911, set of 50, colored and printed **240.00**
Life In A Liner, Churchman's Ciga-
rettes, 1930, set of 25, full color.... **150.00**
The Queen Mary, Churchman's Ciga-
rettes, 1936, set of 50, 1³/₈ x 2⁵/₈",
full color **300.00**
The Story of Ships, Murray Co, 1940,
set of 50, full color............. **42.50**
Polar Exploration, A Series, Player Cigarettes, 1915, set of 25............. **20.00**
Radio Celebrities, A Series, Will's Cigarettes, 1934, set of 50............. **20.00**
School Emblems, Carreras Cigarettes,
1929, set of 50.................. **20.00**
Scottish Clan Series, J & F Bell, 1903, set
of 25 .... **175.00**
Shakespeare Series, Ogden's Cigarettes,
1905, set of 50, numbered......... **325.00**
Stage & Screen Personalities, Premier Tobacco, 1936, brown **2.00**

**Cigarette Card Album, Game Birds of
America, Allen & Ginter, Second Edition,
50 bird cards printed on 12 color litho
plates, c1890, $150.00.**

Tariff Reform Series, Anglo Cigarette,
1909 .... **15.00**
Tennis
Bill Tilden, Ardath Cigarettes, 1935,
full color, 1³/₈ x 2⁵/₈"............ **10.00**
Helen Jacobs, Ogden's Cigarettes,
1936, full color, 1³/₈ x 2⁵/₈" **7.50**
Helen Wills Moody, Phillips Ciga-
rettes, 1935, full color, 1³/₈ x 2⁵/₈" .. **5.00**
Tennis, Ardath Tobacco Co, 1938, set
of 50........................ **35.00**
The Laughing Cavalier, Guernsey To-
bacco Co, 1935, set of 48 .... **35.00**
Woman with Can, theatrical costume,
Sweet Lavender, 1¹/₄ x 2³/₄" **3.00**
Zeppelin, M Santos Dumont Navigating
Airship, Ogden's Cigarettes, 1900–04 **15.00**

VALENTINES

History: Early cards were handmade, often containing both handwritten verses and hand drawn
pictures. Many cards also were hand colored and
contained cutwork.

Mass production of machine–made cards featuring chromolithography began after 1840. In
1847, Esther Howland of Worcester, Massachusetts, established a company to make valentines
which were hand decorated with paper lace and
other materials imported from England. They had
a small "H" stamped in red in the top left corner.
Howland's company eventually became the New
England Valentine Company (N.E.V. Co.).

George C. Whitney and his brother founded a
company after the Civil War which dominated
the market from the 1870s through the first decades of the twentieth century. They bought out
several competitors, one of which was the New
England Valentine Company.

Lace paper was invented in 1834. The 1835 to
1860 period is known as the Golden Age of lacy

cards. Embossed paper was used in England after 1800. Embossed lithographs and woodcuts developed between 1825–40, with early examples being hand colored.

Previously, valentine collectors focused on cards made before 1930, with special emphasis on the nineteenth century. Cards made before 1800 are known, but most are in museums. Beginning in the late 1980s, interest began to shift from nineteenth century cards to those made between 1920 and 1960. Comic sheets, Art Deco, and cards with a streamlined modern motif are part of the reason. Subject collectors also have discovered the world of valentines. Prices for mid–twentieth century valentines still range from 50¢ to a few dollars, but retail value is increasing steadily.

References: Roberta B. Etter, *Tokens Of Love,* Abbeville Press, 1990; Helaine Fendelman & Jeri Schwartz, *The Official Price Guide to Holiday Collectibles,* House of Collectibles, 1991; Ruth Webb Lee, *A History of Valentines,* reprinted by National Valentine Collectors Association; Frank Staff, *The Valentine And Its Origins.*

Collectors' Club: National Valentine Collectors Association, Box 1404, Santa Ana, CA 92702.

Lacy Pullout, three dimensional, diecut decorations, decal-edge, 4¾ x 7⅛", $40.00.

Greeting Card

"A Friendly Valentine," boy in sailboat reading valentine, heart on sail, c1910	**3.00**
Art Nouveau, heart shape	**5.00**
Balloon with cherub and dove, opens to form flower, four tier fold–out, stand–up, emb, c1910	**30.00**
"Best Valentine Wishes," woman wearing winter clothing reading valentine card, c1920	**1.50**
Boy and Girl, strolling in woods, both holding flowers, four tiers, fold–out, stand–up, Germany, c1910	**28.00**
"Cupid's Temple of Love," honeycomb, c1928	**15.00**
Dainty Dimples Series	**5.00**
Diecut girl, emb, silver and gold paper lace, inside greeting, 9" h	**15.00**
"Fly To Me With Love," girl center, diecut paper lace, mounted geometrical shape, c1890	**5.50**
"For My Valentine," boy and girl picking flowers, inside greeting, 4" h, Whitney, USA	**1.50**
"Good Wishes For You," two children framed, diecut lace, emb background, inside greeting, 6" h	**8.00**
"Hearts Are Ripe," children picking heart shape apples	**5.00**
"I'd Make a Bird of a Valentine," parrot, stand–up, 5" h, Germany	**4.00**
"I'd Love To Paint You My Valentine,"	

boy painting a girl's portrait, fold–out, stand–up, 6" h, USA	**3.00**
"It Must Be Fine, To Have A Valentine," Valentine Wishes Series	**10.00**
"Lady Killer," comical, A J Fisher, NY, c1850	**30.00**
Little Lulu and Tubby, stand up	**15.00**
"Loves Message," cupid delivering floral garland to girl, dated 1902	**3.00**
"Loving Greetings," diecut girl and boy sitting on chaise, emb background, fold–out, stand–up, 9" h, Germany	**15.00**
"My Valentine, Think Of Me," boy holding bouquet, c1900	**2.00**
"Remember Me, Yours Forever," paper lace, printed poem, c1900	**2.00**
Religious, flowers, five layers, pull–down, Germany	**50.00**
"Such Is Married Life," mechanical, c1950	**45.00**
"Temple Of Love," Raphael Tuck, Betsy Beauties Series, girl chasing butterfly	**6.00**
"To My Dear Valentine," heart shape, girl portrait center, c1910	**1.50**
"To My Sweetheart," boy playing rugby, wearing striped shirt, c1920	**3.50**
"To My Sweetheart," boy wearing	

golfing outfit, swinging golf club, Germany, c1920 . . . .   **4.00**

"To My Sweetheart," cupid holding package, fold–out, red tissue paper, stand–up, 5" h, USA **7.00**

"To My Sweetheart," two cupids, fold–out, tissue paper, 8" h, USA . .   **7.50**

"To My Valentine," boy and girl holding flowers, blue diecut background, fold–out, stand–up, 6" h, Germany **8.00**

"To My Valentine," boy playing a mandolin, fold–out, stand–up, diecut background, 6" h, Germany . . .   **8.00**

"To My Valentine," girl driving toy car, delivering Valentine, Germany, c1910 . . . .   **4.50**

"To My Valentine," girl holding flowers, fold–out skirt, tissue paper, stand–up, 6¾", Germany **5.00**

"To My Valentine," girl holding envelope, red and pink fold–out, tissue paper, stand–up, 9" h, Germany . . .   **12.00**

"To My Valentine," little ballerina, foldout, cutout, 6" h, Germany **5.00**

"To My Valentine," two young girls peering over fence, boy postman arriving with large valentine, Germany, c1910 . . . .   **3.00**

"True Love," heart shape frame with woman center, floral cluster border, c1890 . . . .   **3.00**

"True to Thee," diecut flowers and girls, blue windmill background, fold–out, stand–up, 5¼", Tuck **10.00**

"Valentine Greetings," heart with girl and landscape illus, emb, c1910 . . .   **2.00**

"Valentine's Greetings," two girls, diecut, Germany **7.00**

"Will You Be My Valentine," boy wearing sailor suit and duck, c1920   **2.00**

"With Love's Greeting," oval frame with boy and girl riding bicycle, vinework dec, c1890 . . . .   **1.50**

Postcard

"A Heart Secret," red heart with lock and key, square frame with woman center upper left corner, verse on bottom, John Winsch **15.00**

"A Valentine Reminder," woman with valentines, red hearts within heart background, verse on bottom, John Winsch **18.00**

"Be My Valentine," girl wearing purple dress, holding bouquet of roses, gold heart and verse background, marked "Whitney, USA," 1930s . . .   **1.25**

Cupid on swing of roses, red hearts and gold scroll work border, marked "E Nash" **1.25**

"February 14th," heart with cupids

shooting hearts and arrows at lovers, green ivy trim, Germany, 1910 . . . .   **1.50**

"Hand it to me straight, Will you be my Valentine?," girl holding bouquet and wearing hat with feather plumes, standing on heart **1.50**

"Love's Greeting," boy and girl, 1922, sgd "Ellen H. Clapsaddle" **5.00**

"My Valentine Think Of Me," two young girls **3.00**

"St. Valentine's Greeting," girl wearing long blue dress and blue hat with bag and umbrella, heart background **5.00**

"St. Valentine's Greetings," girl and boy, sgd "Ellen H. Clapsaddle" **5.00**

"To My Sweetheart," semi–nude boy chef holding platter with steaming arrow pierced heart, John Winsch . .   **20.00**

"To My Sweet Valentine," woman greeting three cupids, sepia tones . .   **1.50**

"To My Valentine," Gibson girl on swing, gilded background **2.00**

"To My Valentine," large heart center with two cupids and flowers **2.50**

"To My Valentine," pumpkin head man and woman sitting on bench, verse on top **5.00**

"To My Valentine," two cupids holding garland of hearts, marked "London, 1910" **1.50**

"To My Valentine," two cupids picking heart shape apples in tree, one cupid standing on ground holding sack of apples open **2.50**

"To My Valentine with Love," portrait of a young girl, emb background . . .   **2.00**

"Valentine Greetings," Dutch boy holding heart **1.50**

Mechanical, little girl stirring kettle, 4 x 6", 1930s, **$6.50.**

"Valentine Greetings," Gibson girl framed by heart, 1916 . . . .   **2.00**
"Valentine Wishes," large heart with message, boy and girl sitting on bench. **1.50**

VIEW BOOKS

History: Escaping from the urban environment, especially during the summer, was an established practice of the wealthy and middle class by the middle of the nineteenth century. A resort industry developed at many beach and mountain communities. Those who could not leave their home or work for an extended period spent a shorter time, ranging from a few days to a week. The concept of an annual vacation developed slowly during the nineteenth century.

Fast, dependable public transportation made escaping even easier. Individuals and families thought nothing of traveling three to four hours to spend a "day at the beach." Many traveled to the "big city" for the first time.

As the nineteenth century ended, Americans developed a historical consciousness, fostered in part by the American centennial celebrations. Visiting important historic sites, from Boston to Gettysburg, became popular.

Many of the individuals who traveled to the beach, big city, historic site, or mountain wanted a souvenir of their visit. One of the most popular souvenirs of the Victorian era was the view book.

Nineteenth and early twentieth century view books were small, hardcover booklets that contained a strip of folded paper that was printed on both sides. The standard bill of fare was a series of sepia toned engravings showing landscape views and prominent buildings. Size varied. The standard size was slightly smaller than a post card.

The cover was often elaborate with embossed and relief designs. The title usually was added with gold leaf. Unfortunately, the quality of the binding left much to be desired. Heavy use resulted in the covers separating from the folded section. The paper generally was of modest quality and had a glossy surface.

As the art of photography developed, the engraved scenic view book was replaced by one that contained actual photographs of the area. By the end of the nineteenth century, the accordion fold format gave way to a small bound book of views. The idea would be resurrected during the linen post card era (1920–1940) when accordion fold post card units were popular.

View books sell best in the locale to which they apply. Collectors prefer photographic view books over those containing engraved views. View books are especially helpful to local preservation groups who use the photographs for research purposes.

Aldershot, headquarters of British Army, 34 pgs **25.00**
Billy Rose's Aquacade, New York World's Fair, 1939, Weissmuller cov   **30.00**
Bisley Rifle Meeting and Camp, shooting headquarters of British Army, c1900, 32 pgs **25.00**
Buffalo & Niagara Falls, early 1900s **3.00**
California, issued by Union Pacific System, 1929, 45 pgs **10.00**
Cathedral of Commerce Woolworth Building, NY, 1918, 31 pgs, color and black and white **7.00**
Century of Progress, Chicago, 1933, 28 pgs, full color illus, orig envelope, 6 x 8¼" **30.00**
Descriptions of the Great Temple–Salt Lake City, 1929 . . . .   **3.00**
Florida, 1936, 32 pgs, 8 x 5½" **8.00**
Glasgow Exhibition, 1901, 44 views and pictures **25.00**
Gloucester, MA, 1905, 8 x 10" **13.00**
Grand Canyon, 1910, 21 color photos, Kolb Brothers **20.00**
History of Finnish Mutual Fire Insurance Co, 1890–1915, 1915, 52 pgs **6.00**
Howe Caverns, NY, 1941, 72 pgs, includes foldout map, 5 x 7½" **10.00**
How to See the Best in the West, Standard Stations, 1940 . . . .   **4.00**
Lexington and Concord, MA, 1903. . . . .   **10.00**
Milan, Italy, 1920s **6.00**
Mohican Trail, Catskill Mountains, NY, 1920s, 40 pgs, 5 x 7" **18.00**
Mt Vernon, 1921, 32 pgs, Beck Engraving Co, Philadelphia **10.00**

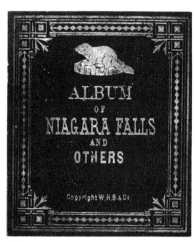

Album of Niagara Falls and Others, copyright W. H. B. & Co., dark green emb. cardboard covers, gold lettering and dec., sepia illustrations, 4⅝ x 5½", c1900, $30.00.

Napoli, 1930, 32 foldout panels, chromolithograph cov, 4½ x 6½" **14.00**

New York World's Fair, 1934, 64 pgs ... **30.00**

New York World's Fair, 1939, Official Souvenir Book, spiral bound, orange and blue cov with Trylon and Perisphere illus, 10 x 14" **50.00**

North Carolina, 1946, 28 pgs, full color, 8 x 5½" **8.00**

Pan–American Exposition, 1901, 100 pgs, illus, 6½ x 9" **28.00**

Pasadena Tournament of Roses Pictorial, 1957 .... **5.00**

Philadelphia, 1964, 128 pgs, dj, 5 x 7" .. **8.00**

Photostint Views of Picturesque Detroit, The Convention City, 1899, sixteen color plates, 9 x 6" **7.00**

Piney Ridge Resort & Round About There, Ludinton, MI, diecut cover, 1890s..................... **12.00**

Portland, ME, views of Portland & vicinity, 1895, 32 pgs **12.00**

Quebec Canada, early 1900s **3.00**

Rome, 1930s, 100 pgs, full color, 10 x 7" **6.00**

Royal Mail Cabin Liners, int. views, 1924 **25.00**

Sights and Scenes of the World, 1899, 19 photos **35.00**

The Adirondacks, 1880s **8.00**

The Call of the Mountains–Vacations in Glacier National Park, 33 pgs, 1925, 8 x 11" **10.00**

The Shasta Route In All Its Grandeur–Scenic Guide Book San Francisco...To Portland, OR, 1915, 25 pgs, 12 x 9½" **16.00**

Touraide, New York World's Fair, 1939, spiral bound, 48 pgs, issued by Conoco, 9 x 12".................. **26.00**

Trail of the Olympian–2000 Miles of Scenic Splender–Chicago to Puget Sound, 1914, 36 pgs, 9½ x 6" **12.00**

Panama Canal, I. L. Maduro's Souvenir Store, Panama, color litho covers, black-and-white photo illustrations, 32 pages, 10 x 8", c1910, $30.00.

Universal Exposition, St Louis, 1904, 81 pgs, emb cov, 12 x 9½" **24.00**

Watkins Glen, NY, 1910, color photos, 5½ x 7" **9.00**

White Mountains, 1938, 20 pgs, 7 x 5".. **10.00**

Worcester, MA, 34 views, 6 x 8", 1915.. **5.00**

World's Columbian Exposition Presented by Mfgrs of Wonderful Lehr Seven Octave Piano Style Organs, Easton, PA, sepia photos **16.00**

Yellowstone National Park, 24 color views, 10 x 13" **20.00**

WRAPPERS, GUM CARD

History: The first wrappers date from the early 1930s and were issued by the Goudey Company. All card companies adopted the practice.

The collecting of gum card wrappers is now firmly established. Remember, the wrapper itself may be 1,000 times more scarce than the cards that it protected. Wrappers were quickly discarded; few were purposely saved. Some wrappers, such as "Horrors of war," are truly rare. Others are in demand and can command prices exceeding $500.

The most desirable wrappers are those based on TV shows, movies, and historical figures. The period of 1965 to 1978 witnessed a large number of gum sets being offered. Wrappers from this era are a good starting point for the novice collector.

Pick a limited topic or theme and concentrate on it. The first wrapper an individual tends to buy is either a cover for a set of cards already in his possession or because he remembers the set from childhood. Before long, he is hooked.

Wrappers may be cleaned of wax build–up and mildew with a cotton swab. Using your fingernail or sharp pointed object runs the risk of tears. Tears can be repaired by putting tape on the back surface of the wrapper. However, don't use tape unless absolutely necessary. Wrappers with portions missing, especially on the front, are greatly reduced in value.

Most collectors display wrappers by placing them in plastic notebook pages. The wrapper is either folded to original pack size or unfolded and laid flat.

The discovery, not uncommon, of unopened boxes of cards in a long–forgotten warehouse can create significant price fluctuation for the cards as well as the wrappers. Collectors must constantly keep the idea that the sudden appearance of a scarce wrapper is a sign that a hoard has been found. Further, collectors have been wrapper conscious since the early 1980s. Everyone now saves the wrappers. The result is that post–1980 wrappers are never likely to reach the value of their pre–1980 counterparts.

Research has begun on wrapper artists. Many

comic book illustrators designed gum card wrappers.

The growing collector interest in the non–sport cards has brought wrappers into the mainstream of non–sport collecting. For years, wrapper collectors viewed themselves as an independent collecting group. Today, *The Wrapper*, the principal publication for wrapper collectors, contains more advertising for cards than it does for wrappers.

To date, the bulk of wrapper collecting has focused on wrappers involved with sport and non–sport trading cards. What about candy and chewing gum wrappers? A small, but dedicated group of collectors has been collecting chewing gum wrappers. The real opportunity appears to be in the area of candy wrappers. Collector interest is minimal at the moment. Alas, so also is survival. Perhaps the growing collectibility of candy boxes will spark interest in candy wrappers. Time will tell.

References: Christopher Benjamin, *The Sport Americana Price Guide to Non–Sport Cards, 1930–1960, No. 2*, Edgewater Book Co., 1993; Christopher Benjamin, *The Sport Americana Price Guide to Non–Sport Cards, Part Two: 1961–1992, No. 4*, Edgewater Book Co., 1993; John Neuer, *Checklist & Prices of U.S. Non–Sport Wrappers*, published by author, 1992.

Periodicals: *Collect*, Tuff Stuff Publications, 2309 Hungary Road, Richmond, VA 23228; *Non–Sport Network*, 19 Lores Plaza, #160, New Milford, CT 06776; *The Non–Sport Update*, Roxanne Toser Non–Sport Enterprises, Inc., PO Box 5858, Harrisburg, PA 17110; *The Wrapper*, PO Box 227, Geneva, IL 60134.

Addams Family, Donruss, 1964	25.00
Alien, 1979	12.00
Andy Gibb, Donruss, 1978	1.00
Annie Album Stickers, Topps, Panini Co, 1982	.35
Antique Autos, Bowman, 1953	65.00
Archie Tattoos, Topps, 1969	15.00
Astro Boy Tattoos	10.00
Astronauts, Topps, 1963	75.00
Autos of 1977, Topps	1.00
Back–Slapper Stickers, Fleer	6.00
Baseball Stickers, Fleer	3.00
Baseball Super Freaks, 1st Series, Donruss	2.00
Baseball Weird–Ohs, Fleer	20.00
Batman, 1966	
Adam West photo	39.00
Batman & Robin	35.00
Three Bat logos	32.00
Battle, Topps, 1965	100.00
Battlestar Galactica, 1978, Topps	.35
Batty Buttons, Topps, c1973	6.00
Bay City Rollers, 1975	5.00

Beatles Movie, A Hard Day's Night, Topps, 1964	25.00
Ben Casey and Dr Kildare, 1962	32.00
Beautiful People	2.00
Believe It Or Not, Fleer, 1970	8.00
Black Hole, Topps, 1979	.35
Bobby Sherman, "Getting Together," Topps, 1971	200.00
Brady Bunch, Topps, 1969	35.00
Bugs Bunny Roadrunner Tattoos, Topps, 1980	.50
Captain Nice, Topps	250.00
Casey & Kildare, Topps, 1962	40.00
Choppers & Hot Bikes, Donruss	4.00
Combat, 1963	32.00
Comic Book Foldees, Topps, 1966	15.00
Comic Cover Stickers, Topps, 1960s	20.00
Crazy Stick–Ons, Bazooka Sugar Free Bubble Gum, 1979	1.00
Cyndi Lauper, Topps, 1985	.35
Daktari, Philadelphia Chewing Gum Company, 1966	35.00
Dark Shadows, 2nd Series, Philadelphia Chewing Gum Company, 1969	20.00
Disgusting Disguises, Topps, 1970	10.00
Doctor Dolittle Tattoos, 1967	15.00
Drag Nationals, Fleer, 1972	8.00
Dukes of Hazzard, Donruss, 1980	.35
Elephant Jokes, L M Becker Company, 1960s	40.00
E T, Topps, 1982	.35
Evel Knievel, Topps, 1974	7.00
Famous Americans, Topps, 1963	50.00
Fiends and Machines, Donruss, 1970	35.00
Flags of the World, Topps, 1970	15.00
Flying Nun, Donruss, 1968	5.00
Frankenstein Stickers, Topps, 1966	15.00
Freddie and the Dreamers, 1966	10.00
Funny Travel Posters, Topps, 1967	7.50
Garbage Pail Kids, Topps	1.00
Giant Size Funny Valentines, Topps, 1961	25.00
Gilligan's Island, Topps, 1965	20.00
Glow Worms & Bed Bugs Tattoos, 1960s	10.00
Gomer Pyle, Fleer, 1965	50.00
Good Guys & Bad Guys, Leaf, 1966	50.00
Green Berets, Philadelphia Chewing Gum Company, 1966	8.00
Gumby and Pokey, Fleer, 1968	15.00
Harry & The Hendersons, Topps	.25
Hogan's Heroes, Fleer	150.00
Hysterical History, 1976	6.00
Idiot Cards, Donruss, 1961	25.00
Insult Post Cards, Topps, 1966	15.00
James Bond 007, Philadelphia Chewing Gum Co, 1965	25.00
Jet Set Stickers, Fleer	2.00
King Kong, 1965	30.00
Kookie Plaks, Topps, 1965	50.00
Krazy People Posters, Topps	35.00
Land of the Giants, Topps, 1968	125.00
Laugh–In, 1968	32.00

Little Shop of Horrors 35
Lost In Space, 1965 . . . . 125.00
Mad Ad Foldees, Topps, 1976 . . . .   1.50
Magic Pictures, Bowman, 1955 . . . . 48.00
Man From U.N.C.L.E., 1965 . . . . 59.00
Marvel Superheroes, 1966 . . . . 28.00
Maya, Topps 15.00
McHale's Navy, 1965 . . . . 32.00
Mickey Mouse, 1930s 140.00
Monkees, Donruss, 1966 . . . . 15.00
Monster Greeting Cards, Topps, 1965 . . 35.00
Munsters, Leaf, 1966, green, black, and
   red design 50.00
My Kookie Klassmates, 1960s 12.00
Nice Or Nasty Valentines, Topps, 1971   8.00
Osmonds, Donruss, 1973 . . . .   6.00
Pac Man, Fleer 35
Partridge Family, Topps, 1971 . . . .   5.00
Pirates Bold, Fleer 125.00
Planet of the Apes, Topps, 1969 . . . . . . 12.00
Quentin, 1969 . . . . 10.00
Rat Fink Greeting Cards, Topps, 1965 . . . 15.00
Rat Patrol, 1967, unopened 42.00
Return of Oz, Topps, 1985 35
Ripley's Believe It or Not, 1970, un-
   opened 42.00
Robert Kennedy, 1968 . . . . 15.00
Rocky Horror Picture Show, 1975 50
Saturday Night Fever, Donruss, 1978 35
School Days Stickers, Fleer 6.00
Secret Wars, Leaf 1.00
Shock Theater, Topps, 1975 . . . . 10.00
Six Million Dollar Man, Topps, 1974 . . . 25.00
Soupy Sales, Topps 25.00
Spook Stories, Leaf Gum, 1963–65, 6 x
   6¼" 50.00
Spook Theater, Leaf, 1961, Frankenstein 65.00

Wrigley's Spearmint Chewing Gum, NRA stamp, dated 1932, $10.00.

Star Trek, Leaf, 1967, photo wrapper . . . 200.00
Stupid Stamps, 1960s 12.00
Superman, 1965, George Reeves 40.00
Super Sneekies, Fleer, 1971 . . . .   4.00
Tarzan, Philadelphia Chewing Gum Co,
   1966 . . . . 30.00
Three Stooges, 1959 . . . . 140.00
Tom & Jerry Tattoos, Topps, 1965 . . . . . . 15.00
Ugly Buttons, 1966 . . . . 15.00
Untouchables, Leaf, 1961 . . . . 15.00
US Presidents, Topps, 1972 . . . . 10.00
Valentine Postcards, 1970 . . . . 10.00
Vote!, 1960s 10.00
Voyage to the Bottom of the Sea,
   Donruss, 1964 . . . . 25.00
Waltons, Topps, 1973 . . . . 75.00
Wanted Posters, 1975 . . . .   6.00
Way Out Wheels, 1970 . . . .   8.00
Wierd–Ohs, 1963, unopened 29.00
World of Stamps, 1960s 8.00
Wrigley's Spearmint–The Perfect Gum,
   unopened, 1916 . . . .   6.00
You'll Die Laughing, Topps, 1973 . . . . .   2.00
Zoo's Who, Topps 3.00

Part III
Collecting Paper
by Subject

AMUSEMENT PARKS

Collectors' Clubs: International Association of Amusement Parks & Attractions, 1488 Duke St., Alexandria, VA 22314; Historic Amusement Foundation, 4410 North Keystone Ave., Indianapolis, IN 46205.

Parks
  Advertising Trade Card
    Atlantic City, multicolored, boardwalk scene, Maizena National Starch Co adv, printed in Germany **75.00**
    Coney Island, Manhattan Beach, timetables, sepia and green tones, American Bank Note Co adv **60.00**
  Booklet, Cedar Point Amusement Park, Breakers Hotel, 25th Annual Outing Convention–Midland Grocery Co, OH, 1922, June, 128 pgs, aerial view **15.00**
  Folder, Coney Island, Brighton Beach Hotel, bathing pavillion, inside text with facts and timetables, yellow and green tones, 1879 . . . . **40.00**
  Photograph, set of 6, Coney Island, 1941 . . . . **17.00**
  Playing Cards
    Disneyland, castle photograph . . . **5.00**
    Dorney Park, Allentown, PA, Alfundo the Clown **5.00**
  Post Card, Dixieland Park, Jacksonville, FL, color view, 1908 . . . . . . **3.00**
  Poster, 39 x 30", Coney Island, Barnum & Bailey–Coney Island Wa-

Souvenir Program and Guide Book, Steel Pier, Atlantic City, NJ, 16 pages, 8½ x 11", 1945, $18.00.

Booklet, Masonite, 1934 World's Fair, color covers, black-and-white illustrations, 8 pages, 4 x 6", $10.00.

    ter Carnival, color, Strobridge Litho, 1898 . . . . **1,500.00**
  Stereograph
    Asbury Park, NJ, buildings, G W Pach, 1870s **10.00**
    Coney Island, NY, #501, trained bears on merry–go–round, H C White **18.00**
  Ticket, Luna Park, Washington, DC, 2½ x 4¼", cardboard, complimentary admission, yellow crescent moon, black lettering, blue ground, c1900 . . . . **20.00**
Rides
  Post Card, Shooting the Chutes, Sylvan Beach, NY, water slide, 1928 postmark **5.00**
  Poster
    C W Parker, Leavenworth, KS, 28 x 21", carousel, steam engine and military band organ vignettes, Japanese mulberry paper backing, framed **825.00**
    Panoramic View, 28 x 41", various rides including The Whip, Ferris Wheel, and Carousel, multicolored, Riverside Print Co, c1910 . . . . **175.00**
    The Jumping Horse Carry–Us–All, 28 x 42", full color, early Parker carousel illus, Riverside Print Co, Milwaukee, c1908 . . . . **1,250.00**
  Sheet Music
    If I Loved You, from *Carousel,* Rogers & Hammerstein, cov with carousel illus, 1945 . . . . . . **10.00**
    Just Take Me Down To Wonder-

land, cov with amusement park
rides illus, 1907 . . . .   **20.00**
Window Card, 11 x 14", Carousels–
Parker's Sublime Creation, carousel company adv, multicolored,
stone litho, angels blowing bugles,
inventor's portrait, c1900 . . . . . .   **90.00**

ANIMAL

References: Juanita Burnett, *A Guide To Easter
Collectibles,* Collector Books, 1992; Ralf
Coykendall Jr., *Coykendall's Second Sporting
Collectibles Price Guide,* Lyons & Burford, 1992;
Ralf Coykendall Jr., *Coykendall's Sporting Col-
lectibles Price Guide,* Lyons & Burford, 1991;
Herbert N. Schiffer, *Collectible Rabbits,* Schiffer
Publishing, 1990; Bob and Beverly Strauss,
American Sporting Advertising, Volume 1, (1987,
1992 value update) Volume 2, (1990, 1992 value
update) published by authors, distributed by L–W
Book Sales.

Periodical: *Moosletter,* 240 Wahl Ave., Evans
City, PA 16033.

Collectors Clubs: The National Elephant Collectors Society, 380 Medford St., Somerville, MA
02145; The Frog Pond, PO Box 193, Beech
Grove, IN 46107.

Domestic
  Advertising Trade Card
    Cow, farmer milking cow for thirsty
    cat, Carnrick's Lacto–Preparata   **35.00**
    Hog, mechanical, Cudahy Packing
    Company **40.00**
  Book, *The Book of Dogs,* National
  Geographic Society, 1919, dj **30.00**

**Children's Book, *Farmyard Friends,* Sam
Gabriel Sons & Co., NY, linenette covers,
12 pages, 10 x 12", 1918, $27.50.**

Bookmark, white rat, Seaside Library,
printed color **3.00**
Diecut
  Cows and milkmaid, 8½ x 10",
  printed color, compliments of
  James Nicholson, Terre Haute, IN   **15.00**
  Farm Animals, two roosters, one
  goat, printed color, 4" l **12.00**
  Rabbits, white, Easter Greeting, four
  layer foldout, printed color, Ernest
  Nister **15.00**
  Rooster, crowing, 7 x 11", printed
  color **25.00**
Envelope, grazing cows, DeLaval
Cream Separator adv, 1932 . . . .   **30.00**
Sheet Music, *If A Rooster Can Love So
Many Little Chickens Can't A Man
Love More Than One,* strutting
rooster surrounded by hens, skyline
background, 1912 . . . .   **20.00**
Window Card, 9 x 7", White Leghorns,
color litho, 1873 . . . .   **35.00**
Extinct
  Big Little Book, *Hal Hardy in the Lost
  Land of Giants,* #1413, R B Winter,
  Tyrannosaurus Rex and Stegosaurus
  on cov, 1938 . . . .   **18.00**
  Coloring Book, *The Valley of Gwangi,*
  Dinosaur on cov **8.00**
  Wrapper, Dinosaur Facts, Topps, 1976   **15.00**
Wild
  Advertising Trade Card
    Alligators, dressed, arguing over
    dinner table, Lustig Clothier. **15.00**
    Caribou, standing by lake, Kellog
    Guns, Rifles & Pistols, New Ha-
    ven, CT, brown and green tones   **25.00**
    Deer, forest scene, heat puzzle,
    John P Lovell & Sons Gun Deal-
    ers, unused. **75.00**
    Elephant, The Sacred White Ele-
    phant, Light of Asia, Forepaugh's
    White Elephant of Siam **25.00**
    Frogs, dressed as sailors, smoking
    pipe and cigarette, Austin, Nich-
    ols & Co, NY **25.00**
    Lion, pulling sulky rake, cherubs
    overhead, three panel folder, A W
    Miner Co, unfolded **150.00**
    Monkeys, metamorphic, triple
    folder, Arm & Hammer Baking
    Soda. **50.00**
    Polar Bear, attacking seal, Henry
    Martin Furs. **15.00**
  Book, *Audubon Western Bird Guide,
  Land, Water & Game Birds,* Richard
  H. Pough, 1957, 316 pgs **12.50**
  Booklet
    Bear shape, diecut, "Bear in Mind,"
    Pettijohn's Breakfast Food, 12
    pgs, color covs **15.00**
    Lyon Brand Auto Supplies, lion

Tobacco Card, Hassan Cork Tipped Cigarettes, White-Bearded Gnu, 2½ x 3¼", 1900s, $5.00.

head on cov, 9 x 12", 16 pgs, printed black and white, 1914 . . . **12.00**
Catalog, Stoddard Tiger Farm Machinery, 16 pgs, color tiger cartoon illus, black and white farm machinery photos **25.00**
Diecut
Elephant, balancing on ball, 5 x 6½", printed color, emb. **20.00**
Giraffes, printed color, emb. **8.00**
Monkeys sitting on board, backs to camera, printed color, emb **8.00**
Label
Leopard Tobacco, prowling leopard, skull foreground, 11 x 11". . . **50.00**
Prairie King Cigars, stampeding bison **65.00**
Playing Cards, Wild Animal Park, San Diego, lion, zebras, elephant, hippopotamus, and rhinoceros, color **6.50**
Post Card
Alligators surrounding black man eating watermelon, Langsdorf . . . **20.00**
Zebra head, "Teddy Zebra," Teddy Roosevelt **24.00**
Poster
Elephant, 36 x 44", "Jumpy? Those Who Keep Their Heads Over Little Things Make The Biggest Headway, Size It Up And Keep Cool!", large elephant scared by mouse, orange, purple, brown, Mathes Company, Chicago, 1929 **225.00**
Fox, 14 x 22", "The Fox Can Transmit Rabies," rabid fox in woods, 1946. . . . . **100.00**
Rhinoceros, 36 x 44", W F Elmes, "Facing Troubles Kills Them," purple, brown, and orange, Mathes Company, Chicago, 1929 **200.00**
Tiger, snarling, 28 x 41", Ringling Bros. Barnum & Bailey Circus, c1942. . . . . **100.00**

Print
Deer, Doe and Fawns, Gary Lucy, 22½ x 17", litho, 1984 . . . . **80.00**
Fox, Red Fox, Louis Frisino, 11¼ x 9" **25.00**
Leopard, Clouded Leopard, Edward J Bierly, 24½ x 32½", 1980 . . . . . **100.00**
Otter, Otter Playground, James Faulkner, 16 x 20" **40.00**
Polar Bear, Midday Moonlight, Fred Machetanz, 23 x 27", 1981 . . . . . **400.00**
Reward of Merit
Rabbits surrounding child, printed color. **15.00**
Zebras, running, printed color. **8.00**
Toy, Bo–Bo the Seal, Ringling Bros. and Barnum & Bailey Circus Toys, #10, punchout and assemble, printed color **10.00**

ARCHITECTURAL

Advertising Cover, envelope, Architectural Iron Works, black on yellow, foundry vignette, c1880 . . . . **50.00**
Book
Architects' & Builders' Handbook, 18th edition, Kidder–Parker, 2315 pgs **25.00**
Radford Architectural Co 25 Low & Medium Priced Houses, 1903, 48 pgs **15.00**
The Architectural Forum, August, 1940, terminal and airport lay–outs **15.00**
Catalog
Aladdin Readi–Cut Homes, 1937, 62 pgs **12.00**

Magazine, *American Builder,* 130 pages, color litho covers, 8½ x 11½", March 1936, $10.00.

Catalog, Blue Ribbon Homes, house plans, black-and-white illustrations, 64 pages, 8½ x 11", 1950s, $15.00.

Curtiss Design Book of Architectural
   Woodwork, Wausau, 1938, 227 pgs   **8.00**
Gordon–Van Tine Fine Homes, 1923,
   128 pgs, 9 x 11½" **9.00**
Hoosier Fence Co, Frankton, IN, No.
   21, 1915, 32 pgs, cemetary, church,
   school, park, and home fences, 5 x
   10" **32.00**
Manchester Iron Works, St Louis, MO,
   1916, 64 pgs, architectural, struc-
   tural, and ornamental iron and steel,
   sidewalk grates, store front columns,
   coal hole rings, balcony support
   brackets, iron railings and window
   guards, fire escapes, etc., 6¾ x
   10¼" **34.00**
Miller–Piehl Homes of Economy,
   c1930, 33 pgs, 10 x 13" **9.00**
Modern Plaster Ornament, Architec-
   tural Decorating Co, Chicago, 1927,
   31 pgs, 9 x 12" **10.00**
Vetter Mfg Co Standard Design Book,
   Stevens Point, WI, 1919, 268 pgs,
   stairways, porches, leaded glass
   windows, etc. **18.00**
William A Radford Home & Garden,
   1925, 16 pgs, house plans, interiors,
   pergolas, 8½ x 11" **17.00**
Willis Manufacturing Co, Galesburg,
   IL, 1937, 32 pgs, fire doors, hardware, and fixtures, 8¼ x 10¾" **20.00**
Magazine, *Architectural Forum,* 1940 . . **5.00**
Periodical, *Academy Architecture & Architectural Review 1903*, Vol 24, 142
pgs, 26 pgs adv, illus, hardbound **8.00**
Plans, C W Hutton & Son, Waterloo, IA,
   small home floor plans, dimensions,
   and pictures, 1930, 63 pgs, 8½ x 11" **40.00**

Poster, The Architect & The Industrial
   Arts, 11th Exhibition of Contemporary
   American Design, Metropolitan Museum of Art, blue, orange, green, and
   black Art Deco motif, silkscreen,
   c1938, 16 x 22" **175.00**
Sign, Frohman, Robb, and Little Archi-
   tects, watercolor on board, Gothic
   church arch image, c1925, 20 x 28" . . **110.00**

AUTOMOTIVE

References: Jim and Nancy Schaut, *American Automobilia: An Illustrated History & Price Guide,* Wallace–Homestead, 1992; John J. Zolomij, *The Motor Car In Art: Selections From The Raymond E. Holland Automotive Art Collection*, Automobile Quarterly Publications, 1990.

Periodical: *Mobilia,* PO Box 575, Middlebury, VT 05753.

Collectors' Club: Veteran Motor Car Club Of America, PO Box 360788, Strongville, OH 44136.

Blotter, Goodyear Tires adv **5.00**
Book, *History of the Studebaker Corpo-
ration,* Albert Russell Erskine, 98 pgs,
   photo every other page, 1918. . . . . . **40.00**
Booklet
   Albany, NY Automobile Show, Feb-
      ruary 8–15th, 1930, 52 pgs **5.00**
   A Complete Description of the Stan-
      ley Steamer Car, 32 pgs, 22nd
      year, prices **30.00**
   Facts & Figures of Automobile Indus-
      try 1927 Edition, National Auto
      Chamber of Commerce, 96 pgs,
      illus **5.00**
   We Drivers, General Motors, 36 pgs,
      illus, 1935 . . . . **4.00**
Brochure
   Alpha Romeo, Giulietta Sprint,
      1955, 4 pgs, two color gravure,
      double page center spread, 8½ x
      12" **65.00**
   Buick, Series 90, 1933, black and
      white photos, 8 x 10" **7.00**
   Oakland Sensible Six, Oakland Mo-
      tor Car Co, 1925, 16 pgs **65.00**
Bubble Gum Cards, Bowman, 1953,
   48 cards, Antique Autos, color, 2 x
   2½" **75.00**
Catalog
   Buick Motor Cars, 1922, 48 pgs **37.00**
   Cadillac, Type 61, emb covs,
      gravures, 1922, 28 pgs, 12 x 10" . . **185.00**
   Ford, Mustang, February, 1964, 12
      pgs, double page foldout, color,
      first catalog, 12 x 11" **75.00**
   Gramm Motor Truck, 1912, illus . . . **40.00**
   Holliday & Co, 1921, automotive
      and garage wquipment, illus. **45.00**

Advertising Post Card, 1970 Impala Custom Coupe, Chevrolet, unused, $5.00.

Mercury, 1952, 36 pgs, accessories, color covs, 8 x 8".............	**25.00**
New Departure Manufacturing Company, 1927, supplies......	**18.00**
Checks, Ford Repair Shop, bound book of 390, unused, M Reardon, Peoria, IL, 1920s.....................	**20.00**
Cookbook, *The Ford Treasury of Favorite Recipes From Famous Eating Places,* Ford Motor Company, 1955, 252 pgs, dj	**17.50**
Folder	
Auto Union Program, color, opens to c1956, 6¹/₂ x 8"..............	**18.00**
Dodge, color, 1952, opens to 30 x 21"...................	**35.00**
Game, En–Ar–Co Auto Game, National Refining Co, Cleveland, OH, copyright 1925, orig envelope.....	**75.00**
Handbook, Ford Thunderbird, 64 pgs, illus, 1955, 6 x 8"	**25.00**
Magazine, *Northern Automotive Journal,* November, 1948	**8.00**
Manual, Volkswagen Owner's Manual Operation and Maintenance, 1971–72 models, 130 pgs, vinyl cov	**10.00**
Map, linen backed, Automobile Map of Central New Hampshire, Automobile Club of North America, routes in red, 40 x 40" open.............	**40.00**
Menu, diecut standup, early yellow sedan, open doors to read selections ..	**25.00**
Newsletter, Lincoln, 1934, 4 pgs, color convertible illus back cov, 8¹/₂ x 11"	**20.00**
Owner's Kit, Plymouth, includes 36 page illus manual, Plymouth service certificate, Chrysler parts leaflet, Mopar radio booklet, and monthly bank payment folder, orig 6 x 9" brown paper folder, 1951........	**20.00**
Owner's Manual	
Cadillac, Type 55, c1925, 104 pgs, 6 x 9"	**100.00**
Chevrolet, 1951, 16 pgs, color, 11 x 8".......................	**35.00**

Essex Motor Cars, Model A, 1921, 62 pgs, 5³/₄ x 8¹/₂"..............	**40.00**
Ford, Model T, 1914.............	**15.00**
Parts Manual	
Cadillac, 1941	**110.00**
DeSoto, 1936, master...........	**45.00**
Photo Album, 1940s, 30 pgs, burgundy leatherette covs, one black and white automobile photograph each page, 11 x 8"..................	**250.00**
Post Card, advertising	
Buick, 3¹/₂ x 5¹/₂", "Best Buick Yet," green four door sedan, 1941 license plate	**10.00**
DeSoto, color, four door sedan, 1939	**4.00**
Poster	
2nd Annual Automobile Club Show, Madison Square Garden, November 1901, stone litho, Gibson style lady driving touring car, pastel colors, 29 x 40"..............	**1,100.00**
Buick, "Kansas City," black and white, 1921–22, 25 x 38".......	**85.00**
Scraps, twelve sheets, four images, autos and people, late 1940s, early 1950s vehicles, Buick, Ford, Olds, and Chevy Bel Air, printed color, emb, 6¹/₂ x 9¹/₂"................	**20.00**
Sheet Music	
He'd Have To Get Under–Get Out and Get Under (To Fix Up His Automobile), cov with man beneath early touring car illus, 1913	**35.00**
In My Merry Oldsmobile, couple in open Olds tourer, 1905, 10¹/₂ x 14"	**60.00**
The Little Ford Rambled Right Along, Model T passing other disabled autos along road, 1914, 11 x 14"	**50.00**
The Motor March, cov with touring car illus, 1906...............	**30.00**
Stock Certificate	
Academy Motor Sales & Service, Inc., green and black, eagle vignette, unissued	**15.00**
General Motors Corporation, $1,000 bond, green, vignette with car, truck, and train, 1954	**8.00**
North Shore Stutz Corporation, Chicago dealership, brown border, eagle vignette, unissued	**25.00**

AUTO RACING

References: William Boddy, *The History of Motor Racing,* G. P. Putnam's Sons, 1977; Roderick A. Malloy, *Malloy's Sports Collectibles Value Guide,* Wallace–Homestead, 1993.

Periodicals: *Collector's World,* NA–TEX Publishing, PO Box 562029, Charlotte, NC 28256;

Racing Collectibles Price Guide, SportsStars Inc., PO Box 608114, Orlando, FL 32860.

Collectors' Club: National Indy 500 Collectors' Club, 10505 N. Delaware St., Indianapolis, IN 46280.

Label, broom, Auto No 8, Windsor Broom Co, brown and yellow racer, red and yellow ground **3.00**

Magazine, *Racing Pictorial*, late 1963, 48 pgs, Richard Petty, A J Foyt, Fireball Roberts, Parnelli Jones, and others, 8½ x 11" **10.00**

Needle Book, multicolored racing scene, Prize Medal Needles, Germany **20.00**

Pass, California Stock Car Racing Association, 1950, 2½ x 3¼" **5.00**

Playing Cards, Indianapolis Motor Speedway, logo and flags, black background **10.00**

Post Card, Indy Speedway, early track image with trees in infield, full length aerial view, postmarked 1935 .... **10.00**

Poster

Automobile Club Show, woman driving touring car around race track, c1905, 20 x 30" **600.00**

Auto Races–Bridgewater Grange, bright red roadster pursued by black car in background, yellow ground, c1933, 29 x 42" **165.00**

Indianapolis 500, 1967, 22 x 14" **35.00**

Program, Indianapolis 500, May, 1947 **90.00**

Puzzle, Crisco Racing, premium, 200 pcs., 17 x 11", $20.00.

AVIATION

References: Trev Davis and Fred Chan, (comps.) *Airline Playing Cards: An Illustrated Reference Guide, Second Edition*, published by compilers, 1987; Richard R. Wallin, *Commercial Aviation Collectibles: An Illustrated Price Guide*, Wallace–Homestead, 1990.

Airlines

Air Sickness Bag, Mexicana Airlines, logo **1.00**

Baggage Label

North American Airlines, oval, airplane image **25.00**

United Air Lines, oval, plane flying above clouds, "Coast–To–Coast Border–To–Border" **10.00**

Book, *Delta–The History of An Airline*, D Lewis & P Newton, 1979, 503 pgs, dj **15.00**

Booklet, National Airlines, 64 pgs, Florida vacations, glossy paper, photos, orig mailing envelope, 1954 postmark, 5¼ x 7¼" **12.00**

Calendar, 1953, TWA, Constellation airplane **25.00**

Catalog, United Air Lines, 1947, airway flight pattern maps, soft cov, blue tone photos, 7 x 9" **15.00**

Certificate, Japan Air Lines, International Dateline Crossing, 1966 .... **12.00**

Coaster, Western Air Lines, paper, logo, scalloped edge .... **.25**

First Flight Cover, Pan Am, first jet flight from Tokyo to Honolulu, 1959 **8.00**

Ledger, flight log, United Airlines, New York to Chicago, flight pattern map, 1931 .... **10.00**

Menu

Pan Am, boat plane **1.50**

TWA, "Gold Plate Service," 1960s **5.00**

Photograph, United Air Lines DC–6 Mainliner 300, color, framed, 19 x 22" **65.00**

Playing Cards, TWA, plane and "TWA" on backs **5.00**

Poster

Colonial Airlines, DC–4 over island of Bermuda, 1950s, 27 x 41" **350.00**

United Air Liner over San Francisco Bay, Clayton Knight, foil printed, silver, black, and blue–green, metal ribs top and bottom, c1940, 15 x 21" **325.00**

Safety Card, US Air, BAC 1–11, airplane in flight, 1970s **2.00**

Timetable

Alaska Star Airlines, prop plane.... **15.00**

United Air Lines, map of United States and bi–plane, 1930s **40.00**

General

Blotter, P51 North American Mustang pursuit plane image, Bond Bread adv, early 1940s, 6¼ x 3½"....... **12.00**

Book

Aeroplane Cut–Outs, Whitman, #W933, 1930, punchout pgs, unused, 9¾ x 14¾" **75.00**

Airports and Airways: Cost, Opera-

tion, and Maintenance, Donald
Duke, 1927, dj **12.50**
Booklet
  Aeronautical Exhibition, Aero Club
  of America, 1912 . . . .   **45.00**
  *Detroit Aero Air Plane Engine
  Model 1911* **35.00**
  Flying Model Airplanes, mid 1930s,
  24 pgs, Curtiss Candy premium,
  stiff paper, blueprints and instruc-
  tions, black and white historic
  aviator photos, 10 x 16" **45.00**
  *We, The Story of Achievement in
  Aviation,* history prior to 1928,
  Coca–Cola adv back cov **20.00**
Catalog, Curtiss Aviation School, early
  1900s **75.00**
Certificate, Certificate of Honor,
  Vought Sikorsky Corsair Shipboard
  Fighter Plane image, blue and
  white, 1942, 6 x 10" **10.00**
Coloring Book, Planes and Jets, Whit-
  man, 1952, partially colored, 11 x
  15" **18.00**
Comic Book, Aviation Cadets, Street &
  Smith, 1943 . . . .   **12.00**
Fan, Douglas DC–3, cardboard, lists
  safety procedures **10.00**
Magazine
  Aerial Age, March 20, 1916, 47 pgs   **30.00**
  Aviation Week, 1940s **50.00**
  Flying Aces, October, 1940 . . . .   **65.00**
  Popular Aviation Magazine, De-
  cember, 1932, 68 pgs, 8½ x
  11¼" **8.00**
Magic Lantern Slides, History of Avia-
  tion, c1910, set of 24, 3½ x 2¼" . . .   **125.00**
Photograph, 1917 Curtiss NJ–4 Jenny
  Biplane, full color glossy, auto-
  graphed by OX5 tank engine inven-
  tor "Frank Tank," c1967, 8 x 10". . .   **18.00**
Print
  The Beauty of Flight, litho, West-
  ernFokker Tri–Motor, 1920s, 8 x
  10" **50.00**
  The Giant Begins To Stir, William S
  Phillips, airplane, 1983, 29¼ x
  23½" **350.00**
Puzzle, jigsaw, Night Bombing Over
  Germany, Victory Series, #315, JS
  Publishing Corp, New York City, full
  color, 1943, 14½ x 21" **18.00**
Sheet Music, *Come Josephine In My
  Flying Machine (Up She Goes!),* cov
  with bi–plane illus, 1910 . . . .   **30.00**
Sign, black man flying early airplane, J
  P Alley's Hambone Cigars, circular,
  two sided, 7" d **25.00**
Stamp Album, 140, 20 pgs, Tydol–
  Veedol Service Stations' premium,
  soft cov, 5½ x 8" **30.00**

Valentine, biplane, printed color, me-
  chanical, "I'm Up In The Air About
  You, Dear Valentine!" **5.00**
Personalities
Byrd, Richard E
  Book, *Alone,* 1934, details Antarctic
  trip, autographed **115.00**
  Game, Admiral Byrd's South Pole
  Game, Little America, c1933, 13
  x 17" **75.00**
  Photograph, black and white semi–
  glossy, Admiral Byrd embarking
  1940s transport plane, auto-
  graphed, 8 x 10" **25.00**
Earhart, Amelia
  Autograph, card, full signature, 3 x
  2" **175.00**
  Book, *The Fun of It,* Amelia Earhart,
  1932 . . . .   **250.00**
  Photograph, black and white, sup-
  plement of Philadelphia Record,
  Sunday, July 11, 193, 7½ x 9½"   **15.00**
  Sheet Music, *Amelia Earhart's Last
  Flight,* 1939 . . . .   **50.00**
Lindbergh, Charles
  Booklet, *Lindbergh in Paris,* 1927,
  24 pgs, souvenir, flight highlights,
  8½ x 11" **50.00**
  Calendar, 1928, Lindbergh with air-
  plane, color **12.00**
  Label, cigar
  Charles Lindbergh, red, white,
  and blue **15.00**
  Spirit of St Louis, green and blue,
  6½ x 7¾" **20.00**
  Playing Cards, National Air and
  Space Museum, Smithsonian In-
  stitute, *Spirit of St Louis* **6.50**
  Post Card, air mail, black and white,
  issued to welcome Lindbergh to
  Milwaukee, August 1927, back
  text endorses air mail, 3¼ x 5½"   **25.00**
  Poster, *Spirit of St Louis* Cigars adv,
  dark blue, light blue, and white, 8
  x 9½" **35.00**
  Sheet Music
  *Like An Angel You Flew Into Ev-
  eryone's Heart,* Lindbergh
  photo cov, 1927 . . . .   **40.00**
  Lindy, Lindy, Wolfe Gilbert and
  Abel Baer, black, white, and or-
  ange cov, 1927 copyright, 9¼
  x 12¼" **20.00**
Miscellaneous
  Book, *Heroes of Aviation,* Laurence
  La Tourette Driggs, 1927, dj **20.00**
  Puzzle Cards, famous aviators, set of
  6 . . . .   **30.00**
Wright Brothers
  Magazine Tear Sheet, *Youth's Com-
  panion,* October 1, 1908, 16 pg

Sheet Music, *NC-4 March*, F. E. Bigelow, black-and-white real photo cover by A. C. Read, blue printed overwash, published by Walter Jacobs Company, 9¼ x 12¼", 1919, $30.00.

article, black and white cov, 11 x 16½" **25.00**
Photograph, first flight, framed, 1903, 31 x 41" **150.00**
Program, Wright family home dedication, autographed by Orville Wright, 1938. . . . . **1,400.00**

BARBER

Reference: Phillip L. Krumholz, *Value Guide For Barberiana & Shaving Collectibles,* Ad Libs Publishing Co, 1988.

Advertising Trade Card, Barber Shop, hair style illus, black and pink **16.00**
Book
   Gillette's Social Redemption, Melvin L Senery, 1907, 783 pgs **60.00**
   Once Over Lightly, Charles DeZemler, c1939, 270 pgs **35.00**
Box
   Allegro Razor Sharpener **3.00**
   Keen Kutter Razor Hone, E C Simmons **5.00**
Business Card, Dendy's Beauty Culture and Barber College **8.00**
Catalog
   Biedermeier, German barber supply, German text, c1910, 48 pgs. **20.00**
   Birmingham Grinding Works, 1920s, 64 pgs **50.00**
   Cattaraugus Cutlery Co, 1925, 81 pgs **70.00**
   Clifford & Co Manufacturing Perfumers, Boston, 1884–85, 62 pgs, printed wrappers, illus, bottles, brushes, clippers, combs, colognes, mirrors, mugs, poles, razors, etc., 3 x 5" **175.00**
   Perfumers' Handbook and Catalog, Fritzsche Brothers Inc, NY, 1944, 266 pgs, cloth backed printed boards, illus, raw materials for floral waters, colognes, powders, bath salts, hair preparations, etc., 5 x 7" **20.00**
   Makerauer Barber Supply Co, 1910, 184 pgs **200.00**
   Noonan's Toilet Specialties, early 1900s. **22.00**

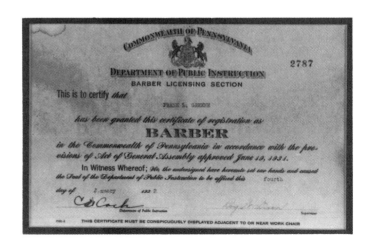

License, Commonwealth of Pennsylvania, Department of Public Instructions, 12½ x 9½" matted size, 1932, $18.00.

T S Simms & Co, Maker of Better
Brushes, 31 pgs 30.00
Display, standup, cardboard, Crescent
Razor Blades, 24 packages, crescent
moon logo, Plexiglas sleeve, 11 x 13″   78.00
Envelope, Hair Net, orig blonde net 3.00
Flyer, Oakland Barber Shop, hair cut and
shave adv, 1930s, 6½ x 5″. 6.00
Golf Score Card, Barbasol premium 5.00
Letterhead, Madison Barbers' Supplies,
c1900 . . . .   10.00
License, c1930, framed. 40.00
Match Cover, Gillette Blue Blades adv,
1930s, unused. 3.00
Pamphlet, Robeson Cutlery Co, 1910, 16
pgs. 35.00
Photograph, barber shop int., 5 x 7″ 40.00
Playing Cards, Gillette, 1905, unused. . .   150.00
Post Card
Barber shop ext., c1900. . . . .   10.00
The Unsafe Safety Razor, comic,
woman shaving man, c1910 . . . . . .   10.00
Receipt Book, Keen Kutter, 1920s. 25.00
Sign
Bickmore Shaving Cream, 1930s,
31″ h 75.00
Damschinsky's Liquid Hair Dye, six
dyed hair samples, c1910, 14 x 19″   175.00
Leukroth's Oriental Hair Tonic, color
litho, 10 x 14″. 200.00
Pinaud Preparations, standup, man
holding bottle, 1940s. 60.00
Window Card, man cutting hair, "The
Newest and Most Sanitary Shop in
Providence," 6 x 3¼″ 10.00

BASEBALL

References: Gwen Aldridge, *Baseball Archaeology: Artifacts From the Great American Pastime,* Chronicle Books, 1993; Mark Allen Baker, *Sports Collectors Digest Baseball Autograph Handbook,* Second Edition, Krause Publications, 1991; James Beckett, *The Sport Americana Baseball Collectibles Price Guide, No. 2,* Edgewater Book Company, 1988; Peter Capano, *Baseball Collectibles with Price Guide,* Schiffer Publishing, 1989; Bruce Chadwick and David Spindel, *The Boston Red Sox,* Abbeville Press, 1992; Bruce Chadwick and David Spindel, *The Bronx Bombers,* Abbeville Press, 1992; Bruce Chadwick and David Spindel, *The Dodgers: Memories and Memorabilia From Brooklyn To L.A.,* Abbeville Press, 1993; Bruce Chadwick and David Spindel, *The Giants: Memories and Memorabilia From A Century of Baseball,* Abbeville Press, 1993; Douglas Congdon–Martin and John Kashmanian, *Baseball Treasures: Memorabilia from the National Pastime,* Schiffer Publishing, 1993; Bruce Kronnick, *The Baseball Fan's Complete Guide to Collecting Autographs,* Betterway Publications, 1990; Mark

Larson, *The Complete Guide to Baseball Memorabilia,* Krause Publications, 1992; Roderick A. Malloy, *Malloy's Sports Collectibles Value Guide,* Wallace–Homestead, 1993; Ron Menchine, *A Picture Postcard History of Baseball,* Almar Press Book Publishers, 1992; Don Raycraft, *Collecting Baseball Player Autographs,* Collector Books, 1991; M. Donald Raycraft and R. Craig Raycraft, *Value Guide To Baseball Collectibles,* Collector Books, 1992.

Collectors' Club: Society for American Baseball Research, PO Box 93183, Cleveland, OH 44101–5183.

Periodicals: *Malloy's Sports Cards and Collectibles,* 15 Danbury Road, Ridgefield, CT 06877; *Sports Collectors Digest,* 700 E. State Street, Iola, WI 54990.

Autograph, 3 x 5″ card
Boggs, Wade 4.00
Campanella, Roy. 75.00
Mathewson, Christy 300.00
Musial, Stan. 4.00
Robinson, Brooks 4.00
Ruth, Babe.   250.00
Williams, Ted 8.00
Book
Babe & I, 1959. . . . .   30.00
Big–Time Baseball, Ben Olan, 1958,
192 pgs, history text, ...   30.00
The Babe Ruth Story, first edition,
1948, 96 pgs, soft cov, 8½ x 11″ . . .   40.00
Bread Label
Fischer Baking, 1951–52, 2¾ x 2¾″,
#23, Mel Parnell, Boston Red Six . .   30.00
#31, Early Wynn, Cleveland In-
dians 50.00
National Tea Company, 1952, 2¾ x
2¹/₁₆″
#2, Yogi Berra, New York Yankees   175.00
#25, Preacher Roe, Brooklyn
Dodgers. 60.00
#34, Gerry Staley, St Louis Cardi-
nals 50.00
Northland Bread, 1953, 2 ¹/₁₆ x 2¹/₁₆″
#5, Clint Courtney, St Louis Browns   20.00
#18, Mannie Minoso, Chicago
White Sox 50.00
Tip Top, 1952, 2¾ x 2½″
#12, Johnny Groth, Detroit Tigers   20.00
#24, Mickey Mantle, New York
Yankees 500.00
Decal
Star Cal, Meyercord Co, Chicago,
1952
#70F, Phil Rizzuto, 4⅛ x 6⅛″. 15.00
#84B, Eddie Lopat and Yogi Berra,
3¹/₁₆ x 4⅛″ 12.50

Topps, 1969
  Hank Aaron **6.00**
  Don Drysdale **2.00**
Dixie Lid
  1937, black and burgundy ink
    Carl Hubbell, New York Giants **40.00**
    Charles Hartnett, Chicago Cubs . . .   **32.50**
  1938, blue ink
    Sam Baugh, Washington Redskins   **20.00**
    Wally Moses, Philadelphia A's **15.00**
  1952, blue tint, 2 1¹/₁₆" d
    Chico Carrasquel, Chicago White
      Sox **35.00**
    Andy Seminick, Cincinnati Reds . . .   **45.00**
  1953, burgundy tint, 2 1¹/₁₆"
    Virgil Trucks, St Louis Browns **12.50**
    Warren Spahn, Boston Braves **30.00**
  1954, sepia tint, 2 1¹/₁₆"
    Al Rosen **10.00**
    Gene Woodling **7.50**
Fan, diecut, Pete Rose, "Ty–Breaker/
  Cobb Buster" **15.00**
Game
  Baseball, Samuel Lowe Co, 1942 . . . .   **25.00**
  Baseball Game, All–Fair, 1930 . . . . . .   **250.00**
  Game of Base Ball, J H Singer, c1890   **250.00**
Magazine
  Babe Ruth Baseball Advice **85.00**
  Baseball Monthly, first issue, Vol 1,
    #1, March, 1962, BRS Publishing
    Co, 64 pgs **30.00**
  Official Baseball Annual, No. 3,
    Whitestone Publications, 1965 . . . .   **25.00**
  Quick, August 4, 1952, Jackie Robin-
    son on cov **25.00**
Magazine Tear Sheet, Bill Dickey, Mel
  Ott, Chesterfield adv, full page, color,
  10¹/₄ x 14" **15.00**

Magazine Tear Sheet, sandlot game image, Kellogg's cereal ad, 10¹/₂ x 16", c1915, $18.00.

Milk Bottle Cap
  Cincinnati Reds, 1¹/₄" d
    Fred Hutchinson **3.75**
    Tommy Harper **2.25**
  Detroit Tigers, 1¹/₄" d, blue player, or-
    ange lettered name, "Visit Tiger Sta-
    dium, See The Tigers More In '64"
    Norman Cash **6.00**
    Dave Wickersham **2.50**
Photograph
  Casey Stengel, autographed **50.00**
  George Brett, autographed **9.00**
  Goose Goslin, 8 x 10", matte finish,
    black and white, black ink signature   **75.00**
  Lou Gehrig, autographed **400.00**
  New York Giants, 1951 . . . .   **45.00**
  Orel Hershiser, autographed **10.00**
  Philadelphia Phillies, 9 x 11", full
    color, team, 1946 . . . .   **25.00**
  Sandy Koufax, autographed **18.00**
  Steve Carlton, autographed **12.00**
  Tom Seaver, autographed **15.00**
  Ty Cobb, autographed **180.00**
  Yogi Berra, autographed **12.00**
Post Card, Perez–Steele, autographed
  Bob Feller **15.00**
  Ernie Banks **20.00**
  Mickey Mantle **150.00**
  Satchel Paige **1,200.00**
  Stan Musial **35.00**
  Willie Mays **45.00**
Poster, repeating multicolored design of
  swinging batter and catcher, gray bor-
  ders, 1950, 45 x 38" **75.00**
Press Pass, 1939 Chicago Cubs, inked
  Western Union employee name, red
  symbol, 2¹/₂ x 3³/₄" **35.00**
Program
  All–Star Game
    Milwaukee, 1955 . . . .   **80.00**
    New York, 1964 . . . .   **30.00**
  Athletics Official Score Card & Pro-
    gram, Philadelphia A's, 1949 . . . . .   **20.00**
  Buffalo Bisons and Jersey City Giants,
    Offermann Stadium, 1940, 16 pgs, 7
    x 10" **18.00**
  Chicago Cubs and New York Giants,
    Wrigley Field, 1947, 6 x 9" **25.00**
  Hagerstown Owls vs. Wilmington
    team, 1945, 4 pgs, 7 x 10¹/₄" **15.00**
  World Series
    New York Yankees and New York
      Giants, 1937, 24 pgs, 9 x 11" **50.00**
    Philadelphia Phillies and Baltimore
      Orioles, 1983, 104 pgs, issued as
      commemorative by Major League
      Baseball Promotion Corp, 8¹/₄ x
      11" **25.00**
    Pittsburgh Pirates and Baltimore
      Orioles, 1971, 72 pgs, 8¹/₄ x 10¹/₂"   **25.00**
Record Book, Rawlings, 1940 . . . .   **15.00**

Program, 1987 World Series, color and black-and-white photographs, 96 pages, 8 x 11", $20.00.

Schedule, Yale University Baseball Association, 1907, 5 x 4" opened **30.00**
Sheet Music
  Bam, It's Going, Going, Gone, Cincinnati Reds cov, 1939 . . . .   **60.00**
  The Baseball, runner and catcher at home plate cov illus, "Dedicated to the Great National Game of America by Johann C Schmid," United States Music Co, blue on yellow, 1915 . . . .   **50.00**
Ticket
  Harvard Baseball Association, green and black, c1880, 4$^1/_2$ x 1$^1/_2$" **45.00**
  Ottumwa Red Sox and Oskaloosa, West End Park, IA, 1930, 1$^1/_4$ x 2" . .   **6.00**
  World Series, 1960, game 2, Pittsburgh Pirates and New York Yankees, Forbes Field, first floor reserved seat **20.00**
Ticket Stub, World Series, 1945, Chicago Cubs and Detroit Tigers, Wrigley Field   **15.00**
Yearbook
  Boston Red Sox, 1972 . . . .   **12.00**
  Brooklyn Dodgers, 1954 . . . .   **50.00**
  Los Angeles Dodgers, 1966, 56 pgs, full color illus of manager Walt Alston on cov, 8$^1/_4$ x 11" **30.00**
  New York Giants, Big League Book Series, 1955, 48 pgs, 8$^1/_2$ x 11" **20.00**
  New York Mets, 1962 . . . .   **50.00**
  Philadelphia Phillies, 1950 . . . .   **50.00**
  Washington Nationals, 1953, 48 pgs, 8$^1/_4$ x 10$^1/_2$" **30.00**

BEARS

References: Dottie Ayers and Donna Harrison, *Advertising Art of Steiff: Teddy Bears and Play-*

things, Hobby House Press, 1990; Linda N. Schoonmaker, *A Collector's History of the Teddy Bear,* Hobby House Press, 1983, third printing.

Real
  Advertising Trade Card
    Esquimaux Rubber Boots, Eskimo hunter and polar bear. **30.00**
    Magic Yeast, diecut sitting polar bear, "Bear in Mind" **20.00**
  Game, Game of Bear Hunt, Milton Bradley, 1923 . . . .   **70.00**
  Poster
    Franklin Park Zoo adv, caged polar bear image, blue, black, yellow, and gray, c1925, 30 x 45" **475.00**
    Willard F Elmes illus, labor incentive, large brown bear standing on rocks image, "Growling keeps at a distance those who could help you along...only friends have friends," Mather & Co, 1929, 36 x 44" **325.00**
Teddy
  Book
    More About The Roosevelt Bears, Seymour Eaton, illus **90.00**
    Mother Goose's Teddy Bears, Frederick L Cavally, color illus, worn edges **365.00**
    The Roosevelt Bears Abroad, Seymour Eaton, illus **100.00**
  Paper Doll
    Teddy Bear and His Friends, Platt & Munk Co, three books, boxed set   **45.00**
    Teddy Bear Paper Doll
      J Ottmann Litho Co, NY **85.00**
      Selchow & Righter **75.00**
    Post Card, Molly and her Teddy Bear, sgd M Greiner **8.00**
Other
  Book, *The True Story of Smokey The Bear,* Big Golden Book, 1950s, 8$^1/_4$ x 11" **15.00**

Advertising Post Card, Bear Brand Hosiery, full color, 1910, $25.00.

Post Card, emb., printed color, International Art Publishing Co., Series 791, Germany, divided back, 3½ x 5½", $30.00.

Children's Book, *The Smokey Bear Book*, Golden Shape Book, Mel Crawford, Western Publishing Company, 24 pages, 8 x 8", 1970, $10.00.

Coloring Book, Smokey the Bear, Whitman, 8 x 10½", 1960s **12.00**
Fan, cardboard, Smokey by campfire, 1950s, 7 x 8" **18.00**
Paper Doll
  The Animated Goldilocks Doll with the Three Bears, Milton Bradley   **20.00**
  The Three Bears' Home, Patten Beard, illus by Violet Moore Higgins, McLoughlin Bros, 1933 . . . .   **35.00**
Puzzle, frame tray, Yogi Bear **10.00**
Stamp Album, Smokey The Bear Golden Stamp Book, Simon & Schuster, 1958, 32 pgs, 8½ x 11" **15.00**

BEATLES

References: Jeff Augsburger, Marty Eck, and Rick Rann, *The Beatles Memorabilia Price Guide, Second Edition,* Wallace–Homestead, 1993; Barbara

Fenick, *Collecting The Beatles, An Introduction and Price Guide to Fab Four Collectibles, Records and Memorabilia, Volume 1* (1984) and *Volume 2* (1988), Pierian Press; Jerry Osborne, Perry Cox, and Joe Lindsay, *The Official Price Guide To Memorabilia of Elvis Presley And The Beatles,* House of Collectibles, 1988; Michael Stern, Barbara Crawford, and Hollis Lamon, *The Beatles,* Collector Books, 1993.

Periodicals: *Beatlefan,* PO Box 33515, Decatur, GA 30033; *Good Day Sunshine,* 397 Edgewood Avenue, New Haven, CT 06511.

Collectors' Clubs: Beatles Fan Club of Great Britain, Superstore Productions, 123 Marina, St Leonards on Sea, East Sussex, England TN 38 OBN; Working Hero Club, 3311 Niagara St., Pittsburgh, PA 15213.

Book, Samuel Leach, *Beatles on Broadway,* Racine, WI, 1964, 32 pgs, illus, orig color picture wraps. **15.00**
Book Cover, black and white, black and white photos, Book Covers Inc, 10 x 13" **5.00**
Box
  Beatles Shampoo, blue and black faces, lettering, and facsimile signatures on white ground, Bronson Products Co, 13 x 8 x 8" **275.00**
  Dubble Bubble Gum, held 480 pcs of gum and free Beatles two ring binder, 12 x 10 x 4½" **75.00**
Calendar, 1964, The Beatles Book, spiral binding, 12 color and black and white photos, Beat Publications, 9 x 11". . . .   **75.00**
Certificate, birth, set of four, reprints of Beatles' orig birth certificates, Davidson's Authentic Documents, orig envelope **45.00**
Clothing Tag, The Beatles Authentic Mod Fashions, cardboard, Ninth St Limited, Los Angeles **3.00**

Store Card, "Hey Kids!!! We're Here!!!", black-and-white photo, red lettering, 1965, $12.00.

Coloring Book, Saalfield, #5240, black and white photos, unused, 8½ x 11".. **40.00**

Computer, slide chart with Beatles text, Capitol Records, 1970, 4 x 9" **30.00**

Display Box, The Beatles Diary, orange, black, and white, H B Langman Co, 8¾ x 2¼ x 4¼" **45.00**

Game, Flip Your Wig, Milton Bradley, 1964 .... **90.00**

Greeting Card, Birthday, Beatles standing in doorway, "Happy Birthday From The Beatles," American Greetings, color, 8½ x 12¼" **15.00**

Hanger, diecut bust photo, black and white, John Lennon, Saunders Ent, 16" h **45.00**

Lobby Card, *Help!*, Beatles playing marching band instruments........ **30.00**

Magazine
   Movie Fan Magazine, 1964, 60 pgs, 8½ x 11" **35.00**
   The Official Yellow Submarine Magazine, Pyramid Publications **20.00**

Notebook, Paul McCartney photo cov, side bound, 8½ x 11" **25.00**

Paperback Book, *The Beatles in a Hard Day's Night,* John Burke, Dell Publishing, 1964, 156 pgs............... **30.00**

Poster, Beatles at "Our World" telecast, Pace International, 1970, 37½ x 24½" **20.00**

Pressbook, *Let It Be,* 6 pgs, 11 x 17" **25.00**

Program, concert at Carnegie Hall, New York, February 12, 1964 .... **150.00**

Puzzle, jigsaw, The Beatles Illustrated Lyrics Puzzle in a Puzzle, orig box, poster, and envelope with puzzle solutions, 33 x 18½" **150.00**

School Report Cover, Beatles' faces and instruments on cov, Select–O–Pak, 9¼ x 11½".................... **50.00**

Stamps, 5 pgs, twenty stamps each page, color, yellow booklet, Hallmark, 7¼ x 4" **20.00**

Ticket, *Help!* movie, Advance Prevue Showing, 8½ x 3¾".............. **15.00**

Wrapper, ice cream, Krunch Coated Ice Cream Bar, Beatle offer on back **80.00**

BEAUTY PRODUCTS

References: Douglas Congdon–Martin, *Drugstore & Soda Fountain Antiques,* Schiffer Publishing, 1991; Alice Muncaster, Ellen Sawyer and Ken Kapson, *The Baby Made Me Buy It!,* Crown Publishing, 1991.

Advertising Trade Card
   Buckingham's Dye for Whiskers, before and after images **15.00**
   Colgate Ribbon Dental Cream, girl at sink brushing teeth, mechanical ... **60.00**

Djer–Kiss Face Powder, set of four, pretty woman image on each **30.00**

Hall's Vegetable Sicilian Hair Renewer, little girl holding huge bottle, "Saved Papa's Hair from turning gray, and falling off, and will save yours."..................... **15.00**

Parker's Hair Balsam, Victorian family in front of fireplace, picture of white–haired husband over mantel, wife says "I never would have married you looking as you do in that portrait"..................... **20.00**

Calendar, 1891, Suchan's Carbolic Soap, full pad **25.00**

Fan, Trix Breath Perfume, frog riding on chick **25.00**

Label, Carnation Toilet Water, floral motif, multicolored, c1900........... **5.00**

Poster
   Elizabeth Arden Face Powders, untrimmed proof, c1937, 25 x 37" **250.00**
   Hoyt's German Cologne, "The Most Fragrant Perfumes," girl surrounded by flowers, matted and framed, 28 x 22"........................ **400.00**
   Ivory Soap, H Granville Smith illus, maid holding bar of soap, "There are many white soaps...Ivory soap is 99 44/100 percent pure," 1900, 11 x 16"...................... **150.00**

Sign
   Ayer's Hair Vigor, woman with long hair standing by table, "Restores Gray Hair to its Natural Vitality and Color"..................... **350.00**
   Florida Water, perfume, couple standing by fountain, L Prang, early 1880s, 10 x 14¼" **495.00**
   Procter & Gamble's Soap, Victorian woman wearing bonnet and lacy scarf, "Purity," 17½ x 22"...... **130.00**
   Satin Skin Powder and Satin Skin Cream, woman holding fan, 1903, 27½ x 41½".................. **400.00**

Booklet, Beauty Culture in the Home, Dr. Miles Nervene, 32 pages, 4½ x 6", 1930s, $5.00.

Window Card, set of three, Gourard's
Oriental Cold Cream, WWI beauties,
tinted portraits, 18 x 9". **95.00**

BICYCLE

References: Frederick Alderson, *Bicycling: A History*, Praeger, 1972; Neil S. Wood (ed.), *Evolution of the Bicycle,* L–W Book Sales, 1991.

Periodicals: *Antique/Classic Bicycle News,* PO Box 1049, Ann Arbor, MI 48106; *Bicycle Trader,* PO Box 5600, Pittsburgh, PA 15207.

Collectors' Clubs: Classic Bicycle and Whizzer Club, 35769 Simon, Fraser, MI 48026; The Wheelmen, 216 E. Sedgewick, Philadelphia, PA 19117.

Advertising Trade Card
    Acme Model 14 Bicycle, black design,
    buff background **20.00**
    Columbia Bicycles, black and orange   **40.00**
    Enameline, paper doll, boy bicycle
    rider, Harvard University. **40.00**
    Hickory Bicycle by Sterling, skeleton
    riding bicycle. **32.00**
    Krakauer Pianos, man and woman rid-
    ing high wheeled bicycle, printed
    color **12.00**
    Pope Manufacturing Co, paper doll,
    woman riding Columbia bicycle,
    1895 . . . .   **50.00**
Application Form, League of American
    Wheelmen, 1896 . . . .   **12.00**
Billhead, Warren Bros Bicycles &
    Sporting Goods, Birmingham, AL,
    printed black and white, 1927, used . .   **20.00**
Book, *The Standard Road Book,* New
    York Series, Book 8, 1897, 70 pgs, lea-
    ther cov, maps, ads for bicycles,
    equipment, and hotels. **40.00**
Catalog
    Bicycle Sundries and Fittings, Ameri-
    can Bicycle Co, Columbia Sales
    Dept, Hartford, CT, 1901, 52 pgs,
    illus, printed green wrappers, 5 x 7"   **35.00**
    Buffalo Tricycle Co, 1880s, 4 pgs, stiff
    card stock **30.00**

**Blotter, Firestone Bicycle Tires, printed
color, 6 x 3", 1920s, $15.00.**

Columbia Bicycles, 1893, 50 pgs,
    illus, cycling vignettes **75.00**
Manufacturers and Jobbers of Bicycles
    and Sundries, Howard Bicycle Sup-
    ply Co, Chicago, IL, 1897, 32 pgs,
    illus, printed wrappers **35.00**
Cover, Badger Cycle Co, blue, 1891,
    used **12.00**
Folder, Overman Wheel Co, bicycles
    illus on front, back with factory and
    Victor Bicycles illus, printed black and
    white **25.00**
Game
    Game of Bicycle Race, McLoughlin
    Brothers, 1891 . . . .   **550.00**
    The Bicycle Race, Chaffee & Selchow,
    1898 . . . .   **550.00**
    The New Bicycle Game, Parker Broth-
    ers, 1894 . . . .   **700.00**
Label, cigar, Royal Finish, George S Har-
    ris & Sons, NY, bicycle race, Cyclist
    Tourist Club logo **20.00**
Letterhead
    Gendron Wheel Co, Toledo, OH, chil-
    dren's bicycles, printed black and
    white, 1918 . . . .   **15.00**
    The Miami Cycle Mfg Co, Middleton,
    OH, High Grade Bicycles, printed
    black and white, 1918 . . . .   **15.00**
Map, Staten Island Drive & Bicycle Road
    Map, white and blue, red routes, 1896,
    12" sq. **20.00**
Poster, The New Great Syndicate Shows
    and Paris Hippodrome, The Most Ex-
    pert and Artistic Bicyclists of the
    World, acrobats on bicycles, 39 x 26"   **400.00**
Ticket
    Charlotte Boulevard Bicycle, Roches-
    ter & Charlotte Turnpike Road Co,
    printed black on orange, 1897. . . . .   **12.00**
    Private Bicycle Riding School, compli-
    mentary lesson, Standard Bicycle
    and Machine Co adv on back, black
    on green, 1896. . . . .   **25.00**

BILLIARDS

Billhead, Stevens Billiard Tables, 1899 . .   **4.00**
Book, *The Science of Billiards with Prac-
    tical Applications,* J T Stoddard, Butter-
    field, Boston, first edition, 1913, cloth
    cov, 160 pgs, cloth cov, illus, 5 x 7" . .   **25.00**
Booklet, Draillib Billiard Cloth, Hyatt
    Pocket & Billiard Balls Wholesale
    Price List, 13 pgs **8.00**
Brochure, *The Home Billiardette Table–
    Rolls Royce of Miniature Pool Tables,*
    1931, 2 pgs, 8½ x 11" **20.00**
Catalog, J Magann & Co, 1917, billiard
    tables, pocket tables, and bowling al-
    leys **22.00**
Label, cigar box sample, American

Champions, Schumacher & Ettlinger, men playing billiards image, 1901 . . .   50.00
Magazine Tear Sheet, *American Review,* Baby Grand Billiard Tables adv, 1914, full page, billiard table illus 8.00
Sign, cardboard, Brunswick–Balke–Collender Co, international billiard experts images, 31 x 41" 400.00
Tobacco Card
Joe Davis, No. 17, Ardath Cork Cigarettes, 1935 . . . .   6.00
Tom Newman, No. 11, Churchman Cigarettes, caricature portrait, 1928   9.00
Walter Lindrum, No. 67, Carreras Cigarettes, oval, 1935 . . . .   3.50

BLACK

References: Douglas Congdon–Martin, *Images In Black: 150 Years of Black Collectibles,* Schiffer Publishing, 1990; Patiki Gibbs, *Black Collectibles Sold In America,* Collector Books, 1987, 1993 value update; Jan Lindenberger, *Black Memorabilia Around the House: A Handbook & Price Guide,* Schiffer Publishing, 1993; Dawn Reno, *Collecting Black Americana,* Crown Publishing, 1986; Darrell A Smith, *Black Americana: A Personal Collection,* Black Relics, 1988; Jackie Young, *Black Collectibles: Mammy and Her Friends,* Schiffer Publishing, 1988.

Periodical: *Black Ethnic Collectibles,* 1401 Asbury Court, Hyattsville, MD 20782.

Collectors' Club: Black Memorabilia Collectors Association, 822 4th ST NE, Apt. 2, Washington DC 20002.

Advertising Trade Card
Fairbanks Cottolene, black lady picking cotton 15.00
Singer Sewing Machine, black women smoking, one using machine, c1890, 3 x 5" 7.50
Arcade Card, Four Mills Brothers, mid 1930s 8.00
Book, *Little Brown Koko,* Blanche Hunt, American Colortype Co, 1952, 96 pgs 20.00
Broadside, Carncross Minstrels, blue and white, Blacks playing banjo and leaning against title, black babies playing instruments, Ledger Job Printing, Philadelphia, c1885, 10½ x 31" 195.00
Comic Book, *Clean Fun Starring Sugarfoots Jones,* 1944 . . . .   130.00
Document, bill of sale, LA, slaves, lists names and ages, 8 x 14" 75.00
Flyer, movie, Amos 'N Andy in *Check and Double Check,* 6 x 15" 25.00
Label, barrel, Sauer Kraut, F A Waidner

Fruit Crate Label, Dixie Boy Brand, black child eating grapefruit, color photograph, 9 x 8½", 1930s, $18.00.

& Co, Chicago, black face peering out through cabbage leaves, 12" d . .   450.00
Magazine, *Saturday Evening Post,* August 28, 1903, black picking cotton on cov 20.00
Newspaper
Chicago Tribune, Underground RR, February 8, 1874 . . . .   15.00
Copperhead, The Crises, Columbus, Oh, October 28, 1863, "Negroes In General Grant's Army & Their Terrible Sufferings" 45.00
Post Card, Skinning A Coon, red necked white man picking pockets of black lady, c1908, unused 15.00
Poster
Hawkins Brothers Comedy Company Banjo Kings, black-and-white photos of brothers playing guitars and banjos, text at bottom, colored stock, c1914, 6 x 14" 65.00

Mechanical Joke, racist, "Toilette," Germany, 2¼ x 3½", c1900, $95.00.

The Sunny South, J C Rockwell's Big City Show, "All Colored People," caricature black man wearing loudly colored mismatched clothing, watermelon watch fob, and monocle, holding binoculars and Jockey Club entry pass, Donaldson Co, c1905, 20 x 30" **300.00**

Toty Musical Excentric Novelty, Harry Gonel illus, black man playing clock shaped violin, Aunt Jemima-style woman playing change in her pockets, another black man playing harmonica and guitar simultaneously, c1890, 24 x 36" **275.00**

Uncle Tom's Cabin, Witherell & Davies Traveling Company, Tom and Eva in plantation garden, multicolored litho, A S Seers Litho, late 1880s, 30 x 26" **375.00**

Program, Duke Ellington & His Orchestra, 1950, drawing on cov **15.00**

Sheet Music
Oh Dat Watermelon, black girl sitting on watermelon, holding watermelon crib **40.00**
They Made It Twice As Nice As Paradise & They Called It Dixieland, elderly black woman with white boy on knees, 1922 . . .   **8.50**
Three Little Words, Amos 'N Andy cov illus, 1930 . . . .   **25.00**

Sign
Gold Dust Washing Powder, Gold Dust Twins doing spring cleaning, 26 x 10" **1,250.00**
Little African Licorice Drops, black and white, alligator sneaking up on crawling baby, c1915, 14½ x 11½" **250.00**

Valentine, "The Craze Has Reached Coonville," multicolored litho, big mama on cycle with poem, 7 x 9" . . .   **65.00**

BOTANICAL

Advertising Trade Card
Bowker Fert'z Co, "Food for Flowers," printed color, hyacinth **5.00**
Goetting's Violet Perfume & Soaps, diecut bouquet of violets, mechanical **30.00**
J F Schuh Hardware, Ann Arbor, MI, roses and violets, printed color . . .   **10.00**
The Keller Bros & Blight Co Upright Pianos, Bridgeport, CT, flowers and fan illus, stock, printed color, emb **9.00**

Billhead, The Stafford Greenhouses, Marquette, MI, floral design, 1900, unused **4.00**

Bookmark, floral bouquet, Eastman's Fine Perfumes, Park Drug Store adv, T Sinclair & Sons Litho, printed color   **6.00**

Catalog
C W Stuart & Co, Nurserymen, 1900–10, 192 pgs, descriptive plate book, oblong, cloth backed, printed wrappers, colored halftones on rectos by Process Color Printing Co of Rochester, NY, texts on versos, flowers, shrubs, bushes, fruits, 7 x 5" **75.00**
Fairview Seed Farms, Syracuse, NY, 1910, 64 pgs, black and white illus, four pgs of color illus, yellow, red, and blue cov, 5 x 7" **20.00**
Jung's Seeds, fruits, flowers, and vegetables illus, 1940, 72 pgs. **8.00**
Mills Catalogue Seeds and Plants, Rose Hill, NY, 1913, 92 pgs, black and white illus, 3 pgs of free premiums, red cov, 5 x 7" **30.00**
Robert Scott & Son, Scott's Roses and Other Beautiful Flowers, Philadelphia, PA, 1889, 56 pgs, black and white illus, full color plate, red and black cov, 5 x 7" **50.00**

Advertising Trade Card, Farmers' Fertilizer Co., color litho front, black-and-white text on back, 4⅝ x 2¾", $5.00.

Cover
  Sunset Seed & Nursery Co, San Francisco, CA, multicolored rose, printed color, 1950, used **5.00**
  Greens Nursery Co, Rochester, NY, printed black and white, unused   **6.00**
Magazine, *The Monthly Family Circle & Parlor Annual,* 1847, hand tinted steel engraved floral print cov, 5¼ x 8½" **10.00**
Manual, *An Illustrated Manual of California Shrubs,* Howard E McMinn, Professor of Botany, Mills College, CA, 1939, 689 pgs, signed by author   **25.00**
Poster, Crosman Bros Choice Flower Seeds, Rochester, NY, color litho, young girl holding bouquet, birds and flowers background, J Ottmann Litho, 1887, 19 x 24" **1,250.00**
Print
  Iris and Orchid, pr, hand colored engravings from *The Botanical Magazine,* sgd and dated, William Curtis, 1789 and 1790, matted and framed, 10¼ x 13¼" **175.00**
  Red Peony, chromolithograph, Pratt, matted and framed, 9⅞ x 12⅞" . .   **105.00**
  Red Camellia, hand colored litho, framed, 8½ x 11½" **55.00**
  Reward of Merit, pansy, "Excelsior, Fifty Merits, 1876," blue and white, gold emb.   **10.00**

BOXING

Reference: Roderick A. Malloy, *Malloy's Sports Collectibles Value Guide,* Wallace–Homestead, 1993.

Periodicals: *Boxing Collectors Newsletter,* 59 Bosson St., Revere, MA 02151; *Malloy's Sports Cards and Collectibles,* 15 Danbury Road, Ridgefield, CT 06877; *Sports Collectors Digest,* 700 East State Street, Iola, WI 54990.

Book, *The Boxer,* John P. Wagner, Orange Judd Publishing, 1950, 282 pgs, dj **12.00**
Flyer, newsprint, "Roar of the Crowd, With the One and Only Joe Louis," movie adv, Louis in ring amid screaming crowd, 1940s, 6 x 13" **20.00**
Magazine
  Boxing Magazine, January 9, 1942, cov with Joe Louis vs Buddy Baer at Madison Square Gardens, color cov, 48 pgs, 9 x 12" **55.00**
  Quick, March 23, 1953, Rocky Marciano on cov **6.00**
  The Ring, January, 1971, "Jail or Title for Cassius Clay" cov story **10.00**
Photograph, black and white glossy, Floyd Patterson, wearing uniform,

Arcade Card, Ted "Red Top" Davis, real photo, green tint, 3⅜ x 5⅜", 1940s, $8.00.

black marker signature "To Stephen, My Sincere Best Wishes For A Healthy And Happy Life, Your Friend, Floyd Patterson," 8 x 9¾" **40.00**
Playing Cards, James J Jeffries Championship, boxer photo image, 1909 copyright, complete deck **100.00**
Poster, boxers in ring, detailed crowd, bold seven color graphics, 1952, 54 x 41" **75.00**
Program
  Joe Louis vs Buddy Baer, Madison Square Garden, January 9, 1942, 4 pgs, heavy stock, main bout and prelims, 6 x 9" **35.00**
  New York Athletic Club Amateur Boxing & Wrestling Championships, 1882, 4 pgs **30.00**
Ticket, World's Heavyweight Championship, Dempsey vs Gibbons, July 4, 1923, O'Toole County American Legion, Shelby, MT **50.00**
Tobacco Card
  Gene Tunney, Churchman Cigarettes, sepia photo, 1938, 1⅜ x 2⅝" **22.50**
  Jim Braddock, Phillips Cigarettes, full color, 1936, 1⅜ x 2⅝" **10.00**

BOY SCOUT

References: William Hillcourt, *Norman Rockwell's World of Scouting,* Harry Abrams, 1977; J. Bryan Putman, ed., *Official Price Guide To Scouting Collectibles,* House of Collectibles, 1982; R. J. Sayers, *Identification & Value Guide To Scouting Collectibles,* Books Americana, 1984; Harry D. Thorsen, *Scouts On Stamps Of The World,* privately printed.

Periodical: *Scout Memorabilia Magazine,* c/o The Lawrence L. Lee Scouting Museum, PO Box 1121, Manchester, NH 03105.

Membership Card, J. C. Leyendecker cover illus., with official BSA envelope, 2¼ x 3¾" folded, opens to 6¾ x 3¾", January 31, 1938, $18.00.

Collectors' Club: Scouts On Stamps Society International, 7406 Park Dr., Tampa, FL 33610.

Certificate, Certificate of Appreciation to Den Mother, red and green printing and illustrations, cub scouts in various activities, dated 1955, signed by Cubmaster, 5 x 7" 5.00
Diary, one year, 1928 . . . .   7.50
Game
    Boy Scout Progress Game, Parker Brothers, 1926 . . . .   150.00
    Boy Scouts, McLoughlin Brothers, c1910 . . . .   200.00
    The Game of Boy Scouts, Parker Brothers, 1926 . . . .   350.00
Handbook, Boy Scouts of America, March, 1937, 506 pgs, Leyendecker cov with two Boy Scouts, one with field glasses, other with signal flag, color, mounted on linen, profuse int. illus 45.00
Magazine
    Boys' Life, February, 1933, Norman Rockwell cov 25.00
    Life, July 24, 1950, Boy Scout cov 3.00
Notebook, Scoutmasters Troop Program Notebook–1940, November, 1939, 128 pgs, soft cov, booklet provided to troops by Boy's Life and the local council, helpful hints, scout activities forms, 4½ x 7" 12.50
Pamphlet, Lone Scout Degree, 1918. . . .   10.00
Photograph, uniformed Boy Scout group and leaders, demonstrating camp cook out procedures, 1938, 8½ x 6½". 20.00
Post Card, photo of Scout in uniform showing Boy Scout sign, c1920. . . . . .   10.00
Poster
    Leyendecker, 1918, 20 x 30" 50.00
    Rockwell, Norman, 1937 National Jamboree, BSA logo, 24 x 40" 65.00
Registration Card, Official Registration Card
    Bi–fold, illustrated by Norman Rockwell, dated February, 1947, color

cov of Boy scout, cub scout and sea scout with flags, scouting trail banner illustrated at the bottom, orig envelope, 5 x 4". 15.00
Tri–fold, illustrated by J C Leyendecker, dated October, 1934, full color cov illustration shows scout signalling with semaphore flags while another scout looks through binoculars, Leyendecker signature in lower left hand corner; center back panel full color illustration of scenes showing scouts providing various services; orig envelope, 4 x 7" open 18.00
Signal Disc, The Pocket Signal Disk, two unit series, double sided, double wheeled device with international morse code signals in one window and semaphore signals in other window, red and black illustrations, orig envelope, Standard Novelty Co, La Jolla California, 1914 copyright, 3¼ x 6" . .   25.00
Stamp, plate block, Boy Scouts of America, 1910–1960, 4¢ stamp, shows boy scout giving scout pledge sign, Norman Rockwell, unused, 2¼ x 4" 8.00

BREWERIANA

References: Donald Bull, Manfred Friedrich, and Robert Gottschalk, *American Breweries,* Bullworks, 1984; Sharon and Bob Huxford, *Huxford's Collectible Advertising: An Illustrated Value Guide,* Collector Books, 1993; Keith Osborne and Brian Pipe, *The International Book of Beer Labels, Mats, & Coasters,* Chartwell Books, 1979.

Collectors' Clubs: American Breweriana Association Inc., PO Box 11157, Pueblo, CO 81001; East Coast Breweriana Association, 2010 N. Broad St., Lansdale, PA 19446; National Association of Breweriana, Advertising, 2343 Mat–tu–Wee Lane, Wauwatosa, WI 53226.

Advertising Trade Card, mechanical, Blue Ribbon Beer, "How Many

Coaster, Sunshine Brewing Company, printed color, "Get a Sunny Thing Going," 3½" d, 1950s, $4.00.

Faces Can You Make?'', three rotating wheels each with facial parts to make eight complete faces	**80.00**
Billhead, Ross's Bottling Guinnesses Stout & Bass's Ale, Sault Ste Marie, MI, printed color, H Gamse & Bro Litho, 1917, used	**12.00**
Blotter, Feigenspan's Half and Half Beer, bottle image.	**60.00**
Calendar, 1906, Grand Rapids Brewing Co, diecut cardboard, emb, girl reading "Dr Hall's Health Hints," 10 x 14½".	**1,000.00**
Certificate, Burlington Brewing Co, unissued, 1937	**4.00**
Diecut, glass of beer, c1950, 13" h . . .	**12.00**
Letterhead, Phillips Best Brewing Co, shows breweries and medals won in 1878 Paris and 1876 Philadelphia, pair of letterheads and cov	**30.00**
Magazine, *TV Guide*, August 27–September 2, 1949, cov with Pat McElroy, Miss Rheingold of 1949. . .	**75.00**
Poster	
Koehler Beer, repeated design of three beer bottles and glasses, "Pour a Koehler Collar Today!," 1956, 35 x 23".	**25.00**
Narragansett Ale, Lester Beall illus, two men wearing suits carry large ale bottles, blue ground, 1937, 30 x 15"	**150.00**
Rolling Rock, four pairs of pony bottles and glasses, 22 x 23".	**100.00**
Sign, Ste Genevieve Brewing and Lighting Association, MO, emb, young lady holding tennis racket and glass of beer, c1915, 11 x 17½"	**700.00**

BUSINESS

References: Leslie Cabarga, *Letterheads: One Hundred Years of Great Designs, 1850–1950,* Chronicle Books, 1992; Bill Yatchman, *The Stock*

& Bond Collectors Price Guide, published by author, 1985.

Periodical: *Bank Note Reporter,* 700 East State Street, Iola, WI 54990.

Collectors' Clubs: American Society of Check Collectors, PO Box 69, Boynton Beach, FL 33425; Bond and Share Society, 26 Broadway, New York, NY 10004.

Document	
Banknote, E B Estes & Sons Wooden Clothespins, New York, Brooks Banknote Co, Springfield, MA, printed color, 1915	**18.00**
Billhead	
A S Barnes & Co Publishers, Wholesale Booksellers & Stationers, NY, printed black and white, 1879 . . .	**8.00**
Ezra Clark & Co, Importers and Dealers in Iron, Steel, Nails, etc., Hartford, CT, printed black and white, 1854	**12.00**
H Childs & Co, Bessemer Shoes, IL, printed color, emb gold and silver, 1897, used	**12.00**
S D Elwood, Commercial & Law Stationer, Detroit, MI, printed black and white, 1861, used	**8.00**
Wyckoff, Seamens & Benedict, Remington, Standard Typewriter, Philadelphia, PA, red seal with typewriter, 1891	**8.00**
Bond, 10 x 15", Transit Warehouse Co, construction bond, printed color, brown and white, eagle logo, with tickets, 1923	**10.00**
Booklet, name card samples	
Ohio Card Co, Cadiz, OH, five parts, four cards, printed color, 5 x 14".	**25.00**

Bill of Lading, New York & Baltimore Transportation Line, via Chesapeake and Delaware Canal and Delaware and Raritan Canal, 8½ x 7", 1871, $12.50.

Ace Cigar Co. Buffalo, N. Y.

Cigar Label, Sunset Club, Ace Cigar Co., Buffalo, NY, brown and red, 10 x 6³/₄", $18.00.

Ray Card Co, North Haven, CT, six parts, six sample cards, printed color, 5¹/₂ x 16¹/₂" 30.00
Business Card, Metropolitan Cabinet-making and Undertaking Co, Branch Parlors, St Johnsville, NY, printed black and white 10.00
Check, Buckley & Douglas Lumber Co, Manistee, MI, Gast Bank Note Co, printed black and white, 1902   8.00
Ledger, Emlen Estate Accounting book, 1809 . . . .   100.00
Letterhead
Baldwin Tool Works, Parkensbury, WV, color label, printed black and white, shovels, spades, scoops, etc., 1917, used 12.00
Baxter Stove Co, Mansfield, OH, black on orange, printed black and white, G H Dunston Litho, 1887, used 8.00
Boone Hardware Co, NC, printed color, in reference to Smith & Wesson gun repair 12.00
Cleveland Cooperative Stove Co, Cleveland, OH, printed black and white, 1887, used 10.00
Keystone Plow Co, New Castle, PA, blue, printed color, 1894, used . .   8.00
Southbend Iron Works, Oliver Plows, black on light blue, printed black and white, 1893, used 10.00
Thomas Manufacturing Co, Thomas rakes, tedders, lawn mowers, etc., Springfield, MA, ¹/₂ sheet, printed black and white, Winters Litho . .   8.00
Worcester Wire Novelty Co, Canton, OH, printed rat traps and baskets, printed black and white, 1914, used 15.00
Wright Steam Engine Works, Newburgh, NY, printed black and white, 1882 . . . .   12.00
Script Note, $2.00, Vermont Glass

Factory, Farmers Bank, Troy, NY, printed black and white, 1814, used   75.00
History, booklet
Bartholomay Brewing Co, Rochester, NY, c1880, company history and operations, 34 sepia prints, three foldout 50.00
John Wanamaker, *Methods of Business,* outlines history from founding to present, 1876, 16 pgs. 85.00
Montgomery Ward, *A Chicago Enterprise,* traces history, black and white sketches, 1891, 10 pgs. 30.00

CAMPBELL

References: David Longest, *Character Toys and Collectibles,* Collector Books, 1984, 1992 value update; David Longest, *Character Toys and Collectibles, Second Series* Collector Books, 1987, 1990 value update.

Periodical: *Kids Illustrated Drayton Supplement* (K.I.D.S), 649 Bayview Drive, Akron, OH 44319.

Book, *Campbell Kids At Home* 15.00
Cookbook, Campbell Soup Kids, 64 pgs   30.00
Display Figure, diecut cardboard, standup 15.00
Magazine Tear Sheet, children illus, full color 6.00
Place Cards, set of 4, diecut, full color, different Campbell Kids illus, c1931, 3 x 4" 50.00

Magazine Tear Sheet, *Woman's Home Companion,* 10³/₄ x 13³/₄", November 1923, $9.00.

Jigsaw Puzzle, The Campbell Kids, Schooltime, Jaymar, Kiddie Puzzle, #319, 28 pcs., 13 x 10", $12.00.

Placemats, The Campbell Kids Eat–O–Mats, Milton Bradley, 1950s, orig box, unused, set of 6, 16 x 11".......... **25.00**

Puzzle, frame tray, cardboard, Campbell Kids in hurdle race, 10 x 13"........ **12.00**

CAMERA

Periodical: *Camera Shopper Magazine,* One Magnolia Hill, West Hartford, CT 06117.

Collectors' Clubs: National Stereoscopic Association, PO Box 14801, Columbus, OH 43214; Photographic Historical Society, PO Box 39563, Rochester, NY 14604.

Advertising Trade Card, Heywood's Mammoth Photograph, Ambrotype Gallery, Boston, MA, 2 x 2¼"....... **15.00**

Billhead, E K Co to Kittell & Co, Kinderhook, NY, monthly statement, 1914 .... **10.00**

Book
  Amateur Carbro Colour Prints, Viscount Hanworth, Focal Press, London, 1950–51, 188 pgs, third edition, dj **20.00**
  Guide to Kodak Retina, Retina Reflex, Signet and Pony, Kenneth S Tydings, 1952, 128 pgs, soft cov **8.00**
  Lecia Guide, W D Emanuel, Focal Press, 1945–53, 112 pgs........ **8.00**

Booklet
  Leitz Close–up and Photomicrography with the Lecia Camera, E Leitz, NY, 48 pgs **15.00**
  Making Titles and Editing Your Cine–Kodak Films, 1931, 30 pgs **20.00**

Box, Eastman's Kodak Developing Powders, "For Use in Brownie Tank Developer," c1900.................. **8.00**

Brochure, Kodak Medalist II, c1949, 24 pgs........................ **20.00**

Camera, Photo–Pac, cardboard, disposable, black, 12 exposure, 1950 ...... **38.00**

Catalog
  Blair Camera Co, Boston, The Hawk–Eye Camera, 1891, 18 pgs........ **25.00**
  Century Cameras, 1909............ **40.00**
  George Murphy Camera, 1917, 192 pgs............................. **25.00**
  Graflex, 1937, 28 pgs **20.00**
  Hyatt's Catalog, c1910, 206 pgs, cameras, parts, equipment, and supplies **35.00**
  Kodak
    1914, 64 pgs **30.00**
    1920, 32 pgs, illus, photo cov **20.00**
  Kodaks and Brownies, October, 1938, 36 pgs **15.00**
  Korona, 1926, 52 pgs **25.00**
  Leica
    1939, 97 pgs **35.00**
    1955, 84 pgs **15.00**
  Poco Cameras, Rochester Camera and Supply Co, Rochester, NY, 1903, 44 pgs.......................... **30.00**
  Schneider Lens, 1930, 20 pgs **20.00**
  Seneca, 1912, 76 pgs, 5 x 8½"..... **40.00**
  Voigtlander, 1930, 28 pgs.......... **30.00**
  Watson and Sons, Ltd, Camera Lenses and Accessories, 1937, 24 pgs..... **20.00**
  Wollensak Lenses and Shutters, 1916–17, 36 pgs **20.00**

Invoice, Horgan, Robey & Co, Boston, graphics with lens, 1895, 6 x 9"..... **10.00**

Magazine
  Kodakery–A Magazine for Amateur Photographers, 1919–21......... **32.00**
  Studio Light, 1917–29, 107 issues ... **200.00**

Manual
  Eastman's No. 2 Eureka Camera, c1899, 18 pgs **20.00**
  Graflex, service and parts, 60 pgs, punched for binder, c1948 .... **15.00**

Magazine Tear Sheet, Kodak adv., $12.00.

Kodak, #4 Folding Pocket Kodak, 1910, 56 pgs **15.00**
Lecia, second edition, first printing . . . **35.00**
Lecia Reflex Housing, 1956, 8 pgs . . . **5.00**
Sound Kodascope FS–10–N, service and parts, 55 pgs, large format, c1947 . . . . **7.00**
Window Display, glossy, "Color Experts," Kodak, 1949, 8 x 10" **30.00**

CANDY

Advertising Cover, envelope
Chase's Candies, brown on orange, factory image, 1941 . . . . **15.00**
Good & Plenty, Quaker City Chocolate & Confectionery Co Inc, pink and blue, display box image, 1936 **30.00**
Advertising Trade Card
Adams Tutti Frutti Gum, Euchre card game **25.00**
Beeman's Pepsi Gum, hold–to–light **18.00**
Huyler's Chocolates, rooster and baby chicks waking sleeping girl **10.00**
Newton Brothers Pepsin Chewing gum, diecut, emb, 1887. . . . . **85.00**
Wrigley's Gum, premium hat rack offer. **15.00**
Book
A Treatise on the Art of Boiling Sugar, Crystallizing, Lozenge Making, Comfits, Gum Goods, and Other Processes for Confectionery, Henry Weatherley, Baird, Philadelphia, 1903, 196 pgs, cloth cov, advertisements. **35.00**
Chocolate and Confectionery, C Trevor Williams, Leonard Hill, London, second edition, 1953, 240 pgs, cloth, halftone plate illus, line drawn vignettes **25.00**
My Candy Secrets; A Book of Simple and Accurate Information Which, if Faithfully Followed, Will Enable the Novice to Make Candies that Need Not Fear Comparison with the Professional Product, Mary Elizabeth Evans, Stokes, NY, 1919, 146 pgs, cloth cov, photo illus **45.00**
Box
Brach's Candy **40.00**
Goff's Atlantic City Salt Water Taffy, woman wearing orange swim suit, holding candy box overhead, wading in ocean, 8⁷⁄₈ x 4⁷⁄₈ x 2¹⁄₂" **7.50**
Maillard Chocolates, cardboard, sq, ext. dec with cloth and linen appliques **65.00**
Brochure, Cracker Jack, "Village Baseball Team," 1920s. **45.00**
Calendar, George Smith & Son Bakers &

Confectioners, 1901, colonial couple, full pad **25.00**
Catalog, Eppelsheimer & Co, New York, NY, chocolate molds, c1928, 34 pgs, 7 x 11¹⁄₄" **48.00**
Cookbook
Art of Home Candy Making, 1915, 89 pgs **15.00**
Hood's Book–Home Made Candies, C I Hood & Co, Lowell, MA, 1883, 16 pgs **10.00**
Flyer, James Salt Water Taffy Co adv, Atlantic City, NJ, color litho, c1930 . . . . **30.00**
Magazine Tear Sheet, *Appleton's Journal,* 1905, Peter's Chocolate, full page **5.00**
Matchbook Cover, Topps 1¢ Gum **20.00**
Photograph, Woolworth's licorice window display, c1930 . . . . **25.00**
Poster, Wrigley's Gum, pioneer woman wearing bonnet gazes over wagon train, "Pioneer Women Helped Build Our Great Country," Otis Shepard illus, c1943, 28 x 11". **100.00**
Sign
Chocolate Alligators, multicolored alligator image, "One Cent Each," 6" sq **30.00**
Wrigley's Chewing Gum, woman selling gum to girl **375.00**
Wrapper, Planter's 5¢ Candy **15.00**

CAT

References: Pauline Flick, *Cat Collectibles,* Wallace–Homestead, 1992; J. L. Lynnlee, *Purrrfection: The Cat,* Schiffer Publishing, 1990; Alice L. Muncaster and Ellen Sawyer, *The Black Cat Made Me Buy It!,* Crown Publishers, 1988; Alice Muncaster and Ellen Yanow; *The Cat Made Me Buy It,* Crown Publishers, 1984; Alice L. Muncaster and Ellen Yanow Sawyer, *The Cat Sold It!,* Crown Publishers, 1986; Silvester and Mobbs, *The Cat Fancier: A Guide To Catland Postcards,* Longman Group, 1982.

Collectors' Club: Cat Collectors, 33161 Wendy Dr., Sterling Hts., MI 48315.

Advertising Trade Card
Dr Thomas Eclectric Oil, kitten emerging from product box **15.00**
Clark's Mile–End Spool Cotton, teacher cat scolding two schoolboy kittens playing with tangled thread **15.00**
Leather Goods, diecut, pallet shape, cat heads **5.00**
Box, Corticelli Sewing Silk, white cat playing with spool of thread, c1925 . . **10.00**
Calendar, Chesapeake & Ohio Railway, 1957, Chessie illus **75.00**

Cigar Label, White Cat, red, blue, and brown, 9 x 7", $12.00.

Card Game, Black Cat Fortune Telling Game, Parker Brothers, 1897 . . . . **65.00**

Children's Book
The Bright Eye Book, Mila Winter, Reuben H Lilja and Co, 1941, sgd, 8¹/₂ x 12" **25.00**

With Louis Wain in Pussyland, Raphael Tuck, c1910 . . . . **250.00**

Christmas Card, diecut, kitten in canopied bed, "With Loving Christmas Greetings," c1900 . . . . **12.50**

Diecut, movable head and legs, text on back, Raphael Tuck and Sons, c1910 **45.00**

Halloween Lantern, cardboard, cat's head, black, orange tissue paper eyes, nose, and mouth, two sided, late 1940s, 11" h **65.00**

Label, cigar, Our Kitties, emb black and white cats on red rug **8.00**

Matchbox, Coats Sewing Cotton adv, teacher cat instructing three kittens. . . **1.00**

Party Set, 40 x 40" tablecloth and four napkins, pumpkin vines and black cats, c1950 . . . . **45.00**

Postage Stamps, block of four, two cats each stamp, designed by John Dawson, issued February 5, 1988. . . . **2.50**

Post Card, cats and teddy bears, #474, artist sgd, Arthur Thiele, divided back **20.00**

Poster
Ideal Classic Adv, white Persian cat cuddling up to radiator heater, Luisa Polo illus, G Ricordi Co, Milan, Italy, c1930, 39 x 53". **475.00**

Nestle's Swiss Milk, two cats sitting on wall, full moon in background, John Hassall illus, c1920 . . . . **125.00**

Puzzle, jigsaw, The Robber Kitten, Parker Brothers, 1920s **35.00**

Scrap, "Cat Show," kittens in cages, Raphael Tuck, c1910. . . . . **75.00**

Sheet Music, *Kitten on the Keys,* white kitten walking on piano keyboard, c1915 . . . . **10.00**

Sign, diecut, two cats wearing Victorian clothes, A & P adv **110.00**

Valentine, diecut, standup, Puss 'N Boots, mechanical, hat swivels to change eyes, Germany **15.00**

CELEBRITY

References: Ted Hake, *Hake's Guide To Presidential Campaign Collectibles,* Wallace–Homestead, 1992; Leslie Halliwell, *The Filmgoer's Companion,* Avon, 1978; Charles Hamilton, *American Autographs,* University of Oklahoma Press, 1983; John Hegenberger, *Collector's Guide To Treasures From The Silver Screen,* Wallace–Homestead, 1991; Ephraim Katz, *The Film Encyclopedia,* Perigee Books, 1979; Leonard Maltin (ed.), *TV Movies and Video Guide,* New American Library, 1987; Keith Melder, *Hail To The Candidate: Presidential Campaigns From Banners To Broadcasts,* Smithsonian Institution Press, 1992; Robert W. Pelton, *Collecting Autographs For Fun And Profit,* Betterway Publications, 1987; George Sanders, Helen Sanders, and Ralph Roberts, *Collector's Guide To Autographs,* Wallace–Homestead, 1990; George Sanders, Helen Sanders, and Ralph Roberts, *The Price Guide to Autographs, Second Edition,* Wallace–Homestead, 1991; Richard De Thuin, *The Official Identification and Price Guide To Movie Memorabilia,* House of Collectibles, 1990; Jon R. Warren, *Warren's Movie Poster Price Guide, 1993 Edition,* American Collector's Exchange, 1992; Dian Zillner, *Hollywood Collectibles,* Schiffer Publishing, 1991.

Periodicals: *Big Reel,* Route 3, PO Box 83, Madison, NC 27025; *Classic Images,* PO Box 809, Muscatine, IA 52761; *Hollywood Movie Archives,* PO Box 1566, Apple Valley, CA 92307; *Movie Collectors' World,* PO Box 309, Fraser, MI 48026; *Nostalgia World,* PO Box 231, North Haven, CT 06473; *The Political Bandwagon,* PO Box 348, Leola, PA 17540; *The Political Collector Newspaper,* PO Box 5171, York, PA 17405.

Collectors' Clubs: American Political Items Collectors, PO Box 340339, San Antonio, TX 78234; Company of Military Historians, North Main Street, Westbrook, CT 06498; Hollywood Studio Collectors Club, Suite 450, 3960 Laurel Canyon Blvd., Studio City, CA 91604; Manuscript Society, 350 N. Niagara Street, Burbank, CA 91505; Universal Autograph Collectors Club, PO Box 6181, Washington, DC 20044.

Entertainment
Bardot, Brigitte, movie press book, *La Parisienne,* United Artists, 8 pgs, Bardot cov portrait, "Oh That Bardot!". **75.00**

Bergman, Ingrid, post card, black and white photo portrait, *Arch of Triumph* movie adv on back **10.00**

Bow, Clara, portrait, lobby card stock, violet and white, early 1930s, 11 x 14" **45.00**

Brando, Marlon, movie press book, booklet, *Julius Caesar*, MGM, 16 pgs, 8 x 12" **15.00**

Cagney, James, movie press book, *Man of a Thousand Faces*, Universal, 20 pgs, "The Lon Chaney Story" **25.00**

Chaplin, Charlie, flyer, Chaplin surrounded by clowns, "Charlie Chaplin in his Greatest Comedy, The Circus," 8 x 11" **20.00**

Davies, Marian, portrait, tinted, *Modern Screen Magazine* premium, *Page Miss Glory* movie, c1932, 8 x 11" **6.00**

De Haviland, Olivia, letter, discussing meeting with Jean Harlow, typed, sgd, autographed photo, 1983 . . . .   **50.00**

Dorsey, Tommy, original art, Richard Waldrep, "Sentimental Gentleman," Big Band Recordings series, Time–Life Inc, colored pencil, dyes, airbrush, and acrylic, sgd, mid 1980s, 20 x 20" **1,500.00**

Eastwood, Clint, greeting card, Christmas, 1959 . . . .   **20.00**

Garland, Judy, brochure, "Judy Garland Community Sing," Victory House, Pershing Square, Los Angeles, October 21, 1942 live performance, 4 pgs, Garland cov, 7 x 10", with 7 x 9" RKO Palace Theater booklet advertising Garland in "Two–a–Day" all star variety show, 1951 . . . .   **60.00**

Joan Crawford, sheet music, *Always and Always,* 9 x 12", 1937, $12.00.

Marx, Groucho, poster, full figure Groucho smoking cigar, "Tune in Groucho in New Fall Series Every Week," DeSoto–Plymouth radio show adv, two sheets, with orig envelope and radio call letter sheets, 1953, 49 x 75" **300.00**

Rogers, Ginger, book, *Ginger Rogers & the Riddle of the Scarlet Cloak,* Whitman, 1942 . . . .   **8.00**

Sinatra, Frank, sheet music, *That Sinatra Swing,* 1944 . . . .   **10.00**

Wyman, Jane, post card, handwritten, sgd, early 1940s **40.00**

Historical

Adams, Andrew, autograph, handwritten document, Chief Judge, dated 1796, 4 x 13" **130.00**

Antoinette, Marie, carte de visite, c1868 . . . .   **18.00**

Blenker, Lewis, Brigadier General, carte de visite, Brady, c1860 . . . . . .   **60.00**

Custer, General George A, carte de visite, Brady, c1865 . . . .   **275.00**

Davis, Jeff, envelope, Civil War, Davis riding backwards on flying goose, "Jeff Sound on the Goose" **15.00**

Franklin, Benjamin

   Advertising Trade Card, Franklin holding box of Quaker Oats **25.00**

   Carte de Visite, C D Fredericks **10.00**

Grant, Lt General Ulysses S

   Label, cigar, Our Chieftain, L E Neuman & Co Litho, Grant portrait   **50.00**

   Photo, albumen, seated on horse, Reed, 1870s **50.00**

Keller, Helen, sheet music, *Star of Happiness,* dedicated to Keller, cov with Keller wearing Grecian gown, 1919, 9 x 12" **30.00**

Lindbergh, Charles, calendar, 1927, commemorative, Lindbergh photo portrait in oval beneath eagle and flags, full pad **60.00**

Napoleon, album, Allen & Ginter Cigarettes, portrait on cov, 24 pgs, chromolithograph **300.00**

Twain, Mark, letterhead, Voigt Milling, Grand Rapids, farm and product images including vignette of Mark Twain Flour sack with Twain's face, c1895 . . . .   **25.00**

Political

Blaine, James G, ballot, jugate portraits, "For President... Blaine/For Vice President...Logan/The Republican Ticket," 6 x 13" **40.00**

Coolidge, Calvin, fan, cardboard, black lettering, "We Will Help To Keep Cool–idge" and "Mifflin County Women's Coolidge Club Lewistown, Pennsylvania 1924," wood handle, 9 x 15" **40.00**

Sheet Music, *President Cleveland's Grand March*, steel engraving, C. H. Dixson Co. Pub., 10½ x 14", c1884, $65.00.

Dewey, Thomas E, booklet, portrait on cov, black and white photos, Dewey, Bricker, and other PA candidates' campaigns, 24 pgs, 2½ x 4" **6.00**

Eisenhower, Dwight D, matchbook cover, inaugural, portraits, unused, 1953 .... **10.00**

Ferraro, Geraldine A, autograph, paperback book, *Official Proceedings of the 1984 Democratic National Convention,* large black signature on cov **35.00**

Garfield, James A, poster, black and white, names below, text identifying Republican candidates for president and vice president, Morgan's Sapolio adv slogan, 1881–85 campaign, 21½ x 28" **125.00**

Goldwater, Barry M, paperback book, *A Texan Looks at Lyndon, A Study In Illegitimate Power,* J Evetts Haley, 256 pgs, "Issued by Citizens For Goldwater Tacoma, WA" stamped on title page, 4½ x 6" **12.00**

Grant, Ulysses S, tobacco card, Blackwells Durham, multicolored, portrait of Tilden and verse, opens to reveal portrait of Grant with verse about accepting nomination, company logo on back, 1876, 3 x 4" ... **40.00**

Nixon, Richard M, Christmas card, full color photo of first family, first name facsimile signatures, orig envelope postmarked 1967, NY return address, 4 x 6" **30.00**

Roosevelt, Franklin, cigar band, "Franklin D Roosevelt Hand Made," black, white, red, and gold, c1933, 3" l................... **10.00**

Roosevelt, Theodore, post card, Teddy in Africa, caricature shaking hands

with baboon, 1909 copyright, unused, 5½ x 3½". **35.00**

Taft, William Howard, post card, "Hellow Bill!," multicolored, opossum dressed as Uncle Sam, eight line verse, unused **20.00**

Truman, Harry S, program, Inaugural Ball, gold cov, blue binding cord, National Guard Armory, portraits of President and Mrs Truman, Margaret, and Barkley, January 20, 1949, 8½ x 11" **35.00**

Willkie, Wendell L, sticker, diecut foil, silver, blue, and red, "Willkie, The Hope of America," 3½ x 6". **10.00**

Wilson, Woodrow, stereoscopic view, with Lloyd George and Clemencea at Versailles **3.00**

CEREAL

Reference: Tom Tumbusch, *Tomart's Price Guide to Radio Premiums and Cereal Box Collectibles,* Wallace–Homestead, 1991.

Periodicals: *Flake,* PO Box 481, Cambridge, MA 02140; *Free Inside,* PO Box 178844, San Diego, CA 92117.

Advertising Trade Card
   AMC Perfect Cereals, horse drawn wagon loaded with cereal boxes ... **35.00**
   Friend's Rolled White Oats, Quaker woman wearing bonnet and factory vignettes **40.00**
   Pettijohn's California Breakfast Food, folder, equestrian woman holding product box, standing next to horse with feedbag, "I Eat Pettijohn's California Breakfast Food, My Horse Eats Oats," black and white....... **20.00**
   Quaker Rolled White Oats, American Cereal Co, diecut box, metamorphic, children sitting at breakfast table int. **30.00**
   Wheatlet Breakfast Food, Franklin Mills, diecut, standup, Uncle Sam standing next to large bowl of cereal on cereal box **90.00**
Blotter, Shredded Wheat, breakfast table setting, beige ground **30.00**
Booklet, Quaker Oats
   Puzzle Pictures, 16 pgs, black and white and color **20.00**
   The Frolie Grasshopper Circus, 16 pgs, color **20.00**
Box
   Clover Farm Regular Cooking Rolled Oats, cylinder, bee and clover flower, 1930s, 10" h **40.00**
   Jersey Corn Flakes, image of family eating cereal on front, multicolored, unopened, 1920s.............. **40.00**

Kellogg's, magazine tear sheet, *The Delineator*, unsgd J. C. Leyendecker illustration, color litho, 9½ x 14½", 1916, $30.00.

Nabisco Shredded Wheat, 1942	**65.00**
Rice Chex, red checkered design, 1950s	**65.00**
Washington Crisps Toasted Corn Flakes, Washington portrait, red, white, and blue flag motif, 9 x 6" . . .	**100.00**
Wheaties, Pete Rose	**15.00**
White Swan Oatmeal, 4 oz	**28.00**
Calendar, Wheatlet Breakfast Food, diecut standup, little girl with cereal box and bowl, standing by open window, no pad, 1899	**50.00**
Magazine Tear Sheet, Pep Cereal, features Our Gang, color	**30.00**
Premium	
Activity Set, Mighty Mouse Merry–Pack, Post Alpha Bits, punchout sheets, c1956	**60.00**
Book, *Dick Tracy*, Quaker Oats, c1939	**25.00**
Card, Roy Rogers Pop Out Card, "Trigger Says His Prayers," unused	**15.00**
Card Game, Space Match, Quaker Quisp, color illus box, 1968	**25.00**
Certificate, Cap'n Crunch Oath of Allegiance, color illus, 1960s, 8 x 10"	**24.00**
Comic Book, Baseball Facts & Fun, Post Sugar Crisp, 52 pgs	**30.00**

Cut–Out, Rocket Firing Star Fighter Jet and Exploding Light Tank, Cheerios, 1950s	**12.00**
Mask, Singing Lady Party Kit, Kellogg's, uncut, 1936	**60.00**
Post Card, Lone Ranger photo and facsimile signature, Cheerios, 1956 . . .	**10.00**
Train–O–Gram, punchout card, Santa Fe Twin Unit Diesel, Shredded Wheat, unused, 1956, set of 3, 4 x 7"	**30.00**
Sign, Washington Crisps, image of product box with George Washington on front	**175.00**
Stereoview, Quaker Oats	**4.00**
Story Album, Shredded Wheat	**75.00**

CHARACTER

References: Ted Hake, *Hake's Guide to Comic Character Collectibles,* Wallace–Homestead, 1993; Maurice Horn and Richard Marshall (eds.), *World Encyclopedia of Comics,* Chelsea House Publications; David Longest, *Character Toys and Collectibles,* Collector Books, 1984, 1992 value update; David Longest, *Character Toys and Collectibles, Second Series* Collector Books, 1987, 1990 value update; Freddi Margolin and Andrea Podley, *The Official Price Guide To Peanuts Collectibles,* House of Collectibles, 1990.

Advertising	
Aunt Jemima	
Cookbook, 1927, 12 pgs, 3 x 6"	**10.00**
Placemat, Aunt Jemima's Kitchen . .	**15.00**
Poster, Aunt Jemima Spice Set adv, 1950, 16½ x 22"	**125.00**
Puzzle Toy, diecut cardboard head and shoulders, red, white, and blue, Aunt Jemima Pancake Flour, early 1900s	**75.00**
Bibendum, Michelin Man	
Poster, Bibendum wearing scarf, snowflakes in background, "Winter Forecast, Join The Move To Michelin, XM–5," round, 1960s–70s, 17" d	**100.00**
Sign, Bibendum mapping in tire, yellow letters, cobalt blue background, "Michelin Tires & Tubes," c1920, 60 x 18"	**450.00**
Buster Brown	
Book, *Buster Brown's Latest,* Buster Brown Hosiery Mills premium, 1909 copyright, 16 pgs, R F Outcault signature on cov art, three different stories	**85.00**
Box	
Buster Brown Shoes	**15.00**
Stockings, color graphics	**40.00**
Fan, framed	**75.00**

Post Card, Buster and Tige, multi-colored, 1906, Tuck. **25.00**

Chiquita Banana

Paper Doll, Kellogg's premium, 1944. . . . . **28.00**

Sheet Music, cov with Chiquita and Calypso musicians, 1947 copyright **12.00**

Doe–Wah–Jack, catalog, Furnaces and Ranges, 1935 . . . . **28.00**

Dutch Boy, paint book, unused, 1907–20 . . . . **25.00**

Exxon Tiger, shopping bag **4.00**

Gold Dust Twins

Calendar, 1933 . . . . **20.00**

Fan, diecut cardboard, color litho, Twins at 1904 World's Fair, wood handle, 7¹/₂" d **150.00**

Sign, orange and black, "Let The Gold Dust Twins Do Your Work," 20 x 13" **90.00**

Nipper, sign, RCA Victor, cardboard, framed **75.00**

Phillip Morris Bellboy

Cigarette Pack, sample, "Guest Package," Johnny on both sides, cellophane seal, unopened, 1930–40, 1¹/₂ x 3" **25.00**

Placecard, Johnny image **15.00**

Reddy Kilowatt

Coaster, black, white, and red image, wax paper backing, unused, set of 20, 3¹/₂" d **15.00**

Matchbook Cover, red, black, white, and silver, Reddy and electric range, Niagara Hudson Power Co, c1930, 1¹/₂ x 4¹/₂". **18.00**

Poster, red, white, and blue, 1960s, 11 x 13¹/₂" **40.00**

Snap, Crackle, and Pop, Kellogg's Rice Krispies

Blotter, multicolored, c1940, 3¹/₂ x 5¹/₂" **5.00**

Song Book, 1937 . . . . **5.00**

Speedy Alka Seltzer

Calendar, 1941, Miles Weather Calendar, red, white, and blue, Alka Seltzer and other Miles products cartoon ads each sheet, 10 x 16". **25.00**

Playing Cards, 100th Anniversary commemorative, 1984, orig 2¹/₂ x 3¹/₂" box **15.00**

Post Card **12.00**

Wrigley's Spearman, booklet, *Wrigley's Mother Goose,* cov with spearman riding flying goose, 4 x 5⁷/₈" **20.00**

Cartoon

Bugs Bunny

Paint Book, Whitman, unused, 1944, 8¹/₂ x 11" **12.00**

Viewmaster Reel, Tru–Vue, #T–54, "TV Trouble," full color, Bugs, Porky, and Petunia, unopened, 1959 copyright **15.00**

Casper the Friendly Ghost, game, Jumping Beans, 1959. . . . . **30.00**

Flintstones

Puzzle, Whitman, 1962, Hanna–Barbera, Fred and Wilma floating on Dino, 14 x 18". **10.00**

Viewmaster Reel, Tru–Vue, #T–58, "Sea Monster," Pebbles and Bam–Bam, unopened, 1964 copyright **15.00**

Jetsons, colorforms set, black and white jet–age airport board, instruction leaflet, 1963 copyright, complete. **35.00**

Mighty Mouse, game, Playhouse Rescue, 1956, unused **50.00**

Popeye

Book

Choose Your Weppins, Saalfield **10.00**

Wash Up, Olive Oyl and Swee'Pea, 1980, 7¹/₂ x 13". . . . **8.00**

Playing Cards, 1938. . . . . **30.00**

Wallpaper, 1930s, 10' roll. **200.00**

Porky Pig, Big Little Book, *Porky Pig and His Gang,* Whitman, #1404. . . **35.00**

Rocky and Bullwinkle, coloring book, Bullwinkle's How To Have Fun Outdoors Without Getting Clobbered, unused **20.00**

Woody Woodpecker

Book, *Woody Woodpecker's Peck of Trouble,* Whitman, 1951, hard cov 6 x 6¹/₂" **5.00**

Christmas Card, Woody surrounded by other Lantz characters, Lantz facsimile signature, c1950, 11 x 15¹/₂" **75.00**

Coloring Set, orig box, 1958 . . . . . . **30.00**

Comic

Andy Gump, calendar, 1913. . . . . . . **65.00**

Barney Google

Book, *Barney Google and Spark Plug,* Cupples & Leon, 1925, 48 pgs **75.00**

Sheet Music, Barney and Spark Plug on cov, 1923 . . . . **22.50**

Valentine, mechanical, diecut, movable feather reveals message, 1940. . . . . **30.00**

Bettie Boop

Decal, 1950s **12.00**

Valentine, mechanical, diecut, movable feather in hair moves eyes and changes message from "Don't Keep Me Waiting For Your Love, Valentine" to "Or I'll Start Looking Around, Valentine," 1940, 3¹/₂ x 4¹/₂". **30.00**

Blondie and Dagwood
Book, *Blondie & Dagwood's Snap-shot Clue,* 1934 . . . .   **45.00**
Coloring Book, Whitman #1121–15, 1950, 92 pgs, 8½ x 11" **15.00**
Cookbook, dj **35.00**
Greeting Card, Dagwood carrying greeting card on front, Dagwood doing dishes inside, 1939, Hallmark, 5 x 6" **12.50**
Paint Book, Whitman, #605 . . . . . .   **25.00**
Stationery, 1950s, orig box **28.00**
Bringing Up Father, poster, George McManus illus, theatrical production adv, Jiggs and friend playing cards on rooftop, New York City skyline and smiling moon and stars in background, color litho, black, red, and yellow, c1915, 41 x 81" . . .   **475.00**
Buster Brown, book, *Buster Brown's Amusing Capers,* 1908, 60 pgs, color, hard cov, 17 x 11" **45.00**
Dennis the Menace, book, *Baby Sitter's Guide by Dennis the Menace,* Hank Ketchum, Henry Holt & Co Publishers, 1954, hard cov, Bob Harman illus, 6 x 9" **10.00**
Dick Tracy
Big Little Book, *Dick Tracy In Chains Of Crime,* Whitman, #1185, 1935 . . . .   **25.00**
Certificate, Secret Service Membership, 1939 . . . .   **25.00**
Felix the Cat, brochure, Eastman Kodak adv, 1920–30 . . . .   **55.00**
Henry, valentine **12.00**
Katzenjammer Kids, poster, theatrical production adv, Mom and Pop Katzenjammer looking at sleeping kids, "Der Little Sveet–hearts, Der Little Stiffs," greens, black, and flesh tones, c1912, 28 x 41" **350.00**
Li'l Abner, coloring book, Saalfield, #209, 1941, 80 pgs, 8 x 11" **30.00**
Little King, poster, full color, Little King on roller skates, queen, son, and court in foreground, Simon & Schuster 1933 copyright, 18 x 26" **75.00**
Little Lulu
Little Golden Book, *Little Lulu,* #203 . . . .   **12.00**
Paper Doll, cardboard display, Kleenex adv, 1951, 10" h **28.00**
Little Nemo, sheet music, cov with Windsor McCay characters, stage production adv, color litho, 1908, 11 x 14" **50.00**
Mutt and Jeff
Booklet, *Mutt and Jeff Songster,* 1905, 8 pgs, music and song hits, cov with large three color Mutt and Jeff image **35.00**

Little Lulu, paper doll book, *Marge's Little Lulu Doll Book,* Whitman Publishing Company, 1970, 6 pages, unused, 7¼ x 15½", copyright 1971, $40.00.

Sheet Music, 1916 . . . .   **18.00**
Pogo, book, *The Pogo Peek–A–Book,* Walt Kelly, Simon & Schuster, first printing, 1955, 92 pgs, 1955, soft cov, 6½ x 10¾" **35.00**
Winnie Winkle The Breadwinner, box, cigar, paper labels on wood, color litho, Winnie images, MM Branner facsimile signature on lid, blue and white banner inscription inside lid, c1930 . . . .   **30.00**
Yellow Kid
Bookmark, diecut cardboard, full color, yellow ground, Yellow Kid depicted as chocolate candy surrounded by other candies, issued by "A No. 1 Candy Company," late 1890s, 2½ x 6¼" **60.00**
Box, cigar **400.00**
Calendar Card, Schierbaum's Hardware adv, March 1912 . . . .   **12.00**
Post Card, Yellow Kid with Buster Brown and Tige, "Over The Bounding Main," 1903 . . . .   **45.00**
Receipt, 4¼ x 8¼" **35.00**

CHICKEN

Advertising Trade Card
Excelsior Poultry Netting, black boy trying to steal chicken **15.00**
Galvanized Steel Wire Netting, chicken coop and yard illus, bold colors **50.00**
Plano Co Twine Binder, two roosters pulling binder, "He Crows Best, Who Crows Last," bold colors **20.00**

Book

Mother Carey's Chickens, Wiggin, 1911, library edition 20.00

On The Rearing And Management Of Poultry; Being The Essay To Which The Prize Of The Royal Agricultural Society Of England Was Awarded, William Trotter, Simpkin, Marshall, London, printed pictorial wrappers, 1852, 51 pgs, illus 40.00

Poultry Diseases; Methods of Preventing and Curing Them, H. H. Stoddard, Hartford, CT, 1891, 72 pgs, printed wrappers 15.00

Booklet

Park & Pollard Co, Boston, 1909, 64 pgs, illus. 5.00

Quaker Oats Ful-O-Pep Feed, "Brooding Chicks," 1930, 30 pgs . .   7.50

Catalog

Columbia Incubator Co, emb hatching chicks on two tone green cov, 1901, 5 x 7" 40.00

Poultry Supplies of Every Description, Cyphers Incubator Co, Toronto, Ontario, 1899, 24 pgs, line and halftone illus, printed wrappers, 5 x 7" 20.00

Flyer, Price List of Choice Fowls and Eggs, Henry Bishop, Springfield, OH, 1871–72, 4 pgs, folded, printed red and black, with insert listing stock. . . .   50.00

Label, asparagus, Chickie Asparagus, fluffy yellow chick, bunch of green asparagus, black background 2.00

Post Card

Advertising, Rhode Island Red Eggs,

Booklet, *Pratts Practical Pointers on the Care of Poultry,* color litho covers, black-and-white illustrations, 64 pages, 5 x 7", 1920s, $18.00.

Book Plate, multicolor litho, "Buff Cochin Cock," Harrison Weir lithographer, 5³⁄₄ x 7¹⁄₂" image, 1873, $35.00.

price list, black and white chicken image, red lettering, divided back, 1910 . . . .   8.00

Artist Signed, Arthur Thiele, Chickens at Party series, #1242, divided back   20.00

Photomontage, giant chicken pulling oversized cart loaded with eggs. . . .   12.00

Print

Portraits of Fowls in the Yards of S I Bestor, A Fancier in Hartford, CT, litho, E C Kellogg lithographer, 1863, 9¹⁄₄ x 12³⁄₈" image 150.00

Silver Laced Wyandottes, color, c1900, 9 x 6¹⁄₂" 45.00

Program, The New York Fanciers' Club, 4th Annual Exhibition of Poultry, Pigeons, Pets and Non–Sporting Dogs, Madison Square Garden, NY, 1886, prize list and regulations, illus printed red wrappers 35.00

Sign, Pratts Poultry, rooster pulling cart carrying chicks and eggs, 16 x 20". . . .   450.00

CHILDREN

Reference: Alice L. Muncaster, Ellen Sawyer and Ken Kapson, *The Baby Made Me Buy It!,* Crown Publishers, 1991.

Advertising Trade Card

Auld & Conger Black–Boards, little girl writing on blackboard, folder . .   60.00

A N & T Coy Linen Netting, diecut standup, little girl wearing net dress, "Fishermen are filled with joy At the sight of Netty Coy" 25.00

Mellin's Food for Infants and Invalids,

baby's face in oval, hold to the light
and baby's eyes open. **20.00**
Sun Life Insurance Co, seashore scene
with little girl wearing red dress and
bonnet, sun setting in background   **30.00**
White Mountain Refrigerator, girl
opening refrigerator door, mechani-
cal **30.00**
Blotter, little boy image, Ceresota Flour
adv, 4 x 7" **3.00**
Booklet, adv
Bordens Condensed Milk Co, *The Best
Ice Cream,* cov with two girls and
boy making ice cream **30.00**
Carnick's Soluble Food, *Our Baby's
First & Second Years,* baby on front
cov, 64 pgs, advice and product in-
formation **20.00**
Calendar
Borolyptol Antiseptic Mouthwash and
Dentifrice, 1895, adv, three chil-
dren in bathroom, oldest boy gar-
gling, September pad **40.00**
Clark's ONT Spool Cotton, 1894, adv,
girl and boy swinging on spool
"swing," full pad **25.00**
Little Folks, 1911, three part, Clapsad-
dle type children, printed color,
emb, 13½" h **35.00**
Canister, Dixie Kid Cut Plug Tobacco,
baby image, cardboard, paper label,
5" sq **550.00**
Catalog, William Deering & Co, Chi-
cago, IL, 1888, 48 pgs, harvesting machinery, children and animals on cov,
7½ x 10¼" **85.00**
Label, cigar
Fifty Little Orphans, fifty little children,
1880s **12.00**

**Advertising Trade Card, Gunther's Chi-
cago Candy, full color, 3 x 4¼", $3.00.**

**Store Sign, "Ten Beautiful Baby Pictures,"
Maude Fangel illustration, *Ladies' Home
Journal,* 11 x 13", 1920s, $40.00.**

Little Rose, young girl holding rose,
1890s **9.00**
Sonny Boy, little boy wearing sailor
suit seated on father's lap **20.00**
Paper Doll, mechanical advertising trade
card, three heads on revolving dial,
text on back **30.00**
Valentine, diecut standup, little girl
wearing Mexican style clothing, play-
ing banjo, "Nita! Juanita!", Tuck **20.00**

CHRISTMAS

References: Ann Bahar, *Santa Dolls: Historical to
Contemporary,* Hobby House Press, 1992; Robert
Brenner, *Christmas Past,* Schiffer Publishing,
1986; Robert Brenner, *Christmas Revisited,* Schiffer Publishing, 1986; George Johnson, *Christmas
Ornaments, Lights & Decorations,* Collector
Books, 1987, 1990 value update; Polly and Pam
Judd, *Santa Dolls & Figurines Price Guide: Antique to Contemporary,* Hobby House Press,
1992; Robert M. Merck, *Deck The Halls,* Abbeville Press, 1992; Nancy Schiffer, *Christmas Ornaments: A Festive Study,* Schiffer Publishing,
1984.

Periodicals: *Golden Glow of Christmas Past,* PO
Box 14808, Chicago, IL 60614; *Ornament Collector,* R.R. #1, Canton, IL 61520.

Advertising Trade Card
E H Dunbar Boots & Shoes, Santa and
campfire scene **25.00**
Old Lion Coffee, child with wreath
around shoulders **7.00**
Santa Claus Soap, diecut, Santa with
package on his back **30.00**
Book
Christmas Book, Christmas Cut Out
Series, Charles Graham and Co **10.00**
Christmas Greetings, Holiday Publish-
ing Co, 1906 . . . .   **6.50**

Miracle on 34th St, Valentine Davies,
Harcourt, Brace and Co, 1947 . . . . .   **10.00**
*Night Before Christmas or A Visit from
St Nicholas,* McLoughlin Bros, 1896   **20.00**
The Christmas Surprise, Grosset &
Dunlap, 1950, pop–up, ten stories   **25.00**
Box, candy, stockings hanging over
hearth, string handle, 1940–50, 3 x 5"   **5.00**
Calendar, 1906, adv, poster, C D Kenny
Co Teas, Coffees, and Sugars, chromo-
lithograph, two girls knocking on
door, holding gifts and wreath, ornate
border with calendar sheets and
ornate gilt holly leaves and berries,
Kaufmann & Strauss, 20 x 28" **525.00**
Catalog
Carson, Pirie Scott & Co, Gift Sugges-
tions, Chicago, 1910, 12 pgs, cloth
backed, stiff pictorial wrappers,
halftone illus **20.00**
Kirkman & Son Inc, Kirkman Products,
Brooklyn, NY, "For a Merry Christ-
mas Save Your Kirkman Coupons,
They Will Bring Joy and Happiness
to the Kiddies," 1920s, 8 pgs, illus,
children's toys and novelties **15.00**
Montgomery Ward Co, Christmas
Book, Kansas City, MO, 1949, 214
pgs, illus, pictorial wrappers **25.00**
Greeting Card
Advertising, Standard Oil Co, printed
color **12.00**
Artist Signed
Prang, "At Christmas time may
Peace o'er shadow you," flowers,
white fringe **15.00**
Raphael Tuck, children and dog
playing in snow, 4 x 2" **6.00**
Bifold, winged bicycle wheel on front,
inside with pop–up scene of six men
on bicycles, "With Best Wishes For
A Bright And Merry Christmas" **75.00**
Magazine Cover, *Harper's Christmas,*
1896, Edward Penfield illus, woman
wearing red coat and black muff walk-
ing dog, 13 x 17" **200.00**
Matchbook Cover, Christmas designs on
matches, 3 1/4 x 4 1/4" **15.00**
Nativity Scene, foldout, emb, standing
figures, Germany, 4 1/2 x 5 1/2" **12.00**
Post Card
"A Merry Christmas," toy soldiers and
cannons **3.00**
"Christmas Wishes," children in sled
pulled by two rabbits, Germany . . .   **4.00**
Poster, "Buy Christmas Seals–Fight Tu-
berculosis," Uncle Sam carrying
Christmas seals pkgs, 1926, 21 x 28" . .   **150.00**
Sign, Wrigley's, Santa holding sack of
gum and toys, red and green, c1910,
6" h **25.00**
Stereoview, children and Santa peeking

**Magazine Tear Sheet, Santa Drinking
Coca-Cola, *Life,* Haddon Sundblom illustration, full printed color, 1936, $20.00.**

at each other through keyhole, Key-
stone View Co, 1899 . . . .   **10.00**
Tree Ornament, two sided, twelve alpha-
bet letters, Germany, orig pkg **10.00**

CIRCUS

Periodical: *Circus Report,* 525 Oak Street, El Cer-
rito, CA 94530.

Collectors' Clubs: Circus Fans of America, Four
Center Drive, Camp Hill, PA 17011; The Circus
Historical Society, 743 Beverly Park Place, Jackson, MI 49203; The Circus Model Builders International, 347 Lonsdale Avenue, Dayton, OH
45419.

Advertising Trade Card
Adam Forepaugh Museum, Menagerie
and Triple Circus, eight circus acts   **55.00**
Lautz Bros & Co's Circus Soap, acro-
batic horseback riders image **30.00**
Book
Barnum, Phineas T.
*Dollars and Sense. Or How To Get
On, The Whole Secret In A Nut-
shell,* W W Denslow illus, Eastern
Publishing, Boston, 1890, red 488
pgs, cloth cov, 5 x 7" **45.00**
*Lion Jack: A Story of Perilous Adven-
ture Among Wild Men and the*

Capturing of Wild Beasts; Showing How Menageries Are Made, Dillingham, NY, 1887, 380 pgs, red cloth cov, gilt and black lettering, 3 x 5" **50.00**

Benton, Joel, *A Unique Story of a Marvelous Career. Life of Phineas T. Barnum. Elegantly Illustrated,* Edgewood, Philadelphia, 1891, 529 pgs, cloth cov, 5 x 7" **25.00**

Kiralfy, Imre, *The Fall of Babylon. The Most Stupendous Open Air Exhibition in the World. At Oakland Garden, Boston,* 1890, 36 pgs, chromolithographic pictorial wrappers, folding 24" l chromolithographic frontispiece, Barnum & Bailey show program, 5 x 7" **50.00**

Otis, James, *Toby Tyler or 10 Weeks With A Circus,* Goldsmith Publishing, c1930, dj **4.00**

Booklet, *The Dog's Circus,* McLaughlin's Coffee premium, 8 pgs, black and white and color, cov with dogs going to circus illus **25.00**

Broadside

Campbell's One Ring Circus, double sided, tent shows, clowns, wild west act, etc., c1920, 11 x 24" **35.00**

Zircus Hippodrom Und Menagerie, German, contortionist wearing spotted tights and other acts, c1920, 9 x 19" **85.00**

Christmas Card

L G Kelly–Miller Bros Circus, pr, 4 pgs, three color, early 1940s, 5 x 7" **20.00**

Ringling Brothers & Barnum & Bailey, Willy Pogony color illus, color and metallic inks, hand sgd at bottom by Dexter W Fellows, 1929, 14 x 10". .   **100.00**

Letter, Ringling Brothers & Barnum & Bailey, publicity, with press releases and complimentary press tickets in orig envelope, 1939 season. **20.00**

Letterhead, Hunt's Three Ring Circus, detailed illus of animals and acts across top and down left margin, printed color, unused **12.00**

Letterhead, Hagenbeck Wallace Circus, color litho, unused, 8½ x 11", $35.00.

Magazine

Ringling Bros & Barnum & Bailey Circus, 1937 . . . .   **25.00**

The Strange Stories of Gargantua and Toto, c1940, 12 pgs, Ringling Circus gorillas article, 9 x 12" **25.00**

Photograph

Al G Barnes Circus Wagon, midget standing by wheel, c1930, 3¼ x 5"   **8.00**

Hollis Riding Act, Melvin and Bessy Hollis, black and white, sgd, inscriptions on reverse, c1930, set of four different poses **90.00**

Sparks Bros Circus, snapshots of performers, some with circus wagons in background or trained animals, set of 12 . . . .   **75.00**

Poster

Christy Bros Big 5 Ring Wild Animal Shows–The Wonder Show, camels, bison, oxen, and deer, vignette of Christy Bros in upper left corner, Erie Litho, c1925, 27 x 41" . . .   **150.00**

Downie Bros Circus, close–up clown's face surrounded by other performing clowns, Erie Litho, c1920, 28 x 41" **200.00**

Hagenbeck–Wallace Circus, acrobatic horseback rider image, "Helen Hudson America's Foremost Rider," Erie Litho, c1928, 28 x 41" **175.00**

Ringling Bros & Barnum & Bailey Combined Circus, panoramic scene, circus train, wagons, and animals, dark blue background, c1935, 41 x 27" **150.00**

Press Story, Barnum & Bailey, Persia, The Thousand and One Nights, illus cov, c1915, 7 x 15" **35.00**

Print Book, *Evelyn Curro's Americana Print Book #5,* Old Circus Parade Wagons, Lark Press, New York, 1954, full color, ornate hardboard portfolio, 9 x 6" **25.00**

Program

Barnum & Bailey, 1918, 36 pgs, 7 x 9"   **25.00**

Billie Rose's Jumbo, 1935, 32 pgs, Henry Clive circus girl cov **20.00**

Charles Sparks Presents Downie Bros Circus, c1930, 8 pgs, sepia illus, 11 x 17" **15.00**

Clyde Beatty–Cole Brothers, 1962, 32 pgs, 9 x 12" **10.00**

Cole Brothers Circus with Clyde Beatty and Ken Maynard, 40 pgs, color cov with Beatty in lion cage, 9 x 12" **25.00**

Hagenbeck–Wallace & Sells Bros Circus, 1935 . . . .   **45.00**

Peary Brothers Great Circus, Australia, c1935, 8 pgs, illus, 6 x 9" **25.00**

Ringling Brothers & Barnum & Bailey, 1953, 60 pgs, 8 x 11" **15.00**

Souvenir Program, King and Franklin Circus, 8½ x 11″, 1947, $15.00.

Sells–Floto Circus, 1932 season, 20 pgs, sepia gravure photos, 6 x 9″ ... **30.00**
Route Book, Sparks Circus, 1922 season, 32 pgs, portrait frontispieces, 4 x 6″. ... **35.00**
Route Card
  Hagenbeck–Wallace Circus, 15th/16th week, 1926, 3 x 6″ **10.00**
  John Robinson's Circus, 26th/28th week, color head, 1926, 3 x 5″ **15.00**
Route Sheet, Cole Brothers Circus with

Sheet Music, *Sheridan's Ride March-Galop*, full color litho cover, A. Hoen & Co., Richmond, VA, 9 x 12″, 1922, $55.00.

Clyde Beatty, color head, 1936, 9 x 16″.......................... **15.00**
Ticket
  Adam Forepaugh Sells Bros, complimentary admission, ornate, numbered, 1910 season, set of four **20.00**
  Buffalo Bill's Wild West, ornate design, c1910 .... **20.00**
  Hunt's Three Ring Circus, annual pass, engraved, hand sgd by Charles A Hunt to "G. A. Hunt and Party," 1933 .... **20.00**
  Ringling Brothers & Barnum & Bailey, press, 1925, unused............ **5.00**
  Sparks Circus, season pass, sgd by Clifton R Sparks, 1926 .... **15.00**

CIVIL WAR

Reference: *North South Trader's Civil War Magazine's Civil War Collectors' Price Guide, 5th Edition,* North South Trader, 1991.

Periodical: *North South Trader,* PO Drawer 631, Orange, VA 22960.

Collectors' Club: The Civil War Round Table, 357 W. Chicago Ave., Chicago, IL 60610.

Bond, Louisiana Reconstruction Bonds on Baby Bonds, 1870s, set of four **75.00**
Book
  Battles For The Union, Captain W Glazier, 1878, 417 pgs **15.00**
  History of the Eighth Regiment Vermont Volunteers, 1861–1865, George N. Carpenter, Boston, 1886, 335 pgs, cloth, 30 plates **95.00**
  Memoirs, With Special Reference to Secession and the Civil War, John H. Reagan, Neale Pub Co, NY and Washington, 1906, 351 pgs, cloth **130.00**
Broadside, reunion and encampment of the Western Union Veterans' Association, at Gunnison, CO, July 1–5, c1900, 15 x 7″ **200.00**
Card, Ladies' Southern Aid Association, solicitation on behalf of "The Family of Jefferson Davis," 1865–70 .... **50.00**
Cartes de Visites
  General Benjamin Alvord, wearing uniform **35.00**
  Libby Prison, Richmond, VA, ext. view **15.00**
  Soldier, amputated left leg.......... **95.00**
Check, August 9, 1865, Philadelphia, red print........................... **8.00**
Document
  Application, Confederate Widow's Application for Pension, 2 pgs, widow of Thomas Green, Spaulding, MS..................... **25.00**
  Appointment, Benjamin F Butler, Union general, appointment of Ma-

jor John Cassels as officer in the National Asylum for Disabled Volun-
teer Soldiers **195.00**
Clothing Requisition, September 30,
1863, 39th Mass Vols, requesting
one wool blanket and one rubber
blanket to Capt Charles Hunt **8.00**
Enlistment Roster, twenty–one indi-
vidual full signatures with county
listed, Harmony Church, KY, Dec
1862 . . . .   **100.00**
Pay Voucher, partially printed, sgd J M
Schofield, Union general, July 31,
1864, 17 x 11" **75.00**
Envelope
Skull and cross bones, black bordered
flag on staff with skull and cross
bones **12.00**
Jeff Davis, Davis going to war and re-
turning, Davis turns into mule **15.00**
Label, cigar
Flor De Monday, soldier wearing uni-
form portrait **45.00**
General Hartranft, general's portrait . .   **8.00**
Letter
Soldier's, Jan 31, 1864, Sunny South,
Dept of the Gulf Hdgs, 75th NY 1st
Brigade Cavl Div, New Orleans . . .   **45.00**
William Sprague, Union BGV, lined
stationery, Camp Clark, July 11,
1861, 8 x 9" **75.00**
Newspaper
New York Daily Tribune, August 11,
1863, Lee reinforced by Polk **15.00**
*The Lutheran and Missionary Newspa-
per,* July 14, 1864, *USS Kearsarge*
sinks the *USS Alabama* **15.00**
Scrapbook, Society of the Army of the
Potomac, contains daily general or-
ders of the 1923–30 annual encamp-
ments **35.00**
Sheet Music, *The Soldiers Return March,*
1865 . . . .   **10.00**
Stereoview, The War of the Union **7.50**

CLOCKS

Collectors' Club: National Association of Watch
and Clock Collectors, Inc., 514 Poplar St., Columbia, PA 17512.

Advertising Trade Card
Ansonia Clock Company, NY, Peep O'
Day Alarm Clock, metamorphic . . .   **20.00**
8th Wonder or Engle Clock, very large
ornate clock image, "Now on Exhibition through the principal cities of
the United States" **15.00**
Catalog, Kienzle Clocks & Parts, 1929–
30 . . . .   **18.00**
Warranty, printed, document for clock

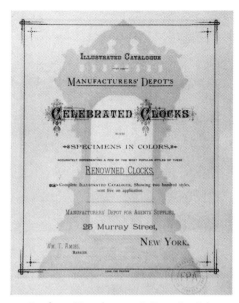

Catalog, Manufacturers' Depot's Celebrated Clocks, 8 pages, 10 x 12¾",
$35.00.

sold by A. Reynolds to Thomas Mc-
Daniels for One Day Brass Clock,
dated 1847, 1¾ x 7" **18.00**

COCA–COLA

References: Shelly and Helen Goldstein, *Coca–
Cola Collectibles,* (four volumes, plus index),
published by author, 1970s; Deborah Goldstein
Hill, *Wallace–Homestead Price Guide To Coca–
Cola Collectibles,* Wallace–Homestead, 1984,
1991 value update; *Goldstein's Coca–Cola Collectibles: An Illustrated Value Guide,* Collector
Books, 1991, 1993 value update; Allan Petretti,
Petretti's Coca–Cola Collectibles Price Guide,
8th Edition, Wallace–Homestead, 1992; Al Wilson, *Collectors' Guide To Coca–Cola Items,* Volume I (1985, 1992 value update) and Volume II
(1987, 1993 value update), L–W Book Sales.

Collectors' Club: The Coca–Cola Collectors'
Club International, PO Box 546, Holmdel, NJ
07733.

Banner
Refreshing, soda bottle in snow, icicles
in foreground, 1950s, 18 x 60" **125.00**
Try Our Coca–Cola 5¢, 1940s **35.00**
Billhead
1905, logo and Coke bottle, Way-
cross, GA, 3¾ x 8½" **50.00**
1923, logo, Augusta, GA, 8½ x 7" **30.00**

Magazine Tear Sheet, *American Boy*, black-and-white photograph, Massengale, Atlanta, 11 x 14", 1904, $35.00.

Blotter
  Greatest Pause On Earth, clown, 1940   **50.00**
  Pure & Healthy, 1915 . . . .   **25.00**
Booklet, *The Truth About Coca–Cola*,
  1912, 16 pgs **35.00**
Bottle Protector, "So Easy To Serve,"
  1942 . . . .   **2.00**
Brochure, Pause For Living, 1957 . . . . . .   **5.00**
Calendar
  1908, "Drink Coca–Cola, Relieves
    Fatigue," woman drinking from
    glass, 7 x 14" **2,500.00**
  1918, June Caprice, 5 x 9" **200.00**
  1931, Huckleberry Finn type boy,
    Norman Rockwell illus **525.00**
  1933, Village Blacksmith, full pad, 17
    x 30" **375.00**
  1942, "Thirst knows no season,"
    young couple building snowman . .   **100.00**
  1959, "The pause that refreshes,"
    young people at basketball game . .   **30.00**
Coaster, hand putting bottle in rack,
  1940s, 3¹/₂" d **4.00**
Coupon, two sided, "Is The Best,"
  1890s, 1¹/₂ x 3³/₈" **175.00**
Diecut
  Cherub holding tray, easel back,
    1908, 14³/₄" h **2,000.00**
  Girl holding tray, 1926, 11¹/₂ x 14"   **350.00**
Display, cardboard, seated boy fishing,

dog watching, Norman Rockwell
  illus, Snyder & Black, 1935, 13 x 36" **1,200.00**
Fan, little girl picking flowers, 1920 . . . .   **28.00**
Letterhead, logo, red and green printing,
  1903 . . . .   **90.00**
Magazine Tear Sheet, *Housewife,* 1910,
  ladies and dog at fountain, 16 x 22". . .   **120.00**
Map, North America, 1940s, 36 x 30". . .   **40.00**
Matchbook   Cover,   "Delicious,
  Refreshing," 1936 . . . .   **5.00**
Menu, cardboard, "Sign of Good Taste,"
  1950s **50.00**
Playing Cards
  Girl holding bottle, 1961, orig box . . .   **35.00**
  WW II enemy aircraft **60.00**
Post Card, Coca–Cola Hemisfair, 1968
  World's Fair Coke pavilion **6.00**
Score Pad, 1940s, 4 x 7¹/₂". **10.00**
Sheet Music, *My Coca–Cola Girl,* 1915,
  10³/₄ x 13³/₄" **325.00**
Sign
  Joan Crawford, cardboard, 1934, 24 x
    14" **425.00**
  Man holding soda bottle and hotdog,
    1929, 30 x 10" **375.00**
  Phil Rizzuto, cardboard, "Coke's a
    Natural!", 1950s, 12 x 10". **200.00**
  Soda bottle and hamburger, card-
    board, 1934, 30 x 14" **125.00**
Soda Fountain Card
  A Friendly Place to Meet! Drink Coca–
    Cola, two couples greeting each
    other, 1950s. **20.00**
  Hot dog! and Coke, 1960s. **6.00**
Tablet, "Drink Coca–Cola," orig pencil   **8.00**
Ticket, salesman's delivery, 3³/₄ x 5¹/₂" . .   **30.00**
Visor, cardboard, 1960s **6.00**

COIN OPERATED

References: Nic Costa, *Automatic Pleasures: The History of the Coin Machine,* Kevin Frances Publishing, 1988; Bill Enes, *Silent Salesmen: An Encyclopedia of Collectible Gum, Candy & Nut Machines,* published by author, 1987; J. Krivine, *Juke Box Saturday Night,* The Bucklebury Press, 1977, out of print.

Periodicals: *Classic Amusements,* 12644 Chapel Road, PO Box 315, Clifton, VA 22024; *Coin Machine Trader,* 569 Kansas SE, PO Box 602, Huron, SD 57350; *Coin–Op Newsletter,* 909 26th St., NW, Washington, DC, 20037; *Gameroom Magazine,* 1014 Mt. Tabor Rd., New Albany, IN 47150.

Date Book, Seeburg Juke Box, cov with
  emb juke box, 1955. . . . .   **15.00**
Magazine Tear Sheet, Wurlitzer Juke
  Box, party setting, Albert Dorne illus,

Magazine Tear Sheet, Butter-Kist Pop Corn Machine, *The Saturday Evening Post*, 11 x 14", 1917, $10.00.

Saturday Evening Post, 1940s, color, full page, 11 x 14"	**12.00**
Newspaper Headline, *Ohio Republican News,* "House Outlaws Slot Machines"	**1.50**

COLLEGE/UNIVERSITY

Advertising Trade Card, Princeton University, diecut boy baseball player, Enameline adv	**40.00**
Book, *Stanford, The Story of A University,* Edith Mirriles, 1959, 255 pgs, sgd by author	**17.50**
Broadside, Roanoke College, Eighth Annual Contest, gold lettering, 1861, 10 x 5"	**25.00**
Calendar, 1916, University of Wisconsin, Madison, cov with tinted Bascom Hall photo, different campus building photo each month	**100.00**
Class Pass, Harvard University, pathological anatomy, 1862.	**25.00**
Directory, The Signet, National College Directory Phi Sigma Kappa, 1911, 128 pgs	**5.00**
Folder, Yale Athletic Association Fall Meeting, three panels, lists twelve events, black lettering, violet ground, 1874	**40.00**
Freshman Admittance, Polytechnic College, PA, black lettering, orange ground, 1868.	**20.00**

Commencement Program, University of Iowa, steel engraving, 3 pages, 5 x 5¼", 1891, $10.00.

Magazine, *College Humor,* Vol 1, 1931	**2.00**
Matriculation Card, University of Pennsylvania, 1820–21.	**60.00**
Photograph, Berkeley, CA, Zeta Psi Fraternity, men sitting on front steps, each holding sports equipment, 1880s, 11 x 14"	**150.00**
Program, Amherst College Class Day of 1863	**8.00**
Score Card, Yale, baseball, set of three, Yale vs Trinity, Harvard, and Princeton, bifold, 1878	**40.00**
Ticket, pr, Harvard Class Day, lettering superimposed over Memorial Hall image, 1886.	**25.00**
Yearbook, University of Texas at Austin, 1918, 480 pgs	**12.00**

COUNTRY WESTERN

Reference: House of Collectibles, *Official Price Guide To Music Collectibles,* Sixth Edition, House of Collectibles, 1986.

Bumper Sticker, Jimmie Davis, "Davis for Governor"	**15.00**
Greeting Card, Loretta Lynn, sgd and inscribed.	**12.00**
Letter, Wilf Carter, typewritten, sgd, c1975	**8.00**
Lobby Card, Tex Ritter, 27 x 41"	**100.00**
Map, Nashville, TN, sgd by Roy Acuff and other country western performers, c1948	**115.00**
Photograph	
Elton Britt, snapshot, pr, one sgd	**15.00**
Rex Allen, black and white, glossy, sgd, 8 x 10".	**15.00**
Post Card, Cliff Carlisle photo	**4.00**
Poster, Bradley Kincaid performance . . .	**20.00**
Record Jacket, Chet Atkins, sgd.	**35.00**
Sheet Music	
Al Dexter, *Pistol Packin' Mama,* sgd . .	**18.00**

Folder, Meet the Radio Folks, Keystone Barn Dance programs, black-and-white photos, 12 pages, 1930s, $8.00.

Cowboy Copas, *Filipino Baby*, sgd . . .	30.00
Songbook Album, Flatt & Scruggs, sgd by band, July 28, 1963, Hillbilly Park, Newark, OH	50.00
Ticket Stub, Willie Nelson concert, c1977	15.00

COW

Reference: Emily Margolin Gwathmey, *Wholly Cow!*, Abbeville Press, 1988.

Periodical: *Moosletter*, 240 Wahl Ave., Evans City, PA 16033.

Advertising Trade Card
Carnick's Lacto Preparata & Soluable Food, man holding child on knee milking cow	45.00
Domestic Sewing Machine Co, $30,000 Jersey Cow image, printed color	6.00
Dwight's Saleratus, black, white, and gold, cow image on front, text on back, 1890s, 3¼ x 5¼"	15.00
Eclipse Halter, tethered cow, "Cannot be slipped by any cattle"	30.00
Swift's Jersey Butterine, folder, milkmaid and cow image one side	40.00
Blotter, Cow Brand Baking Soda adv, blue and white, c1920, 9¼ x 4"	10.00
Book, *Herd Book*, Holstein Breeder's Assoc, 1884, 684 pgs, cov with engraved and litho cow and bull illus	18.00
Box, Country Dairy Butter, cows image, dated 1917, 3½" d, 3" h	3.00
Calendar, 1912, Sharple's Separator, girl using machine, cow at window	120.00
Post Card, Walkover Shoes adv, boy with cow, printed color, divided back.	6.00
Poster, Evaporated Milk–Pure Cow's Milk, black and white cows, green background, 1940	8.00

Magazine Tear Sheet, Auction Sale of Pure Bred Registered Holsteins, 10 x 13¾", 1921, $10.00.

Scrap, holstein, diecut, emb, printed color, 4" w	8.00
Sheet Music, *Cow Cow Boogie*, Swing Symphony, Leeds Music, illus of cow playing piano on cov	2.50
Sign	
American Stock Food, Uncle Sam with farm animals in barnyard	375.00
Sharples, milkmaid and cows, matted and framed, 19 x 12"	220.00
Well's Richardson & Co's Improved Butter Color, boy and cow, 20 x 26"	350.00

COWBOY HEROES

References: Joseph J. Caro, *Collector's Guide to Hopalong Cassidy Memorabilia*, L–W Book Sales, 1992; Lee J. Felbinger, *The Lone Ranger Pictorial Scrapbook*, published by author, 1988; Theodore L. Hake and Robert D. Cauler, *Six Gun Heroes: A Price Guide To Movie Cowboy Collectibles*, Wallace Homestead, 1976; Robert Heide and John Gilman, *Box–Office Buckaroos*, Abbeville Press, 1989; Dave Holland, *From Out Of The Past: A Pictorial History of the Lone Ranger*, Holland House, 1988; David Rothel, *The Gene Autry Book*, Empire Publishing, 1988; David Rothel, *The Roy Rogers Book*, Empire Publishing, 1987.

Autry, Gene

Big Little Book, *Gene Autry in Special Ranger Rule*, Whitman, #1456, 1945 . . . . 30.00

Book, *Gene Autry Goes to the Circus*, Whitman, Tell–A–Tale series, 1950, 28 pgs, hard cov, 5½ x 6½" . . . 20.00

Bread Label, color photo scene, series No. 5, #6–8, early 1950s, set of 3, 2¾" sq 55.00

Coloring Book, Whitman, #2953, 1956, 40 pgs, 6¾ x 7½" 14.00

Comic Book, Gene Autry Comics, Vol 1, #20, Dell, October 1948. . . . . . . 18.00

Lobby Card, *Red River Valley*, full color action scene, 11 x 14" 18.00

Magazine, *Movie Mirror*, cover story, 1940 . . . . 30.00

Photograph, black and white glossy, sgd "To Elizabeth from Gene Autry," 1939, 8 x 10" 125.00

Post Card, photo 10.00

Program, The Gene Autry Show, c1950, 8 pgs, traveling show souvenir, 8½ x 11" 32.00

Puzzle, frame tray, Whitman, 1953, 11½ x 15" 25.00

Sheet Music, *Red River Valley*. 20.00

Tablet, cov with Gene and Champion and facsimile signature, "Gene Autry, Columbia Pictures," lined paper, unused, c1950, 8 x 10" 24.00

Brown, Johnny Mack

Lobby Card, *Range Law*, 14 x 11" 25.00

Poster, *Black Trail*, 27 x 41". 35.00

Benson, Bobbie, coloring book, Bobbie Benson's B–Bar–B Riders, Whitman, 1950 . . . . 20.00

Cisco Kid

Face Mask 30.00

Photo Card, Tip Top Bread premium 12.50

Program, Cisco Kid Rodeo, Wrigley Field, Chicago, stiff paper folder, glossy, early 1950s, 8½ x 11" 25.00

Puzzle, frame tray, Duncan Renaldo and Diablo portrait, Saalfield, Doubleday & Co, 1951, 10½ x 11½". . . 35.00

Cody, Buffalo Bill

Photo Card, black and white, facsimile signature, 1890–1900, 4¼ x 6½" 60.00

Poster, Cody on horseback, wearing fringed buckskin jacket, "Col. W. F. Cody 'Buffalo Bill,' " 1908, 40 x 60" 1,500.00

Earp, Wyatt

Big Little Book, *Hugh O'Brien TV's Wyatt Earp*, Whitman, #1644, 1958, 276 pgs 15.00

Color and Stencil Set 135.00

Hopalong Cassidy

Birthday Card, photo pinback button insert 35.00

Card Game, Hopalong Canasta, Hoppy and Topper image on cards, Pacific Playing Card Co, double deck, 1950 copyright. 85.00

Coloring Book, 1938 . . . . 50.00

Comic Book, Vol 5, #29, Fawcett, March 1949 . . . . 55.00

Milk Carton, waxed cardboard, red, white, and blue, 5½ x 11½" 12.00

Party Plates, Hoppy on Topper, white ground, unopened cellophane pkg, set of six 20.00

Post Card, Hopalong Cassidy Savings Club, Hoppy image, 1950 . . . . 3.00

Poster, *Riders of Deadline*, 27 x 41" . . 40.00

Stationery, Buzza Cardoza, orig box . . 175.00

Tablet, lined paper 25.00

Magazine Tear Sheet, Joel McCrea, Quaker Puffed Wheat comic strip adv., 11 x 8", 1950, $12.00.

Coloring Book, *Lone Ranger,* Whitman Publishing Co., unused, 8 x 11", 1974, $17.50.

Wrapper, gum 45.00
Jones, Buck
  Big Little Book, *Buck Jones and the Night Riders,* Gaylord DuBois, Hal Arbo illus, Whitman, #4069, 1937, 316 pgs, hard cov, 7½ x 9½". 90.00
  Manual, Buck Jones Rangers–Cowboys Collection, #1, 1932. . . . 65.00
  Sheet Music, *Hidden,* Phantom Rider, 1936 . . . . 25.00
Lone Ranger
  Blotter, Bond Bread adv. 10.00
  Book, *The Lone Ranger,* Little Golden Book, Simon & Schuster, 1956, 24 pgs, 6½ x 8". 12.00
  Coloring Book, Tonto, Whitman, 1957 15.00
  Magazine, *Golden West,* Lone Ranger cov. 10.00
  Map, Frontier Town, four sections. . . . 135.00
  Membership Card, Lone Ranger US Savings Bond Peace Patrol, Moore portrait. 20.00
  Paint Book, 1940 . . . . 30.00
  Photo Card, Clayton Moore, black and white glossy, facsimile Lone Ranger signature, 1956–57, 3½ x 5½" 35.00
  Sheet Music, *Hi Yo Silver, The Lone Ranger's Song,* 1938 . . . . 80.00
Maynard, Ken
  Cigar Band, diecut, emb, red, gold, and black design, black and white photo, 1930s, 1 x 3". 20.00
  Lobby Card, red, white, blue, flesh, and brown, Universal, 1933, 14 x 22". 50.00
McCoy, Tim, Big Little Book, *The Prescott Kid,* Whitman, #1152, Columbia Pictures, adapted by Eleanor Packer, 1935, 160 pgs, hard cov, soft spine, 4⅝ x 5¼" 25.00
Mix, Tom
  Arcade Card, photo, red, brown, and white, 6½" h 60.00
  Big Little Book, *The Range War* 30.00

Book, *The Fabulous Tom Mix,* Olive Stokes Mix, Eric Heath assistant, Prentice–Hall, 1957, 178 pgs, hard cov, dj, 6 x 8½" 15.00
Box, boots, Mix and horse image, 1930s. 50.00
Brochure, Tom Mix New Premium Catalog, mystery ring, pens, pocket knives, etc., order blank, c1938, 8 x 10" 30.00
Comic Book, #3, Ralston premium, Jan 1941. . . . . 60.00
Dixie Lid, brown and white, photo, "Miracle Rider" rim inscription, 1935, 2¼" d 25.00
Label, cigar, Mix portrait, full color, emb, early 1930s, 6 x 5" 12.00
Manual, 1941 . . . . 45.00
Poster, *Tom Mix Circus & Wild West Show,* 28 x 42". 200.00
Route Card, Tom Mix Circus, color poster images of Mix beside circus tent, 1934 season, set of 12, 3 x 6". . 125.00
Route Sheet, Tom Mix Wild West and Sam B Dills Circus, cov with Tom Mix portrait, 1934, 9 x 12" 30.00
Sheet Music, *The Old Spinning Wheel,* Straight Shooters cov photo, 1933 copyright 30.00
Tobacco Card, cigarette pack insert, black and white photo, #350, series D, Orami Cigarettes, Germany, c1930, 1½ x 2" 10.00
Oakley, Annie, Little Golden Book, *Annie Oakley Sharpshooter,* 1956 . . . 10.00
Ranger Joe, ranch money, Ranger Joe Cereal premium, "One Buck," 1952, 4¾ x 2½". 25.00
Rifleman, book, Whitman, color photo cov with Connors and Crawford, hard cov. 10.00
Rogers, Roy
  Book, *Roy Rogers on the Trail of the Zeros,* Whitman, #1501, 1954, 282 pgs, hard cov, 5½ x 8" 28.00
  Cereal Box, Quaker Oats, cardboard cylinder, litho paper label with Rogers' branding iron ring premium adv, c1948, 7¼" h. 75.00
  Coloring Book, Trigger and Bullet, Whitman, #2958, 1959, 6½ x 7½" 25.00
  Display Box, yo-yos, full color, 4½ x 2½ x 7" 135.00
  Membership Card, Roy Rogers Riders Club, buff color, black and white Roy and Trigger photo surrounded by red lasso design, facsimile signature, nine rules for club members on reverse, 1948–50, 2½ x 4⅛". 30.00
  Paint Book, Whitman, #1158, 1948, 48 pgs, unused, 11 x 15" 60.00
  Paint By Number Set, MIB 65.00

Paper Doll, Roy and Dale, Whitman, 1954 . . . .   **35.00**
Poster, *Spoilers of the Plains*, Republic Pictures, full color, 1951, 27 x 41"   **80.00**
Puzzle, jigsaw, family portrait, Roy, Dale, and Dusty, Whitman, orig box, mid 1950s, 15 x 21" **25.00**
Sky King, photograph, black and white glossy, Kirby Grant, autographed "For Cheryl, Sky King," c1950, 7 x 9" **65.00**
Wayne, John
Poster, *Rooster Cogburn* **40.00**
Tablet, color photo cov with facsimile signature, c1950, 5½ x 9" **30.00**
Wild Bill Hickok, Breakfast Game Score Card, Kellogg's cereal boxes and messages from Guy Madison and Andy Devine on front, mid 1950s, 8 x 10" . .   **25.00**

CREAM OF WHEAT

Reference: Dave Stivers, *The Nabisco Brands Collection of Cream of Wheat Advertising Art*, Collectors' Showcase, 1986.

Magazine, *Needlecraft*, #3, 1917, inside cov adv **15.00**
Magazine Tear Sheet
Chef Rastus and Miss Muffet, full color, 1910, 7 x 9" **20.00**
Chef Rastus and Old King Cole, color, 1902 . . . .   **30.00**
Old Santa Knows, E B Bird illus, full page, December 1920 . . . .   **6.00**
Map, Jolly Bill and Jane on the Moon, radio premium, black and white, 1933, 21 x 28" **50.00**
Note Pad, leather cov with Chef Rastus, image and "Don't Forget Cream of Wheat," c1910, 4 x 6". **30.00**
Poster, Uncle Sam holding health bill, reading Cream of Wheat billboard, "Well, You're Helping Some!", c1915, 5¼ x 8¼". **20.00**

DEERE, JOHN

Advertising Trade Card
Mansur Corn Planters, three panel folder, planters and factory illus panels, text inside **40.00**
No. 9 Planter, planter on front, text on back, Rawlings Implement Co Agents **25.00**
Plows, color, barefoot woman watering horse, plow and chicks in foreground, "Largest Plow Manufactory In The World" **35.00**
Reindeer Cultivator, folder, one panel with squirrel sitting on fallen log, manicured fields in background,

Catalog, Syracuse Plows, black-and-white illustrations, 32 pages, 4 x 9", 1916, $37.50.

other panel with cultivator illus, text inside, color. **30.00**
Book, *John Deere Model A Tractor Instructions and Parts List*, 1936 . . . .   **28.00**
Catalog
Hay Tools, 1940s, color and black and white illus **50.00**
Parts, 1948. . . . .   **25.00**
Manual, John Deere Self Dump Rake . . .   **10.00**
Payment Coupon, John Deere Plow Co, Sailor Springs, IL, revenue stamp with Deere logo, 1922, 4 x 9½" **7.50**
String Tag, cardboard, "John Deere, Pioneer Manufacturer of Steel Plows, Moline, Ill" rim inscription, red and white, 1890s, 3" d **35.00**

DENTAL

Reference: Bill Carter et al., *Dental Collectibles & Antiques*, Dental Folklore Books of K.C., 1984.

Advertising Trade Card
Colgate Dental Cream, mechanical, folder, girl brushing teeth at sink . . .   **50.00**
Dr Carman's Dentalaid, black and white, 1882 American Institute exhibit image, text on back **40.00**
J Ralph Phelps Dentist, real photo, text on back **20.00**
Mennen's Borofoam Tooth Powder, folder, product tin illus **24.00**
York Dental Parlors, "Originators of Vitalized Air for Painless Extracting," red printing, white ground, upper plate image. **20.00**
Box, Dentone Tooth Paste, 1915–20, unused. **4.00**

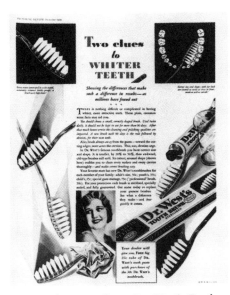

Magazine Tear Sheet, Dr. West's Tooth Brush, 10½ x 13½", 1929, $15.00.

Catalog, Dentist's Supply Catalogue, Lee S Smith & Son, Pittsburgh, 1915, 982 pgs, illus, hard cov. **65.00**
Chart, "Why Do Teeth Ache?," multi-colored, Bristol–Myers Ipana Tooth-paste adv, 1941, 19¼ x 26½" **12.00**
Document, account statements, S S White Dental Mfg Co, Philadelphia, c1900 . . . . **2.00**
Journal, *Dental Items of Interest,* October, 1924. . . . . **10.00**
Letters and Documents, S S White Dental Mfg Co, Philadelphia, 1904–1907, lot of 16 . . . . **30.00**
Poster, If Your Teeth Work More The Dentist Will Work Less, pastel portrait, young woman with apple **20.00**
Textbook, *Practical Dental Metallurgy,* Hodgen, 1914, 366 pgs, illus, used at Pitt Dental School **15.00**

DIRIGIBLE

References: Walter Curley, *The Graf Zeppelin's Flights to South America,* Spellman Museum, 1970; Arthur Falk, *Hindenburg Crash Mail,* Clear Color Litho, 1976; Sieger, *Zeppelin Post Katalog,* Wurttemberg, 1981, in German.

Collectors' Club: Zeppelin Collectors Club, c/o Aerophilatelic Federation, PO Box 1239, Elgin, IL 60121–1239.

Book, *The Scientific American War Book,* 1916, 335 pgs, 572 illus, chapters on zeppelins **6.00**

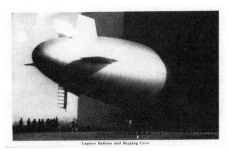

Captive Balloon and Rigging Crew

Post Card, black-and-white photo, "Captive Balloon and Rigging Crew," divided back, 5½ x 3½", 1940s, $20.00.

Flight Cover
  Hindenburg, first North American flight, 1936 . . . . **20.00**
  U.S.S. Akron, tactical training flight from Lakehurst, August 1932. . . . . . **7.50**
Flyer, New Jersey Central Railroad, To See The *Graf Zeppelin,* October 14, 1928, 5 x 14" **25.00**
Lobby Card, *The Hindenburg* movie, 1975, set of 8 . . . . **30.00**
Needle Book, airship image **12.00**
Newspaper, *Chicago Daily News,* May 7, 1937 *Hindenburg* crash headline story. **105.00**
Photograph, *Macon* Zeppelin, black and white, factory, executives, and families with skeletal zeppelin framework in background, 1927, 8 x 10" **14.00**
Playing Cards, Airship No. 909, Standard Playing Card Co, Chicago, orig box, 1894 . . . . **40.00**
Post Card
  Graf Zeppelin photo, postmarked Stuttgart, 1933. . . . . **25.00**
  Hindenburg. **35.00**
Puzzle, jigsaw, *The Hindenburg* movie, 15½ x 18" **20.00**
Sheet Music
  Come Take a Trip in My Airship **20.00**
  Take Me Up With You Dearie, cov with couple in airship cupola illus, 1909 . . . . **20.00**
  Wreck of the Shenandoah. **18.00**
Timetable, German Zeppelin Transport Co/American Zeppelin Transport Inc, March 15, 1937, sailings and rates . . . **100.00**

DISNEY

References: Marcia Blitz, *Donald Duck,* Harmony Books, 1979; Robert Heide and John Gilman, *Cartoon Collectibles,* Doubleday & Co., 1984; Bevis Hillier, *Walt Disney's Mickey Mouse Memorabilia,* Harry Abrams, 1986; David Longest and Michael Stern, *The Collector's Encyclo-*

pedia of Disneyana, Collector Books, 1992; Leonard Maltin, The Disney Films, Crown Publishers, 1973; Richard Schnickel, The Disney Version: The Life, Times, Art and Commerce of Walt Disney, Avon Books, 1968; Michael Stern, Stern's Guide to Disney Collectibles, First Series (1989, 1992 value update) and Second Series (1990, 1993 value update), Collector Books; Tom Tumbusch, Tomart's Illustrated Disneyana Catalog and Price Guide, Volume 1 (1985), Volume 2 (1985), Volume 3 (1985), Volume 4 (1987), Tomart Publications; Tom Tumbusch, Tomart's Illustrated Disneyana Catalog and Price Guide, Condensed Edition, Tomart Publications, 1989.

Periodicals: Mouse Club Newsletter, 2056 Cirone Way, San Jose, CA 95124; Storyboard Magazine For Disneyana Collectors, 2512 Artesia Blvd., Redondo Beach, CA 90278; Storyboard/The Art of Laughter, 80 Main St., Nashua, NH 03060.

Collectors' Club: National Fantasy Club For Disneyana Collectors, PO Box 19212, Irvine, CA 92713.

Album, souvenir, Snow White & The Seven Dwarfs, song lyrics and music, 14 pgs, black and white illus	25.00
Blotter, Sunoco adv	
Donald Duck, 1939	12.00
Mickey and Minnie Mouse, as bride and groom in convertible	25.00
Book	
Little Red Riding Hood & Big Bad Wolf, David McCay Pub Co, 1934, illus	4.00
Mickey Mouse Fire Brigade, Whitman, 1936, hard cov	15.00
Story of Pinocchio, Whitman, 1939, soft cov	12.00
The Adventures of Mickey Mouse; Book 1, Walt Disney, David McKay Co, Philadelphia, first edition, 1931, color illus	750.00
Booklet	
Donald Duck Sells Motor Oil, 1941, 8 pgs, Sunoco Motor Oil adv, color cov with Donald and other characters, 9 x 5"	25.00
Join Mickey Mouse In His Lucky Seven Birthday Party, September 28, 1935, 29 pgs, promotional material and birthday buttons included, 9 x 11"	95.00
Coloring Book, Mickey Mouse, 1931, unused	75.00
Comic Book	
Walt Disney Presents Zorro, #7, September, 1967	10.00
Walt Disney's Comics, Donald Duck, Vol 8, No. 11, August, 1948	13.00
Decal, Snow White and Seven Dwarfs, 1940s, 4" h	4.00

Game Wheel, Walt Disney World Fun Flight Game Match Ups, Eastern Airlines, full color, 6¾" d, 1980, $7.50.

Dry Cleaning Bag, white paper, cutout Zorro costume, printed black, red, and orange, dry cleaner adv and "Walt Disney Studios Presents Zorro on ABC–TV" printed on bag, c1960, 23 x 36"	35.00
Greeting Card, Easter, diecut, Donald Duck, flocked body, Hallmark, 1942	25.00
Magazine	
Disney: Stage Magazine, February, 1938, color cov with Grumpy illus, Adventures of Snow White article by Monroe Leaf, 9 x 12"	60.00
Walt Disney Magazine, Vol. II, No. 5, 1956, 42 pgs, full color photo cov, includes articles, games, and puzzles, 8½ x 11"	20.00
Map, Disneyland, 1970s	12.00
Non–Sport Trading Card, Bassett & Co Confectionery, 1977, 50 cards, Disney character action scenes, text relates health and safety tip related to picture, 1⅜ x 2⅝"	25.00
Paint Book, Pinocchio, Whitman, c1939, 48 pgs, 11 x 15"	60.00
Post Card, castle, 1970s	20.00

Walt Disney's Magazine, Mickey Mouse Club fan magazine, Volume 11, 8th issue, color photo cover, June 1957, $20.00.

Poster, *Snow White and the Seven Dwarfs* movie, head illus each dwarf, one sheet, 1937 . . . . **1,870.00**

Press Sheet, Mickey's Man Friday, mats, posters, and stills illus, orig mailing cov, c1935, 9 x 12" **55.00**

Program, souvenir
Disney on Parade, 1973 . . . . **10.00**
Fantasia, Walt Disney, 1940. . . . . . . **12.00**

Puppet, cardboard, Mickey Mouse, punchout, Donald Duck bread premium, unpunched, 1950s **15.00**

Puzzle, jigsaw, Three Little Pigs at Work and Play, orig box, 1940s **15.00**

Recipe Card, Mickey Mouse image, Recipe Scrapbook, Weber Baking Co adv on back, set of 4 . . . . **35.00**

Sheet Music
Brazil, from *Saludos Amigos* film, Donald Duck cov, 1942 . . . . **18.00**
Der Führer's Face, cov with Donald Duck throwing huge tomato at Hitler caricature, 1942 . . . . **40.00**
The Dwarf's Yodel Song, L Morey, F Churchill, Snow White and Dwarfs cov illus, 1938 . . . . **18.00**

Stamp Book, *Animals of Africa,* Walt Disney, Simon & Schuster, 1956, 32 pgs, 8½ x 11" **30.00**

Valentine, mechanical, Goofy holding net, movable arm, 1939, 3 x 5". **28.00**

DIXIE

Box, Dixie Kid Cut Plug Tobacco, cardboard, black baby on label, 4½" sq . . . **275.00**

Label
Broom, Dixie, seated black man playing banjo **1.00**
Grapefruit, Dixie Boy, black child eating grapefruit **2.00**

Post Card, "Greetings From Dixieland," folding, blacks, Ashville PC Co **7.50**

Sheet Music
And They Call It Dixieland, Whiting, 1916 . . . . **15.00**
I'll Be In My Dixie Home Again To–Morrow, R Turk, J R Robinson, Barbelle cov illus, 1922. . . . . **7.00**
When It's Night Time Down In Dixieland, Berlin, 1914 . . . . **15.00**

DOG

Reference: Alice L. Muncaster and Ellen Sawyer, *The Dog Made Me Buy It!,* Crown Publishers, 1990.

Periodical: *The Wee Scots,* PO Box 1512, Dept. 92–5, Columbia, IN 47202.

Collectors' Club: Canine Collectibles Club of America, 736 N. Western Ave., Suite 314, Lake Forest, IL 60045.

Advertising Trade Card
Kenyon Hat and Fur Co, diecut dog, standup, front legs fold out to form stand, holding sign in mouth, two sided, front and back of dog **20.00**
New Home Sewing Machine, diecut, racing greyhound, girl in Victorian dress riding on back, "Light Running" **25.00**
Speaking Dog Bank adv, "$1.00 Each," L H Mace & Co. **500.00**
Va–Li–Na, diecut dog, standup, begging dog holding card in mouth, "For Chapped Hands and Sweating Feet" **15.00**

Book
Dogs of Today, Harding Cox, illus, 1931 . . . . **5.00**
Elias Vail Trains Gun Dogs, Ella B Moffit, pointing breeds, spaniels, and non–slip retrievers, 1937, 219 pgs **12.00**

Booklet, *Handling Your Hunting Dog,* Ralston Purina, 1947, 64 pgs. **5.00**

Calendar, 1949, Morrel Circus, collie, wolfhound, poodle, and terrier performing tricks, 8½ x 11" **15.00**

Catalog
Dog Furnishings, 1920 . . . . **24.00**
Ladies Kennel Club of Massachusetts, Third Open Air Dog Show, 1906, 100 pgs, woman judging small breeds cov illus **20.00**
New England Kennel Club, 16th Annual Dog Show, 1900, 98 pgs, photos, advertisements **35.00**
St Louis Kennel Club, Third Annual Dog Show, 1899, 110 pgs, photos, color cov with woman and St Bernard **40.00**

Label Cigar
Kennel Club, dog dressed in clothing, 1880s, 4½ x 4½". **12.00**

know your
SCOTTISH TERRIER

Book, *Know Your Scottish Terrier,* Earl Schneider editor, The Pet Library Ltd., 64 pages, 5½ x 7⅞", 1970s, $7.50.

Cigarette Card, dogs wearing top hats, "Where, Oh! Where Do I Live?", De Reszke Cigarettes, Real Photographs 6th Series of 27, No. 18, 1³/₈ x 2⁵/₈", 1920s, $8.00.

Shep, collie and little girl, sample inner lid label, American Litho Co, 1901 . . . . 40.00
Two Friends, lady petting St Bernard 6.00
Grape, Thorobreds, grapes, boxer dog image, 13 x 4" 1.00
Little Golden Book, *Rin–Tin–Tin and Rusty*, 1955 . . . . 8.00
Non–Sport Trading Card, 1961, 48 cards, various breeds, full color, 1³/₈ x 2⁵/₈" 20.00
Print, "Hunting Dog Puppies," E H Osthaus, 9 x 12". 75.00
Sign, cardboard, Old Boston Beer, dog image, 23" sq 25.00
Stock Certificate, dog vignette, Osborn Mills, Fall River, MA, 1910 . . . . 30.00

EDUCATION

References: Steven Heller and Steven Guarnaccia, *School Days*, Abbeville Press, 1992; Lar and Sue Hothem, *School Collectibles of the Past*, Hothem House, 1993.

Advertising Trade Card
Allen & Thomas, NY, school supplies, children building snowman on front, text on back, 3¹/₂ x 5¹/₄" 8.00
H M Crider, York, PA, sample reward of merit card on front, adv text on back, 2¹/₂ x 4". 10.00
Announcement, opening, Parker Run School House, printed, black and white, 1888, 3¹/₄ x 5¹/₂" 20.00
Arithmetic Tables, multiplication one side, addition, subtraction, and division other side, 7 x 9¹/₄" 18.00

Book, *The New American First Reader*, J H Butler & Co, Philadelphia, 1871, 4¹/₄ x 7¹/₄" 10.00
Booklet, Barnes's Vertical Penmanship, 1898 . . . . 8.00
Catalog
McClurg's School & Office Supplies, Chicago, 304 pgs, 1949–50, 10 x 12" 9.00
Practical Drawing Co, Dallas, TX, school supplies and art materials, 120 pgs, 1924, 5³/₄ x 8¹/₂" 17.00
Certificate of Promotion, printed black and white, 1890, 5 x 7" 7.50
Diploma, Wisconsin School for the Blind, 1918 . . . . 5.00
Flash Cards, Iroquois Number Box, Iroquois Pub Co, Inc, Syracuse, NY, orig 2³/₄ x 5⁷/₈ x 1" box 25.00
Honor Card, cardboard, printed, ornate borders, 4¹/₄ x 6" 35.00
Learning Wheel, Presidents of the United States, Rossig Educational Charts, early 1930s, 10" d 25.00
Magazine, *Teacher's Institute & Practical Teacher*, 48 pgs, April 1893 . . . . 10.00
Map, United States, retractable, wood case 35.00
Photograph, albumen, school children posed in front of one room schoolhouse, c1880, 6¹/₂ x 8¹/₂" 10.00
Register
New Class Register and Recitation Record, hard cov, c1910, 5¹/₈ x 9". . 8.00
White's New School Register, American Book Co, c1910, 9 x 11³/₄" 12.00
Reward of Merit
Bank of Industry, hand colored, banknote motif, two paper, two card stock, dated 1856 and 1865, set of four 30.00

Child's Drawing Book, *Our Country*, Sprague Warner & Co., Chicago, 12 pages, 5¹/₄ x 6", c1903, $17.50.

Lobby Card, *The Little Red Schoolhouse*, Chesterfield Picture, 14 x 11", 1930s, $12.00.

Bank of Merit, blue printing, hand colored, stock certificate motif, "Five Shares of Stock to the Holder" 8.00

Maxim Reward Card, colorful scenic add–on in center, "Do nothing you would wish to conceal," printed graphic design, Colton, Zahn & Roberts, NY 25.00

Reward of Merit, printed, hand colored design, school children and book, C Magnus, NY 20.00

Souvenir Booklet, student roster, c1900, 3¼ x 5½". 10.00

Vocabulary Card, animal illus and related words on front, fill–in–the–blank sentences on back, 5½ x 9" 5.00

ELECTRICAL APPLIANCES

Reference: Gary Miller and K. M. Scotty Mitchell, *Price Guide to Collectible Kitchen Appliances*, Wallace–Homestead, 1991.

Catalog
  Catalogue and Price List of Electrical Appliances, Elliot Shaw and Co, Philadelphia, PA, 48 pgs, 1889 . . . .   38.00
  Glenwood Ranges, Weir Stove Co, Taunton, MA, 8 pgs 15.00
  Majestic Electric Refrigerator, 15 pgs, color photos, specifications, 1930s   8.00
  Westinghouse Electric Kitchens, 1936, 20 pgs, 8½ x 11" 10.00
Cookbook, *Rival Crock–Pot Cooking*, 208 pgs, 1975 . . . .   7.00
Magazine Tear Sheet
  Hotpoint Irons, *Good Housekeeping*, full page, July 1929 . . . .   10.00
  Norge Rollator Refrigerator, WWII image with startled husband and wife standing in front of cylindrical refrigerator with Army gunner and two machine guns protruding from top, text applauds American housewife for going without new appliance until after war, full page, 1943 . . . .   18.00
  Sunbeam Mixmaster, "Making Rationed Foods Go Further," free Victory recipe cards, full page, 1943 . .   15.00
  Virginia Sweet Pancake Griddle, *Good Housekeeping*, Nov 1929 . . . .   8.00

ELSIE, THE BORDEN COW

Reference: Ted Hake, *Hake's Guide To Advertising Collectibles*, Wallace–Homestead, 1992.

Booklet, 108 World's Fair Recipes From Borden's," 32 pgs, 1939–40 New York World's Fair, 6½ x 9½". 30.00

Box, Elsie Takes A Bath soap, brown and white, Elsie peeking out from shower curtain design on front, silhouette Elsie behind curtain other three sides, 1942, 2½ x 3 x 5½" 12.00

Calendar, 1943 With Elsie the Borden Cow, color, Elsie cartoon each page, 8 x 14" 50.00

Cartoon Book, 16 pgs, early 1940s, 3¼ x 4" 20.00

Coloring Book, 1957. . . . .   15.00

Cookbook, 374 pgs, hard cov, 1952, first edition 30.00

Display, diecut, Borden's Ice Cream, full color, Elsie's head above strawberry soda, c1950, 14 x 19" 20.00

Game, Elsie and Her Family, 1941, Selchow & Righter Co 75.00

Jigsaw Puzzle, Elsie Puzzle Box, Selchow & Righter, color, 16 x 8" orig box, set of three 40.00

Placemat 15.00

Post Card, Elsie sitting on perisphere, "From Moo To You–With Love Elsie," from New York World's Fair Borden exhibit, 1939–40, unopened package, 3½ x 6", set of 5 . . . .   35.00

Blotter, "That Christmas May Live On! Buy Extra War Bonds," 6 x 3", 1940s, $5.00.

ELVIS

Reference: Jerry Osborne, Perry Cox and Joe Lindsay, *The Official Price Guide To Memorabilia of Elvis Presley & The Beatles,* House of Collectibles, 1988.

Collectors' Club: Graceland News Fan Club, PO Box 452, Rutherford, NJ 07070.

Album, Official Elvis Presley Album, pub by *Movie Teen* Magazine, 1956	10.00
Book, *Elvis Portrait Portfolio,* Sean Shaver, Timus Pub, 304 pgs, black and white photos, first edition, sgd and numbered, #554 of 1956, 1983	125.00
Booklet	
Dial E!–I Love You, 1962	15.00
Elvis Presley–Man or Mouse, privately printed by Chaw Mank, 1960	15.00
Calendar Card, Elvis portrait, 1963	8.00
Christmas Card	
Elvis, wearing Army uniform, 1959	15.00
Graceland scenes, sepia and blue tones, 1970s	30.00
You Too, The World Wide Elvis Presley Fan Club, 1958	20.00
Christmas Ornament, paper, Blue Hawaii, 1961	35.00
Fan Booklet, "Elvis, Yesterday, Today & Always," Triton Press, 1980	5.00
Hat, Army, "GI Blues," 1960	35.00
Letter, Tom Diskin of Col Tom Parker Management, concerning Elvis tour, 1973	10.00
Magazine	
Elvis Monthly, April 1961	12.00
Fans' Star Library, "Elvis in the army" cov, 1959	15.00
Pyromania, Elvis cov, British, 1976	10.00
Screen Stories, 1976, December, Elvis and Priscilla Presley	10.00
Menu, Las Vegas Hilton souvenir, 45	

Magazine Cover Story, ***National Police Gazette,*** **10½ x 13¼", December 1958, $35.00.**

rpm record shape, cov with Elvis bust pose and signature	1,250.00
Newspaper, *Memphis Press–Scimitar,* death of Elvis, front page banner headline and color photo, related articles and photos inside, August 17, 1977	30.00
Photo Card, Elvis wearing red checkered jacket, late 1950s	10.00
Pictorial, color, supplement to *Milwaukee Sentinel,* 1977	8.00
Post Card, "Easter Greeting, Elvis Presley," 1967	20.00
Poster	
"Easy Come, Easy Go," adv, 1967	40.00
"Give Elvis For Christmas," RCA adv, 1959	40.00
"Welcome Home Elvis," Billy Joe Burnette tribute song, 1979	15.00
Poster Book, Vol 1, 20 posters, 1977	20.00
Schedule, tour dates, orig Thomas A Parker Management envelope, 1974	10.00
Sheet Music	
You Don't Know Me, young Elvis photo cov, 1955	10.00
Wooden Heart, 1960	12.00
Songbook, 34 pgs, portrait on front and back covs, 1970s	18.00

ENVIRONMENTAL

Manuscript, concerning waterway rights beneath Boston road, "doing as little hurt or spoil as may be to the land," 1738, 2 pgs, 12 x 7½"	15.00
Poster, conservation	
"Light Consumes Coal, Save Light, Save Coal, United States Fuel Administration," Cole Phillips illus, glowing yellow light bulb against blue and red ground, black borders, mauve lettering, 1917, 20 x 28"	1,450.00
"Save Gasoline, It's a WAR necessity," Ray Greenleaf illus, broadside motif, 1917, 20 x 30"	125.00
"Save the products of the Land, Eat more fish–they feed themselves," United States Food Administration, Charles Livingston Bull illus, golden bass fish swimming through green tone water and plantlife, mauve lettering, c1918, 20 x 30"	225.00

FARM EQUIPMENT

References: Francis Blase, Jr., *Hebner & Sons: Pioneers of Farm Machinery in America 1840–1926,* published by author, 1984; R. Douglas Hurt, *American Farm Tools from Hand–Power to Steam–Power,* Sunflower University Press, 1982.

Advertising Trade Card, J I Case Steam
Tractor........................ **8.00**
Billhead, pr, Curtis Manufacturing Co
Agricultural Implements, green and
red plow vignettes, 1874.......... **30.00**
Booklet
Johnson Harvester Co, *They Cheered*
the Chief, 7 page color illus story, 5
pgs with products and descriptions **30.00**
New American Manure Speader, We
Say, They Say, American Harow Co,
Detroit, MI, 1902, 16 pgs........ **20.00**
Brochure, Vulcan Plows, multicolored.. **5.00**
Calendar
C M Conant Co Pumps, 1922, pump
illus, full pad, 16¾ x 47¼"....... **110.00**
De Laval Cream Separators, 1917, girl
and collie, full pad, 12 x 23"...... **325.00**
E L McClain Manufacturing Company,
Success Horse Collars, 1889, 15½ x
20½"........................ **410.00**
Empire Cream Separator, 1910...... **350.00**
Johnston Harvester Company, 1913.. **95.00**
Walter Wood Harvesting Machines,
1890, booklet **40.00**
Catalog
Boggs Manufacturing Co, Standard Po-
tato Graders, Onion Graders and
Warehouse Equipment, 1928, 24
pgs......................... **25.00**
Caledonia Bean Harvester Works, Ag-
ricultural implements, Caledonia,
NY, c1925, 40 pgs.............. **15.00**
Case Cultivator, 400 Series Tractors,
1961, 53 pgs **10.00**
D M Osbourne Farm Machinery,
1900, 32 pgs, color illus **30.00**
Farm Barns, Beatty Bros, Fergus, Ontario, c1920, 352 pgs, illus, barns,
tools, equipment **14.50**
Louden Machinery, 1917, 224 pgs,
illus, hay, dairy, horse, etc., hard
cov......................... **15.00**
Check, Coggan & Sons, Farm Implements, Sailor Springs, IL, cancelled,
ornate design, 1924.............. **5.00**
Photograph, Strangeland & Halverson
Farm Implements Co, front view,
c1890, 7 x 5".................. **12.50**
Post Card, adv, Jones of Binghamton
Scales, "Weighing the Baby," weighing calf on platform scale.......... **25.00**
Poster
Lean Manufacturing Co, horse, ox,
and camel–drawn harrows, 21¼ x
27½"........................ **325.00**
Sandwich Baling Presses, farm ma-
chinery image, 24 x 29".......... **100.00**
Sign
New Way Large Bale Hay Press, horse
team and hay press illus, 24 x 18".. **140.00**
Nye's National Self–Dumping Rake,

rake illus, Milton Bradley Co Lith,
15½ x 12½".................. **135.00**
Pirate Plows, 1890, 20½ x 26½" ... **1,625.00**

FARM LIFE

Almanac
The Farmer's Almanack, Robert B
Thomas, 1818................ **25.00**
The Farmer's Calendar or Utica Al-
manack for the Western District of
the State of New York for...1807,
Utica, Andrew Beers, printed by
Asahel Seward, 1807 .... **28.00**
Book, *American Farmer's Pictorial Cy-*
clopedia of Live Stock . . . Including
. . . Dogs and Feed; Being Also a
Complete Stock Doctor, Jonathan
Periam and A H Baker, NY & St Louis, 1,232 pgs, pictorial cloth cov,
illus, chromo plates, two folding
charts, 1888, 5 x 7"............ **55.00**
Booklet, *80 Pictures of Farm Experi-*
ences, Celotex Insulation Corp,
1936, 35 pgs.................. **5.00**
Calendar
Lister's Animal Bone Fertilizers,
1899, woman holding wheat, farm
scene background, factory
overprint on full pad, 13 x 23" ... **140.00**
Youth's Companion, 1904, "Spring-
time," color litho, three panels,
center panel with farmer, wife,
and child in field with flowers,
birds on other panels, 22 x 11½" **200.00**
Catalog, Case Cultivator, 400 Series
Tractor parts, 53 pgs, 1961........ **10.00**
Certificate, Stockman Protective Association, Oklahoma, three large farm
vignettes, 1926................. **6.00**

Almanac, *Studebaker Farmers' Almanac,*
11th edition, 48 pages, 1910, $25.00.

Document, insurance policy, Ohio
Farmers Insurance Co, two vignettes,
one with farm scene with burning
barn, other of farm animals, 1875 .. **12.50**
Magazine
Farm Journal Magazine, 1935 ..... **2.00**
The Farmer's Wife, 1929 .... **12.00**
Poster
Adriance Buckeye Harvesting Ma-
chinery, barefoot farm girl image,
horse–drawn farm equipment vi-
gnettes, 1897, 20½ x 28" **385.00**
Ferry's Seeds, 1910, 20½ x 27½". ... **60.00**
Granite Iron Ware, woman carrying
milking pail, cow, 12½ x 28" **575.00**
International Stock Food, pig eating
corn, 21½ x 28" **145.00**
Print
Seed Time and Harvest, Grant
Wood, artist sgd, dated 1937 .... **1,900.00**
The Western Farmer's Home, Currier
& Ives, hand colored litho, framed,
13½ x 17½" **375.00**
Sign
American Stock Food, Uncle Sam at
barnyard, feeding horse **425.00**
Capewell Horsenail Co, family eat-
ing dinner, horse reaching through
door being hand fed by mother,
"One of the Family," framed,
c1910, 19 x 25". **215.00**
International Stock Foods, farmer
feeding calves, 20¾ x 26½". **110.00**
Rice's Seeds, man with cabbage, 24
x 12" **75.00**
Stock Certificate, Reading Fair Co, PA,
vignettes of cows, horses, and barns,
1916 .... **15.00**

FASHION

Patterns
Booklet
Construction Hints, dresses of the
time, illus every page, 1905 ..... **10.00**
How to Make Children's Clothes,
Singer, 1930, illus **8.00**
Catalog
Butterick, 1922, needle art, color
illus **20.00**
Domestic Sewing Machine Co,
Winter Styles, A Domestic Cata-
logue of Fashions, NY, 1876, pa-
per patterns **20.00**
McCall's Patterns, 1904, 48 pgs ... **38.00**
Pattern Book, *Shirt Waists,* Mrs E D
Barnard, Rochester, NY, 1901, 12
pgs, large folding plate for waist,
sleeve, and collar measuring and
cutting **25.00**
Styles
Book, *Fashion–From Ancient Egypt to*

Pattern, Simplicity #6208, doll clothes,
copyright Ideal Toy Co., 5½ x 8¼" envelope, 1965, $18.00.

the Present Day, Mila Contini, Odyssey Press, NY, 1965, 322 pgs, 8 x
11½" **15.00**
Catalog
Boggs and Buhl, Fashion Review,
1888, 72 pgs, Spring and Summer **50.00**
Boston Store, women's fashions,
1911, 96 pgs, Fall/Winter **60.00**
Charles A Stevens & Bros, 1892, 52
pgs, Spring and Summer, fashion-
able lady on cov, silk dress goods,
waists, ribbons, laces, and para-
sols. **40.00**
Charles William Stores, New York
Styles, 1915, 344 pgs **75.00**
Dannenbaum's Sons and Co, Latest
Styles in Hat and Bonnet Frames,
Philadelphia, PA, 1907, 30 pgs,
Fall/Winter **18.00**
Franklin Simon Co, correct dress for
women, misses, girls, infants,
men, and boys, 1921, 130 pgs,
Fall/Winter **50.00**
National Cloak & Suit Co, men's,
women's, and children's fashions,
1909, 140 pgs, Fall/Winter **100.00**
Perry Dame Co, ladies' and chil-
dren's New York fashions, 1917,
149 pgs **65.00**
Flyer, La France Shoes, high button
shoes, c1910, 8 pgs **12.00**
Label, cigar, Peg, high top shoe image,
gold trim red ground **6.00**
Magazine, *Home Book of Fashions,*
Autumn, 1921, published by *Ladies'
Home Journal,* 48 pgs, color and
black and white, Lillian Gish on
back cov **8.00**
Poster, Arbell Shoes, Werler illus, silhouette profile of woman's face,
brightly colored shoes floating
against dark blue ground, c1955, 45
x 59". **300.00**

FAST FOOD

References: Ken Clee and Suzan Hufferd, *A Collector's Guide To Fast–Food Restaurant Kid's Meal Promotions (Other Than McDonald's),* SKI Publishing, 1991; Gary Henriques and Audre DuVall, *McCollecting: The Illustrated Price Guide to McDonald's Collectibles,* Piedmont Publishing, 1992.

Periodicals: *Collecting Tips Newsletter,* P.O. Box 633, Joplin, MO 64802; *For Here or to Go,* 2773 Curtis Way, Sacramento, CA 95818.

Collectors' Club: McDonald's Collectors Club, 2315 Ross Dr., Stow, OH 44224.

Activity Book, Adventures of the Big Boy, No. 241, May, 1977, 7 x 10"	20.00
Book, McDonald's, *Let's Eat Out!,* 28 pgs, commemorates 10th anniversary, 1965, 7 x 9"	30.00
Bookmark, Burger King, cardboard, sheet of 5, 1970	4.00
Box	
Carl's Jr meal, cardboard, Star Flyer, flying saucer, 1985	2.50
Dairy Queen, kid's meal, Hot Diggity, Dennis the Menace image	1.50
Howard Johnson's Candy, salt water taffy, multicolored	.50
Kentucky Fried Chicken, Colonel's Kids meal, Foghorn Leghorn featured, 1987	2.00
Wendy's, kid's meal, The Good Stuff Gang, 1988	1.50
Calendar, 1980, Burger King, Olympic Games	2.50
Colorforms, McDonald's, premium, 1986	2.00
Contest Sheet, McDonald's, "$1,000,000 Menu Song," glossy paper, jukebox design, instructions on back, with 33⅓ rpm vinyl record, 1988, 9 x 10½"	15.00
Coupon, Hardee's, roast beef sandwich special, old style buildings illus	.25
Crown, Burger King, cardboard, jewelled design, "Have It Your Way"	7.00
Decals, A & W Root Beer, Root Beer Bear and A & W logo, single sheet, 1977	2.50
Dixie Cup, Shoney's Big Boy, waxed paper, full color Big Boy image, late 1960s, 11" h	40.00
Matchbook, Big Boy, 1950s	8.00
Menu	
Bob's Big Boy, cardboard, bifold, die-cut front cov, full color, 1949, 5½ x 8"	30.00
Denny's, child's games and activities, 1978	2.00
Napkin, Pizza Hut, logo	.50
Notebook, Shoney's Big Boy School Notebook, lined paper, 1980s, 8½ x 11"	5.00
Placemat, Sambo, tiger image	.75
Poster, McDonald's, ET with raised finger, 1985	6.00
Puzzle, jigsaw, frame tray	
Burger King, cartoon illus with king in helicopter flying over restaurant, 1973, 8½ x 10"	10.00
Kentucky Fried Chicken, bucket of chicken image, 1954, 7 x 9"	15.00
Sticker, Carl's Jr, Happy Star, puffy, wiggly eyes, 1984	1.50
Straw, A & W Root Beer, paper wrapper, 1970s	4.00
Sunglasses, Carl's Jr, cardboard, star shape, no lenses, 1983	2.50
Valentine, Burger King, King image, 1977, sheet of 6	4.00

FIRE

Advertising Trade Card	
Buckeye Force Pumps, Springfield, OH, black man pumping water to extinguish house fire	25.00
German American Insurance Co, multicolored harbor fire scene	40.00
Phoenix Fire Insurance Co, diecut, two sided, fireman image, color	55.00

Broadside, White Castle Meal, $12.00.

Silsby Manufacturing Co Fire Engines, detailed vignette **260.00**
Booklet, American Fire Extinguisher Co, Boston, 1967, 60 pgs............. **45.00**
Book
  Brief History of the Massachusetts Charitable Fire Society, Sprague, 1893 .... **36.00**
  1917 New York Fire Dept History, 218 pgs, hard cov, 8 x 10"........... **5.00**
  The Mickey Mouse Fire Brigade, Whitman, 1936, multicolored hard cov, black and white illus, 7 x 10"...... **80.00**
Bubble Gum Card, Bowman's Firefighters, No. 9, Ward LaFrance, three Stage Booster, full color, 2½ x 3¾" **1.75**
Catalog
  Byron Jackson Co, 1930, 36 pgs, pumps, fire truck, and fire boats, fire engine cov................... **10.00**
  Harden Star Hand Grenade, Harden Hand Grenade Fire Extinguisher Co, Chicago, IL, c1885, 64 pgs, testimonials, illus wrappers............. **60.00**
  The Babcock Improved Self–Acting Chemical Fire Apparatus, Babcock Mfg Co, New York, NY, c1885, 24 pgs, fire engines and extinguishers, illus **200.00**
  The Neccessity of the Age, United States Fire Alarm Mfg Co, New York, NY, c1890, 16 pgs, endorsements.. **30.00**

Sheet Music, *Midnight Fire Alarm, March & Two Step,* E. T. Paull, full color litho by A. Hoen & Co., Richmond, VA, 10½ x 14", 1900, $60.00.

Label
  Cigar, Round–Up, cowboy at campfire dreaming of sweetheart, 9 x 6"   **6.00**
  Firewood, Storytime Firewood, hearth scene, pioneer family seated by fireplace, sgd James Dowlen, dated 1977 .... **1.00**
Letterhead, Hartford Fire Insurance, deer logo, 1890..................... **6.00**
Post Card, Chemical and Hose Co No. 2, Johnstown, PA, horse–drawn pumper, fire house in background.......... **12.00**
Poster, Hydropult–Most Efficient Fire Engine in the World, Palace Garden fire scene, October, 1860, 11 x 14", framed........................ **175.00**
Program
  Firemen's Convention, 1927........ **4.00**
  Fireman's Dance, logo on front, unprinted int., emb color........ **6.00**
Sheet Music
  Fire Drill, Harry Lincoln, cov with three horses pulling steam pumper, 1909 .... **11.50**
  Midnight Fire Alarm **60.00**
Sign, fire scene, B & L Tobacco adv, paper on cardboard, 1895, 21 x 28" **275.00**

FIREARMS

Reference: Ralf Coykendall Jr., *Coykendall's Second Sporting Collectibles Price Guide,* Lyons & Burford, 1992; Ralf Coykendall Jr., *Coykendall's Sporting Collectibles Price Guide,* Lyons & Burford, 1991; Ted Hake, *Hake's Guide To Advertising Collectibles,* Wallace–Homestead, 1992; Jim and Vivian Karsnitz, *Sporting Collectibles,* Schiffer Publishing, 1992; Bob and Beverly Strauss, *American Sporting Advertising, Volume 1* (1987, 1992 value update), *Volume 2* (1990, 1992 value update), published by authors, distributed by L–W Book Sales.

Accessories
  Advertising Cover, envelope, Remington UMC, full color, flying turkey and two shells, 1930s, 6 x 3½"   **40.00**
  Advertising Trade Card, Charles Folsom Dealer in Fire Arms, Ammunition & Cutlery........... **40.00**
  Billhead, Atlas Powder Co, c1910 ..   **15.00**
  Brochure, Weaver Telescope Sights, W R Weaver Co, El Paso, TX, c1950, 10 pgs, sights for target and hunting rifles, illus **20.00**
Calendar
  Austin Powder Company, 1900, 21½ x 38" **1,200.00**
  The Peters Cartridge Company, 1930, wall, full color, 20 x 40"   **350.00**

Catalog, Western Ammunition Handbook, Western Cartridge Co., East Alton, IL, black-and-white illustrations, 72 pages, 5½ x 7¾", 1930, $25.00.

Catalog
  Gun Sights, C W DuBois, Tacoma, WA, c1918, 36 pgs, illus **75.00**
  Modern Firearms and Ammunition, Remington Arms Co, New York, NY, 1923, 190 pgs **85.00**
Counter Display
  Peters Cartridge Co, diecut cardboard, standup, running deer and bullet images, "Peters the Old Timer's standby," 1930s, 14 x 18" **75.00**
  Remington Arms, heavy cardboard, standup, color, details bullet components, 1968 . . . . **20.00**
Label
  Golden Pheasant Gun Powder, E I DuPont, printed color **8.00**
  Indian Rifle Gun Powder, E I DuPont De Nemours Co, printed color, 1908 . . . . **8.00**
  Poster, UMC Cartridges, hunter shooting at charging bear, "In a Tight Place, Shoot UMC Cartridges," c1900, 16 x 24½" **175.00**
  Scorecard, Remington UMC, Nitro Club shell cut-away view, c1910, 3½ x 6" **30.00**
  Sign, Infallible Shot Gun Powder, multicolored woman with gun and dog, 10 x 15" **225.00**
  Window Card, Remington UMC Steel Lined Shot Shells, cardboard, full color, cartoon bears examining shells, 1910, 7 x 10" **50.00**
Handguns
  Advertising Trade Card, Colt Patent Firearms Co, mechanical, burglar looking through window, another man's arm raises holding pistol. . . **375.00**
  Booklet, Colt Guns, c1950, 44 pgs, illus, sgd and inscribed by Joe Bodrie, "The Fastest Gun Alive" **20.00**

Broadside, Merwin, Hulbert & Co System Automatic Revolvers, handgun illus, c1880, 9 x 12" **100.00**
Catalog, Colt Revolvers and Automatic Pistols, Colt's Patent Fire Arms Mfg Co, Hartford, Ct, 1929, 36 pgs, with price list **75.00**
Rifles and Shotguns
  Advertising Cover, envelope, Hibbard, Spencer, Bartlett Co, shotgun vignette on back, 1902 . . . . . . **25.00**
  Calendar, Winchester Repeating Arms Co, 1897, hunter with horse, aiming at deer in distance **650.00**
  Catalog
    Catalog 1929–30 High Grade Fire Arms & Accessories, Kennebec Supply Co, Lynn, MA, 28 pgs, Colt, Iver–Johnson, Winchester, Smith & Wesson, and Harrington & Richardson, illus **60.00**
    Catalogue—Firearms Collection, United States Cartridge Co, Lowell, MA, c1905, 140 pgs, matchlocks, carbines, revolvers, crossbows, etc., photos and illus, unpriced **150.00**
    Fine Single–Shot Target and Sporting Rifles, Pistols, Sights, etc., J Stevens Arms and Tool Co, Chicopee Falls, MA, 1900, 128 pgs, prices **50.00**
    Guns, Rifles, Fishing Tackle, Pittsburgh Fire Arms Co, Pittsburgh, PA, 1885, 60 pgs, illus. **200.00**
    Robert Abels Antique Firearms And Edged Weapons, No. 29, 1950s **15.00**
  Letterhead
    Iver Johnson Arms & Cycle Works, Fitchburg, MA, printed black and white, with bill, 1916, used **15.00**
    J Stevens Arms Co, Chicopee Falls, MA, printed black and white, 1916 . . . . **12.00**
    Laften & Taylor, Gun and Locksmith, Jacksonville, FL, orange illus, 1927 . . . . **12.00**
    The Marlin Firearms Co, New Haven, CT, printed black and white, 1914, used **15.00**
  Poster
    Marlin Repeating Rifles and Shotguns, two ducks falling in water, hunter in background, "The Gun for the Man Who Knows," 16¼ x 24¾" **200.00**
    Remington Guns and Ammunition, shooting exhibition by Ken Beegle, black and white photo of Beegle holding rifle, 1930s, 13¾ x 18¼" **75.00**

Sign
  Colt Firearms Co, cowboy on
    horseback, c1890, 23 x 27".... **1,250.00**
  Remington UMC 22 Cal. Repeat-
    ing Rifle, cardboard, full color,
    duck hunter, 1930s, 9 x 13" ... **150.00**
  Sketch, Remington Rifle, orig artist's
    rendering, color pastels, .222
    Remington–Mauser action, wal-
    nut stock, 20 x 25"............. **35.00**

FIREWORKS

Advertising Trade Card
  Aetna Fireworks, Hyde & Co, "Ocean
    Fireworks at the Point of Pines," fire-
    works over ocean illus, text on back **75.00**
  Fire Works!, for sale by Lancaster
    grocer, flag image **26.00**
  Walsh's Old time Birch & Root Beer,
    children setting off fireworks, Patri-
    otic scene.................... **16.00**
Box, firecrackers
  Doughboy Salute, cardboard, six fire-
    crackers, 4½ x 3".............. **50.00**
  Hitts Thunder Flashcracka, 1930s.... **20.00**
  Tipp Musical Salutes, Tipp Fireworks
    Co, Tippecanoe City, OH, 3½ x
    2¼".......................... **25.00**
  Trojan, six jumbo magic black snakes,
    string of tied firecrackers, Japan, 2⅜
    x 1⅝"........................ **15.00**
Catalog
  All Colored Fireworks, Balloons, Flags,
    Lanterns, Torpedos, Toy Pistols,
    etc., Scharff–Bernheimer Grocery
    Co, St Louis, MO, c1898, 8 pgs,
    numerous fireworks patterns and
    trails illus **200.00**
  Descriptive Catalogue and Price List of

**Firecracker Label, Gorilla Brand, brown,
blue, and yellow, $35.00.**

Fireworks, Masten & Wells, Boston,
    MA, 1887, 72 pgs **125.00**
  Our Own Make of Fireworks, Heyer
    Brothers, Boston, MA, c1890, 4 pgs,
    lists fireworks, rockets, and candles,
    prices, trick pistol illus back page .. **90.00**
  Spencer Fireworks, 1940s.......... **25.00**
Envelope, George Miller & Son Co, Im-
    porters of Mandarin Firecrackers, Fire
    Works, etc., Philadelphia, PA, black
    and white, postmarked June 20, 1907 **50.00**
Game, Go Bang Game, Milton Bradley,
    9 x 9" **75.00**
Letterhead, I Rambo Fireworks, Reading,
    PA, 1912 .... **10.00**
Magazine Cover, Life, Fourth of July fire-
    works display illus, July 4, 1955 ..... **3.00**
Playing Cards, Washington Monument,
    Washington, DC, monument and fire-
    works........................ **6.50**
Post Card, red firecrackers spell "4th of
    July," Germany **2.00**
Poster, Columbia figure igniting rocket
    held by Chinaman, fireworks display
    over New York skyline in background,
    New York newspaper The Sunday
    World adv for "8 Funny Pages," July
    12, c1900, 12 x 18".............. **95.00**

FISHING

Reference: Ralf Coykendall Jr., *Coykendall's Second Sporting Collectibles Price Guide,* Lyons &
Burford, 1992; Ralf Coykendall Jr., *Coykendall's
Sporting Collectibles Price Guide,* Lyons & Burford, 1991.

Advertising Trade Card
  Candee Rubber Boots, man dressed in
    suit fishing in lake, sepia tones,
    "Now here's fishing superfine!
    Here's the angler's joy complete!
    Four–pound trout upon your line,
    'Candee' Boots upon your feet" ... **25.00**
  Fleischman's Yeast, emb, fishermen in
    boats, bringing in nets, int. diecut
    net **25.00**
  Gold Medal Cotton Netting, diecut,
    standup, Gold Medal Kid with fish
    in one hand, hat in other, "Fishes no
    matter how deeply they've hid Are
    Caught in the Net of the Gold Medal
    Kid"......................... **25.00**
Book
  Bait Casting, Wm C Vogt, 1928, 104
    pgs, first edition **15.00**
  Fresh–Water Bass, Ray Bergman,
    1942, New York, illus and color
    plates by Fred Hildebrandt, ¾ green
    morocco gilt, board slipcase, sgd by
    author, with envelope containing
    extra suite of 10 color plates of flies **357.00**

Magazine Cover, *Hunting and Fishing*, 8¼ x 11¼", May 1938, $18.00.

With Fly, Plug, and Bait, Ray Bergman, 1947, New York, illus by Edgar Burke and Ivin Sickels, second edition, ½ morocco, board slipcase, sgd by author, with envelope containing extra suite of 6 color plates of flies **330.00**

Calendar, Oakwood Market, OH, 1906, man fishing, 8½ x 5½" **90.00**

Catalog

C Farlow & Co, London, UK, Catalogue of High Class Fishing Tackle, 1920, 250 pgs, heavy paper wrappers, 12 pgs of color plates of trout and salmon flies **125.00**

Harley–Wickham Co, Erie, PA, Harley's Catalog of Sporting Supplies— No. 51, c1930, 4to **40.00**

H D Folsom Arms Co, New York, NY, Sporting Goods, Fishing Tackle, Catalogue No. 45, c1935, 240 pgs, equipment and clothing, illus **50.00**

Horton & Co, Bristol, CT, 1910, 72 pgs, illus, cardboard wrappers with watercolor print illus by Olive–Kemp...................... **85.00**

Iver Johnson Sporting Goods Co, fishing tackle, 1920s **22.00**

Parker's Fishing and Hunting Catalog, 1960, 160 pgs, reels and rifles, 8½ x 5½" **15.00**

South Bend Co, What Tackle and When, 1931, 76 pgs, fishing equipment, black and white and color photos, 5 x 7"................. **60.00**

Weller Deluxe Tackle, 1963, 89 pgs, punched for binder, 8 x 10½" **20.00**

Chart, Creek Chub Bait Co, full color, 31 lures with names, 8½ x 11"........ **25.00**

Cookbook, *Magic Yeast Recipes,* multi-colored cov with little girl going fishing image, 12 pgs................. **15.00**

Label, orange, Golden Trout, orange trout leaping from water, Orange Cove   **2.00**

Letterhead, Crocker & Winsor, Fish of All Kinds, Boston, MA, printed color, blue on white, fishing ship, 1902 .... **10.00**

Magazine, *Fly Fisherman,* 1975 .... **2.50**

Poster

Canadian Pacific adv, Ewart illus, silkscreen design, hooked rainbow trout, "Canada For Game Fish," c1935, 24 x 35"............... **325.00**

United Airlines adv, Jos Binder illus, casting fisherman illus, airliner overhead, c1953, 25 x 40" **300.00**

FLORAL

Advertising Trade Card, J Temple Co, Thomaston, CT, clothing sale, floral design front, adv back, 1880s, 5½ x 4"   **5.00**

Book, *Wild Flowers of New York,* Homer D House, Albany, NY, 1923, second printing, two volumes, color plates, green cloth cov, 8 x 10"........... **110.00**

Booklet, *Our National Flower Which Shall It Be?,* nationwide campaign to select national flower, printed by L Prang & Co, color centerfold of two choices, 1889, 12 pgs, 7½ x 6" **28.00**

Calendar, woman holding bouquet of roses, Orange County Brewery adv, 28 x 15" **450.00**

Catalog

Robert Scott & Son Scott's Roses and Other Beautiful Flowers, Philadelphia, PA, 1889, 56 pgs, illus, black and white cuts, one full page color plate, red and black pictorial wraps   **45.00**

The Livingston Seed Co, Columbus, OH, 1902, 48 pgs, wholesale price list of "True Blue" seeds for flowers and vegetables, 7 pgs florist and garden requisites, 7½ x 9¾"........ **16.00**

Label

Cigar

Daisies, bouquet of daisies, 9 x 6" .. **7.00**

La Rosa De Florida, emb pink rose, gold highlights, 1899, 9 x 6" **9.00**

Vuelta Abajo, emb chrysanthemums, 9 x 6" **5.00**

Orange, Symbol, California poppies, maple leaf, wrapped Sunkist orange, Riverside **2.00**

Post Card, adv

Allen Nursery Co, roses, printed color   **6.00**

Dinger & Conard Co, Leading Rose Growers of America, West Grove, PA, undivided back, 1901–07..... **8.00**

La Moreaux Nursery Co, seed catalog, printed color, divided back, 1913 .. **9.00**

Poster

Bouquet of Roses, Red Rose Brand Raisins adv, Rosedale Raisin Vine-

Seed Packet, Gomphrena, multicolor, Huth Seed Co. Inc., San Antonio, TX, No. 625, 2³/₄ x 3¹/₂", $5.00.

yard Co, Bakersfield, CA, 1920s, 8¹/₂ x 13" 20.00
Floral Bouquet, glass of beer, and cigar stand, Jacob Hoffman Brewing Co adv, J Ottmann Litho Co, c1900, 21¹/₂ x 31¹/₂" 30.00

FOOD

References: Al Bergevin, *Food and Drink Containers and Their Prices,* Wallace–Homestead, 1988; Douglas Congdon–Martin, *America For Sale: A Collector's Guide to Antique Advertising,* Schiffer Publishing, 1991; Ted Hake, *Hake's Guide To Advertising Collectibles,* Wallace–Homestead, 1992; Sharon and Bob Huxford, *Huxford's Collectible Advertising: An Illustrated Value Guide,* Collector Books, 1993.

Advertising Cover, envelope, Home Pie Company, color pie illus, 1945 . . . . . . 20.00
Advertising Trade Card
  Cornish, Curtis & Green, Butter and Cheese Makers, factory vignette one side, text other side, black and white   15.00
  Hecker's Buckwheat, hold to the light, Man in the Moon eating pancakes   20.00
  Heinz Cooked Spaghetti, diecut pickle   20.00
  Maryland Biscuit Co, Oyster Crackers, ship's deck, sailor pulling cargo from hold, flyer attached to rope . . .   30.00
  The Milk Council, Inc, Chicago, IL, diecut milk bottle, offset printed, two sided 15.00
  William Heyser Oyster Packer, Baltimore, MD, Fruit and Produce Dealer, orange pineapple vignette   15.00
Blotter, Franklin Peanut Co adv, 1920 . .   2.00
Book, *The Grocer's Encyclopedia: A Compendium of Useful Information Concerning Foods Of All Kinds, How*

They Are Raised, Prepared and Marketed, How To Care For Them In The Store And Home, How Best To Use And Enjoy Them – And Other Valuable Information For Grocers And General Storekeepers, NY, 1911, 748 pgs, cloth cov, color and black and white illus 75.00
Booklet, *Home Canning,* U S Dept of Agriculture, 1917, 43 pgs, instructions for canning, labeling, and inspecting 9.00
Box
  Hoosier Poet Brand Rolled Oats, cardboard cylinder, 4" d, 7¹/₂" h 55.00
  Log Cabin Brownies, coardboard, log cabin shape, 3¹/₂ x 2³/₄ x 3" 60.00
Calendar
  A C Stram Groceries, URMA Brand, Green Bay, WI, 1930, full pad, 10 x 16" 20.00
  A & P Tea Company, cardboard, shopkeeper, customers, and food products, 1903, full pad, 10 x 13³/₄" 110.00
  Best Baking Co, Milk Bread, 1896, cardboard, family seated at dinner table, 12 x 14¹/₂" 350.00
  Fleischmann's Yeast, 1906, cardboard, 10¹/₄ x 14¹/₄" 120.00
  Grand Union Tea Co, 1905, 29 x 9¹/₂" 275.00
  New Process Gas Range, 1898, cook holding loaf of bread, full pad, 14¹/₂ x 22¹/₂" 220.00
Catalog
  Charles & Co, New York, NY, 1932, 386 pgs, Depression era fine foods, hard cov, 4 color plates, packaged foods, cigar, and cigarette ads 35.00
  George's Codfish Blocks, Andrews & Co, Gloucester, MA, 1885, 4 pgs, fish caught and brought to market in Gloucester, description of Codfish Block grades 15.00
  Grocer's Bulletin—Vol. XII, No. 8, G Thalheimer, Syracuse, NY, 1913, 70 pgs, illus advertisements 30.00
  Swift Illustrated, Swift & Co, Chicago,

Coffee Label, Hilo Roasted Coffee, color litho, red-and-blue on tan ground, 6¹/₂ x 11¹/₂", $18.00.

IL, 1900, 16 pgs, color plates, chromolithographs of meat products' processing **40.00**

Wholesale Provision Dealers, William G Bell & Co, Boston, MA, meats, pickles, and canned goods, 1866, 4 pgs **50.00**

Cookbook, *Chiquita Banana's Recipe Book,* 1950, 24 pgs, color covs and illus, 6 x 9" **6.50**

Display, counter

Junket Desserts, diecut cardboard, standup, three dimensional, interior dining room scene, girls eating Junket Desserts, cook standing in background, 13¼ x 8½ x 5" **300.00**

Wedding Bell Coffee, diecut cardboard, standup, seasonal illus, "Serve Cold When Hot/Serve Hot When Cold," 27½ x 16½" **220.00**

Flyer, The Truth As an Answer to the Bombastic Advertising of Royal Baking Powder, Cleveland Brothers, Albany, NY, 1884, 2 pgs, rebuttal of claims made by Royal Baking Powder Co . . . **15.00**

Handbook, *Preserving of Fruits,* Dr D Jayne & Son, Philadelphia, PA, 1916, 32 pgs, printed color paper wrappers **20.00**

Label

Grapes, Valley Beauty, girl, bunch of grapes, and two hands holding wine glasses, red ground . . . . **.50**

Tomatoes, Dana's Jardiniere Canned Tomatoes, Dana Canned Goods Co, Belpre, OH, jardiniere and tomato design, c1910, 4¼ x 10¾" **5.00**

Newspaper, *The Milling Engineer,* United States Miller, Milwaukee, WI, 1891, 15 pgs, devoted to flour and milling industry, illus, ads, folio **25.00**

Poster, bread, multicolored, space at bottom for brand name, 1930s, 14 x 30" **4.00**

Sign

Beech–Nut Peanut Butter, cardboard, "For Kids & Grown–ups," framed, 24½ x 14½" **125.00**

Ceresota Flour, boy slicing loaf of bread, 16½ x 21½" **325.00**

Heinz, round, pickle center, "Pure Food Products, estd 1869, 57 Varieties," 17" d **30.00**

Tally Card, Voigts Crescent Flour, figural, flour sack shape, printed color, crease at top **5.00**

Window Card, Voigts Royal Flour, red, white, and black, 1910s, 11 x 4" **2.50**

FOOTBALL

Reference: Roderick A. Malloy, *Malloy's Sports Collectibles Value Guide,* Wallace–Homestead, 1993.

Guide Book, Detroit Lions, Amoco Oil Company giveaway, 60 pages, black-and-white photos, 4½ x 6½", 1981, $9.00.

Advertising Trade Card, diecut football player, Yale letter emblem on sweater, Enameline adv **40.00**

Book

American Football, Walter Camp, New York, 1891, plates, first edition of first book on American football . . **660.00**

A Scientific and Practical Treatise on American Football for Schools and Colleges, A Alonzo Stagg and Henry Williams, New York, 1894, revised to date, play diagrams, dj **300.00**

King Football; The Vulgarization of American Colleges, R Harris, Vanguard Press, 254 pgs, first edition **6.50**

Booklet

Football Book Schedules & Information, 1940, college and professional teams, Hires Root Beer premium . . . **15.00**

Gulf Football Manual, Gulf Oil premium, 1933, 24 pgs **5.00**

Catalog

A G Spalding & Bros Fall and Winter Sports—Catalogue 101, New York,

Program, West Reading vs. Wilson, Coca-Cola centerfold, 7¾ x 10½", October 9, 1948, $15.00.

Score Keeper, heavy cardboard, six movable score wheels, Albert Richard Sportswear adv., 6½ x 2⅜", 1948, $22.00.

NY,1893, 40 pgs, predominantly football equipment and uniforms .. **75.00**
A J Reach Fall & Winter Catalogue, Philadelphia, PA, 1912–13, 32 pgs, illus, football and other sporting equipment **25.00**
Magazine
Illustrated Football Annual, 1938 . . . . **40.00**
Stanley Woodward's Football, 1953 . . **4.00**
Magazine Cover, *Life,* black and white photo cov with West Point's All–American co-captain runningbacks Glenn Davis and Felix (Doc) Blanchard, September 16, 1946, 10½ x 14" **15.00**
Paperback Book, *How Champions Play Football,* 1948, 98 pgs **10.00**
Post Card, inset photo of Knute Rockne above Rockne Memorial, Notre Dame University, CA, color, unused, 1940 . . **7.50**
Program
1945, *Philadelphia Inquirer* Charities 8th Annual Classic, Eagles vs Packers, September 13, Municipal Stadium **18.00**
1949, Lincoln University vs Howard University **15.00**
1966 NFL Championship, Green Bay vs Dallas **200.00**
1970 AFC Division, Baltimore vs Cincinnati **28.00**
Ticket
1967 AFL Championship, Oakland vs Houston **22.00**
1976 AFC Wild Card, Houston vs Miami **10.00**
1978, Ohio State, seating diagram on back **1.50**
Wrapper, Bowman's Football, waxed paper, 1954, 5 x 6¼" **8.00**
Yearbook
1965 Naval Academy, Roger Staubach's junior and senior years **75.00**
1974 Green Bay Packers, autographed by coaches and most players **17.00**

FOUNTAIN PEN

Reference: Glen B. Bowen, *Collectible Fountain Pens,* L–W Book Sales, 1982.

Collectors' Club: Pen Fancier's Club, 1169 Overcash Drive, Dunedin, FL 34698.

Advertising Cover, envelope
Century Double Feed Fountain Pen, Century Pen Company, Whitewater, WI, pen image, 1908 . . . . . **40.00**
Swan Pens, red, blue, and green printing both sides, 1910s **35.00**
Advertising Trade Card
Aikin, Lambert & Company Gold Pens, black and white, fountain pen image **40.00**
Spencerian Pens, young girl sitting at desk, writing with pen, dog watching **40.00**
Blotter
Wahl–Eversharp Persona–Point Fountain Pens, fountain pen image, sepia tones, c1930 . . . . **25.00**
Waterman's Ideal Fountain Pen, hand holding pen, multicolored, c1912 . . . . **18.00**
Booklet, Moore Pen Company, "Moore's won't leak," safety pen adv, c1920 . . . . **12.00**
Calendar, Mabie, Todd & Bard Gold Pens, New York, 1878 . . . . **40.00**

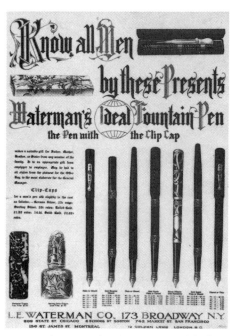

Magazine Tear Sheet, Waterman's Ideal Fountain Pen, Christmas motif, multicolor litho, 10 x 13", 1906, $20.00.

Catalog
  Harvey Stylographic Fountain Pens,
  Harvey Manufacturing Co, North-
  ampton, MA, 1904 . . . .   10.00
  Richter & Phillips Co, 1939, 400 pgs,
  jewelry and fountain pens, color
  illus 10.00
  Waterman's Ideal Fountain Pen, L E
  Waterman Co, New York, NY, No.
  55, c1892, color cov, black and
  white illus 15.00
Instruction Sheet, Parker Vacuumatic
  Pen, black and white, 1 pg 3.00
Letterhead, Waterman's "Ideal" Foun-
  tain Pen, black and white, pen illus,
  1885 . . . .   8.00
Magazine Advertisement, *Appleton's
  Journal,* Waterman's Ideal Fountain
  Pens, 1905 . . . .   5.00
Poster, Waterman's Ideal Fountain Pen,
  Uncle Sam at Treaty of Portsmouth,
  early 1900s, 41½ x 19½" 2,530.00
Sign, Parker Lucky–Curve Pens, diecut
  cardboard, multicolored, 1920s. . . .   25.00

FRATERNAL

Advertising Trade Card, Miss M E Taylor,
  Knight Templar Plumes a Specialty,
  black and white, hat illus 10.00
Bible, Masonic, c1931, 1,200 pgs, illus,
  leather binding, 22 kt gold stamping,
  9½ x 11½ x 2½" 65.00
Book
  Encyclopedia of Freemasonry, published by Masonic History Co, two
  volumes, 1919, 943 pgs, black cov,
  gold trim 50.00
  Mackey's Revised Encyclopedia of

**Lodge Book, Solar Lodge, 171, I.O.O.F.,
lists members and officers, emb. color
covers, 20 pages, 2½ x 4½", 1913, $4.00.**

  Freemasonry, two volumes, 1929,
  1,217 pgs, illus 55.00
  National Memorial, Benevolent & Pro-
  tective Order of Elks, 1931, hard cov   30.00
Booklet
  Knights of Honor, promotional, elf im-
  ages on cov and int., 10 pgs 15.00
  Odd Fellows Pillar Encampment,
  1905, 50 pgs, rules, practices, and
  member information 11.00
Bookplate, Masonic Library 3.50
Catalog
  Blue Lodge supplies, Morgan, Puhl &
  Morris, Detroit, MI, 1898, 72 pgs,
  fully illus, paraphernalia needed for
  Masonic rituals, illus paper wrap-
  pers 90.00
  Costumes & Supplies of the Ancient
  Accepted Scottish Rites of Free Ma-
  sonry, Henderson–Ames Company,
  Kalamazoo, MI, 1896, 80 pgs, two
  color pgs with costume illus 85.00
  IOOF Costumes & Regalia, C E Ward
  Co, New London, CT, No. 41,
  c1910, 73 pgs, 8 color pgs 75.00
  IOOF Costumes, Regalia, & Supplies,
  Cat. No. 2, Ward–Stilson Co, An-
  derson, IN, c1915, 122 pgs, color
  and black and white, orig price list
  in inside front cov pocket, order
  forms attached 100.00
  Rathbone Sisters, Costumes and Sup-
  plies, Cat. #214, Pettibone Bros Mfg
  Co, Cincinnati, OH, c1900, 24 pgs,
  Women's Auxiliaries of Knights of
  Pythias organizations. 45.00
Certificate
  Independent Order of Odd Fellows,
  eight vignettes, 1927 . . . .   10.00
  Masonic
  Belfast, Ireland, engraved, c1813 . .   150.00
  Maine, membership in Lodge 86,
  ornate, red printing 15.00
Chart, Masonic symbols and illus, Hatch
  & Co, Trinity Bldg, Broadway, NY,
  1865, 19 x 24" 40.00
Invitation, Odd Fellows, Arcanus #102
  Lodge Chicken Fry, Elmwood, IL,
  1903, 4 x 7" 9.00
Label, cigar box
  Elks Temple, emb, multicolored and
  gold 25.00
  Infinity, Masonic symbols 45.00
  Tun Tavern, colonial view of Ameri-
  can Masonic Lodge 40.00
Letterhead, Independent Order of Odd
  Fellows, Canal Lodge No. 48,
  Searsmont, ME, 1840s, 7½ x 9¾" 8.00
Magazine, *Masonic World,* War Unity
  issue, September, 1942 . . . .   10.00
Matchbook Cover
  Elks 2.25

Loyal Order of Moose 3.25
Membership Card, Supreme Lodge
  Knights of Pythias, vignettes at top,
  1916, 8 x 10" 8.00
Post Card
  Elks Club Reception Hall, Honolulu,
    c1910 . . . .   8.50
  Knights of Columbus Hut, U S Train-
    ing Station, Newport, RI, Albertype
    Co, Brooklyn, NY 3.50
  Souvenir Book, Knights of Templar,
    1895, 160 pgs, adv 30.00

FREAKS

Advertising Trade Card, Millie Christine
  Two Headed Lady, black lady version,
  adv and promotional text on back 35.00
Autograph, pitch card photo, Pete Moore
  sitting on stool with deformed legs, sgd
  "Pete Moore, Cumberland Valley
  Shows," 3¹/₂ x 5¹/₂" 20.00
Book
  *A True Life and an Interesting History
    of Che–Mah the Celebrated Chinese
    Dwarf, Smallest of All Dwarfs,* auto-
    biographical, New York Popular
    Publishing, NY, 1882, 14 pgs, color
    pictorial wrappers, 3 x 5" 40.00
  *History of the Wide World's Wonder,
    Eli Bowen,* New York Popular Pub-
    lishing, NY, 1879–80, 15 pgs, man
    born with feet but without legs, self
    exhibited and with Forepaugh's Ag-
    gregation, blue pictorial wrappers, 3
    x 5" 50.00
  *Isaac W Sprague, The Living Skeleton.
    A Wonderful Curiosity,* Rockland
    Standard Press, Rockland, MA, 15
    pgs, exhibited with P T Barnum,
    plain pink wrappers 50.00
Envelope, pictorial, entitled "The Tom
  Thumb Gift, Containing the Life, Ad-

**Post Card, circus freaks, black-and-white
real photo, undivided back, 3¹/₂ x 5¹/₂",
1900s, $25.00.**

FRANCES
Half Man -:- Half Woman

**Publicity Card, "Frances, Half Man/Half
Woman," black-and-white real photo,
printed in Toronto, Canada, blank back,
3¹/₂ x 5¹/₂", 1900s, $35.00.**

ventures, and Marriage of General
  Tom Thumb, with a Cut of Himself and
  Wife, and a Picture of the Baby,"
  printed, red and black, three page bi-
  ography, six vignette illus, 1864 . . . . .   150.00
Magazine, *Bob Hermines Magazine of
  Midgets,* 1945, 17 pgs, World's Small-
  est People, 5¹/₄ x 8¹/₄" 20.00
Pamphlet, Mr & Mrs Al Tomaini–
  World's Strangest Married Couple, 4
  pgs, 5¹/₂ x 8¹/₂" 14.00
Photo Card, midget parents with baby,
  "Mr & Mrs G B Reader & Son, Grover,
  Jr," 3¹/₂ x 4¹/₂" 11.00
Photograph, 3 x 4¹/₂", Jack Stretch, "The
  Rubber Skin Man," set of 3 different
  poses 35.00
Pitch Card
  Col Jerry Lipko, State Fair Freaks, Pre-
    sents Stella the Bearded Lady, auto-
    graph back, 5 x 7" 38.00
  Frank A Lentini, standing showing
    three legs, four feet, sixteen toes,
    and two bodies, "Please show this
    photo to your friend" on bottom, 6 x
    3" 28.00
Post Card, Ripley's Official Post Card,
  1933 World's Fair, Chicago, Paul
  Desmuke photo, "The Armless Won-
  der Throwing Knives With His Feet" . .   15.00

FUNERARY

Advertising Trade Card, Geo A Cunley
  Monumental & Granite Works, cem-
  etary scene, black and green 50.00
Blotter, Magical 999 Embalmer Formula,
  c1900 . . . .   5.00

Book

Champion Expanding Encyclopedia of Embalming, Champion Chemical Co, Springfield, OH, 1923–28, monthly additions, approx 30 pgs each month, 9 x 12". **32.00**

Embalmer's Daily Memorandum for 1896, William Owen and Co, Fulton St, NY. **75.00**

Booklet, Incineration, John B Beugless, United States Cremation Company, Ltd, 14 pgs, front cov with Portland vase image, 9³/₄ x 6". **18.00**

Calendar, A G Lundberg, Artistic Memorials in Granite & Marble, Westford, MA, 1926, 10 x 14". **20.00**

Catalog

Caskets & Funeral Supplies, Sunbury, PA, 188 pgs, leather cov, 5 x 9¹/₂" . .   **45.00**

Derma Surgery with Complete Catalog of Embalmer's Supplies, H S Eckels and Co, Philadelphia, PA, c1927, 324 pgs, 9 x 12". **35.00**

Cemetary Pillars, Mausoleums, Statues, Headstones, etc., Flint Granite Co, Albany, NY, 1900s, 49 pgs **20.00**

Oliver Johnson, Inc., Chicago, IL, 1930, 31 pgs, illus, grave digger tents, decorations, markers, ground thawer, lawn equipment, etc., prices. **22.50**

Springfield Metallic Casket Co, 24 pgs and wrappers, folding casket carriages and pedestals, 6¹/₄ x 9¹/₄". . . .   **30.00**

Fan, adv, cardboard

Sisler Bros, Inc, Fine Monuments, garden and mountain scene, full color, text on back, wooden handle, 8¹/₂ x 7¹/₂". **25.00**

Swallow Funeral Home, four panel, folding, floral bouquet, text on back   **30.00**

Funeral Invitation, printed, black and white, 5¹/₄ x 3¹/₄", 1931, $7.50.

Funeral Notice, black bordered card and envelope, Farmersville, OK funeral, 1914 . . . .   **8.50**

Painting, mourning, watercolor, matted and framed, 1810, 8³/₈ x 10³/₈" **65.00**

Playing Cards, The Campfield–Hickman Funeral Home, Barberton, OH, funeral home illus, yellow ground, 1954. . . . .   **15.00**

Post Mortem

Albumen Photo, child in flower–filled coffin, eyes open, mounted, 4³/₄ x 8"   **25.00**

Cabinet Card

Corpse lying in open coffin under evergreen trees, boat shape coffin, close–up, c1890. . . . .   **50.00**

Deceased child in mother's arms. . .   **20.00**

Register, undertaker's, lists information and costs of funerals from 1891 to 1895, Toledo, OH. **10.00**

Remembrance Card, diecut, gold lettering and illus, black ground, 1888, 4¹/₈ x 6³/₈". **6.00**

Sheet Music, *Funeral March,* Eclipse Publishing Co, Philadelphia, PA, c1914 . . . .   **12.00**

FURNITURE

Advertising Trade Card

Burger & Co Furniture Manufacturers, furniture illus **42.00**

H R Plimpton's Ottoman & Sofas, black and white, factory and sofa images **40.00**

Book

A Completed Century 1826–1926, Printed at the Merrymount Press, Heywood–Wakefield Company, Boston, MA, 1926, 112 pgs, company history, hard cov, illus. **100.00**

Furniture, As Interpreted By the Century Furniture Co, Century Furniture Co, Grand Rapids, MI, 1929, 158 pgs, stiff board cov, traces history of furniture in Europe. **50.00**

Simple Colonial Furniture, Gottshall, 1931, diagram illus, hard cov **6.75**

Catalog

Bagby Furniture Co, Baltimore, MD, Special Short Line Catalogue, 1914, 36 pgs, utilitarian wood bedroom furniture. **30.00**

Decorators Supply Co, Chicago, IL, Illustrated Catalogue of Period Ornaments for Furniture, Catalogue 117, 1924, 148 pgs, furniture hardware   **50.00**

Merriman Hall & Co, 1898, 46 pgs, ash and oak furniture **60.00**

Piedmont Red Cedar Chest Co, Piedmont Old Fashioned Moth Proof Red Cedar Chests, Statesville, NC, 1921, 48 pgs. **18.00**

Billhead, Glazier & Witt-feld, Manufacturers & Dealers in Cabinet Furniture, receipt, 8½ x 4½", 1867, $18.00.

Catalog, H. C. Valentine & Co., Antiques, beds, four-part folded cover with nine loose illustrated sheets, 6 x 9", 1929, $40.00.

Flyer
   Bagby Furniture Co, Baltimore, MD, Christmas Furniture Sale, 1902, 6 pgs, inexpensive furniture with imitation wood finishes, folio **25.00**
   Charles Hollander & Sons, Baltimore, MD, Supplemental Sheet #33, c1900, 6 pgs, illus, oak, wicker, and upholstered furniture, folio **15.00**
Letterhead
   Fort Smith Couch & Bedding Company, Ft Smith, AR, chaise lounge vignette on cov, 1907 . . . .   **8.50**
   The Dappy Furniture Co, Conneautville, PA, ornate printed cov, 1898 . . . .   **10.00**
Magazine, *Furniture Trades Magazine,* December 25, 1893, The Furniture Worker, Chicago, IL, 50 pgs, Stickley and other prominent manufacturers adv. **15.00**
Plates, set of 24, string–tied, Indian Head Table Co, Nashua, NH, heavy cen-

Catalog, Lincoln Chair and Novelty Co., colonial furniture, sepia photo illus., 32 pages, 9 x 12", 1932–1933, $45.00.

Catalog, The West Branch Cedar Chests, West Branch Novelty Co., Milton, PA, orange, black, and white, 15 pages, 12 x 9", Spring 1928, $30.00.

terpost tables for living rooms, clubs, etc., with 1913 price list, oblong 8vo   **35.00**

GIRLIES

Reference: Denis C. Jackson, *Men's Girlie Magazines: The Only Price Guide, Newstanders, Third Edition,* published by author, 1991.

Blotter, Penn Securities, Earl Moran figure and July–September 1948 calendar, 4 x 9".....................   **12.00**
Calendar
   1953, half New Year's nude girl popping out of January calendar, body and fender shop adv, 12 complete pgs, 9½ x 14"................   **30.00**
   1960, Figure Calendar, Sizzle, scantily clad brunette sitting on bed, 8¼ x 11"........................   **25.00**
Magazine
   Gorgeous Girls, #8, 78 pgs, 1968, Jaybird Enterprises.............   **6.00**
   Lasses & Glasses, Vol 1, #1, 1968, Parliament...................   **12.00**
   Modern Man Annual, Vol 1, #1, 1960s......................   **12.00**
   Rascal, Vol 1, #1, 1963, Camerarts Publishing **10.00**
Matchbook Cover, Royal Flash Set, Convention theme **5.00**
Poster
   Lorna, black and white photo image, Lorna Maitland, nude holding towel in front of her, 1964 ....   **125.00**
   "Una Nuova Veste," nude blonde girl ready to pull on T–shirt, Winchester Repeating Arms Co, 13⅜ x 26⅜" ..   **300.00**
Print, "Bewitching Eyes," blonde girl, color, Zoe Mozert, 1930s, 8 x 10" **10.00**
Puzzle
   Bathing Beauties, George W Brelsford,

Magazine, *Adam,* Vol. 3, No. 3, 8¼ x 10¾", 1959, $6.00.

Magazine, *Gallant,* Vol. 1, No. 1, 8½ x 11", May 1959, $5.00.

   180 diecut cardboard pcs, 1930s, 12 x 9¾" **12.00**
   Nude sitting on window sill, lake scene background, hand cut pressboard, 250 pcs, 9½ x 11½" **15.00**
   Playboy Playmate, American Publishing Co, copyright 1967, 297 diecut cardboard pcs, metal canister **18.00**
Sign, Penn Beverage Co adv, bathing beauty and floating beverage case, framed **85.00**
Sticker, sexy cowgirl, scantily clad with guns, titled "Home on the Range," 1940s........................   **5.00**

GIRL SCOUT

Reference: Mary Degenhardt and Judy Kirsch, *Girl Scout Collector's Guide,* Wallace–Homestead, 1987, out–of–print.

Book
   Juliette Low and The Girl Scouts, Choate & Ferris, 1928 ....   **15.00**
   Lady From Savannah, The Life of Juliette Low, Schultz & Lawrence, Lippincott, 1958, first edition **10.00**
   The Girl Scouts Rally, Katherine Keene Galt, Saalfield, 1921 ....   **15.00**
Booklet, *Girl Scouting & the Jewish Girl,* 1944 ....   **6.00**

Calendar
  1953, full color photo, full pad **20.00**
  1954, full color photo, penciled notes,
    8½ x 10" **15.00**
Catalog
  Brownie Equipment, 1950, 16 pgs, 8 x
    8" **8.50**
  Camp Fire Girls, 1916, 50 pgs, well
    illus, Camp Fire Girls Co, NY, 8¾ x
    12" **20.00**
Certificate, Daisy Girl Scout, vining floral
  border with birds and butterflies, Girl
  Scout emblem **5.00**
Charter, tan textured paper, dark brown
  inscription and design, inked signa-
  tures, dated January 1921, 9 x 14¾" . . **22.00**
Comic Book, *Daisy Lowe of the Girl
  Scouts*, full color, history text, 16 pgs,
  1954 copyright, 6½ x 10" **15.00**
Diary, Girl Scout Diary, 1929, orange
  cov with black silhouette, 3¼ x 5¼" . . **12.00**
First Day Cover, "50 Years of Girl Scout-
  ing," Burlington, VT, July 24, 1962
  cancel, Ken Boll cachet **4.00**
Handbook
  Brownie Scout Handbook, 8th printing **5.00**
  Girl Scout Handbook
    4th edition, 1st printing, 1933 . . . . . **5.00**
    7th edition, 1st printing, 1953 . . . . . **3.00**
  How Girls Can Help Their Country,
    1917, first edition **35.00**
  Scouting For Girls, 1927, 464 pgs,
    Girls Scouts, Inc, NY **15.00**
Magazine, *The American Girl*, June,
  1934, 52 pgs, 8½ x 12" **8.00**
Manual, *Scouting For Girls*, 1920, 557
  pgs **20.00**
Letter, June 6, 1938, Girl Scouts of

Book, **The Girl Scouts' Rally,** Girl Scout
Series, Vol. 2, Katherine Keene Galt,
Saalfield Publishing Co., Chicago, IL, hard
cover, dj, 5 x 7½", 1921, $15.00.

Houghton, Houghton, MI letterhead,
  accepting resignation of director, orig
  Girl Scout envelope **12.00**
Sheet Music
  Girl Scouts Together, Gladys Cornwell
    Goff, illus cov **6.00**
  No Man Is An Island, 1950 . . . . **3.00**

GLASS

Advertising Trade Card, Vasa Murrhina
  Art Glass Co, factory vignette on re-
  verse **22.00**
Book
  Faber, William Frederic, *Stained Glass
    Windows, An Essay With A Report
    To The Vestry On Stained Glass
    Windows For Grace Church,
    Lockport, NY*, 1900, 41 pgs, 3 x 5" **35.00**
  Heckler, Norman C, *American Bottles
    In The Charles B Gardner Collec-
    tion*, 1975, hardbound, auto-
    graphed **85.00**
  Hunter, *Steigel Glass*, Boston, 1914,
    272 pgs, black and white illus, pic-
    torial cov, 7 x 10" **300.00**
  McKearin, G, *Two Hundred Years Of
    American Blown Glass*, Bonanza,
    NY, 382 pgs, dj, 8 x 11" **40.00**
  Skelley, Leloise Davis, *Modern Fine
    Glass, the Work of the Leading Art-
    ists and Designers and of the Most
    Famous Glass–Making Houses
    Here and Abroad*, Garden City Pub-
    lishing Co, 1942, 144 pgs, dj, 9 x
    12" **65.00**
  Warman, Edwin G, *American Cut
    Glass*, E G Warman Publishing Inc,
    1978, 11th printing **30.00**
Box, Libbey Glass, cocktail glass, silver,
  Libbey's logo center, originally held
  four glasses, 16 x 4" **1.50**
Catalog
  Fostoria Glass Co, Manufacturers of
    Decorated Lamps, Globes and
    Shades, Crystal Glass Lamps, Table
    Glassware, and Glass Novelties,
    Moundsville, WV, 1890–95, 24 pgs **250.00**
Magazine, *The Magazine of Old Glass*,
  1938–39 . . . . **30.00**

GOLF

References: Roderick A. Malloy, *Malloy's Sports
Collectibles Value Guide*, Wallace–Homestead,
1993; John M. and Morton W. Olman, *Olman's
Guide To Golf Antiques & Other Treasurers of the
Game*, Market Street Press, 1992; Beverly Robb,
Collectible Golfing Novelties, Schiffer Publish-
ing, 1922; Shirley & Jerry Sprung, *Decorative Golf
Collectibles: Collector's Information, Current
Prices*, Glentiques, 1991.

Collectors' Club: Golf Collectors' Society, P.O. Box 491, Shawnee Mission, KS 66201.

Advertising Trade Card
  Enameline, diecut, Vassar student girl golfer **40.00**
  Humphries Witch Hazel Oil, full color woman golfer. **25.00**
  Spalding Bros, golfer, "Spalding's Golf Player," diecut, standup **90.00**
Blotter, litho lady golfer image, Retona Health Restorer adv **25.00**
Book
  Bateman, H M, *Adventures at Golf,* 1st edition **155.00**
  Collett, Glenna, *Ladies in the Rough* . .   **50.00**
  Haultain, *The Mystery of Golf,* 2nd edition, 1912 . . . .   **70.00**
  Martin, John S, *The Curious History of the Golf Ball,* 1968 . . . .   **155.00**
  Metz, Dick, *The Secret of Par Golf,* 1935, 10¼ x 13", orig dj **10.00**
  Morrison, Alex J, *A New Way to Better Golf,* 1931 . . . .   **35.00**
  Schoor, Gene, *Babe Didrikson, The World's Greatest Woman Athlete,* Doubleday, 1978, first edition. **20.00**
  Travis, W J, *Practical Golf,* 1902 . . . . .   **35.00**
Booklet, Resorts In The Canadian Rockies, men and women playing golf at Banff Golf Course, 1920s, 8 x 11" **20.00**
Box, smiling lady golfer, 1920–30 . . . . .   **25.00**
Brochure, The Chautauqua Golf Club, 1915–20, 6 pgs, 3¹/₁₂ x 7" **8.00**
Calendar, 1951, Byron Nelson's Winning Golf, John C Larkin Insurance Co   **18.00**
Comic Book
  Mickey Mouse, Dell Comics, #30, 1953, Mickey swinging golf club and golf course scene **10.00**
  New Terrytoons, Heckle and Jeckle, #17, Whitman, golf scene, 1972. . .   **8.00**

Cookbook, *Golfer's,* Iarrobino, 1968, 91 pgs **3.00**
First Day Cover, The Country Club, Brookline, MA, 1913 US Open Championship, Francis D Ouimet, America's First Golf Hero, June 13, 1988 cancel stamp, Margaret Lowery autograph **50.00**
Game
  Amateur Golf, Parker Brothers, Inc, 1928, 52 cards with golfer scene on back, multicolored litho golf course on board, adv sheet, and instruction sheet, golf scene on box cov **65.00**
  Golf Bug, paper game board, cards and markers, orig box, 1915 . . . . . .   **75.00**
Greeting Card
  "A Happy Easter," two rabbits playing golf, emb, unused, c1917 . . . .   **12.50**
  "May every Christmas joy be Yours!," golf scene.   **50.00**
Handbook, *Golfer's Handbook,* Bob MacDonald and Les Bolstad, orig boxed set of 4. . . . .   **45.00**
Magazine
  Golf Digest, 1963, 12 issues **15.00**
  Golfing, March, 1952 . . . .   **8.00**
  Golf World, April 13, 1951, Valerie Hogan cov **15.00**
  Sports Illustrated
    1958, August 25, Pine Valley Golf Course **7.75**
    1961, January 23, Crosby Golf Tournament. **5.50**
    1964, April 6, Jack Nicklaus cov . . .   **13.50**
  The American Golfer,
    1928, December **15.00**
    1932, March **8.00**
Magazine Cover
  Harper's Weekly, December 28, 1900, illus titled "The End of the Season," framed **35.00**

Jigsaw Puzzle, Goofy Golf, Sty Mee in Chinee, Richfield premium, No. 4, orig. envelope with Alex Morrison's golf lesson on back, 7 x 9", 1933, $25.00.

Sheet Music, *Follow Thru,* green, black, and white covers, De Sylva, Brown, and Henderson, Inc., 9 x 11¾", 1928, $4.00.

Life, August 8, 1955, Ben Hogan, autographed, framed **200.00**
Magazine Tear Sheet
  Advertisement
    Ivory Soap, woman swinging golf club, man and caddy looking on, 1906. . . . . **15.00**
    Mennen's Borated Talcum Toilet Powder, inset circle scene of women, golf clubs and golf bag, c1906, matted and framed. **35.00**
    Wescott Soles, The Gathering Place of Fashion, woman swinging golf club, May, 1927, framed **25.00**
  Article, Teeing Off With Babe Ruth, *Collier's,* April, 1929, matted and framed **100.00**
  Illustration
    Life, golf scene, R M Crosby, full page. **10.00**
    Time, January 10, 1949, full color sketch of Ben Hogan **35.00**
Manual, *Diemil–Vardon Golf Manual,* Western Golf Publishing, USA, 1927 **150.00**
Paperback Book, *How to Hit a Golf Ball,* Slammin Sammy Snead, 1950, 74 pgs **12.00**
Photograph
  Arnold Palmer, An American Legend, Palmer with Darrel Brown, NBC publicity release **20.00**
  J S Lockwood, set of 6, each with different golf scene, 1900, 5 x 4" **65.00**
Playing Cards
  Animal Snap, cartoon golfing illus, Hong Kong, 1960 . . . . **8.00**
  Zweifel Card Golf, 1932, orig box. . . . **25.00**
Post Card
  Humorous cartoon golf scene **10.00**
  Lady Golfer, pyrography, 1930–40. . . **5.00**
  Rules of Golf, Crombie, set of 9 . . . . . . **30.00**
  Silence is Golden, "It's Good Policy to Leave a Few Things Unsaid," bird with broken golf club, c1900. . . . . . **10.00**

St Andrews, 24 sepia views, c1900 . . . **145.00**
Poster, movie, *Follow The Sun,* real life love story of Valarie and Ben Hogan, Ben Hogan autograph, 1951, framed **350.00**
Print
  Blackheath Golfers, c1950, framed. . . **150.00**
  Golf Swinging, A B Frost **100.00**
  The First Tee, Dendy Sadler, colored etching. **30.00**
  The Golf Girl, Howard Chandler Christy **100.00**
Program
  Bob Hope Desert Classic, 1967. . . . . . **15.00**
  Bryon Nelson Golf Classic, April 22–28, 1968, Preston Trail Golf Club, Dallas, TX, cov with Arnold Palmer autograph **75.00**
  Fort Worth Open Golf Championship, First Annual, 1945, Glen Garden Country Club, Fort Worth, TX **100.00**
Puzzle
  Goofy Golf, No. 1, A Swiss–ituation, Richfield Gasoline, golfer shooting from eagle's nest, paper envelope with golf lessons, 1930s. **25.00**
  Joe Palooka Jigsaw Puzzle, supplement of *Sunday Inquirer,* Philadelphia, 1933 copyright, golf scene, 8 x 10". **15.00**
Sheet Music, *Button Up Your Overcoat,* golf scene cov, 1928 . . . . **8.00**
Stereoviews
  The Argument, Keystone View Company, USA, 1906 . . . . **8.00**
  The Embryo Golfer, A C Co, 1925. . . . **15.00**
Tobacco Card
  Ball, J, Churchmann's Cigarettes, 1927, 1st Series, #1. . . . . **120.00**
  Gillies, Harold, No. 6, Will's Cigarettes, 1930 . . . . **50.00**
  King, S L, Larger Cigarettes, 1936–39 **5.00**
  Perkins, T P, Churchmann's Cigarettes, 1928, caricature illus. **10.00**
Valentine, pop–up
  Valentine Greetings, little golfer wearing knickers, 1900–20. . . . . **45.00**
  You're the one FORE me Valentine, 1940–50 . . . . **30.00**
Yearbook, *USGA,* 1931 . . . . **25.00**

GONE WITH THE WIND

Reference: Patrick McCarver, *Gone With The Wind Collector's Guide,* Collector's Originals, 1990.

Book
  Gone With The Wind, Margaret Mitchell, 1940, 391 pgs. **25.00**
  Gone With The Wind Trivia Book, P Bartel **12.00**

Cookbook, *Gone With The Wind, Famous Southern Recipes* Pebeco Toothpaste **45.00**
Folder, tinted sepia portrait illus, text biography, and production statistics, Loew's Theatre imprint on back, $8^{1}/_{2}$ x $10^{1}/_{2}$" **75.00**
Magazine Article
  Doll World, October, 1981, paper doll sets from the movie, 6 pgs **20.00**
  Life, December 19, 1939, movie article and David O Selznick, 8 pgs ... **45.00**
  Time, December 25, 1939, Vivien Leigh cov **75.00**
Paper Doll, Vivien Leigh **12.00**
Poster, folded, multicolored, c1970, 27 x 41" **35.00**
Program, buff paper, brown illus, 1939, $6^{1}/_{4}$ x $9^{1}/_{2}$" **50.00**
Souvenir Book, color, 1939 .... **35.00**

HOCKEY

References: James Beckett, *The Official Price Guide To Hockey Cards,* House of Collectibles, 1992; Roderick A. Malloy, *Malloy's Sports Collectibles Value Guide,* Wallace–Homestead, 1993.

Periodical: *Sports Collectors Digest,* 700 East State St., Iola, WI 54990.

Advertising Trade Card, image of Victorian men playing ice hockey, A & P adv **25.00**
Book, *Official 1932 Field Hockey Guide,* Spaulding's Athletic Library **15.00**
Bubble Gum Card
  Bowman, 1990–91
    Complete Set **15.00**
    1, Jeremy Roenick **2.50**
    188, Mike Modano .... **.50**
    208, Kevin Stevens **1.25**
  O–Pee–Chee, 1968–69
    16, Bobby Hull **42.50**

Magazine Cover, *Collier's,* $10^{1}/_{2}$ x $13^{1}/_{2}$", December 6, 1941, $15.00.

29, Gordie Howe **50.00**
Topps
  1961–62, complete set **650.00**
  1964–65, Pierre Pilote SP, 59 ..... **110.00**
  1966–67, Bobby Orr, 35 .... **750.00**
Magazine, *Sports Illustrated*
  1960, January 25, Hockey in Russia .. **5.00**
  1967, December 11, Bobby Orr cov .. **15.50**
  1969, April 7, St Louis Hockey cov ... **6.50**

HOLIDAY

References: Juanita Burnett, *A Guide To Easter Collectibles,* Collector Books, 1992; Helaine Fendelman & Jeri Schwartz, *The Official Price Guide To Holiday Collectibles,* House of Collectibles, 1991.

Periodical: *Trick or Treat Trader,* P.O. Box 499, 4 Lawrence St., Winchester, NH 03470.

Birthday
  Bag, favor, lithographed paper, "Happy Birthday," mid 20th C **3.00**
  Hat, Sweet Sixteen, crown type, cardboard, silver covered, glitter dec, 1930 .... **5.00**
  Paper Doll, Dolly Dingle's Birthday Cards, uncut, early 20th C **15.00**
  Post Card, emb floral design **8.00**
  Puzzle, post card type, Birthday Wishes, German, c1909, dove, heart, florals, and anchor, perforated cardboard pcs **8.00**
Christmas
  Book, *A Christmas Sermon,* Robert Louis Stevenson, Charles Scribner & Sons, NY, 1919 .... **4.00**
  Box, candy, cardboard, Christmas scenes, 1930s, 3 x 5 x $1^{1}/_{2}$" **5.00**
  Greeting Card, "A Merry Christmas," three children wearing winter clothing, huddled beneath umbrella, Wolf & Co, NY **2.50**
  Label, cigar, untitled, Christmas tree and child on sleigh **45.00**
  Post Card, "A Merry Christmas," Father Christmas outside lighted house, wearing green robe, c1910, Germany **5.00**
  Puzzle, Santa Claus Puzzle Box, Milton Bradley Co, c1910, set of 3 hand cut cardboard puzzles, 9 x $12^{1}/_{2}$", orig box **175.00**
Easter
  Advertising Display, cardboard, Easter bunny holding colored food dyes .. **25.00**
  Book
    Peter Cottontail, 1940 .... **10.00**
    The Tale of Peter Rabbit, Edna M Aldredge and Jessie F McKee, Harter Publishing Co, 1931 ..... **18.00**

Box
  Candy, litho cardboard, chicks and
    bunnies, ribbon dec on neck **12.00**
  Kauffman's Egg Dye, early 1900s . .   **75.00**
Greeting Card
  Booklet, 10 pgs, The Cabbage Land
    Pupils, 1920s, 3½ x 6" **15.00**
  Mechanical, bunny drinking soda,
    soda flows through straw, 1920s   **8.00**
Nut Cup, yellow crepe paper, card-
    board cutout rabbit, name tag, 1940   **5.00**
Post Card
  "Easter Greetings," boy and girl
    carrying flowers, emb, early
    20th C **5.00**
  "Happy Easter," four chicks and
    flowers, one chick emerging from
    egg shell **10.00**
Sheet Music, *Easter Parade* **10.00**
Father's Day, sign, "Father's Day Spe-
    cial," Winchester Arms, 1966 . . . .   **12.00**
Fourth of July
  Bottle Carrier, Coca–Cola, July Fourth,
    six box wrapper, c1935 . . . .   **70.00**
  Box, candy, shield shape, red, white,
    and blue, 2¼ x 2½" **10.00**
  Post Card, "Wishing You a Glorious
    4th of July," children, dog, fire-
    crackers, and flag, emb **10.00**
  Sheet Music
    Stars and Stripes Forever **10.00**
    Yankee Doodle Dandy, James
      Cagney, 1931 . . . .   **20.00**
  Tablecloth, printed red, white, and
    blue flags and Liberty Bell,
    Dennison **10.00**
Halloween
  Advertising Display, cardboard, A &
    W Rootbeer, Happy Halloween
    from the Munsters **50.00**
  Apron, crepe paper, orange and black,
    ruffled edge **25.00**

**Halloween, cat, honeycomb body, card-
board head, chest, legs, and tail, 4 x 9",
1930s, $20.00.**

**Halloween, witch face hanger, emb. card-
board, black, orange, and white, 6 x 6½",
1930s, $18.00.**

Bag, trick or treat, litho pumpkin head,
    "Happy Halloween," 1940 . . . .   **18.00**
Book, *Charlie Brown's Pumpkin Car-
    ols,* mid 20th C **10.00**
Booklet
  How To Entertain On Halloween,
    Dennison Mfg Co, 36 pgs, 1926   **15.00**
  Pranks and Parties, 1927 . . . .   **18.00**
Fan, litho, two black cats, arched
    backs, wood handle, marked
    "DRGM Germany" **15.00**
Game, party type, Cat and Witch,
    Whitman, 1940s, MIB **50.00**
Magazine, *Liberty,* November 8,
    1941, colorful Halloween cov **6.00**
Nut Cup, crepe paper and cardboard,
    jack–o'–lantern, 1940 . . . .   **35.00**
Photograph, children's costume party,
    1940s **30.00**
Post Card
  "Halloween Greeting," woman
    bobbing for apples, jack–o'–
    lantern border, E C Banks, 1909   **12.00**
  "Happy Halloween," witch riding
    on broom, early 20th C **10.00**
  "Wishing You a Merry Halloween,"
    black cat driving jack–o'–lantern
    carriage, pulled by six mice,
    checked border, 1912 . . . .   **15.00**
  Wall Decoration, jack–o'–lantern,
    cardboard, cutout, orange tissue
    dec, double sided, 2 x 6" **55.00**
Memorial Day, post card, "Memorial
    Day Greetings," flag, draped red,
    white, and blue curtain, soldier's hat,
    crossed swords, gun, and bugle, fort
    scene background, 1909 . . . .   **6.00**
Mother's Day, magazine tear sheet,
    Whitman's Chocolates and Confec-
    tions adv, Pioneer woman statue illus   **8.00**
New Year's
  Banner, "Happy New Year," silver
    border, 1930 . . . .   **10.00**

Centerpiece, cardboard, Father Time, scythe, emb "New Year's Greetings" **25.00**

Children's Book, *Miss Flora McFlimsey And The Baby New Year,* Mariana, Lothrop, Lee & Shepard, 1951, dj **22.00**

Hat, cone shape, cardboard, crepe paper dec, cutout silver foil, 1928 .... **12.00**

Invitation, litho paper, Father Time, package, 1930 .... **7.00**

Menu, New Year's Eve, Fountainbleau, Miami Beach, litho paper, 1957 .... **10.00**

Noisemaker, horn, paper over cardboard, silver and black, 1930 ..... **5.00**

Photograph
  Copacabana Night Club, New York City, New Year's Eve party, 1948, framed **35.00**
  Times Square, New York, New Year's Eve, 1953 .... **15.00**

Post Card
  "Happy New Year," baby surrounded by flowers, emb, German, early 20th C **5.00**
  "New Year's Greetings," Kewpie ringing bells, Rose O'Neill, 1910 **35.00**

Ticket, admission to New Year's Eve Festival, Concord, NH, festival vignette, blue printing, white background, 1858 .... **50.00**

St Patrick's Day

Hat, top hat, cardboard, foil covered, shamrock dec **20.00**

Nut Cup, crepe paper, green and white, double frill, cardboard shamrock **5.00**

Place Card, leprechaun, pot of gold and name tag **5.00**

Post Card, "The Charm of the Morn to You, Here's Wishing You A Bright and Happy St Patrick's Day," girl holding flower bouquet, 1916 ..... **15.00**

Sheet Music
  Danny Boy, 1940s **5.00**
  When Irish Eyes Are Smiling, 1930s **10.00**

Tablecloth, printed leprechauns and shamrocks, green and white, orig cellophane package, mid 1900s ... **10.00**

Thanksgiving

Advertising Trade Card, "Thanksgiving Greetings," emb, Acme Stove Co adv, 1936 .... **7.00**

Book, *Thanksgiving,* Dennison, 1930 **10.00**

Greeting Card, "Happy Thanksgiving," turkey, mid 20th C **5.00**

Menu, Hotel Astor, Thanksgiving dinner, early 20th C **10.00**

Napkin, printed, Pilgrims and Indians, cellophane package, 1940s **5.00**

Paper Dolls, newspaper sheet, *Boston*

  Sunday Globe, table and family, 1895, 9½ x 8" **40.00**

Photograph, grade school play, Landing of the Pilgrims, 1940 .... **15.00**

Post Card
  Corn cob design, emb, 1910 ...... **6.00**
  Turkey and pumpkin, printed **4.00**

Print, Landing of the Pilgrims, Currier and Ives, 13 x 17" **85.00**

Puzzle, Thanksgiving, Jig of the Week, No. 8, 1932, 300 diecut cardboard pcs, 10¼ x 13½", orig box **15.00**

Tablecloth, Pilgrims and Indians at feast, matching napkins, set....... **25.00**

Valentine's Day

Banner, "Happy Valentine's Day," printed paper, mid 20th C **15.00**

Box, Valentine greeting cards, 1950 .. **15.00**

Candy Box, heart shape, cardboard, red satin and gold lace dec, center with doves **35.00**

Cookbook, *Valentine Queen of Hearts,* Jell–O, early 20th C **18.00**

Diecut, cherubs and flowers, orig package, early 20th C **35.00**

Greeting Card
  Easel Back, girl, birds, flowers, and hearts, Tuck **35.00**
  Fold–out, lace dec, cartouche of woman, 1940............... **15.00**
  Mechanical, boy on skis, winter scene, verse **25.00**

Sheet Music, *My Funny Valentine* **5.00**

Wall Decoration, cardboard, emb cherub with quiver **15.00**

HORSE

Reference: Jim and Nancy Schaut, *Horsin' Around Horse Collectibles,* L–W Book Sales, 1990.

Advertising Trade Card
  Emory's Family Pills, horse–drawn carriage **5.00**
  Galena Axle Grease Co **5.00**
  Grant & Besse Clothiers, two horses and man, farm scene **12.00**
  Lion Coffee, lady riding horse **12.00**
  Star Cough Drops, horsehead **4.00**

Almanac, August Flower and German Syrup, 1913, man on horse, 6¾ x 9".. **15.00**

Book
  A Treatise On The Horse And His Diseases, 1880, 90 pgs **20.00**
  Old Bones the Wonder Horse, 1918 .. **10.00**
  The Black Stallion, Walter Farley, first edition, dj **15.00**

Booklet
  How To Ride & Train the Saddle Horse **5.00**
  Introductory Mail Course in Horsemanship, Jesse Beery, 1913 .... **8.00**

Box, Kendall's Spavin Cure, imp horse
  motif, 8½ x 10½ x 8½" **80.00**
Calendar
  1889, horse seated at desk, E L Mc-
    Clain Mfg Co, Greenfield, OH, 15 x
    20" **140.00**
  1907, cardboard, cowgirl on horse,
    Dousman Milling adv, 10 x 20" **50.00**
  1935, Lone Ranger and Silver illus . . .   **75.00**
  1950, Dodge Stables and Castleton
    Farm. **45.00**
  1952, Mobil Oil, flying red horse **8.00**
Catalog
  American Horse Goods, Detroit,
    1910, 108 pgs **45.00**
  American Shearer Manufacturing Co,
    Nashua, NH, 1892, 84 pgs, horse
    clipping devices. **65.00**
  Horse Buggy, 1910 . . . .   **65.00**
  Neverslip Horseshoe Co, Boston,
    1885, 48 pgs **18.00**
  S D Myres Saddle Co, Fine Stock Sad-
    dles, Ranch Supplies and Art Lea-
    ther Goods, El Paso, TX, c1930, 80
    pgs **50.00**
Coloring Book, Hi–Yo Silver, Silver illus
  on cov, cutout and coloring book,
  1953, 8½ x 11" **20.00**
Flyer, Professor Beery's Horse Breaking
  Outfit, 1913, 12 x 18" **6.00**
Label
  Apple, Blue Winner, Washington state
    apples, cowboy on horseback,
    rodeo scene **4.00**
  Cigar, Bohemian and Kate Sparks, two
    horses pulling buggy **75.00**
  Lemon, Gateway, two horseback
    riders, redwood forest, dark blue
    background, Lemon Grove **2.00**
  Pear, Diamond S, California **7.00**
Magazine
  Life, December 22, 1952, Midget
    Horse **5.00**
  Saddle and Bridle, 1931 . . . .   **5.00**
  Western Horseman, Volume 1, #1,
    1935 . . . .   **15.00**
Magazine Tear Sheet, adv, Cream of
  Wheat, "Where The Mail Goes–
  Cream of Wheat Goes," man on
  horseback delivering mail, framed . . .   **25.00**
Post Card
  Coca–Cola, horse and delivery
    wagon, c1900 . . . .   **95.00**
  Three draft horses, head illus, Ger-
    man, early 1900s **5.00**
Poster
  Anheuser Busch, 50th Anniversary,
    1933–83, Clydesdales horses **8.00**
  Kendall's Spavin Cure adv, litho illus   **400.00**
  Prescott Rodeo, 100th Anniversary,
    June 30th–July 4th, Prescott, AZ,
    1988 . . . .   **25.00**

Cigar Label, Nebraska Girl, green, red, and gold, 10 x 6", $30.00.

Saddle Horse Contests, Beer Exhibi-
  tions, Dayton OH Fairgrounds,
  1913, framed **300.00**
Print
  Currier and Ives, Celebrated Trotting
    Horse Henry **195.00**
  Hagerman, Kurt, Kentucky Tradition–
    The Derby, Churchill Downs, etch-
    ing, sgd in pencil lower right, titled
    in pencil lower left, 6½ x 9" **50.00**
Prize List
  National Horse Show Association,
    19th Annual Exhibition, Madison
    Square Garden, entry blank, cov
    with black and gold lettering on red
    ground, 1903 . . . .   **25.00**
  Norfolk Horse Show Association, Sec-
    ond Annual Exhibition, entry form,
    cov with team of horses pulling
    coach **20.00**
Puzzle
  Follow Your Dream, Springbok, A
    Mini Jigsaw Puzzle, Pegasus illus . .   **5.00**
  Jingle Bells, horse–drawn sleigh,
    Strauss, 1960s **15.00**
  Old Dobbin Scroll Puzzle, Milton
    Bradley Co, 1920s, set of 2 diecut
    cardboard 7½ x 10¼" puzzles, 15
    pcs, orig box **12.00**
  Wild Horses, Jig of the Week, #5,
    1933 . . . .   **25.00**
Reward of Merit, horse with dog illus,
  Bufford, poem on back, issued by Mas-
  sachusetts Society for the Prevention
  of Cruelty to Animals, 96 Tremont St,
  Boston, MA, 3 x 5⁵⁄₁₆" **55.00**
Sheet Music
  A Little White Gardenia, All the King's
    Horses, Famous Music Corp, man
    on black horse illus on cov **5.00**
  *Never Swap Horses When You're
    Crossing a Stream*, Woodrow Wil-
    son on horseback portrait, 1916 . . .   **15.00**
Sign
  Belgian Stallion, cardboard, 1935, 12
    x 16". **15.00**

Dr A C Daniels Horse Medicine, horse
head illus, 17 x 22" **395.00**
Long & Alistatter Rakes and Cultiva-
tors, various horse–drawn equip-
ment scenes, 16 x 23" **500.00**
Stock Certificate, Weaverville and Shasta
Wagon Road Company, 1860, three
shares, litho vignette of horse drawn
covered wagon **225.00**

HORSE RACING

References: Willis Ackerman (Comp.), *Dan Patch
Mass Merchandiser,* published by compiler,
1981; Roderick A. Malloy, *Malloy's Sports Collectibles Value Guide,* Wallace–Homestead,
1993.

Advertising Trade Card, Arbuckle Coffee,
horse racing view on back, 1892. . . . .   **3.50**
Book, *The American Racing Manual,*
1947, 978 pgs, track diagrams, photos,
and record **15.00**
Bumper Sticker, Carolina Cup, 1969, 9½
x 4". **2.50**
Cabinet Card, woman sulky driver hold-
ing buggy whip, dated 1892 . . . .   **40.00**
Catalog
Gilliam Manufacturing Company,
Gilliam Horse Boots and Racing
Specialties, Canton, OH, 1903, 40
pgs. **100.00**
John Middling, Middling Two
Wheelers, 1910, 34 pgs, harness
racing sulkies, six different models,
prices and descriptions **50.00**
Game
Derby Day, 72" foldout playing board,
six wood horses and hurdles, Parker
Brothers, 1959 copyright **40.00**
Kentucky Derby Racing, Whitman, 1938   **18.00**
The Derby Steeple Chase, multi-
colored litho race track board, four

**Wine Label, Tote, blue and red, "The
Sportsman's Tonic," 3¼ x 4¼", $3.50.**

wood counters, 18 wood chips, and
spinner, orig box, c1890 . . . .   **85.00**
Label, cigar
Alcazar, race horse, colorful grand-
stand background **8.00**
La Diana, female jockey, horse race
scene **15.00**
Sport of Kings, race horses. **5.00**
Magazine
Sports Illustrated
1955, January 10, Santa Anita Horse
Race. **8.00**
1955, February 28, Hialeah Horse
Race. **10.00**
1958, April 28, Silky Sullivan **10.00**
TV Guide, June 10–16, 1950, Thor-
oughbred Horse Racing cov **40.00**
Photograph
Portrait, race horse, black and white,
c1920 . . . .   **15.00**
Saratoga Finish, horse and buggies,
track, and people standing by picket
fence, 1870s **15.00**
Program
Arlington Park, Chicago, June 23,
1943, 4 x 8½" **15.00**
Delaware Park, June 29, 1945. . . . . . .   **5.00**
Kentucky Derby, May 4, 1963, 4 x 9"   **18.00**
Sheet Music, *Dan Patch March,* photo on
cov. **50.00**
Sign, Dark Horse Cigar adv, two trotting
race horses, 12 x 23" **65.00**
Ticket, Kentucky Derby, Saturday, May
2, 1936, 2¼ x 3½". **8.00**

HOUSEHOLD

Reference: Linda Campbell Franklin, *300 Years
of Housekeeping Collectibles,* Books Americana,
1992.

Advertising Trade Card
Acme White Lead & Color Works,
Granite Floor Paint **5.00**
Berry Bros Hard Oil Finish, emb, Un-
cle Sam, 7 x 4" **45.00**
Conqueror Clothes Wringer, fold up . .   **12.00**
Easy Washer, mechanical **10.00**
Fairbank's Scouring Soap, mech-
ancial, lady's arm moves down
scouring pan **40.00**
Freese's Clementine Glue, two illus,
1885 . . . .   **5.00**
Gold Dust Twins, "Makes Housework
Easy," diecut, washing dishes **60.00**
Hartshorn Shade Rollers, baby pulls
down shade, mother napping in
chair. **4.00**
Hunters Sifter, Fred S Myer's Mfg Co,
lady wearing cap and apron, sifting
flour into bowl **4.00**

Luca's Co, Paints and Varnishes, factory scenes on both sides 6.00
New Household, White Warner & Co Stoves & Ranges, woman and children, kitchen scene 14.00
Sapolio, Enoch Morgan & Sons, boy wearing fancy clothes 2.50
Van Stan's Stratena Glue, black man lecturing, 1880s 32.00
Webb's Superior Stove Polish, green on gold 2.00
Box
  Eagle Asbestos Stove Lining, cardboard, 2³⁄₄ x 3³⁄₄" 8.00
  Honor Bright Soap, cardboard, 2¹⁄₂ x 3³⁄₄" 5.00
  Reynold's Rat Driver Poison, cardboard, c1900, 3¹⁄₂ x 7" 5.00
Brochure
  Gold Dust Brite Spots, 16 pgs, black lettering, yellow ground, 3⁷⁄₈ x 6" . .   25.00
  Grandpa's Wonder Soap, 3 x 5" 5.00
  Magic Yeast, 3 x 5" 4.00
Calendar, 1929, Clothesline, full pad . . .   60.00
Catalog
  Buffalo Mfg Co, Water Filters, Water Coolers, Buffalo, NY, July, 1903, 128 pgs, spittoons to bathroom fixtures, chafing dishes to water coolers 100.00
  Day and Night Solar Heating Co, c1912, 8 pgs, fold out type, shows homes equipped with solar water heating device 50.00
  Incandescent Light and Stove Co, Make Home Homelike by Using the F–P Home Lighting and Cooking Plant, Cincinnati, OH, 1905–15, 36 pgs 12.00
  James McCutcheon & Co, New York, NY, ND, CA, 1929, 16 pgs, housekeeping linens, 7¹⁄₂ x 10¹⁄₂" 16.00
  Kirkman & Sons, Kirkman Premiums, 1925, 16 pgs, soap box coupons for household premiums 20.00
  National Washboard Company, c1925, 36 pgs, color illus of washboards 100.00
  Puritan Lamp & Shade Co, Puritan Lamps and Shades, Special Reference #2, 1925, 20 pgs, floor lamps and shades 50.00
  Rathbone and Sard & Co, New Acorn Parlor Stove for 1887, Chicago, IL, 1887, 8 pgs 15.00
  Savage Arms Corp, Freedom from All Washday Bondage, Utica, NY, c1930, 16 pgs, washer/dryer combination 35.00
  The Holmquist & Co, Chicago, IL, No. 12, 1905, 40 pgs, Curtain Stretchers, Ladders, Woodenware, Sundries,

black and white product illus, 3¹⁄₂ x 6¹⁄₂" 15.00
United Lighting Fixture Co, c1914, 4 pgs, lamps and lighting fixtures 85.00
Walker & Pratt Mfg Co, Trade Price List of Walker–Crawford Furnaces, Boston, MA, 1910, 22 pgs, coal and wood burning furnaces 30.00
Label, broom
  Capitol, Washington DC, capitol building 50
  Dixie, black man seated on bench, playing banjo 1.00
  Winner, lady holding torch 50
Magazine, Good Housekeeping, 1920–29 . . . .   8.00
Magazine Advertisement
  Preston's Braided Wire Carpet Whip, Hollow Cable Mfg Co, Hornell, NY, House Furnishing Review, December, 1910 . . . .   8.00
  Silver's Patent Broom, C A Clegg & Co, NY, Harper's Weekly, April 11, 1869 . . . .   12.00
  Sweeperette Co, Grand Rapids, MI, woman holding broom, Century, December, 1895 . . . .   10.00
  The Heaven Air Purifier Company, Chicago, IL, Century, May 1883 . . .   15.00
Napkin, crepe paper, cocktail size, cream, scalloped diecut edges, printed

Magazine Tear Sheet, Nesco Oil Cook Stove Royal Enameled Ware, graniteware adv., *Woman's World*, 10 x 13" trimmed, 1920s, $12.00.

borders, red, green, yellow and blue dots, orig cardboard box of 48, early 1930s. **5.00**
Sign, Dixon's Stove Polish, 6 x 8" **65.00**
Sticker, New York Housewares, Atlantic City, emb, blue and white, Art Deco design, 1940 . . . . **5.00**

HUNTING

References: Ralf Coykendall Jr., *Coykendall's Second Sporting Collectibles Price Guide*, Lyons & Burford, 1992; Ralf Coykendall Jr., *Coykendall's Sporting Collectibles Price Guide*, Lyons & Burford, 1991; Jim and Vivian Karsnitz, *Sporting Collectibles*, Schiffer Publishing, 1992; Bob and Beverly Strauss, *American Sporting Advertising, Volume 1* (1987, 1992 value update), *Volume 2* (1990, 1992 value update), published by authors, distributed by L–W Book Sales.

Almanac, black and yellow hunting vignettes on cov, Burdock Blood Bitters promotional, 1887 . . . . **20.00**
Book
  Curtis, P, *Game Shooting*, 1927, 279 pgs. **8.50**
  Fur Trapping: A Book of Instructions; To Trap, Snare, Poison & Shoot, 1934, 180 pgs, illus **15.00**
  Koller, Larry, *The Treasury of Hunting*, New York, 1965, first edition. **20.00**
  O'Connor, Jack, *The Art of Hunting Big Game in America*, New York, 1967, first edition. **25.00**
  Van Dyke, Theodore S, *The Still Hunter*, New York, 1943, dj **45.00**
  Whelan, Townsend, *The Hunting Rifle*, Harrisburg, PA, 1940 . . . . **40.00**

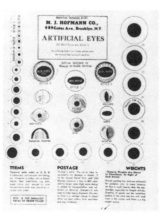

Catalog, Artificial Eyes, M. J. Hofmann Co., taxidermists' supplies, orange-and-black covers, illustrated black and white, 28 pages, 8½ x 11", 1959, $17.50.

Jigsaw Puzzle, Madmar, double-sided, hunting scene one side, The Mayflower Compact other side, 10 x 8", $25.00.

Calendar
  1919, United States Cartridge Company, hunter with bag of ruffled grouse **300.00**
  1921, Hercules Powder Company, titled "Outnumbered," three boys hunting rabbit, Arthur Fuller **150.00**
  1923, Peters Cartridge Co, titled "Outpointed," hunter, dog, and porcupine, Goodwin. **200.00**
  1930, Winchester Arms Company, hunter holding calendar pages **300.00**
Catalog
  Howe Fur Co, Coopers Mills, ME, 1945, 72 pgs, trapping and hunting equipment, 8¼ x 10". **25.00**
  The Archers Company, Fine Bows and Arrows, Pinehurst, NC, 1932, 32 pgs. **25.00**
Label, cigar box, Hunters Return, winter hunting scene **75.00**
Magazine
  Field & Stream, 1955. . . . . **8.00**
  Hunter, Trader, Trapper, August, 1923, hunter sitting on top of alligator on cov, 7 x 9" **8.50**

Manual, Gentleman Beer, hunting and
trapping, 1947 . . . .   **28.00**
Paperback Book, *Lynch's Scientific
Methods of Trapping*, 1928, 104 pgs,
illus **12.00**
Poster
Remington, hunters approaching bear,
N C Wyeth **350.00**
Union Metallic Cartridge Company,
hunter, hound, and mountain lion
scene, Johnson, 1906 . . . .   **350.00**
Sign, "No Gunning or Trespassing, Pri-
vate Property, No Entering or Hunting
Allowed," white cardboard, black let-
tering, Pennsylvania law, 1943, 10 x
13" **30.00**

ICE CREAM

Collectors' Club: The Ice Screamers, P.O. Box
5387, Lancaster, PA 17601.

Advertising Trade Card
American Machine Co Ice Cream
Freezer, children playing around
freezer **4.00**
Dairylea Ice Cream, diecut, mechani-
cal, boy with cap, rolls eyes, Ger-
many **30.00**
Gem Freezer, The Best In The World,
girl and ice cream freezer illus **12.00**
Reid's Ice Cream, "She had but one
tooth! And that was for Reid's Ice
Cream," old lady with one tooth . . .   **15.00**
Semon Ice Cream, diecut, frog, printed
both sides **25.00**
Book, *Theory and Practice of Ice Cream
Making,* Hugo Sommer, 1938 . . . .   **25.00**
Booklet
Eskimo Pie, premiums, 2 pgs, 1952 . . .   **15.00**
White Mountain Ice Cream, woman
making ice cream **25.00**
Box
Bing Crosby Ice Cream **5.00**
Cool Farm Ice Cream, unused and
unfolded, set of 3 . . . .   **17.00**
Catalog
Frank A Beeler, Ice Cream Maker's
Formulary & Price List, 1910–15 . . .   **25.00**
Thos Mills & Bros, Inc, Philadelphia,
Ice Cream Manufacturers' Equip-
ment, #31, early 1900s, 60 pgs,
black and white illus, 5³⁄₄ x 8³⁄₄" . . .   **65.00**
Cookbook, Dainty Dishes For All Year
Round, Shepard's Lightning Freezer,
Mrs S T Rorer, 1899, ice cream recipes
and kitchen tool illus, 64 pgs, 7 x 4" . .   **15.00**
Greeting Card, Christmas, Breyer Ice
Cream, c1920 . . . .   **20.00**

Catalog, Thomas Mills & Bro., Inc., Philadelphia, PA, Ice Cream Manufacturers'
Equipment, printed black on orange
covers, black-and-white product illustrations, No. 31, 60 pages, 5¹⁄₂ x 8³⁄₄",
$35.00.

Hat, Rich Valley Milk–Ice Cream, paper,
overseas service type, red and white . .   **5.00**
Paper Doll, Carnation Ice Cream, 1950s,
doll and three outfits **5.00**
Playing Cards
Dolly Madison Ice Cream, Dolly Mad-
ison Quality Checked Selected Ice
Cream, blue, red, and white graph-
ics, yellow background **5.00**
Kemply Ice Cream Co, stemmed dish
of ice cream, geometric border **5.00**
Post Card
Bodle's Ice Cream Store, diecut. **8.00**
Telling's Ice Cream **1.50**
Poster, Lemon Flake Ice Cream, 1945–
50, large dish of ice cream illus, 12 x
21" **25.00**
Sheet Music
*I Scream, You Scream, We All Scream
for Ice Cream,* Howard Johnson,
Billy Molly, and Robert King **15.00**
Oh My Eskimo Pie **25.00**
Sign
Banquet Ice Cream, Brunette Beauty
Sundae, cardboard, Walter Neilly &
Co, 25 x 13" **200.00**
Eskimo Pie 10¢, cardboard, igloo, es-
kimo, and polar bear scene, 1922,
19¹⁄₄ x 9¹⁄₂".   **150.00**
Snappy Pac–kit–Ice Cream, Ready to
Carry . . . 10¢, 18¹⁄₂ x 7¹⁄₂" **10.00**

INDIAN

References: Dawn E. Reno, *The Official Identification and Price Guide to American Indian Collectibles,* House of Collectibles, 1988, Robert Ward, *Investment Guide To North American Real Photo Postcards,* Antique Paper Guild, 1991.

Advertising Trade Card, Magnolia Ham, Indian theme **18.00**

Booklet

Cheyenne River & Standing Rock Indian Lands, 1909, 12 pgs, issued by Dept of Interior **6.50**

Epochs of US History, Indian chief image on cov, Chase & Sanborn adv, 8 pgs, 1914 . . . .   **15.00**

Calendar

1922, Ulmer Installment Co, Round Oak Stoves & Ranges, emb, Indian calling mouse, full pad, 21 x 11" . . .   **160.00**

1924, Hupmobile, Indian, people, and sedan illus, 12 x 36" **145.00**

Check, Seneca Nation of Indians, Brant, NY, Bank of North Collens, NY, April 26, 1897, payable to Wm Mohawk . . .   **18.00**

Cookbook, *Delightful Cooking with the Three Great Products from Corn,* Corn Products Refining Co, NY, full color cov with Mazola Indian maiden and three products, 64 pgs, c1920, 5 x 6½"   **12.50**

Document

1828, House of Representatives, report on emigrating tribes of Southeastern Indians, lists eight tribes moving west of Mississippi, 3½ pgs   **18.00**

1836, House of Representatives, Choctaw land claim, 1 pg **10.00**

1900, bank draft, Whitewood Baking Co, Whitewood, SD, Indian roping buffalo vignette, black printing, blue paper, red documentary stamp on front **75.00**

Drawing, Indian girl, pen and ink, Charlie Bear, 1975, 8 x 6" **18.00**

View Card, Cherokee Indian Reservation, NC, 12 card color foldout, 4¼ x 6" folded, 1936, $5.00.

Label

Apple, Skookum, smiling Indian, cartoon face, red and blue apples, green background **1.00**

Cigar Box, Red Queen, Indian maiden with bow and arrow **35.00**

Newspaper, *Lynn News,* October 29, 1852, Sioux Warrior's Race for Life headline **28.00**

Painting

Becker, Frederick W, Desert Hot Wells, oil on board, dated on back "1966," framed, 9 x 12" **250.00**

Sweezy, Carl, War Chief, oil on board, titled and sgd, framed **425.00**

Poster, Great Pueblo Revolt, Tri-Centennial 1680–1980, three Pueblo Indians on top of adobe buildings, Parker Boyiddle, 24 x 16" **20.00**

Premium, puzzle, Straight Arrow Indian Jigsaw, Nabisco, 1949, orig envelope   **145.00**

Print

Kiowa Warrior, Parker Boyiddle **20.00**

The Deer Slayer, Austin Deuel, Indian hunter holding bow and arrow, rocky snow covered scene, numbered and sgd lower left, 23¾ x 17½" **30.00**

Puzzle

Jack and Ann Visit Old Chief–Tan, Chief–Tan Shoes, 18 pcs, 1930s, 3¾ x 6½" **15.00**

Keeping the Tryst, Indian maiden, canoe, and lake scene, Muddle series, Santway Photo–Craft Co, Inc, Watertown, NY, orig box, 15 x 11" **12.00**

Sign, Indian Medicine Co, Indian medicine man illus, matted and framed, 24 x 15" **100.00**

INSURANCE

References: Ted Hake, *Hake's Guide To Advertising Collectibles,* Wallace–Homestead, 1992; Sharon and Bob Huxford, *Huxford's Collectible Advertising: An Illustrated Value Guide,* Collector Books, 1993.

Advertising Cover, Ohio Armers Insurance Co, blue window, 1885, orig envelope **40.00**

Advertising Trade Card

Home Insurance Co, girl standing by tree. **4.00**

Metropolitan Life Insurance, mechanical, titled "The Lost Jap," movable wheel, solve puzzle **115.00**

North American Fire Insurance Co, Continental Banknote Co, engraved, black and white ferocious bear attack scene **200.00**

Blotter, Great American Insurance Company, NY, printed, red on white, 9 x 4", 1929, $5.00.

Phoenix Insurance Co, yellow and gold **14.00**
Prudential Life Insurance Co, salesman at door **8.00**
United States Mutual, diecut, fold to form box **38.00**
Booklet
Four Wheel Fun, issued by Fireman's Fund Insurance Co. **15.00**
The Metropolitan Mother Goose, Metropolitan Life Insurance, color illus, 1920s........................ **25.00**
Broadside, Hanover Fire Insurance, engraved, green printing, black background, text on back, 1875, 9 x 5½" .. **30.00**
Calendar
1889, Metropolitan Life Insurance Co, color illus of children and winter scene, 4¾ x 6¼" **8.00**
1890, Aetna Insurance Co, cardboard, framed, 26 x 19". **290.00**
1896, Hartford Fire Insurance **12.00**
1898, John Hancock Insurance **25.00**
1899, Metropolitan Life Insurance, eight children, framed, 12 x 20" ... **85.00**
1904, Equitable Life Insurance **25.00**

1930–31, New York Life Insurance .. **10.00**
1958, National Life Insurance Co, bear illus **10.00**
Certificate, earnings, Atlantic Mutual Insurance Co, large eagle vignette, Root & Anthony, NY, revenue stamps **35.00**
Cookbook
Teddy Bears, Prudential Insurance, little girl serving two teddy bears tea illus on cov, 1910 .... **25.00**
The Family Food Supply, Metropolitan Life Insurance, 1934, 23 pgs **5.00**
Document
Aetna Insurance Co, 1868, policy, Treasury stamps, eagle vignette.... **15.00**
Peoples Equitable Mutual Fire Insurance Co, 1867, 7½ x 9" **8.00**
Needle Book, The National Life and Accident Insurance Co, shield shape, WSM Radio adv on int. cov, 1930s ... **10.00**
Pass, Waiting Room Privileges, New York Life Building, Omaha, NE, printed, black and white **5.00**
Sign, Teutonia Insurance Co, Teutonian hordes crushing Roman warriors, ornate border, c1872, 24 x 19" **350.00**
Stock Certificate, Harmonia Fire Insurance, 1927..................... **15.00**

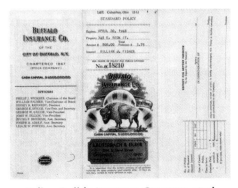

Policy, Buffalo Insurance Company, steel engraved logo, 2 pages, 3⅝ x 8⅜" closed size, 1948, $8.00.

INTERIOR DECORATING

Advertising Trade Card
Atkinson & Co House Furnishings, Boston, parlor scene **12.00**
C Wood & Co, Paper Hangings, Taunton, MA, black and white, Hancock sketch................ **10.00**
Kilborn's Health Bath, black and white his and her tub on front, adv with price on back.................. **32.00**
Vincent, Barstow & Co, beautiful room scene **50.00**
Book, *Ladie's Home Journal Book of Interior Decorating,* E Halsey, 1959, 224 pgs.......................... **15.00**

Booklet
Interior Decorating Home Study, set of
12, 1928 .... **20.00**
Sherwin–Williams On Home Deco-
rating, 1935, 32 pgs, 7 x 8" **8.50**
Catalog
C A Schmidt, Book of Designs, Uphol-
stery, Drapery, Fancy Drapery and
Mantel Trimmings, NY, 1877, 34
pgs **300.00**
Johnson Co, SC, Suggestions For
Parquetry Floors, 1893, 16 pgs **75.00**
Lowe Brothers, Paints and Varnishes,
Practical Hints on Painting and Dec-
orating with Pictorial Color Sugges-
tions, Dayton, OH, 1935, 62 pgs,
color interior schemes **20.00**
Montgomery Ward & Co, 60th Anni-
versary Style Book, Chicago, IL,
1932, 84 pgs, wallpaper **75.00**
Olson Rug Company, The New Olson
Duo–Velvety Rugs, Chicago and
NY, 1928, 32 pgs.............. **15.00**
Sherwin Williams Co, Stencils & Stencil Materials, Cleveland, OH, 1912
40 pgs **15.00**
Standard Textile Products Co, Sanitas
Modern Wall Covering and Its Uses,
NY, 1915–20, 28 pgs, int. cov
pocket with two wallpaper samples
and four color printed samples
sheets showing variety effects **35.00**
Upholstery Supply Co, Milwaukee,
c1920, 171 pgs, 11 x 8"......... **5.00**
Vetter Mfg Co Standard Design Book,
1919, 368 pgs, sash and door,
stairways, built-ins, porches, leaded
window sections **18.00**
Wheeling Corrugating Co, No. 313,
Wheeling Ceilings, Wheeling, WV,
1914, 270 pgs, wide variety of
pressed metal ceilings **100.00**

Catalog, Color Perfect Wallpaper, Sears Roebuck and Co., portfolio with samples, 7¹⁄₄ x 9", 1940, $35.00.

Sign, Dobson Carpets, cardboard, factory scene, orig frame, 28 x 38"...... **90.00**

JEWELRY

Reference: Lillian Baker, *Twentieth Century Fashionable Plastic Jewelry,* Collector Books, 1992; Roseann Ettinger, *Popular Jewelry: 1840–1940,* Schiffer Publishing, 1990; Harrice Simons Miller, *The Official Identification and Price Guide To Costume Jewelry,* House of Collectibles, 1990; Penny Proddow, Debra Healy, and Marion Fasel, *Hollywood Jewels: Movies, Jewelry, Stars,* Harry N. Abrams, 1992.

Advertising Trade Card
Boss Pat Cases, Frear, Jeweler **15.00**
Giles Brothers, Manf'g Jewelers diecut,
gold and black design, beige back-
ground **25.00**
Mermod and Jaccard Jewelry Co, St
Louis, diamond ring illus **20.00**
T B Hagstoz & Co Diamonds, Philadel-
phia, business card style **20.00**
W Forsyth Jewelers, 1861, black and
white printing **30.00**
Book
Cut–Steel and Berlin Iron Jewelry,
Anne Clifford, South Brunswick, A S
Barnes, 1971, 95 pgs, dj, 6¹⁄₂ x 8¹⁄₂" **65.00**
*Engraved Gems: Their History and an
Elaborate View of Their Place In Art,*
Maxwell Sommerville, Philadel-
phia, 1889, gilt maroon cloth cov .. **300.00**
The Crown Jewels of England, Sir
George Younghusband and Cyril
Davenport, 1919, London, limited
edition, gilt red cloth cov......... **50.00**
The Cultured Pearl, Jewel of Japan,
Norine C Reece, Rutland, Charles
Tuttle, 1958, 107 pgs, 5 x 7¹⁄₂".... **20.00**
Catalog
A C Becken Co, Chicago, IL, c1926,
414 pgs, 8¹⁄₂ x 11" **37.00**
Daniel Low & Co, Inc, Salem, MA,
1926, 164 pgs, 9¹⁄₂ x 6¹⁄₂" **30.00**
Irons & Russell, Illustrated Catalogue
of Solid Gold Society Emblems,
Pins, Buttons, Charms, Providence,
RI, 1895, 246 pgs.............. **85.00**
Jason Weiler & Sons, Jewelers, 1920.. **22.00**
Providence Jewelry Co, St Louis, MO,
1887, 208 pgs, 6³⁄₄ x 9³⁄₄" **115.00**
R Chester Frost & Co, Chicago, IL,
1890, 147 pgs, 6¹⁄₄ x 9¹⁄₄" **70.00**
Richter & Phillips Co Jewelry Catalog,
1939, 400 pgs, color photos **10.00**
Sigler's Jewelery Fashions, Cleveland,
OH, 1907, 4 pgs **15.00**
Stephen Lane Folger, Manufacturing
Jeweler, NY, 1910, 20 pgs, club and

Catalog, A Treasure House of Charms, Charm and Treasure, Inc., NY, 138 pages, black-and-white photos, 9 x 12", 1950s, $20.00.

college pins and rings, gold and silver medals, watches, diamonds, and jewelry...................... 35.00

T W Lind Co, Jewelers' Findings, Galleries, Ornaments, Settings, Pin Stems, Providence, RI, c1915, 32 pgs........................ 50.00

W Green & Co, Inc, Illustrated Catalogue of Jewelers' Supplies, New York, NY, 1911, 563 pgs, tools and supplies for jewelry making and repair 250.00

Magazine, *Life,* November 24, 1952, Jewelry in Fashion............... 5.00

Magazine Cover, six strand rhinestone collar, Pauline Trigère, *Harper's Bazaar,* November, 1962 .... 12.00

Magazine Tear Sheet, adv, Trifari Jewelry, *Mademoiselle,* August, 1948.... 9.00

Newspaper Advertisement, Napier Jewlery, *New York Times,* April 2, 1929 .... 6.00

JUDAICA

Album, Yiddish Theatre, Zalme Zylberzweig, Yiddish and English text, illus, gilt stamped cloth cov, 1937.... 75.00

Book
Aspects of Jewish Power in the US, Vol 4, Dearborn Publishing, 1922 ..... 5.00

The Jews in Philadelphia, Hyman P Rosenbach, Edward Stern and Co, 1883, first edition, cloth cov 132.00

The Manners and Customs of the Jews and Other Nations Mentioned in the Bible, George Stokes, first American edition, cloth cov............... 165.00

Booklet, The Shadow that Haunts the Jew, Malbert, 1920 .... 4.00

Calendar, 1766–67, columned information on weekly Torah and Haftorah

readings, festival celebrations, monthly equivalents of secular calendar........................... 190.00

Cookbook, *Council Cookbook,* published by San Francisco Section of the Council of Jewish Women, stamped cloth cov...................... 350.00

Diecut, Von Stufe zu Stufe, Fuld & Co, NY copyright, 3⅝ x 2⅞".......... 10.00

Certificate, L'Shanah Tovah Shipskaart, entitles bearer blessings for New Year, Yiddish print, 1920s 140.00

Letter
1937, to Solomon Joseph Sher from Shalom Eliezer Halberstam, approbation for a book, 1 pg........... 550.00

1949, October 17, to Mr William Houseman of *Look* magazine from Eddie Cantor, complimenting him on Israel article 100.00

1954, November 17, Israeli Embassy stationery to Mr Daniel Mich, reply to questions for poll conducted on UN efforts for peace............ 150.00

Magazine, *Life,* June 13, 1955, Judaism article 5.00

Manual, *HaDibbur Halvri,* M Krinsky, book for Hebrew beginners, illus, 1905 .... 80.00

Map, Historical Map of Palestine Or The Holy Land, engraved, published by Augustus Mitchell, framed, 1849 .... 250.00

Newspaper
Naye Arbeiter Velt, 1926, Yiddish text, Department of Education stamp ... 50.00

The Jewish American, Detroit, July 13, 1906, 8 pgs, Jewish related news and adv 12.00

Post Card, Prayer Lesson For Confirmation, 1910 .... 4.50

Poster
Jewish National Fund, 1950–63, colorful scene of children farming on Kibbutz, 19 x 13"............... 40.00

Jewish Welfare Board, "Civilian When We Go Through This We Need All

**Diecut, red, yellow, and blue, 4 x 2⅞",
$20.00.**

the Help and Comfort You Can Give," soldier calling out with raised left hand and Star of David, blue and brown illus, cream background, 1918 . . . . **150.00**

Scrapbook, contains 1,000 post cards, Jewish images and traditions, color pictorial dj, 1897–1917 . . . . **145.00**

Songbook, Blau–Wiess Liederbuch, Jewish folksongs, 1914 . . . . **75.00**

Stock Certificate, The Jewish Colonial Trust, five shares, issued to Dr Chamitzer, blue border, red seal, Palestine life and industry vignettes, 1900 **385.00**

Tobacco Card, Jewish Reader, Churchmann Cigarettes, 1938, full color, 1³/₈ x 2⁵/₈" **5.00**

KELLOGG'S

References: Ted Hake, *Hake's Guide To Advertising Collectibles*, Wallace–Homestead, 1992; Tom Tumbusch, *Tomart's Price Guide to Radio Premiums and Cereal Box Collectibles*, Wallace–Homestead, 1991.

Periodicals: *Flake*, PO Box 481, Cambridge, MA 02140; *Free Inside*, PO Box 178844, San Diego, CA 92117.

Activity Book, "Kellogg's 75th Anniversary Fun Book," c1980, 48 pgs, color and black and white, 8¹/₂ x 11" **10.00**

Advertising Trade Card, Rice Krispies, triple folder, Snap, Crackle, and Pop images, Vernon Grant illus, artist sgd, 1932 . . . . **15.00**

Almanac, The Housewife's Almanac, distributed by Kellogg's All–Bran, color adv, 1938 . . . . **8.00**

Blotter, The Sweetheart of the Corn, color, woman and cornstalk illus, 1910, 3¹/₂ x 6¹/₄" **12.00**

Booklet
  Funny Jungleland Moving–Pictures, color, horizontal flaps create various bizarre animals, 1909, 7 x 9". . . **35.00**
  Kellogg's Funny Jungleland Book, movable flaps change animals' faces, color, 1932 . . . . **12.00**
  Mother Goose, c1935, 18 pgs, nursery rhymes "as told by Kellogg's Singing Lady," story and cov art by Vernon Grant, 5 x 6". **25.00**

Cookbook, 1978 . . . . **6.00**

Display, cardboard
  Doll Clothes Patterns, "1 Free with 2 Packages Kellogg's Wheat Krispies" **140.00**
  Replica Cereal Box, Rice Krispies one side, Corn Flakes other side, c1958, 5 x 14¹/₂ x 20¹/₂" **75.00**

Folder, "Premiums," color, illus, lists

Magazine Tear Sheet, Shredded Krumbles, *The Delineator*, sgd. Andrew Loomis illustration, 14¹/₂ x 19¹/₂", 1920, $30.00.

premiums, Vernon Grant cartoon art, 1930s, opens to 18" l **20.00**

Mask, set of three, Snap, Crackle, and Pop faces, Rice Krispies premium, stiff paper, 1933, 11 x 14" **75.00**

Playing Cards, Kellogg's Frosties, Tony the Tiger eating cereal, "They're G–r–r–reat!", 1978–80 . . . . **5.00**

Premium Wheel of Knowledge, mechanical, rotating dial, facts about United States **30.00**

KENNEDY, JOHN F.

Reference: Ted Hake, *Hake's Guide To Presidential Campaign Collectibles*, Wallace–Homestead, 1992.

Collectors' Club: Kennedy Political Items Collectors, PO Box 922, Clark, NJ 07066.

Book, *A Pictorial Biography of John F. Kennedy*, 40 portrait cards, cardboard, includes wedding, school, press conference, throwing baseball at season opener, etc., orig box, 3 x 5" **45.00**

Brochure, John F Kennedy For U.S. Senator, red, white, and blue, JFK's face, 1952, 6¹/₂ x 9" **75.00**

Bumper Sticker, "Kennedy For President," JFK's face, 1960, 17½ x 4" 8.00
Business Card, "John Fitzgerald Kennedy, United States Senate, Massachusetts," emb gold eagle upper left corner, 1950s, 3¾ x 1¾" 75.00
First Day Cover, JFK Inaugural, Kennedy photo, postmarked Washington, DC, January 20, 1961, sgd by ceremony participants Marian Anderson, Richard Cardinal Cushing, Archbishop Iakovos, John Barclay, and Rabbi Nelson Gluck 65.00
Magazine
 Berliner Illustrite, Kennedy assassination, special edition, German 18.00
 Life, December 19, 1960, JFK, Jackie, and JFK Jr cov, christening 5.00
Newspaper
 L.A. Times, November 23, 1963, Kennedy assassination, photos of Kennedys in car before shooting, Johnson taking oath of office 18.00
 The Philadelphia Inquirer, November 23, 24, 25, and 26, 1963, four issues, covs Nation's tribute to JFK . . .   20.00
Periscope, cardboard, "Souvenir of Washington D.C. Inaugural," green and white, JFK's face and Capitol building illus, 1961, 16" h 45.00
Post Card, photographic, color portrait, "Vote For John F. Kennedy," 1960 . . .   10.00
Poster, portrait, red, white, and blue striped ground, "Kennedy For President, Leadership For The 60's," 1960, 13 x 21" 45.00
Program, memorial, bound copy of 1961 Kennedy–Johnson Inaugural Program,

copy No. 40, gold lettering identifies as Speaker of the House John W McCormack's copy 175.00
Record Jacket, Kennedy speeches, color, 1963, 12" sq 3.50
Window Card, "Out Of Respect For John F. Kennedy We Will Remain Closed Until Noon, Monday, November 25, By proclamation of the Fort Atkinson City Council President," heavy cardboard, black lettering, wide black mourning band border, white ground, 11 x 8½" 4.00
Window Sticker, Kennedy–Johnson, red, white, and blue, 3¼ x 8¼" 4.00

KITCHEN

References: Linda Campbell Franklin, *300 Years of Kitchen Collectibles,* third edition, Books Americana, 1991; Gary Miller and K. M. Scotty Mitchell, *Price Guide to Collectible Kitchen Appliances,* Wallace–Homestead, 1991.

Periodical: *Kitchen Antiques & Collectibles News,* 4645 Laurel Ridge Drive, Harrisburg, PA 17110.

Advertising Trade Card
 Agate Iron Ware, "The Crowning Triumph," color, woman placing crown on giant coffeepot, other women dancing around base 20.00
 Enterprise Meat and Food Chopper, product clamped to table illus 8.00
Booklet
 Ringen Stoves, Buster Brown, c1905   30.00
 The Cheapest Way to Cook–90 Cent Gas, Public Service Gas Co, 1890s, 48 pgs, tinted black and white photos of gas appliances including lamps, irons, and stoves 38.00
Bookmark, Acorn Stoves adv 6.00
Catalog
 Erie Hollow Ware, 1890, 16 pgs, foldout, black and white, prices 15.00
 General Electric Co, Schenectady, NY, "Freedom", The Joy of Living Electrically–The Health Kitchen, Refrigerators, Stoves, Dishwashers, etc., 1933, 28 pgs, color illus, 5½ x 8" . .   22.00
 Kalamazoo Stove Co, Kalamazoo, MI, 1928, 88 pgs, cast iron ranges in porcelain enamel, color and black and white illus, 8½ x 11" 18.00
 National Enameling and Stamping Co, Milwaukee, 1920–30, cooking ware, milk cans, wash boilers, pantry sets, well buckets, etc. 20.00
 Prizer Stoves, Ranges, Furnaces, Reading, PA, No. 10, 48 pgs, illus 20.00
 Washburn Co, 1924, 116 pgs, kitchen utensils. 50.00

Card of Appreciation, Kennedy funeral, from Mrs. John Kennedy, printed, black and white, black bordered envelope with printed signature, 5½ x 3⅜" card, 1963, $18.00.

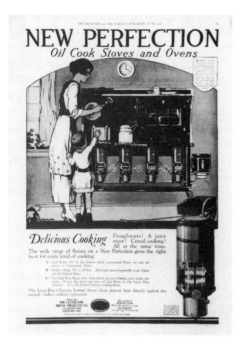

Magazine Tear Sheet, New Perfection Oil Cook Stoves and Ovens, *Designer and the Woman's Magazine*, sgd. Wetteroy illustration, June 1920, $10.00.

Cookbook
Dainty Dishes For All Year Round,
 1899, 64 pgs, Shepard's Lightning
 Freezer adv, kitchen tool illus, illus
 cov, 7 x 4" **15.00**
 Granite Ironware adv, c1880, 64 pgs   **15.00**
Coupon, Mirro Aluminum Bake Pan,
 printed, black on pale orange, two
 sided, 20 cents off a 55¢ bake pan,
 Lundt & Co, Moline, IL, 1920s, 6 x 3"   **3.00**
Flyer, Westinghouse Automatic Range
 adv, color illus, c1920, 8½ x 11". **7.00**
Label
 Lemon, Household, woman in 1940s
 kitchen setting, Porterville, 12½ x
 8¾" **1.00**
 Yam, Vitamin, kitchen scene, mother
 feeding son vitamins **1.00**
Playing Cards, 1950s kitchen scene,
 Hotpoint All–Electric Kitchen **17.50**
Puzzle, jigsaw, diecut cardboard, General Electric Portable Appliances,
 kitchen scene, c1960, orig plastic bag
 and guide picture, 10½ x 15" **8.00**
Sign, Kitchen Kleanzer, cardboard, product illus **45.00**
Toy, paper, Kitchen Furniture, No. 78,
 Built–Rite **55.00**

KNIVES

Reference: Bernard Levine, *Levine's Guide To Knives and Their Values,* Third Edition, DBI Books, 1993.

Periodicals: *Edges,* PO Box 22007, Chattanooga, TN 37422; *Knife World,* PO Box 3395, Knoxville, TN 37927.

Collectors' Clubs: American Blade Collectors, PO Box 22007, Chattanooga, TN 37422; National Knife Collectors Association, PO Box 21070, Chattanooga, TN 37421.

Cutlery
 Advertising Trade Card
 Briddell Cutlery Factory, 1930s. . . .   **2.00**
 John Russell Cutlery, bifold, factory
 vignette on front, Centennial Expo
 buildings inside **65.00**
 Catalog
 Lamson & Goodnow Mfg Co, New
 York, NY, Household Cutlery,
 Butchers, Painters, Paperhangers
 Tools, 1930, 48 pgs, specialty
 knives and tools for specific
 trades **50.00**
 Seattle Hardware Co, Seattle, WA,
 Universal Carvers, Kitchen Cutlery, Pocket Knives, Shears &
 Scissors, 1924, 48 pgs **35.00**
 Playing Cards, Frank's Kutlery Kuts,
 USPC, 52 cards, one joker, and two
 extra cards, boxed set, c1900 . . . . .   **30.00**
 Sign
 Remington, cardboard, "Knives that
 Bite," woman carving ham, full
 color, 1929, 7 x 10½" **30.00**
 Winchester Cutlery Tools, litho,
 split image, mother and daughter
 in kitchen, father and son in garage, 16 x 21" **240.00**
Pocket
 Advertising Trade Card, Lion Coffee
 "Pocket–Knife Free" premium offer, color boy and dog portrait, blue
 and white pocket knife illus, c1895,
 5½ x 3½" **10.00**
 Catalog
 H & D Folson Arms Co, New York,
 NY, Catalogue No. 31, 1929–30,
 142 pgs, color and black and

Box, Boy Scout Knife, $2.00.

white illus, sporting goods includ-
ing pocket knives **75.00**
Home Supply Co, Illustrated Cata-
logue, New York, NY, c1898, 32
pgs, misc boys' items including
pocket knives **40.00**
Remington Arms Co, New York,
NY, Catalogue C–5 Remington
Pocket Knives, c1915, 64 pgs,
hundreds of full–size pocket knife
illus **185.00**
Von Lengerke & Antoine, Chicago,
IL, Guns Ammunition, Cutlery,
1914, 120 pgs, illus, guns, pocket
knives, and sporting goods, paper
wrappers **35.00**
Poster, Keen Kutter, 1950s, 15 x 22" . . **8.00**

LARKIN

Advertising Trade Card
Mauch Chunk, PA and Mount Pisgah,
J L Larkin Co **16.00**
Ottumwa Starch **3.00**
Pinacles in the Grand Canyon, J L
Larkin Co **14.00**
This Mississippi at Burlington, J L
Larkin Co **12.00**
Brochure, Larkin Soap, 1885 . . . . **15.00**
Catalog
1895, 20 pgs, self pictorial printed
wrappers, illus **50.00**
1919, 184 pgs, The Larkin Factory–to–
Family Plan, Spring & Summer,
illus, products and premiums **25.00**
1922, 204 pgs, Fall and Winter, No.
88 . . . . **60.00**
1923, 196, pgs, The Larkin Factory–
to–Family Plan Catalog No. 90, pre-
miums, illus, six color plates **35.00**
1926, 235 pgs, Spring and Summer,

**Catalog, The Larkin Plan, No. 79, 188
pages, color covers, black-and-white and
color illustrations, 8 x 11", Spring & Summer 1918, $45.00.**

eight color plates, printed color cov,
9 x 12" **40.00**
1930, 222 pgs, The World's Greatest
Premium Values–Catalogue 103,
illus, premiums include household
goods, clothing, and toys **35.00**
Post Card, adv, two card foldout, multicolored factory image **30.00**

LEGAL

Arrest Warrant, NY, 1850s **50.00**
Book
Commentaries on American Law,
James Kent, NY, first edition,
1884, four volumes **275.00**
*General Laws Passed By the Legisla-
ture of Wisconsin,* 1860s, hard
cov **10.00**
*Law Dictionary, Adapted To The
Constitution and Laws of the
United States,* John Bouvier, sixth
edition, 1856, revised and en-
larged, Philadelphia, two volumes **30.00**
*Patent Law & How to Obtain Letters
Patent,* 1873, 120 pgs **9.00**
Certificate, inspection, Rectified Whis-
key, 1868, 8½ x 14" **8.00**
Document
Deed, NH land sale, 1783 . . . . **30.00**
Estate Inventory, handwritten, 1783 **30.00**
Henderson Circuit Court, KY, 1820,
5 pgs, sgd by John James Audubon **1,000.00**
Land Grant
Philadelphia, PA, 300 acres of
land to Thomas Morgan, 1769 **45.00**
Texas, emb seal, 1858, 13 x 15" . . **75.00**
Tax, $2.00 duty on carriage, NH,
1814, 8 x 13" **40.00**
Ledger, Court Fees and Summons
Served and Charges, New Hamp-
shire, handwritten, 1885 to 1858 . . . **35.00**

LINCOLN

Advertising Trade Card, Lincoln sketch,
Larkin & Co, Sweet Home Soaps adv,
Buffalo, NY, text on back **15.00**
Ballot, Union Ticket, Lincoln/Johnson,
ship *Kearsarge* sinking the *Alabama*
image, 1864, 3 x 7½" **150.00**
Book, Little Leather Library, *Speeches
and Addresses of Abraham Lincoln,* 96
pgs, 3 x 4" **20.00**
Carte de Visite, bust portrait, T R Burn-
ham, Boston imprint on back **25.00**
Envelope, "Honest Abe," campaign, en-
graved portrait upper center, used. . . . **20.00**
Label
Cigar
Los Immortales, portraits of Washington, Lincoln, and Grant, 1890s **20.00**

Magazine, The Century Illustrated Monthly Magazine, Lincoln Centennial Number, The Century Co., Union Square, NY, Vol. 77, No. 4, printed black and yellow covers, color frontispiece miniature portrait, 134 pages, black-and-white photographs, color plates, 7 x 10", February 1909, $25.00.

Old Abe, portrait, 2¼ x 2½"	.50
Oranges, Lincoln, multicolored portrait, orange ground, Riverside, 10 x 11"	2.00
Letterhead, A A Waterman & Co Lincoln Fountain Pen, Lincoln's head next to fountain pen image, 1904	35.00
Newspaper	
Daily Alta California, San Francisco, April 18, 1865, four pgs, assassination articles, black mourning lines and borders	225.00
New York Herald, November 20, 1863, Gettysburg Address, speech delivered the previous day	110.00
Photograph, albumen, sepia, portrait, ornate brass frame, 1864, 1½ x 2"	500.00
Print	
A E Hilton, "Gettysburg Address," colorful portrait, illumin by J R Rosen, emb "Talio–Chrome," c1944, 11½ x 17"	16.00
Kellogg, "Abraham Lincoln," portrait, 1860, 10 x 14"	300.00
Post Card, portrait in oval in center, White House above, log cabin below	5.00
Songbook, *The Republican Campaign Songster Co. 1,* American Publishing House, Cincinnati, OH, 48 pgs, black and white portrait on title page, 4 x 5½"	100.00
Souvenir Book, *Abe Lincoln In Illinois,* Raymond Massey as Lincoln, Norman Rockwell illus	15.00
Stereoview, funeral procession passing through Philadelphia	175.00

LIQUOR

Reference: Sharon and Bob Huxford, *Huxford's Collectible Advertising: An Illustrated Value Guide,* Collector Books, 1993.

Advertising Trade Card	
Capital Fine Kentucky Whiskey, colorful view Washington Capital	**75.00**
Kingston's Rum and Marie Brizard & Rodger's Cognac Fine Champagne, colorful illus, gold background, 1890 calendar reverse	**26.00**
Blotter	
Old Forester Whiskey, "Old Forester, $29.50 Delivered, Brown–Forman Distillery," green and blue lettering, pink ground, 7 x 4"	**3.00**
Old Grand–Dad Whiskey, whiskey bottles, "Bottled in Bond," 6 x 3" . .	**10.00**
Book	
Economic Aspects of the Liquor Problem, 12th Annual Report of the Commissioner of Labor, Washington, 1898, 275 pgs	**12.00**
Melrose: Honey of Roses, Stirling Graham, 1944, 95 pgs, History of the Records and Goldsborough Co, Melrose brand whiskey, third printing	**8.00**
Coupons, U S Internal Revenue Special Tax, Retail Liquor Dealer, vignette of man with jug, 1875, set of 12	**7.00**
Display, diecut cardboard, emb, Hartman's Family Liquor, girl and cherub in boat, framed, 16 x 14"	**150.00**
Football Guide, Kessler Whiskey premium, professional and college teams statistics, 1972	**4.00**
Label	
Hunter Bourbon, hunter and dog illus, 4½" sq	**1.50**
Napa Rock, Tom Collins mixer, mountain scene, conifers, stream, 2½ x 4¼"	**.25**
Old Crow, sepia distillery scene, 3½ x 4½"	**.75**
Rocking Chair, old Mr Boston and rocking chair image, 3¼ x 5"	**1.50**
Superior Bourbon Whiskey, diecut, multicolored, Southern gentlemen illus	**20.00**
Matchbook, Carstairs White Seal Blended Whiskey, oversized, blue, gold, and red, seal balancing ball on cov and matches, 1940s, 3½ x 4½", unused	**10.00**
Order Form, Wollstein Mercantile Cedar Point Whiskey, multicolored, bottle, brewer, text, and prices on front, reverse with order blank, c1900, 5½ x 8"	**30.00**

Magazine Tear Sheet, Glenmore Distilleries Co., Inc., Louisville, KY, Christmas motif, 10½ x 13½", 1941, $7.00.

Playing Cards
Early Times Kentucky Straight Bourbon Whisky (sic), whiskey bottle, yellow ground, "Just Mention My Name" **8.00**
Johnnie Walker Black Label Scotch, yellow logo, black ground, "12 Years Old" **5.00**
Post Card, adv, Kinsey Pure Rye Whiskey, Angelo Myers Distillery, Inc, color, hunter and dog in farmer's field facing farmer holding large stick, "No Trespassing" sign on fence post **15.00**
Poster
Clark & Sons Liquor Merchants, Victorian lady in garden, 35 x 25" **400.00**
Hannis Distilling Co, Hannisville Dis-

tillery, Martinsburg, WV, factory scene, matted and framed, 20 x 18"   **450.00**
Sign, Old Guckenheimer Rye Whiskey, cardboard litho, farmer in rye field points to whiskey bottle, "Best Rye in the Field," framed, 11 x 15" **250.00**
Stamp, US Internal Revenue Tax, series 1882, boy with whiskey barrels and still **4.00**

MAGIC

Collectors' Club: Magic Collectors Association, 19 Logan St., New Britain, CT 06051.

Big Little Book, *Houdini's Big Little Book of Magic,* premium, "Compliments of Am Oil Co" **25.00**
Book
Chemcraft Chemical Magic, 1940, 31 pgs **15.00**
Life of Robert Houdini, King of the Conjurers, translated from French, Rochester Pub, 1859 . . . .   **60.00**
Magicians Handy Book of Cigarette Tricks, 1933, 36 pgs. **15.00**
Booklet
Bag of Tricks, Weatherbird Shoes premium, 1932, 64 pgs, wraps **20.00**
Easy Magic For Everyone, c1920, 16 pgs, pub by Arthur Felsman, Chicago, photos and drawings **15.00**
Tricks With Cards, Hoffman, c1890, 145 pgs plus ads, explains card tricks, c1890 . . . .   **30.00**
Bubble Gum Cards, Magic Trick Bubble Gum, Philadelphia Chewing Gum Co, 1953, 24 cards, Harry Blackstone magic tricks, bifold, folders explain various magic tricks, 2⁷/₁₆ x 3½" **90.00**
Catalog
Illustrated and Descriptive Catalogue of New and Superior Conjuring Wonders, Martinka and Co, NY, 1898, 144 pgs **55.00**
Leroy's Mammoth Pictorial 20th Cen-

Store Sign, Schenley Distilling Co., red and white, black ground, 7 x 3", c1940s, $10.00.

Cigar Label, Wizard, blue, green, and gold, 10 x 6½", $30.00.

tury Up–To–Date Illustrated Catalogue: Conjuring Wonders, Magic, Second Sight Illusions, etc., W D Leroy, Boston, MA, 1905–10, 212 pgs.......................... **50.00**

Nelson Enterprises Magic Catalog #22, 1948, 162 pgs, soft cov...... **12.00**

Flyer, Ferrante–The Prince of Magic, adv, black and white, photo illus, c1890, 3¼ x 7½"................ **8.00**

Handbill, "Parlour Magic Without Apparatus, Souvenir U.S. Centennial, 1876, Invented and Manufactured by Robert Nickle," two sided **35.00**

Manual, *Hermann's Wizards Manual,* 1915, 66 pgs **10.50**

Paperback Book, *Hermann's Art of Magic,* Professor Hermann, early 1900s, 95 pgs, 5 x 7".................... **20.00**

Poster, George The Supreme Master of Magic **210.00**

MEDICAL

References: Douglas Condon–Martin, *Drugstore and Soda Fountain Antiques,* Schiffer Publishing, 1991; Sharon and Bob Huxford, *Huxford's Collectible Advertising: An Illustrated Value Guide,* Collector Books, 1993; Lillian C. and Charles G. Richardson, *The Pill Rollers: Apothecary Antiques and Drug Store Collectibles,* Second Edition, Old Fort Press, 1992.

Collectors' Club: Medical Collectors Association, 1300 Morris Park Ave., Bronx, NY 10461.

Advertising Trade Card, Lydia E Pinkham's Vegetable Compound, color, scenic, text on back, 1890s, 3 x 4½"......................... **10.00**

Almanac, Dr D Jayne's Medicine, 1915 **4.00**

Book
McClellan's Regional Anatomy, Vol. 2, 1894, color illus.............. **18.00**

Merck's 1907 Index: An Encyclopedia for the Chemist, Pharmacist and Physician, 472 pgs.............. **12.00**

Obstetrics, Manual for Students & Practitioners, 1903, 265 pgs, 82 engravings..................... **6.00**

The People's Medical Lighthouse, Dr Harmon Knox, New York, 1854, 470 pgs, illus, lists and describes various diseases............... **20.00**

Booklet
Alka–Seltzer Song Book, c1935 ..... **2.50**

Walsh's Physicians' Combined Call–Book And Tablet, 1878, 150 pgs, leather cov, 4½ x 7¼".......... **10.00**

Bookmark, Climax Catarrh Cure, woman wearing fur coat, color **10.00**

Broadside
Dr M McHenry's Soothing Syrup, "Stomach Bitters, Oil For Burns, & Popular Liniments," framed, 11 x 14"........................ **120.00**

Indian Sovereign Remedy for Palpitation of the Heart, ornate border, 1840s...................... **28.00**

Catalog
Brewer & Co, pharmaceutical, 1938. . **20.00**

Feick Brothers Co, Pittsburgh, PA, Surgical Instruments, Office Equipment, Artificial Limbs–8th Edition, 1929, 458 pgs, hard cov, price list. . **60.00**

Tilden & Co, New Lebanon, NY, Prices Current Tilden & Co's Medicinal Preparation, 1872, 32 pgs, paper wrappers **40.00**

Wilson Ear Drum Co, Louisville, KY, Wilson's Common Sense Ear Drums, c1894, 32 pgs, illus, testimonials **40.00**

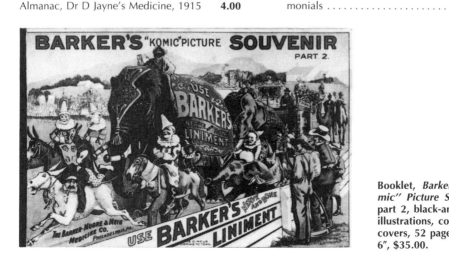

Booklet, *Barker's "Komic" Picture Souvenir,* part 2, black-and-white illustrations, color litho covers, 52 pages, 9½ x 6", $35.00.

Cookbook, *Dr Ward's Medical Co Cook Book,* illus, tonics and patent medicines, c1920 . . . .   **3.00**
Coupon, Dr Blumer's products premiums, floral dinnerware, 2¼ x 4" . . .   **.25**
Display, Smith Brothers Cough Drops, diecut cardboard, Smith Brothers figures, 34 x 12", pr **150.00**
Document, August 30, 1792, town of Boston asking doctor to tend a poor family, 7¾ x 3½". **11.50**
Imprint, "Synopsis and Nosology, Being and Arrangement and Definition of Diseases," William Cullen, MD, 1792   **50.00**
Label
    Mosquito Repellent, Skidoo Skitoes, blue and white, 2¼ x 7". . . . .   **.50**
    Pill Box, Dr Blumer's Torpedo Pellets, two owls, yellow and brown, 7 x 4½" **1.00**
Letter, woman doctor, formulas for cure of Morphine, tobacco, and whiskey habits, 1882, 5 pgs. **35.00**
Magazine, *The Medical Record,* "A Weekly Journal of Medicine and Surgery," New York, 1885, four issues. . .   **20.00**
Note Book, World's Dispensary Medical Association of Buffalo, NY, illus, information and claims, 1887 calendar . . .   **20.00**
Pamphlet, Medical Eclectic, 1877, 110 pgs, 5½ x 9". **9.00**
Photograph, black and white, nurses wearing uniforms, posing on steps of

Shenandoah Valley Hospital, 1895–1905, 4½ x 3¾" **20.00**
Poster
    Dr D Jaynes Expectorant, woman wearing bodice and cape, "Remedy For Worms, Debility, and Dyspepsia," 29 x 13". **425.00**
    Health Habits, National Child Welfare Association, Roy Williams, 1920, 17 x 28" **35.00**
Prospectus, "College of Pharmacy of City of New York, Session 1893–1894," 68 pgs, 20 pgs advertisements, illus **5.00**
Sign
    Dr B J Kendall's Tonic And Blood Purifier, Pectorial Elixir, Blackberry Balsam, 1890, 5½ x 24" **17.00**
    Dr Haile's Ole Injun System Tonic, color litho, Indian wearing headdress, "Kidneys, Liver & Stomach," 1940, 13 x 20". **50.00**
    Red Star 5¢ Cough Drops, waxed cardboard, shelf strip, 1905 . . . .   **2.50**

MILITARY

References: Ray A. Bows, *Vietnam Military Lore: 1959–1973, Volume I,* Bows & Sons, 1988; Jack H. Smith, *Military Postcards: 1870–1945,* Wallace–Homestead, 1988 out–of–print; George Sanders, Helen Sanders and Ralph Roberts, *The Price Guide To Autographs,* Second Edition, Wallace–Homestead, 1991.

Periodicals: *Military Collector Magazine,* PO Box 245, Lyon Station, PA 19536; *Military Collectors News,* PO Box 702073, Tulsa, OK 74170.

Collectors' Club: Company of Military Historians, N. Main St., Westbrook, CT 06498.

Branches
Air Force
    Cookbook, *Stove Pilot,* compiled by Air Force pilots' wives, 1940s **25.00**
    Invitation, 44–H Army Air Forces Pilots Class Graduation, Fredrick Army Air Field, Fredrick, OK, emb bomber on cov, Sep 1944 . . . .   **7.00**
    Label, vegetable, Dominator, fighter plane illus, 7 x 9" **2.00**
    Post Card
        B–25 Bomber, flying above clouds, photographic **5.00**
        "Keep 'em Flying, Greetings from Jackson, Miss.," plane flying over sea, full moon in background, Curt Teich & Co **3.00**
    Poster
        Aviation Cadets – US Army Air Forces, fighter pilots looking sky-

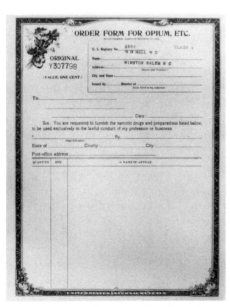

Order Form, doctor's order form for opium, etc., red bordered duplicate copy, unused, 8½ x 11", $20.00.

Aeronautics Recognition Guide to Operational War Planes, Issue 7 and 8, National Aeronautics Council, Inc., edited by L. C. Guthman, Lieutenant (j.g.) U. S. Naval Reserve, illustrated with black-and-white photographs, 178 pages, 5³/₄ x 9", 1943, $25.00.

ward, orange and red ground, tinted photomontage, 1943, 25 x 38" 150.00
Fly For Her Liberty and Yours – US Army Air Forces, fighter pilot and girlfriend, Howard Chandler Christy, 1944, 25 x 38" 600.00
Sheet Music, Mechs of the Air Corps, cov with aviator wings, red, white, and blue, dated 1942 . . . . 10.00
Yearbook, Tinker Field Air Service Command, Oklahoma City, personnel roster, photos, history of AAF, emb cov, 1944 . . . . 25.00
Army
Book, Exciting Experiences in the Mexican War, Marshall Everett, Bible House, Chicago, 318 pgs 75.00
Cabinet Photo, GAR veteran, wearing uniform holding sword 25.00
Catalog, Bannerman Co Military Goods, 1940, 287 pgs 100.00
Cookbook, Army Food & Messing, 1942 . . . . 15.00
Manual, Instructions In Military Signaling For The Use Of The Regular & Volunteer Army, 1899, 64 pgs, illus, 1899 . . . . 10.00

Army-Navy Insignia Guide, mechanical wheel with branch insignia, cardboard, printed multicolor, 4 x 5¹/₂", 1942, $18.00.

Post Card, large "V" and "United States Army," red, white, and blue, unused 4.00
Poster, reward, for "The Arrest and Delivery of a Deserter," July, 1911, 9¹/₂ x 12" 10.00
Scoring Chart, USFET, "Athletic Office Presents GI World Series, Nurnberg Soldiers Field, September, 1945," 4 pgs, unused 45.00
Sheet Music
Army Air Corps, 1942, red, white, and blue aviator wings on cov . . . 7.00
My Gal 'Yond the Rock–Rock–Rockies, cov with Army uniform image, 1945 . . . . 10.00

Book, The U. S. Army, A Guide to Its Men and Equipment, Fletcher Pratt, Whitman Publishing Co., hard cover, lithographed color covers, 53 action pictures by David Pattee, 62 pages, 5¹/₂ x 3¹/₂", 1942, $15.00.

What Do You Do In The Infantry, marching song, 264th Infantry Reg, 1943 . . . .   **9.00**

Stamps, plate block set of ten, US Army/Navy, catalog #785–94 . . . .   **40.00**

Toy, paper, Army Camp, No. 16, Built–Rite, 1936 . . . .   **70.00**

Coast Guard

Poster

  Always Ready–Join The US Coast Guard–Remember Pearl Harbor, Coast Guard flag, yellow ground, silkscreen, c1943, 22 x 28" **110.00**

  Hit Back–Enlist in the Coast Guard–Remember Pearl Harbor, PBY airplane bombing U–boat, silkscreen, c1942, 22 x 28" **200.00**

Marines

Book, *Fix Bayonets!,* John W Thomason Jr, 1926 . . . .   **10.00**

Photograph, 161st Platoon, San Diego, CA, black and white group photo, 1946, 6½ x 9½" **5.00**

Placard, recruitment, "The Marines Want You!, Apply Elm St. Manchester, NH," marine beckoning to recruits, 1910s, 11 x 14" **125.00**

Post Card, Machine Gun Nest, Camp Lejeune, Marine Base, New River, NC, photographic, Curt Teich & Co   **5.00**

Poster, Enlist Now US Marine Corps, Iwo Jima image, Tom Lovell, 1945, 29 x 40" **275.00**

Navy

Book, *U.S. Navy Photographs,* Steichen **75.00**

Business Card, Wayne Hardin, Naval Academy Athletic Association, assistant football coach, 1960s **12.00**

Certificate, Apprenticeship, US Navy Dept, to Arthur Donna, "Term of 4 years at Naval Torpedo Station, Newport, RI," aircraft carrier vignette, 1939 . . . .   **20.00**

Christmas Card, Annapolis, sailing ship illus, color, orig mailing envelope, 1920, 8 x 10" **20.00**

Cookbook, US Navy, 1944 . . . .   **12.00**

Document, discharge papers, war service certificate, two uniform photos, and newspaper story about one of the first women to enlist in Navy, WAVE Mabelle Clinton, discharge dated 1919 . . . .   **125.00**

Flyer, Continental Digest, cov with black and white photo of Commander Gene Tunney shaking hands with navy recruit, published by Continental Optical Co, Nov/Dec 1941 . . . .   **8.50**

Ledger Sheet, Bureau of Navigation,

Needle Book, The Army and Navy Needle Book, printed color cover, front with war ship, back with eagle, Japan, 5 x 2¾", 1930s, $12.00.

payment for services to the *U.S.S. Tuscarora,* 1874 . . . .   **10.00**

Photograph, US warship *Maine,* sunk in Havana, February 15, 1898 . . . . .   **10.00**

Program, Navy vs Notre Dame, Philadelphia Stadium, October 1960 . . .   **15.00**

Ticket, Pacific Coast Army vs Navy, La Coliseum, American Legion/Armistice Day, Navy side, patriotic sailor/soldier, November 11, 1940, 3 x 4" **15.00**

Toy, paper, Navy Battle Fleet and Coast Artillery Gun, No. 60, Built–Rite **45.00**

Personalities

Autograph, typed letter, Herman Nickerson Jr, Lt General, USMC, sgd, 1 pg **30.00**

Envelope, General Mark Clark, cartoon style, sgd by Clark, purple imprinting, postmarked May 7, 1945   **35.00**

Lobby Card, *Patton* movie, tanks and troops illus, 1970 . . . .   **18.00**

Magazine

  Life, August 7, 1954, color cov with General Patton in tank turret **12.00**

  War News Illustrated, August, 1943, MacArthur article **5.00**

Newspaper, General Douglas MacArthur, *Allentown Chronicle,* PA, September 21, 1951, "Welcome General MacArthur, Popular Hero Given Roaring Greetings on Arrival in Allentown," red and blue headline lettering **12.00**

Photograph, General Omar Bradley, wearing four–star uniform with mourning band, inscribed and sgd, 1945 . . . .   **125.00**

Poster, General Douglas MacArthur, "He's Counting On Us," photomontage bust of MacArthur, orange ground, Miller Studios, c1943, 22 x 33" **100.00**

MINING

Advertising Trade Card, Tunnel Coal Co, miners with headlamps vignette, black and white. **60.00**

Annual, *The Coal Trade,* Frederick E Saward, compendium of statistics and facts on coal mining and production, prices, 1902, 150 pgs **7.00**

Bond

Dexter Mining Co 6% Gold Bond, Wyoming, 1906, uncut sheet, 40 coupons. **25.00**

Massachusetts New Mexico Mining Co, eagle and factory vignettes, 13 coupons, 11½ x 14" **20.00**

State of Colorado, Bandora Mining and Milling Co, gold bond payable in gold coin, ten 30¢ coupons attached, 1892 . . . . **45.00**

Book

Getting Gold: A Gold Mining Handbook for Practical Men, 1897, 204 pgs, hard cov **35.00**

Reports Upon The Mineral Resources of the United States, Washington, 1867, 360 pgs **25.00**

Booklet, Potash Mining, Kali Works, Chicago, 1912, 72 pgs, mining photos . . . **8.00**

Brochure, Pneumatic Machine Co, Syracuse, NY, Pneumatic Coal Puncher, 1911, 40 pgs, illus, electric coal mining machine, several views of coal mine cuts. **40.00**

Catalog, Union Iron Works, San Francisco, CA, Catalogue #3, 1896, 204 pgs, illus, mining machinery, double page color plate of San Francisco Bay with ships in harbor, front and back cov with color views of Bay area **250.00**

Check, Yellow Aster Mining & Milling, Los Angles, Ca, 1908, gold mine vignette. **5.00**

Document, draft, from The Office of The Quincy Mining Company, revenue stamp, 1865. . . . . **10.00**

Label, tobacco, Welcome Nugget, gold miner holding up giant nugget, stone litho, 1880s **65.00**

Letter, Tennessee Consolidated Lead Mining Co to Directors of company, sgd by four engineers, 3 pgs, 1850 . . . **25.00**

Magazine, *Life,* Gold Rush cov and article, April 27, 1959. . . . . **3.00**

Magazine Tear Sheet, *Harper's,* May 6, 1876, miner holding miner's lamp and two picks over shoulder, 11 x 16" **8.00**

Newspaper

Daily Alta California, San Francisco, CA, February 10, 1853, Gold Rush articles and adv **30.00**

Daily Evening Bulletin, San Francisco, CA, March 22, 1856, Gold Rush paper edited by James King **35.00**

Harpers Weekly, 1897, Klondike Gold Rush article, three issues **25.00**

The Silver State, Winnemucca, NE, August 19, 1875, Nevada Silver Rush paper. **12.00**

Photograph, albumen, Kimberley Diamond Mine, men, mules, horses and wagons, sluice boxes, and buckets with cables, 1870s, 5½ x 8" **45.00**

Post Card, "Off for the mines," armed men, stagecoach, and horses in western town, J J Harris & Co building in background, 1903 . . . . **10.00**

Receipt, $25.00, 100 shares of Manhattan Gold Mining Co of Colorado, 1864 **10.00**

Stock Certificate

Coalition Mines Co, New York, vignette of miners at top, 1917 . . . . . . **6.00**

Cooperative Gold Mining Company, 1,000 shares at 5¢ each, Spanish American war stamp, ornate, vignette of woman with flag, May 1900 . . . . **38.00**

Western Utah Copper Co, top vignette of miner with drill **6.00**

Yucca Cyanide Mining & Milling Co, Arizona Territory, three vignettes at top of working miners and smoking mill, gold seal and body print, 1903 **20.00**

Cigar Label, King Coal, red, black, and gold, 9 x 6½", $35.00.

MARILYN MONROE

References: Richard De Thuin, *The Official Identification and Price Guide To Movie Memorabilia,* House of Collectibles, 1990; Denis C. Jackson, *The Price and Identification Guide to Marilyn Monroe,* published by author, 1989.

Collectors' Club: Marilyn Monroe International Fan Club, PO Box 7544, Northridge, CA 91327.

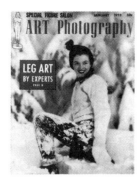

Magazine, *Art Photography*, Marilyn Monroe cover, 8½ x 11", January 1952, $40.00.

Autograph, placemat, Waldorf Astoria coffee shop, pencil message and signature, matted and framed with color photo 2,500.00
Book, *My Story by Marilyn Monroe*, Stein & Day, 1974, 141 pgs, dj 25.00
Calendar, 1955, full pad, 10 x 17" 25.00
Magazine
  Focus, color cov with Monroe photo, November, 1955 . . . .   7.50
  Ladies Home Journal, July, 1973, color photo cov, article 18.00
  Life, November 9, 1959, Monroe cov 25.00
  Modern Man, November, 1953, cov with Marilyn in swimsuit on beach, story and photos 25.00
  Movie Life, December, 1956, black and white Monroe pictorial 12.00
Movie Press Book, *Bus Stop*, 96 pgs, Monroe cov, British promotional, 6 x 8" 45.00
Post Card, *Bus Stop,* French version, sexy Monroe photo 15.00

Magazine, *Life*, 10½ x 13½", August 17, 1962, $35.00.

Sheet Music, song from *Bus Stop,* Monroe cov, 1956 . . . .   25.00

MOTORCYCLES

Collectors' Club: Antique Motorcycle Club of America, 14943 York Road, Sparks, MD 21152.

Advertising Trade Card, Harley–Davidson, motorcycle, green background 22.00
Blotter, Indian Scout Motorcycle, motorcycle image, ornate border, brilliant colors 40.00
Calendar, 1984, Easyrider 4.00
Catalog, Harley Davidson, Showroom Catalog, 1927, 16 color pgs motorcycle 130.00
Letterhead and Envelope, Heffner & Jarrett Motor Cycles, both with large blue vignette of Excelsior Motor Cycle, early 20th C. 20.00
Magazine
  Harley Davidson Enthusiast, 1934 . . .   4.00
  The Enthusiast, 1946, October 15.00
Manual, Harley–Davidson Service Manual, 1976 . . . .   5.00
Photograph
  Harley Davidson cycle and rider, 1921, 3 x 5" 15.00
  Man and woman with Indian motorcycle, house in background, side view of cycle, three black and white snapshots, 1930s 12.00
  Man standing next to woman seated on c1911 Harley Davidson, albumen, 4 x 3¼" 25.00
Post Card
  Harley Davidson, order blank for ordering 1926 catalog 5.00
  Photographic, two children on motorcycle photo 25.00

MOVIE

References: Richard De Thuin, *The Official Identification and Price Guide To Movie Memorabilia,* House of Collectibles, 1990; Tony Fusco, *The Official Identification and Price Guide To Posters,* House of Collectibles, 1990; John Hegenberger, *Collector's Guide To Movie Memorabilia,* Wallace–Homestead, 1991; Leslie Halliwell, *The Filmgoer's Companion,* Avon, 1978; Ephraim Katz, *The Film Encyclopedia,* Perigee Books, 1979; Leonard Maltin (ed.), *TV Movies and Videos Guide,* New American Library, 1987; John Margolies, *Palaces of Dreams: Movie Theater Postcards,* Bulfinch Press, 1993; Patrick McCarver, *Gone With The Wind Collector's Price Guide,* Collector's Originals, 1990; Edward R. Pardella, *Shirley Temple Dolls and Fashions: A Collector's Guide To The World's Darling,* Schiffer Publishing, 1992; Jay Scarfone and William Stillman, *The Wizard of Oz Collector's Treasury,* Schiffer Publishing, 1992; Patricia R. Smith, *Shirley Temple Dolls and Collectibles,* (1977, 1992 value update), *Second Series,* (1979, 1992 value update), Collector Books; Jon R. Warren, *Warren's Movie Poster Price Guide, 1993 Edition,* Collector's Exchange, 1992; Dian Zillner, *Hollywood Collectibles,* Schiffer Publishing, 1991.

Periodicals: *Big Reel,* Route 3, PO Box 83, Madison, NC 27025; *Classic Images,* PO Box 809, Muscatine, IA 52761; *Hollywood Movie Archives,* PO Box 1566, Apple Valley, CA 92307; *Movie Collectors' World,* PO Box 309, Fraser, MI 48026; *Nostalgia World,* PO Box 231, North Haven, CT 06473.

Collectors' Club: Hollywood Studio Collectors Club, Suite 450, 3960 Laurel Canyon Blvd., Studio City, CA 91604.

Arcade Card, Leslie Howard, 1930s...	**4.00**
Autograph	
Orson Welles, *Citizen Kane,* c1975	**250.00**
Ray Bolger, sgd photo, the Scarecrow from *Wizard of Oz*	**85.00**
Book	
Gable and Lombard, hard cov, dj...	**30.00**
Frankenstein, Grosset & Dunlap, movie edition of Shelley book, four movie scene illus, 1932, 240 pgs, hard cov, 6 x 9"	**50.00**
Hollywood and the Great Fan Magazines, M Levin, NY, first edition, 1970	**5.00**
Box, Bing Crosby Ice Cream, full color portrait, 1953, 3 x 3 x 4"	**2.50**
Brochure, "Let's Go to the Movies," No. 62, 1932, 48 pgs, features fa-	

Magazine, *Life,* Elizabeth Taylor and Richard Burton cover, with intact Post Cereal baseball cards #5 Mickey Mantle and #6 Roger Maris, April 13, 1962, $175.00.

mous Hollywood stars including Dietrich, Chevalier, Hopkins, Arlen, Sydney, etc., black and white photos, Reed Publishing Co, 4 x 6"	**12.50**
Calendar, 1950, "Movie Star Calendar For 1950," 11 x 17"	**22.00**
Cigarette Card, Clark Gable, No. 46, Park Drive Cigarettes	**25.00**
Cocktail Napkins, Groucho Marx, comic scenes and 1955 De Soto adv, orig box.....................	**35.00**
Coloring Book, June Allyson, c1952, 11 x 15", some pgs colored........	**35.00**
Cookbook	
Gone With The Wind, Pebeco premium	**45.00**
Yul Brynner, first edition, dj, 1983 ..	**18.00**
Dixie Lid, Joan Crawford	**190.00**
Insert	
Johnny Eager, Robert Taylor, Lana Turner, 1941.................	**45.00**
Three Little Words, Fred Astaire, Vera Mills, 1950	**25.00**
Tonight and Every Night, Rita Hayworth, 1944	**70.00**
Up Goes Maisie, Ann Southern, 1946......................	**20.00**
Label, cigar, Rudolph Valentino, portrait, wood grained ground	**20.00**
Lobby Card	
Kid Galahad, Elvis Presley, 1962, pair	**50.00**
The Hindenberg, George C Scott, 1975, set of 8................	**20.00**
Magazine	
Life, November 15, 1954, Gina Lollobrigida	**3.00**
Motion Picture, June, 1974, cov with Robert Wagner and Natalie Wood	**8.00**
Movie Life, October, 1951, cov with Ava Gardner and Frank Sinatra...	**15.00**
Movie Stars, August, 1962, cov with Elizabeth Taylor, Natalie Wood, and Janet Leigh	**10.00**
Screenland, February, 1966, cov with Hayley Mills and Peter Noone....................	**10.00**
Screen Stories, October, 1951, cov with Van Johnson and June Allyson	**12.50**
Paperback Book	
A Dictionary of the Cinema, Peter Graham, 1964, Louise Brooks on cov	**15.00**
Karloff, the Man, the Monster, the Movies, D Gifford, 1973, 350 pgs	**15.00**
Photograph	
Carole Lombard, Paramount Pictures promo, automatic pen signature, 1938	**6.00**
Humphrey Bogart, black and white glossy, upper body portrait, red	

ink signature and inscription, June
19, 1952, 8 x 10"............... **2,700.00**
Poster
  Dorothy Lamour, wearing sarong,
    Royal Crown Cola adv, 1940s, 19
    x 36".................... **35.00**
  Marshall of Gunsmoke, Tex Ritter,
    1943.................... **25.00**
  Old Overland Trail, Rex Allen, 1952,
    27 x 41".................. **95.00**
  Rancho Grande, re–release, Gene
    Autry, 1940.............. **65.00**
  Springfield Rifle, Gary Cooper,
    c1952, 14 x 22"........... **45.00**
  Tucson Raiders, Wild Bill Elliott as
    Red Ryder, 1944........... **35.00**
  Willard, 1971.............. **7.50**
Program, *Gone With The Wind,* sepia
  tones, 4 pgs, production facts...... **50.00**
Sheet Music
  As Time Goes By, cover with Bogart,
    Bergman, and Henreid, *Casa-
    blanca,* 1942............... **100.00**
  Gone With The Wind, four pcs..... **60.00**
  I'll Sing You A Thousand Love Songs,
    Clark Gable cov............ **10.00**
  Let's Face the Music and Dance,
    Fred Astaire and Ginger Rogers
    cov, from *Follow The Fleet,* 1935 **10.00**
  Some Sunday Morning, Errol Flynn
    dancing with Smith cov, 1945 ... **20.00**
  Wooden Heart, Elvis Presley, cov

Sheet Music, *Love Walked In,* Goldwyn
Follies, Chappell & Co., real photo, tan
wash, 9 x 12", c1938, $25.00.

photo of Presley wearing Army
  uniform.................... **7.50**
Title Card, *Tarzan Escapes,* with six
  lobby cards and two duplicates,
  1936....................... **450.00**

MUSIC

Reference: House of Collectibles (eds.), *The Official Price Guide To Music Collectibles, Sixth Edition,* House of Collectibles, 1986, out–of–print.

Book, *How to Tell the Nationality of Old
  Violins,* pub by Balfour & Co, London,
  1901, enlarged second edition, red
  cloth cov, recto pgs only paginated
  through 28, verso pgs with drawings or
  photos of violins.................. **22.00**
Booklet, *How Music Is Made,* C G Conn
  Co, 1927, 56 pgs, illus............ **5.00**
Broadside, Sohmer & Co Piano–Fortes,
  four part, New York store on front,
  1861, 12 x 18".................. **25.00**
Cabinet Photo, bandsman in uniform
  with brass instrument, 1892 .... **25.00**
Catalog
  Baldwin Piano, c1910, 84 pgs, 7 x 10" **12.50**
  Conn Co, Band & Orchestra Instru-
    ments, 1940, 56 pgs............ **50.00**
  Frank Holton & Co, Elkhorn, WI,
    Holton's Harmony Hints, 1937, 30
    pgs, illus, band instruments, price
    list.......................... **60.00**
  Kagan & Gaines, 1938, 32 pgs, violins,
    violas, cellos, etc. **30.00**
  Lyon & Healy, Chicago, IL, 1911, 102
    pgs, violins, photographic plates, 5
    x 10"....................... **85.00**
  Steinway Piano, 1920, 36 pgs, 4¼ x 6" **15.00**
  William Lewis & Son, Stringed Musi-
    cal Instruments and Accessories,
    1930, 96 pgs **80.00**
  Wing Pianos, 1913, large format,
    twelve full page color plates **40.00**
Flyer
  C Bruno & Son, New York, NY,
    Sousa's Band Harmonicas, single
    sheet, two sided, yellow ground,
    harmonicas one side, violin strings
    other side, c1915.............. **20.00**
  Mason & Hamlin, Cambridge, MA,
    Mason & Hamlin's Melodeons, 8
    pgs, illus, testimonials, descriptions,
    and prices, c1864 .... **60.00**
Invitation, music instructions by Mr G W
  Morgon, lists rates, Sep 1871........ **9.00**
Label
  Apples, Boy Blue, little boy blowing
    horn, blue ground, 10½ x 9" **1.00**
  Cigar, Huyler Cigars, musician image,
    5 x 5" **4.00**

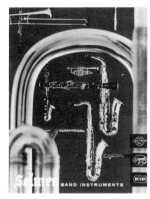

Catalog, Selmer Band Instruments, 28 pages, color covers, black-and-white photos, 8½ x 11", 1958, $20.00.

Manual, The Kamikl Ukulele Method, 1915, 64 pgs 5.00
Photograph, violinist, seated bald man wearing double–breasted coat, stiff pointed collar, and paisley tie, holding violin upright in lap, 1880s, 4½ x 6½, mounted on 7 x 9" card 28.00
Playing Cards, Black playing trumpet, "New Orleans," Delta Air Lines adv . . 10.00
Post Card
    American Music Hall, "The Show Place Of Chicago," full color Music Hall image 6.00
    Count Basie, mutoscope, black and white 5.00
Poster, Wilcox & White Organ Co, woman holding player piano roll, 27 x 23" 150.00
Program, Johnny Mathis, 1970, 10 x 13" 10.00
Sheet Music, *Great Western Band,* cov with photo of band members with instruments, 1898. . . . . 12.00

Vocal Score, *Miss Bob White,* Pastoral Comedy Opera, words and music by Willard Spenser, 9¼ x 11¾", 1901, $15.00.

Sign, Everett Piano Co, factory scene, pianos on horse–drawn wagons, 22 x 38". 200.00

NABISCO
Booklet
    Cook Out With Sky King, photo and logo on front cov, premium, 1950s, 3 x 7" 25.00
    National Biscuit Company, Maxfield Parrish cov with close–up of chef holding sign "Bug Biscuit Baked by National Biscuit Company," color, 1920, 6 x 3" 20.00
    75 Desserts, color photos, product illus on cov 10.00
Premium
    Card, Straight Arrow's 72 Injun–Uities Secrets of Indian Lore and Know–How, 1951 . . . . 20.00
    Puzzle, jigsaw, Straight Arrow Indian, orig envelope, 1959. . . . . 10.00

"Uneeda Bakers"

Magazine Tear Sheet, Uneeda Bakers' Boy with Yellow Slicker, Sugar Wafers adv., *Ladies' Home Journal,* 10 x 14", September 1930, $12.00.

NATURAL DISASTER
Advertising Trade Card, Johnstown Flood, screaming cat under shower endorses umbrellas, "No Johnstown flood for me...," Steiner & Swartz Lady's and Gent's Furnishing Goods. . 15.00

Book
History of the Johnstown Flood, Willis
    F Johnson, 518 pgs, illus, 1889 . . . .   **15.00**
New England Flood of November,
    1927, American Railway Engineer-
    ing Association Bulletin, Vol III
    #308, 112 pgs, adv, Aug 1928 . . . .   **7.50**
1945 Flood Pictures of the Point and
    the Surrounding Areas, Louisville
    Flood, 20 pgs, soft cov, approx 150
    photos of flood damage **25.00**
San Francisco's Horror of Earthquake,
    Fire, and Famine, memorial volume,
    illus, dated April 18, 1906 . . . .   **15.00**
Booklet, Pictorial Story of the Flood of
    Southern Tier, New York State, 1925,
    32 pgs, photos and captions **6.00**
Newspaper
    Alaskan Earthquake, *News Tribune,*
        Duluth, MN, March 29, 1964, arti-
        cles on earthquake and rebuilding   **7.50**
    South Carolina Earthquake, *News &*
        Courier, Charleston, SC, 1886, 8 pgs **100.00**
    San Francisco Chronicle, April 22,
        1906, San Francisco Earthquake and
        Fire. **45.00**
    San Francisco Earthquake and Fire,
        San Francisco Chronicle, April 22,
        1906, top banner headline "Force
        Of The Fire Is At Last Spent," 6 pgs,
        six photos of ruins and bread lines
        following disaster, ...   **45.00**
Photograph, set of 4, San Antonio flood,
    albumen, San Antonio river at flood
    stage, one with people and trolley on
    bridge over swollen river, 1900. . . . . .   **20.00**
Sign, cardboard, cyclone image, Cy-
    clone Twister Cigars **50.00**
Stereoview
    Boston Fire, ruins, Soule, 1872 . . . . . .   **10.00**
    Galveston Flood, ruins, Graves, 1900   **5.00**
    Johnstown Flood, real photo, large flat
        mount card, Webster & Albee, titled
        and dated, c1889, set of 8 . . . .   **95.00**
Sheet Music, San Francisco Earthquake
    and Fire, *San Francisco's Cry,* illus
    cov, 1906 . . . .   **20.00**

NATURAL HISTORY

Book
    Natural History, c1800, 596 pgs, 38
        black and white plates **10.00**
    Natural History of Remarkable Birds,
        printed by William Espy, Dublin,
        1821, 171 pgs, full page engravings,
        leather cov, 3½ x 5½" **25.00**
    Mineral Resources of the U.S., 1920,
        1923, GPO, fold–out maps **7.00**
Catalog, The Naturalist Advertiser,
    American Naturalist Salem, #5, 1873,

**Trade Card Jigsaw Puzzle, Turkish Tro-
phies, zebra, No. 2, 3¼ x 2½", 1910,
$8.00.**

80 pgs, natural history books and taxi-
    dermy speciments, adv **25.00**
Guide, Visitor's Guide to the Collection
    of Birds in the American Museum of
    Natural History, Manhattan Square,
    NY, 1888 . . . .   **5.00**
Handbook, *A Report Of The Cruise Of*
    The Revenue Steamer 'Corwin' In Arc-
    tic Ocean, 1885, 1887, color plates
    and woodcuts on Eskimos and land-
    scapes, two maps of Alaskan rivers . . .   **120.00**
Print
    Alexander Pope Jr, "Blue–Billed
        Duck," *Upland Game Birds and*
        Water Fowl of the United States,
        NY, 1877–78, 14 x 20" **150.00**
    Thomas Doughty, "American Sparrow
        Hawk," *The Cabinet of Natural His-*
        tory and American Rural Sports se-
        ries, hand colored litho, 1830–32,
        3½ x 11" **60.00**

NAUTICAL

Book, *The Galley Guide: A Purely Hu-*
    manitarian Work, Planned Out Of
    Consideration For The Digestive Ap-
    paratus Of Those Who Cruise – The
    Thing, After All, Upon Which Success
    Or Failure Largely Depends, Alex W
    Moffat, Motor Boat Publishing, NY,
    1923, 145 pgs **20.00**
Brochure, Cruising With Safety, 1947, 76
    pgs, sailboat and motorboat photos,
    glossy stiff covs, third edition. **10.00**
Catalog
    Marine Hardware, P & F Corbin, New
        Britain, CT, c1920, 278 pgs, loose–
        leaf format, illus, brass and bronze
        hardware **35.00**
    Nautical Almanac, Riggs & Brother,
        Philadelphia, PA, 1910, 154 pgs,
        nautical instruments, includes par-
        tially used ship's log. **125.00**

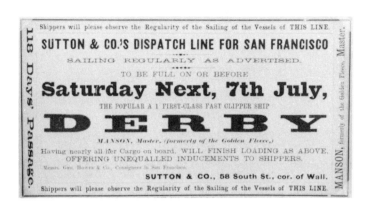

Clipper Ship Card, *Derby*, Sutton & Co.'s Dispatch Line for San Francisco, blue lettering, white ground, printed by Nesbit & Co., Printers, NY, 6⅜ x 3⁹/₁₆", $300.00.

Steamship and Yacht Ranges, Bramhall, Deane Company, New York, NY, c1910, 16 pgs, illus, nautical supplies, includes list of boats outfitted by Bramhall, Deane Company, oblong 8vo 40.00

Clipper Ship Card, passage to California, *Golden Fleece,* vignette of three masted sailing ships 950.00

Document
Bill of Lading, Cromwell, NYNO Steamship Line, shipped from New Orleans to Providence via steamship *New Orleans,* logo on red flag, 11 x 8" 24.00

Bill of Sale, "U.S. of America Bill of Sale of Enrolled Vessel," parchment, sailing ship vignette, 1893 . . . 15.00

Insurance, brig *Betsy,* total loss of brig and cargo, Eben Ricker late master, N F Marine Insurance Co, 1805, 12 x 7" 14.00

Pay, brig *Private,* 1801, bearer to be paid seven dollars, handwritten, 8½ x 3½" 12.00

Shipping Order, Cromwell Lines, shipped 28 bales of cotton on steamship *Knickerbocker,* green paddle boat vignette, 11 x 8½" 32.00

Label
Cigar, Cutter Cigars, sailing yacht flying US flag, 1887, 5 x 5" 32.00

Vegetable, Defender Tomatoes, two sailing ships along coastline, 9 x 3½" 2.00

Poster, Central Hudson Line, couple with camera and binoculars standing at ship's rail, artist sgd "WG," 1918–20, 45 x 30" 190.00

Stock Certificate, Pioneer Steamship Co, steamship vignette, ornate border, 1914 . . . . 20.00

Receipt, *Medford,* Harbour Masters Office, New Orleans, black and white, printed by L Dillard, 1842 . . . . 10.00

Sea Chart, Chart of the North and Baltic Seas, J Thomson, outline colored, 1816, 23 x 19" 35.00

OCCUPATION

Bus Driver
Brochure, Greyhound Bus, foldout, route maps, bus pictures, full color, 1930s 10.00

Schedule, Travel by Motor Coach Richmond Fredericksburg, Washington, 1927, blue and white 8.00

Doctor, magazine tear sheet, dentist promoting Sunkist Oranges, 10½ x 13½", 1934, $10.00.

Fireman

References: Chuck Deluca, *Firehouse Memorabilia: A Collector's Reference,* Maritime Antique Auctions, 1989; Mary Jane and James Piatti, *Firehouse Collectibles,* The Engine House, 1979.

Collectors' Club: Fire Collectors Club, PO Box 992, Milwaukee, WI 53201.

Blotter, Fire Your Orders At Us, Seneca
   Castle, NY, firemen putting out burn-
   ing house **4.00**
Book
   Fires and Firefighters, John V Morris,
     Little, Brown, & Co, Boston, 1953,
     387 pgs **30.00**
   *Our Firemen, History of New York Fire
     Departments,* A E Costello, 1887,
     first edition **225.00**
   The American Firemen, H S Champlin,
     Regan & Cashman, Boston, 1875,
     256 pgs **80.00**
   *The Story of the Volunteer Fire Depart-
     ment of the City of NY,* G W
     Sheldon, Harper & Brothers, NY,
     1882, 575 pgs **100.00**
   The Young Firemen of Lakeville, Frank
     V Webster, Cupples & Leon Co, NY,
     1909, 204 pgs **18.00**
Bubble Gum Card, Bowman's Firefight-

Firemen, magazine tear sheet, Beech-Nut Gum, color, 8 x 11½", 1930s, $10.00.

   ers, #4, Airport Crash Truck, 2½ x
   3¾" **1.75**
Cabinet Photo, fireman, Lowell, MA, full
   length view **8.00**
Catalog
   Darley Municipal–Fire Protection
   Everything For Fire Prevention & Fire
     Protection, American La France,
     1910, 306 pgs **35.00**
   Fire Department Supplies, James Boyd
     & Bros, Philadelphia, PA, 128 pgs . .   **20.00**
   Modern Fire Fighting Equipment, #38,
     American La France, 1938, 144 pgs   **15.00**
Certificate, Fireman's
   Active Member, Florida, NY, Decem-
     ber 5, 1898, Cairns & Bros, 143
     Grants St, NY, colored illus of chem-
     ical wagon, steamer, extinguisher,
     hose cart, ladder truck, hose reel,
     fireman, hydrant, and hose **75.00**
   City of Paterson, February 21, 1879,
     litho photo **65.00**
Children's Book, *Fred Fireman,* Joe Kauf-
   man, Golden Press, NY, 1968 . . . .   **4.00**
Coloring Book, Fire Department Pic-
   tures, #734, M A Donahue & Co, Chi-
   cago, 1917 . . . .   **20.00**
Magazine
   Fireman, 1940–50 . . . .   **5.00**
   *Volunteer Firemen–Prof Journal of Vol
     Firemen's Section of National Fire
     Protection Association,* 1935–37 . .   **15.00**
Post Card
   Chemical Engine No. 2, Scranton, PA,
     photo, horse–drawn engine **40.00**
   Crack Fire Team, Beaver Falls, PA,
     photo, horse–drawn engine, 1909   **75.00**
   Fire Truck No. 1, Providence, RI,
     horse–drawn photo **30.00**
   Hose Truck, driving to fire, emb,
     printed color, silver highlights,
     P1400 series, Germany, 1908 . . . . .   **35.00**
   Life of a Cleveland Fireman, Cleve-
     land, OH, black and white photo of
     firemen fighting fire **5.00**
   Our Brave Fire Laddies–The Rescue,
     color photo of fireman saving
     woman from burning building **8.00**
Poster, Silver Springs Brewery, 1910, full
   color fireman, 16" d **30.00**
Print, Always Ready, Nathaniel Currier
   dressed as fireman, pulling hose reel
   out of fire house, Currier & Ives, 1858   **250.00**
Program
   Firemen Convention, 1927 . . . .   **30.00**
   Fireman Dance, logo on front, emb
     color **6.00**
   44th Annual Parade, Middletown Fire
     Department, October 9, 1902 . . . . .   **5.00**
Puzzle
   Ed Wynn Fire Chief, wearing helmet,
     holding axe, steamer background,

Viking Manufacturing Co, Boston, MA........................ **18.00**
Five Little Firemen, Little Golden Picture Puzzle, Series No. 1, Whitman, 1949, cartoon firemen fighting burning house, orig box.......... **8.00**

Sheet Music
Eagle Quick Step, 1843, firemen and engine leaving burned barn....... **18.00**
Midnight Fire Alarm.............. **20.00**
The Fire Master, 1908, firemen fighting fire in street scene........... **15.00**

Stereo View, #8232, Burning of the Cold Storage Building, Fifteen brave firemen lost their lives, July 10th, B W Kilburn, Littleton, NH 1893 copyright **8.00**
Ticket, Fourteenth Annual Picnic & Reception of the Mystic Club of Philadelphia, Wednesday, July 4th, 1883, steamer illus.................... **5.00**
Valentine Card, To My Valentine, boy cupid wearing fireman's hat and boots putting out burning heart with hose, Ethel Dewees artist.............. **4.00**

Policeman

Reference: Monty McCord, Police Cars: A Photographic History, Krause Publications, 1991.

Periodical: Police Collectors News, RR 1, Box 14, Baldwin, WI 54002.

Book, Knots Untied: Or Ways and Byways in the Hidden Life of American Detectives by Officer George S McWatters, Late of the Metropolitan Police, NY, 665 pgs, 1871.......... **35.00**
Booklet, The ABC of Practical Pistol Instruction For Home Guards, Police Auxilary, c1920, 27 pgs, NRA of America....................... **4.25**
Brochure
Plymouth Police Cars, Best On Any Beat, 1957, closeup face of policeman...................... **8.00**
The New 1953 Ford Police Car, police badge shape outline with policemen riding in police car on front cov.... **12.00**
True Stories About the Car that Stands up Best, Plymouth, 1938, policeman and car photo on front cov.... **15.00**
Catalog, Edward K Tryon Co, Philadelphia, PA, 1924, 400 pgs, 12 pgs of police goods................... **100.00**
Game, Rival Policeman, McLoughlin Bros, 1896, policeman chasing man on box cov, 23 pcs and playing board **275.00**
Label, cigar, Yellow Cab, policeman and yellow taxi cab, 2 x 5½".......... **8.00**
Magazine, Police Gazette, January, 1959, 10½ x 13"................. **40.00**

Nurse, magazine cover, *The Saturday Evening Post*, sgd. J. C. Leyendecker illustration, printed red and black, 96 pages, 11 x 14", March 30, 1918, $45.00.

Photograph
Motorcycle squad, three policemen posed on motorcycles in front of station No. 6, Kansas City, MO...... **10.00**
Parade, six policemen riding in open patrol wagon, Detroit, MI, 1917... **12.00**
Three Los Angeles police officers sitting in horse–drawn patrol wagon, ornate "Police Patrol" on wagon, 1880s...................... **15.00**

Post Card
The Seat of Trouble, policeman approaching two children......... **3.00**
You'd keep the peace, were you a police, I love a brave, bold man like you, boy dressed as police officer holding billy club, E Curtis artist... **5.00**
You'll be Copped, boy dressed as police officer holding billy club, FSM artist....................... **4.00**

Postman
Advertising Trade Card, Celluloid Collars & Cuffs adv, postman holding mail bag, US map and flag illus.... **20.00**

Book
Postal Laws & Regulations of USA, 1897, 597 pgs................. **10.00**
US Official Postal Guide, 1876, 266 pgs...................... **8.00**

Catalog
Morrill Bros, Complete Price List of Printed Post Office Supplies, Fulton, NY, 1889, 12 pgs.............. **45.00**
Riverside Tailoring Co, Mail Carriers' Uniforms, 1938, 12 pgs.......... **35.00**

Game
The Letter Carrier, McLoughlin Bros, c1890, 117 playing pcs, multicolored litho playing board, postman delivering letters to woman on box lid.................... **95.00**

The Postman Game, Parker Brothers, c1895, multicolored litho board, four wood markers and die **15.00**
Little Golden Book, *Seven Little Post-men,* Tibor Gergely, M W Brown and E T Hurd **10.00**

OCEAN LINER

References: John Adams, *Ocean Steamers: The History of Ocean Going Steam Ships,* New Cavendish Books, 1992; Karl D. Spence, *How To Identify and Price Ocean Liner Collectibles,* published by author, 1991; Karl D. Spence, *Oceanliner Collectibles,* published by author, 1992.

Collectors' Clubs: Steamship Historical Society of America, Inc., Suite #4, 300 Ray Drive, Providence, RI 02906; Titanic Historical Society, PO Box 51053, Indian Orchard, MA 01151.

Booklet, 1937 Cruise of the SS Reliance Around The World, Hamburg-American Line, North German Lloyd, printed black, blue, and gold covers, foldout map of cruise, 32 pages, black-and-white photographs, 8½ x 11", $18.00.

Book
  A Century of Shipping–The History of The Royal Netherlands Steamship Company 1856–1956, Ger H Knap, 136 pgs, black and white and color photos, various ships and company history, 7½ x 10½" **35.00**
  Wreck of the Titanic, Everett, 320 pgs   **30.00**
Booklet
  Alcoa Line, Arcadia and Saint John, Bermuda service, March 10, 1941, sailing schedule **8.00**
  Britannic, March 1955, 12 pgs, first class deck plans, color photos, 9 x 12" **16.00**
  Cunard, September, 1953, 23 pgs **10.00**
  Booklet, *RMS Queen Mary* **25.00**
  Royal Interocean Lines, May 1965, 12 pgs, color photos of ships, 7 x 9" . . .   **12.00**
  White Star Line, "Our Cabin Liners," November 1933, 24 pgs, 1st class accommodation photos for *Georgic* and *Britannic* **70.00**
Brochure, Cunard Line, Round The World "Carinthia" Southern Hemisphere Cruise, 64 pgs, black and white ship photos, maps, and visitation sites, 1933 . . . .   **30.00**
Check, Old Colony Steamboat Co, July 25, 1881, canceled **6.00**
Deck Plan, White Star line Triple Screw RMS Titanic, 45,000 Tons, December, 1911, 40 x 30", black and white **250.00**
Letter Card, Cunard *RMS Queen Mary,* fold–out, color illus, 1930s, 6½ x 4" . .   **18.00**
Letterhead, *Empress of Australia I,* Round the World Cruise, 1929–30 . . . .   **2.00**
Magazine
  Canadian Pacific Princess, 16 pgs, travel type **4.00**

  Colliers, May 4, 1912, Titanic survivors **35.00**
  Life, August 6, 1956, *Andrea Doria* sinks **10.00**
Magazine Tear Sheet, *Harper's,* monthly, 1913, black and white view of "New Olympic–virtually two ships in one," sister ship to *Titanic,* 6 x 9" **8.00**
Matchbook Cover, Holland–American Lines **1.75**
Menu
  Bremen, Welcome Aboard First Class Dinner Menu, July 17, 1936, hard emb board cov, raised compass rose   **25.00**
  Carinthia, third class dinner menu, July 6, 1939, village scene **6.00**
  RMS Queen Mary, dinner, June 7, 1936 . . . .   **15.00**
  RMS Rotterdam, Lido Restaurant, Art Deco cov, 1937, 4 x 5½" **10.00**
  SS Chiyo Maru, March 1909, 6 x 9" . . .   **30.00**
  Statendam, farewell dinner, July 23, 1935, Frans Hals on cov, ship on back cov **8.00**
Menu Card, set of 4, engraved ship *Berkshire,* Merchants & Miners Transportation Co **15.00**
Newspaper, *RMS Queen Mary, Ocean Times,* June 6, 1936 . . . .   **15.00**
Pamphlet, Ward Line, New York and Cuba Mail Steamship Co, 24 pgs, 1926   **24.00**
Photograph
  Carnival, color aerial view **1.50**
  Duchess of Bedford, black and white view **4.00**
Playing Cards
  Boheme, ship in ocean, coastline background **15.00**
  Delta Line, aerial view of ship in ocean   **17.50**

Dance Card, *Europa*, Nord Deutscher Lloyd Bremen Line, printed, black and white, gold emb. logo, 3½ x 6", 1930s, $8.00.

SS Milwaukee Clipper, ship in ocean
scene **12.50**
Post Card
Andrea Doria, multicolored **16.00**
Aquitania, sepia photo, portside view,
5½ x 10¾".................. **20.00**
Empress of Britain II, port broadside
view, sepia.................... **8.00**
Time of Arrival, black and white ships,
1906, 3½ x 5½"............... **18.00**
Poster
Queen Elizabeth II, "For Once In Your
Life, Live," ship and skyline view .. **22.00**
Queen Mary, docking at Southampton, sepia tone, c1938, 20 x 30" ... **125.00**
SS Washington, 1933, 25 x 30" **150.00**
Program
Queen of Bermuda, February 7, 1959 **14.00**
Samaria, Shore Programme at Singapore, Golden Jubilee Cruise, March
1923, 7 pgs **8.00**
Sheet Music, *Mandalay, USS Leviathan,*
jazz band on deck scene on cov, red,
white, and blue dec border, 4 pgs **9.00**
Toy, *Rigby's Book of Model Ships,* 1953,
punchout, unused **50.00**

OFFICE PRODUCTS

References: William Aspray, *Computing Before Computers,* 1989; *The Business Machines and Equipment Digest 1927,* Chicago, 1927; NCR, *Celebrating the Future, 1884–1984,* published by company, 1984; Michael R. Williams, *A History of Computing Technology,* Prentice Hall, 1985.

Periodicals: *The Typewriter Exchange,* 2125 Mt. Vernon St., Philadelphia, PA 19130; *Typewriter Times,* 1216 Garden St., Hoboken, NJ 07030.

Collectors' Clubs: Early Typewriter Collectors Association, 2591 Military Ave., Los Angeles, CA 90064; Internationales Forum Historische Buro-

welt e.w. (IFHB), PO Box 50 11 68, D–5000 Koln 50, Germany.

Advertising Trade Card
Simplex Typewriter, diecut, Santa
Claus holding typewriter, 1913 .... **20.00**
Smith Premier Typewriter Co, diecut,
silver, black, and green **40.00**
Booklet
Blickenderfer Typewriter, 1901, 4 pgs,
women using typewriters illus, Pan–
American Exposition giveaway **30.00**
Panama–Pacific Exposition, 1915, 30
pgs, compliments of Remington
Typewriter Co, illus cov.......... **25.00**
Smith Premier Typewriter Co, diecut
typewriter shape, 6 pgs **30.00**
The Typewriter, A Short History, Zellers, 1873–1948 .... **7.00**
Brochure, foldout, Oliver Co, Chicago,
IL, New Model 9 typewriter, 1922, 8½
x 10½" opened **8.00**
Catalog
Globe–Wernicke Co, Cabinet Supplies, Cincinnati, OH, 1907, 60 pgs,
cutting edge of office technology... **40.00**
Invincible Steel Business Furniture,
Manitowoc, WI, 1940, 80 pgs..... **5.00**
Oliver Typewriter Co, Chicago, IL,
c1902, 24 pgs **75.00**
Wood Filing Equipment, 1923, 60 pgs **65.00**
Yawman & Erbe Mfg Co, Rochester,
NY, c1900, 68 pgs, card filing sys-

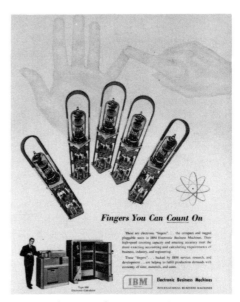

Magazine Tear Sheet, IBM, "Fingers You Can Count On," type 604 electronic calculator adv., 10 x 13", 1950s, $15.00.

tems, photo of girl using Fisher Book
  Typewriter **40.00**
Display, American Pencil Co, cardboard,
  roadster shape **85.00**
Sign, Dixon's American Graphite Pen-
  cils, Jos Dixon Crucible Co, little girl
  holding comical drawing of pencil,
  framed, 29 x 15" **450.00**

OIL COMPANIES

References: Scott Anderson, *Check The Oil,* Wallace–Homestead, 1986; Mark Anderton, *Gas Station Collectibles,* Wallace–Homestead, 1993;
Ted Hake, *Hake's Guide To Advertising Collectibles,* Wallace–Homestead, 1992; Sonya Stenzler
and Rick Pease, *Gas Station Collectibles,* Schiffer
Publishing, 1993; Michael Karl Witzel, *The
American Gas Station,* Motorbooks International,
1992.

Periodical: *Hemmings Motor News,* Box 100,
Bennington, VT 05201.

Collectors' Club: International Petroliana Collectors Association, PO Box 1000–F, Westerville,
OH 43081.

Advertising Trade Card
  A W Harris Oil Co, diecut, oil barrel   **20.00**
  Beacon Oil Co, family scene, multi-
    colored **60.00**
Broadside, Merchant's Oil, three color
  illus, framed, 27 x 12" **1,500.00**
Photograph, The Standard Oil Co,
  Ohio filling station, c1920 . . . .   **10.00**
Playing Cards
  Jenkel Oil Co, Inc, white and red de-
    livery truck and printing, blue and
    gold border **10.00**
  Marathon, The Ohio Oil Company,
    white with red, white, and blue
    Marathon logo center, red and
    gold border **7.50**
  Sinclair Oils, white, red and gold
    border, oil well and refinery center   **5.00**
  Sorenson Oil Co, Phillips 66 logo,
    white, green and gold top and bot-
    tom border **6.50**
  Standard Oil, dark red, gold border,
    white circle center with name. . . .   **2.50**
Score Book, Soho Oil, Cleveland In-
  dians, 1947 . . . .   **18.00**
Stock Certificate
  Blue Ribbon Oil & Development Co,
    OK, 1920, oil field and smoking
    refinery vignettes, green printing   **15.00**
  Texas–Atlantic Oil Co, TX, 1921,
    Texas map, oil wells, workers,
    trains, and tanks vignette, green
    and beige printing, gold seal **15.00**
  The Union Oil, Gas & Refining Co,
    Arizona Territory, 1902, oil field,

**Needle Book, Compliments of Your Esso
Dealer, five needle packages, double fold,
printed color, red and black on white,
Japan, 5 x 3½", 1950s, $10.00.**

  buildings, and tank vignette, gold
    seal **20.00**
  Union Consolidated Oil Co, WV,
    1902, rope border, eagle with pa-
    triotic symbols, buffalo, train, and
    steamboat vignette, ornate banner
    with title **50.00**

OLYMPICS

Reference: Roderick A. Malloy, *Malloy's Sports
Collectibles Value Guide,* Wallace–Homestead,
1993.

Book
  Illustrated History of the Olympics,
    Dick Schaap, third edition, dj, 1975   **8.00**
  19 Olympiad, 302 pgs, Spanish and
    American text, 1968 final results, dj,
    9 x 12" **18.00**
  1936 Olympic Games, Sonja Henie
    and other world athletes photos . . .   **450.00**
Coaster, paper, 1972, "Munscher Bier,"
  Munich, Germany, double sided **25.00**
Magazine, *Sports Illustrated,* November
  19, 1956, Summer Olympic article . . .   **15.00**
Manual, Olympic Edition, 1936, 48 pgs,
  issued by Shell Petroleum, 3¼ x 6¼"   **15.00**
Poster, XIV Winter Olympics, 1984
  Sarajevo, ski jumper **15.00**
Program
  1948, Summer Olympic Trials, 20 pgs,
    weight lifting trials, 8 x 10½" **15.00**
  1952, 72 pgs, rowing tryouts **20.00**
Ticket
  X Olympiad, Los Angeles, CA, 1932,
    Track and Field, 2½ x 4½" **15.00**
  XXII Olympics, 1980, Moscow, USSR,
    pr, unused **8.00**
Tobacco Card
  B Fiske, Kings of Speed, Churchmann
    Cigarettes, 1939, bobsled **20.00**

Jigsaw Puzzle, 1932 Olympic Games, Toddy premium, color litho, orig. envelope, 75 pcs., 13 x 10", $30.00.

C Cooledge, Sporting Events and Star, Senior Service Cigarettes, Churchmann Cigarettes, 1939 . . . .   **10.00**
Johnny Weissmuller, Boguslavsky Cigarettes, 1925, full color, 1³/₈ x 2⁵/₈"   **6.00**
R Johnson, Record Holders of the World, Cadet Sweets, 1962 . . . .   **10.00**
Sonja Henie, Drapkin Cigarettes, 1930, black and white photo, 1³/₈ x 2⁵/₈ **8.00**

OPERA

Reference: House of Collectibles (eds.), *The Official Price Guide to Music Collectibles,* House of Collectibles, Sixth Edition, 1986, out–of–print.

Advertising Trade Card
  Harlem & Westchester Clothing, man at opera scene **7.00**
  Lancaster Opera Co, *Pinafore,* folder, band on cov, text int **20.00**
Brochure, Opera Co, sgd by Regina Resnick, c1952 . . . .   **10.00**
Check, 1969, sgd by Cesare Siepi **25.00**
Document, contract, opera company, sgd by Patrice Munsel **20.00**
Label, cigar, Madame Butterfly, opera scene, butterflies, and ship **28.00**
Letter, Enrico Caruso, c1915, 2 typed pgs, sgd **155.00**
Magazine, *Opera News,* Justino Diaz photo on cov **30.00**
Magazine Cover, *Opera News,* Birgit Nilsson photo, sgd **18.00**
Magazine Tear Sheet
  Article, Zinka Milanov, sgd in blue pencil **25.00**
  Photo of John Brownlee, sgd and in-

scribed, mounted on stiff paper, 5 x 7¹/₂" **20.00**
Pamphlet, Los Angeles Opera House, Compliments of OW Childs, May 27, 1884, 5¹/₂ x 5" **75.00**
Photograph
  Adler, Kurt, sgd and inscribed, 8 x 10" **20.00**
  Caruso, Enrico, wearing costume from *Girl of the Golden West,* matted, 8 x 10" **75.00**
Poster
  Metropolitan Opera House, 1900– 10, unillustrated **50.00**
  Three Penny Opera, Paul Davis, 1976, two panels, 41 x 81" **275.00**
Program
  A Masked Ball, Metropolitan Opera House, 1940, Knabe Piano adv on back **8.00**

Cigar Label, Madame Butterfly, red, blue, and gold, 8¹/₂ x 6¹/₂", $28.00.

German Comic Opera, 1881, cupid
and butterfly dec, black and white,
engraved by Bailey, Banks, and
Biddle **8.00**
Metropolitan Opera, sgd by Frances
Alda **35.00**
Record Jacket, Montserrat Caballe, sgd
and inscribed **50.00**
Scrapbook
Enrico Caruso, photos, news clip-
pings, tickets, etc. **1,800.00**
James Melton, 150 press clippings
relating to his career, vinyl cov . . .   **75.00**

OUTER SPACE & SPACE EXPLORATION

Reference: Stuart Schneider, *Collecting the Space Race,* Schiffer Publishing, 1993.

Periodical: *SpaceLog,* PO Box 533, Alamogordo, NM 88310.

Autograph
Beregovoi, G T, cosmonaut, Soyuz 3,
unrelated cov, bold black ink signa-
ture, 1968 . . . .   **30.00**
Irwin, James, astronaut, 3 x 5" card . . .   **30.00**
Resnick, Judy, astronaut, 3 x 5" card . .   **85.00**
Shepard, Alan, astronaut, 8 x 10" pho-
tograph, c1962 . . . .   **45.00**
Swigert, Jack, astronaut, envelope, ink
signature, Man on the Moon stamp,
canceled Kennedy Space Center,
April 11, 1970 . . . .   **45.00**
Book
Into Space With the Astronauts, Won-
der Book, 1965, 48 pgs, 8 x 11" **15.00**
Keeping Up With The Astronauts,
Grosset & Dunlap, 1963, 92 pgs, 9 x
11½" **20.00**
Man in Flight, Saalfield, 1962, 48 pgs,
8 x 11" **18.00**
*Rockets, Missiles and Space Travel
With Sputnik Data,* Willy Ley, re-
vised edition, 1957, 528 pgs, dj. . . .   **15.00**
The Exploration of Space, Arthur C
Clarke, Temple Press Ltd, London,
1951, 198 pgs, color illus, 6 x 9" . . .   **40.00**
Victory In Space, Otto O Binder, 1962,
212 pgs, 6 x 9" **15.00**
We Seven, authored by original seven
astronauts, Simon and Schuster,
1962, 474 pgs, black and white
photos, 6 x 8½" **20.00**
Booklet, Saturn V, official NASA publica-
tion, 1967 copyright **25.00**
Calendar, 1969–70, September to Au-
gust, commemorates Apollo 11, moon
landing illus, spiral bound, 9½ x 11"   **15.00**
Coloring Book
Rockets and Space, Treasure Books,
1960s, 65 pgs, unused **15.00**

Apollo/Man on the Moon, Saalfield,
1969, moon landing illus cov,
unused, 8½ x 11". **15.00**
First Day Cover, Apollo VIII, December,
1968, 3¾ x 6½" **10.00**
Game
Apollo Moon Flight, Jones Publishing
Co, 1969, red, white, blue, green,
and yellow board, Saturn V rocket
shape playing cards, wood playing
pieces, dice, orig box. **40.00**
Moon Flight, Avon Products, 1970,
orig box **20.00**
Rocket Race to Saturn, Lido Toy,
c1950, 9½ x 13" board, four rocket
playing pieces, orig box. **40.00**
Little Golden Book, *Exploring Space,*
Rose Wyler, Tibor Gergely **8.00**
Magazine
Life, July 4, 1969, Off to the Moon
article. **12.00**
Look, February 21, 1956, 6 pg article
and photos on Lt Col Frank K
Everest, Date with Outer Space cov   **10.00**
Photograph
Alan Bean and spacecraft, "Apollo 12
On The Moon–November 19,
1969," color, 8 x 10". **40.00**
Apollo XVI, NASA, 1972 liftoff and lu-
nar view, 8 x 10" **12.00**
Charles Conrad, wearing space suit,
color, 8 x 10" **30.00**
Jim Irwin, spacecraft, and land rover,
white border with "Astronaut Irwin
Salutes Flag At Apollo Hadley–
Apennine Landing Site," color, 8 x
10" **75.00**
Playing Cards, Space Shuttle, Kennedy
Space Center, Florida, USA, shuttle
taking off from launch pad. **6.50**
Premium, Lipton Lunar Space Map, full
color, 20 x 24" **15.00**

PATRIOTIC

References: Boleslow and Marie–Louis D'Otrange Mastai, *The Stars and Stripes: The American Flag As Art And As History from the Birth Of The Republic To The Present,* Alfred Knopf, 1973; Robert Ward, *Investment Guide To North American Real Photo Postcards,* Antique Paper Guild, 1991.

Collectors' Club: North American Vexillological Association, PO Box 580, Winchester, MA 01890.

Advertising Cover, Uncle Sam and
world globe, White Mountain Refrigerators, color design front and back,
orig envelope, 1906 . . . .   **100.00**
Advertising Trade Card
Anheuser Busch Brewing Assoc,

1893, flag draped woman holding glass of beer 30.00

Brooks Oil Co, Cleveland, OH, Bunker Hill Harness Oil, Uncle Sam illus 6.00

Emmert Proprietary Co, Uncle Sam Harness Oil 5.00

F Branca Milan, colorful eagle and shield scene, 1894 testimonial ... 46.00

Frank Millers Blacking, Uncle Sam shaving with straight razor, using polished boot as mirror, eagle looking at reflection 25.00

Henry Mayo Minced Codfish, Uncle Sam's Award 15.00

Home Light Oil, Uncle Sam supplying world 30.00

Hub Gore Makers of Elastic For Shoes, It Was Honored at the World's Fair of 1893, Uncle Sam holding shoe, 3½ x 6¼" 15.00

Pillsbury's Best Flour, Uncle Sam giving flour to people of world ... 33.00

Blotter, large flag image, gold highlights, "Victory," Follansbee Brothers Co Roofing Tin adv, June 1898 calendar inset 15.00

Catalog, Davis Sewing Machine, c1899, 20 pgs, "Old Abe" War Eagle perched on draped American flags on cov, product illus, techniques, and testimonials 30.00

Game

Heroes of America, Games of the Nations Series, Paul Educational Games, 1920s, box with flag illus 22.00

Old Glory, Parker Brothers, 1899, card game, multicolored US flag and US military heroes on backs, 52 cards and 2 adv cards 18.00

Label, cigar

American Citizen, George Washington, American eagle and shield .. 6.00

Companita, patriotic lady and winged man over shield 30.00

Don Alfonsa, US Miss Liberty greets Cuban counterpart, 1890s 10.00

Cigar Label, American Glory, red, white, and blue, 10 x 6", $25.00.

First Banner, George Washington, US shield and American eagle ... 18.00

Foreign Exchange, patriotic lady gesturing to clipper ship, 1890s 12.00

Magazine, *Life,* June 21, 1906, James Montgomery Flagg centerfold 10.00

Paper Doll, Uncle Sam's Little Helpers Paper Dolls, Ann Kovach, 1943 .... 15.00

Playing Cards

Delta Air Lines, Washington, color illus of American flag, capitol building, and Abraham Lincoln .. 10.00

Evinrude, patriotic emblem with printed "Evinrude," blue, white border 18.00

Post Card

American Flag, banner type sheet music for *Star Spangled Banner,* and stars illus, Int Art Co, NY 5.00

For the Sake of Old Glory, military officers and flags 3.00

George Led The World's Dance In His Day, H B Griggs 10.00

Greetings for February Twenty–Second, Washington and old woman, landscape scene, draped red, white, and blue banner, 1916 4.00

Honor The Brave, crossed flags, eagle, and stars and stripes shield... 5.00

Souvenir of Decoration Day, draped red, white, and blue curtain with stars and stripes, soldiers guns, drum, and knapsack, ships in background, 1909 .... 5.00

The Day We Celebrate, When in the course of human events, young George Washington giving speech, American flag, C Bunnell and Chapman 6.00

Theodore Roosevelt, 1910, multicolored Uncle Sam, GOP elephant, and Taft dancing on dock 35.00

Uncle Sam, wearing pair of Taft campaign buttons on lapels, 1908 copyright..................... 35.00

United States of America, lady holding flag and eagle illus, G Howard Hilder 7.00

Poster

Defend Your Country, Enlist Now in the Army, Uncle Sam pulling up his sleeves, 26 x 38" 100.00

First Call–I Need You In The Navy This Minute!, full color Uncle Sam illus, James Montgomery Flagg, 10 x 11" 275.00

Great Atlantic & Pacific Tea Co, multicolor Uncle Sam, woman, and grocer, matted and framed, 8 x 10" 250.00

Save Seed Corn Now, An Alarming Shortage Exists, Uncle Sam with arm around farmer, 1918, 21 x 31" 115.00

The Navy Is Calling–Enlist Now, L N

Britton, large American eagle, shield on chest, towering over Naval crew **200.00**

Poster Stamp, Wm Horstmann Co, Philadelphia, 100th Anniversary, 1916, Miss Liberty design **9.00**

Sheet Music

Any Bonds Today, National Defense program theme song, Uncle Sam on cov, copyright 1941, 6 pgs, 9 x 12" **15.00**

Father of the Land We Love, George M Cohan, George Washington illus, James Montgomery Flagg artist, copyright 1931 . . . . **6.00**

Heaven Born Banner, Vincent Bryan & Gertrude Hoffman, 1905, red, white, and blue design cov **20.00**

Our Flag, 1859, Clark **25.00**

Peace and Liberty, 1917 . . . . **15.00**

Stars and Stripes Forever, John Philip Sousa, 1897 . . . . **35.00**

Star Spangled Banner, Bufford, 34 star US flag and French flag. **30.00**

Sign

Battle Axe Plug Tobacco, Let Us Have Peace, cardboard, litho of Uncle Sam and two men, diamond shape, framed, 12 x 12" . . . **250.00**

Peters' Weatherbird Shoes, litho, Uncle Sam teaching bird students, classroom scene, orig frame, 22 x 30" **1,500.00**

Tanlac Medicine, cardboard, diecut, Uncle Sam holding package, world background, 30 x 20" **115.00**

Union Leader Cut Plug, The National Smoke & Chew, Uncle Sam holding product, sailing ship background, c1899, framed **4,900.00**

White House Coffee, cardboard, patriotic oval with elderly man, coffee can with White House, 11 x 20" **65.00**

PEPSI

References: Ted Hake *Hake's Guide To Advertising Collectibles,* Wallace–Homestead, 1992; Everette and Mary Lloyd, *Pepsi–Cola Collectibles,* Schiffer Publishing, 1993; Bill Vehling and Michael Hunt, *Pepsi–Cola Collectibles, Vol. 1,* 1990, (1993 value update), *Vol. 2,* 1990, and *Vol. 3,* 1993, L–W Book Sales.

Collectors' Club: Pepsi–Cola Collectors Club, PO Box 1275, Covina, CA 91722.

Bookmark, feather and bottle cap, 1940s, 3 x 12" **35.00**

Comic Strip, Pepsi and Pete, full color, 1940, 12 x 9" **35.00**

Cookbook, Pepsi–Cola, 1940, soft cov . . **14.00**

Six Pack Carton, 8 x 9 x 5", 1960s, $25.00.

Coupon, fold–over, Pepsi–Cola Free Coupon Offer, Worth 25¢, 1940s, 6 x 7" **75.00**

Cup, cardboard, 12 oz, allover Pepsi logo, c1960 . . . . **10.00**

Display, cardboard, diecut, standup, 1960s **45.00**

Fan, cardboard, McPherson Beverages, Inc, Bottlers of 7–Up & Pepsi–Cola, wood handle, 10 x 10", 1940s **75.00**

Hat, vendor's, 1940s, 12 x 5" **50.00**

Letterhead, Pepsi–Cola, Greensboro, NC, 1916, 8½ x 11" **100.00**

Magazine, *Pepsi World,* The Steele Years, 1959, 8½ x 11" **10.00**

Matchbook, 1950s **20.00**

Menu, one sheet, Pepsi glass and bottle cap, 1940s, 8 x 11" **50.00**

Newspaper Advertisement, 1938, Pepsi bottle illus **4.00**

Photograph, soda fountain int. view with Pepsi sign, c1910, 10 x 8" **100.00**

Playing Cards, red, white, and blue Pepsi logo **7.50**

Poster

Counter Spy, radio thriller, Pepsi logo, 1940s, 8 x 19" **18.00**

Pepsi–Cola, Pepsi's Best . . . Take No Less, woman sitting on beach holding Pepsi, 1940s, 36 x 24" **475.00**

Program, 1951 National Convention, bottle cap illus on front cov, 1954, 8½ x 11" **35.00**

Sign

Be Sociable, Have A Pepsi, trolley, cardboard, 1950s, 28 x 11" **85.00**

Pepsi–Cola, cardboard, 1950s, 11 x 27" **110.00**

Stock Certificate, Pepsi–Cola Bottling Co of California, 1936, framed, 11 x 8½" **25.00**

Ticket, Russell Bros Circus, Pepsi–Cola adv, 1930s, 5 x 3" **50.00**

PHONOGRAPH

Reference: Robert W. Baumbach, *Look For The Dog: An Illustrated Guide to Victor Talking Machines,* Stationery X–Press, 1990.

Periodical: *The Horn Speaker,* PO Box 1193, Mabank, TX 75147.

Collectors' Club: Antique Phonograph Collectors Club, 502 E. 17th St, Brooklyn, NY 11226.

Advertising Trade Card, Edison Phonograph, old couple listening with amazement **6.00**
Catalog
John A McVickar Radio Home Recorder and Reproducer, NY, wax disc system attaches to phonograph **35.00**
Thomas A Edison Inc, Manufacturing Laboratories and Executive Offices, Orange, NJ, 1920, 29 pgs, plate line drawings illus **25.00**
Label, cigar, Edonsia, It Speaks For Itself, 1910, full color, emb phonograph illus, 6 x 8" **15.00**
Manual, Edison Diamond Disc Phonographs, Orange, NJ, 1920, 12 pgs, setting up and operating models **35.00**
Photograph, little girl standing on stool by phonograph with hand to ear, 4 x 6" **20.00**
Stock Certificate, Montana Phonograph Company, 1889, Helena, MT, two phonograph vignettes, black border, unissued **8.00**

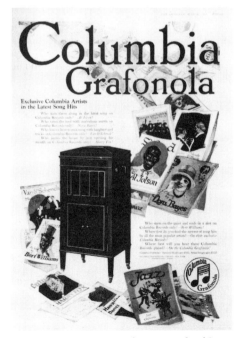

Magazine Tear Sheet, Columbia Grafonola, *The Designer,* sgd. Emil illustration, color litho, 9½ x 15½", March 1920, $20.00.

PHOTOGRAPHY

References: Stuart Bennett, *How to Buy Photographs,* Salem House, 1987; William C. Darrah, *Cartes de Visite in Nineteenth Century Photography,* published by author, 1981; B. E. C. Howarth–Loomes, *Victorian Photography: An Introduction for Collectors and Connoisseurs,* St. Martin's Press, Inc., 1974; O. Henry Mace, *Collectors' Guide to Early Photographs,* Wallace–Homestead, 1990; Lou W. McCullough, *Card Photographs, A Guide To Their History and Value,* Schiffer Publishing, 1981; Floyd and Marion Rinhart, *American Miniature Case Art,* A. S. Barnes and Co., 1969; Susan Theran, *Leonard's Annual Price Index of Prints, Posters and Photographs, Volume 1,* Auction Index, Inc., 1992; Susan Theran, *Prints, Posters and Photographs: Identification and Price Guide,* Avon Books, 1993; John Waldsmith, *Stereoviews: An Illustrated History and Price Guide,* Wallace–Homestead, 1991.

Periodical: *The Photograph Collector,* 163 Amsterdam Ave. #201, New York, NY 10023.

Collectors' Clubs: American Photographical Historical Society, 520 West 44th St., New York, NY 10036; Photographic Historical Society of New England, Inc., PO Box 189, West Newton Station, Boston, MA 02165; Western Photographic Collectors Association, PO Box 4294, Whittier, CA 90607.

Advertising Trade Card
Cope & Day Portrait View Photographers, black and white **35.00**
Heywood's Mammoth Photograph, Boston, MA, 2 x 2¼" **15.00**
Book
Fine Art of Photography, Anderson, 1919, 316 pgs, illus **15.00**
Kodak Reference Handbook, binder with twelve booklets, 1950–60 . . . . **25.00**
Booklet
Leitz Close–up and Photomicrography with the Lecia Camera, 48 pgs **15.00**
Picture Taking With The Brownie Camera No. 3, July 1901, 48 pgs . . . **8.00**
Brochure, Voitlander Rangefinder Bessa Model 2, 6 pgs **4.00**
Catalog
Bass Still Camera, 1939, 72 pgs **6.00**
Catalog of Photographic Apparatus & Supplies, 1920, 176 pgs, Hulburt Photo Supply Co, Springfield, MO **15.00**
Eastman Kodak Co Kodaks and Kodak Supplies, Rochester, NY, 1924, 64 pgs **15.00**
George Murphy Inc, Catalogue of Photographic Materials, NY, 1940, 272 pgs, illus **15.00**
Document, invoice, Horgan, Robey &

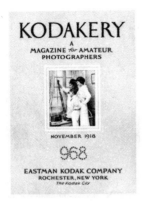

KODAKERY
A
MAGAZINE *for* AMATEUR
PHOTOGRAPHERS

NOVEMBER 1918

968

EASTMAN KODAK COMPANY
ROCHESTER, NEW YORK
The Kodak City

Booklet, "Kodakery, A Magazine for Amateur Photographers," Eastman Kodak Company, Rochester, NY, printed black and gray covers, black-and-white illustrations and photographs, 32 pages, 5¼ x 7½", 1918, $12.00.

Co, Boston, 1895, graphics with lens, 6 x 9"	10.00
Magazine	
Kodakery–A Magazine for Amateur Photographers, 1919	15.00
The Camera, July, 1937	10.00
Manual, Pallard/Bolex Camera, 22 pgs. .	8.00

PIN–UP

References: Denis C. Jackson, *The Price and Identification Guide To Alberto Vargas And George Petty, Second Edition,* published by author, 1987; Denis C. Jackson, *The Price and Identification Guide To Coles Phillips,* published by author, 1986.

Blotter	
Bubblegirl, 1950s, 4 x 9"	3.00
"Going My Way," girl standing in rubber raft while hitch hiking, sea plane overhead, sgd by Del Masters, Laony Motor Services, Inc, Chicago adv, 4 x 9"	4.50
Booklet, World's Smallest Pin–up Book, 1955–60, 16 fold out photos of nude nymphs, vinyl bound.	5.00
Calendar	
1938, DeVorss, woman wearing bathing suit, full pad, 9 x 14".	40.00
1940, Petty, Petty girl for each month, Old Gold Cigarette adv, 18 x 10". . .	55.00
1941, Earl Moran, Out In Front, complete pad, 11 x 23	80.00
1942, *Esquire,* Varga Girl, 8½ x 12", plastic spiral binding, 12 pgs, horizontal format, verses by Phil Stack	90.00

1944	
MacPherson, artist sketch pad, poetry on each month, plastic spiral hanger, 9 x 14".	75.00
Petty, A Good Hook–Up, full pad, 15 x 8"	60.00
1945	
Moran, Earl, Starlight, full color blonde, nude, dark green drape, black ground	47.00
Vargas, *Esquire,* orig envelope	90.00
1946	
DeVorss, Jeanne, full pad, 16 x 33"	95.00
Vargas, complete, orig mailing envelope, excellent condition	125.00
1947	
Armstrong, Rolf, See You Soon, salesman's sample, September pad, 11 x 23"	45.00
Munson, artist sketch pad, spiral plastic hanger, mint condition, 9 x 14".	75.00
Petty, spiral bound, orig envelope, Fawcett Publications, 9 x 12". . . .	70.00
1948	
Moran, Earl, Reflection, nude woman, full pad, 11 x 23"	110.00
Pogony, Willie, "Gone With The Wind," nude at seaside with one foot on inflatable horse, black Scottie looking on, 12 x 19"	75.00
Unknown artist, artist sketch pad, little poetry, pin–up boy for April	90.00
1949, Petty, Come On Along, full color art, unused, 7½ x 16"	65.00
1950, Medcalf, artist sgd, adv Ditzler Paint Auto Body, blonde with Scottie dog splashing foot in ocean, Dec only, 14 x 45".	55.00
1952, Elvgren, full color glossy art, spiral bound, Brown & Bigelow, 8½ x 13"	90.00
1954	
Golden Dreams, nude Marilyn Monroe, full color, 9 x 15"	75.00
Petty Girl, 12 pgs, vertical format, verses, 8¼ x 11".	60.00
1955, Stepping Out, December pad, 16 x 33"	85.00
1956	
MacPherson, color drawing, 9½ x 12½"	35.00
Marilyn Monroe, 8 x 14", four full color pictures	200.00
1956, Petty girl, *Esquire,* full color, 11 x 8".	45.00
1988, Chippendale Revue.	8.00
Calender Top, no pad	
Daisy, DeVorss, nude woman, 22 x 30".	110.00
Double Exposure, Elvgren, woman with towel, 16 x 20".	55.00
Fresh Breeze, Elvgren, standing	

brunette with low cut flowered blouse, holding flowers in raised skirt, 16 x 20″ **32.50**

Card, c1940, 3½ x 5″, set of 3
Earl Moran, red ground **22.00**
Zoe Mozert, full color **18.00**

Christmas Card, MacPherson, tan, red, black, and blue, 5½ x 8″ **25.00**

Date Book, *Esquire* color cov, spiral binding, full color pin–up photos, copyright 1943, George Hurrell, 5 x 7″ **40.00**

Diecut, Earl Moran, Hot–cha Girl Cutouts, full color, c1945, 10″ h **10.00**

Folder
Albine Calendar and Novelty Co, Chicago, IL, pin–up art tops, twelve illus, 1948 . . . . **18.00**
Petty Girl Revue, from Dec 1941 issue of *Esquire*, double sided, verses, different girl in each drawing, four 3¾ x 8½″ drawings, six 5 x 7⅝″ drawings, one 6½ x 5½″ drawing **65.00**
Sally of Hollywood & Vine, cardboard, sliding insert changing from dress to underwear to nude **40.00**

Magazine
Hollywood Tales, Vol 1, #36, 1930s, 24 pgs, full color art **30.00**
Marilyn Monroe Pin–Ups, 1953, 8½ x 11″, 32 pgs, black and white and full color photos **70.00**
Movieland Pin–Ups, Anita Ekberg cov, 1955 . . . . **16.00**

Match Book Cover
Cowgirl **3.50**
Petty, "Its In The Bag," Martins Tavern, Chicago, late 1940s **5.00**

Note Pad, pastel, 1944 calendar on back, 3 x 4½″ **6.00**

Playing Cards
Bob Elson's Petty Pippins, 52 cards, dressed as bride **45.00**
Elvgren
Hats Off, double deck, seated brunette wearing green hat and red gloves on one deck, other with kneeling blonde wearing black hat and gloves, unused, black and gold sliding titled box **60.00**
Having a Bang–Up Time, 1940s, full color art, orig box and flyleaf **50.00**
Petty Pippins, cowgirl leaning against fence, c1940, orig box **62.50**
Royal Flushes, nudes, large size, orig box **15.00**
Vargas
Girl Drawings, 53 cards, different illus, plastic coated, mfg by Creative Playing Card Co, St Louis, green box **150.00**
Gorgeous Girls, c1950, Creative Playing Card Co, full color art, orig box **75.00**

Blotter, Armstrong Girl, Brown & Bigelow adv., $10.00.

Post Card, nude woman from waist up, arms folded over chest, divided back **10.00**

Poster
Martin Senour Paint, "If It's Worth Covering, It's Worth Martin Senour Synthol Enamel," woman removing robe to reveal sheer underwear, 22 x 40″ **100.00**
Raleigh Tobacco, beautiful brunette, 1939–41, full color **15.00**
Walt Otto, full color, woman in shorts walking wire hair terrier, c1951, 17 x 33″ **50.00**

Print
Armstrong, Rolf, brunette in bibbed shorts, yellow blouse, matted and framed, 11 x 14″ **30.00**
Elvgren
Adoration, woman on bed with scarf, 15 x 19″ **60.00**
Thar She Blows, framed, 8 x 10″ . . . **25.00**
La Gatta, John, The Ziegfeld Girl of 1941, 9 x 12″ **8.00**
Moran, Earl, Dreaming, blonde woman stretched across purple background, printed by Brown and Bigelow, gold frame **185.00**
Petty, Calendar Girl, F Warde Traver, Gray Litho Co, NY, 1903, 10 x 12½″ **10.00**
Vargas, *Esquire,* Phil Stack verse, WWII, matted, framed, 11 x 14″ . . . **65.00**
Unknown Artist, woman sitting on red bench, marked "Copr C Moss 1947 Litho in USA" **50.00**

Program, Skating Vanities of 1947, Vargas, blonde roller–skater wearing pink outfit, 8 x 11″ **32.50**

Punchboard Label, 3¾ x 8″, Elvgren, unused **14.00**

PLANTERS PEANUTS

Reference: Richard D. and Barbara Reddock, *Planters Peanuts Advertising And Collectibles,* Wallace–Homestead, 1978, out–of–print.

Collectors' Club: Peanut Pals, PO Box 4465, Huntsville, AL 35815.

Peanut Bag, wax paper, red and blue Mr. Peanut, pennant logo, and lettering, 2¹/₂ x 5¹/₂", 1920s, $18.00.

Jigsaw Puzzle, Playboy Playmate Puzzle, American Publishing Corporation, AP110, 1967, $15.00.

Advertising Trade Card, c1935, wild animals, pr, 2 x 2¹/₂"	6.00
Bookmark, cardboard, diecut, 1920–30	20.00
Box, cardboard, red and black, logo on sides, 8 x 9"	30.00
Card, Planter's Cocktail Peanuts can, "For The Boys In Service, Send A Few Of These Vacuum Cans Today," silhouette of bugler, c1918, 21 x 11"	75.00
Coloring Book, Mr Peanut & Smokey the Bear, 1973	15.00
Cookbook, *Cooking the Modern Way*, 1948, 40 pgs	22.50
Display, cardboard	
Figural, Mr Peanut, diecut, standup, 48" h	18.00
Mr Peanut in nut shell canoe, girl with parasol, 1920s, 6 x 9"	450.00
Paintbook	
Colorful Story of Peanuts as Told by Mr Peanut, 1957, 28 pgs, 7¹/₂ x 10¹/₂"	30.00
Presidents Paint Book, 1953	45.00
Seeing the USA, 48 states, 1950	35.00
Poster, Mr Peanut, 1980 Winter Olympics, 18 x 26"	8.00
Premium, Planter's Pennant Brand Salted Peanuts bag, red and blue printing, translucent paper, Mr Peanut holding red pennant, late 1920s, unused, 3 x 6"	12.00
Punchboard, Planter's Peanuts, peanut logo, 5¢ punch	30.00
Sign, cardboard, 1939 World's Fair, 1939, 7"	15.00

PLAYBOY

Reference: Jack Bramble, *The Playboy Collectors Guide & Price List, Sixth Edition,* Budget Enterprises, 1984.

Book	
Playboy Jazz Festival, 1959, hard cov	12.00
Twelfth Anniversary Playboy Reader, 1966, 874 pgs, hard cov	25.00
Calendar	
1961, desk type, Playmate, MIB, 5¹/₂ x 6¹/₂"	45.00
1964, spiral bound, different photo each month, 8¹/₂ x 12¹/₂"	25.00
1969, desk type, easel back, Playmate photos each month, unused, orig envelope, 6 x 8"	22.00
1973, spiral bound, full color glossy Playmate photos each month, 8¹/₄ x 12¹/₂"	18.00
Magazine	
1955, September, black and white Marilyn Monroe photos	300.00
1957	4.00
1961, January–December, set of 12	75.00
1966	3.00

Magazine, Vol. 18, No. 9, 8¹/₄ x 11¹/₄", September 1971, $2.50.

Puzzle
  1967, Miss October, Majken Haugedal, cardboard canister **40.00**
  1970, blonde Playmate centerfold on white airbag cushion, red carpeting, cardboard canister **25.00**

POLITICAL

References: Richard Friz, *The Official Price Guide To Political Memorabilia,* House of Collectibles, 1988; Ted Hake, *Hake's Guide To Presidential Campaign Collectibles,* Wallace–Homestead, 1992; Keith Melder, *Hail to The Candidate: Presidential Campaigns From Banners To Broadcasts,* Smithsonian Institution Press, 1992.

Periodicals: *The Political Bandwagon,* PO Box 348, Leola, PA 17540; *The Political Collector Newspaper,* PO Box 5171, York, PA 17405.

Collectors' Club: American Political Items Collectors, PO Box 340339, San Antonio, TX 78234.

Advertising Trade Card
  A G Pollard & Co, full color photo of salesman and President and Mrs. Cleveland **8.00**
  Barton's Boots & Shoes, Newburyport, MA, "Vote for the Best Man," Cleveland, Thurman, Harrison, and Morton photos, red, white, and blue flag design **12.00**
  George Attwood, dealer in boots, shoes & rubbers, Auburn, ME, engraved Benjamin Harrison **8.00**
  Johann Hoff's Malt Extract, color oval print of McKinley, brown background. **15.00**
  McBride Co, Jewelers and Opticians, President Harrison, bust photo, $4^1/4 \times 6^1/2$" **20.00**
  Neutraline, J A Hoitt Co, Nashua, NH, black and white Grover Cleveland sketch **12.00**
  The Ale and Beef Company, Cleve-

Cigar Label, Cleveland-Hendricks, blue, gray, and red, 7 x 4½", $75.00.

land And Stevenson, sepia photos, 1892 . . . .   **25.00**
Autograph
  Hubert Humphrey, photo, "To Jess Rand Best Wishes Hubert Humphrey" **25.00**
  Richard Nixon, black and white photo, "To Jess Rand with Best Wishes Richard Nixon," 8 x 10". .   **75.00**
Book
  A Political Text Book for 1860, view of Presidential nominations and elections **75.00**
  Leslie's Pictorial History of Garfield, 1881 . . . .   **15.00**
  Proceedings of the 1876 Republican National Convention **45.00**
  Republican Campaign Textbook for 1892, Republican National Committee, 263 pgs **12.00**
  Republican National Convention, San Francisco, 1964, 160 pgs **22.50**
  The Heroic Life of William McKinley, DeWolfe, Fiske & Co, Boston, 1902, 28 pgs, $7^1/2 \times 9^1/2$" **15.00**
Booklet, Republican Party Platform 1932, 24 pgs, jugate photos on cov   **20.00**
Box, Bubble Gum Cigars, cardboard, cigar box style, int. cov with "I Like Adlai," portrait, and inscription, c1952, $4^1/5 \times 8^1/2 \times 3$" **25.00**
Broadside, A Proclamation from the Governor declaring Thursday September 19, 1901 a day of mourning for President McKinley, Groton, MA, September 17, 1901, 5 x 10" **35.00**
Brochure
  About Vietnam, Nixon re–election, six panels **2.00**
  The Winning Ticket Goldwater/Miller, Vote Tuesday November 3, 1964 . . . .   **3.00**
  Why Women in the AFT Should Support Walter Mondale, 1984, $3^1/2 \times 9$". **20.00**
Bubble Gum Card, Johnson vs Goldwater, Topps, 1964, 66 cards **45.00**
Card
  Beacom and McCauley for State Treasurer and Auditor General, Republican candidates' portraits and slogans, election day handout, 1897 . . . .   **20.00**
  "Important–Order Wrigley's Campaign Button Gum Now," Pepsin Chewing Gum and Roosevelt button illus, 1906. . . . .   **100.00**
Catalog, Campaign Products Catalog, Votes Unlimited Corp, 1972, black, white, and purple cov, 5 x 8" **40.00**
Coloring Book
  John F Kennedy, 1962, unused **25.00**

Pamphlet, anti-FDR, "Promise and Performance," red and blue on white, 16 pages, 4 x 8¾", 1936, $15.00.

Lyndon Johnson, 1964 campaign issues, Louis Welk illus 8.00
Watergate Coloring Book/Join The Fun/Color The Facts, 1973, 48 pgs, 8 x 11" 15.00
Envelope, addressed to Abraham Lincoln, endorsed "Respectfully submitted to the Attorney General A Lincoln," March 31, 1862 .... 4,350.00
Fan, Franklin Roosevelt, cardboard, litho, photo, Boyd School advertising on back, 7½ x 10½" 20.00
Game
    Game of Politics, Parker Brothers, Uncle Sam, elephant, donkey, and white house illus on box lid 20.00
    Reaganomics, 1981, red, white, and blue box 12.00
    Roosevelt at San Juan, card game, 1899, multicolored box 150.00
Invitation, Eisenhower Inauguration, 1957, 6¼ x 10" 15.00
Label, cigar
    American Protectorate, James Monroe portrait 5.00
    Memorata, President McKinley portrait, commemorating death 16.00
Letter, August 22, 1968, Lester Maddox to supporter in Scarsdale, NY, governor's letterhead 42.00
Manual, *Open a Political Boutique,* Women for Humphrey, how to publication by United Democrats for Humphrey 25.00
Matchbook
    Goldwater for President, 1964, blue and white, 1½ x 2" 3.00
    Lyndon B Johnson and Hubert Humphrey, pictorial 5.00

Menu, Harry S Truman, 70th Birthday Dinner, May 1954, full color photo   15.00
Newspaper
    Chicago Tribune
        Dewey Defeats Truman, Nov 3, 1948 .... 800.00
        Ford Seeks Nominees for Vice Presidency, August 11, 1974, Ford photo on front page...... 8.00
    New York Times, April 13, 1945, President Roosevelt Is Dead, four column article and photo 16.00
    Los Angeles Times, November 23, 1963, Kennedy assassination 18.00
    The Philadelphia Inquirer, March 29, 1969, Eisenhower Dies, US World Mourn 10.00
    The Washington Sunday Star and Daily News, January 21, 1973, Nixon Sees New Era of Peace, full color photo, Nixon taking oath... 15.00
Pamphlet, Dewey Gets Things Done...The Man Who Gave New York State a Housecleaning, Republican National Committee, c1944, 16 pgs, 3¼ x 6¼" 8.00
Paperback Book, *The Republican Campaign Text Book for 1880* 35.00
Paper Doll, First Family, Ronald and Nancy Reagan, book, Dell, 1981, 9 x 12" 15.00
Photograph, Richard Nixon shaking hands with Congressman George Bush, black and white 12.00
Post Card
    Bryan & Kern, "Shall the People Rule," black and white jugate photos, full color Capitol photo .. 18.00
    John F Kennedy, "Vote for John F Kennedy President November 8, 1960," color photo............ 10.00
    Theodore Roosevelt, "Delighted," Gutman, c1907............... 20.00
    Warren Harding, "Marion County Presents the name of Warren G Harding as a Republican Candidate for Nomination for United States Senator," sepia photo..... 50.00
    William Howard Taft & James Sherman, "The Nation's Choice," black and white jugate photos, ornate design of flags and eagle .. 7.50
Poster
    Barry Goldwater, "A Choice ... Not An Echo," 1964, red, white, and blue, 14 x 21" 15.00
    Blaine/Logan, "The Republican Candidates For 1884," black and white, 22½ x 28" 300.00
    Dukakis/Bentsen, cardboard, blue and white, Texas Democratic Party, 15 x 11"................ 8.00

For President Charles E Hughes, 1916, sepia tone photo, 16 x 21"   30.00

James A Garfield, 1881–85, black and white, Morgan's Sapolio slogan, 21½ x 28" 125.00

Landon For President, 1936, brown and white, 11 x 16" 25.00

Roosevelt/Truman campaign, 1944, jugate, black and white bust portraits, red lettering, black stars, 14¾ x 11" 60.00

Stevenson, 1956, cardboard, red, white, and purple, 8½ x 22" 75.00

Voter For Jimmy Carter, 1976, green and white, 14 x 22" 8.00

Print, Johnson seated by mountain of paper and ink bottles, 18 x 24" 2,200.00

Program

Centennial National Republican Convention, 1956, 160 pgs, black, white, and orange cov, Ike and Lincoln portraits, 9 x 12" 30.00

Democratic National Convention, 1936, 394 pgs, 11 x 14" 20.00

Dewey Celebration, 1899, grand reception at NY harbor, colorful cov, black and white photographs, advertisements, 90 pgs, 7 x 10" . . .   25.00

Eisenhower/Nixon Inaugural Ball, January 1957. . . . .   20.00

Official Program, Democratic National Convention, 1948, 80 pgs, 9 x 12" 45.00

Taft/Sherman 1909 Official Inaugural Program, 32 pgs 50.00

Puzzle

Playing Possum with Taft, 1909, Duplex Puzzle, orig multicolored box 125.00

Roosevelt and Garner, Together To Revive Prosperity, 1933, red, white, and blue 35.00

Sheet Music

A March to Eisenhower, Souvenir of Inauguration 1953, 4 pgs, red, white, and blue cov, 8 x 11" 10.00

Garfield's Funeral March, 1881, 6 pgs, bold black cov, 9½ x 12½" . .   12.00

Keep Cool with Coolidge, 1924, red, white, and blue cov, 9 x 12" 40.00

Nation's Prayer For The President/ Dedicated To Franklin D. Roosevelt, 1933, black and white, 9½ x 12½" 15.00

Wilson March, 1912, red, white, blue, and brown, Wilson photo, 10 x 13½" 25.00

Ticket

Boise Penrose for Senator, admission to endorsement meeting, multicolored, 1896 . . . .   15.00

Cleveland/Hendricks Inaugural Ball,

March 4, 1885, black and white jugate bust portraits, 7 x 9½" 10.00

Franklin D Roosevelt 1937 Inauguration, 2½ x 6" 40.00

Republican National Convention, June, 1900, engraved 18.00

RADIO

References: Anthony Slide, *Great Radio Personalities In Historic Photographs,* The Vestal Press, 1982; Vincent Terrace, *Radio's Golden Years: The Encyclopedia of Radio Programs 1930– 1960,* A. S. Barnes & Co., 1981; Tom Tumbusch, *Tomart's Price Guide To Radio Premium and Cereal Box Collectibles,* Wallace–Homestead, 1991.

Periodicals: *Hello Again,* Box 4321, Hamden, CT 06514; *Old Time Radio Digest,* 4114 Montgomery Rd., Cincinnati, OH 45212.

Collectors' Club: Oldtime Radio–Show Collectors Association, 45 Barry St., Sudbury, Ontario P3B 3H6 Canada.

Album, Breakfast Club Family Album, Chicago, Don McNeill, c1941, 96 pgs, jokes and skits from radio show 18.00

Book

Book of Radio Stars, 1930, Eveready Flash Light Batteries, Groucho Marx, Jack Benny, and George Burns illus 38.00

Floyd Gibbons: Knight Of The Air, Douglas Gilbert, 1930, 96 pgs. 8.00

Is It A Fraud, Special Investigator, 1947, 40 pgs, Mutual Network, Commercial Credit Corp, orig mailing envelope, 5 x 7½" 15.00

Cigar Bag, Sophie Tucker adv, Roi-Tan Cigars, Chevrolet adv. on reverse, 4 x 6½", $10.00.

Sheet Music, Pepsodent Hour theme, *The Perfect Song,* Amos & Andy black-and-white real photo, red printed color ground, Chappell & Harms Pub. Co., 9 x 12", 1929, $40.00.

Radio's Truth or Consequences Party Book, 1940, Ralph Edwards 8.00

The 1954 Breakfast Club Yearbook, Don McNeill, spiral bound 8.00

WOR Radio 1922–1982, 60 pgs, photos and stories, soft cov 10.00

Booklet
All About Amos 'n Andy, 1929, 128 pgs, photos and scripts. 50.00
Deluxe Picture Portfolio WWVA Friendly Folks, WV, c1947, black and white photos, 8½ x 11". 7.00
Edison Hours with Famous Composers, 1928 radio shows, photos, and drawings, 1929, 60 pgs, 5 x 7" 20.00
Official 1936 Secrets For Silver Star Member, Radio Orphan Annie's Secret Society–Strictly Confidential #47447 .... 22.00
QST Amateur Radio Book, March 1935 .... 5.00

WMBD Radio Personalities, Peoria, IL, 1939, 24 pgs 12.00
Coloring Book, Sergeant Preston, Whitman, 1943, 32 pgs, unused, 8½ x 11½" 20.00
Game
Amos and Andy, Acrobat Ring and Disk, 1930s 95.00
Professor Quiz, Radio Game, 1939, orig mailer 25.00
Quiz Kids Own Game Box, Parker Brothers, Inc, 1940 .... 12.50
The Merry Game of Fibber McGee And The Wistful Vista Mystery, Milton Bradley, 1940, By Arrangement with The National Broadcasting Co Inc 20.00
Magazine, *Radio Mirro,* December, 1939, Judy Garland cov. 12.00
Map, Young Forty–Niners, 1930s, used to follow broadcast adventures 50.00
Menu, Kate Smith cov, A & P, 8 pgs, 8½ x 11¾". 4.00
Post Card, Red Skelton, radio show cast photo, matte finish, 1948 post mark .. 20.00
Poster, Eddie Cantor, 1935–36, movie and radio show, New Pebeco Tooth Paste adv, 11½ x 19". 70.00
Premium, script, Death Valley Days, April 11, 1935, Pacific Coast Borax. . . 48.00
Program, The Woman In White, Radio Soap Opera, 1938, 12 pgs, sponsored by Pillsbury, 12 x 9½" 15.00
Sheet Music
Little Orphan Annie's Song, compliments of Ovaltine & Radio's Orphan Annie, 1931, Annie and Sandy drawing on cov 20.00
Three Little Words, Amos and Andy, 1930 .... 25.00
Ticket, CBS Radio Show, Welcome Lewis Singing Bee, Saturday, February

Birthday Card, console radio shape, bi-fold, printed, brown, satin ribbon dec., Buzza Craftacres, 4⅜ x 5½", 1940s, $7.00.

Certificate, $50.00 Radio Certificate, Great Lakes Radio Corp., hand sgd. by cashier, printed green and black on white, 8½ x 6¼", dated May 31, 1930, $12.50.

22, 1941, set of 4, orig envelope,
unused. **25.00**

RADIOS

Reference: Philip Collins, *Radios: The Golden Age,* Chronicle Books, 1987; Alan Douglas, *Radio Manufacturers of the 1920's, Volume I,* (1988) and *Volume 2* (1989), *Volume 3* (1991,) The Vestal Press; David and Betty Johnson, *Guide To Old Radios–Pointers, Pictures, and Prices,* Wallace–Homestead, 1989; Scott Wood (ed.) *Evolution Of The Radio,* L–W Book Sales, 1991, 1992 value update.

Periodicals: *Antique Radio Classified,* PO Box 802, Carlisle, MA 01746; *Radio Age,* 636 Cambridge Road, Augusta, GA 30909.

Collectors' Clubs: Antique Radio Club of America, 3445 Adaline Drive, Stow, OH 44224; Antique Wireless Association, 59 Main St., Bloomfield, NY 14469.

Book, *1938 Radio Dictionary,* Gernsback's Educational Library #5, 32 pgs,
list terminology **5.00**
Brochure, Philco Radio, fold–out type,
1936 . . . . **5.00**
Catalog
Allied Radio, Chicago, 1937, 152 pgs,
6 x 9" **12.00**
Baltimore Radio Corp, NY, 1933, 88
pgs, radios and parts **15.00**
Hallicrafters Radios, 1944–45, 31 pgs **8.00**
Lafayette Radios, Wholesale Radio
Service, NY, 1935, 190 pgs, 7 x 10" **15.00**
Philco Radio & Phonograph, 1942,
illus and parts list **30.00**
Manual
Atwater Kent, 1931, service, parts
price list, factory binder. **25.00**
Duston's A C Radio Manual, 1928, 60
pgs, 8 x 11". **15.00**
Poster
Phillips Radio, "Magic With Four
Hands," c1950, magicians and
floating portable radios, pink and
blue background, 23 x 31½" **150.00**
Zenith Radio Tubes, c1930, large radio tube superimposed over female tightrope walker carrying portable radio, black background,
Italian, 39 x 53". **1,500.00**

RAILROAD

References: Stanley L. Baker, *Railroad Collectibles: An Illustrated Value Guide, Fourth Edition,* Collector Books, 1990, 1993 value update; Phil Bollhagen (comp.), *The Great Book Of Railroad Playing Cards,* published by author, 1991.

Periodicals: *Key, Lock and Lantern,* PO Box 65, Demarest, NJ 07627; *U. S. Rail News,* PO Box 7007, Huntingdon Woods, MI 48070.

Collectors' Clubs: Railroad Enthusiasts, 456 Main Street, West Townsend, MA 01474; Railroadiana Collectors Association, 795 Aspen Drive, Buffalo Grove, IL 60089; Railway and Locomotive Historical Society, PO Box 1418, Westford, MA 01886.

Advertising Trade Card
Chicago & North Western Railway,
blue and gold, lists of stops adv on
back. **20.00**
Michigan Central and Great Western
Railways, suspension bridge over
Niagara Falls, Great Central Route
adv on back **15.00**
Album, The Western Pacific RR, Feather
Canyon Route, Salt Lake City to San
Francisco Bay, 1923, 6½ x 8½" **35.00**
Blotter, Lehigh Valley Railroad **5.00**
Book
*C & NWRR Co, Rules...Operating
Dept,* 1928. . . . . **5.00**
History of Burlington Route, Overton,
NY, 1965, 1st edition. **30.00**
*History of Pennsylvania RR, 1846–
1946* **65.00**
*The Official Guide of Railways &
Steam Navigation Lines of the
United States, Puerto Rico, Canada,
Mexico & Cuba,* 1929, includes
timetables **100.00**
Booklet
*Claremont–The Great Terminal of the
World's Great Port,* Lehigh Valley,
c1920, 7 x 10" **18.00**
Northern Pacific RR, 1913. . . . . **30.00**
Oregon and Idaho Railroad, locomotive on cov **20.00**
Southern California Mid–Winter Ex-

Dinner Napkin, Chessie, printed, blue on white, 4 x 8½" folded, 1960s, $8.00.

cursion, Salt Lake Route, four panels, February, 1913 . . . .   8.00
The Erie Limited, June, 1929, three panels, equipment views, blue and white cov 15.00
The Pacific Northwest and Alaska, published by Union Pacific, 1931, 48 pgs, black and white photos, three rail route maps 7.00
Broadside, Mr. England's Patent Self–Acting Car Coupler, endorsed by B & O Railroad, April, 1856, 8½ x 11". . . .   20.00
Brochure
  Pennsylvania Railroad, 1943, 48 pgs   7.00
  Santa Fe Railroad, 1936, 78 pgs 12.00
Calendar
  CNW Railroad, 1949. . . . .   35.00
  GN Railroad, 1934 . . . .   50.00
  Maine Central, 1949, passenger train, pocket type 3.50
  Pennsylvania Railroad, pocket type, colorful train and mountain scene. .   8.00
  Union Pacific Railroad, 1960 . . . .   10.00
Calendar Sheet, Great Northern Railroad, 1928, April, 10 x 22" 55.00
Calling Card, Railway Express Agency, black and red. 115.00
Catalog
  American Steel & Wire Co, Chicago, IL, 1928, 167 pgs, railroad bonding of rails and tracks, 6 x 9" 20.00
  Baldwin Locomotive Works, Philadelphia, PA, 1902, 35 pgs, 70 years of locomotive building, 6 x 9" 37.00
  Burnham, Parry, Williams & Co, Narrow Gauge Locomotives, Philadelphia, PA, 1877, 38 pgs. 300.00
  Males Co, Locomotives, Passenger, Freight, Contractor Cars, Steam Shovels, Cincinnati, OH, c1908, 32 pgs. 45.00
  Pullman Coach Co, 1920 . . . .   16.00
  Safety Car Heating and Lighting Co, The Generator on the Car Body, New York, NY, 1915, 14 pgs 25.00
Discount Card, Western Union Telegraph Co, 1909, to send messages for Atchison, Topeka & Santa Fe Railway, Inter Banknote Co, printed, black and white 10.00
Document
  Draft, Rockville Railroad Company, 1863 . . . .   6.00
  Employment Application, Pennsylvania Railroad, 1906, telegraph operator, 8 x 14" 5.00
  Receipt, Boston & Providence Railroad Co, #485 Light Engine Co, 1835, 6 x 4¼" 15.00
Greeting Card, Christmas, diecut train car, standup three dimensional train, pink celluloid windows, Germany . . .   75.00

Label, cigar, The Overland, SS Pierce Co, steam locomotive image 35.00
Letter, Toledo, Wabash, & Western Railway Co, 1870, August 20, concerning Republican Convention, signed by Robert Anderson 12.50
Magazine
  Ballou's Pictorial, Boston Railroad Depots on cov, March 8, 1856. . . . . . .   9.00
  Burlington Bulletin, 1962, 7 pgs, 9 x 12". 3.50
  Railway Conductor, May 1945, Roosevelt on cov 5.00
  Saturday Evening Post, May 8, 1943, Norman Rockwell illus, "A Night on Troop Train," 2 pgs of sketches 50.00
  Tracks, May 1956, Chesapeake & Ohio RR, presidential issue, Eisenhower on cov. 12.00
Magazine Tear Sheet, illus, train leaving Grand Central Depot, NY, *Harper's Weekly,* October 9, 1875 . . . .   10.00
Manual, Pennsylvania Railroad Manual of Instructions to Railroad Conductors, Ticket Collectors & Baggagemen, 1945, 120 pgs, 4½ x 9" 6.50
Map, Union Pacific Railway, 1886, tourist folder. 18.00
Matchbook
  Central Vermont Railway 7.50
  Delaware/Hudson. 10.00
  Rock Island Railroad, red and black logo 2.00
  Soo Line 12.00
  Tennessee Central 10.00
  Union Pacific Railroad 15.00
Menu
  B & O Railroad, child's, train form, 4 x 18" opened 15.00
  Burlington Route, Chuckwagon/Denver Zephyr, 6 x 9". 8.00
  Canadian Pacific Railroad, 1928. . . . .   6.00
  Great Northern, 1944 . . . .   12.50
  Lehigh Valley Railroad, c1950, A la Carte breakfast, lower corner logo   3.75
  Santa Fe, dinner, 6 x 9" 16.00
  The New York Central RR, dining car service, 1917, color, printed by Bailey, Banks & Biddle Co, Philadelphia 18.00
Pamphlet, Burlington Route, The Cody Road to Yellowstone Park, 1931, color   10.00
Photograph
  Cement Laboratory of Pennsylvania Railroad, March 12, 1906, int. view, 6 x 7½" 10.50
  Train Trestle, parked locomotive and five dump cars, c1880, mounted, 6½ x 8½". 10.00
Playing Cards
  C & O Railroad, Peake Chessie's "Old Man" 5.00

Chicago, Milwaukee & St Paul, 1919,
scenic views, orig box **40.00**
New York, New Haven & Hartford
Railroad, orig wrapper and box **65.00**
Southern Pacific Railroad **20.00**
Post Card, Reading, PA railroad depot . . **3.00**
Poster
Chicago Aurora & Elgin Railroad, Bad
Order, placard, 3½ x 8" **1.50**
Put Railroads Ahead of the Game—
Victory is Dependent Upon Efficient
Transportation, red, white, and
blue, 12 x 18" **39.00**
Receipt, Toledo, Wabash, & Western
Railway Co, delivery of 14 bushels of
apples, 1867 . . . . **10.00**
Rule Book, Northern Pacific Railway,
1922 . . . . **8.00**
Sheet Music, *Hail to the Baltimore &
Ohio,* 1927, engraved B & O engine . . **20.00**
Stock Certificate
Baltimore–Ohio Railroad Co, NY,
1893, 50 shares, train vignette **30.00**
Boston–Providence Railroad Co,
1883, boats, railroads, and factories
vignettes **20.00**
Chicago–Burlington and Quincy Rail-
road Co, Chicago, IL, 1899, train vi-
gnette **20.00**
Cincinnati & St Louis RR Co, Novem-
ber 25, 1882, waterfront vignette
with ships and train **15.00**
Erie–Lackawanna Railroad Co, 1960s **6.00**
Erie Railroad Co, 1950s **8.00**
Missouri, Kansas & Texas Railway
Company, 100 shares, cow vignette,
cherubs in corners, green border, 8
x 11½" **15.00**
Northern Railroad, Boston, 1864, 25¢
Brown Stamp, red seal **30.00**
Old Colony Railroad Co, 1896,
$1,000, trains, horse, and wagons
vignettes **30.00**
Philadelphia Railroad Co, State of PA,
1980, woman vignette **6.00**
Toledo, Delphos & Burlington Rail-
road Co, June 3, 1882, locomotive
and coal tender vignette **15.00**
Western Railroad, 1955, train station
and locomotive vignette **10.00**
Ticket
Boston & Maine RR, 1947 . . . . **5.00**
Southern Pacific Lines, Railroad
Boosters, Ojai–Ventura County
Railway Trip, 1939 . . . . **10.00**
Time Table
Chesapeake & Ohio RR, 1964, passen-
ger train **5.00**
Lackawanna, 1947, New York City,
Buffalo, Cleveland, Detroit, Chi-
cago, 16 pgs, 8 x 9" **8.00**
Pennsylvania Railroad System, 1923,

THE PULLMAN COMPANY—Passenger's
Check. To identify accommodations purchased.
~LOUISVILLE to NASHVILLE, Tenn.
TRAIN   SEAT   CAR
M
Property taken into car will be entirely at owner's risk.
OFFICE **14-1**   FORM **17**   **$0.80**
1313

Ticket, The Pullman Company, Louisville
to Nashville, TN, $6.00.

Chicago, St Louis, Pittsburgh,
printed black and white **10.00**
Popular Excursions to Sylvan Beach,
Oneida Lake, Via West Shore Rail-
road, NYC & W Railways, black
printing, blue ground **12.00**
Union Pacific Railroad, 1937, 48 pgs,
8 x 9" **16.00**
View Book
Montreal, Canadian Pacific, 1915 . . . . **8.00**
Rocky Mountain Views on the Rio
Grande Railroad from San Francisco
to Salt Lake City, 1944 . . . . **8.00**
Views Along the Line of the Western
Pacific Railroad from San Francisco
to Salt Lake City, 1944 . . . . **8.00**

RCA

References: Robert W. Baumbach, *Look for the
Dog: An Illustrated Guide to Victor Talking Ma-
chines,* Stationery X–Press, 1990; Ted Hake,
Hake's Guide To Advertising Collectibles,
Wallace–Homestead, 1992.

Book, *Victor Book of the Opera,* 1912 . . **15.00**
Catalog
RCA Victor, 1917, record and per-
former photos, leatherette cov **40.00**
Victor Hawaiian Records, 1916, full
color illus, 8 x 11" **20.00**
Victor Records, 1922 . . . . **25.00**
Fan, cardboard, record shape with
woman's face, black, white, red, and
brown, wood handle, 1930s, 8" d **75.00**
Leaflet, Victor–Victrola, c1915, four pgs,
Nipper on front cov **20.00**
Letterhead, Victor Talking Machine, en-
velope **30.00**
Manual, RCA Receiving Tube Manual,
1937 . . . . **10.00**
Pamphlet, New Victor Records February
1919, 20 pgs, color cov, 5 x 6¾" **23.00**
Post Card, 1907, hold–to–light type **10.00**
Poster, New Victor Records In Foreign
Languages, 1919, records available in
eleven different languages, 13½ x
17½" **40.00**

Sign, cardboard, RCA Nipper dog illus,
  framed 20.00
Souvenir Folio, RCA Victor Records Car-
  avan, 1954, 16 pgs, full page adv on
  back for New RCA Victor 45 Extended
  Play record and Victrola 45 player, 8¹/₂
  x 11" 45.00

REGIONAL

Advertising Trade Card
  Adirondack scene, Burrow–Giles Li-
    tho Co 20.00
  Melville Garden, Boston Harbor Re-
    sort, black and white clam bake
    scene 20.00
  Starin's Glen Island, Victorian swim-
    ming scene, sepia 50.00
  West Brighton Beach Hotel, Coney
    Island, beachfront and hotel scene   75.00
Book
  A Guide to Travelers Visiting The Falls,
    Niagara Falls, 1835, H A Parsons,
    hard bound cov 95.00
  Florida: Empire Of The Sun, 1930, de-
    scribes advantages of living in Flor-
    ida, hard bound cov 20.00
  Hawaii, William Graves, National
    Geographic Society, 1970, 204 pgs,
    dj 20.00
  Hawaii As The Camera Sees It, sixth
    edition 5.00
  The Illustrated History of Hackensack,
    NJ, 1898, The Bergen County Dem-
    ocrat, 130 pgs, hard bound, gilt
    edges 25.00
  Yonkers, NY, Philpse Manor Hall,
    1912, 255 pgs 5.50
  8th report of US Geographical Survey,
    1889, 1064 pgs, illus, color maps . .   15.00
Booklet
  Ayer, MA, 1902, 120 pgs, industries
    and principle buildings, 6 x 9¹/₂" . . .   12.00
  Daytona, FL, 1916, Compliments of
    the City of Daytona, 6 x 3¹/₂" 6.00
  Life Worth Living on the Chesapeake
    Bay and Its Tributaries, Elliott Y Mc-
    Daniel Co, c1910, 32 pgs, black and
    white illus 17.50
  Your Long Beach Home, Long Beach,
    CA, 1925, 36 pgs, photos and ads
    on benefits of moving there 10.00
Brochure
  Los Angeles County, CA, 1933, 9 x 12"   8.00
  Niagara to the Sea, Canada Steamship
    Lines, 100 pgs, foldout map 6.00
  Shell's New England Tour Trips, 1937   4.00
  The Great Smoky Mountains National
    Park, 1928, 80 pgs 6.00
  Yellowstone National Park, WY, 1938,
    38 pgs, foldout map 4.00
Directory, San Francisco, 1903, 2300
  pgs, Crocker–Langley 45.00

Guide Book
  Lafayette, Indiana 1893 Book of Infor-
    mation 6.00
  The Great Temple–Salt Lake City,
    1929 . . . .   4.00
  Yellowstone National Park, Union Pa-
    cific RR, 1924 . . . .   4.00
Magazine, *National Geographic,* 1916,
  two bound volumes 25.00
Map
  Map of the General Government
    Roads in the Territory of Minnesota,
    1854, 13 x 19" 18.00
  Wake Island, February 11, 1943, US
    Government, 34¹/₂ x 47" 25.00
  West Indies, Mitchells Geography,
    1852, hand colored 18.00
Newspaper
  The Daily News, McAlester, 1907, In-
    dian Territory 30.00
  Tombstone Epitaph, 1880, Arizona
    Territory 165.00
  Weekly Independent, October 7,
    1875, Helena, Montana Territory
    headline, 8 pgs 30.00
Playing Cards, Yellowstone National
  Park, Haynes Inc, copyright 1935, orig
  box 45.00
Viewbook
  Atlantic City, 1907, 48 pgs, 8 x 10" . . .   22.50
  New York, The Empire City, early
    1900s, 50 views, 10 x 9" 12.00
  San Francisco Bay Area, 1938 . . . . . .   12.00
  Silver Springs Florida's International
    Attraction, 1937 . . . .   8.00
  The Beauties of the State of Washing-
    ton, 1915, 112 pgs, photos, 6 x 9¹/₄"   15.00
  The New England Seashore, 1896,
    photos of beaches in MA, NH, and
    ME, Boston & Maine Railroad, 6 x 8"   14.00
  Wisconsin, Kilburn & The Dells, Chi-
    cago, Milwaukee, and St Paul Rail-
    way, 1907, 6 x 9" 12.00
  Yellowstone National Park, Haynes
    Inc, 24 color views 35.00

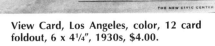

**View Card, Los Angeles, color, 12 card
foldout, 6 x 4¹/₄", 1930s, $4.00.**

RELIGIOUS

Advertising Trade Card, Brooks Paints, St
Peters Cathedral **10.00**
Book
   History of Society of Friends, Wm R
   Wagstaff, 1845, 400 pgs and *History
   of the Rise, Increase, and Progress of
   the Christian People Called
   Quakers,* Wm Sewell, 1844, two
   bound volumes **40.00**
   Sinner's Complaint To God, London,
   1707, 518 pgs **15.00**
Card, First Communion, mechanical,
   opens to three dimensional altar
   scene, Germany **30.00**
Catalog, The Globe Furniture & Mfg,
   Northville, MI, 28 pgs, pews, communion rails, pulpit, altar chairs, al-
   tars, hymn boards, baptismal fonts . . .   **37.00**
Cookbook, *Presbyterian Cookbook,* First
   Presbyterian Church, Dayton, OH,
   tenth edition, 1886 . . . .   **20.00**
Game, Game of Bible Characters,
   Zondervan Publishing House, 1939,
   Verita V Blair Head, ...   **17.50**
Label, Lemon, Vesper, people going to
   church, maroon background, Por-
   terville **1.00**
Letter, Edward Everett Hale, church sta-
   tionery, 1881 . . . .   **95.00**
Magazine, *Life*
   1955, December 26, Christianity . .   **5.00**
   1958, November 10, Pope John
   XXIII **10.00**
Manual
   Representation of the Ordinance of
   Baptism, Samuel Wilson, London,
   1772, 32 pgs, $4^{1}/_{2}$ x $6^{1}/_{2}$" **25.00**

**Advertising Card, The Famous North Car-
olina Gospel Singers, Mt. Carmel Baptist
Church, Philadelphia, PA, 7th Anniversary show, black-and-white photograph
on cardboard, 6 x $7^{1}/_{2}$", 1920s, $30.00.**

Manual of Biblical Geography, c1887,
   25 pgs, maps, diagrams, and foldout
   panorama of Jerusalem **30.00**
Newspaper
   Sunday School Advocate, NY, 1846,
   Methodist Episcopal Church **4.00**
   Times and Seasons, Nauvoo, IL, Octo-
   ber 15, 1843, Mormon, history of
   Joseph Smith **55.00**
Painting
   The Virgin Adoring the Infant Christ,
   gouache on paper, Armitage–Smith,
   20th C, $39^{1}/_{2}$ x $25^{1}/_{4}$" **850.00**
   The White Church, oil on board,
   Pauline Palmer, 1867–1938, $19^{1}/_{2}$
   x $23^{1}/_{2}$" **1,400.00**
Pamphlet, *The Devil's Theology,* Wil-
   liam Lloyd Clark, 1900, Milan, IL,
   Anti–Catholic content, stapled **5.00**
Ticket, Centennial Celebration, Presbyte-
   rian Church of Frankford, Philadelphia, history of church, addresses, music, reminiscences, black and white,
   May 4, 1870 . . . .   **35.00**

ROCK 'N' ROLL

Reference: Paul Grushkin, *The Art of Rock–
Posters From Presley to Punk,* Abbeville Press,
1986; David K. Henkel, *The Official Price Guide
to Rock And Roll,* House of Collectibles, 1992;
Hilary Kay, *Rock and Roll Collectables,*
Sotheby's; Karen and John Lesniweski, *Kiss Col-
lectibles; Identification And Value Guide,* Avon
Books, 1993.

Book
   James Dean, William Bast, Ballantine
   Books, 1956, 150 pgs **15.00**
   Woodstock 69, Joseph J Sia, 1970, 124
   pgs, Scholastic Book Services **25.00**
Songbook, *The Golden Era of Rock &
   Roll,* Words & Music **10.00**
Box, gum, Monkees, Donruss, 1966, full
   color illus, 4 x 8 x $1^{1}/_{2}$" **25.00**
Game
   Duran Duran Into The Arena, Milton
   Bradley, 1985 copyright **15.00**
   Kiss on Tour, Aucoin Management,
   1978 copyright, 17" sq board with
   full color photos. **45.00**
Magazine
   Creem, Kiss Creem Special Edition,
   1978, black and white photos **25.00**
   Post Card, Rolling Stones, ''The Roll-
   ing Stones Exile On Main Street,
   Scene 1 and Scene 2,'' c1972, per-
   forated **15.00**
Poster
   Doors, full color, green bottom border,
   white Doors logo, copyright 1968
   Doors Production Corp, 24 x 36". . .   **20.00**

Bail Bond, The Doors, issued to James Douglas Morrison following Miami concert, stamped "Nov. 12, 1969, J.F. McCracken, Clerk," matted and framed with "Wanted" poster and descriptive plaque, $15,000.00.

Fabian, "Teen Dreams," 1950s, full color, orig sealed bag, 11 x 14" **25.00**

Family Dog, February 2–4, 1968, Avalon Ballroom, full color illus, 14 x 20" **75.00**

Fleetwood Mac, January 1970 concert, Deutsches Museum, Munich, West Germany, full color, 33 x 46" **30.00**

Grateful Dead Fan Club, "The Golden Road To Unlimited Devotion," late 1960s, gold and blue, black and white photo, 14 x 20" **50.00**

James Gang, October 2, 1971, Curtis Hixon Hall, Tampa, FL, 14 x 22" . . . **15.00**

Jefferson Airplane, April 11–13, Fillmore concert, shiny silver Statue of Liberty illus, black background, 1960s, 13 x 9" **50.00**

Miller Blues Band, January 10–15,

Sheet Music, *(We're Gonna) Rock Around The Clock,* Bill Haley and the Comets, $5.00.

1967, Fillmore West concert, orange, blue, and red, copyright 1967 Neon Rose, 14 x 20" **50.00**

Moody Blues, April 1, 1970 concert, Terrace Ballroom, Salt Lake City, UT, stiff paper, 18½ x 25½" **50.00**

Yard Birds, Civic Auditorium, 1967, red, white, and blue, 14½ x 23½" . . **50.00**

Program

Kiss, 1977–78 World Tour, 11 x 17" . . **15.00**

The Who, 8½ x 11", photo biography of each member, English concert, late 1960s, 8½ x 11" **12.50**

Puzzle, American Publishing Corp, 1977 copyright, Love Gun album scene, orig box, 11 x 17" assembled. **15.00**

Sheet Music

Bill Haley and the Comets, *Green Tree Boogie,* greentone photo on front, 2 pgs music and lyrics, copyright 1955 Myers Music, 9 x 11" **20.00**

Purple People Eater, purpletone photo of Sheb Wooley, 2 pgs lyrics, copyright 1958 Cordial Music Co, 9 x 12" **15.00**

The Who, *Substitute,* 2 pgs, bluetone group photo on cov, copyright 1966 Fabulous Music Ltd, 8½ x 11" **12.50**

Tour Book, Bob Dylan, c1977, 28 pgs, 10 x 14" **25.00**

Yearbook, Dick Clark Official American Bandstand Yearbook, c1950, 40 pgs, color and black and white photos, 9 x 12" **25.00**

ROGERS, WILL

Reference: Dian Zillner, *Hollywood Collectibles,* Schiffer Publishing, 1991.

Jigsaw Puzzle, State Fair, Movie Cut-Ups Co. Inc., No. 10, Janet Gaynor, Will Rogers, Lew Ayres, and Sally Eilers, orig. box, 13½ x 10", $20.00.

Book
The Writings of Will Rogers, Series I and II, six different titles, Oklahoma State University Press, Stillwater, orig dust jackets or pictorial cloth cov........................ **120.00**
Will Rogers Ambassador of Good Will, Prince of Wit, P O'Brien, 1935   **15.00**
Calendar, 1942, Rogers seated looking out window, holding newspaper, William Fawcett Funeral Home give–away **15.00**
Fan, color photo of Rogers, Boyd Roland Funeral Home adv on back **12.00**
Lobby Card
Mr. Skitch, Fox, 1933 .... **35.00**
The Story of Will Rogers, Warner Brothers, 1952................. **20.00**
Magazine, Radio Stars, September, 1933, Rogers on cov **20.00**
Magazine Tear Sheet, Screen Book, adv for They Had to See Paris, Fox Film, 1929 .... **5.00**
Newspaper, Tulsa Tribune, August 16, 1935, Will Rogers, Wiley Post Instantly Killed as Plane Crashes in Alaska headline................. **100.00**
Post Card, photo, Hotel Last Frontier, Las Vegas, NV, empty saddles and Will Rogers painting, c1949, unused **8.50**
Poster, Handy Andy, close–up of Rogers' face, Tooker litho, 1934, 27 x 41".... **100.00**
Puzzle, State Fair scene, 1933, orig box   **25.00**

ROYALTY

Reference: Lincoln Hallinan, British Commemoratives: Royalty, Politics, War and Sport, Antique Collectors' Club, 1993; Peter Johnson, Royal Memorabilia: A Phillips Collectors Guide, Dunestyle Publishing, 1988; John May, Victoria Remembered, A Royal History 1817–1861, Heinemann; David Rogers, Coronation Souvenirs and Commemoratives, Latimer New Dimensions, 1975; Jack H. Smith, Royal Postcards, Wallace–Homestead, 1987; Geoffrey Warren, Royal Souvenirs, Orbis, 1977; Audrey B. Zeder, British Royal Commemoratives, Wallace–Homestead, 1986, out–of–print.

Calendar, Princess Elizabeth, 1949, 8½ x 4¾" **40.00**
Christmas Card, Prince Philip and Queen Elizabeth emb seals and entwined initials, 1961 .... **195.00**
Game, Royal Game of Kings and Queens, McLoughlin Brothers, 1890, 17 x 11¼" game board, 40 playing pieces **65.00**
Label, orange, Sunkist, Victoria portrait **15.00**
Magazine
Country Life, Charles and Diana wedding **25.00**
Everybody's, Elizabeth Coronation ... **25.00**
Life
1955, February 21, Princess Margaret cov **8.00**
1961, February 3, Queen Elizabeth **5.00**
Radio Times, Elizabeth 60th Birthday **20.00**
Magazine Cover, Collier's, Edward VII Coronation, Lyendecker **35.00**
Newspaper, Coronation of Elizabeth II headline **8.00**
Paper Doll
Princess Diana, Golden, 1985 ...... **10.00**

Cover Story, *TV Guide*, The Royal Wedding: What It Means To Us, multicolor sketch of Charles and Di, black-and-white and color photos, 144 pages, 5 x 7½″, July 25–31, 1981, $15.00.

Queen Elizabeth I, Bellerophon, uncut **5.00**
Photograph, Elizabeth Jubilee, Elizabeth and Philip, black and white, 6 x 8″ ... **15.00**
Playing Card
  Andrew and Sarah, 1986 Wedding, color photos, Waddingtons, double deck...................... **30.00**
  Edward VIII, 1919 Canada Visit, color portrait, C Goodall & Co **75.00**
  Elizabeth II, 1977, Jubilee, sepia photos, Waddingtons............... **25.00**
  George V and Mary, 1911 Coronation, color photos, double deck........ **75.00**
Post Card
  Coronation of George V, 1911, black and white **5.00**
  Edward VII and Alexandra, riding in horsedrawn carriage **15.00**
  George V and Queen Mary, multicolored, Tuck.................. **20.00**
  Princess Diana, 30th Birthday **10.00**
  Queen Alexandra, address to nation of Edward VII death **5.00**
  Queen Elizabeth, 40th Anniversary, multicolored **10.00**
  Queen Mother, 90th Birthday, Enterprise........................ **5.00**
  Queen Victoria Eugenia, Spain, royalty dress.................. **15.00**
  Victoria, 1897 Jubilee, Art Deco railway building **15.00**
Print, Princess Charlotte, 19th C, black and white, 4½ x 7″ **25.00**
Program
  Charles Investiture, 1969. .... **25.00**
  Coronation of Her Majesty Queen Elizabeth, 39 pgs **10.00**
Puzzle, Andrew and Sarah wedding, Waddington, tin box **45.00**
Souvenir Book, The Royal Wedding,

Prince Andrew and Sarah Ferguson, 32 pgs **15.00**

SAILING AND SAILING SHIP

Advertising Trade Card
  F A Leavitt Yacht and Boat Sails, blue and white **33.00**
  Yankee Sailing Ships, three volume set, color clipper ship illus, State Street Trust Co............... **100.00**
Book, *David Sails The Viking Trail,* D. B. Putnam, 1931, 155 pgs, first edition **5.00**
Catalog
  Boston & Lockport Block Co, Catalogue of Tackle Blocks, Boston, MA, 1888, 94 pgs, used on both sailing ships and steamships **135.00**
  Geo B Carpenter & Co, Tents, Flags, Awnings, Ship's Sails, Wagon Covers, Chicago, IL, 1910, 82 pgs **125.00**
  Kalamazoo Canvas Boat Co, Kalamazoo Canvas Folding Boat, Kalamazoo, MI, c1943, 8 pgs, canvas boats, adaptable for sailboats, canoes, and motor boats......... **25.00**
  Marine Model Company, Models I Have Built Series 5, New York, NY, 1939, 34 pgs, models of sailing ships **40.00**
  Merriman Bros, Boston, Yacht Blocks, Deck Spar, Rigging Equipment, and Wire Rope Rigging Services, 1939, 80 pgs **15.00**
  William J Wild, Ship Model Making, How to Make A Clipper Ship, New York, NY, 1943, 64 pgs.......... **35.00**
Clipper Ship Card, Storm King, Neptune above clipper ship, black and gold lettering, Coleman's California Line to San Francisco **1,000.00**
Document
  Insurance, total loss of brig *Betsy* and cargo, Eben Ricker late master, N F Marine Insurance Co, 1805, 12 x 7″........................ **15.00**
  Second Exchange, Merchants Bank, NY, 1840, vignette of woman and sailing ship **35.00**
  US of Am Bill of Sale of Enrolled Vessel, 1893, parchment, sailing ship vignette..................... **25.00**
Game, Yacht Race, Milton Bradley, multicolored litho board with ships and sailboat scenes, five pcs, orig box with large sail boat illus **30.00**
Label, lemon, Schooner, sailing vessel, sky background, Goleta **2.00**
Stereoview, Aboard Ship, New York Harbor, two large sailing ships, 1891 **28.00**

SANTA CLAUS

Reference: Ann Bahar, *Santa Dolls: Historical To Contemporary,* Hobby House Press, 1992; E. Willis Jones, *The Santa Claus Book,* Walker, 1976; Helaine Fendelman and Jeri Schwartz, *The Official Price Guide Holiday Collectibles,* House of Collectibles, 1991; Polly and Pam Judd, *Santa Dolls and Figurines Price Guide: Antique to Contemporary,* Hobby House Press, 1992.

Advertising Trade Card
Bank of Newberry, PA, bell, Santa head dec, 6" h 5.00
Dundee Smart Clothes, Allentown, PA, Santa, pack on back 4.00
First National Bank, Bloomsburg, PA, Santa, pack on back, train at feet, 7" h 4.00
Greenpoint Savings Bank, Brooklyn, NY, Santa, pack on back 4.00
Santa Claus Soap, Santa, tree over shoulder, child and doll at feet, 1899 . . . .   15.00
Star Soap, Schultz & Co, Zanesville, OH, Santa by chimney with toys, 5½ x 7½" 15.00
West Haven Savings and Loan, Hazelton, PA, Santa, pack on back, 7" h 4.00
Woolson Spice Co, Father Christmas, Santa and reindeer 12.00
Book
Around the World with Santa Claus, McLoughlin Bros, NY, 1900 . . . . . .   25.00
How Santa Filled the Christmas Stockings, Stecher Litho Co, Rochester, NY, 1916 . . . .   12.00
Old Saint Nicholas, Chicago, Homewood Publishing Co 15.00
Watching for Santa Claus, Hurst & Co, NY, 1912 . . . .   15.00

Post Card, emb, green suit, red ground, Germany, 3½ x 5½", 1900s, $12.00.

Box
Candy, cardboard, rect, Santa face on all sides, 1950s 7.50
Sticker, cardboard, emb Santa portrait on cov seal, white ground, Dennison, c1925, 1 x 1½ x 1½" 8.00
Card Holder, paper, fold–up Santa and reindeer, Hallmark, 1940s 18.00
Children's Book, adv giveaways
L L Stearn's Dept Store, Williamsport, PA, *Santa Claus Book,* color illus, 1920s 12.50
Snellenberg's Dept Store, Philadelphia, PA, *Snellenberg's,* Santa and children cov, 1930s 10.00
Diecut, Santa riding donkey with Christmas tree, c1900, 5½" h 8.00
Display Stand–Up, Pepsi–Cola Santa, cardboard, one leg raised, bottle in hand, 60" h 65.00
Figure, cardboard, Santa holding tree, black cardboard platform, 4" h 7.00
Game
Game of The Visit of Santa Claus, McLoughlin, c1899, multicolored litho board with Santa and workshop scene, 38 pcs, orig box with Santa at chimney illus 250.00
Santa Claus Game, Milton Bradley, 1920–24, five pcs, multicolored litho board on bottom of box, orig box with Santa illus 85.00
Greeting Card
"Christmas Greetings In My House," house shape, Santa with tree inside, 1930s 3.00
"Christmas Greetings," Santa cutout, poem inside, 1930s 3.50
"Merry Christmas," foldout, Santa on front, pictures to trace inside, 1930s   3.00
Label, lemon, Santa, full color, 1928, 9 x 12" 5.00
Magazine Tear Sheet, "Merry Old Santa Claus," Thomas Nast, *Harper's Weekly* 100.00
Playing Cards, Santa Clausland, Santa Claus, IN, color santa illus 7.50
Post Card
"A Merry Christmas," Father Christmas, blue coat, presents, tree, Germany 6.00
"A Merry Christmas To You," Santa beside donkey loaded with toys, 1904 . . . .   5.00
"Christmas Greetings," Father Christmas, putting toys through window, Germany 7.00
"Christmas Greetings," Santa driving three wheeled motorbike, 1909 . . .   10.00
"Happy Christmas Wishes," Santa steering ship's wheel, Germany. . . .   5.00

"Joyful Christmas," Father Christmas
face, two children, 1913 . . . . **4.50**
"Loving Christmas Wishes," emb, Fa-
ther Christmas face, surrounded by
holly **4.00**
"May your Christmas be Merry and
Gay," Father Christmas photograph,
peeping through doorway, Ger-
many **6.00**
Santa Trio, cloth and cardboard bod-
ies, paper and celluloid faces,
1950s, Japan, 5–7" **45.00**
Poster, Santa, RC Cola adv, 28 x 11" **40.00**
Print, The Marriage of Santa Claus, 1928,
framed **32.00**
Puzzle, Santa Claus Puzzle Box, Milton
Bradley, 1924–26, three multicolored
litho puzzles, orig box with Santa and
toys illus. **95.00**
Sign, Royal Crown Cola, 1950s, full
color Santa holding bottle, 6 x 7¼" . . . **5.00**

SCIENCE

Collectors' Club: The Oughtred Society, 8338
Colombard Court, San Jose, CA 95135.

Booklet, Half Hour Experiments with
Plants, Burbank, 1922 . . . . **12.00**
Catalog
Arthur D Thomas Company, Laboratory Apparatus and Reagents, Philadelphia, PA, 1921, 816 pgs, instruments and apparatus for chemical,
metallurgical, and biological labo-
ratories **175.00**
Carl Zeiss, Astronomical Instruments,
Altazimuth Telescopes For Astronomical and Terrestrial Observations, Comet Finders, 1915–20, 22
pgs **50.00**
Edward N Kent, Descriptive Catalogue
of Chemical Apparatus, Chemicals
and Pure Reagents, NY, 1846, 40
pgs **300.00**
Eugene, Dietzgen Co, Drafting & Sur-

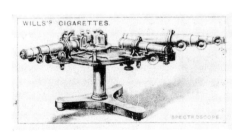

**Cigarette Card, Will's Cigarettes, Famous
Inventions series, No. 10, Spectroscope,
2⅝ x 1⅜", $3.00.**

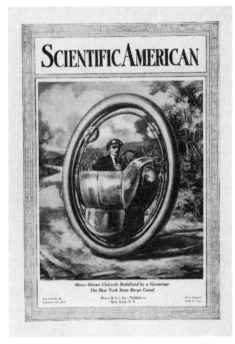

**Magazine, *Scientific American*, Vol. CXI,
No. 24, 14 pages, black and white, 11 x
16", December 12, 1914, $15.00.**

veying Supplies, Twelfth Edition,
Chicago, 1926, 490 pgs **25.00**
F Weber & Co, Supplementary Cata-
logue and Price List of Richter Math-
ematical Instruments, Philadelphia,
1915–20, 16 pgs **20.00**
Handbook and Illustrated Catalogue of
The Engineers, and Surveyors, Instruments of Precision, Boston,
1900, 212 pgs, cloth backed stiff
paper wrappers **100.00**
Johnson Service Co, Thermometers,
Barometers, Hygrometers, Milwau-
kee, WI, c1920, 32 pgs **50.00**
L E Knott Apparatus Co, Boston, 1921,
scientific instruments, 326 pgs, sci-
entific instruments, 8 x 10½" **35.00**
Ward's Natural Science Establishment,
Ward Collection of Meteorites and
Specimens for Sale, Rochester, NY,
1892, 72 pgs **50.00**
Magazine
Popular Science, October, 1936 . . . . . **8.00**
Science and Invention, September,
1929 . . . . **5.00**
Paperback Book, *Zodiac & Its Mysteries,*
Prof Seward, 1915, over 250 pgs, in-
cludes 48 pgs illus catalog **12.00**

SCIENCE FICTION

References: Sue Cornwell and Mike Kott, *The Official Price Guide Star Trek and Star Wars Collectibles,* Third Edition, House of Collectibles, 1991; Christine Gentry and Sally Gibson–Downs, *Greenberg's Guide To Star Trek Collectibles, Volumes I–III,* Greenberg Publishing, 1992; Stephen J. Sansweet, *Star Wars: From Concept To Screen To Collectible,* Chronicle Books, 1992; Don and Maggie Thompson, *The Official Price Guide To Science Fiction and Fantasy Collectibles,* Third Edition, House of Collectibles, 1989; T. N. Tumbusch, *Space Adventure Collectibles,* Wallace–Homestead, 1990; Bruce Lanier Wright, *Yesterday's Tomorrows: The Golden Age of Science Fiction Movie Posters 1950–1964,* Taylor Publishing, 1993.

Paperback Book, Ace Books, Inc., Double Novel Books, D-362, two novels, *Edge of Time,* David Grinnell, and *The 100th Millennium,* John Brunner, 256 pages, 4¹/₄ x 6¹/₂", 1959, $5.00.

Art, original
  Amazing Adventures #18, War of the
    Worlds, Neal Adams, pencil layout,
    translucent paper 40.00
  Beyond Imagination–Do You Remember Lemuria?, newspaper art, 10 x
    13" 40.00
  Journey Into Mystery #1, Jim Starlin
    and Mike Ploog 40.00
Big Little Book
  *Maximo The Amazing Superhuman
    And The Crystals Of Doom,*
    Whitman, #1444 . . . .   20.00
Book
  Adams, Douglas, *The Restaurant at the
    End of the Universe,* 1981, hard cov   2.00
  Asprin, Robert Lynn, *The Cold Cash
    War,* 1977, hard cov 5.00
  Bain, F. W., *A Digit Of The Moon,*
    Putnam, NY, 1906 . . . .   30.00
  Battlestar Galactica, hard cov 5.00
  Biggle, Lloyd Jr., *This Darkening Universe,* first edition, Doubleday, NY,
    1975 . . . .   80.00
  Boyd, John, *The Girl With The Jade
    Green Eyes,* Viking Press, NY, 1978   17.00
  Gail, Otto W., *By Rocket to the Moon,*
    Dodd, Mead and Co, NY, 1950 . . . .   23.00
  Maine, Charles E., *The Isotope Man,*
    Book Club Edition, undated 3.00
  Piserchia, Doris, *Spaceling,* Book Club
    Edition, undated 4.00
  Rohmer, Sax, *Brood Of The Witch
    Queen,* A L Burt, undated 14.00
  Sacranie, Raj, *Stories From Outer
    Space,* Chartwell, 1979 . . . .   8.00
  Sherwood, Martin, *Maxwell's Demon,*
    first edition, Thomas Nelson, NY,
    1976 . . . .   14.00
  Smith, George O., *Nomad,* first edition, Prime Press, Philadelphia,
    1950 . . . .   42.00
  Train, Arthur and Robert Williams

  Wood, *The Man Who Rocked The
    Earth,* first edition, Doubleday Page,
    NY, 1915, pictorial cloth binding . . 165.00
Bubble Gum Cards, Alien, Topps, 1979,
  84 cards 10.00
Calendar, Star Trek, 1970s 8.00
Game
  Escape from Death Star, Star Wars,
    Kenner, 1977 copyright, orig box . .   15.00
  Twilight Zone, Ideal, 1964 . . . .   35.00
Playing Card, Star Trek the Wrath of
  Khan, complete deck, full color photos, orig box 7.50
Post Card, Captain Kirk, Lincoln Enterprises, full color, 5 x 7" 60
Poster, movie
  Cat–Women Of The Moon, Astor Pictures, 1954, 14 x 36" 30.00
  Crack in the World 20.00
  Creature With The Atom Brain,
    Columbia Pictures, 1955, 22 x 28"   34.00
  Destination Inner Space 18.00
  Fiend Without A Face, 1958, 27 x 41"   40.00
  Incredible Shrinking Man, Universal
    Pictures, 1957, 14 x 36" 120.00
  Journey To The Center Of The Earth,
    Twentieth Century–Fox, 1959, 22 x
    28" 27.00
  Plague Of The Zombies, Twentieth
    Century–Fox, 1966, 14 x 36" 22.00
  The Alligator People 40.00
  The Earth Dies Screaming, Twentieth
    Century–Fox, 1964, 22 x 28" 15.00
  The Man With the X–Ray Eyes, 1963,
    27 x 41" 50.00
  The Space Children 65.00
  The Thing That Couldn't Die, Universal Pictures, 1958, 14 x 36" 18.00
  They Came From Beyond Space 12.00
  War Of The Satellites, Allied Artists,
    1958, 14 x 36" 27.00

Pulp, *Amazine Stories, Fact and Science Fiction*, Vol. 36, No. 9, Ziff-Davis Publishing Co., 146 pages, 5½ x 7¾", May 1962, $3.00.

Catalog, Seed Annual, D. M. Ferry & Co., Detroit, MI, color litho cover, 4 litho color plates, black-and-white illustrations, foldout order sheet, 168 pages, 5¾ x 8¾", 1882, $40.00.

Press Book
   City Beneath The Sea, Universal Pictures, 1953, 14 pgs **12.00**
   The Day Mars Invaded Earth, Twentieth Century–Fox, 1962, 12 pgs **6.00**
Puzzle, 2001: A Space Odyssey, MGM's Fabulous Four **20.00**

SEEDS

Advertising Trade Card, La Moreaux Nursery Co, 1913, seed catalog, printed, color, divided back **9.00**
Catalogs
   Benson & Burpee, Priced Catalogue of Fine Stock Reliable Seed, Philadelphia, PA, 1877, 24 pgs. **50.00**
   Burgess Seeds & Plants for 1933, 128 pgs **12.00**
   D M Ferry & Co, Detroit, MI, 1917, 105 pgs, 7 x 9¾" **22.00**
   Fairview Seed Farms, Syracuse, NY, 1910, 64 pgs **20.00**
   Ferre, Batchelder & Co, Catalogue of Seeds, and Vegetable and Flower Garden Manual, Springfield, MA, 1869, 84 pgs **40.00**
   Germain Seed Co, Seeds and Plants, Los Angeles, CA, 1908, 96 pgs **60.00**
   Great Northern Seed Co, Catalogue for 1900, Rockford, IL, 64 pgs, wood cut illus **35.00**
   Holmes–Letherman Seed Co, Holco Seeds, Canton, OH, 1928, 80 pgs, color printed wrappers **15.00**
   John A Salzer Seed Co, 1940, 127 pgs **8.00**
   Joseph Breck & Son, Catalogue of Vegetable Seeds, For Sale At The New England Agricultural Warehouse and Seed Store, Boston, MA, c1860, 20 pgs **50.00**

Joseph Harris Co, Inc, Harris Seeds, Coldwater, NY, 1934, 96 pgs **15.00**
J W Jung Seed Co, Jung Quality Seeds, Randolph, WI, 1925, 52 pgs, black and white illus, color paper wrappers **15.00**
Kendall & Whitney's Seed Catalog, 1931 . . . . **55.00**
Luther Burbank Co, Burbank Seed Book, San Francisco, CA, 1914, 80 pgs, printed wrappers **125.00**
Marshall's Matchless Seeds, 1933. . . . **18.00**
Mills Catalogue Seeds and Plants, Rose Hill, NY, 1913, 92 pgs, red pictorial wrappers **30.00**
Mills Seed Catalogue, Rose Hill, NY, 1901, 80 pgs, red, green, and yellow pictorial wrappers **22.50**
Montgomery Ward Co, Growing Flowers from Seed, #87–136, 13 pgs **18.00**
Robert and James Farquhar, Illustrated Catalogue of Reliable Seeds, Plants,

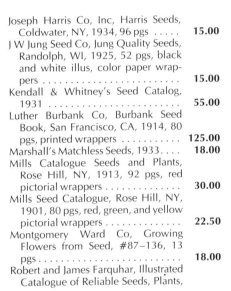

Peas, Card Seed Co., green and black, 3¼ x 5", $5.00.

Bulbs and Garden Requisites, Boston, 1883, 56 pgs, printed wrappers **25.00**
Sutton & Sons, Seed Catalogue, 1927, 192 pgs, color plates **45.00**
Templin–Bradley Co, Penny Packet Seeds, Cleveland, OH, c1925, 24 pgs **20.00**
Trustworthy Garden Field, Flowers, Seeds, 1931, 24 pgs, orig envelope **21.00**
Sign, D M Ferry & Company Seeds, man sitting outside shack, 1907, 22½ x 32" **340.00**

SEWING

References: Joyce Clement, *The Official Price Guide To Sewing Collectibles,* House of Collectibles, 1987, out–of–print; Estelle Zalkin, *Zalkin's Handbook of Thimbles and Sewing Implements,* Warman Publishing Co., 1988.

Advertising Trade Card
Clark's ONT Spool Cotton, woman holding spool of cotton talking to man **15.00**
Domestic Sewing Machine, black caricature illus **26.00**
Gray & Grace's Sewing Machines, 1858 . . . . **42.00**
Home Sewing Machine Co, woman looking in mirror seeing herself and sewing machine. **20.00**
Household Sewing Machine Co, spirit of '76 scene, dated 1885 . . . . **6.00**
J P Coats Spool Cotton, metamorphic, fish getting away from broken line, fish caught with Coats thread when opened. **46.00**
Singer Sewing Machine, women sewing, machine illus on back, 1890s, 3 x 5". **7.50**
Standard Sewing Machine Co, rotary shuttle in bicycle form **20.00**
Wheeler and Wilson, family watching sewing machine delivery. **4.00**
White Sewing Machine, metamorphic, foot pedal sewing machine and youthful family scene **8.00**
Book
Florence Home Needlework, Nontuck Silk Co, 1887, 96 pgs. **15.00**
History of the Sewing Machine, James Parton, c1867, 44 pgs, 13 pgs illus and prices for Howe Sewing Machine **35.00**
The Singer Drawing Book For Young Artists, 1930s, 3¼ x 5½" **10.00**
Booklet
Construction hints, dresses of the time, pictures on every page, 1905. . . . . . **10.00**
Florence Sewing Machines, 1873, 16 pgs, engraved illus **12.00**

Needle Book, Fashion Quality Needle Book, printed color covers, 115 needles, Japan, 6¾ x 4¼", 1950s, $8.00.

How to Make Children's Clothes, Singer, 1930, illus **8.00**
Shakespeare Boiled Down, New Home Sewing Machine, 1890s, 30 pgs **20.00**
Singer Manufacturing Co, 1893 Chicago World Columbian Exposition exhibit photos, full color cov, 8 pgs **25.00**
Singer Sewing Machines, 1912, 32 pgs, engraved illus **10.00**
Singer the Universal Sewing Machine, diecut, Pan–Am Expo, 1901 . . . . . . **65.00**
Brochure, Gearhart Knitting Machine Co, Gearhart's 1914 Family Knitters, Clearfield, PA, 1914, 8 pgs, six examples of knitted material done by machine **50.00**
Calendar, Singer Sewing Machines, 1904, Indian on diecut animal skin, 16¼ x 20½" **85.00**
Catalog
C B Barker & Co, Price List of Genuine Sewing Machine Parts, New York, NY, c1870, 144 pgs, replacements parts for sewing machines **75.00**
Davis Sewing Machine Co, Dayton, OH, 1893, 24 pgs, The Davis Vertical Feed Sewing Machine **40.00**
F M Van Etten, Trade Circular and Price List for 1877, Chicago, IL, 1877, 96 pgs, sewing machines and parts **75.00**
King Sewing Machine Co, Buffalo, NY, 1909, 56 pgs **40.00**
New Home Sewing Machine Co, Orange, MA, c1905, 16 pgs. **25.00**
Th. de Dillmont Embroiderer's Alphabet–Letters, Figures, etc, Mulhouse, FR, c1905, 64 pgs, illus of patterns for letters and dec for embroidery . . **50.00**
Victor Sewing Machine Co, Middletown, CT and Philadelphia, c1880, accordion style, eight panels **20.00**
Wheeler & Wilson Mfg Co, Sewing

Machines, Bridgeport, CT, 1860s, 31 pgs, yellow pictorial wrappers . .   **50.00**
White Co, Eldridge Special Sewing Machines, Boston, 1906, 16 pgs . . .   **20.00**
Youth's Companion, Boston, 1928, 20 pgs. **20.00**
Engraving, Clark's ONT Spool Cotton Factory, hand colored image, matted   **30.00**
Envelope, Singer Co, 1901, Pan–American Exposition, color, all over design, unused **80.00**
Folder
Singer Sewing Machine, four panels, color, 1800–1900 historical vignettes **15.00**
White Sewing Machine, eight panels, product illus. **20.00**
Manual, Howe Sewing Machine, NY, 1872, 20 pgs, blue printed wraps with factory view and Elias Howe steamboat on back, machines and parts illus   **25.00**
Needle Book, diecut, logo shape, Red Owl Food Stores adv **5.00**
Pamphlet, *How to Make Children's Clothes The Modern Singer Way,* 1928, Singer Service Library No. 3 . . .   **5.00**
Post Card, Singer Sewing Machine Store, photo of employees and sewing machines, 1909 . . . .   **38.00**
Print, little girl, red and pink roses, San Diego Sewing Machine Co adv, Compliments of the New Home Sewing Machine Co, early 1900s, 10 x 41" . . .   **50.00**
Puzzle, Singer Buffalo Puzzle, full color, 50 pcs, 1900, 7 x 10" **35.00**
Sewing Needle Book, Elsie the Cow, mounted sewing needles, 4³/₄ x 5¹/₄" . .   **6.50**
Sign
Clark's ONT Spool Cotton Thread, 1890s, roll down type, woman and child, orig metal strips top and bottom, 14¹/₂ x 25" **250.00**
Singer Sewing Machines, grandmother and child at sewing machine, 14 x 24". **410.00**

SOCIAL CAUSE

Advertising Trade Card, American Red Cross, 1901–07, Santa and Father time, printed, red and silver, undivided back. **20.00**
Book, *Prisoners Of Poverty: Women Wage Workers, Their Trades And Their Lives,* Helen Campbell, Little, Brown, and Co, Boston, 1900, 257 pgs, red cloth cov **40.00**
Booklet
The House That Rum Built, National Temperance Society Publication House, 1884, 24 pgs, woodcut cov and illus. **25.00**

WCTU Parlimentary Rules, c1880 . . .   **10.00**
Calendar, American Red Cross, 1919, 28 x 10¹/₄". **35.00**
Flyer, Temperance, Dr Walker's Vinegar Bitters adv, extols virtues of product, 4 pgs, illus, 8 x 11" **6.00**
Journal, *The Official Organ of the White Ribbon Army,* WCTU, 1887 . . . .   **12.00**
Letter, Red Cross, 1904, 4 pgs, signed by Mabel T Boardman **50.00**
Magazine, *Life,* September 25, 1950, Swedish Red Cross girl on cov. **5.00**
Membership Card, Bangor Association for Prevention of Cruelty to Animals, Organized April 22, 1869, life membership, card stock, blue and red lettering, gold border. **100.00**
Post Card
Anti–Prohibition, c1930, "Why I Like The Orient," liquor bottles and gambling dice view **16.50**
Prohibition Demonstration, Onaway, MI, crowd listening to speaker and band. **32.00**
Poster, National Prohibition–The Saloon Must Go–Vote Straight Prohibition Ticket, eagle and patriotic motif, banner with "National Prohibition," c1910, 12 x 19" **185.00**

SODA

References: Q. David Bowers, *The Moxie Encyclopedia,* The Vestal Press, 1985; Ted Hake, *Hake's Guide To Advertising Collectibles,* Wallace–Homestead, 1992; Sharon and Bob Huxford, *Huxford's Collectible Advertising; An Illustrated Value Guide,* Collector Books, 1993; Tom Morrison, *Root Beer: Advertising and Collectibles,* Schiffer Publishing, 1992; Frank N. Potter, *The Book of Moxie,* Collector Books, 1987.

Collectors' Club: Moxie Enthusiasts Collectors Club of America, Route 375, Box 164, Woodstock, NY 12498.

Advertising Cover, envelope, Chero–Cola Bottling Co, bottle image, 1923   **20.00**
Advertising Trade Card
Belfast Ginger Ale, black and white   **25.00**
Hires Improved Root Beer, full color, 1889, 4 x 6". **25.00**
Learn To Drink Moxie, diecut, full color, c1910, 7" l **30.00**
Baseball Score Card, Moxie, red and white, 3" d **15.00**
Book, *Puzzle Book of Unnatural History,* Hires, full color, diecut pgs, c1910, 3 x 4¹/₂". **30.00**
Booklet, *Hires Magic Story,* Hires Root Beer, 1934, 8 pgs, color **25.00**

Advertising Stringer, "Cheer Up," green bottle, red label, double sided, hanger, unused, 2½ x 8½", $15.00.

Calendar
  Dr Pepper, 1949, full pad **50.00**
  Hoods Sarsaparilla, 1888, diecut, little girl's face, framed, 18 x 11" . . . **325.00**
  Nehi, 1936, girl's portrait illus, full pad, 11½ x 23. . . . . **200.00**
  NuGrape, 1949, 6 pgs,15 x 25" **30.00**
  RC Cola
    1946, Diana Lynn, full pad, 11½ x 25". **60.00**
    1951, Ann Blyth, October–December, 11½ x 25". **50.00**
  Squirt, 1948, 6 pgs, 16 x 22½" **30.00**
  Sun Crest Cola, 1957 . . . . **28.00**
Carrier, Pure Rock Sparkling Club Soda, holds six 12 oz bottles, 8¼ x 12¼". **15.00**
Fan, Dr Pepper, cardboard, six pack of Dr Pepper, red and green **50.00**
Matchbook Cover, Drink 7–Up It Likes You, black, white, and red, 1940s, 1½ x 2" **10.00**
Newspaper Advertisement, Hires Root Beer, 1902, two corked bottles illus, 8¼ x 10½" **12.00**
Playing Cards, 7 Up, Fresh Up **12.00**
Post Card, Hires, Alice, full color, 1912, 3½ x 5½" **10.00**
Poster
  Canada Dry Spur, 16 x 26½" **75.00**
  Hires Root Beer, cardboard, woman holding glass of root beer, 39 x 24" **500.00**
  Moxie, cardboard, Enjoy A Lift The Healthful Way, Drink Moxie, father and son picnicking after hunt, 31 x 40". **105.00**
  Pepsi, Counter Spy, 19½ x 8" **40.00**
  RC Cola, Joan Caulfield, 28 x 11" . . . **50.00**
  7–Up, cardboard, plate of food and bottle of soda, 1960, 10 x 17" **15.00**
Sign
  Add 7–Up For A Real Treat, cardboard, diecut, full color, easel

back, 1940s, 9½ x 13½". **20.00**
Boone Cola, cardboard, Daniel Boone on bottle, 15 x 5" **35.00**
Canada Dry Ginger Ale, cardboard, Ginger Sparkling Ale, Lemon–Lime Rickey, fizzing glasses and bottles **40.00**
Cherry Smash, Drink Cherry Smash, paper, litho, colonial dressed man, framed. **160.00**
Frosty Root Beer, Everybody Loves Frosty, cardboard, diecut, animated figure holding sign, 13 x 21" **25.00**
Hires R–J Root Beer, cardboard, diecut, full color, 1930s, 9½ x 14". . . **30.00**
Hoods Sarsaparilla, cardboard, diecut, litho, little boy sitting on box, holding soda, framed, 19 x 11" . . . **1,000.00**
Kist Orange, Get Kist Here, Orange & Other Flavors, cardboard, diecut, standup, pretty girl displaying product, 12 x 14" **55.00**
Ma's Root Beer, Drink Old Fashion Ma's Root Beer, cardboard, 1940s, 12 x 10". **5.00**
Moxie, diecut, Ellen Percy, 9" h **30.00**
Nehi, Genuine Nehi In This Bottle Only, paper litho on artist board, bottle and woman's leg, 19 x 40" **130.00**
NuGrape, A Flavor You Can't Forget, Had Yours To–day?, cardboard, bottle in center **30.00**
Raser's Root Beer, girl on floor writing on slate, 25 x 25". **600.00**
Snyder's Beverages, They Are the Best Beverages, Battle Creek, MI, oval with seated girl, matted and framed, 23 x 18" **85.00**
Wynola Soda, Drink Wynola, Good Anytime, soda bottle cradled in 5¢ symbol, 1950s, 9 x 20" **22.00**
Zesto, cardboard, 10½ x 6¼" **25.00**

Magazine Tear Sheet, Royal Crown Cola, *Life*, printed color, sgd. Miller illustration, 10¼ x 14", 1955, $18.00.

SODA FOUNTAIN

References: Douglas Congdon–Martin, *Drugstore and Soda Fountain Antiques,* Schiffer Publishing, 1991; Paul Dickson, *The Great American Ice Cream Book,* Galahad Books, 1972; Sharon and Bob Huxford, *Huxford's Collectible Advertising: An Illustrated Value Guide,* Collector Books, 1993; Ray Klug, *Antique Advertising Encyclopedia, Volume I,* 1978, 1992 value update, *Volume II,* 1985, 1989 value update, L–W Promotions; Tom Morrison, *Root Beer: Advertising and Collectibles,* Schiffer Publishing, 1992; Ralph Pomeroy, *The Ice Cream Connection,* Paddington Press, 1975.

Collectors' Club: The Ice Screamer, PO Box 5387, Lancaster, PA 17601.

Advertising Trade Card, Coca–Cola, At Your Soda Fountain, punched for hanging display **125.00**
Brochure, White Mountain Ice Cream, woman making ice cream **25.00**
Box, Pepsi, cardboard, 10½" paper straws, box of 500, c1950 . . . . **40.00**
Catalog, Dean Foster Co, 1908, soda counter goods **48.00**
Diecut, heavy card stock
   Banana Split, glass boat dish with ice cream, walnuts, cherries, and other toppings, c1950, 12" l **15.00**
   Sundae, dish with vanilla ice cream and chocolate syrup, glass pitcher with chocolate syrup, c1950, 11" h   **12.00**
Fan, Lee's Drug Store, Natrona Heights, PA, cardboard, diecut, sundae, candy, fruit, and milkshake illus **75.00**

Syrup Label, Red Bud Brand Strawberry Fountain Syrup, blue and red, 5 x 6", $3.00.

Menu, Hook's Dependable Drug Store Fountain Menu, 1920–30 . . . . **35.00**
Photograph, int. soda fountain view, front counter service, c1905 . . . . **10.00**
Poster
   Chocolate Chip Ice Cream, 1950s, colorful, 13 x 20" **10.00**
   Chocolate Shakes and Shakers, repeated designs of shakes and aluminum shaker canisters, Anon, c1950, 25 x 11" **30.00**
   Emerson's Ginger–Mint Julep, paper, 20¼ x 4½" **35.00**
   Hanging Out At The Fountain, six repeated designs of couples leaning against fountain stools, eating from sundaes and floats, Anon, 1950, 54 x 41" **175.00**
   Trio O' Shakes, three images of hand gripping frothy chocolate shakes, Anon, 1947, 29 x 22" **25.00**
   7–Up Float, cardboard, bottle and Art Deco glass, 1948, 8½ x 11" **10.00**
Sign
   Cherry Cheer, cardboard, 7 x 11" **125.00**
   Drink Cherry Blossoms, cardboard, cherry blossom shape, girl face sipping drink with straw, 8¾ x 6" . . **60.00**
   Mission Orange Soda, paper, 1940– 50, 20 x 26¼" **50.00**
   Orange Julep, cardboard, 7¾ x 11" . . . **75.00**
   Way·Up Lemon & Lime Fruit Flavor, cardboard, 5 x 7" **45.00**
   Whistle Soda, cardboard, standup, diecut, elf and bottle, 1940s **20.00**
Thermometer, Puritas Ice Cream, cardboard, c1923, 12½" h **35.00**

SOUVENIR

References: Diane Allmen, *The Official Identification and Price Guide To Postcards,* House of Collectibles, 1990; Frederic H. Megson and Mary S. Megson, *American Advertising Postcards: Sets and Series 1890–1920,* published by authors, 1985; John Waldsmith, *Stereoviews: An Illustrated History and Price Guide,* Wallace–Homestead, 1991; Robert Ward, *Investment Guide to North American Real Photo Postcards,* Antique Paper Guild, 1991; Jane Wood, *The Collector's Guide To Post Cards,* L–W Promotions, 1984, 1993 value update.

Periodical: *Travel Collector,* PO Box 40, Manawa, WI 54949.

Collectors' Club: Antique Souvenir Collectors News, Box 562, Great Barrington, MA 01230.

Album, New Orleans photos, 1885 . . . . **10.00**
Book
   Guy & Dolls, broadway/stage, 1950s   **30.00**

Booklet, Souvenir of the Panama Pacific Exposition San Francisco 1915, Lowney's Chocolates giveaway, color litho, 8 pages, 6⅛ x 4¼", $18.00.

Ohio Centennial, 1903	**20.00**
Booklet, Yosemite Visitor's Guide, 32 color photos	**8.00**
Card Folder, Yellowstone National Park, 1928	**5.00**
Playing Cards	
Adventureland, Des Moines, IA, pale yellow, caboose illus, train track border	**5.00**
Chicago, Sears Tower, World's Tallest Building, color aerial view, yellow border	**10.00**
Disneyland, castle illus, white background	**5.00**
Grand Ole Opry House, color aerial view	**7.50**
Knott's Berry Farm, CA, six different illus, red background	**5.00**
Little Italy Festival, Outtio Stagioni Fountain, Clinton, IN, white, brown illus, green border	**10.00**
Mount Rushmore, SD, color illus of four president's mountain, yellow border	**12.50**
Pro Football Hall Of Fame, Canton, OH, building illus	**7.50**
Post Card	
Bismark Garden, Chicago, Marigold Room	**5.50**
Georgian Hotel, Athens	**2.00**
National Bank of the Republic, Chicago, Souvenir American Bankers Convention, October 20–23, 1903	**3.00**
New York World's Fair, 1964	**12.00**
The Lake Mohonk House, The Testimonial Gateway, NY	**3.50**
The Touraline Hotel, Boston, hotel view	**4.00**
Program, Rose Bowl Parade, 1940	**20.00**
View Book, Mohican Trail, Catskill Mountains, NY, oval cutout, Indian	

cov, forty–one scenes and map, heavy stock, 5 x 7" **18.00**

SPACE ADVENTURERS

References: Sue Cornwell and Mike Kott, *The Official Price Guide To Star Trek and Star Wars Collectibles,* Third Edition, House of Collectibles, 1991; Christine Gentry and Sally Gibson–Downs, *Greenberg's Guide To Star Trek Collectibles, Volumes I–III,* Greenberg Publishing, 1992; Don and Maggie Thompson, *The Official Price Guide To Science Fiction and Fantasy Collectibles,* Third Edition, House of Collectibles, 1989; Stephen J. Sansweet, *Star Wars: From Concept To Screen To Collectible,* Chronicle Books, 1992; T. N. Tumbush, *Space Adventure Collectibles,* Wallace–Homestead, 1990.

Periodical: *Galaxy Patrol Newsletter,* 22 Colton St., Worcester, MA 01610.

Autograph, photo, Star Trek, television series, black and white glossy, 8 x 10"	**100.00**
Big Little Book	
Buck Rogers and the Depth Men of Jupiter, Whitman, #1169, 1935 . . .	**65.00**
Flash Gordon in the Water World of Mongo, Whitman, #1407, 1937 . . .	**70.00**
Catalog, Space Patrol	**175.00**
Certificate, membership, E. T.	**4.00**
Coloring Book	
Darth Vader and Stormtroopers, Kenner	**5.00**
Tom Corbett, Space Cadet, Saalfield, 1952	**30.00**
Comic Sheet, Sunday, Buck Rogers, 1930–65 . . . . , ...	**20.00**
Game	
Adventures of R2–D2, Kenner	**18.00**
Battle of The Planets, Milton Bradley	**6.00**
Buck Rogers Adventures In The 25th Century, Trans–O–Gram	**33.00**

Star Trek, birthday card, punch-out Captain Kirk figure, tri-fold, Random House Greetings, 5 x 10" folded size, 1976, $15.00.

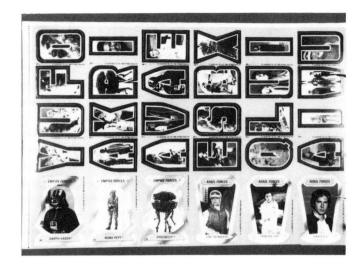

Star Wars, proof sheet, *Empire Strikes Back* **bubblegum card stickers, yellow ground, 15½ x 10¾", 1980, $30.00.**

Star Trek, Hasbro, 1974, orig box	50.00

Greeting Card
Flash Gordon, Christmas, orig envelope, 1951 . . . . — **10.00**
Star Trek, Random House, 1976, "This is your Captain speaking...Have a far–out birthday," punch out items — **15.00**
Handbook, *Space Patrol Handbook,* 1950s, 16 pgs, black and white illus, 4½ x 6" . . . . — **90.00**
Magazine Tear Sheet, Buck Rogers Strat–O–Sphere Balloon adv, 1935 . . . . — **35.00**
Map, Buck Rogers Map Of The Solar System, bright colors, Cocomalt premium, 18½ x 25½" . . . . — **425.00**
Photograph, Captain Video . . . . — **10.00**
Poster, movie
Captain Video . . . . — **325.00**
Flash Gordon, *Flash Gordon Conquers the Universe,* 1973, black, white, and red, 27 x 41" . . . . — **50.00**
Star Wars . . . . — **90.00**
Program, Star Trek, International Convention, 1973 . . . . — **55.00**
Puzzle
Alien Jigsaw Puzzle, H G Toys, 1979 — **20.00**
Buck Rogers, Marauder series, #3, Milton Bradley, 1979 copyright, orig box . . . . — **15.00**
Tom Corbett, Space Cadet, Saalfield, 1952 . . . . — **22.00**
Sheet Music
Main Theme Star Trek II The Wrath Of Khan, James Horner, Famous Music Corp, 1982. . . . . — **3.00**
Space Patrol. . . . . — **35.00**
Toy, figure, Buck Rogers, cardboard, newspaper premium . . . . — **45.00**

SPORTS

Reference: Roderick A. Malloy, *Malloy's Sports Collectibles Value Guide,* Wallace–Homestead, 1993.

Periodical: *Sports Collectors Digest,* 700 East State Street, Iola, WI 54990.

Book
Handbook of Wrestling, Hugh F Leonard, 1897, 265 pgs . . . . — **12.00**
How To Improve Your Basketball, Phog Allen, Bud Foster, and Ed Hickey, 1950, 80 pgs. . . . . — **5.75**
Booklet
Beadle's Dime Book of Croquet, 1866, 28 pgs, illus . . . . — **25.00**
D & M Official Rules for 1926, baseball, lawn tennis, field hockey, and hand ball . . . . — **20.00**
Sports Secrets, National Biscuit Co, 1937 . . . . — **25.00**
Catalog
A J Reach, Philadelphia, PA, 1912, 32 pgs, fall athlete equipment. . . . . — **25.00**
Bradford & Anthony, Wholesale Price List of Winslow's Skates and Skate Straps, Boston, 1869, 16 pgs, pictorial wrappers . . . . — **125.00**
Gymnasium Apparatus, c1920, 148 pgs, gymnastics, indoor sports, track and field, basketball nets, and playground equipment . . . . — **40.00**
Hood Rubber Co, basketball and sneakers, 1939, 44 pgs . . . . — **9.00**
Spauding, A G & Bros, Fall &7 Winter Sports, 1907, 128 pgs, variety of sports equipment . . . . — **100.00**

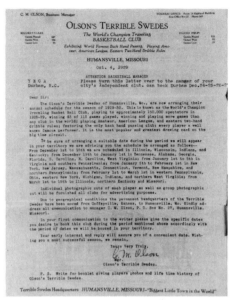

Basketball, promotional flyer, Olson's Terrible Swedes, black and white, 8 pages, with manager's letter, 8½ x 11", 1929, $20.00.

W Bingham Co Sporting Goods, 1952,
   150 pgs, 8½ x 12" **15.00**
Winslow's Ice Skates/Roller Skates,
   Worcester, MA, 1906, 2 pgs **20.00**
Wright & Pitson Victor Co, Springfield,
   MA, 1920, 38 pgs, football, basketball,
   and other winter sport uniforms and
   accessories **35.00**
Game
   Bowling, A Board Game, Parker Broth-
   ers, 1896, multicolored litho board,
   instructions on back of box, orig box   **45.00**
   Sports, Milton Bradley, c1910, multi-
   colored litho board, three pcs, orig
   box. **40.00**
Letterhead, Northland Ski Manufacturing
   Co, skier and children on toboggan vi-
   gnettes, 1926. . . . .   **20.00**
Magazine
   Century, October, 1903 . . . .   **30.00**
   The Woman's Magazine,, 1909,
   women's basketball article, en-
   graved ads **12.00**
Manual, How To Play Croquet, A New
   Pocket Manual of Complete Instruc-
   tions for American Players, Boston,
   Adams & Co, 1865, 47 pgs **25.00**
Photograph
   Basketball player wearing uniform
   holding ball, 1931, 6 x 8". **6.00**
   Bowling, men's team holding sign
   "Misfit Bowling Club," 1910, 4¾ x
   3½" **12.00**

Poster
   5th Avenue, John J Hayes, Winner of
   the Marathon Race, red, white, and
   black silhouettes, Fred G Cooper,
   1926, 20 x 29" **425.00**
   The High Diver, German swimming
   exhibitions, Anon, Arthur Albrecht
   & Co, c1910, 27 x 29" **325.00**
   The A1 American Girl Plays Hard, basketball motif, 1918 . . . .   **50.00**

Boxing, arcade card, Ruffy Silverstein, sepia tint, real photo of wrestler, 3⅜ x 5⅜",
1940s, $6.00.

Program
Harlem Globetrotters, 1951–52, 18
pgs, wraps, 7¾ x 10¾" **8.00**
Super Bowl XI **30.00**

STATUE OF LIBERTY

Advertising Trade Card
Brainerd Armstrong Co, statue holding
spool of thread **25.00**
Holmes & Coutts Sea Foam Wagers,
"Liberty Feeding the World" **40.00**
New Easy Lawn Mower, harbor scene
with man cutting grass, statue back-
ground **20.00**
Parisian Sauce, colorful, presented to
Columbia in New York harbor,
statue background **40.00**
Pratts Astral Oil, statue with sunset
scene **16.00**
Blotter, L A Pugh Hardware, Butler, IN,
statue motif, 1918 . . . . **6.00**
Book, *Liberty Enlightening the World*,
c1890, hard bound blue cov **15.00**
Playing Cards, 606, US Playing Card Co,
Cincinnati, OH, statue and flags, gold
edges, orig box **18.00**

**Booklet, savings bond drive, "Treasured
Possessions," printed, black and white,
color centerfold, Division of Savings
Bonds, Treasury Department, 5½ x 8",
1930s, $12.00.**

Poster
New York–The Wonder City of the
World–New York Central Lines,
panorama night city scene, illumi-
nated statue, c1930, 27 x 41" **350.00**
Save Your Child From Autocracy,
statue and baby illus, 30 x 40" **50.00**
That Liberty Shall Not Perish, statue in
flames, Pennell, 20 x 30" **150.00**

TELEPHONE

References: Bob Alexander and Mike Bruner, *A
Collectors' Guide To Telephones, Telegraphs &
Express Co. Advertising*, Guard Frog Books, 1992;
Kate Dooner, *Telephones: Antique to Modern*,
Schiffer Publishing, 1992.

Collector's Clubs: Antique Telephone Collectors
Association, Box 94, Abilene, KS 67410; Tele-
phone collectors International, Inc., 19 North
Cherry Dr., Oswego, IL 60543.

Almanac
AT&T, Telephone Almanac, 1930. . . . **15.00**
Bell Systems Telephone, 58th anniver-
sary issue, 1934 . . . . **14.00**
Blotter, A T & T adv, Bell logo, "Don't
Write – Talk, Local and Long Distance
Telephone," red, white, and blue,
c1916, 8 x 4" **20.00**
Booklet, Alexander Graham Bell biogra-
phy, Bell Telephone, 32 pgs, Bell por-
trait on cov, 1951 . . . . **6.00**
Broadside, Atlantic Telegraph, "Triumph
of Science," 6 x 9" **20.00**
Calendar, Tri–State Telephone Co, Dec
1916 . . . . **25.00**
Catalog
J H Bunnell & Co, Catalog of Supplies,
No. 7, illus, cov with factory image,
1885 . . . . **75.00**
Western Electric Co, New York, NY,
Inter–Phones and Accessories, 60
pgs, wholesale and retail price lists,
illus, 1916 . . . . **50.00**
Fan, Bell System, logo, dark blue and
white, ... **12.00**
Journal, Canadian Telephone Journal,
phone illus, cov with black and white
hockey player, Jan 1938 . . . . **6.00**
Magazine
*General Telephone Co of Wisconsin
News Lines*, July 1956 . . . . **8.00**
Telephony, 1955 . . . . **2.00**
Memo Pad, Southern New England Tele-
phone Company, simulated leather
cov with black lettering and red good
luck stamp, blue Bell System logo on
back **20.00**
Playing Cards
Bell System, gold logo, dark blue

Blotter, candlestick telephone, "Phone for a full supply today," Shields Lumber and Coal Co., red and black, 6½ x 3½", $5.00.

ground, gold and black striped border	**7.50**
Telephone Pioneers of America, dark blue and white, Bell logo	**3.00**
The Telephone, One Hundred Years of Service, 1876–1976, light blue and white	**5.00**
Post Card	
Santa talking on candlestick telephone, sign on desk reads "Christmas Shopping Simplified By telephone, Use the Bell," Bell Telephone Co adv, full color, text on back, c1910, 3¼ x 5½"	**30.00**
"The Party Line," old man talking on wall telephone, Successful Farming Publishing Co	**20.00**
Receipt, E S Greely & Co Railway, Telegraph and Telephone Supplies, dated 1885	**35.00**
Sheet Music	
Call Me Up Some Rainy Afternoon, cov with woman making phone call and man walking in rain, 1910	**10.00**
Who Are You With To–Night?, couple talking on candlestick telephones, 1910	**15.00**
Sign, cardboard and tissue paper, standup, Santa talking on candlestick telephone, American Tissue Mills adv, 19½ x 18¾"	**75.00**
Stock Certificate, American Telegraphone Co, District of Columbia, 1907	**13.00**
Telephone Index, " 'Home' Telephone Index," cardboard, hangs on mouthpiece of candlestick telephone, 8" h . .	**65.00**
Valentine, Love's Telephone, mechanical, turn wheel to move woman to and from telephone, messages change at second wall phone	**40.00**

TELEVISION

References: Jefferson Graham, *Come On Down!!!–The TV Game Show Book,* Abbeville Press, 1988; Ted Hake, *Hake's Guide To TV Collectibles,* Wallace–Homestead, 1990; David Inman, *The TV Encyclopedia,* Perigee Book, 1991; Brian Paquette and Paul Howley, *The Toys From U.N.C.L.E.: Memorabilia And Collectors Guide,* Entertainment Publishing, 1990; Neil Summers, *The Official TV Western Book, Volume 4,* The Old West Shop Publishing, 1992; Vincent Terrace, *Encyclopedia Of Television–Series, Pilots, And Specials, 1937–1973,* 3 volumes, Zoetrope, 1986.

Periodicals: *Filmfax,* PO Box 1900, Evanston, IL 60204; *The TV Collector,* PO Box 1088, Easton, MA 02334.

Activity Book, Dr Kildare Punch–Out Book, Golden Funtime, 1962	**20.00**
Big Little Book, Gunsmoke, 1958	**15.00**
Book	
Flight of Fear, Land of the Giants, Carl Henry Rathjen, Whitman Pub, #1516, 1969, 212 pgs, hard cov, 5¼ x 8"	**18.00**
The Munsters and the Great Camera Caper, Whitman, #1510, 1965, 212 pgs, 6 x 7½"	**15.00**
Book Cover, Welcome Back Kotter, unused	**12.00**
Box, candy, Ozzie and Harriet, Mounds, Nelson family cartoon illus, 1957	**98.00**
Bubble Gum Card, Man From U.N.C.L.E., complete set, 1960s	**60.00**
Card Game, Archie Bunker Card Game, All in the Family, 1972	**25.00**
Christmas Card	
Clint Eastwood, Rawhide, 1959	**20.00**
Rick Nelson, Ozzie and Harriet fan card, 1964	**30.00**
Colorforms, Flipper, Standard Toykraft, 1966	**50.00**
Coloring Book	
Addams Family, Saalfield, #4595, 1965, 8½ x 11"	**35.00**
Land of the Giants, Whitman, #1138, unused, 1969, 8 x 10"	**25.00**
Rin–Tin–Tin, Whitman, #1257, 1955, 8¼ x 11"	**15.00**
Wagon Train, Whitman, unused, 1959	**30.00**
Comic Book, Gunsmoke, 1958	**12.00**
Disk, Howdy Doody, cardboard, "Clarabell Says..." and portrait on front, Wonder Bread adv on back, attached pin and string, 1¾" d	**10.00**
Fan Club Card, I Love Lucy, Lucille Ball/ Desi Arnaz, 1950s	**15.00**
Journal, Richard Chamberlain Fan Club, 1960s	**15.00**
Letter, Buffalo Bob Smith, relates favorite prayer, one pg, 1956	**25.00**
Magazine, *TV Guide,* Lucille Ball cov, April 30, 1966	**10.00**

Handbook, *TV Time '79*, Peggy Herz, Scholastic Book Services, NY, color photo covers, black-and-white photos, 92 pages, 5⅛ x 7½", $20.00.

Magic Slate, Sea Hunt, 1960 . . . .   **60.00**
Paint By Number Set, Maverick, unused, orig box with James Garner on lid **125.00**
Paperback Book, *The Wild, Wild West*, Signet Books, first printing, 1966 . . . . .   **25.00**
Paper Toy, Grandfather Clock Punch–out, Captain Kangaroo, diecut cardboard, punch–out clock pieces, moving eyes, mouth, and secret panel, Buster Brown premium, Keeshan–Miller Enterprises, 1956 . . . .   **25.00**
Placemat, Howdy Doody, set of 8 . . . . . .   **45.00**
Post Card
   The Addams Family, color, 1964 . . . .   **10.00**
   The Life of Riley, fan response card, 1955 . . . .   **5.00**
Puzzle
   Cheyenne, boxed set of three **15.00**
   Gunsmoke, frame tray **10.00**
   Happy Days, 1976 . . . .   **15.00**
   Howdy Doody, frame tray, amusement park ride image, Whitman, 1953, 11½ x 15" **25.00**
   Maverick, frame tray, Whitman, gunfight image, 1959, 11½ x 14½" **22.00**
   Ramar of the Jungle, boxed set of four   **65.00**
   Starsky & Hutch, 1976 . . . .   **15.00**
Sticker Book, Fat Albert and the Cosby Kids, Whitman, #2865–66, unused, 1973, 8½ x 11" **17.50**
Wrapper
   Bubble Gum, Munsters, waxed paper, Leaf, 1966, 6" sq **50.00**
   Ice Cream, Howdy Doody Fudge Bar, 1950s **3.00**

TELEVISIONS

References: Harry Poster and John Sakas, *1990 Price Guide To Vintage TVs and Collectible Radios*, Sight, Sound, Style, 1990; Scott Wood (ed.)

Classic TVs With Price Guide: Pre–War thru 1950s, L–W Book Sales, 1992.

Collectors' Club: Antique Wireless Association, 59 Main St., Bloomfield, NY 14469.

Booklet, America's First Television Tour, NBC, 1939, 32 pgs, speculates television's role in the future **20.00**
Brochure, American Television Inc, Television and You, 1946, 25 pgs, equipment illus, int. and ext. building views, show set–ups, historical figures **20.00**
Magazine Tear Sheet
   Admiral, "The Shape Of Things To Come," TV of the future with elevating television screen, war text and war bonds stamp, *Collier's*, November 14, 1942 . . . .   **18.00**
   General Electric, closeup image of boxer Joe Louis on screen, 1947 . . .   **12.00**
   Sparton Cosmic Eye Television, television set on football field, "So real it's like a seat in the stadium!", 1953 . .   **8.00**
   Zenith "Gotham," console with circle screen television, Twin Cobra Record Changer, and FM–AM radio combination, 1949 . . . .   **10.00**
Playing Cards, Magnavox, gold lettering and logo, dark green ground, gold and white border **3.50**
Stock Certificate, Television Associates of Rhode Island, 100 shares **6.00**

Magazine Tear Sheet, Sparton TV, color, *Collier's*, 10½ x 13½", March 31, 1951, $9.00.

TEMPLE, SHIRLEY

References: Edward R. Pardella, *Shirley Temple Dolls And Fashion: A Collector's Guide To The World's Darling,* Schiffer Publishing, 1992; Patricia R. Smith, *Shirley Temple Dolls And Collectibles, Series 1,* 1977, 1992 value update, and *Series 2* 1979, 1992 value update, Collector Books; Dian Zillner, *Hollywood Collectibles,* Schiffer Publishing, 1991.

Autograph, letter, "Dear Mr Editor, Here
  are the pictures I promised to take for
  Look. Some of them are a little fuzzy. I
  hope *Look* likes them. Love, Shirley
  Temple," portrait on letterhead,
  docket stamp 1939 on verso 50.00
Book
  My Life & Times by Shirley Temple,
  1936 . . . .   25.00
  Rebecca of Sunnybrook Farm, Random House, full color Temple cov,
  movie photos 35.00
  Shirley Temple Through The Day,
  Saalfield Publishing, 1946. . . . .   10.00
Christmas Card, Hallmark, 1935, 4 x 5"   12.00
Cigarette Card
  Carreras Cigarettes, Temple portrait,
  full color, 1936, 1³/₈ x 2⁵/₈" 7.00
  Gallaher Cigarettes, Temple and Gary
  Cooper, full color, 1935, 1¹/₂ x 2¹/₂"   7.50
Clothes Hanger, cardboard, blue, 1930s   10.00
Clothing Tag, black and white photo,
  endorsed by Temple, orig string cord,
  1930s, 3 x 5" 12.00
Drawing Book, Saalfield, #1725, 1935,
  hard cov. 35.00
Fan, RC Cola adv, *I'll Be Seeing You* 25.00
Lobby Card, *Adventure in Baltimore,*
  RKO, 1949.   12.00
Magazine
  Photoplay, Temple cov, September,
  1939 . . . .   12.00

Magazine Cover Story, *Life,* 132 pages, 10¹/₂ x 14", March 30, 1942, $25.00.

Screenland, Temple cov, October,
  1944 . . . .   15.00
  This Week of Milwaukee Sentinel, December 28, 1941, cov photo 5.00
Movie Still
  Captain January, 1936, 8 x 10" 15.00
  Little Miss Marker, Paramount Films,
  1934, 8 x 10" 20.00
Paper Doll
  Gabriel Co, 1958. . . . .   25.00
  Saalfield, #1765, life size, 1936 . . . . .   90.00
Party Invitations, 1973, package of ten . .   4.00
Pattern, Shirley Temple Doll outfits, Simplicity #2717, 1958 . . . .   18.00
Photograph, sepia tones, 8 x 10" 10.00
Playing Cards, Temple wearing duck
  dress, 1930s. 45.00
Post Card, *Captain January* scene, sepia
  tones, glossy, 1936, 3¹/₂ x 5¹/₂" 15.00
Scrapbook, Saalfield, 1937, 11 x 15" . . .   25.00
Sheet Music
  Animal Crackers In My Soup, Temple
  cov, 1935.   20.00
  Goodnight My Love, from *Stowaway*   18.00
  Good Ship Lollipop, 1934 . . . .   12.00
  When I'm With You, from *Poor Little
  Rich Girl,* Temple wearing band
  uniform cov, 1936 . . . .   16.00
Sign, cardboard, "Shirley Temple Loves
  Quaker Puffed Wheat," 19 x 30". 90.00
Souvenir Book, grand marshal, Tournament of Roses Parade, 1939, 32 pgs, 9
  x 12" 25.00
Tablet, color, 1935, 5¹/₂ x 9" 20.00
Toy, stage, cardboard, litho red cardboard curtains, yellow cords, early
  1970s, 10 x 24 x 36" 50.00

TENNIS

Reference: Roderick A. Malloy, *Malloy's Sports Collectibles Value Guide,* Wallace–Homestead, 1993.

Periodical: *Sports Collectors Digest,* 700 East State Street, Iola, WI 54990.

Advertising Trade Card, diecut, female
  tennis player, Enameline adv. 40.00
Cigarette Card, Helen Jacobs, full color,
  Ogden's Cigarettes, 1936, 1³/₈ x 2⁵/₈"   7.50
Photograph
  Don Budge and Ellsworth Vines, rackets at net, 1939, 7 x 9" 12.00
  Ethel Arnold and James Sharp, wearing
  tennis outfits, holding rackets, black
  and white, 1935, 6 x 8" 7.50
Playing Cards, Arzy's Tennis Shop, Beverly Hills adv, black and white tennis
  player and banner logo, white ground,
  gold and red border 5.00

Magazine Cover, *The Saturday Evening Post,* **$18.00.**

Poster
Grays of Cambridge, tennis racket and ball, "The Light Blue Tennis Ball," green and blue background, Affiches Marci, c1947, 24 x 39" ... **225.00**
Philadelphia Sunday Press, red headed female tennis player image, blue striped background, c1896, 16 x 22" **125.00**
Play Helps Study, tennis motif, 1924, 17 x 28½" **20.00**
Sign, Victorian lady tennis player, Ste Genevieve Brewing and Lighting Association adv, emb paper, 1910–19, 11 x 17½".......................... **700.00**

THEATER

Reference: Frederic and Mary Megson, *American Advertising Postcards: Sets and Series 1890–1920,* published by authors, 1985.

Advertising Trade Card
Boston Bijou Theater, audience scene, advertising *The Beggar Student,* multicolored **90.00**
Madison Square Theater, folder, outside view of theater, *Young Mrs. Winthrop* details **85.00**
Autograph, photograph, Dorothy Kirsten, 8 x 10" **60.00**
Book
A History of the American Theatre, William Dunlap, NY, cloth cov, 1832, tall 12mo **385.00**
Dramatic Life As I Found It, Noah Ludlow, 1880, 733 pgs, St Louis ... **400.00**
How To Stage A Minstrel Show, A Manual For The Amateur Burnt Cork Director, Jeff Branen and Frederick G Johnson, illus by Harlan Tarbell,

Denison, Chicago, 1921, 64 pgs, printed wrappers, illus.......... **20.00**
Stage Effects, How To Make and Work Them, Second Impression, A Rose, Routledge, London, 1915–25, 60 pgs, includes effects for sun, rain, thunder, lightning, fire, water, wind, snow, collapsible chair, and conflagrations **25.00**
Stage Scenery and Lighting, first edition, "Handbook for Non–professionals," 1931, 398 pgs photos and illus, hard cov **10.00**
Broadside, "Last Week of the Grand Performance of Shakespeare's Comedy...Tempest," 8½ x 20¾" **40.00**
Catalog
A M Buch & Co, Philadelphia, PA, Hair Goods, Theatrical and Street, Wigs & Toupees, c1910, 24 pgs, theatrical wigs and make–up **40.00**
Appleton Publishing Co, Omaha, NE, 1916, 184 pgs, theatrical equipment, 7½ x 10½". **25.00**
Cleon Throckmorton Inc, NY, Catalog of the Theatre, Scenery, Lighting, Hardware, Painting, Costume, Make Up, 1932, 72 pgs, pictorial wrappers, line drawn illus **25.00**
Monarch Moving Picture Machine, Leader Calcium Light and other Theater equipment **85.00**
Stage & Scenery, 1893, 8 pgs **45.00**
Cigarette Card, brown and black Venie Clancy portrait, Between the Acts, Bravo Cigarettes, text on back, Heppenheimer Litho, NY, 2 x 4" **25.00**
Label, cigar, Clint Ford, bust portrait and two vignettes in costume.......... **6.00**
License, entertainment, City of Providence, RI, orders *Star Spangled Banner* played at every performance, 1919... **15.00**
Magazine Cover, sgd by Joan Sutherland **30.00**
Newspaper, *The Stage,* New York, Volume 11, Number 1, February 9, 1871, 16 x 11" **20.00**
Playbill
Grease, Royale Theatre, February, 1978 .... **10.00**
Hammerstein's Victoria Theatre, NY, Houdini performance adv, 1914... **85.00**
Ziegfeld Theatre, Brigadoon adv on back with Williams, Musial, and DiMaggio endorsing Chesterfield Cigarettes, 1948 .... **15.00**
Playing Cards, New Amsterdam Theatre, shepherd and sheep vignette, multicolored **15.00**
Poster
Absurd Person Singular, sgd by cast members, NY, 1974............. **120.00**
Ashes, woman lying on bed, covered

Program, "Up in Mabel's Room," color litho covers, black-and-white and color advertisements, Comiskey Park home game schedule on inside cover, 16 pages, 5¼ x 7¾", 1919, $35.00.

with sheet, New York Shakespeare Festival production, 1977, three sheet, 81 x 41" 125.00

Maude Banks Theater, 1872, 78 x 40½" 100.00

The Missouri Girl, Victorian actress bowing toward audience, "Daisy Grubb (in Sassiety)," litho, Donaldson Co, 41 x 80" 200.00

Uncle Tom's Cabin, "No, No I Ain't Going Let," Lincoln and Stowe portraits in upper corners, Ackermann–Quigley, 30 x 20" 80.00

Program

Ben–Hur, photo plates with lettered tissue guards, pictorial wrappers, silk tied, NY, 1900 . . . . 100.00

B F Keiths Theater, Washington DC, April 24, 1922 . . . . 10.00

New York Hippodrome, 30 pgs, *A Yankee Circus on Mars,* and *The Hindoo Princess,* illus, ext. views, sets, actor portraits, full page adv for Luna Park, color cov with lady on horse, 1905, 8 x 12" 35.00

Plymouth Theater, Boston, MA, *Abes Irish Rose,* November 15, 1943 . . . . 10.00

Romeo and Juliet, Pillar of Fire, and *Gala Performance,* S Hurock, Metropolitan Opera House, Apr 20, 1944, 20 pgs 5.50

The Tzigane, Tremont Theatre, Boston, MA 18.00

Scrapbook

Cabinet Cards, stage actors and actresses, late 19th C 190.00

Newspaper Clippings, New York the-

ater, includes James J Corbett, Maud Adams, and Mary Pickford, 1887–1918, 40 pgs 20.00

Souvenir Book, *You Can't Take It With You,* 1937, 15 pgs, Pulitzer Prize Play 7.00

THREE STOOGES

Activity Book, punch–out, Golden Press, 1962, 7½ x 13" 75.00

Autograph, photograph, sgd by each, 8 x 10" 275.00

Bubble Gum Cards, Fleer, 1965, 66 cards 65.00

Colorforms, 1959 . . . . 200.00

Movie Still, Curly in "X–Ray Fluoroscope" machine, flanked by Larry and Moe, 1938 . . . . 45.00

Paperback Book

Stooge Mania, Tom Hansen with Jeffrey Forrester, Contemporary Books, 1984 . . . . 10.00

The Stooge Chronicles, Jeffrey Forrester, Contemporary Books, 1981 12.00

Script, *Snow White and The Three Stooges,* 1960, 132 pgs 75.00

Title Card, *The Three Stooges In Orbit,* Columbia Pictures, 1962 . . . . 18.00

Comic Book, Gold Key, No. 38, Western Publishing Co., "Larry, Moe and Curly-Joe discover the hide-out of the Abdominal Snowman," color real photo cover, 32 pages, 6¾ x 10¼", March 1968, $18.00.

TITANIC

Collectors' Clubs: Steamship Historical Society of America, Inc., Suite #4, 300 Ray Drive, Providence, RI 02906; Titanic Historical Society, PO Box 51053, Indian Orchard, MA 01151.

Book

Story of the Wreck of the Titanic, Memorial Edition, Marshall Everett, 1912 . . . . 20.00

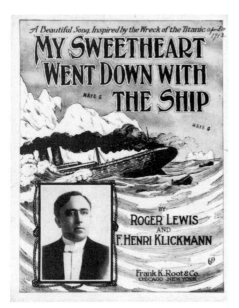

Sheet Music, *My Sweetheart Went Down With the Ship*, Roger Lewis and F. Henri Klickmann, Frank K. Root & Co., Chicago, IL, greentone cover illustration, 10¼ x 13½", 1912, $55.00.

The Tragic Story of the Empress of Ireland and Other Sea Disasters, Logan Marshall, 1914, 351 pgs, hard cov   45.00
Voyage of the Iceberg, Richard Brown, 1983, hard cov, dj 12.50
Brochure, World's Largest & Finest Steamers: New Triple Screw *Olympic* and *Titanic,* int. views 500.00
Newspaper, headline story, "Crippled Titanic's Passengers Saved," *The Daily News,* San Francisco, April 15, 1912   175.00
Paperback Book, *The Titanic, End of a Dream,* Wyn Craig Wade 5.00
Photograph, *Titanic,* April 3, 1912 . . . . .   25.00
Postal Cover, 75th Anniversary, limited edition, print of ship, sgd by survivor B Dean 25.00
Post Card, black and white, starboard quarter, memorial card, 5½ x 3½" . . .   7.00
Poster, *A Night To Remember,* 30 x 48"   75.00
Press Kit, *Titanic* Historical Society, 1982 convention 20.00
Print, color, *Titanic* image, Bagley 18.00
Puzzle, *New York Times* headline edition, front pg image, Parker Brothers . .   25.00
Sheet Music
    The Band Played 'Nearer By God To Thee' As The Ship Went Down, Beam & Jones, large format, 1912 . .   35.00
    The Wreck Of The Titanic, cov photo

of sinking *Titanic,* William Baltzell, 1912 . . . .   **75.00**
Stationery, ship's name **100.00**

TOBACCO

References: Philip Collins, *Smokerama: Classic Tobacco Accoutrements,* Chronicle Books, 1992; Douglas Congdon–Martin, *America For Sale: A Collector's Guide To Antique Advertising,* Schiffer Publishing, 1991; Joe Davidson, *The Art of the Cigar Label,* Wellfleet, 1989; Sharon and Bob Huxford, *Huxford's Collectible Advertising: An Illustrated Value Guide,* Collector Books, 1993; Tony Hyman, *Handbook of American Cigar Boxes,* Arnet Art Museum, 1979; Murray Cards International, Ltd. (comp.), *Cigarette Card Values: 1992 Catalogue of Cigarette & Other Trade Cards,* Murray Cards International Ltd., 1992.

Collectors' Clubs: Cigarette Pack Collectors Association, 61 Searle St., Georgetown, MA 01833; International Seal, Label & Cigar Band Society, 8915 East Bellevue St., Tucson, AZ 85715.

Chewing
    Advertising Trade Card, Grand Cut Plug Tobacco, woman wearing green dress, 10 x 6" 20.00
    Booklet, Honest Scrap Tobacco, 12 pgs, color illus, "An Everyday Scrap" 30.00
    Box, Lyon Tobacco, women sorting tobacco image, 1870s. 95.00
    Calendar, 1918, Chiquez Le Tebac Stag, "Invincible," sailor, framed, 22 x 39" 150.00
    Display, Mail Pouch Chewing Tobacco, diecut cardboard, standup, parading bass drummer and dog, 1930s. 475.00
    Display Box, cardboard, Blue Tiger Chewing Tobacco, tiger image, holds 5¢ packages, 11 x 8 x 6". 225.00
    Label, carton, Big John Tobacco, The Mild Cut Plug Tobacco, horizontal   50.00
    Package, Cincy Chewing and Smoking Tobacco, red, white, and blue, unused. 30.00
Sign
    Brown's Mule Tobacco, mule reaching in window pulling blanket off man 175.00
    Climax Plug, Black man on mule, framed, 19 x 34" 1,200.00
    Crusader Tobacco, c1900, 13 x 7"   25.00
    Happy Thought Wave Line Plug Tobacco, sailor image, Wilson & McCallay Tobacco Co, framed, 28 x 39" 2,000.00
    Red Jacket Tobacco, cardboard, baseball scene, 22 x 28". 125.00

Pouch, Yankee Girl Chewing Tobacco, Scotten, Dillon Co., reinforced paper, red and blue, 4¾ x 7", 1920s, $12.00.

Seal of North Carolina Plug Cut, "Wash Day," women doing wash at river, full color image, black border, 7½ x 12½" **75.00**

Time Plug Tobacco, cardboard, 12" sq **25.00**

Cigar

Advertising Trade Card

A T Co Battle Ax, diecut, cartoon man smoking huge cigar **30.00**

Dude Cigars, Simmons & Co, 1882 **20.00**

Havana Perfectos, triple folder, cigar box shape, opens to box of cigars, opens again to promotional text from Associated Importers of Havana Cigars **40.00**

Orange Tea & Coffee Co, Earth smoking cigar held by chef **20.00**

Box, cardboard, Marksman Cigars, two men shooting guns, 5¢, 3 x 5 x 1" **25.00**

Calendar, 1910, Q & Q Perfectos,

Quinn Bros Makers, Troy, NY, framed, 30 x 20" **2,200.00**

Catalog

American Electrical Nov. & Mfg. Co. Ever Ready Portable Electric Cigar Lighters, 1925, 8 pgs. **30.00**

United Cigar Stores, 1916, 48 pgs, int. store photo **12.00**

Cigar Box Label Proof, I Should Worry cigars, man smoking cigar, relaxing in easy chair, Moehle Litho, 1914 . . **75.00**

Display, Blue Ribbon Cigars, cardboard standup, logo on green and white ground **35.00**

Document, Internal Revenue Tax, Retail Dealer Tobacco, vignette of woman holding cigar box, twelve coupons, 1879 . . . . **7.00**

Label, Lydia Havana Cigars, large cigar image surrounded by sun rays . . **7.00**

Playing Cards, pinochle deck, Royal Lancer Cigars, adv text on aces, orig box **25.00**

Poster

Bachelor Cigars, "A Whirlwind Quarter," two trotters, framed, 1903, 24 x 30" **250.00**

Bengal Cheroots, H Ellis & Co, Baltimore, MD, tiger head and cigar box, Isaac Friedenwald Litho, Baltimore, MD, c1885, 15½ x 23½" **700.00**

General Cigar Co, National Brands, factory vignettes, 23½ x 34½" . . . **300.00**

Cigarette

Advertising Trade Card, Vanity Fair Cigarettes **40.00**

Album, cigarette cards

Allen & Ginter, "Paris Exposition," 15 chromolithographed pgs. **275.00**

W Duck & Sons, Terrors of America **50.00**

Booklet, Camel Cigarettes, "Know Your Nerves," 1934, 3 x 4" **20.00**

Brochure, promotional, Guido Cigarette Machine Co Inc, 1910, 8 pgs. . **20.00**

Carton, Chesterfield Cigarettes, litho,

Cigarette Pack Label, The Waldorf-Astoria, American Tobacco Co., black on silver, 6¼ x 3½", 1930s, $12.00.

Christmas motif, servicemen, Santa, and crowd at train station going home for holidays 15.00

Cigarette Card, De Reszke Cigarettes, real photo, puppies 3.50

Decal, Lucky Strike, full size Lucky Green pack, dated 1931, 6" sq. 15.00

Display, Lucky Strike, standup, woman with cartoon horse and dog, holds single cigarette 6.00

Magazine Tear Sheet
Advertisement, Old Gold Cigarettes, "We're Tobacco Men Not Medicine Men, Old Gold Cures Just One Thing: The World's Best Tobacco," tops of hundreds of cigarettes, 1950s, 10 x 14" 12.50
Article, *Fortune,* October, 1949, Phillip Morris Comeback, 5 pg article with photos 15.00

Playing Cards
Camel Cigarettes 18.00
Marlboro Cigarettes, black, red, and white logo 9.00

Poster
Kool Cigarettes, smoking penguin, c1933, 12 x 18" 35.00
L & M, Gunsmoke testimonial 65.00
Old Gold Cigarettes, Indian maiden wearing headdress, holding bow

and arrow, product package lower right corner, sgd by George Petty, c1940, 31 x 43" 350.00

Zig–Zag Cigarette papers, pretty girl wearing red dress and straw hat, surrounded by product packages, chromolithograph, c1903, 17 x 21" 325.00

Printer's Proof, Perfection Cigarettes, cigarette package and woman wearing red hat, dark blue ground, light blue border, framed, 1900s, 23 x 29" 375.00

Score Card, Bridge Hands, Lucky Strike, six different cards 20.00

Sheet Music, *A Story Of Two Cigarettes,* cov with two Chesterfield cigarettes resting is ashtray, Mickey Stoner, Fred Jay and Leonard K Marker, Chesterfield Cigarettes adv, 1945 . . . .   15.00

Sign, Lucky Strike Cigarettes, cardboard, couple kissing by Lucky Green tin, 1930s, 30 x 35" 550.00

Wrappers, early 20th C, set of 6 . . . . .   15.00

Pipe
Advertising Trade Card, diecut, pipe shape, theatrical adv, Montgomery Phister's *A Soap Bubble,* text on back 15.00

Magazine Tear Sheet, Camel Cigarettes, R. J. Reynolds Tobacco Co., nurse smoking cigarette, "You like them FRESH? So do I!", *Pictorial Review Magazine,* 10½ x 13½", March 1932, $15.00.

Magazine Tear Sheet, Prince Albert, man smoking pipe, "P. A. for pipe grouches," $9.00.

Catalog, Lorillard P, Co, New York, NY, 1916, 128 pgs, pipes and to-bacco advertisements **35.00**

Folder, Dills Best Smoking Tobacco, diecut, box shape, pipe cleaners at-tached to inside pocket **15.00**

Sign

Bull Durham Tobacco, cardboard, woman smoking pipe at General Store, framed, 1880–1900. . . . . . **300.00**

Granger Pipe Tobacco, cardboard, butler, child, and tobacco canis-ter, 29 x 45" **100.00**

Pogue's Patent Plug, Durham, NC, man smoking pipe, riding bro-ken–down horse, Empire Litho & Eng Co, 1880s, 7 x 10" **300.00**

Union Leader Cut Plug, cardboard, Uncle Sam smoking pipe, 18 x 26" **900.00**

TOY

References: Jurgen and Marianne Cieslik, *Lehmann Toys,* New Cavendish Books, 1982; Richard Friz, *The Official Price Guide to Collect-ible Toys, 5th Edition,* House of Collectibles, 1990; David Longest, *Character Toys and Col-lectibles, First Series,* 1984, 1992 value update and *Second Series* 1987, Collector Books; David Longest, *Toys: Antique & Collectible,* Collector Books, 1990, 1992 value update; Charlie Mack, *Lesney's Matchbox Toys: Regular Wheel Years, 1947–1969,* Schiffer Publishing, 1992; Albert W. McCollough, *The New Book Of Buddy L Toys, Volume I,* 1991, and *Volume II,* 1991, Greenberg Publishing Co.; Kevin McGimpsey and Stewart Orr, *Collecting Matchbox Die Cast Toys: The First Forty Years,* Major Productions Limited, 1989; Richard O'Brien, *Collecting Toys: A Collector's Identification and Value Guide, Sixth Edition,* Books Americana, 1993; Maxine A. Pinsky, *Greenberg's Guide To Marx Toys, Volume I* Greenberg Publishing Co., 1988; Harry L. Rinker, *Collector's Guide To Toys, Games, and Puzzles,* Wallace–Homestead, 1991; Gerhard C. Walter, *Metal Toys From Nuremberg: The Unique Me-chanical Toys Of The Firm Of Georg Kellerman & Co. Of Nuremberg 1910–1979,* Schiffer Publish-ing, 1992; James Weiland and Edward Force, *Tootsie Toys, World's First Die Cast Models,* Mo-torbooks International, 1980; Blair Whitton, *Paper Toys of the World,* Hobby House Press, 1986.

Periodicals: *Antique Toy World,* PO Box 34509, Chicago, IL 60634; *Collectible Toys and Values,* Attic Books, Inc., 15 Danbury Road, Ridgefield, CT 06877.

Advertising Trade Card, cartoon Black riding horse and carriage pull toy, "Big 4" Morris Theater adv, 1883 . . . . **30.00**

Catalog, Toy O Rama, multicolor, in-cludes Ny-Lint, A. C. Gilbert, Revell, Tonka, Mattel, Ideal, and Structo, 40 pages, 7 x 10¼", 1955–56, $40.00.

Booklet, Erector Set, Gilbert Co, 1938, 44 pgs, 10 x 7" **18.00**

Catalog

A C Gilbert Co, New Haven, CT, How to Make 'Em Book – The New Erec-tor, 44 pgs, illus, orig wrappers, price list **40.00**

Magazine Tear Sheet, Meccano Co., Eliza-beth, NJ, black, white, and red, 10 x 14", 1929, $15.00.

Barbie and Ken Fashion Catalog,
1962, 56 pgs **35.00**
Dent Toy Co, Cast Iron Toy Catalog,
c1910 . . . .   **45.00**
FAO Schwartz, Christmas
1956 . . . .   **75.00**
1972 . . . .   **50.00**
Schmid Brothers, Lancaster, PA,
Wheel Toys – The Growing Line,
c1925, 16 pgs, toy wagons, walkers,
tricycles, and small bicycles, illus,
price list **75.00**
West & Lee Co, Worcester, MA, Illus-
trated Catalogue of Chivalrie, 1874,
32 pgs, woodcut illus, game equipment and rules, orig mailing enve-
lope **200.00**
Magazine Tear Sheet, article, *Fortune,*
January, 1946, Louis Marx toys, color
illus **10.00**
Manual, Daisy Air Rifle instructions,
1950s, folds out to 11 x 16" **4.00**
Photograph, black and white, boy play-
ing with shovel, pedal car and tin toy
truck in foreground, c1920, 3½ x 4½"   **18.00**

TOY TRAINS

References: Paul V. Ambrose, *Greenberg's Guide
to Lionel Trains, 1945–1969, Volume III, Sets,*
Greenberg Publishing, 1990; Susan and Al
Bagdade, *Collector's Guide To American Toy
Trains,* Wallace–Homestead, 1990; Bruce C.
Greenberg (ed.), *Greenberg's American Flyer Cat-
alogues, 1946–1955,* Greenberg Publishing,
1991; Bruce C. Greenberg, *Greenberg's Guide To
Ives Trains, 1901–1932, Volume II,* Greenberg
Publishing Co., 1992; Bruce Greenberg, (edited
by Christian F. Rohlfing), *Greenberg's Guide To
Lionel Trains: 1901–1942, Volume 2,* Greenberg
Publishing Co., 1988; Greenberg Publishing Co.,
Inc., *Greenberg's Lionel Catalogues, Volume V:
1955–1960,* Greenberg Publishing Company,
Inc., 1992; Greenberg Publishing Co., Inc.,
Greenberg's Marx Train Catalogues: 1938–1975,
Greenberg Publishing Company, Inc., 1992; John
Hubbard, *The Story of Williams Electric Trains,*
Greenberg Publishing Co., 1987; Lionel Book
Committee Train Collectors Association, *Lionel
Trains: Standard of the World, 1900–1943, Sec-
ond Edition,* Train Collectors Association, 1989;
Eric J. Matzke, *Greenberg's Guide To Marx
Trains, Volume II,* Greenberg Publishing Co.,
1990; Robert J. Osterhoff, *Greenberg's Guide to
Lionel Paper and Collectibles,* Greenberg Pub-
lishing, 1990; Alan R. Schuweiler, *Greenberg's
Guide to American Flyer, Wide Gauge,* Green-
berg Publishing Co., 1989.
Note: Greenberg Publishing Company, Inc.,
(7543 Main Street, Sykesville, MD 21784) is the
leading publisher of toy train literature. Anyone

interested in the subject should write for their
catalog and ask to be put on their mailing list.

Periodical: *Classic Toy Trains,* PO Box 1612,
Waukesha, WI 53187.

Collectors' Clubs: Lionel Collector's Club of
America, PO Box 479, La Salle, IL 61301; The
National Model Railroad Association, 4121
Cromwell Road, Chattanooga, TN 37421; The
Toy Train Operating Society, Inc., 25 West Wal-
nut Street, Suite 308, Pasadena, CA 91130; The
Train Collector's Association, PO Box 249,
Strasburg, PA 17579.

Catalog
George D Stock, Philadelphia, PA, HO
Model Railroad Supplies, 1947, 12
pgs, illus, prices **20.00**
Lionel Corporation, New York, NY
1926, 47 pgs, Lionel Trains, color illus   **75.00**
1937, 48 pgs, Lionel Model Trains, full
color, trains, sets, and accessories,
oblong 4to **85.00**
1947 . . . .   **35.00**
Magazine Cover, *Saturday Evening Post,*
December 19, 1953, boy playing with
model trains **5.00**
Manual, Lionel trains, 1949, 56 pgs, ex-
tra sheets **15.00**
Stock Certificate, Lionel Corp, 1968, vi-
gnette of boy and trains, company logo   **10.00**

**Magazine Tear Sheet, Lionel Electric
Trains,** *Popular Science Monthly,* **8 x
11½", November 1928, $12.00.**

TRANSPORTATION

Reference: Robert Ward, *Investment Guide To North American Real Photo Postcards,* Antique Paper Guild, 1991.

Blotter, Southern Steamship Company, Philadelphia, PA, Christmas motif, coaching scene, 1922 calendar, 7³/₄ x 3" **18.00**
Bond
    Arkansas Highway Bond, $10,000, State House vignette, green border, 1931 . . . .   **10.00**
    British Motor Cab Co, light brown, emb tax stamp, coupons attached, c1914 . . . .   **38.00**
    Constantinople Bus Bond, wine and black, attached coupons, 1910 . . . .   **30.00**
    New York City Rapid Transit, Indian engraving, orange, $1,000, 1961 . .   **8.50**
Book
    Motorbus Transportation, 1930, four volume set, illus. **18.00**
    Trolley Car Treasury, Frank Rowsome, 1946, 200 pgs, over 300 photos, dj   **30.00**
Booklet
    NY Subway Rapid Transit, Moses King, photos. **20.00**
    Rules & Regulations–Interborough Rapid Transit Co, Manhattan Railway Division **15.00**
Calendar, 1949, Rapid Transit Co Inc, Jewett City, CT. **10.00**
Catalog, H A Moyer Carriage Co, Syracuse, NY, 1900, 82 pgs, 7 x 8¼" **145.00**
Document
    Bill of Lading, Mississippi River steamboat *DuBuque,* steamboat illus, 1848, 10 x 8" **20.00**
    Waybill, Holbrook & Fort Apache Stage Line, 1904, 7 x 17" **35.00**
Envelope, Yellow Cab, taxi image, c1910, 2 x 4½" **4.50**
Label, cigar
    Pacific Highway, stagecoach image, simulated wood ground. **6.00**
    Yellow Cab, old time policeman and 1910s yellow taxi cab, 2 x 5½" **8.00**
Photograph
    Barge *Jackson* loaded with cotton, 8 x 10". **6.00**
    Riverboat, *Washington Irving,* side view, old buses waiting at dock, black and white, c1915, 9³/₄ x 7³/₄"   **16.00**
    Riverboat Pilots, professional, albumen, five riverboat pilots posed before tent, large Victorian home in background, gold edge, c1880, 8 x 10". **30.00**
Playing Cards
    Norwalk Modern Transportation, sil-

Timetable, New England Transportation Company bus schedule, 3 x 4½" folded size, 1955, $12.00.

ver streamlined images of airplane, ocean liner, train, bus, and truck, red ground, silver border **5.00**
    Seashore Trolley Museum, Kennebunkport, ME, two trollies, multicolored on yellow ground **7.50**
Poster
    The Greyhound Lines, streamlined Greyhound bus shooting down Southern road amid plantation house and trees, leaping greyhound dog in foreground, Walt Brownson, c1938, 20 x 20" **150.00**
    Trolleybus to Kingston, doubledecker bus and cityscape image, Greg Brown, c1930, 25 x 40". **385.00**
Scrip, Chesapeake and Delaware Canal Company, mortgage loan, black and white, 1887 . . . .   **7.50**
Sheet Music
    Crossing on the Ferry, Newcomb, 1869 . . . .   **20.00**
    Mister Whitney's Little Jitney Bus, Clarence Gaskill, 1915 . . . .   **20.00**
    Riding On The Elevated Railroad, Sam Devere, 1890. . . . .   **15.00**
    Take Me 'Round In A Taxicab, Mel J Gibeon 1908 . . . .   **18.00**
    That St Louis Jitney Bus "That Busted Bus", Mellinger, 1915 . . . .   **15.00**
    Upon The Trolley Line, Gus Edwards, 1905 . . . .   **20.00**
Sign, "Call A Checker Taxi" and "Extra Passengers Free, Also Cadillac Limousines," early taxicab illus, 11 x 7" **75.00**
Stock Certificate
    Boston Elevated Railway Co, 1929 . . .   **8.00**
    Highley Automatic Sulky Company,

eagle vignette, gold seal, black and gold, unissued **4.50**

Old Colony Steamship Company, paddlewheeler image, black and white, 1888 . . . . **45.00**

Philadelphia Transportation Company, angel vignette, brown border, 1948 . . . . **5.00**

Trolley Sign, cardboard litho, Tuxedo Tobacco adv, George M Cohan portrait and product image, 11 x 21" **700.00**

UNION

Advertising Trade Card, United Garment Workers of America, "The Swastika A Good Luck Charm" text on back, red and black lettering, buff ground **20.00**

Book, *The Flivver King–Ford America,* Upton Sinclair, United Auto Workers, 1937, 119 pgs **24.00**

Brochure, The Fifth Freedom–Freedom to Work, anti–union message prepared by S A Woods Machine Company, Boston, 28 pgs **12.00**

Calendar, 1985, International Association of Machinists and Aerospace Workers, Appointment Calendar, Earth on cover, several illus of Shuttle and other space crafts on monthly pgs, full color **5.00**

Contract, carbon, AFTRA, Desi Arnaz for appearance on the Andy Williams Show, sgd by Arnaz **115.00**

Letter, AFL letterhead, one page, sgd by labor leader George Meany, typed, thank you message, 1957 . . . . **27.00**

Letterhead, Bux–Mont Credit Union, Sellersville, PA, matching envelope, membership card, unused **1.00**

Membership Book, 1092 Lodge of International Association of Machinists, complete with stamps, c1960 . . . . . . **2.00**

Newspaper, *The Machinist,* 1958 . . . . . . **3.00**

Notepad, Union Cigar adv, celluloid cov, black and white union anti–trust text, blue facsimile Union Cigar label on each side, c1901 . . . . **35.00**

Pamphlet, The Closed or Open Shop–Which?, Elbert Hubbard, Roycrofters Pub, 1910 . . . . **12.00**

Playing Cards

Credit Union, red sign post, "Save–Borrow at your Credit Union," white ground, red and white border **12.00**

Retail Clerks International Association, International Headquarters, Lafayette, Ind, brown, gold, and beige, logo center. **3.00**

Sign

Big Ben Smoking Tobacco adv, "Union Made," 14 x 20" **120.00**

Membership Card, Amalgamated Society of Carpenters and Joiners, black and white, folded, 4¹/₄ x 2³/₄" open size, 1887, $15.00.

Union Store, Retail Clerks Union, logo center, "The Property of and Issued By the Retail Clerks International Protective Association," 10 x 8" . . . **50.00**

Ticket, lottery, black and white, George Washington, woman, and three workers with raised hands holding numbers, "Mechanics Art Union," c1800, 2 x 5" **20.00**

VOLUME ONE, NUMBER ONE

References: David K. Henkel, *Magazines: Identification and Price Guide,* Avon Books, 1993; Denis C. Jackson, *The Masters Price & Identification Guide to Old Magazines,* published by author, 1985; Denis C. Jackson, *Men's Girlie Magazines: The Only Price Guide!: Newstanders, Third Edition,* The Illustrator Collector's News, 1991; Frank Zawacki, *Famous Faces: Price Guide and Catalog for Magazine Collectors,* Wallace–Homestead, 1985 (Prices outdated, but accurate issue listing information).

Periodical: *Malloy's Sports Collectibles,* Attic Books, 17 Danbury Road, Ridgefield, CT 06877.

Comic Books

DC

Action No. 1, June 1938 . . . . **75,000.00**

The Atom, June–July, 1962 . . . . . **535.00**

Captain Atom, March 1987 . . . . **5.00**

Gangbusters, December–January, 1947–48 .... **300.00**

Hopalong Cassidy, February 1954 .... **150.00**

Mystery in Space, April–May 1951 .... **1,500.00**

Shazam, February 1973 .... **5.00**

Star Trek, February 1984....... **10.00**

Teen Titans, First Series, January 1966 .... **135.00**

Wonder Woman, Summer 1942 **3,500.00**

Dell Publishing, Wyatt Earp, November 1957............... **30.00**

Gold Key

The Lone Ranger, September 1964 .... **22.00**

Man From U.N.C.L.E., February 1965 .... **85.00**

Star Trek, Planet of No Return... **250.00**

Marvel

Adventures on the Planet of the Apes, October 1975 .... **3.50**

Amazing Spider–Man, March 1963 .... **8,400.00**

Captain America Comics, May 1941, Timely/Atlas **20,000.00**

Conan the Barbarian, October 1979 .... **185.00**

Dazzler, March 1981 .... **4.00**

Fantastic Four, November 1961 **7,200.00**

Incredible Hulk, May 1962..... **3,700.00**

Punisher, January 1986........ **50.00**

Strange Tales, June 1951....... **1,050.00**

2001: A Space Odyssey, December 1976 .... **2.50**

Mirage Studios, Teenage Mutant Ninja Turtles

First Printing **325.00**

Third Printing **40.00**

Warren Publishing Co., Vampirella, September 1969 .... **125.00**

Magazines

Baseball, May 1908 .... **2,500.00**

Baseball Digest, August 42, Elmer Valo cov **75.00**

Complete Baseball Magazine, Spring 1949, DiMaggio/Musial/ Williams cov................ **45.00**

Inside Sports, October 1979, cov featuring Lemon wearing Yankees hat.................. **30.00**

Life, November 23, 1936, Fort Peck Dam cov **110.00**

Look, February 1937, Germany's Wilhelm Goering on cov **50.00**

Newsweek, February 17, 1933, combination cov of Nazi Troops, Franklin D. Roosevelt, Stalin, and others **75.00**

Northern Lights, January 1867, only 11 issues printed, contributions from leading U.S. literary figures **35.00**

Life, black-and-white photo cover, 96 pages, 10½ x 14″, November 23, 1936, $110.00.

Playboy, December 1953, Marilyn Monroe centerfold and cov..... **1,500.00**

Saturday Evening Post, January 1, 1900, illustration of gentleman at dinner on cov **45.00**

Sport Magazine, September 1946, Joe DiMaggio and Little Joe on cov **450.00**

Sports Illustrated, August 16, 1954, Eddie Matthew cov and baseball card insert................. **250.00**

Time, March 3, 1933, Joseph G. Cannon cov................. **100.00**

TV Guide, April 3, 1953, Desi Arnaz, Jr., cov **100.00**

Newspapers

Boston, Massachusetts, Gleason's Pictorial, May 3, 1851, first illustrated weekly newspaper printed in America **75.00**

Racine, Ohio, The Tribune, April 13, 1887 .... **20.00**

Rochester, New York, December 20, 1936, The Rochester Weekly Flash, reform paper........... **25.00**

The Beatles Personality Annual, 68 pages, 8¼ x 11″, 1964, $40.00.

Rhode Island, Smithville Intellectual Cultivator, August 19, 1846, first and perhaps only issue of educational paper from Smithville College, view of school on masthead **35.00**

WATCHES

Collectors' Club: National Association of Watch & Clock Collectors, 514 Poplar Street, Columbia, PA 17512.

Advertising Trade Card
  Aurora Watch Co, smiling girl listening to ticking pocket watch **20.00**
  Brown & Keller Watches, Clocks, & Jewelry, text on front, invoice on back, 1868. . . . .   **25.00**
  Hampden Watches, color, little girl holding watch to grandmother's ear, dark blue ground **25.00**
  Illinois Watch Co, two sided, envelope design, emb postage stamps **30.00**
Book, *The Perfected American Watch*, Waltham Watch Co, Waltham, MA, 1907 reprint, 44 pgs, 5$^1/_2$ x 8$^1/_2$". **8.00**
Booklet, The Secrets of Switzerland, Omega Watch Centennial, history of Omega, 1950 . . . .   **18.00**
Box
  Gene Autry Six Shooter Watch **225.00**
  Hopalong Cassidy Watch, saddle stand shape display **175.00**
  Popeye Watch, Sheffield **50.00**
Catalog, Accurate Time–By Astronomy–by Wireless–by Illinois Springfield Watches, 1915, 30 pgs **10.00**
Sign, Elgin Watches, Father Time holding pocket watch and scythe, "The World's Standard," 17 x 24$^1/_2$" **250.00**
Stock Certificate, Elgin National Watch Company, engraved, green, two vi-

gnettes, eagle holding pocket watch, Old Father Time, issued and canceled, 1930s. **18.00**

WAYNE, JOHN

Reference: Dian Zillner, *Hollywood Collectibles,* Schiffer Publishing, 1991.

Periodical: *The Big Trail: A Newsletter of the Films of John Wayne,* 540 Stanton Ave., Akron, OH 44301.

Arcade Card, c1950 . . . .   **2.00**
Autograph, 3 x 5" card. **50.00**
Coloring Book, Saalfield, #2354–15, 1951, 32 pgs, 11 x 15". **50.00**
Jigsaw Puzzle, diecut cardboard, 1951, 15 x 11$^1/_2$" **15.00**
Lobby Card
  Blood Alley, Wayne and Lauren Bacall, Warner Brothers, 1955 . . . .   **25.00**
  Blue Steel, movie scene, Monogram Pictures, 1934 . . . .   **45.00**
Magazine, *TV Guide*
  #891, Wayne and Raquel Welch cov, April 25–May 1, 1970 . . . .   **10.00**
  #975, Wayne, Bob Hope, and others on cov, December 4–10, 1971 . . . .   **7.00**
Magazine Cover
  Life, August 11, 1969. . . . .   **6.00**
  Look, four pg article and black and white photos of making of movie *Flying Tiger,* full color cov photo, October 6, 1942, 9 x 12" **35.00**
Movie Still, black and white, 8 x 10". . . .   **5.00**
Photograph, black and white glossy, on horseback, wearing Western clothes, US flag and courthouse in background, inscribed "Good Luck, John Wayne," dated Nov 1977 on verso, 7 x 9$^1/_2$". **350.00**
Poster, *The Spoilers,* Wayne, Marlene

Business Card, D. Oppenheimer & Bro., wholesale watches, diamonds, and jewelry, Baltimore, MD, steel engraved, 5 x 3", 1890s, $8.00.

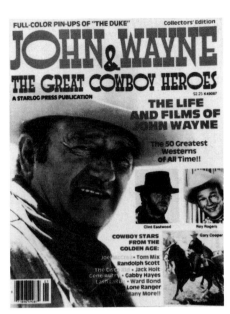

Magazine, *John Wayne & The Great Cowboy Heroes,* Starlog Press Publication, 84 pages, 8 x 11", 1979, $25.00.

Dietrich, and Randolph Scott, Universal Pictures, 1942, 27 x 41" **175.00**
Sheet Music, *Put Your Arms Around Me, Honey,* 4 pgs, Wayne, Martha Scott, and Dale Evans black and white cov photo, 1937, 9 x 12" **18.00**
Stationery, single sheet with black and white illus, envelope **2.50**
Tablet, color photo and facsimile signature on cov, c1950, 5½ x 9" **30.00**
Window Card, *The Dark Command,* Wayne and Claire Trevor, Republic Pictures, 1940, 22 x 28". **18.00**

WEST, MAE

Arcade Card, color, *My Little Chickadee,* West and W C Fields **18.00**
Autograph
 Card, 3 x 5" **30.00**
 Photograph, inscribed "Come Up and See Me Sometime," sgd and dated April 12, 1939, 8 x 10". **75.00**
Book, *Mae West,* Ells & Musgrove, hard cov, dj, 1982 . . . . **5.00**
Magazine Tear Sheet, *Song Hits,* August, 1935, article, full page photo **25.00**
Magazine Cover, *Life,* April 18, 1969 . . . **3.00**
Photograph, black and white glossy, half length pose, wearing white furs, inscribed and sgd in purple ink, 8 x 10" **60.00**
Sheet Music, *Good–Night Nurse,* 1912,

Cigarette Card, Player's Cigarettes, film stars, #47, printed color, 1⅜ x 2⅝", 1930s, $18.00.

6 pgs, West wearing nurse's uniform on cov, 11 x 13½" **40.00**
Song Book, *The Ideal Songster,* c1930, West cov **12.00**

WESTERN

References: Warren R. Anderson, *Owning Western History: A Guide To Collecting Rare Documents, Historical Letters And Valuable Autographs From The Old West,* Mountain Press Publishing, 1993; Bob Ball, *Western Memorabilia and Collectibles,* Schiffer Publishing, 1993; Robert W. D. Ball and Edward Vebell, *Cowboy Collectibles And Western Memorabilia,* Schiffer Publishing, 1991, 1993 value update; Michael Friedman, *Cowboy Culture: The Last Frontier Of American Antiques,* Schiffer Publishing, 1992; Bill Macklin, *Cowboy and Gunfighter Collectibles,* Mountain Press Publishing, 1989.

Periodical: *The Spur,* PO Box 3098, Colorado Springs, CO 80934.

Collectors' Club: Western American Collectors Society, PO Box 620417, Woodside, CA 94062.

Book
 Guidebook of the Western United States, four volumes: *The Northern Pacific Route, With a Side Trip to Yellowstone Park, The Overland Route, With a Side Trip to Yellowstone Park, The Santa Fe Route, With a Side to the Grand Canyon of the Colorado,* and *The Shasta Route and Coast Line,* US Geological Survey, GPO, Washington, first edition, cloth cov, foldout maps, 1915 . . . . . **85.00**
 How I Know, Or Sixteen Years

Eventful Experience Embracing Service On The Battle–Fields Of The South, Thrilling Adventures, Narrow Escapes, And Dire Disasters On The Western Frontier, Life Among The Mormons, The Miners, and The Indians, James Swisher, published by author, second edition, 1881, 584 pgs, dec cloth cov **50.00**

Tales of the Colorado Pioneers, Alice Polk Hill, Denver, first edition, 1884, 319 pgs, cloth cov **75.00**

The Pioneers, A Tale of the Western Wilderness, R M Ballantyne, 1872 **80.00**

Catalog, Leroy Shane Novelties, Authentic Western Merchandise, Indian Craft, Hit Toys, 1949, 48 pgs. **12.00**

Display, diecut cardboard, cowgirl on horseback lighting cigarette for cowboy, Helmar Cigarettes adv, 21 x 29" **125.00**

Label, cigar, Sam Houston Cigars, Houston wearing flat Texas hat, holding walking stick **8.00**

Newspaper
New York Herald, October 28, 1881, Gunfight at the OK Corral–Three Cowboys Killed **200.00**
Virginia Chronicle, Virginia City, NE, 1884, 4 pgs, mine image in masthead, 15½ x 22½". **15.00**

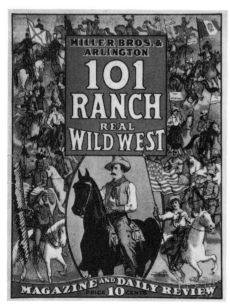

Program, Miller Bros. & Arlington 101 Ranch Real Wild West Magazine and Daily Review, 40 pages, color litho covers, black-and-white photos and illustrations, 7¼ x 9¾", 1915, $60.00.

Sheet Music, *Home on the Range,* Ray Noble and His Orchestra, 9 x 12", 1933, $8.00.

Photograph
Cowboy, mounted, wearing ornate cuffs and holstered pistol with mother–of–pearl grips, hills and barn in background, extremely clear image, albumen, c1900, 3 x 3" **35.00**
Cowboys roping and branding cattle on prairie, c1920, 6 x 4" **22.50**
Group on horseback descending canyon trail, guide wearing ten gallon hat and kerchief, black and white, dated 1925, 7 x 5" **10.00**
Outlaws, four mounted men, heavily armed, tents pitched in background, Riley Ridge, OK, text on back identifies three of the men as Daltons, 4 x 7½" **175.00**
Western Prairie County Homestead, family sitting outside house, c1890 **8.50**

Playing Cards, cowboy riding bucking bronco, red and white background, Rodeo Awards, Winston Cigarettes adv. **20.00**

Post Card, photo
Arizona Bill, 5th Cavalry scout, a.k.a. Raymond Hatfield Gardner, wearing buckskins, with rifle and burro, with biography **50.00**
Branding Calves, emb and tinted. **8.00**

Post Card Folder, Bronco Busters, Wild West Cowboys Souvenir Folder, full color, 20 panels, unused **18.00**

Program
Tucson, AZ Rodeo, February, 1939, 36 pgs, illus, large format, folding map **20.00**
World Championship Rodeo, 1944, Roy Rogers photos **15.00**

World's Championship Rodeo, 1941,
 Gene Autry photo **10.00**
Scrapbook
 Southwestern post cards, snapshots,
 and other travel ephemera, 1940s–
 50s. **50.00**
 Western and Hillbilly Stars, 1952, 52
 pgs **15.00**
Sheet Music, *The Utah Trail*, Bob Palmer
 and Tex Ritter, 1928 . . . .   **6.00**

WINCHESTER

References: Ralf Coykendall Jr., *Coykendall's Sporting Collectibles Price Guide,* Burford, 1991; Ted Hake, *Hake's Guide to Advertising Collectibles,* Wallace–Homestead, 1992; Sharon and Bob Huxford, *Huxford's Collectible Advertising: An Illustrated Value Guide,* Collector Books, 1993; Bob and Beverly Strauss, *American Sporting Advertising, Volume 1,* 1987, 1992 value update, and *Volume 2,* 1990, 1992 value update, published by authors, distributed by L–W Book Sales.

Booklet, Rules of the Winchester Junior
 Rifle Corps, c1915, 5¼ x 3¼" **30.00**
Calendar
 1889, grizzly bear attacking hunter,
 28 x 20".   **1,000.00**
 1896, hunters and moose, framed, 14
 x 26". **900.00**
 1914, hunter and dogs in cornfield, 30
 x 15". **100.00**
Catalog
 1918, Catalogue 81, Winchester Repeating Arms Co, New Haven, CT,
 216 pgs, rifles, shotguns, and ammunition, price revision slip pasted
 in front, illus, 8vo **100.00**
 1950, Arms & Accessories, 60 pgs,
 color illus. **60.00**
 1965, 48 pgs, color illus **16.00**
 1968, Winchester Firearms, 19 pgs. . .   **10.00**
Display
 Hanger, color, "Hunting Time–Stop
 em!–Go With–Winchester & West-
 ern," late 1960s. **15.00**
 Standup, cardboard, jacketed bullets,
 lead bullets, cartridges, wads, prime
 shells, and primers illus, color, 21 x
 27" **22.50**
Envelope
 Model 1912 Light–Weight Hammer-
 less Repeating Shotgun, color, two
 hunters and dog, c1920, 6½ x 3½"   **40.00**
 Rifles and Cartridges, two hunters,
 c1920, 6½ x 3½". **40.00**
Handbook
 Salesman's, 1956, 84 pgs, black and
 white and color illus **80.00**

Magazine Tear Sheet, Winchester Rifle, Eagle Scout comic, "Billy and Wes Learn About Upland Shooting," *Boy's Life*, 10½ x 13½", May 1959, $15.00.

Winchester Ammunition Handbook,
 first edition, 1950, 112 pgs, illus . . .   **15.00**
Playing Cards, red lettering, blue and
 white flying duck, blue ground, white
 border **18.00**
Post Card, adv, Winchester Repeating
 Arms Co, Boston, MA, gun dealer adv,
 rifles illus, 1881 . . . .   **15.00**
Print, "Texas–Frontier of Freedom,"
 Bernie Fuchs, commissioned by Win-
 chester Arms, c1970, 14 x 28" **12.00**
Sign
 Rifles and Shotguns for Sale Here, two
 dogs, logo and shells around border,
 H R Poore, 32 x 42" **650.00**
 Winchester, chromolithograph, bear
 and dogs, H R Poore, Philadelphia,
 orig oak frame, 32 x 42". **525.00**
Window Card, Leader Paper Shot Shells,
 box shape, color, c1910, 8" sq **100.00**

WIZARD OF OZ

Reference: Jay Scarfone and William Stillman, *The Wizard of Oz Collector's Treasury,* Schiffer Publishing, 1992.

Collectors' Club: The International Wizard of Oz Club, 220 N. 11th St., Escanaba, MI 49829.

Booklet
Little Wizard Stories, back cov with Scarecrow and Tin Woodsman carrying large Jell–O mold, radio show premium, 1933–34 . . . .   **25.00**
The Wizard of Oz Special Edition, 22 pgs, each page with photo from MGM motion picture, 1970 television broadcast promotional, MGM Merchandising and Singer Sewing Machine Co **30.00**
Box, Dunkin' Donuts' Munchkins Donut Hole Treats, *Return to Oz* motif, 1985 . . . .   **5.00**
Calendar, 1989, 50th Anniversary Commemorative Edition, twelve color photos, spiral bound **18.00**
Coloring Book, Judy Garland as Dorothy in The Wizard of Oz Coloring Book, Aero Educational Products, Ltd, 1977 . . . .   **15.00**
Display, Jell–O, cartoon Oz characters, promotes radio show, 1933 . . .   **25.00**
Insert, Garland, Morgan, Bolger, Lahr, and Haley, MGM, 1939, 14 x 36". . .   **4,500.00**
Magazine Tear Sheet, *Wizard of Oz* adv, *Photoplay Magazine,* September, 1939, 2 pgs **12.00**

Magazine Tear Sheet, Metropolitan Life Insurance Co., color tinted, 6½ x 9½", 1954, $12.00.

Movie Still
Cowardly Lion, MGM, 1939 . . . . . .   **25.00**
Tin Man, Dorothy, and Scarecrow on the yellow brick road, MGM, 1939 . . . .   **35.00**
Paint Book, Whitman, #663, 1939 . . .   **35.00**
Party Plates, Hallmark, c1975 . . . .   **10.00**
Photograph, Margaret Hamilton, sgd and inscribed **65.00**
Press Book, 2 pgs, 1972 re–release . . .   **8.00**
Puzzle, frame tray, scenes from MGM movie, Jaymar, 1960s, set of 4 . . . . .   **125.00**
Script, 113 pgs **50.00**
Sheet Music, *Over The Rainbow,* E Y Harburg lyrics, Harold Arlen music, Leo Frist, NYC publisher **15.00**
Stationery, Whitman, The Wizard of Oz Children's Writing Paper," ten sheets and envelopes, orig box, 1939   **175.00**
Window Card, Garland, Morgan, Lahr, Haley, and Bolger, MGM, 1939, 14 x 22" **3,750.00**
Valentine, diecut, standup, Glinda the Good Witch of the North, "I Witch You Would Be My Valentine," American Colortype Co, 1940–41 . .   **20.00**

WOMEN'S ISSUES

Autograph, letter, Susan B Anthony, Women's Suffrage Association letterhead, May 11, 1885, 2¼ pgs **350.00**
Book
Prisoners Of Poverty: Women Wage Workers, Their Trades And Their Lives, Helen Campbell, Little, Brown, Boston, 1900, 257 pgs, red cloth cov **40.00**
Tell It All: A Woman's Life in Polygamy, Mrs Stenhouse, 623 pgs, hard cov **15.00**
The Intelligent Woman's Guide To Socialism and Capital, Bernard Shaw, Brentanos, 1928, 495 pgs **22.00**
Newspaper
The New Northwest, Portland, OR, Womans' Suffrage paper published by Abigail Scott Duniway, May 1, 1874 . . . .   **25.00**
Women's Christian Temperance Union, November, 1877 . . . .   **8.00**
Photograph, albumen, "My Catch!," woman trapper, holding coyote by two steel traps, 1880s, 6 x 8" **40.00**
Post Card
"Ambition," girl conducting suffragette meeting with her dolls, sepia tones, postmarked Kansas, 1910   **25.00**
"Them pesky suffragettes wants everything for themselves," man standing at lady's room door, 1912 . . . .   **18.00**
"Ven Vimmens Get Their Rights,"

Dutch girl pulling boy in wagon, 1907 .... **12.50**

"Women's Rights," three girls and boy swimming, sepia tones, postmarked 1919 .... **20.00**

Poster

It's A Woman's War, Too – Join the WAVES, WAVE telegraph operator, black background, John Falter, 1940s, 28 x 42" **175.00**

Jenny on the Job, set of eight safety and health posters designed for female factory workers, full color, US Public Health Service, 1943, 10 x 14" .. **200.00**

Program

Stage Women's War Relief Fund, benefit, Houdini performance at Hippodrome Theatre, NY, wrappers, Apr 14, 1918 .... **450.00**

Woman's Relief Corps, benefit, *Ladies Minstrels*, 1896, 8 pgs, sepia tones, 6 x 9½" **15.00**

Song Book, *Equal Suffrage*, women's suffrage, Eugenie M Raye–Smith, Richmond Hill, NY, 1912, 16 pgs, 22 songs to be sung to popular tunes, 5 x 7" **40.00**

WORLD'S FAIRS & EXPOSITIONS

References: *American Art, New York World's Fair, 1939*, Apollo Books, 1987; Carl Abbott, *The Great Extravaganza: Portland and the Lewis and Clark Exposition*, Oregon Historical Society, 1981; S. Applebaum, *The New York World's Fair 1939–40*, Scottwall Associates, 1989; Kurt Krueger, *Meet Me In St. Louis–The Exonumia of the 1904 World's Fair*, Krause Publications, 1979; Frederick and Mary Megson, *American Exposition Postcards, 1870–1929: A Catalog and Price Guide*, The Postcard Lovers, 1992; Larry Zim, Mel Lerner, and Herbert Rolfes, *The World Of Tomorrow: The 1939 New York World's Fair*, Main Street Press Book, Harper & Row, 1988.

Periodical: *World's Fair*, PO Box 339, Corte Madera, CA 94976.

Collectors' Club: World's Fair Collectors' Society, Inc., PO Box 20806, Sarasota, FL 34276.

Bond, 1901 Buffalo Pan–American Exposition, Pan–American Exposition Company First Mortgage Bond, $500.00, brown and white, gold seal, four coupons at bottom, 17 x 11" **100.00**

Book

Jamestown Expo 1907, Tributes and Toasts 1607–1907, Julia Wyatt Bullard, J Ball Co, 196 pgs, hard cov, black and white photos **30.00**

Booklet

1893 Chicago World Columbian Exposition, Fairbank's Cottolene Shortening adv, 8 pgs, color cov entrance to exhibit image **25.00**

1915 Panama–Pacific Exposition, photos and map, Chicago–Northwestern Line Railroad issue .. **15.00**

1926 Sesqui–Centennial International Exposition, Philadelphia, Flags of America from the Time of Columbus to the Present Day, Sesqui edition, 30 pgs, 67 color flag images, John Wanamaker adv **10.00**

1935 California Pacific International Exposition, San Diego, "National Parks of the West," Standard Oil premium, black and white photos by western photographers, 16 pgs, orig mailing envelope, 5 x 8" **3.50**

Brochure, 1909 Hudson–Fulton Celebration, State of New York Education Dept, 64 pgs, history, photos........ **30.00**

Cabinet Card, 1893 Chicago World Columbian Exposition, "Big Tree," full story on reverse **10.00**

Calendar

1876 Philadelphia Centennial, Home Insurance Co adv, card stock, color litho, 12 pgs, patriotic and Centennial scenes, Kronheim & Co, 7½ x 5½" **200.00**

1893 Chicago World Columbian Exposition, stock, chromolithograph, World's Fair Manufacturers and Liberal Arts Building, R H Jones Liquors, Reading, PA adv, full pad, pink cov paper................ **60.00**

Calling Card, diecut, hand and flowers around central vignettes of Electrical and Fisheries Buildings, "With Loving Greeting," 2 x 3" **20.00**

Catalog

1876 Philadelphia Centennial, Official Catalogue of the United States International Exhibition 1876, 4 pgs, exhibition buildings illus, folio **85.00**

1926 Sesqui–Centennial International Exposition, Philadelphia, Illustrated Catalog Department of Fine Arts, 126 pgs, first 60 pgs photos of art on exhibit, lists exhibits by name, place, and country, cross referenced by art form **25.00**

1939 New York World's Fair, Stoeger's Catalog and Handbook of Arms and Ammunition, Jubilee Issue **150.00**

Cover

1884 Twelfth Cincinnati Industrial Exposition, all over brown adv on back, 2¢ rate to Chicago, Gibson House corner card............. **100.00**

Advertising Trade Card, 1893 Columbian Exposition, Machinery Hall, color litho, G. L. Winter Wholesale Mfg., Hagerstown, MD, 6 x 4", $28.00.

1898 Reading Sesqui–Centennial, all over adv features Indians, railroad, courthouse, and allegorical figure, Sticher Hardware corner card **90.00**

1904 Louisiana Purchase Centennial, multicolor cachet, 1903 . . . . **125.00**

Engraving, woodcut, 1853 New York Exposition, "Bird's Eye View of The Crystal Palace," panoramic view of buildings, crowds, flags, and skyline, *Illustrated News* supplement, foldout, dated July 23, 1853, 20 x 14". **35.00**

Envelope, Souvenir Weather Map Pan–American Exposition, full color flags image, unused **40.00**

Guide Book

1893 Columbian Exposition, "The Big Four World's Fair Route To Chi-cago," Cleveland, Cincinnati, Chicago, and St Louis Railway Co, folding map, lithoprint views of Expo buildings, int. views. **20.00**

1939 New York, guide to General Motors Highway and Horizons Exhibit **7.00**

Label

Ale, 1876 Philadelphia Centennial, Continental Brewing Co, Burton Ale, "Centennial Exhibition 1876 highest Premium Awarded," oval, black on salmon **15.00**

Cigar

1893 Chicago World Columbian Exposition, Exposition Cigars. . . . **15.00**

1904 St Louis, Temple Cigars, full color Temple building and people **16.00**

Magazine, *Texaco Star,* 1939 New York

Poster Stamps, 1939 New York World's Fair, unopened package of 54, orange-and-white envelope with Trylon and Perisphere, $25.00.

World's Fair, 26 pgs, color photo of Petroleum building on cov, 8 x 11" . . . **35.00**

Map

1876 Philadelphia Centennial, Centennial Views, foldout, hand colored, green, blue, pink, and yellow, center views surrounded by four black and white vignettes of various buildings, matted and framed, 20 x 22". **300.00**

1939 New York World's Fair, fairgrounds and map of New York City, Trylon and Perisphere, 20 x 28". **25.00**

Matchbook, 1939 New York, Wrigley Spearmint Chewing Gum adv **2.00**

Needle Book, 1933 Century of Progress, full color, no needles. **5.00**

Newspaper, *Frank Leslie's Illustrated Historical Register of the Centennial Exposition 1876,* Frank Norton editor, NY, 320 pgs, nearly 800 illus, 1877, elephant folio **50.00**

Pamphlet, 1933 Century of Progress, Durkee Famous Foods, 16 pgs. **5.00**

Photograph, 1893 Chicago World Columbian Exposition, south entrance of the Art Gallery and entrance to Transportation Building, pr **25.00**

Post Card

1907 Jamestown Exposition, novelty, Mule Barometer, hair tail moves with weather conditions, Norfolk, VA Exposition Station 1907 cancel **50.00**

1926 "Greetings To You From Philadelphia, The Sesqui Centennial," full color illus of Liberty Bell, garland, shields, divided back with blue Sesqui Centennial seal, unused **15.00**

1934 Century of Progress, real photo, "Smallest Woman in the World". . . **12.00**

Poster

1876 Philadelphia Centennial, "1776 Centennial International Exposition 1876," black and sepia tones, Main Exhibition Building in center, twelve historical vignettes in border, pub by H Schile, NY, 23 x 30" **700.00**

1939 New York, "Go By All Means, World's Fair of 1940," stylized image of family riding high wheel bicycle, scooter, and running to fair, S Ekmar, 13 x 20" **95.00**

Poster Stamps, 1939 New York World's Fair, orig pkg **25.00**

Print, woodcut, 1884 Cincinnati Industrial Exposition, *Harper's Weekly,* September 20, 1884, full page, H F Farney **15.00**

Program, 1939 New York World's Fair, April 30, opening day, 16 pgs, Trylon and Perisphere on cov, 6 x 9" **75.00**

Tijuana Bible—8 Pager, Jitterbug Bug Contest at the World's Fair, green and black covers, 4¼ x 3⅛", $20.00

Scrapbook, 1893 Chicago World Columbian Exposition, ephemera includes more than 100 adv trade cards in addition to Enterprise Congress World's Fair set of 15 . . . . **600.00**

Sheet Music

King Cotton March, 1895 Atlanta Cotton States and International Exposition, John Phillip Sousa, black and white **30.00**

New Orleans Exposition Grand March, black and white cov, vignettes of five buildings, 1884 . . . . . **50.00**

The World's Fair Quick Step, 1851 London International Exposition, William Dressler composer, Hall & Son, NY, color litho building and grounds, 6 x 12". **150.00**

Souvenir Book, Louisiana Purchase Exposition, 64 pgs, day and night scenes, blue and gold cov **35.00**

Stationery, 1914 Anglo–American Exposition, official stationery, color, unused. **15.00**

Ticket, 1876 Philadelphia Centennial, Exhibitor Pass, photo, emb seal, most dates punched **100.00**

View Book, 1939 New York World's Fair, 64 pgs, World of Tomorrow, linen type paper, printed color of Trylon and Perisphere on cov, black and white photos, 7 x 10" **45.00**

WORLD WAR I

Periodicals: *Military Collector Magazine,* PO Box 245, Lyon Station, PA 19536; *Military Collectors News,* PO Box 702073, Tulsa, OK 74170.

Book

Operation & Tactical Use of Lewis Automatic Machine Gun, Colonel I N

Lewis, Van Nostrand Pub, 1917, 149 pgs, illus, cloth cov **35.00**
Pictorial History of 26th Division, 1920, 320 pgs **23.00**
The Plattsburger, souvenir Plattsburg Training Camp, NY, Mutt and Jeff comic art, 240 pgs, hard cov, 8½ x 12" **75.00**
Certificate, Liberty Loan, multicolored, 9½ x 12½" **25.00**
Flip Book, soldier, sailor, and Uncle Sam presenting the Colors, Pledge of Allegiance, Liberty Bond promotion, 1917 copyright, 2 x 2½ x ¼" **25.00**
Magazine Cover, *The Literary Digest,* March 30, 1918, US Army Supplies in France **25.00**
Map, published in the *Boston Sunday Advertiser,* color, Jan 1918 . . . .   **12.00**
Photograph
 8th Battalion, 154th Brigade, troops with weapons, identified on back, 8½ x 6½" **15.00**
 German Submarine *U–53,* crew on deck, US steamer in background, albumen, Waterman, RI, 8 x 10" **25.00**
Post Card
 Battle Photo, *Chicago Daily News* . . .   **3.00**
 Soldier's Dispatch, diecut, 10½ x 3" . .   **25.00**
Poster
 Can Vegetables, Fruit, And The Kaiser, Too, John Paul Verees, humorous image of unhappy Kaiser in jar of Kaiser Brand Unsweetened Vegetables **150.00**
 For Home & Country–Victory Liberty Loan, Alfred Everitt Orr, American Litho Co, 1918, 20 x 30" **35.00**
 Help Uncle Sam Stamp Out The Kaiser–Buy US Government Bonds, Harry S Bressler, large foot ready to step on tiny Kaiser, bright yellow ground **185.00**
 Some Backing! The Empire State Needs Soldiers, Join The New York State Guard!, James Montgomery Flagg **195.00**
Sheet Music
 Over There, Cohan, Norman Rockwell cov illus **45.00**
 When The Kaiser Does The Goose Step To A Good Old American Flag, 4 pgs, 1917, 10½ x 13½" **20.00**
Stereoview, doughboys at the front **4.00**
Tablet, eagle and flag illus and "Victory" on glossy paper cov, 8 x 10" **7.50**
Window Card, Navy, "Man From This Home Now Serving His Country" **18.00**
Yardlong, USS Sibenoy Arriving At US Naval Base, August 8, 1919, framed . .   **125.00**

WORLD WAR II

Reference: Stan Cohen, *V For Victory: America's Home Front During World War II,* Pictorial Histories Publishing Company, 1991.

Periodical: *Military Collectors Magazine,* PO Box 245, Lyon Station, PA 19536. *Military Collectors News,* PO Box 702073, Tulsa, OK 74170.

Atlas
 Global Atlas of the World At War, Mathews–Northup, 1944 . . . .   **12.00**
 Liberty World Atlas, Pictorial History of World War II, Hammond, cutout globe assembly **20.00**
Aviation Combat Planes, set of 32, British, Russian, German, Italian, and Japanese, orig envelope **16.00**
Blotter
 Insignia Guide, color, 1942, 4 x 9" . . .   **6.50**
 National Wartime Nutrition Program adv, early 1940s **8.00**
Book
 A Photographic Record of All the Theaters of Action Chronologically Arranged, pictorial history, Wm H Wise & Co, Inc, NY, dark blue dec cov, pictorial end papers, 1944, 7 x 10" **125.00**
 World War II in Headlines and Pictures, Philadelphia, *Evening Bulletin,* soft cov, 1956, 10½ x 14" **32.00**
Broadside, What To Do In Blackouts, Civil Defense do's and don'ts, black and white, 1942, 28 x 43" **75.00**

V Mail Packet, stationery, 12 sheets and envelopes, unopened, 1940s, $9.00.

Envelope, Iwo Jima flag raising scene, G
F Hadley artist, Aug 29, 1945 . . . .   **20.00**
Guide Book, Uniform and Insignia
Pocket Guide, U S, China, United
Kingdom, USSR, and Poland **20.00**
Magazine, *Time,* April 6, 1942, WWII
coverage **27.50**
Manual, *Recognition Pictorial Manual,*
Bureau of Aeronautics, Navy Depart-
ment, Washington, DC, silhouettes
and technical information on Allied
and Axis aircraft, June, 1943, 80 pgs,
black and white, 6 x 10" **75.00**
Matchbook, Remember Pearl Harbor . . .   **4.00**
Newspaper, Nazi, *Deutsche Bug–
Zeitung,* October 10, 1942, large
spread eagle on wreathed swastika in
masthead **20.00**
Post Card, Vultee P–66, Keep Them Fly-
ing, Longshaw **7.00**
Poster
Help Buy This Gun By Buying Stamps

Or Bonds, GI manning anti–aircraft
gun, sgd "Jos Popa," 36 x 47" **18.00**
Let's All Fight, Buy War Bonds, soldier
wearing pith helmet, holding rifle
with bayonet, production workers in
background, dark blue ground,
1942, 28 x 22" **110.00**
Think American, Our Hearts, Heads,
and Hands are United, marines,
sailors, and workers standing before
huge draped American Flag, silver
ground, 1944, 20 x 27" **300.00**
Propaganda Leaflet, Hans Frank photo
below quotes from Roosevelt's speech
about war crimes, gummed back, writ-
ten in Polish, 1943, 9½ x 6½" **50.00**
Ration Book, two sets of coupons **10.00**
Scrapbook, 60 pgs, newspaper clippings   **30.00**
Sheet Music, *He's 1–A in the Army,*
Redd Evans, Valiant Music Co, blue
and white cov **5.00**

INDEX